The Biblical Seminar
76

this be from Heaven...'

'If this be from Heaven...'

Jesus and the New Testament Authors
in their Relationship to Judaism

Peter J. Tomson

www.SheffieldAcademicPress.com

Published by
Sheffield Academic Press Ltd
Mansion House
19 Kingfield Road
Sheffield S11 9AS
England
www.SheffieldAcademicPress.com

Typeset by Sheffield Academic Press
and
Printed on acid-free paper in Great Britain
by The Cromwell Press
Trowbridge, Wiltshire

British Library Cataloguing-in-Publication Data

A catalogue record for this book is available
from the British Library

ISBN 1-84127-196-9

CONTENTS

PREFACE

Every book has its history, a poet once wrote, referring to the reactions of the readers, but the history of a book really begins long before that, and it precedes even the exertions of the author himself. For historiographers the question of where to draw the boundary between eras and histories is a common one. For me, the history of this book began with the request of the Foundation for Scientific Research into Christian Literature on Jews and Judaism (Stichting Wetenschappelijk Onderzoek van Christelijke Literatuur over Joden en Jodendom). I am obliged to the Foundation for the trust expressed in their request and for the challenge involved, without which the book would not have been conceived of.

Nonetheless, the reader may be interested in knowing something about my motives, and perhaps these can be shown best by means of an anecdote. A friend invited me, as a freshman student of theology, to attend a lecture by a rabbi that took place in the Anne Frank House in Amsterdam. The lecture was about the Hebrew verbs in the creation story and the significances that rabbis traditionally have heard in them. The lecture burgeoned, and thus the 'budding' and 'bearing fruit' of the trees in paradise became key words in a process of learning that continues on into the present. The teacher was Yehuda Aschkenasy, offspring of an ancient rabbinical line who had survived Auschwitz and had completed his rabbinical studies only after much wandering. In that particular lecture, and later many times again, he made it clear that only one who becomes a student can teach others well.

In the course of his studies, the student naturally also became acquainted with Christian doctrine. Karl Barth's insight that the church can only teach if it also learns struck a familiar chord; nonetheless, I was often confused by the disparity between Christian theology and the teachings of the rabbis, with which I began to feel more and more at home. Aschkenasy pointed out negotiable paths to me. In the first place, it was not Aschkenasy's intention that Christian theologians became whole or half Jews, but better Christians. In the second place, he taught his students the trust necessary in order not to repress unanswered questions, nor to patch them up by providing them with the semblance of an answer, but to leave them open, whereby space is created for a process of learning from which in time a new perspective can emerge.

The present book concentrates on the one hand on the painful question which was then legible to the students on their teacher's face: *where does the unmotivated hate for the Jews come from?* We had no answer; we felt guilty and were silent. Quite rightly so. When one cannot speak, one should be silent. The biblical tradition, however, does not reckon with collective guilt. Children are not responsible for the deeds of their parents. The feeling of guilt can be better interpreted as a motivation to do things differently. But in which way different, and different from what? Without conscientious connection to tradition, no renewing can take place; likewise, tradition cannot continue without renewal. Thus we realized that we belong to an unusual generation. We are privileged to be witnesses of and participants in a process of change that knows no equal in the history of Christianity: *the reassessment of the Jewish roots of Christian tradition*—the other main theme of this book.

The title is borrowed from the plea of the Pharisee Gamaliel to let the followers of Jesus go, since every human judgment of a community like theirs would be but provisory (Acts 5.39). The expression is adapted to the related question posed by Jesus to the temple administrators in Jerusalem: 'The baptism of John, was it from Heaven or from men?' (Mk 11.30). 'Heaven' is here a discrete designation for God, as in rabbinic Hebrew usage.

Methodology, style and spelling are accounted for at the end.

In conclusion, those who made this publication possible deserve thanks. The Board of the Foundation, and especially its secretary, Dr J. Wieberdink, are to be credited not only for their indefatigable energy and stimulus but also for their attentive reading of the Dutch manuscript. In addition, they made provision for the English translation. The translator, Dr Janet Dyk, has done an exceptional job in rendering a complex and in more than one sense intertextual Dutch original into elegant English. The numerous biblical passages, which were often adapted to the specific context, presented an additional challenge in the translation. Finally, I am much obliged to those responsible at Sheffield Academic Press for accepting the book in their series.

The book can now be launched into its history with its readers. May its shortcomings and inaccuracies not hinder a joyful process of learning.

ABBREVIATIONS

AB	Anchor Bible
ASTI	*Annual of the Swedish Theological Institute*
BETL	Bibliotheca ephemeridum theologicarum lovaniensium
BHT	Beiträge zur historischen Theologie
CD	Damascus Document
CRINT	Compendia rerum judaicarum ad Novum Testamentum
EKKNT	Evangelisch-Katholischer Kommentar zum Neuen Testament
EvT	*Evangelische Theologie*
HNT	Handbuch zum Neuen Testament
HTKNT	Herders theologischer Kommentar zum Neuen Testament
ICC	International Critical Commentary
JSP	*Journal for the Study of the Pseudepigrapha*
MeyerK	H.A.W. Meyer (ed.), *Kritisch-exegetischer Kommentar über das Neue Testament*
NovTSup	*Novum Testamentum*, Supplements
RB	*Revue Biblique*
SNTSMS	Society for New Testament Studies Monograph Series
VCSup	*Vigiliae christianae*, Supplements
WUNT	Wissenschaftliche Untersuchungen zum Neuen Testament
ZTK	*Zeitschrift für Theologie und Kirche*

Introduction

READING THE NEW TESTAMENT ANEW

Jews, Anti-Semitism and the New Testament

Two apparently mutually exclusive insights concerning the New Testament have progressively surfaced in the general consciousness, namely, that the New Testament manifests anti-Judaism or hatred for the Jews *and* that the New Testament can only be understood from the context of the Judaism of its day. Some would allege simply that the New Testament is *a Jewish book*, while others conclude just as easily that the New Testament is *an anti-Jewish book*. Both theses are defensible and both are equally true or untrue. To rise above this stalemate, insight into the relationship of the one to the other must be acquired. For those readers prepared to consider these two insights seriously, this book offers itself as a companion through the diversified and at times seemingly contradictory evidence from ancient times.

Undoubtedly because of the process of awareness brought about by the Shoah or Holocaust, quite recently *both* insights are becoming common knowledge. That the cognizance of both aspects has grown simultaneously is in itself intriguing. In pondering the remarkable relationship of Christianity and Judaism, it can even be difficult to distinguish which of the two had precedence—the realization that Christian antipathy for Jews has been particularly profound and intense, or the dawning consciousness that Jewish roots are essential for Christianity. Since the nineteenth century, both facets have been brought forward by individual Jewish and Christian historians and theologians, often separately, sometimes in conjunction with one another. Only recent happenings, however, have challenged many minds to further contemplation.

New insights into ancient texts result from changes in the reader's world. There is a complex but direct relationship between the process of reflection taking place after Auschwitz and the renewed study of the

Jewish origins of Christianity. Closer consideration, however, reveals that it is not Auschwitz or the Shoah *alone* that is responsible. During the nineteenth century, the emergence of historical research, which in turn was related to a new form of society and a renewed concept of humankind, has produced innovating perceptions whose ramifications are bewildering. What connections are there between the Enlightenment, revolution, emancipation, democracy, secularization, nationalism, historiography, imperialism, anti-Semitism, world wars, mass murders and theological reflection? The links are multiple and multifarious. We find ourselves in a radical process of change of such magnitude that for the past two centuries the foundations of western civilization have been churning. Millions of victims have been called for. Still, besides the resulting horror, profound new insights have surfaced. Our simultaneous reconsideration of both the Jewish origins of Christianity and the Christian roots of deep aversion for the Jews is but one facet of this whole process.

Incidentally, the conviction that Christianity and Judaism are of entirely different orders and unrelated to each other has remained alive as well. Orthodox Christians who cling to this persuasion do not easily tend to reconsider the ties between their faith and Judaism, choosing rather to go no further than emphasizing the distinctions. Given their dreadful lot within Christian Europe, the case is fundamentally different for the Jews. Nonetheless, the attitude of a practising Jew who maintains that neither Christianity nor its founder is of any consequence whatsoever to Judaism is comparable to the orthodox Christian attitude just mentioned. Both think in terms of two mutually exclusive religious worlds.

I am not writing to pass judgment on such beliefs, nor to address these positions. My point of departure is the empirical fact that Christianity and Judaism are interwoven. Christian hatred of the Jews cannot be explained without also taking into account the Jewish origins of Christianity, nor can the Jewish roots be discussed without awareness of the bitter fruits that they have borne.

In general, there can be three different specific motivations for reading this book. One reader primarily involved with the New Testament could be curious as to its Jewish background and be concerned particularly about the traces of anti-Judaism within it. A second reader could be basically indignant about hostility towards the Jews and anti-Semitism, but realize as well that it is necessary to know more about the roots thereof in the New Testament in interaction with the Jewish context of that time. A third reader could be involved in Judaism but, in spite of Christianity's poor reputation, be curious as to what of value the New Testament could contain. The diversity in orientation implies that readers will not derive the same conclusions from what they are exposed to. In all cases, however, the major emphasis is on rereading, on discovering unknown aspects of a well-known text.

Reading

The process of reading is more complicated than is often assumed. One always 'reads', that is, understands a written text from a preconception of what one expects to find written there. The Greek word for 'reading' reflects this quite simply: *anaginōskein*, literally 'recognize'. Externals influence this perception even before the content is noted: the black border of an obituary notice, the pastel colours of a birth announcement, the official envelopes and seals of important communications, and the brazen gaudiness of unimportant messages. We abstain from reading certain items because so-and-so has written them, while we appreciate others *only* because they have been recommended to our attention in one way or another. In this we could easily be led astray, and the predisposition about what we expected to read could turn into prejudice. It is important, therefore, that we become aware of our preconceptions concerning what we read and that we learn to open ourselves to new information.

One never reads the New Testament without bias, probably not even in our secularized society. The mere mention of the names of 'Paul' or 'Christ' is enough to repel some people. Others nod affirmatively at an allusion to 'John' or 'Matthew'. Both negative and positive reactions are a priori. To what extent does one in this way do justice to a text from nearly two thousand years ago out of a completely different culture whose view of humankind varies entirely from ours?

A long time ago, the so-called average Bible reader was unmasked with mild humour by Hillel, a wise Pharisee teacher. The issue in question was whether the 'written Torah', the five books of Moses, was sufficient in itself or whether an 'oral Torah', a tradition of explanation and application, such as was developed by the Pharisees, was also necessary:

> A case of someone who came to Shammai the Elder. He asked: Master,
> how many Toras have been given from heaven? The latter answered:
> One in writing and one in the mouth. He said: I believe you concerning
> the one which was given in writing, but I do not believe you concerning
> the one given in the mouth. He [Shammai] then became angry and sent
> him on his way with a scolding.
>
> He then came to Hillel, and he asked: Master, how many Toras have
> been given in heaven? This one answered: One in writing and one in the
> mouth. He said: I believe you concerning the one which was given in
> writing, but concerning the one given in the mouth, I do not believe you.
> Then he [Hillel] wrote the alphabet down and asked: What is this? An
> 'A', answered he. And this? a 'B'. Then he asked him: And who tells
> you that this is an 'A' and that is a 'B'? The man answered: I have
> accepted that on faith. Then [Hillel] said: Just as you have accepted that
> on faith, so you will accept this on faith (*ARN*, B29.31a-b).

In other words, nobody reads without tradition or 'canon', without an a
priori understanding within which that which is read is situated. Reading is always interpreting. In the sense of the Pharisee Hillel, this
involves *discussion* in which the one explanation, or 'another explanation', or both, are allowed their rightful place. The discussion represents
a compromise between that which is read and the preconception one
had about it.

The implication is that, in spite of all the author's scholarly reading,
the present book is not more than a 'reading' of the New Testament and
related texts. On many important points there will be some, many, or
even a great majority of scholars who promote a different reading, they,
too, being not more than well-read readers of the New Testament.
Instead of despairing about this fallibility of the experts, the reader is
invited to *read along*. This book contains many extensive quotations
from New Testament and Jewish sources, always with an explanation,
whereby the reader is given insight into the relationship between the
sources and their interpretation, and thereby also into the learned preconceptions of the author himself.

Reading Historically

A reader's preconceptions are influenced both by personal circumstances and by changes in the surrounding society. We read differently
from our grandparents, differently than was read in the Middle Ages or
in antiquity, differently *after* the Second World War than before it.

Such shifts in conceptions do not take place automatically. This is particularly true of reading a book like the Bible, in which one seeks support for belief, for dogma, for cherished convictions anchored in experience. In defiance of this practice, one can contrarily search the Bible for evidence *against* belief and dogma. The latter alternative promises an equally poor chance of truly attentive reading. What is needed is a constant reform, a continuously renewed reshaping of our thinking, of the preconceptions with which we approach the Bible.

Finding a new, contemporary manner of reading not infrequently involves a painful process of change that is never simply deduced from historical happenings nor merely constructed from new-fashioned ideas. The emergence of a new interpretation, of a reformation, from the birth pangs of the age is a vulnerable miracle that, not without reason, has always been seen in relation to divine inspiration or the Holy Spirit. In this sense as well, there are no 'ordinary' Bible readers. Nonetheless, illumination does not come by inspiration alone: even the invention of an electric light bulb took 99 per cent perspiration, according to Edison. Diligent study is needed, concentrated contemplation of the tradition of transmitted knowledge and information. It has never been otherwise. The dawn of a new interpretation was preceded by Daniel's study of prophecy (Dan. 9.2), by Paul's 'zeal for the law', by Augustine's restless searching, by Luther's thirst for true knowledge. Even Jesus, prior to his public appearance, remained in the wilderness for 40 days and 40 nights, sustaining himself solely on the words of Scripture.

The unfathomably profound reshaping of thought in which we find ourselves has been brought about by the emergence of *historical consciousness*. This developed in the era of Enlightenment and Revolution that began in the eighteenth century and appears to have run its course by the end of the twentieth century. Historical consciousness is also *human self-awareness*. The collective sum of all that is human is the product of historical development and is subject to change; furthermore, on the basis of recognized interests, humans have the right to change the results of the past. During this process, the value of human dignity has been rediscovered and formulated in the Declaration of Human Rights. The highly theoretical status of this declaration has become all too apparent, if only in the inhuman aspect of successive revolutions. Surprisingly, in spite of this, the Declaration has heralded a new *consciousness of equality* that has persisted and gained ground step by step. Slavery, first rejected by the French Revolution but reintroduced by

Napoleon, was later irrevocably abolished. Likewise, the emancipation of women, proclaimed by individuals during the Revolution and, if possible, even more rapidly swept under the carpet again, appears ultimately to persevere due to successive 'waves' of feminism.

Becoming aware that things are changeable and that they are continuously changing goes hand in hand. There is no invulnerable human authority, for the latter is a historical development. Political or religious powers that sanction inequality eventually are forced to forfeit their own authority. The insight that humankind is a historical entity and that we can understand ourselves only within our own historical determination applies also to religion as an aspect of human culture. Religious movements come into being, split off or die out; holy books are written in the language and culture of a certain era; faith flowers and withers with the fluctuations of life; each dogma, each reformation proceeds from its own juncture in time. Thus it is that in the age of historical research, the origins of the Old and New Testament were also made an object of study, which in turn became the occasion for church schisms and a lapse in attendance. Nonetheless, an honest thinker can no longer deny that discrepancies between Exodus and Numbers or between Mark and John provide evidence of historical development.

How could one, however, still *read the Scriptures in good faith* in the age of Enlightenment and Revolution, in the awareness that all insight and authority are determined by historical circumstances? A silent and fundamental crisis reigns. What is the relationship between revelation and history, between religion and society, between faith and reason? The revolutions turned against the sovereignty of the throne and the altar, of the pulpit and the clerk. All too often the altar and pulpit had incurred hatred as supporters and confederates of the established disorder. Today, such are banned to the private domains of denominations and sects. The separation of church and state objectified the gap between faith and historical insight. New, more individualistic forms of religion strive to fill the gap thus created. These cannot conceal the fact that the ancient culture of the Bible was about all peoples, the whole earth, the entirety of the nation, justice and injustice. The question is, What does the believer signify as a member of modern society? How can one understand oneself within one's historical determinedness and simultaneously lead an upright religious life? Such questions have been discussed for more than two centuries, and the answers thus far are no more than provisional.

Within this book, the Bible will consistently be approached from a historical point of view. Questions will be posed concerning the circumstances and causes, taking note of nuances in correspondences and distinctions, making judgments as to authenticity and plausibility. Besides the reasons already given, this approach is inescapable because of what has taken place between Christians and Jews: we read differently after the Second World War than we did before it. This issue will be pursued further later on. If we are not obliged to assume that anti-Judaism and anti-Semitism are essential characteristics of Christianity, then they must have originated at some point in history. If we are to know where and how this came about, historical research must be undertaken.

Within this approach, we will view each of the New Testament writings first individually, without presuming a harmonious whole. Differences and discrepancies are often the most informative when investigating historical development. Precisely in reference to the Jews and Judaism, great disparities will become apparent. Through the contrasts the individual character of each writing can be recognized more clearly. Further, the internal texture—the layers from which the text could have been constructed—will be noted. This is particularly applicable to such texts as the Gospels, which were produced by and intended for a community of believers. Finally, we will keep in mind the text as the unity into which it has developed, both each text individually and the New Testament as a whole.

The question as to the possibility of genuine faith and an honest religious life is not hereby resolved. Everything in due time.

Reading after Auschwitz

In this same era of Enlightenment and Revolution, events took place that can only be understood in terms of Obscuration and Reaction: the conscious attempt to exterminate the Jewish people, using instruments not only of modern science and technology but also of church and theology. Thereafter nothing could be the same again. One wanting to read the Scriptures sincerely cannot but inquire about the historical causes of these events and search for means to rise above them.

To begin with one must be aware of what 'Auschwitz' stands for. Auschwitz is the German name for the Polish village Oświęcim, where a concentration camp for Russian and Polish prisoners was located, with a large expansion in the barracks at Brzezinka (Birkenau). Besides the tens of thousands of Poles, one and a half million Jews were murdered here in specially developed mass extermination installations. This was but the organizational acme of a network of camps of destruction and of slaughters in the open field, in which another four million Jews were annihilated, alongside six million Polish, Russian and other prisoners. For Central Europe the goal set for the *Endlösung*, the 'final solution', of the Jewish question, was hereby accomplished. Practically nothing is left of the Jewish communities in Germany and Poland; in the surrounding countries, only a small remnant remains. A ghastly emptiness reigns in the heart of Europe.

It is not out of line to associate this cataclysm with a grave failure on the part of European Christianity. Not only did a minority actively collaborate, but more specifically the majority maintained a massive silence. Church leadership as a rule was horrifyingly mute. When this silence was broken, it was usually on behalf of *baptized* Jews; rarely did one risk one's neck for the 'perfidious infidel'. Even courageous protest movements like the *Bekennende Kirche* in Germany or the *Betere Weerstand* in the Netherlands found it advisable to modify their plea for the Jews by making mention of their lack of obedience to Christ. Immediately after the war, when on all sides hands were joined for rebuilding society, there was a peculiar reserve, even in these circles, towards all that was Jewish. It is atrocious to realize how the survivors, carrying in body and soul the testimony to the unimaginable, were confronted with a chilling wall of incomprehension.

The reticence of these Christians, the silence of the majority, and the active collaboration of the minority did not appear out of thin air. There is a long tradition of Christian hostility towards the Jews, which in its classical form manifested itself in the church of antiquity and of the Middle Ages, which received a new, somewhat spiritualized form in the churches of the Reformation and which resulted in the various forms of participation in modern, secularized anti-Semitism, including National Socialism.

It is necessary to clarify terminology here. Classical, religiously motivated hatred for the Jews can best be termed *anti-Judaism*, because it is aimed against Jewry or *Judaism*. In contrast, *anti-Semitism* does not pretend to be motivated by religious grounds, but by ethnic ('Semitic') or racial factors. Although under the surface of so-called secular, scientific anti-Semitism various religious motives play a role, this does not alter the fact that the anti-Semite sees and presents himself or herself as though there were no religious links. This 'modern' attraction of anti-Semitism can assume an even more deceptive imago of youthful energy and national liberation, hereby gaining a foothold by taking advantage of the shortcomings of Zionism. In order to avoid such modern subtleties, we will often use the simple words which indicate what it is about: aversion or hatred of the Jews. In the final chapter we will go into the specific motives for this hatred.

In its classical form, the breeding ground for the remarkably strong aversion for the Jews by Christians lies undeniably in the feeling of being both *indebted to* and *exalted above* the Jews. Christians read the Jewish Bible, borrow the essentials of their religious vocabulary and social apparatus from the synagogue, and have fixed their hope on the God of Israel. In the Christian view, however, the Jews are blind to that hope in its true form, behave themselves religiously and socially aberrantly and read the Bible solely for the commandments it contains. The image of the church as the 'new Israel', heir of and victor over the Jews, summarizes this characteristic Christian ambivalence towards the Jews.

Careful consideration shows that one must rather speak of an *essential duality*. Christians have adopted the Scriptures, the language of the faith and the ethics of the Jews, while they cannot help but provide a divergent content to this on numerous points. Two aspects are thus at the core of the Christian feeling of identity: an inherent affinity with and an essential distinction from the Jews.

The difference lies in the Christian confession that Jesus is the Messiah. In the first place, this was a point of dispute among the Jews themselves, as can be read in the Acts of the Apostles. For centuries there have been Jewish-Christian groups. From Paul's viewpoint and that of his consorts, the establishment of 'churches of non-Jews' was not intended for the exclusion of the Jewish brothers and sisters. To confess Jesus to be the Messiah did in no way signify that one turned against the Jews; nonetheless, precisely the latter attitude gained swift prominence. At the end of the first century the bishop of Antioch, a city where Paul and his co-workers often resided, wrote that 'to speak of Jesus Christ and to live Jewishly is not compatible' (Ignatius, *To the Magnesians* 10.3), whereby the Christian creed is related directly to the rejection of Judaism. Such a position represses the affinity with the Jews, and we must speak of *Christian anti-Judaism*. This standpoint became exemplary for the later majority church.

After Auschwitz, after the shocking events of the twentieth century, Christians are forced to ask themselves whether it is not possible to assume a different attitude. Can the dual relationship to the Jews be accepted without lapsing into the antagonism that has been transmitted through the ages, that is, the anti-Judaism or deep-rooted aversion for the Jews as the reverse side of the creed? Can Christians respect their affinity with the Jews as well as the differences?

Posing such questions entails in fact searching again for the roots of Christianity. The relationship to the Jews is for Christians not just one point among many on the agenda, but it touches the very foundation of their existence and identity. 'Auschwitz' signifies for many the moral bankruptcy of European Christianity. If this be the case, these questions can also bring about the possibility of a positive development. For Christians it could be the opportunity for a progressive reshaping of their thinking. By recalling the ghastly emptiness, by daring to recognize the long tradition of Christian hatred for the Jews, and by embracing the double nature of their relationship to the Jews, it is possible that space be created for a renewed vision of the basis of the church's existence and a regenerated realization of its identity.

One thing to be learned from 'Auschwitz' is the disproportionate significance of the exception. Not all Christians collaborated the whole time during the war, nor in the Middle Ages, nor in antiquity. In contrast to Ambrose, the bishop of Milan, who forced the emperor in 388 to forego the compensation of damages to the Jews whose synagogue had been burned by Christians, there is John, the bishop of Speyer. During the first Crusade in 1096, which ended in a massacre among the Jews in the Rhineland, John defended the Jews of his city with his own troops. In the time of the Nazis, in contrast to the Christians in Germany and elsewhere who allowed themselves to be made to toe the line, there were church members like Dietrich Bonhoeffer who directly risked his own life by pleading for the Jews and fighting against evil. As of old, Christians today are faced with the choice whether to follow the majority on the way that leads unto death, or to follow Jesus and remain on the side of his faith in the God of Abraham, Isaac and Jacob, who liberates the captive and calls the dead unto life.

Liturgical Reading

As mentioned, in this book a historical or, more precisely, a *historical-critical* approach is chosen. The New Testament writings will each be studied individually, tracing historical components and drawing ancient manuscripts into the discussion. Readers who cherish the New Testament could become uneasy: how can they escape ending up with unlimited fragmentarization? If thus approached, will the New Testament still be found to contain a coherent line, can then the renewing of faith ever be given a chance?

In reaction to such qualms, some emphasize that each Gospel, each text, should be read only as an integral whole. Historical developments should not be taken into account, for otherwise the unique message of each text would not be brought out clearly. Some would go even further and apply this approach to the New Testament as a whole. In isolation, such a method provides, however, no real answers. The historically developed whole of the New Testament is a *unity of contradictions*, not in the least where our focus of attention—the relationship to the Jews—is involved, and this multiformity is also observable within each Gospel. Taking both the Jewish origin of Christianity and the development of the hatred towards the Jews seriously necessitates looking penetratingly at these differences.

Where can Christians find a firm footing when confronted with such a plurality of attitudes? Are Christians able to listen to the New Testament writings as a unity without denying the historical multiplicity and diversity? Is there a method of approach or a situation in which that is possible?

The answer is positive: there is, and it has always been there, but Christians must rediscover it in the midst of this era of Enlightenment and Obscuration, of Revolution and Reaction. The method of approach and the situation where the New Testament can be heard as a credible unity is the continued and recurrent reading of the Scriptures in the liturgy. In the liturgy, while being read and explained, the Scriptures of both the New and the Old Testaments are related one to another in ever new discoveries of meaningful connections.

This is what is meant by *liturgical reading*: the reading of passages of diverse natures so that they are heard together because of their appropriateness to the day of the liturgical calendar or because of a thematic relatedness. There is thus no denial of the differences or contradictions between the passages or the books from which the readings are taken. These divergent texts are here read together—a *many-voiced reading*. In this liturgical polyphony, resonances and harmonies are produced that would not be heard, or perhaps not even be allowed, in the historical approach. How indirect, if even at all existent, is the historical relation between the story of the resurrection of Jesus and that of the liberation from Egypt, or between the pouring out of the Holy Ghost and Psalm 68? Nonetheless, these portions are read together liturgically as an essential unity at the celebrations of Easter and Pentecost, respectively.

This manner of reading is, of course, not novel, but was adopted from the synagogue, where at set times various portions of the Scriptures are 'read together' and expounded as contextually related. Where historical analysis must observe a multiplicity, the liturgy of the synagogue and of the church read a unity. We could even say that liturgical reading is specifically the place where the unity of the Scriptures, or of the *canon*, is created. We will return to this in the final chapter, after having broadened and deepened our historical insight into the diversity of the New Testament.

'Church' and 'Synagogue'

In this context it is fitting that we clarify our preference for the word 'church' as a term here. We intend it flexibly, both in the sense of the local meeting and of the congregation of all places and all times. What defines it are two basic characteristics: *the Scriptures are read aloud*, and these are read *at set times*. The difficulty is, of course, that the term has been monopolized to signify a unique, exclusive institute of salvation, so that, for example, Protestants often prefer to speak of a (local) 'congregation'. The drawback to the latter usage is that the universal aspect is not reflected. A look at the history of the word could be helpful.

The New Testament uses the Greek word *ekklēsia*. This originates, like so many ancient Christian words, from the Septuagint (see pp. 34-35), where it consistently is used to render the Hebrew word *qahal*, 'community meeting' or 'public gathering' (Deut. 23.1-8; cf. Acts 7.38; 19.32). This word has a synonym in the Bible which occurs more often: the Hebrew word *'ēdâ*, 'congregation', and in Greek *sunagōgē*—not by accident also the usual indication for the Jewish congregation in the Graeco-Roman world. In the Talmud the *'ēdâ* is explained as the 'official gathering', that is, of minimally ten members (*b. Meg.* 23b; *b. Ber.* 6a).

Following the 'synagogue', the 'ecclesia' (*èglise, iglesia, chiesa*) is of old an open community that through the ages reads the Scriptures, but meets at different times than the synagogue: not on the seventh day, but on the first day of the week. The word 'church' (*kerk, kirk, Kirche*) refers to this custom and is derived from the old Greek-Christian usage, where *kuriakē* (*hēmera*) indicates '(the day) of the Lord'. The emphasis is upon the *set time* in which one congregates and upon the *name* in whose remembrance this is done. Certainly, the ancient Christian celebration of the Sunday was, to put it mildly, in competition with the Jews, but that was not its origin. Already in New Testament times, Christians meet 'upon the first day of the week' (Lk. 24.1; Acts 20.7; *Did.* 14.1; cf. p. 389), without interfering with the Sabbath and other Jewish feast days (Lk. 23.56; 24.1; Acts 20.6; 18.4).

It is in this line of thinking that the word 'church' is used here: a community with both local and universal dimensions, which reads the Scriptures through the ages, that is, a liturgical–eschatological community. We also speak of Jewish churches in antiquity, that is, local communities of Jews who, besides the Torah reading, recited as well the gospel tradition.

Chapter 1

JUDAISM IN THE GRAECO-ROMAN WORLD

Jesus came from a specific Jewish milieu that did not coincide with the well-known groups of his time. The Judaism of that day came in many hues and tints, probably more numerous and differentiated than we can retrieve. In this first chapter we will endeavour to acquire an overview of this diversity, as broad and differentiated as possible, on the basis of transmitted and rediscovered sources. Later an attempt can be made to situate the specific environments of Jesus and of his followers within that reconstructed variegation.

To begin with, however, a brief survey of the historical context of Judaism itself is needed—the ancient world, which was defined by *Greek culture* and *Roman supremacy*. In this we can distinguish between contexts, which can be depicted graphically as a concentric system. The broadest setting of the New Testament is the Graeco-Roman world; within this Judaism forms a more direct context; the most immediate environment is the specific Jewish milieu of Jesus himself. Conversely stated, we approach Christianity as a movement that came forth out of Judaism within the Graeco-Roman world; the New Testament is the oldest collection of writings from that movement.

The Graeco-Roman World

To clarify what is meant by 'the Graeco-Roman world', we begin with a short military and political survey. In 334 BCE the young Macedonian general Alexander, later called 'the Great', began a long-prepared campaign against the Persians. Within ten years' time he had subdued their entire gigantic empire from the Nile to the Indus, from the Aegean Sea to the Persian Gulf. After his untimely death in 323 BCE his kingdom fell apart and his generals divided the fragments. The most important and stable of these Macedonian kingdoms were the Egyptian kingdom under the royal line founded by Ptolemy and the Seleucidan kingdom under the dynasty of Seleucus, which comprised Syria, large portions of Asia Minor, and for a long time also Babylonia and Persia.

From the second century BCE onwards the power of Rome began to expand in an easterly direction, until the death of the legendary Cleopatra VII in 31 BCE sealed the fate of the Ptolemies, the last remaining Macedonian dynasty. The victor, Octavian, was proclaimed 'Caesar', emperor, with the addition 'Augustus', the illustrious. For the Jews, as for so many other peoples, Macedonian-Greek dominion was now universally replaced by Roman sovereignty, so that in the sources that will occupy us the most, at a certain point we read of 'a decree that went out from Caesar Augustus'.

The victories of Alexander and Augustus confront the historian of ancient culture and religion with a nasty complication. Changes in religion and culture do not usually keep pace with politico-military eras. We are accustomed to neatly dividing up history according to the governing periods of rulers and dynasties. The official royal chronicles kept in antiquity were already fashioned in this manner. The problem is that from such a lofty vantage point, only the history of the victors is recorded, while that of the dominated does not enter the picture. The images of sovereigns immortalized in stone or on paper usually teach us little about the religious life and cultural feelings of ordinary people.

Recent European history as well demonstrates that the religious life of the people changes at a different pace than does the progress of political history. France, with its centralized government under Louis XIV, was fully dedicated to Roman Catholicism and treated the Protestant Huguenots as an intolerable aberration. In spite of the politics of oppression, the Huguenots survived in inhospitable regions as a proud minority, a position which they, by the way, shared with the Jews. More than a century later the Revolution came and the Roman Catholic Church in turn became the target of 'centralistic' oppression, now under the banner of the ideals of humanistic equality. Here again it would be a mistake to conclude from the radical replacement of regimes that a fundamental transformation of religious life and thought had taken place. Traditional Roman Catholicism kept flourishing in France, even though it had lost its comfortable position of power, and Protestantism remained a well-founded minority. The profound crisis for churches and all religions that was brought on by the era of Enlightenment and Revolution was much longer in coming.

Similarly, the fact that the battles and changes of government of the

Macedonian and the Roman empires caused worldwide political changes says little indeed about the evolution of the cultural and religious life of their subjects in the various lands and language communities. Influences from preceding eras continued to be in effect for a long time, and developments which later would cause sensation had already been going on unnoticed for a considerable period.

The rule of Alexander and his successors is denoted as *Hellenism*. This is a fully appropriate term as long as it is applied only to the politico-military aspects. Difficulties arise when one tries to delimitate thereby a period in the development of culture and religion, which, as we have seen, has a completely different rhythm. Several simple facts can illustrate this. The elite of the Roman Empire showed the remarkable tendency of acting as the heirs and prolongators of Greek literature and sculpture. In addition, it was Greek and not Latin that for centuries was the language of official and colloquial use in the Roman Empire. Did not a well-known promulgator of the new faith around 56 CE write a letter to his spiritual kinsmen in Rome about good news for 'Jews and Greeks'—in Greek?

The exaggerated influence that has often been ascribed to 'Hellenism' as a cultural-religious entity complicates matters even further. The enthusiastic rediscovery of Greek civilization around 1800 led to a flowering of the study of the classical languages and to the 'discovery' of Hellenism as a historical-cultural term (J.G. Droysen, 1836). All things Greek were romantically idealized, as was languishingly rendered by Hölderlin's *Hyperion*. In this climate arose both modern *historiography* and *nationalism*. There was, however, a dark reverse side, as became apparent after 1806. Already at that time, Jewish participants in this movement had painfully to discover that the nationalistic glorification of the Greek, German or French 'genius' often contained an 'instinctive' aversion to Jewish culture and religion. In less extravagant form, these sentiments circulated in the halls of science. The history-of-religions approach to the New Testament, which emerged at the end of the nineteenth century, had an enthusiastic and almost exclusive focus on the 'Hellenistic' influence upon early Christianity, while the descriptions of Judaism displayed noticeable antipathy. Of more recent date is the subtler theory that Judaism itself was profoundly influenced by 'Hellenism' and that thereby the way was paved for Christianity. The latter is another example of the exaggeration of the 'Hellenistic' influence, combined with an underrating of the resilience of Judaism.

Did Greek culture then have no influence upon the Jews? Undoubt-edly it did. During the successive Greek and Roman empires, an inter-national and diversified climate reigned, in which Greek was the *lingua franca*. This brings us to the essence. In the first place, the Greek word *hellēnismos* means no more and no less than the coveted ideal of *speak-ing Greek*. This could produce quite remarkable Greek, just as 'inter-national' English nowadays can be grating to the 'real' Englishman. But why should Pakistani or Caribbean English be considered less authentic than London or Irish English, not to mention North American English? The Greek of the Septuagint and of the New Testament is of a com-parable authenticity, bearing the stamp of Judaism and its traditional language Hebrew; nonetheless, both writings witness to Greek as an ideal. In addition to the language, Greek art, literature and science were considered enviable attributes of the Graeco-Macedonian rulers, at least by their educated subjects. The question is what precisely this signified for people in general, especially in countries where Greek was not the vernacular.

Alongside this tendency, there was also a *counter-reaction*. A covert protest against the Greek and later Roman supremacy was widespread. Paradoxically, this could take on a typically 'Hellenistic' form. As early as the third century BCE, Babylonian and Egyptian priests began to describe the respectable history of their own peoples and cultures, but for this they employed the language and style techniques of the Greek historians. In addition, the Jews, for example, traditionally had a critical view of other religions and cultures that precluded indiscriminate bor-rowings. The Babylonian and Egyptian example was soon followed in Jewish circles, and the historical works of Flavius Josephus are a mel-lowed product of this. Christians, too, followed suit, as the historio-graphical work of 'Luke' and the church history of Eusebius (beginning of fourth century CE) show. Of no less significance is the military reac-tion. The successful revolt of the Maccabeans against the religious uni-formity politics of Antiochus Epiphanes, the Macedonian–Syrian ruler, is a monument to Judaism's widespread resilience rooted in the people. The Romans in turn were to be confronted with this.

There is yet another factor which is often neglected: the immense, long-lived influence of Persian occupation and culture. Disregard for this is remarkable and only partially to be justified by the scarcity of sources. The Persian Empire did not only precede Alexander's brilliant campaign, but also precipitated it. The centuries-long Persian occupation of their north-eastern inhabited areas challenged the Greeks to military action, of which the triumphant Macedonian campaign was merely the decisive phase. This places the self-assuredness with which the Greek propagated their language and culture in a different, more militant light. There are telling ancient Persian reports of the persecution of Zoroastrian priests by Greek soldiers. The expansion of Hellenism evidently had an anti-Persian bias, which must have had effect for a long time.

Nonetheless, the inherited rivalry between the Greeks and the Persians had positive sides as well, as is apparent from the infrastructural continuity between the two empires. The administrative organization of the Hellenistic empire was in many aspects based on that of the Persians, for example, the *satrapies* (provincial governments) and the postal service. Contrary to what is often thought, the international climate of cultural exchange that so characteristically influenced Judaism was not an innovation of the Hellenistic period: something of this nature had already arisen under the Persians. On many points one wonders whether what is generally taken as Hellenistic influence does not go back as well to the persistent effect of the Persian period. Previous to the worldwide domination of Greek came that of Aramaic, the lingua franca of the Persian Empire. The stamp that Aramaic left upon the Jewish culture was at least as important as that of Greek, and, in distinction to the latter, has continued up to the present day.

There are still more elements in early Judaism that reveal the continuation of Persian influence, for example, the terminology derived from the Persian administrative milieu. Among the important functions in the temple, there were two that carried Persian names: *amarkal*, 'officer', and *gizbar*, 'keeper of the treasury' (*m. Šeq.* 5.2). From this milieu as well, in which other language influences besides Aramaic were also at work, derive also such frequently used rabbinic terms as *turgeman*, 'translator', *dat*, 'law', and *hazzan*, 'supervisor', and probably also *halakah*, 'rule' (see pp. 78, 87). It is logical to associate these observations with the reorganization of Judaism under Ezra, who, besides being priest and scribe, was also the officially authorized Persian agent for the Jewish religion (Ezra 7). Noticeable sympathy towards the Persian rule is apparent in the title of Cyrus (*Koresh*) as God's 'anointed one' (Isa. 45.1; cf. Ezra 1.1-2). Persian influence comes to the fore in a number of central beliefs of postexilic Judaism, particularly in the apocalyptic elements, which begin to appear only in the later parts of the Old Testament: angels and demons, the resurrection of the dead, the final judgment and a cosmic dualism. Such traces of the submerged influence of Persian domination admonish one to caution in speaking about the influence of 'Hellenism'.

An important reason for prudence in this matter is, finally, the complex and amorphous nature of 'Hellenism' itself. In so far as it represented a cultural unity, it signified at best a climate of international openness with a universal everyday language and relatively brisk means of communication, more an organization than an essence. In this the Persian era was unmistakably carried on, and one could call this a 'Persian–Hellenistic period' in which the boundaries between cities, countries and peoples became indistinct. Not all boundaries disappeared, however. It was typically 'Hellenistic'—as it had been typically 'Persian'—to emphasize one's own non-Greek ancestral tradition. It is in this area that the Jews excelled, as Josephus naturally did not forget to underscore. Another interesting case are the Stoics, a popular school of thought characteristic of the Hellenistic era in its accentuation of the kinship of all persons. It was the Stoics in particular who showed themselves to be receptive to oriental and especially Iranian concepts, such as the cyclic rebirth of the world from fire. Finally, the popularity of the Egyptian and oriental religions, such as the worship of Isis and Mitra besides Dionysus and Demeter, show again the amorphous complexity of 'Hellenism'.

All this must be kept in mind when denoting the broadest historic context of the New Testament as being 'the Graeco-Roman world'. Within that vast context, scattered throughout the Roman Empire and under the continuing cultural influence of the former Hellenistic and Persian eras, the Jews lived and thought. Their social environment and their way of thinking are the topics upon which we wish to shed more light.

Jewish Places of Residence, Languages and Writings

To get an overview of the variegation within Judaism in antiquity, we will take a tour past the different Jewish domiciles and languages, while likewise taking note of the writings that arose from these. This approach deserves some explanation. Our information on the various Jewish living environments in antiquity is acquired primarily from literary sources, that is, from the writings handed down through the ages and those discovered later. On the other hand, the information we seek can be derived from these writings only if they are seen within their original environment. We are thus forced to work in a circle—the so-called *hermeneutic circle*. In order to escape a *closed* circuit it is essential to make comparisons with other sources as much as possible from the same period and circumstances. It is equally important that all those sources and milieus be treated within a single, coherent approach, in which not only the similarities but also the variety of differences are brought out as much as possible.

There is no short cut. Books that promise the reader direct access to 'the facts', for example, by means of newly discovered manuscripts, are misleading. The same is true of scientific treatises with the unfounded pretence of providing an 'objective account'. Each rendering is an interpretation and each interpretation is in principle disputable. Progress, that is, getting closer to the reality of that time, can only be made if we gradually learn to accommodate our representation of that reality more adequately to what the sources bring to light in all of their concrete diversity.

Alexandria: The Septuagint, Philo and Hatred of the Jews
As in more recent times, in antiquity as well probably the majority of the Jews lived outside the Holy Land, in what in Greek is called the *diaspora*, 'dispersion', and in Hebrew the *galût*, 'exile'. Both of these are biblical–prophetic concepts that express the anomaly of living outside of the land of the fathers (e.g. Jer. 24.5; Deut. 30.4 LXX). Just as today, one did not necessarily have to feel 'dispersed' or 'exiled' in one's remote domicile; nonetheless, in antiquity as well there was not a single Diaspora community whose survival could be taken for granted.

Around the beginning of the Christian era, the largest and most prosperous Diaspora community was located in Egypt, especially in Alexandria at the mouth of the Nile. This 'metropolis', adorned with the name of the legendary general, was a paragon of Greek culture, not only because of her millions of inhabitants, but also because of her magnificent architecture, art and science. Greek was spoken in any case in the prominent circles of the cities, while among the poorer inhabitants and the rural population, Egyptian (Coptic) remained in use. Until a short time previously, the Macedonian dynasty of the Ptolemies had immortalized the cultural fame of the capital, together with its own art-loving name. One of the wonders of the world was the *Mousaion*, the temple of the Muses founded by Ptolemy II (beginning of the third century

BCE), which contained by far the largest library in the world. Such treasures did not, of course, materialize out of the blue. The Ptolemies, skilled not only at war and politics but also at business, had developed Alexandria into an unrivalled centre of world commerce.

Jews had long lived in the ancient cultivated area of the Nile (cf. Jer. 44). In the metropolis, they numbered perhaps up to a million souls around the beginning of the Christian era, and they generally lived quite at ease. When around 40 CE problems with the local Greeks about civil and religious rights arose, the Jews did not hesitate to send a delegation to the emperor. In this an important role was played by Philo, about whom we will hear more later. According to a rabbinic tradition, the synagogue of Alexandria, 'the one with the double colonnade', was so immense that it was necessary to wave a sash to indicate the principal liturgical moments (*t. Suk.* 4.6). The Alexandrian Jews maintained close ties with the Holy Land, pilgrimages to Jerusalem were undertaken, and mutual consultations on questions concerning the Scriptures were made.

The Jews contributed to the literary flowering of Alexandria. Many of their works have been lost, but two portions that have been preserved are of great significance to both Jews and Christians: the Septuagint and the writings of Philo. The Septuagint, a Greek translation of the Old Testament, was the Bible of Greek-speaking Jewry. The Scripture reading in the synagogue, as well as the prayers, was conducted in Greek. A Jewish legend emphasizes the venerability of the translation by ascribing it to the literally identical and, therefore, divinely inspired work of 72 (or 70) translators who had especially come over from Jerusalem, 6 from each tribe (*Letter of Aristeas* 32–51; *b. Meg.* 9a; Josephus, *Ant.* 12.57). The appellation derives from the Latin name: *septuaginta*, 'seventy'. The translation is said to have been commissioned by Ptolemy II for the library of his *Mousaion*, expressing that from a Jewish standpoint the Holy Scriptures are of universal significance In reality, there were different versions of the Greek Old Testament in circulation, which must have come into being in connection with their use in separate synagogues. The Greek of the standard text often follows the Hebrew closely and must have sounded strange to Greek ears. Non-Jews had little interest in it, except for those who felt attracted to the Jewish faith and Jewish manner of life, the so-called God-fearers (see Chapter 2), and those who were annoyed by it.

Non-Jewish interest in the Septuagint increased enormously when the

Greek-speaking churches adopted it as Holy Writ, a function which it still has in the Greek Orthodox Church. A late rabbinic tradition registers this change as expropriation: 'The peoples of the world will translate the Torah and read it in Greek, and then they say: We are Israel!' (*Tanḥ ki tisa* 34, 147a). The reaction was evidently precipitated by the polemic attitude of the orthodox, non-Jewish church of the fourth century or later, but such polemics were already exhibited by the church father Justin (±150 CE; *Dial.* 11.5; 135.3). This was, however, not a necessary development, nor the only possible one. Through the synagogal Scripture readings, not only Jews but also innumerable non-Jewish 'God-fearers' had for centuries become familiar with the Greek Bible text. Thus the Greek–Jewish Old Testament became the cradle of Christian theological language usage. In the New Testament we find not only many quotes, but also numberless half-conscious or unconscious borrowings from biblical Greek. The same applied as well to the liturgy and the language of prayer.

Of great significance for Christian theology were the works of *Philo of Alexandria*. Coming from a prosperous Jewish family, he discharged important offices in the Jewish community, such as leading the delegation to Rome, as mentioned. We know him best, however, from his philosophy and Torah study. He appears to have been just as devoted to the primal source of all Jewish thinking, the Torah, as he was at home in the philosophical salons that abounded in Alexandria. For modern readers this represents the Gordian knot: was he a Jewish Greek or a Greek Jew? Did he exercise exegetical philosophy or philosophical exegesis? Philo himself would not have understood these questions: for him, theology and philosophy were one.

Philo's scriptural interpretation is characterized by allegory or spiritualization (see pp. 84-85). This approach was to become an integral element of Christian theology, particularly through the great Christian theologian Origen. Origen grew up in Alexandria at the end of the second century CE and later worked in Caesarea. Through Origen's interest in it, Philo's work was preserved for posterity, as were also the Septuagint and other Greek–Jewish writings. There is bitter irony in the fact that, like the Septuagint, Philo was used to prove that the Christians were right as opposed to the Jews. The influential writings of Eusebius (beginning of the fourth century), bishop of Caesarea and successor to Origen, show this with particular clarity. Through this development, Philo became a stranger to the Jews.

Nonetheless, Philo has a lasting effect on the Jewish culture and history as well, though more indirectly. Rabbinic Judaism did not preserve his works, nor the Septuagint or other Greek–Jewish literature. The oft-repeated explanation that the rabbis rejected philosophy and Greek as being exponents of a foreign culture is not sufficient. Mediaeval Judaism proved quite the opposite, as can be seen in the figure of Maimonides. Not only a great Talmud scholar, but also a philosopher and physician, Maimonides also wrote many of his works in a 'foreign' tongue, namely, Arabic. Another explanation emphasizes the rivalry between Jews and Christians: the Christian annexation of Philo and the Septuagint would have brought the rabbis to withhold their recognition of these writings. Indeed, the Greek Bible translation was the starting point of debate and polemics. The old Alexandrian translation became so much an arsenal for Christian counter-arguments that the rabbis let another translation be made. This rabbinic–Greek translation, however, was again preserved not by the Jews, but by Origen and Eusebius!

The fact that the Greek Bible translation and Philo's works were not preserved by the Jews must, therefore, have other arguments than those based on content. It would seem logical to look for external causes. When we observe from a greater distance, the attention is arrested by the concurrence of this with another enigma, namely, the disappearance of Greek-speaking Jewry. Both phenomena can be related to the blow that the Jewish community in Alexandria received at the beginning of the second century CE and from which it never recovered. Scattered reports indicate that in 115–17, under Emperor Trajan, the Jews in North Africa revolted after years of growing tensions, resulting, among other things, from the war in Judaea. It ended in a catastrophe for the Jews. Many survivors must have left Egypt for good and probably settled in other Greek-speaking Jewish communities. Further on in our survey it will appear to be plausible that these communities as well eventually disappeared, and with them their literature.

About a thousand kilometres to the west of Alexandria lay Cyrene, in the horn of contemporary Lybia. A prominent Jewish community that left its traces even in the New Testament was located here. The only Diaspora Jew that is mentioned by name in the Gospels is Simon of Cyrene (Mk 15.21). Further we hear of the 'synagogue of the Cyrenians', which, alongside that of the 'Alexandrians' and of the 'Cilicians' (from the area beyond Antioch), in Jerusalem determined the contours of the Diaspora (Acts 6.9). Some of the writings produced there are at our disposal. The *Second Book of the Maccabees* is a summary of the five books which a certain Jason of Cyrene wrote about the Maccabean revolt (2 Macc. 2.23). The work testifies not only to an elevated culture but also to good relations with the Jewish motherland. The war of 115–17 possibly broke out in Cyrene, and with it this Jewish community must have disappeared. The five books of Jason were lost, but the summary was preserved—by Christians—as a part of the Septuagint.

The downfall of such vigorous Jewish communities compels serious consideration of the risks involved in contact with non-Jews. As already mentioned, troubles broke out in Alexandria around 40 CE and this recurred regularly. The issue was the civil rights of the Jews, who, in spite of their century-long residence in the city, did not have equal rights with the Greeks—that is, 'Greeks' in the ethnic sense. This should be distinguished from the so-called 'privileges' of the Jews, the rights obtained in Alexandria to exercise one's own religious worship and to remain free from obligations that were contrary to this. The Greeks, however, were not willing to share their civil rights and created a great turmoil when the Jews and other non-Greeks insisted upon them. Besides two writings of Philo on the matter, there is also an excavated papyrus with a decree from Emperor Claudius from 41 CE. He admonishes that there be order, but nonetheless confirms the inferior position of the Jews, perhaps not so much from antipathy as from the habitual conservatism of the Roman administrators. The outbreak of war in Judaea in 66 led to the deployment of Roman soldiers and hence to a massacre (Josephus, *War* 2.487-98). The revolt of 115–17 was merely the fatal climax.

How is this growing antipathy for the Jews to be appraised? The word *anti-Semitism* lies on the tip of the tongue. Within the framework of this book, the relevant question is to what extent there was a pagan, non-Christian hatred of the Jews in antiquity. The situation in Alexandria was in any case one of fluctuating tensions between rival groups. As in so many similar situations, 'hatred of the Jews' had a parallel 'hatred of the Greeks', and the two parties were well-matched in this regard. As long as the Jews were not ascribed exceptionally negative qualities or some exalted role in which they were bound to disappoint, the aversion to them was not much different from aggravated envy. Clearly, the Jews were given such a role in later Christianity, namely, that of the disobedient or rejected people of God. In Alexandria this was, of course, not the issue.

Nonetheless, there was more involved in Alexandria. In ancient literature a specific Egyptian-Greek tradition of negative representation of the Jews can be discerned. Important examples are the priest Manetho, one of the first Egyptian-Hellenistic authors, and Apion, an Egyptian orator who acted as lawyer of the Greeks against the Alexandrian Jewish delegation to the emperor. Years later Flavius Josephus wrote a challenge to Apion's arguments and those of his predecessors (*Against Apion*), from which most of our information about them derives. Apion brought forward three types of recriminations against the Jews: (1) physical inferiority (they were to have been chased out of Egypt as lepers), (2) an absurd religion, and (3) an unjustified pursuit of equal civil rights. The third accusation reflects, of course, the actual motivation for this argumentation. Just as clearly, the first two serve to give a universal foundation to the rejection of granting civil equality: Jews are physically and religiously inferior. Perhaps Manetho's statements (beginning of the third century BCE) were among to the first reactions to the Septuagint. In all events, they form a cynical derision of the Jewish consciousness of being a people who are God's 'own possession' (Exod. 19.5).

The above makes it nearly certain that during the Alexandrian troubles, besides the normal rivalry and social irritation, specific anti-Jewish motives played a role. Though it is preferable to avoid the anachronistic term *anti-Semitism*, the designation *hatred of the Jews* can hardly be evaded. Incidentally, by itself this could not have led to the ruination of North African Jewry, the conditions for which were only created by the politico-military constellation of the Roman Empire. In antiquity as well as later, it was only in combination with material forces and movements that ideas became operational. To that extent— not more and not less—it is meaningful to combat malicious ideas, as Josephus did.

Multilingualism in the Holy Land

We continue our exploration of Jewish domiciles by way of an imaginary exodus. Though perhaps not the largest, certainly the most important location for the Jews in the first century was the Holy Land, called by the Romans 'Judaea' or 'Palestine' and by the Jews 'the land of Israel', a name also occurring in the Bible (Ezek. 40.2; Mt. 2.20-21). The practically unchallenged centre of worldwide Jewish national existence was indeed the temple in Jerusalem with its daily offerings and prayers and the annual cycle of pilgrims' festivals. To this very day, the

Jews enunciate their most important prayer with their faces turned towards the temple in Jerusalem. The significance of the Holy Land is
related as well to the fact that such a large proportion of the ancient
Jewish literature known to us originated there.

Particularly during Passover and other pilgrims' celebrations, the
population of the Holy City swelled exponentially; in quieter times it
was, in comparison to Alexandria, merely a provincial town with a conspicuously large temple. Most of the Jews lived as farmers and trades-
men in numberless scattered villages and settlements in the country.
There were three primary Jewish areas of dwelling: *Judaea* or the region
around and southernly to Jerusalem; *Galilee* in the north; and the *Peraia*
or the 'Other Side' (of the Jordan—*Ever ha-Yarden*). Furthermore, a
series of cities founded or refounded by Hellenistic and Roman monar-
chs were strewn along the coast and in the Jordan Valley, such cities as
Ashkelon, Caesarea (the Roman centre of government), Ptolemais
(Acco), Scythopolis (Bet Shean), Neapolis (Nablus) and Tiberias. Mention must also be made of the Samaritan territory lying between Judaea
and Galilee. In most respects the Samaritans counted as Jews according
to the law, but they lived on an uneasy footing with the Jews.

The destruction of the temple in 70 CE, besides being a great spiritual
shock, meant material disaster for all priests and Levites who derived
their sustenance from it. The catastrophe that resulted from the second
Jewish war against Rome (132–35 CE) had a much more general impact.
Many villages in Judaea were laid in ruins, cultivated agricultural lands
were destroyed, and the Jews were banned from Jerusalem. From then
on Galilee became the centre of Jewish life in the Holy Land, with the
highest rabbinic council being in Tsippori (Sepphoris) and later in
Tiberias. This was not a step backwards in all respects. Although some
chauvinistic Jerusalem scribes looked down upon them, before this time
Galilean Jewry was already known for their distinct devoutness and
dedication to the Torah. Around the end of the second century CE, during the salubrious reign of the orientalizing dynasty of the Severi,
Jewish Galilee attained great economic and spiritual prosperity. To this
testify not only the richly decorated Galilean tombstones, but also the
fact that the Mishnah was then committed to writing.

The Mishnah brings us to the topic of the literary creations of the
Jews of the Holy Land. In order to acquire a valid conception of these, a
survey of the various movements of that time is needed. A separate
section will be dedicated to this, but here a summary is given. Three

types of writings from Palestinian Jewry have been preserved: those of
the sect or sects from *Qumran*, those of the *rabbis* and the portion of
the so-called *apocryphal and pseudepigraphic* writings that came from
the Holy Land. The latter were transmitted in or together with the Old
Testament—by Christians, for whom they apparently were important.

A fourth group of texts, which should at least be mentioned, certainly
within this book, are those parts of the New Testament that originated
in the Holy Land. In the treatment of the sources, Bible scholars and
historians customarily maintain the traditional division in which the
New Testament counts as 'Christian' and hence not 'Jewish'. The earliest phase of Christianity, however, took place entirely within Judaism,
so that this division of the sources is not valid: note, for instance, the
Jewish-Christian epistles of James and Jude, which were probably written in the Holy Land. This group of writings is treated in Chapter 8.

An important question is: in what languages were all these works written? For the Apocrypha and Pseudepigrapha this is often difficult to
determine. Many were preserved only in translation, or in translations
of translations. Greek was an important intermediary as the trade language of the Hellenistic and the (Eastern) Roman Empire. It is plausible
that often the original language was Hebrew or Aramaic. For some of
these works, this has been confirmed: a Hebrew text of the greater part
of Jesus Sirach or Ben Sira was recovered, and in Qumran Aramaic fragments were found of two pseudepigrapha—the Apocalypse of Enoch
and Jubilees. Furthermore, the characteristic writings of the sect at
Qumran are all in Hebrew, although Aramaic and Greek writings were
also found in their library. The main part of rabbinic literature is likewise in Hebrew. As spoken Hebrew became limited to prayers and
scholarly discussions, later rabbinic texts were drafted in Aramaic.
Large sections of the populace did not understand Hebrew, as is apparent from the *targum*, 'translation', that accompanied the Torah reading
in the synagogues. Aramaic, a language intermediate between Hebrew
and Arabic, was, as already mentioned, the lingua franca of the Persian
Empire, which also included the Holy Land. Many Jews in the Holy
Land, just as in Babylonia and other eastern regions, evidently continued to use Aramaic as a colloquial language.

From this it can be deduced that Palestinian Jewry in the first century
was multilingual. Certainly among the educated and the city dwellers,
many had mastered Greek. With numerous pilgrims in Jerusalem, Greek
was spoken, and particularly in the cities and coastal regions Greek was

used for prayers and readings in many synagogues (see p. 178). If the epistles of Jude and James indeed originated in the Holy Land, then excellent Greek was written there as well. The tombstones of the third and fourth centuries are mostly written in Greek only. In contrast, the somewhat older ossuaries and the synagogue inscriptions are often bilingual—Greek and Aramaic. Aramaic was the language that bonded the Jews with the East, and that was used in daily life in Galilee and on the eastern bank of the Jordan. The uniquely Jewish language remained Hebrew, called by the rabbis 'the holy tongue' (*lāshôn ha-qodeš*). Remarkably, practically all prayers from Qumran and in the rabbinic tradition are in Hebrew. This is also true of all parables, a consistent element in the sermons for the people, preserved by the thousands in the Talmud. Excavated texts confirm that at the beginning of the second century CE Hebrew was used as a language of correspondence and government in Judaea. The letters of the leaders during the second Jewish war (132–35 CE) and the archives of Babata, a well-to-do woman, are illustrative: the documents, dealing with everyday subjects, are composed in Aramaic, Hebrew, Greek and Nabataean (a language related to Arabic).

This multilingualism must be kept constantly in mind as the ancient Jewish and Jewish-Christian documents are interpreted. With the Greeks texts the possibility that the writer or translator also had Hebrew or Aramaic syntax in mind must be taken into account. What for us appear to be completely divorced spheres—ancient Jewish literature in Hebrew and in Greek—were for many Jew but two visages of one world of life and thought.

We will return to the Jews in the Holy Land and their writings after we have completed our tour past other Jewish places of residence.

Antioch, Asia Minor, Greece, Babylonia, Rome
Travelling northwards by land one arrived in *Antioch* on the Orontes, the present-day Antakia close to the Turkish 'bend'. In the Hellenistic period this was the capital of the kingdom of the Seleucides that stretched to Babylon and further eastward. For that time, it was a large city and, besides being the seat of government, it was also an important crossroads for merchants between Syria and Asia Minor, Egypt and Greece. Its prominent Jewish community had equal civil rights and lived in a remarkably open relationship with the non-Jewish fellow citizens (Josephus, *War* 7.43-45). Undoubtedly this contributed significantly to

the fact that Antioch became the first centre of Christianity outside of the Holy Land (see Acts 11–15); the distance from the latter was after all only a couple of days' travel.

Most Antiochians probably spoke Greek, although there are indications that the Aramaic of the Syrian–Babylonian hinterlands was also used. There is little more to report than that Jews lived in Antioch. We have no Jewish writings from the many cities northwards and westwards from Antioch where important Jewish communities were, such as *Tarsus*, *Miletus*, *Ephesus* and *Sardis*, unless we count the few letters that Paul possibly wrote in Ephesus, or the Revelation of John recorded on the Isle of Patmos, offshore from the same city (1 Cor. 16.8; Rev. 1.9). Even from the western Asia Minor *Pergamum*, which after Alexandria possessed the largest library of the Hellenistic world, we know of no Jewish writings. Across the Aegean Sea lies the ancient abode of the Greeks where there were many Jewish communities, as is apparent, for example, from the New Testament. In Corinth, the inscription 'Synagogue of the Hebrews' has been recovered (third century CE or later).

One could also travel in an easterly direction from Antioch. Following the caravan route, one first came past *Edessa* and *Nisibis* in present-day Syria, where Jewish communities of some reknown were situated. Somewhat more southerly was *Doura Europos*, where in the third century a synagogue was decorated with extensive frescos. The excavation of these murals provided surprising insight into the existence of a flowering Jewish iconographic tradition that reflects many links with the imaginative Scripture interpretation in rabbinic and other ancient Jewish writings.

Further towards the east and south, on the Euphrates and the Tigris in present-day Iraq, were Diaspora communities in the region of ancient *Babylon* and *Seleucia*, a former Greek colony. These Diaspora communities are important in that they remained outside of the Graeco-Roman sphere of influence during the period that concerns us. The Middle Persian or Parthian Empire (from the second century BCE on) and especially the New Persian Empire of the Sassanids (from the third century CE on) brought a powerful anti-western and later also anti-Christian climate. Greek disappeared definitely and Aramaic remained the medium of communication for the Jews. The rabbinic academies that functioned in Babylonia from the third century CE onwards gained in importance when the Jewish communities in the Holy Land were weakened by the opposition from the Christian empire. From the eighth century onwards, the Babylonians acquired the spiritual leadership of the Jews, which explains the decisive significance of the Talmud version that emerged from Babylonia. For the same reason, the Palestinian Talmud and many Palestinian Jewish midrashim slipped into a mediaeval oblivion and were rescued from this only by modern Jewish scientific endeavours.

These considerations bring us back for a moment to the disappearance of Greek-speaking Jewry and its literature. Palestinian and Babylonian Jewries demonstrate clearly the extent to which the lot of Jewish communities and writings was dependent on external factors. This strengthens our suspicion that something of the same nature affected Greek-speaking Jewry. Possibly an important role was played by two successive, contrasting fields of power: antipathy for the empire, which in the meantime had become Christian, and, a couple of centuries later, the influence of the Arab conquest. Undeniably, the position of the Jews in the Roman Empire deteriorated after Emperor Constantine pronounced Christianity as the privileged religion at the beginning of the fourth century. It is thus understandable that the Jews hailed the Arab conquest of the largest part of the Byzantine (East Roman) Empire in the seventh century as a liberation. This meant not only the installation of Islam in previously Christian areas, but also the suppression of Greek by Arabic.

Possibly the disappearance of Greek as a Jewish means of communication and literature was hereby determined. From the eighth century onwards we see in the east and in Spain the emergence of a new written language for the Jews—Arabic. Philosophical interests were given ample attention. The classical philosophical texts were made available in Arabic by the intermediary of multilingual Syriac Christians. Here we glimpse the total eclipse of Greek as international language of culture, until its rediscovery in the Renaissance. It becomes more and more understandable that the Jews did not preserve their Greek writings, in contrast to those in Hebrew, Aramaic and Arabic.

We pursue our tour once more to end in the capital of the Roman Empire, where emperor and senate resided. When the apostle Paul arrived in Rome in approximately 60 CE (Acts 28), there was already a large and prominent Jewish community there. Jewish cemeteries from several centuries later witness to a great number of Jews and to the importance that they placed in tradition. In the Talmud we hear of diverse travels by prominent rabbis from the Holy Land to Rome, no doubt to settle religious, juridical and financial matters for the community. We get the impression that it was a large, and at least partially traditional, law-observing Jewish community.

Apparently, a portion of the historical works of Joseph ben Mattityahu originated in Rome where he came to be called *Flavius Josephus* after his patron, Vespasian of the house of Flavii. Coming from a prominent priestly family of Jerusalem, he became a local commander in the revolt against Rome, but capitulated quickly and ended up in the court of the Roman general and later emperor Vespasian. The latter treated him royally and gave him a house in Rome and an allowance (*Life* 423). He was, thus, not a Jewish war hero, and perhaps his writings serve to compensate for that fact. In any case he wrote prolifically: first a report on the war, quite shortly after the event and, according to his own statement, originally in Aramaic (*The Jewish War*, see 1.3, 6); about ten years later a general survey of the whole of Jewish history (*Jewish Antiquities*); thereafter, an autobiography with again much attention given to his own conduct (*Life*). A fourth work that has been preserved is the already mentioned apologetic for the Jews against anti-Jewish allegations like those of Apion. His later works were completed under Emperor Domitian (81–96 CE, see *Life* 429). The unpropitiousness of later years of this emperor's reign for the Jews and even more so for the Christians (see pp. 243, 373) could have given Josephus extra impetus to defend the Jews and his own person.

Though Josephus's need for self-justification must be taken into account, his works are of great significance for at least three reasons. First, he wrote his later works in Greek, and if he did indeed do that in Rome, this speaks volumes concerning the importance of Greek in the Roman Empire at the end of the first century. Secondly, he wrote for a non-Jewish public, which thus exposed the exceptional position of the Jews within the empire. Thirdly, and most importantly, he provides a treasure of information on the war, the Jewish community and the world of his day. In particular his information about the different movements within the Holy Land will occupy our attention later.

The works of Josephus, as those of Philo, have been preserved by Christians. Augustine was the first to use the expression that the Jews were the 'librarians' of the Christians: they granted them the Scriptures, the Old Testament (*Enarr. in Ps.* 56.9). To this is attached the implication that, having fulfilled their commission, they could be dismissed.

In any case, in turn the Christians became archivists for the Jews. Without the writings of Josephus and Philo, the Septuagint and the pseud-epigrapha preserved by Christians, our knowledge of ancient Judaism and Jewry would be significantly less.

Jewish Movements and Writings in the Holy Land

We return to the Holy Land and continue there on a smaller scale our tour of Jewish milieus and their literary productions. In the previous section, we could not do justice to an important characteristic of the Palestinean Jewry of that day, namely, the multiplicity of movements and parties. This is essential to the understanding not only of ancient Jewish writings, but also of the New Testament. A complicating issue is connected to this. In the first place, our sources are both fragmentary and prejudiced. The characterization given of a competing group could vary considerably depending on how the group wishes to portray itself. It is an intricate puzzle of which we have only a few pieces and these are, furthermore, disformed and tainted. Yet this is not the whole picture.

Not only are the pieces of this puzzle discoloured, but the vision of the puzzler is also distorted. Significant pieces have been passed down in the one religious community or the other as normative texts: the New Testament within Christianity and rabbinic literature within Judaism. To a lesser extent this is also true of many ancient Jewish writings that have been transmitted within Christianity and have there become familiar (Septuagint with the Apocrypha and Pseudepigrapha, Philo and Josephus). Such a centuries-long reading within a certain community has shrouded the texts with authoritative interpretations determinant for the image of one's 'own' party and 'the other' party. In so far as each reader is formed within one of the two religious traditions, he or she has received an accompanying prejudiced image of 'the other party'. We must therefore check critically the use that we make of the sources, especially of the most familiar sources. We must even be critical of our self-criticism: well-meaning reactions against traditional prejudices can have a distorting effect as well. One could, as a well-meaning Christian, idealize everything Jewish, or as a 'self-critical' Jew give priority to anything that diverges from the Talmud.

A critical use of sources is not novel. What is new in our days is the awareness of the involvement of the researcher. It is not sufficient to investigate whether a writing gives a misshapen representation of a certain group: we are obliged also to inquire as to how we ourselves stand in relation to that image, in relation to that group or that writing. Concretely: from a Christian or a Jewish background, how is the negative image of the Pharisees in the New Testament and their generally positive image in the Talmud to be dealt with? How are we to relate to the negative image of Christianity in the Talmud and its positive image in the New Testament? If one were to pause here for a moment, one could realize that primary feelings of identification with or aversion to one's own spiritual forefathers play a role. Traditional distortions are related to this. In order to read in a purer manner, we should see through our own vilifying or idealizing feelings towards our 'own' party and 'the other' party and allow each its rightful place. The idealization of 'former enemies' is just as untrustworthy a compass. Were not *some* Pharisees indeed formalistic and rigid in their faithfulness to the law? Were there not from the beginning *certain* Christians who viewed the law as done with and Judaism as an outmoded fallacy?

Less clearly, the same mechanisms are at work as well in the interpretation of newly discovered sources, such as the Essene scrolls from Qumran or the Gnostic writings from Nag Hammadi. The joy of discovery can even at times lead to comical exaggeration. In the excited publicity over the inexplicably slow publication of a number of scrolls, tales even circulated about a conspiracy between the Vatican and the orthodox rabbinate. The actual causes were primarily competition and jealousy between scholars, who in the end are only human. In all the commotion, it is essential to remain extra alert to the mentioned mechanism. How easy is it to use the new sources to strengthen the familiar image of one's 'own' and 'the other' party and thus from the very start fail to see the unique significance of these sources! Even stronger, if possible, is the tendency to ascribe an invulnerable authority to the newly discovered sources, as though they were an alternative revelation or Holy Writ.

This accentuated warning to be critical and self-critical in reading is fitting now that we are going to deal with the main currents of Judaism of the first century. Our information on these comes in the first place from Josephus, who repeatedly speaks of a threesome: *Essenes, Sadducees* and *Pharisees* (*War* 2.119-66; *Ant.* 13.171-73; 18.11-22; *Life* 10). Is this set division into three not too schematic? Are there no movements outside of Josephus's field of vision? Do other sources, for example, the New Testament, perhaps tell about these? We will hold on to these questions while first listening to what the various sources tell us about the three main movements.

Qumran and the Essene Writings
Because of their well-circumscribed dating and the specific site where they were found, as well as their excentric position in relation to the other ancient Jewish writings, the scrolls which have been found since 1947 at Qumran by the Dead Sea are a good starting point. Only the characteristic writings of the group that resided there will be discussed and not the many biblical texts and texts from other already known sources that were also there in large numbers.

One of the typical sectarian writings, the *Manual of Discipline* or *Community Rule*, has been recovered in fragments of as many as 12 copies and was apparently considered to be an extremely important document. In it the distinctive features of the group are described in terms of strong contrasts to the outside world, and strict rules are given for the admission of new members and for the punishment of offenders. The goal is 'to be a unity with respect to the Torah and to possessions' (1QS 5.2). The *Damascus Document* or *Zadokite Document* comprises a collection of rules of conduct that in form strongly resemble rabbinic halakah, but which consistently diverge from the latter in strictness. Of importance is also a *halakic letter* in which the correct rules and laws are pointed out to people from outside of the sect (4QMMT); in this the calendar plays an important role (see pp. 79-80). A fourth text, the *Temple Scroll*, paraphrases a portion of the Torah and provides commentary to the biblical rules for the priest by making them stricter in a characteristic manner. Qua form it is a rewriting of the Torah revealed to Moses. A collection of *Psalms of Thanksgiving* has been found whose hallmark is the feeling of sinfulness and total dependency upon the will of God. Mention must also be made of the so-called *War Rule*, a detailed description of the great battle at the end of time, in which the members of the community stand in the vanguard facing the hosts of Darkness. Of importance is, finally, the genre of the *pesher*, 'interpretation', in which passages from the prophets are consistently given an unequivocal, historical explanation.

From these writings a spiritual movement is depicted that lived in community of goods and who viewed the world in a *dualistic* or literally black-and-white manner, which correctly may be called 'sectarian'.

By virtue of divine predestination, the community members count as 'children of light' and are led by the angels of light; the rest of the Jews and of humanity fall under the ruler of darkness and his cohorts. Thus we read at the beginning of the *Manual of Discipline*:

> In order to observe God's laws in the covenant of grace, to be one in the counsel of God and to walk perfectly before his presence...and to love all the children of light, each according to his lot in the counsel of God, and to hate all the children of darkness, each according to his guilt to the vengeance of God... (1QS 1.7-10).

The use of the verbs 'to love' and 'to hate' in combination with 'the children of light' and 'the children of darkness' is striking. Such dualism is not to be found in the Old Testament and must go back to other roots. The influence of the Iranian religion via the period of Persian domination (539–330 BCE) seems the most likely. The dualistic portrayal of mankind and of the world is dramatically delineated in the strict admission and punishment procedures that demarcate the sect from the rest of the Jews and of humanity. These procedures are structured as a set of concentric circles differentiated by a gamut of rules of purification and of punishments. Theologically the leaders of the sect considered themselves to be the vanguard of the imminent end times. The approach to the Scriptures is characterized by an *apocalyptic* manner of thought: the course of history is full of enigmas and secrets that, however, are communicated by revelation to the chosen.

All of these traits resemble strongly the description of the sect of the *Essenes* given by Josephus and Philo. They lived unmarried, without personal belongings, in community of goods, and according to strict rules of purification. Dressed in white, they were conspicuous wherever they went. Their centre was in the desert, but they also lived in small groups scattered throughout the country. Moreover, they maintained some variety in their living customs and there was a minority that did not reject marriage (Josephus, *War* 2.119-62).

There are also differences between what is depicted in Qumran writings and the descriptions of Josephus and Philo, but the importance of these should not be exaggerated. The sect was extremely impenetrable and kept its writings secret so that the information of Philo and Josephus can not be taken as indisputable. Furthermore, during the more than two centuries of its existence and through the scattered manner of living, shifts could have taken place. The excavated scrolls themselves also exhibit variations in details. Even the Essenes apparently did not form a monolithic movement. They lived in different locations, of which the most important was Qumran, and they did not maintain a completely uniform lifestyle. A further unknown group about which Philo writes idealizingly, the 'Therapeuts' (Philo, *The Contemplative Life*), also indicates that there was variation. These lived by a lake in the neighbourhood of Alexandria and, like the Essenes, divided their time between praying, Bible study and labour. As did the latter, these lived soberly, but the group comprised women and men who together participated in the liturgy.

A matter of particular significance is the *interpretation of Scripture* in Qumran. All indications point to a strict and straightforward attitude towards the written text. The essence of the *pesher* is to give the only correct interpretation of a prophetic text in view of the contemporary situation. This becomes even clearer in comparison to the Pharisaic–rabbinic tradition in which 'another interpretation' can always be offered. The same is true of the interpretation of legal texts. The Temple Scroll paraphrases the laws of the Torah as indicated, making them stricter, without allowing for other interpretations. Probably partially for this reason, it appears, the Essenes from Qumran thought up the nickname 'interpreters of slippery things' for the Pharisees (4QpNah 1.2; 2.4-6). 'Slippery things', in Hebrew *halaqôt*, could be an intentional misrepresentation of *halakôt*, the Pharisees' legal rules. In this context the expression *talmud šᵉqārim*, 'explanation of lies', is striking, evidently a scoffing distortion of the Pharisaic interpretation or *talmud* (4QpNah 2.8).

It is remarkable that the Essenes are not mentioned, or perhaps only indirectly, in the New Testament and in rabbinic literature. Philo and Josephus, on the contrary, describe the Essenes extensively and admiringly, while they themselves have more or less affinity with the Pharisaic–rabbinic way of thinking and are at least as temperate as the New Testament authors were. Why the difference? One must keep in mind that Philo and Josephus attempt to give a intriguing and respectable portrayal of Judaism to a partially non-Jewish audience. The intended readership was accustomed to the practice of Hellenistic writers to write extensively about exotic customs and notions, and giving the Essenes thorough attention fits into this. The New Testament and rabbinic literature, in contrast, are intended for insiders and hardly have the pretence of intriguing the well-read outsider. Even Luke and Acts involve the reader in the Palestinian–Jewish context and its manner of life. Thus the

impression is given that the Essenes, who considered the rest of the
Jews to be apostates or unbelievers, and who kept their own teachings
anxiously secret, were in turn avoided by the majority of the Palestinian
Jews and were intentionally ignored.

Nonetheless, the importance of the Qumran scrolls for the understanding of the New Testament was uncontested as soon as they were
discovered. All kinds of expressions previously ascribed to non-Jewish
influences were encountered in these scrolls in a specific Jewish context. Taboo would have prevented the New Testament authors from
directly quoting from Essene sources. We must therefore conclude that
there was a sort of intermediate area where more or less Essene-tinted
ideas circulated without actually coinciding with the Essenes. Thus we
get a better idea of the significance of terms like 'the light of the world',
'the prince of darkness', 'the children of light', 'the works of the law',
'to be justified' (before God) and 'the New Covenant'. While previously scholars had ascribed many of these terms to direct Hellenistic
influence, it was now apparent that they derived from particular Jewish
milieus. External influences upon the New Testament—not to be forgotten, the Iranian—are certainly possible but usually these will have
come via contemporary Judaism.

For the interpretation of rabbinic literature, the Qumran scrolls are
also of great significance. In the first place, early traditions can be dated
better by comparison to the scrolls whose age is archaeologically determined. Further, contrast with the sect produces a sharper picture of
the social position of the Pharisees. Third, the Essene combination of
apocalyptic thinking with strict legal practice saves us from the traditional fallacy of contrasting 'apocalyptic' and 'legalistic Pharisaic'
Judaism. In short, the Qumran scrolls enable us to arrive at a more
nuanced representation of the diversity of the rabbinic tradition in its
historical development.

The Pharisees and Rabbinic Tradition

The Pharisaic–rabbinic tradition deserves special attention. In the first
place, this tradition is the main source of contemporary Judaism and
is, therefore, of great religious and theological importance to Jews and
Christians alike, whatever stance is assumed. Secondly, rabbinic literature, in which the traditions of the Pharisees are incorporated, is the
largest and thematically the most multifaceted collection of ancient
Jewish writings and is therefore indispensable for studying ancient

Jewish texts and history. Thirdly, both because of its volume and diversity and because of particular intrinsic correspondences, this literature is a first-class source for the historical background of the New Testament.

Using rabbinic literature for studying the first century CE saddles us, however, with serious difficulties. Because rabbinic literature was only committed to writing at a late date, a trustworthy dating of older traditions is dependent on external sources. More particularly, the transition from the 'Pharisaic movement' to rabbinic Judaism was accompanied by extensive alterations. Rabbinic information on the period before 70 CE must thus be verified by external sources. An especially bothersome problem is, for example, that the name 'Pharisee' is used diversely in various sources and evidently did not have the same meaning in all milieus. Specifically in reference to the term 'Pharisee' we must pay close attention to the hidden interplay between the images that the sources offer and those that we as readers already have in mind. This important and complicated part of our puzzle can best be approached by observing the relevant pieces separately.

Rabbinic literature began to acquire its fixed written form from the third century BCE onwards. As regards content, however, it identifies itself explicitly with the teachings of leading figures from the time antedating the destruction of the temple, teachers such as Hillel, Gamaliel and Yohanan ben Zakkai. Rabbinic literature only rarely uses the term 'Pharisees' for these leaders and their followers. The word means 'separatists' and is seldom used to refer to a certain fixed faction. An exception is formed by the succinct and seemingly ancient report about debates between 'the Pharisees' and other groups, including the Sadducees, about parts of the law (*m. Yad.* 4.6-7). The account must antedate the destruction of the temple because after that point the Sadducees are heard of no more. The likelihood of this dating is confirmed by the close correspondence in content with the halakhic letter from Qumran (4QMMT). The significance of this exceptional communication is that the rabbinic tradition identifies itself with the 'Pharisees' by the fact that the important rabbinic leader Yohanan ben Zakkai expressly, although not without irony, acts a spokesman for 'the Pharisees'.

In contrast, after the destruction of the temple, rabbinic literature uses the standard designation 'rabbi' for Torah teachers. From the end of the first century CE onwards this was used as the title of an officially ordained scribe. This distinction functions very precisely: previous

Torah teachers are not called 'rabbi'; thus we find 'Shammai and Hillel' and never 'rabbi Shammai and rabbi Hillel', although these count as 'fathers of the world' (*m. 'Ed.* 1.4). The designation 'rabbi' with which Jesus is incidentally addressed was of a non-institutional nature (Mk 9.5; Jn 1.38, provided with a translation!). It was a respectful form of address, corresponding to its literal significance: 'my master'. Only later was this employed for the designation of an ordained 'rabbi'. In short, although the movement of Shammai and Hillel and the group of Yohanan's disciples before 70 CE had no fixed designation in the rabbinic literature, the very same group thereafter bears the title 'rabbi', and we can correctly denote the works created by them as 'rabbinic literature'. We will return later to the difficulty that, simultaneous with this change, the 'Pharisaic' movement and tradition went through radical modifications.

There are two other groups of writings from the first century that employ the designation 'Pharisee' extensively: the writings of Josephus and the New Testament. Usually the authors of these writings use the term as though they themselves were outsiders. This happens, however, in various ways, and the difference can be traced within the New Testament. Within the Gospel of *Matthew*, the Pharisees are obvious opponents. Together with the scribes, they are attacked as 'hypocrites' who 'place heavy loads...upon the people' but who pursue honour and wealth for themselves (Mt. 23.2-7; see p. 273). In the two works *Luke and Acts*, which belong together, the situation is quite different: Pharisees warn Jesus concerning the enmity of Herod Antipas and 'are in honour among the whole people', and Paul boasts of his Pharisaic education from Gamaliel (Lk. 13.31; Acts 5.34; 22.3). In *Josephus* as well, the Pharisees do not have a negative reputation. He relates that the Pharisees enjoy much support among the people, and that all prayers as well as temple rituals should be executed according to their interpretation (*Ant.* 13.298; 18.15). In his autobiography addressed to non-Jewish readers, Josephus declares that in his youth he had finally decided to live his life according to the tradition of the Pharisees (*Life* 12).

How is this contradictory use of the term 'Pharisee' to be explained? The most obvious would be to say that originally it was an extraneous term, not in the first place used by the group itself, nor by the rabbinic writings that identified with them. The reports of the debates with the Sadducees confirm, however, that the term does refer to the predecessors of the rabbis. Taking into account the ironic distance with which Yohanan ben Zakkai applied the appellation to himself, it could be that the designation was understood to be one used by those outside of this group.

The connotations and denotations of the term itself could strengthen this presupposition. The Greek *pharisaioi* derives from the Aramaic *parishaya* which equals the Hebrew *p^erûšîm*, literally 'separated ones'. The verbal root *paraš* in the term is also found in an adage of Hillel, as well as in the halakhic letter from Qumran. The maxim used to be rather inscrutable: 'Hillel says, *do not separate yourself* from the community' (*m. Ab.* 2.4). The halakhic letter from Qumran throws new light on this, where, with reference to certain legal rules, it states: 'We, however, *have separated ourselves* from the majority of the [people…]' (4QMMT 92).

Similar statements are to be found elsewhere in rabbinic literature. The same word is explicitly used for *separatists* who 'have separated themselves from the ways of the community' (*t. Ber.* 3.25; *S. 'Ol. R.* 3.9a). Thus the group to which Hillel and Yohanan ben Zakkai belonged did not accept the designation 'Pharisees' for themselves, but used it for 'separatists' like the Essenes. The expression 'the plague of the Pharisees' ascribed to R. Yoshua (end of first century; *m. Soṭ.* 3.4) is extremely negative. Further, there is an anonymous and apparently ancient tradition that lists seven different sorts of 'Pharisees'. The first five of these are ridiculed as uncongenial, and only the last one is praiseworthy: 'the Pharisee out of love' (*y. Ber.* 9.7, 13b). This list of seven hardly expresses enthusiasm about the lifestyle of the 'Pharisees'.

How can it be that the 'Pharisees' are designated by Josephus and in the New Testament by a name that they themselves use negatively? We get the impression that it is a kind of nickname, which, just like *gueux*, 'beggars', the nickname for the disorderly liberators of Den Briel in the south of Holland in 1572, later became an honorary designation. In reference to the Pharisees, there is a possible connection with the rabbinic tradition about the rules of admission to the 'fellowship' (*ḥabura*) in which in particular regulations concerning tithes and cleanliness played a role (*t. Dem.* 2.2-5; cf. p. 350). There appears to have been a system of concentric demarcations within the group reminiscent of the Qumranic rules of admission, but in a less strict form. The kernel of this tradition impresses one as being ancient and could antedate 70 CE, given the affinity with Qumran. This core has to do with apparently semi-permanent groupings for keeping special rules for tithes and purity. The general goal was undoubtedly communal eating, praying and studying, just as in Qumran (1QS 6.1-3). The regulations involved could be identified in rabbinic literature as characteristic of the predecessors of the rabbis, that is, the 'Pharisees'. This is confirmed by recriminations in the Gospels about the typical 'Pharisaic' emphasis on tithes and purity (Lk. 11.39). On the other hand, the rabbinic tradition about praiseworthy and uncongenial Pharisees could indicate that there was disagreement about the general applicability of these regulations. There are also other grounds for the impression of discord within the Pharisaic movement.

It could be that moderate or conservative opponents labelled the keeping of these special regulations as 'separatism'. They likely would have ignored the internal 'Pharisaic' discussion about the extent of the applicability of these regulations and lumped all 'Pharisees' together. Writers like Josephus and Luke, who wrote for non-Jewish outsiders, could apparently use this title without uncharitable intentions. In contrast, the Gospel of Matthew, which shows signs of a sharp confrontation with the 'Pharisees', carries on the negative use of the name.

In summary, Hillel, Gamaliel and Yohanan ben Zakkai and other predecessors of the rabbinic tradition belonged to a group that Josephus and the author of Luke and Acts affably designate as 'Pharisees'. According to both authors, these were held in high regard by all; furthermore, according to Josephus, community prayers and temple worship were carried out according to their tradition. This is confirmed by comparison with the halakhic letter from Qumran and the discussion between the Sadducees and the Pharisees in the Mishnah.

The tradition of the Pharisees and the rabbis is of a special nature. In contrast to the Sadducees, they maintained only an oral tradition of Scripture interpretation and clarification of the law. The reasons for this are difficult to fathom, but respect for the written letter of Scripture plays an important role, as well as the realization that the vicissitudes of life and society demand a flexible legislation. This flexibility aroused the irritation not only of the Sadducees, but apparently also of the Essenes (see above p. 49). A document like the Temple Scroll demonstrates further that the Essenes had no objection to committing their scriptural and legal interpretations to writing, which could even assume the form of an imitation of the Torah. From the Pharisaic–rabbinic tradition eventually rabbinic literature arose, which we will discuss at the end of this chapter.

The Sadducees

As far as our sources go, the Sadducees come off badly. None of their own writings have been preserved and we have to go on reports passed on by their opponents. It is difficult to arrive at a coherent image of them.

The opponents of the Sadducees express themselves, for example, in rabbinic literature, where we also hear of the 'Boethusians', a family of high priests who evidently had a leading role among the Sadducees (cf. *ARN* A5 and B10.13b). Along with certain other powerful high priestly families, they are charged with greediness and exploitation of the offerings and temple goods (*t. Men.* 13.18-21). These high priestly families were not too popular to start with because two generations earlier they were hoisted into the saddle by Herod, a bloodthirsty despot of dubious lineage (Josephus, *Ant.* 15.320-22). The Sadducees and Boethusians were further criticized because of their uncompromising severity in penal law and their adherence to the literal and rigid interpretation of the Scriptures, as is testified in the following excerpt from the rabbinic commentary to *Megillat Ta'anit*, an old list of feast days during which one may not fast or bury:

> 'Upon the fourth of Tammuz the Book of Decrees became defunct'. For a Book of Decrees was written down and deposited with the Sadducees: 'These are to be stoned, these are to be burnt, these are to be decapitated, these are to be strangled'. Were one to ask them during the session, then they showed the book; were one to ask for argumentation...then they knew not how to answer. The Sages said to them: Is it not written, 'According to [literally: to the *mouth* of] the Tora which they teach you' (Deut. 17.11)—that teaches us that halakhot are not to be written down. Another interpretation: 'The Book of Decrees'. For the Boethusians were accustomed to saying: 'An eye for an eye, a tooth for a tooth' (Exod. 21.24)—if someone hits another's tooth out, then he must hit one of his out; if someone makes another's eye blind, then he must make his eye blind, so that they are equal (*Megillat Ta'anit*, 4 Tammuz, p. 331).

There were evidently two different traditions concerning the meaning of the ancient 'Book of Decrees'. In any case it is possible to deduce that the Sadducees and the Boethusians were linked in some way and that with their rigid and cruel jurisdiction they rejected the Pharisees' dynamic and more humane oral interpretation of Scripture. This is confirmed by Josephus (*Ant.* 13.297). Their approach contrasted with the Pharisaic–rabbinic tradition, in which the following is passed on as a most ancient proverb: 'Be temperate in judgment' (*m. Ab.* 1.1). Furthermore, it is told that Sadducean and Boethusian high priests who wanted to conduct temple ritual in a manner that diverged from the Pharisaic rites were publicly derided by the people (*b. Suk.* 48b; *Ant.* 13.372; cf. p. 63).

In the *New Testament* as well, opponents of the Sadducees express themselves. Even the author of Luke and Acts, who for the remainder approaches Jewry in a nuanced manner, consistently describes the Sadducees as opponents of the Pharisees and as enemies of Jesus and his apostles. This writer confirms explicitly the connection with the temple and the circles of the high priest: '...the high priest and all who were with him, that is the party of the Sadducees' (Acts 5.17). These are the ones who time and again seek to execute Jesus' apostles and persecute his disciples (Acts 4.9). Their intolerance of apocalyptic themes, such as angels and the resurrection of the dead, which were highly important to the Pharisees (Lk. 21.27-40; Acts 23.1-9), makes them conspicuous. This is the same group that apparently condemned Jesus to death on the basis of his apocalyptic words: 'From now on shall the son of man be seated on the right hand of the power of God' (Lk. 22.66-71).

The picture given by rabbinic literature and by the New Testament is fully confirmed by *Josephus*. Naming the Sadducees several times as one of the three 'schools' of the Judaism of that time, he describes them as elitist, cruel in penal justice, fairly ignorant concerning the Scriptures, and sceptical of God's providence and care for creation. Futhermore, they formed a rich aristocracy hated by the people and forced, through the support of the people, to follow the Pharisaic rites in temple rituals (*Ant.* 13.294, 298; 18.16-17). We will return to their attitude towards Christians later.

An important point concerns the *liturgical calendar*. Certain notions of the Sadducees on this are remarkably akin to the principles adhered to in Qumran, in marked contrast to the Pharisaic tradition. The same is true concerning a number of other aspects of the temple ritual (pp. 81, 93). Though several elements give reason to reconsider the connections between the Sadducees and the Qumran scrolls, the vast difference in world view between the two groups excludes the possibility of a close affinity. The Sadducees were wary of anything having to do with eschatology and apocalyptics, while these were central issues for the Essenes. It is more probable that both groups adhered to the same ancient priestly tradition, while for centuries each group went its separate way.

The consensus of the diverse reports concerning the Sadducees is remarkable. It is unfortunate that our information on them comes from their opponents, in which respect as well, this rich elite suffered no lack... The depiction is consistently that of a hated oligarchy that, supported by the Romans, derived its riches from its power over the high priesthood and the temple activities. They also had a reputation of cruelty in penal jurisdiction that fell under the leadership of the high priest. On the other hand, they were forced in temple ritual to follow the popular customs such as formulated by the Pharisees. Their aversion to apocalyptic notions was proverbial and did not contribute to their popularity. With some irony apparently directed towards the Sadducees, it is stated in the Talmud that he who does not believe in the resurrection of the dead will not participate in it (*b. Sanh.* 90a). No more is heard of the Sadducees after the fall of the temple in 70 CE: the basis of their power had been razed.

Pious Individuals in between the Pharisees and the Essenes
It is necessary to return to Josephus's three-way division. A closer look reveals that, while the three groups indeed assumed a prominent place in first-century Judaism, the whole exhibited more subtilities and variegation.

There are two points where Josephus's schema does not hold. In the first place, following one of his standard references to *three* movements, he mentions a *fourth*, about which he says, 'While they share the opinions of the Pharisees in everything, they have an invincible urge for freedom because they have accepted God as sole lord and sovereign' (*Ant.* 18.23). From other details it becomes apparent that he is referring to the political activists against Rome, elsewhere denoted as 'Zealots' (*War* 2.651). These evidently formed less of a 'party' than did the fixed trio. What distinguished them was only the fact that they drew political conclusions from ideas that were common among the Pharisees. This matter will be taken up later when the Pharisaic schools are discussed. Perhaps the introduction of a fourth stream was intended to exonerate the Pharisees from having an anti-Roman attitude. Given the tensions under Domitian (see above p. 44), this is quite imaginable. The three-way division evidently was not crucial for Josephus, and one wonders whether perhaps he had borrowed it from one of his sources.

In the second place, that Josephus's presentation is schematized is apparent from his nearly total silence on the Christians. This is even more striking given their notorious fate in Rome, both under Nero and under Domitian during whose reign Josephus wrote his final works. On the other hand, his report on John the Baptist (see below) contains detailed information about the context from which Jesus emerged. Furthermore, in two accounts he mentions Jesus himself by name. In the first, Jesus is called 'a wise man, if he can be called a man', who was crucified by Pilate but on the third day again 'appeared alive', after whom 'the line of Christians is called' (*Ant.* 18.64). This could have an authentic core but in its present form must derive from the Christians who preserved Josephus's work for us. The other account is accepted as authentic by most scholars. It has to do with the Sadducean high priest Ananus (Hananya), who took advantage of a vacuum in the Roman goverment in the following manner:

> He called the sanhedrin of judges together and brought the brother of Jesus, the so-called Anointed One, whose name was James, before them, with certain other ones, and after having charged him with an infraction of the law, he delivered him over to be stoned. But all in the city who count as being the most moderate and specialized in the knowledge of the law had serious objections to this (*Ant.* 20.200-201).

The designation of James as 'the brother of Jesus' is detailed, while 'certain others'—evidently referring to the Christians—sounds conspicuously vague. It seems that Josephus had information about the Christians, but preferred not to call them by name. This could also be related to the difficulties under Domitian. Incidentally, this report does confirm the Sadducees' antagonism towards Jesus and his followers, in contrast to the moderate attitude of the Pharisees, evidently the ones referred to as the 'moderate law specialists'.

The three-partite division of Josephus should thus not be taken strictly. It refers to three obvious groups in the midst of a much larger society in which everything was shifting. Josephus's remarks about their size and influence point to the same conclusion: he mentions 4000 Essenes and 6000 Pharisees (*Ant.* 17.42; 18.20), while the elite Sadducees were certainly less numerous. Their limited numbers were not in proportion to the influence that he ascribed to them. The power of the Sadducees was, of course, backed by the foreign occupational forces, which was not the case with the Essenes and the Pharisees. Josephus declares repeatedly that the Pharisees were supported by the people upon whom they in turn had a determinant influence (*Ant.* 13.288). Josephus does not report such mutual sympathy with respect to the Essenes; however, the attention devoted to them is not adequately explained by their exotic attractiveness for non-Jewish readers. Philo, too, is expansive about the Essenes, and he mentions the same number of more than 4000 members (*Omn. Prob. Lib.* 75); nonetheless, his apologetic interest is again not sufficient reason for the attention he gives to them. The Essenes apparently had a greater 'radiation' than their actual numbers would seem to warrant.

This all means that outside of the 10,000 Essenes and Pharisees which Josephus mentions, there must have been countless sympathizers of both movements, and to that extent as well the three-partite division is not valid. In the case of the Pharisees, we wonder how correct the depiction is of an organization with limited membership in the first century. The widely enjoyed sympathy of the people consistently reported by Josephus points in any case to another aspect of the Pharisees, namely, their popular character, to which we will return later. A general consideration is that most people never join anything, and that a well-founded movement is by definition a small minority. In the case of the Pharisees we get the ambivalent impression of a popular movement that also had a more 'distinct' appearance. Perhaps this should be related to the 'fellowships' with special rules concerning tithes and purity, as well as to the noted disagreement within the Pharisaic circles as to the extent to which such rules were obligatory.

There is thus every reason to attempt to acquire more information about the vast grey areas outside of the main movements of the first century. In doing so, alertness is essential to recognize traces of sympathy for or kinship with the Essenes and the Pharisees outside of the writings ascribed to one movement or the other.

The first ones to attract attention are the pious individuals that do not fall under one of the three main movements, for example, John the Baptist, mentioned by Josephus in a report that is taken by most scholars to be trustworthy (*Ant.* 18.116-19). Just as in the Gospels, John is depicted as an ascete from the desert who preached a baptism of repentance and forgiveness of sins, and who did not spare himself by refraining from criticizing the governor because of his infringement of the Jewish law (see Chapter 2, pp. 99-100). Josephus's reports and the

Gospels confirm further the relative affinity of John to the environment of Jesus and his followers. Jesus let himself be baptized by John, and after his own time of preparation in the desert Jesus took over John's preaching and later defended him, although he also maintained a certain distance (Mt. 3–4; 11; Lk. 7). In spite of correspondences with the Essenes, such as asceticism, baptism by immersion and dwelling in the desert, John does not seem to have belonged to them. Towards the Pharisees as well John apparently maintained a critical attitude (Mk 2.18; Jn 1.24). John and his followers thus must have belonged to a border area between the Essenes and the Pharisees. The same must have been true of Jesus and his followers.

Josephus tells about yet another ascetic desert preacher, Bannus, by whom he himself had been instructed in his early years and who, like the Essenes, attached great importance to immersion (*Life* 11). Although the relationship to John, Jesus and the Essenes is otherwise unclear, this report strengthens the impression of there having been a large intermediate area in which such pious individuals operated.

Significantly, rabbinic literature also reports such figures, calling them the 'earlier *hasidim*'. There are reports of more than 20 of such *hasidim* between the first century BCE and the third century CE. One of the best known, Honi or Onias, is also mentioned by Josephus (see Chapter 3, p. 138). They are known for their emphasis on mercy instead of on Torah study, and on prayer rather than on rules of purity. In particular, miracles and healings brought about by prayer are ascribed to them. There was a mutually felt distance between them and the Pharisees, but no enmity. Although their piety perhaps entailed that during prayer they avoided the presence of women, women were given explicit attention, in marked contrast to the Essenes. Even in the few statements of them that have been preserved, the correspondences with Jesus are remarkable, the more so since almost all of these figures come from Galilee. Finally, there is a certain congruence between these *hasidim* and the so-called *Derek-Erets literature* that has been passed down within rabbinic tradition (see below).

We thus have two rough coordinates of the socio-religious context of Jesus and his disciples: the desert preachers, such as John the Baptist and Bannus, and the hasidim from rabbinic literature, all of whom operated in the intermediate area between the Essenes and the Pharisees. A further colouring of this area can come from the anonymous writings to which we now turn.

Apocrypha and Pseudepigrapha

A few more pieces of our puzzle are provided by the Apocrypha and Pseudepigrapha, Jewish writings preserved by Christians in or along-side the Old Testament. Only in their distinction from the rest do these writings appear to belong together, but in form and content they differ extensively. They can be roughly divided into two groups.

The first, called 'Apocrypha' in the Protestant tradition, stands closest to the Holy Scriptures. Though not included in the Hebrew Bible, they did become a part of the Septuagint. In part, this reflects the situation before 70 CE when there was as yet no consensus as to the compass of the Scriptures and, furthermore, no demand for such. This does not apply to the five books of the Torah, which had already fully settled into their fixed place several centuries BCE. That the canon of the prophetic books was not yet determined is apparent from the differences between the final Hebrew and Greek canons in the structure and sequence of the books. Even more marked differences are present in what later became the third division of the Hebrew Bible, the so-called *ketuvim*, 'Writings', containing such books as Esther, Chronicles, Proverbs, Song of Solomon and Ecclesiastes. Evidently, that portion of the Old Testament is involved that was last to be formed. One must keep in mind the gradual acceptance of certain writings in the synagogue reading practice. The formation of this portion of the Hebrew canon was apparently a slow process of growth. Although the discussion was formally rounded off towards the end of the first century CE, a century later prominent rabbis still differed about the application of the discussion to Song of Solomon, Ecclesiastes and Proverbs (*m. Yad.* 3.5). Books like Judith, 1 Maccabees and Jesus Sirach were eventually not counted by the rabbinic tradition as books to be read aloud as Holy Scripture, although they are quite akin in nature.

This same discussion was repeated later in Christian circles. The Roman Catholic Church follows the canon of the Septuagint and reads certain books in the liturgy that Protestants, following the rabbis, consider as books that should not be read aloud publicly. The difference is indicated by the ancient church appellation 'apocryphal', 'hidden'—books that are not to be read in the congregation. The Roman Catholic tradition calls them *deutero-canonical* books and reads from them during the summertime of the liturgical year.

From these books only one collection of wisdom proverbs stems from an author known by name, Yeshua ben Sira (Sirach). This prominent man lived in Jerusalem at the beginning of the second century BCE, attached much importance to the temple, and was averse to all extremism. He shows himself to be a kindred spirit not only to late biblical wisdom literature, but also to the Pharisees who arose as a movement some time after him. The same is true as well of the other Apocrypha whose authors are unknown. In style, Tobith, Judith and 1 Maccabees differ little from the canonical books, while in their manner of thought they are not unlike the rabbinic literature. The mutual sympathy between the Pharisees and the people in general witnessed to by Josephus is hereby indirectly confirmed.

The second remaining group of writings forms less of a unity. These are designated as 'Pseudepigrapha', 'quasi-attributed books', because part of them have the pretence of being a revelation recorded by such biblical figures as Enoch, Baruch, Ezra and Moses. A clear effort is made to exhibit connections with the biblical tradition, while on the other hand the writer observably, thus incompletely, hides himself behind his biblical hero. Another part of these writings supplements what later generations missed in the biblical account: exciting or touching biographical details, orations, prayers or letters. Here again perceptible compensations are involved.

In manner of thinking, many of these pseudepigrapha as well do not vary much from rabbinic literature. Their form, however, clashes with the characteristic Pharisaic respect for the written Bible text: these books observably and purposefully imitate a biblical pattern. Something comparable can be found in the *Temple Scroll* from Qumran that professes to be a revelation to Moses.

Some of these works exhibit in content a telling kinship to the Essene scrolls, particularly to the *Book of Jubilees*, which must be even older than the Qumran writings. Its basic form must have emerged in a separate movement of Judaism within which the Essene faction later was formed. Of direct importance to the New Testament is the *Apocalypse of Enoch* (*1 Enoch*), a compilation about angels, cosmic relations and visions of the end times. Hebrew and Aramaic fragments of *Jubilees* and *Enoch* have been found in Qumran, where they assumed an important place. There is explicit reference to a 'book of the divisions of times into their jubilees and heptades' (CD 16.3-4), a reference strongly reminiscent of the *Book of Jubilees*, referring to the solar calendar, which not only in *Jubilees* and *Enoch* but also in the Qumran community played a crucial role (see p. 80).

Although the Pseudepigrapha did not in the least form a unity, they can be roughly placed in the amorphous area between the periphery of the Essenes and the nucleus of the Pharisees. A minority is closer to the Essenes, the majority closer to the Pharisees, but in their written form they all digress from the characteristic Pharisaic oral tradition. It is a telling fact that the production of these writings gradually stopped after the end of the first century CE, when the spiritual leadership fell to the Pharisees and the Essenes and Sadducees disappeared from the scene.

Before 70 CE, apparently one could be mentally akin to the Pharisees without adhering to their principle that commentary on the Scriptures must remain oral. One could, in other words, be sympathetic to the movement, even actively if necessary, without identifying oneself with it. There were uncounted gradations possible as to form and content, on a scale that went from the perimeter of the Essenes to the core of the Pharisees. With this sketch in mind, we can also better situate Greek-writing Diaspora Jews, such as Josephus and Philo. Although related in thinking to the 'Pharisaic middle', Josephus even being a declared adherent, these Diaspora Jews could write unhindered their histories and Bible commentaries and in no way come to the fore as representatives of the Pharisaic movement. Our historical reconstruction is hereby confirmed. The Pharisees and their legal tradition enjoyed the general trust of a greater portion of Jews in the Holy Land and in the Diaspora. In their specific rules of the fellowships, however, they formed but a small minority alongside or opposite the Essenes and the Sadducees. After 70 CE, this multiformity ended: the spiritual authority of the Pharisees became formalized among a large portion of the people and rabbinic Judaism emerged; this will be treated further later.

Certain pseudepigrapha show an unusual relatedness to the earliest Jewish-Christian tradition. In particular the so-called *Testaments of the Twelve Patriarchs* contains a type of moral and ethical admonition strongly resembling the Sermon on the Mount and other passages of the teachings of Jesus, as well as the Epistle of James and the *Didache*. This affinity localizes the context of earliest Christianity within the scale sketched. The cradle of Christianity and the sources of the preaching of Jesus and his disciples must have been at approximately equally great 'socio-religious distance' from the Essenes as from the Pharisees. In this connection, the rabbinic *Derek-Erets* treatises should be mentioned—short tractates of ethical and moral admonitions and unusual piety—as well as the work called *Seder Eliyahu Rabba*. In their exceptional devoutness and ethics these texts distinguish themselves from the whole of the rabbinic literature and betray kinship with the environment of Jesus and other 'pious individuals'.

Based on the information of a century ago, exegetes came to presume that there was a movement that applied itself to revelations or 'apocalypses'. The movement was viewed in particular as being behind the then just rediscovered apocalypses, such as that of Enoch and Baruch. This hypothetical apocalyptic Judaism was distinguished sharply from the legalistic, Pharisaic–rabbinic Judaism. In one fell swoop, the Qumran scrolls have made this division obsolete since this Essene community can be typified as both 'legalistic' and 'apocalyptic'.

Shammaites, Hillelites and Rabbinic Judaism
A final refinement of the picture of Palestinian Judaism in the first century can be gained from a further consideration of the Pharisaic movement, which also entails a further correction of Josephus's schematic tripartite division. Thereafter, rabbinic literature, the collection of writings that form the most important source in this matter, will be discussed.

Internal differences among the Pharisees are of primary importance. Mention has already been made of the fellowships that in one way or another were connected to the Pharisaic movment, the internal criticism of the immoderate attitude of certain Pharisees, and the tension between the popularity and the 'separateness' of their movement. The impression of diversity among the Pharisees is strengthened when note is taken of the two schools that, according to rabbinic literature, swayed the sceptre until the destruction of the temple—the schools of followers of Shammai and of Hillel. Besides theological disputes, such as on the question of whether or not the creation of man was a blessing, hundreds of debates between the Shammaites and the Hillelites concerning the correct interpretation of the law are reported (cf. *b. 'Erub.* 13b; *m. Ber.* 8; *M. 'Ed.* 1).

Two distinct basic attitudes are expressed: in contrast to the more conservative and strict approach of the followers of Shammai, Hillel's followers exhibit a more pliable and imaginative attitude. The sources give the impression that in the years antedating the war against Rome, the Shammaites were in the majority. Particularly due to the flexibility of the Hillelites, and in accordance with Hillel's rule that one should not 'separate oneself from the community', the relationship between the two schools remained congenial in spite of differences of opinion (*t. Yeb.* 1.10). Probably particularly inspired by the Hillelite legacy, the Pharisaic–rabbinic tradition highly values differences of opinion and the discussion in which each party possesses at most but a finite portion of divine truth.

There are, however, also reports of an incident at the beginning of the war against Rome in which tensions mounted so high that the Shammaites took up arms and precipitated a carnage among the Hillelites. Apparently, in this instance a number of foodstuffs of non-Jews, such as oil, bread and cheese, were declared forbidden (*y. Šab.* 1.3c). Other sources seem to corroborate the impression that the Shammaites belonged to the hard core of the revolt usually denoted as the Zealots. The incident was a radical aggravation under circumstances of war, but it should warn us not to underestimate the seriousness of the differences which must have existed in order for such to occur.

The Zealot attitude of the Shammaites is perhaps partially the reason for their later minority position. There is a rabbinic legend about a heavenly voice that pronounced a decision in the discussion between Shammaites and Hillelites as follows: 'Both are words of the living God, but the halakah is according to the school of Hillel' (*y. Ber.* 1.3b; see Chapter 9, p. 418). This paradoxical explanation is appealing, but nonetheless legendary. The simplest assumption is that the Shammaites, due to their greater participation in the catastrophic defeat, came to be a minority. The war had even more disastrous consequences for the Sadducees and the Essenes who thereafter disappear from our sources. Incidentally the reason for the slaughter among these two groups must have been different. Perhaps the Sadducees were victimized by the Zealots because of their close relations to the Romans. To judge from their writings, the Essenes were more likely to have fought against the Romans. There are indications that the Essenes were involved in the heroic suicidal defence of the last Jewish fortification on Massada (see Josephus, *War* 7.252-401).

When peace returned, the leadership of Palestinian Jewry fell to the only group that still functioned and that besides could count on the general support of the people. For lack of a better term, we designate them as the 'Pharisees'. In their ranks as well much was altered by the war. Initially under Yohanan ben Zakkai and thereafter under the centralistic leadership of Gamaliel II, a series of consolidating measures were enacted from the new seat of legal instruction and jurisprudence, Yavne

(Yamnia). Mention has been made (pp. 51-52) of the institution of the title 'rabbi' for ordained teachers. Another measure concerned the reformulation of the so-called 'benediction of the heretics' in the main prayer, with the intention now of barring Jewish Christians as well (*b. Ber.* 28b), a measure whose repercussions are perceptible in the New Testament (see pp. 324-25). Further, there was the formal decision in the long-debated issue over the scope of the Holy Scriptures, at least over certain 'Writings' concerning which there were still differences of opinion (*m. Yad.* 3.5). Gradually the more flexible attitude of the Hillites towards the Scriptures and the law gained dominance and determined the contours of rabbinic tradition and literature.

The complicated relationship between the Pharisees and rabbinic literature can be summarized as follows. The preserved rabbinic writings, with the Mishnah and Talmud as central texts, are an elaboration of the Hillelite tradition, which originally represented a minority within the group designated by Josephus and the New Testament as 'the Pharisees'. The mildness of the Hillelites resulted in consistent reporting of the opinion of the Shammaites (*m. 'Ed.* 1.4).

The outcome was a different Judaism. The diversity antedating the war, in which the Pharisees were but one party among many and besides were internally divided, was now strongly reduced. When this group acquired the leadership, it developed a tendency towards uniformity and consolidation. Internal dissension decreased as well because of the disappearance of most of the Shammaites, whereby the Hillelites became dominant. From this new configuration came into being what is now known as rabbinic Judaism. Because there is nonetheless a certain continuity with the tradition of the Torah teachers from before 70 CE, in this book at times the term Pharisaic–rabbinic tradition will be used.

Rabbinic Literature
The situation after 70 CE evidently gave reason to the 'Pharisees' to create order in the multiplicity and multiformity of oral traditions that had circulated up to that time. The oral transmission of laws, Scripture interpretations and stories was an exclusive custom of the Pharisees that was continued for several centuries by the rabbis. The custom must have originated from a great respect for texts in written form, especially for the 'Holy Scriptures' whose authority was exalted above all. In contrast everything that was said later, all interpretation and complementation of the Bible, was in principle subject to correction and, therefore, must remain oral. This essential flexibility was felt to be

positive: instruction must be creative and constantly self-renewing, just as life itself and society continuously change. The difference with the Essenes and Sadducees on this point has already been pointed out.

In the context of this oral manner of transmission, the rabbis at Yavne began to collect systematically the extant Pharisaic legal traditions, in particular those of the Shammaites and the Hillelites, and to arrange and sort them. On many points decisions were taken and whole new areas were developed. The texts thus created and fixed were repeated as often as necessary and learned by rote by especially gifted scholars who functioned as walking textbooks. Such an oral method of passing down information on is not unique to ancient Judaism but is also reported, for example, of the followers of Zarathustra in Iran and of certain African cultures. The word *mishnah*, which originally indicated all forms of 'teachings' and later referred to the basic collection of law texts, is related to this practice. It comes from the verb *shana*, 'to repeat'. A main role in this reformulation process was reserved for R. Akiva (d. 135 CE) and his pupils R. Meir, R. Yehuda, R. Shimon and R. Yosi.

Nonetheless, after about four generations of working on reformulating, R. Yehuda the Prince, the 'patriarch' and descendant of Hillel, considered the main collection, the Mishnah, to be ripe enough to be committed to writing (220 CE). The lengthy process was begun in which large portions of the widely ramified oral tradition became fixed in writing; we shall never know which portion that was and how much was lost. The Mishnah was followed first by the Tosefta and the Tannaic Midrashim (mid third century). The process continued until the Middle Ages, with as climax the writing down of the Palestinian Talmud and the Babylonian Talmud (fifth–seventh century). While the rabbinic texts were thus only written down from mid third century onwards, the incorporated traditions date from several to many generations earlier. The rudimentary basis of the Mishnah dates, for example, from the end of the first century CE and can, if used critically, throw light on the New Testament.

The *targumim*, Aramaic translations of the Hebrew text of the Torah and the Prophets that were declaimed in the synagogue along with the reading, were also written down (see p. 78), and, only from the seventh century onwards, the rabbinic prayers for individuals and for the congregation.

Though neglected until recently, there are also reports within rabbinic literature of mystic traditions and explicitly *mystic writings*. The latter

were arranged under the 'small' or 'external treatises' to which also
Derekh-Erets literature and related works belong; the name indicates
that these did not constitute a part of the Mishnah or the Talmud.
Important documents among these are the so-called *Hekhalot* texts
(from *hekhal*, 'throne room'), *Sefer Yeṣira* (the 'book of formation'),
and the Hebrew *Apocalypse of Enoch* (*3 Enoch*). Just as the midrash
collections, these represent the committment to writing of as a rule
much older traditions. Within rabbinic literature this phenomenon is
traced back to the first century. One account reports a chain of mystic
tradition between the leading figures of the three first generations of
rabbis, Yohanan ben Zakkai, R. Yoshua and R. Akiva (*t. Ḥag.* 2.2).
Besides the public tradition of law and Scripture interpretation, the
Pharisees and rabbis were thus also acquainted with an esoteric tradition with a mystic-apocalyptic tendency, solely accessible to the initiated. Again it is obvious how deficient the traditional divisions of ancient
Jewish literature are. The Hebrew *Enoch* shows clear correlations with
the Ethiopian *Enoch* (*1 Enoch*) and related works. The Pharisaic–rabbinic milieu was not strictly divorced from 'apocalyptic' circles.

This general picture is confirmed by the New Testament. Before his
conversion, Paul counted as a Pharisee both in his own viewpoint and
in that of others (Phil. 3.5; Acts 23.6), but he also gives evidence of
having had apocalyptic experiences and insights (e.g. 2 Cor. 12.1-5;
1 Thess. 4–5). Jesus, too, was ascribed not only faithfulness to the law
but also mystical experiences and apocalyptic conceptions (Mk 9.2-8;
Mt. 24). Thus one must conclude that apocalyptic traditions did not
occur only among the Essenes, but also among the Pharisees and practically everywhere else among the Jews, including in the early Christian
context. The exceptions to this have already been indicated: Philo and
certain related Greek-speaking Jews, and the Sadducees.

This leads us back once more to the enigma of the selectivity of
rabbinic tradition. Although in their own circles the rabbis transmitted
mystic and apocalyptic traditions, the Christians preserved most of the
Apocrypha and Pseudepigrapha. The same is true of the Septuagint and
the writings of Philo and Josephus, although these, too, differed little
from the Pharisaic–rabbinic literature as far as outlook goes. The simplest assumption is that the rabbis, apart from the Hebrew canon of
Holy Scriptures, passed down that which was central in their own public
instruction. Evidently, Greek–Jewish writings, biblical stories retold
and apocalypses did not belong to this. The loss of the Greek–Jewish

literature is to be ascribed to shifts in the political and military scene, by which first the northern African and later the rest of the Greek-speaking Diasporas disappeared. In the end the rabbinic-, Aramaic- and Hebrew-speaking Jewry preserved only the Hebrew Bible, the Aramaic Targums, the synagogal prayers, the Pharisees' and rabbis' 'public' tradition of instruction, and a number of 'marginal', specifically pious and mystic-apocalyptic treatises.

Chapter 2

JEWISH RELIGIOUS LIFE

How do we perceive Judaism? How do we view religion in general? Before initiating a survey of Jewish religious life in antiquity, a few critical remarks about ourselves are necessary, in the first place concerning our own day and age.

Modern society is based on a principle that profoundly and usually unconsciously determines our perception of religious matters: the *separation of church and state*. Exercised within the church, synagogue, mosque, or some other building, religion and faith are private matters, only indirectly related to public life. This reduction of religion to a non-essential, individual trait was unimaginable in antiquity, where religious worship was an inseparable part of life. As a member of an (extended) family, as an inhabitant of a city or village, and as a subject of a king or an emperor, one was always confronted with religious ritual, particularly on public occasions. Religion was an important part of one's personal status. However one might think about the creed, one belonged to a religious community. The category 'non-religious' did not occur in official terminology. Forming no exception to this, Jewish life was always also Jewish religious life.

A second issue can be summarized as the paradox of change and continuity. Jewish worship is not a matter of the past alone. Sundry prayers from antiquity have been preserved and continue to be used in the tradition of rabbinic Jewry, and one speaks of these most correctly in the present tense. On the other hand, the rabbinic reorganization after the destruction of the temple involved so many shifts that the former situation, including its pluriformity, has been practically eclipsed behind this. Particularly in the area of feasts and rituals—the core of religious life—there were sharp contrasts between the Sadducees, Essenes and Pharisees. Rabbinic literature, however, is redacted with a later, more uniform situation in mind, so that we have to rely on other ancient Jewish sources to correct this. In this presentation, the present tense will be employed for elements that continue to exist in contemporary synagogal practice and the past tense for aspects that are characteristic of the first century. This will occasionally entail shifts between past and present tense within one or two sentences.

A third matter involves the topics that our survey should cover. The focus is on aspects of Jewish life in antiquity that are significant for the New Testament. Overviews of this material have often been written from a limited, negative outlook on Judaism. The relevance of Judaism to the New Testament then becomes negative, in so far as the New Testament personages are placed on a higher plane than their Jewish contemporaries. Who can guarantee that the themes relevant for the New Testament are just as significant for Judaism itself? In this book, it is assumed that Jesus and his first followers were raised as Jews and lived as Jews, that they respected the commandments in the customary manner, attended some synagogue or another on Saturday, and that there they heard the words of the Torah and interpreted them in their own fashion (Lk. 4.16; Acts 17.2). The fact that the latter often brought them into conflict with their fellow Jews is a different matter to which we will return later. Nonetheless, the subjects of the disputes, the assumptions that were made, and the positions that were chosen were all important elements of the Jewish life of that time.

Finally, in the survey we must be aware of the distinction between the various locations of ancient Jewish worship—temple and synagogue—as well as of the difference between the diverse social contexts—the prayers of the congregation and of the individual. These locations and social contexts are not totally distinct, but can overlap.

Temple and Synagogue

In Rome, Alexandria and Athens, in Jerusalem, Caesarea and Capernaum—in all places since ancient times the Jews have gathered for prayers and for the study of the Torah on the Shabbat, the more devout additionally on Mondays and Thursdays. It would, however, be a modern mistake to think that the synagogue was only a house of prayer in antiquity. The word *sunagōgē* means 'gathering', 'congregation', and the oft-recurring designation 'synagogue of the Jews' stood for everything that a 'Jewish community' comprised (cf. Acts 14.1; 17.1, 10). Besides for communal prayers, people gathered there for the treatment of legal and penal cases, administration and registration, school and study, and the care of the needy. If these aspects are not pursued further here, it is because they do not have a direct bearing on the New Testament, except when concerning the aforementioned disputes (2 Cor. 11.24; Mt. 10.17). However that might be, the 'synagogue' was the centre and the soul of the Jewish community, both in the Holy Land and in the Diaspora.

This amounts to stating that for the average Jew in ancient times the 'synagogue' was more important than the temple. Although above the temple worship was called the centre of worldwide Jewish national existence, it is necessary now to be more precise: the temple was the priestly and sacrificial focal point. Innummerable synagogues constituted, however, the local centres of community life and were much closer to the people, even when the temple still functioned. The assumption that, as an institute, the synagogue only arose after the destruction of the temple is incorrect, although after 70 CE the full weight came to rest upon it.

The temple liturgy was based upon the priestly prescriptions from the Torah, and therefore reflected the situation of the Old Testament period, in which the priests laid down the rules. Apart from the individual offerings, ordinary people were only involved in the worship via a special representative. The biblical instruction to 'appear before the Lord three times a year' in the temple (Exod. 23.17) was not taken too literally in the first century. Usually one went only if a special ritual needed to be performed, such as following a birth or the like, and then one often used the opportunity to combine this with a pilgrims' feast, such as Passover.

An important part of the temple worship was constituted by the daily morning and evening offerings, as well as extra offerings for Shabbat, new moon and feast days. These various offerings were accompanied by communal prayers, which were also said in the synagogue and by individuals, and which later developed into the main prayer called 'Eighteen Benedictions'. Here locations, contexts and times overlap: there is change and continuity in one. The prayers were said in the temple and in the synagogue, by the community and by individuals, they were said in former times and today as well, in an altered form— without temple. Communal prayer has always preserved a symbolic tie to the temple worship.

Nonetheless, the rabbis came to regard communal prayer as an independent entity. A well-known proverb about Shimon the Righteous, who must have lived in the first or second century BCE, has been passed down: 'The world stands upon three things: on (the study of) the Torah, *on the worship service* and on deeds of mercy' (*m. Ab.* 1.2). He no doubt included temple worship in 'worship service', *'abōdâ*, but perhaps not that alone. An anonymous tradition, which the Talmud ascribes to someone from the second century CE, indicates that at that time at the latest *'abōdâ*, 'worship service', came to be identified with prayer. The topic of discussion is the prayer for rain, incorporated during the winter into the communal prayers:

> But why exactly in the Prayer? It has been taught: '[And if you hearken, yea, hearken to my commandments...] by loving the LORD your God and serving Him with all your heart and with all your soul' (Deut. 11.13)—*What is then the service with the heart?* You must say: *That is prayer.* And thereafter it is written: '...then I shall give your land's rain in its time, early and later rain' (Deut. 11.14) (*b. Ta'an.* 2a).

True worship is that of the heart: the prayers of the community and of the individual.

In addition to this, from the Talmud and the New Testament it can be inferred that among the Pharisees and in extensive layers of the population there was an aversion to the temple commerce and to the priestly elite who were in charge there. This is related also to the differences between the Pharisees and the Sadducees (see pp. 64-65). The following story, referring to the time shortly after 70 CE, can be placed against this background:

> It happened that Our Master Yohanan ben Zakkai [±80 CE] was travelling when R. Yoshua walked along behind him and said: Woe to us, for the House has been lost, and with it the place where our sins were atoned! He answered: Fear not, we have another atonement in its place. He asked: Then what? He said to him: 'I desire mercy and not sacrifice' (Hos. 6.6) (*ARN* B8.11b; cf. A4.11a).

Yohanan ben Zakkai is known for his peaceableness and for the importance he attached to the spiritual or allegorical interpretation of the commandments. From his answer, we get the distinct impression that the destruction of the temple had relieved him of a problem.

We return later to the temple in connection with purity regulations and other customs that concerned pilgrims. For the moment we pursue further the synagogue and communal prayer.

The synagogue leadership is in the hands of elders chosen by the community. In the Graeco-Roman world, these were often prosperous members for whom it was an honour and a duty to let the community share in their riches. Their names are found in Greek, Aramaic or Hebrew inscriptions and mosaics from excavated synagogues. With reference to the first century, we need not always picture a separate building for the synagogue, but more often a room in the home of such an affluent person, as was apparently also the case among Pauline churches (Rom. 16.5; 1 Cor. 16.19; Col. 4.15; Phlm. 2).

A Jewish congregation is not constituted by its material or spiritual leadership, but by the members themselves. The rabbi as Jewish 'priest' dates only from the Middle Ages. The minimum for a congregation is ten, that is, traditionally, ten adult male members of the congregation, later called the *minyan* (literally: 'counting' or 'quorum'). When ten are present, the community prayers can be said and the Torah can be read (*m. Meg.* 4.3; cf. CD 13.1-2). When fewer are present, these may pray, but only individually.

Given this unadulterated patriarchal principle, it is remarkable that some inscriptions also mention women as administrators. They, too, therefore could have a certain amount of social influence. The scope of this influence, however, should not be overestimated. Even if women participated in the worship service, this did not mean that they led in prayers, Scripture reading or preaching. According to the average Jewish outlook, which was parallel to the traditional Greek and Roman ideas in this matter, a woman should not meddle in community affairs, certainly not in public (*t. Meg.* 3.11). The possibilities were somewhat more favourable for women in Hellenistic Egypt, probably due to the example of the self-assured Macedonian queens. The hesitancy of the synagogue on this point was taken over in unabridged form by the church (1 Cor. 14.34-35; 1 Tim. 2.11-12). In this as well, Christianity is heir and successor of Judaism.

The average ancient Jewish view on women is not very encouraging, but there was some variety. The most restrictive standpoint was held again by the Essenes. In their centre at Qumran, there was no place for women, and a piece of wisdom literature excavated there depicts the woman as a source of sin and temptation (4Q184). The comments on women by moderate Jews like Philo of Alexandria and of well-known rabbis also sound negative to us. Nevertheless, in Pharisaic–rabbinic circles it is assumed that women participate in the worship service. This is also reflected in a midrash cited by Paul in which explicit mention is made of God's 'sons *and daughters*' (2 Cor. 6.18). The rabbis discussed the question whether women should be allowed to study the Torah. One opinion was, 'One is obliged to teach his daughter Torah,' but others said, 'He who teaches his daughter Torah, teaches her licentiousness,' or, 'The wisdom of the woman is in her spindle' (*m. Soṭ.* 3.4; *y. Soṭ.* 3.19a; *b. Yom.* 66b). The few women of whom the rabbinic tradition passes on words of wisdom are the exceptions that confirm the rule. Perceiving this as a social injustice is, of course, modern. Contemporarily, in Jewish circles there is a strong attempt to overcome traditional impediments to full-fledged participation by women.

There were synagogues in all Jewish places of residence. No matter what language was used in daily conversation, the Scriptures were read and prayers said on Saturdays and on festivals. Through this a communal context was continually created that aligned the thinking and cultural expressions of the Jews in their diverse places of residence. Even when, for example, the Scripture interpretation differed drastically in form between Palestine and Alexandria, there was still this underlying structural correlation. When studying the various sorts of ancient Jewish literature, it is, therefore, important to keep the overarching function of the liturgic setting in mind.

Liturgy and Calendar

Ever since some time before the common era, community prayers—the 'normal worship service'—comprise three main elements: the *Shema*, the 'Prayer', and the Torah reading. The distinction between the prayers of the individual and those of the community, that is, of ten or more members, plays an important role in this.

The first essential element of the service is called *Shema Yisrael*, 'Hear, Israel!' The designation derives from the opening words of one of a series of Torah texts (Deut. 6.4-9; 11.13-21; Num. 15.37-41) recited evenings and mornings, or, as phrased in the texts themselves, 'when you lie down and when you arise'. The Shema, which may also be recited individually, is a mixture of prayer and Scripture recitation, in which the devotional aspect of reading the Scriptures is brought to the fore in an exemplary manner. By the recitation of these texts, the community and the individual place themselves daily before God, as of yore the people at Sinai did, in thankfulness for the privilege of being able to hear and observe the Torah.

This custom must be ancient indeed, but it has not been immune to changes. One of these is the omission of the Ten Commandments, which, according to archaeological and literary evidence, preceded the Shema as late as the first century CE. According to a comment in the Mishnah, the 'Ten Words' and the Shema were also recited at the daily offering in the temple (*m. Tam.* 5.1).

The recitation of the Shema is embedded in prayers or blessings, *berakot*, in which God is praised for the daily renewed privilege of receiving the Torah and the Commandments. According to the comment in the Mishnah just mentioned, this also took place in the first century, in any case in the temple. All Jewish prayers consist of such *berakot*. Other prayers include the blessings for the wine and the bread at the beginning of a festive meal, and the blessings that encase the study of the Torah.

The second essential element of the service is 'the Prayer' (*Tefillah* or *Amidah*), comprising a fixed series of the blessings. In a discussion that must have taken place at the end of the first century, this was designated according to a certain tradition as 'the Eighteen Benedictions', after the ideal number of prayers. According to parallel traditions, however, one could suffice with a 'short prayer' or a 'summary of the eighteen' (*m. Ber.* 4.3-4; *t. Ber.* 3.11). At the beginning of the first century, there was thus probably more pluriformity than later. Among other things, correspondences in its content make it possible that the Lord's Prayer was intended as one such 'short prayer' (cf. p. 388). The structure of the eighteen benedictions gradually became normative for daily prayers so that we can speak of the 'Eighteen Benedictions', even though eventually the total was nineteen.

Community prayer originally had a connection to the offerings in the temple, of which a few traces have been preserved. Thus, the prayer is still prayed facing the former location of the altar, respectively, the place where the temple once stood or, from abroad, in the direction of the Holy Land (cf. 1 Kgs 8.28-29, 44, 48). Further, on ordinary days it is recited at least twice, according to the number of daily offerings, with an optional third time, while on the Shabbat and on feast days extra repetitions are added, in analogy to the extra festive offerings. Furthermore, the conclusion of the prayer is inspired by the priestly blessing from the temple (Num. 6.24-26).

The middle portion of the prayer for weekdays contains prayers for forgiveness, sustenance, healing and preservation from evil—notions that bring to mind the second part of the Lord's Prayer—and further for the 'ingathering' of exiles, the expulsion of evil's tyranny, and the coming of the Son of David. The Eighteen Benedictions is recited by the individual, concentrated and in silence, as 'worship of the heart'. In the synagogue, it is thereafter repeated aloud by the leader, the 'representative of the community', an important function that in antiquity could be filled by any member of the community.

The third essential element of the synagogue liturgy is the public Scripture reading, for which a quorum of ten commuity members is required. A liturgic element in its own right, it is surrounded by various rituals and is the most specific characteristic of the Jewish worship service. While prayers are also said alone and in family circles and, in former times, accompanied the offerings in the temple—not to mention the many types of prayers resounding in the sanctuaries of other peoples—the weekly reading of the Torah aloud is a unique creation of the synagogue. This typically Jewish custom was later followed by Christianity and, in another manner, by Islam. Thus it was that Jews, together with Christians, were counted in the Koran as 'the people of the Scriptures' (3.65; 5.68), and the Koran itself came to be seen as 'Scripture' (2.2). In the Roman Catholic and Eastern Orthodox worship services, Scripture reading is an independent liturgic event to which one listens as an act of devotion. Behind this lies the core of the synagogue service—the public reading of the Torah.

In former days, the Scripture lesson without exception included a passage from the Torah. It is not clear whether at all times and in all places a portion from the prophets was read as well. The Bible commentaries of Philo, which appear to originate in synagogue expositions, do not once divert to the prophets. Given the many commentaries on the prophets in Qumran, it is plausible that the prophets were read publicly there. According to rabbinic tradition, one does read from the prophets, and the New Testament provides evidence that in the first century this was not out of the ordinary in a Galilean or Asian Minor synagogue (Lk. 4; Acts 13.15). As these texts indicate, any member of the congregation could be invited to read aloud, and a travelling teacher could thereafter take over to give a homily. As the evangelist explicitly reports, the speaker sat down for his address (cf. also Mt. 5.1). According to rabbinic custom, different persons are invited consecutively for the Torah reading, each reading a portion. As with all liturgic proceedings, these readings are accompanied by prayers of blessing.

In the previous chapter, mention was made that the Torah reading was accompanied by a *targum* or translation, several verses at a time. Written forms of such 'simultaneous translations' have been preserved only in Aramaic; we can only speculate about Greek versions. The rabbinic custom was that the Torah reading itself was done from a written book, but that the translation must be done 'orally', that is, by heart. This is again an expression of the characteristic Pharisaic–rabbinic respect for the written Word of God: every rendering was viewed as an interpretation. The translation was, of course, not improvised but followed conventions, with the possibility of variation. The interpreter was called by a Persian–Akkadian term *turgeman* (*m. Meg.* 4.4), also Hebraized as *meturgeman*. The phenomenon of oral simultaneous translation derived apparently from the international aspect of the Persian Empire. Such an interpreter was also in vogue accompanying the sermon and in academies, where he acted as a 'loudspeaker' who spared the teacher the necessity of raising his voice.

The oral rendering of the Hebrew text shows also what value was placed upon having the Torah reading in Hebrew, if at all possible; however, not only in the Diaspora but also in many synagogues in the Holy Land the reading was also done in Greek (cf. Acts 6.1, 9; 9.29). From the Mishnah it is apparent that the rabbis endorsed this practice, and we can assume the same of the Pharisees. After citing an apparently older rule according to which the Torah could be written in every language, R. Shimon ben Gamliel (±150 CE) declared that the Torah books, besides Hebrew, could be written only in Greek (*m. Meg.* 1.8), which implies that at that time the Torah was read aloud in Greek. In other places in rabbinic literature as well, a certain predilection for Greek is noticeable (*b. Soṭ.* 63b).

The Babylonian Talmud and later Jewish tradition follow an annual reading cycle. From one New Year's celebration to the next, the entire Torah is read through to the end. In sources from the Holy Land there are, however, indications that the reading cycle lasted three years there. There are also traces of a cycles of three-and-a-half years, a time span apparently going back to a half of the seven-year rhythm that is prescribed in the Torah itself, that is, the reading aloud of 'this law' on the Feast of Tabernacles at the beginning of each Seventh Year (Deut. 31.10; cf. Neh. 8). In any event there was a plurality of reading practices in the Holy Land, and it is plausible that the one-year cycle, that is, the later characteristically Babylonian cycle, originated in Palestine as well. Attempts to explain New Testament writings on the basis of synagogal Scripture reading must take this pluriformity into account.

In addition to the Shabbat, services are also held in the synagogue on feast days. The liturgic calendar begins in the autumn with the New Year's celebration (*Rosh ha-Shanah*), followed ten days later by the Day of Atonement (*Yom Kippur*). The intervening ten days are characterized by contemplation and penance. Four days later the cheerful Feast of Booths or Tabernacles (*Sukkot*) begins, during which for a week all meals are eaten outside in a hut with a roof of leaves, decorated with autumn fruits. In mid-winter, *Hanukkah*, the eight-day feast of lights, commemorates the rededication of the temple after the Maccabean revolt. In early spring *Purim* is celebrated, at which time the scroll of Esther is read aloud in preparation for Passover that follows four weeks later.

The Passover Feast (Easter) is called *Pesah* in Hebrew and *Pasha* in Aramaic. The latter form is used in the Gospels (Mk 14.1) and from there it was adopted in many European languages. The celebration begins with a 'Seder night' in family circles. *Seder* means 'order', named after the 'order of service' of the liturgy for this evening celebration. The story of the Exodus is told, embedded in explanations and songs of praise around in a special meal. Certain customs are explicitly reminiscent of the manner in which the meal was eaten before the destruction of the temple. An essential difference is that since the sacrificial service was discontinued, the Passover offering is no longer eaten. The celebration lasts a week, during which time no leavened bread or other yeast products are consumed. From Passover seven weeks are counted until the celebration of 'Weeks' (*Shavuot*), which the Greek-speaking Jews in that time, counting the first day as well, called the Fiftieth Day or *Pentēkostē* (Acts 2.1; 1 Cor. 16.8). The word 'Pentecost', just as the celebration itself, is a legacy of Judaism in its Greek form.

Regarding the *liturgical calendar* and the dating of the feasts, there were fundamental differences between the various groups in the first century, especially between the Essenes and the Pharisees, the latter probably representing the most widespread custom. This point is of great significance for the New Testament, in particular concerning the date of Jesus' last supper and his trial by the Sanhedrin (see pp. 165-66, 310-12).

The *Pharisaic calendar*, which still regulates the synagogal year, comprises 12 lunar months and is supplemented about once in 3 years by an intercalary month, thus completing the solar year. Since one lunar month has 29½ days, and 12 of these add up to 354 days, there are 11½ days per year too few. Passover and Sukkot always begin on the full moon, thus on the fifteenth of the seventh, respectively, the first, lunar month. This can, of course, be any day of the week, including a Shabbat, so that the feast offerings had to be slain on Shabbat as well. Rabbinic literature preserves a story in which Hillel with authority and humour proves that for Passover, the sheep could be slain also on Shabbat—in full accord with the customs of the people, for 'if they are not prophets, then they are in any case the children of the prophets' (*t. Pisha* 4.13-14).

The *Essene solar calendar* explicitly served to avoid such flexibility and thus to protect the Shabbat (cf. CD 11.17). It must be of ancient origin indeed and appears also to lie at the basis of the priestly portions of the Old Testament. It is appropriately called an 'ancient priestly calendar'. A number of Qumran texts testify to the fact that the observance of this calendar occupied a central place there (4QMMT; 4Q320). In pseudepigraphic writings, such as *Jubilees* and *1 Enoch*, which are not typically from the Qumran sect, this calender is assumed as well. The calendar was thus both older and more widespread than the community of Qumran alone; nonetheless, for the sake of convenience we will speak hereafter of the 'Essene calendar'.

Besides safeguarding the Shabbat, the Essene calendar aimed at following the fixed times laid down in creation, particularly the coming and going of the sun. The lucid solution for both problems was a year of 364 days, divided into four seasons each comprising 91 days or 3 months of 30 days plus 1 intercalary day. In this way there were 1¼ days per year too little, and this, too, must have been supplemented by some intercalary system. Apart from that, the system was perfect. Because 91, the number of days in a quarter of a year, equals precisely 13 times 7, all feast days fell on a fixed day of the week. The first day of each quarter was on a Wednesday, and thus also the fifteenth of the first and the seventh months, the days for Passover and the Feast of Tabernacles. In this manner, the Day of Atonement was always on a Friday, New Year on a Wednesday, while the Feast of Weeks or Pentecost, the fiftieth day after Passover, was always on a Sunday. Sunday,

Wednesday, and Friday were preferred days for feasts. This fact is of great significance for early Christian calendar questions.

The consequence of having the Essene and Pharisaic calendars existing side by side is that the one group worked and did business on days that were holy to the other group. The bloody reality of the situation becomes apparent from a furious outburst from Qumran against a high priest, evidently of Pharisaic persuasion, who 'on the feast day, on the rest of the Day of Atonement, appeared to devour them, to make them stumble on the fast day, the Shabbat of their rest' (1QpHab 11.6-8). Additionally, the flexibility with which the Pharisaic exegetes declared offerings and other rituals to be possible on Shabbat aroused the perpetual fury of the Essenes. Probably this was one of the reasons that they called the Pharisees 'interpreters of slippery things' (see above p. 49).

It is significant that elements of the 'Essene' calender were followed in *Sadducean* circles as well. Sadducean and Boethusian priests had objections to waving the *lulav*, the festive bundle of branches, at the Feast of Tabernacles when that fell on a Shabbat (*t. Suk.* 3.1). Thus also in these circles people thought that the Feast of Weeks, in which the *omer* or sheaf of grain is waved, should always fall on a Sunday (*Meg. Ta'an.* 8 *Nisan*, p. 324; see Lev. 23.15). From various souces it appears, however, that this tradition could not be enforced because the Pharisaic position was supported by the majority of the people (Josephus, *Ant.* 18.12-17; *t. Kip.* 1.8). Between the Sadducees and Essenes there are more correspondences in the area of rituals; however, given the great socio-political and ideological differences between the two groups, it is not probably that they influenced each other. More likely, both preserved the same ancient priestly tradition.

The Preaching or Scripture Interpretation

Much indirect information on the sermon or exposition can be found in the ramified section of rabbinic literature tradition devoted to the interpretation of the Scriptures, called *midrash*. The word *midrash* derives from the stem *darash*, 'ask' or 'seek', and signifies 'explanation' or 'perusal, investigation'. The expression *midrash ha-Torah*, 'explanation, perusal, or study of the Torah', occurs in Qumran (1QS 8.15), and *bet midrash*, 'house of learning', in the Hebrew text of Ben Sira (51.47; Greek 51.23)—both from one or two centuries BCE. Many parts of the midrash collection are apparently condensed sermons, and in later Hebrew the sermon came to be called by the cognate term *derasha*. The interplay between sermon and midrash is cardinal to understanding ancient Jewish literature.

In the ancient synagogue service the sermon followed the Scripture reading or preceded it, by way of introduction. Ingenious rhetorical forms were developed, such as stringing together and 'juggling' Bible texts, which the average modern reader may not always appreciate. On the whole, in antiquity rhetoric was a favourite part of general education. While employing rhetorical techniques, the sermon nonetheless remained closely related to the Scripture reading. In addition it aimed at edifying and encouraging the audience, for which the *parable* was a favourite form of expression.

Rabbinic midrash embodies a specific approach to the Bible based on great familiarity with the text. This can be conceived of as a house in which both the speaker and the audience were raised to move about with complete freedom. The familiarity of this space allows for much ingenuity in dealing with the text, a playfulness and humour that could at times give reason to the non-initiated to wonder whether there is any respect for the Holy Scriptures at all. That respect was indeed not lacking becomes apparent when playfulness suddenly gives way to profound gravity, and joy to sorrow. The interested listener must develop an attentive ear for written detail, as well as for the succinctness with which an entire viewpoint or teaching can be summarized. Both that which is expressed and that which is suppressed play an essential role, as well as the polysemy with which the Bible text is heard and is capable of being heard ever anew.

Some examples from different centuries can express the 'soul' of rabbinic midrash better than discursive explanation.

> (1) Rabbi Yohanan said: wherever you encounter the omnipotence of the Holy One, blessed be He, you find his humility. This is written in the Torah, repeated in the Prophets and a third time in the Writings.
> It is written in the Torah: 'For the LORD your God is the God of gods and the Lord of lords, the great, powerful, awe inspiring God, who knows no respect of persons', and directly thereafter, '...who does justice to the orphan and widow and loves the stranger' (Deut. 10.17-18).
> It is repeated in the Prophets: 'Thus says the High and Exalted One, who dwells in eternity and whose name is holy: in the high and holy I dwell', and directly thereafter, '...and with the broken and humble of heart' (Isa. 57.15).

A third time in the Writings: 'Make broad the way for Him that rides upon the clouds, with his name, LORD', and directly thereafter: 'the Father of orphans, the judge of widows' (Ps. 68.5-6) (*b. Meg.* 31a).

R. Yohanan (first half of the third century) strings together texts from the Torah, the Prophets and the Writings, the three parts of the Hebrew canon. This was a favourite technique, here employed to communicate the profound and encouraging message that God's exaltedness is always intimately bound to his attentiveness to humankind. In this there is also a lesson for our own behaviour: if *He* in all his sublimity behaves thus, how much more should *we*, the neighbour of the enslaved and orphaned...

> (2) Rabbi Akiva used to say: Beloved is humankind, for they are created in the image (of God); even greater love: it has been made known to them that they are created in the image, for it is said: 'In the image of God did he make man' (Gen. 9.6).
> Beloved is Israel, that they are called children of the Eternal One; even greater love: it has been made known to them that they are children of the Eternal One, for it is said: 'Children you are of the Lord your God' (Deut. 14.1).
> Beloved is Israel, that they have been given a desirable object; even greater love: it has been made known to them that they have been given the desirable object with which the world is created, for it is said: 'For I have give you good instruction, my Torah, forsake it not' (Prov. 4.2) (*m. Ab.* 3.14)

This is another type of threefold, exegetical proverb. In a complex manner, R. Akiva (beginning of second century) describes a progression that is both ascendant and circular. The circularity lies in the fact that it begins and ends with creation. The ascendant aspect lies in the advancement from that which is general, that is, humankind created after God's image, to the specific, that is, Israel as the one chosen to receive the Torah.

> (3) Hillel was going somewhere. His pupils asked him: Hillel, where are you going?—I am going to fulfil a religious commandment.—Which?—I am going to the (Roman) bathhouse.—Is that then a religious commandment?—Certainly! do not the kings of flesh and blood set their images everywhere, and do they not appoint special personnel to clean and maintain them up for a yearly salary and for being received among the great ones of the kingdom? How much more we ourselves, who are created in His image... (*Lev. R.* 34.4; p. 776-77; cf. Gen. 9.6)

This story about Hillel (end of first century BCE) is anecdote, parable and Scripture interpretation all in one, illustrating both the playfulness and the succinctness of this approach. The content of the story reflects the fearless self-confidence characteristic of Hillel: he teaches the profound and humane lesson that a person honours both himself and his Creator by taking care of his own body.

The flexible manner of interpreting Scriptures exhibited in these examples is characteristic of the rabbis and their predecessors, the Pharisees. In comparison, the Essenes and the Sadducees had a rigid, 'one-dimensional' exegetical method; it is plausible that in this they consciously differentiated themselves from the Pharisees. Gradations lying between Essenes and Pharisees must be taken into account as well. The Scripture interpretation of Jesus and his earliest followers, for example, is to be situated somewhere in the area in between. Furthermore, differences within the Pharisaic movement, as discussed at the end of the previous chapter, also played a role. The Hillelite tradition practised a supple and humane approach to Scriptures, while the Shammaites adhered somewhat more strictly to the letter. Due to the majority of the Hillelites after the destruction of the temple, their versatile midrash eventually came to represent rabbinic literature.

The philosophical Bible commentaries of Philo of Alexandria lack the simple charm of the Pharisaic–rabbinic explanation of Scripture, but share many motifs. The following fragment gives an impression of the profound lucidity that he can achieve:

> The holy word wants to convince us surpassingly that the food of the soul is not earthly but heavenly: 'See, I will make bread to rain upon you from heaven, and the people shall go out and gather it, that of the day for the day, in order that I may try them whether they will walk in My law or not' (Exod. 16.4). You see that the soul is not fed with earthly and perishable matters, but with the words which God causes to descend from the exalted, pure spheres which He calls 'heaven'.
>
> Let the soul then gather 'that of the day for the day', so that it does not proclaim itself but the generous God to be the preserver of that which is good. And it seems to me that the instruction was given for the following reason: the day is the symbol of light and light stands for the development of the soul. Now many have appropriated such light for the soul for the sake of night and darkness, not for dawn and light; thus, for example, (the pursuit of) all kinds of elementary instruction, the so-called 'encyclia', or philosophy itself, for the sake of riches or power as rulers do. But the sensitive person acquires the day for the sake of the day, light for the sake of light, beauty for the sake of beauty. That is why

he added: 'in order that I may try them whether they will walk in My law
or not' (*Allegorical Commentary on the Law* 3.160-67)

In this fragment, Philo, following Hellenistic customs, provides 'primitive' details from the old narratives with an allegoric or spiritual explanation. The bread that the hungry people saw falling from heaven
cannot be intended merely literally; it must contain a deeper significance. Indeed, does not careful reading teach us that the story of
Exodus itself revolves around instructing the people to learn to walk
according to the Torah? Philo concludes that heavenly sustenance for
the soul is involved: the study of the Torah, the highest goal towards
which a person can strive. The 'heavenly bread' is not intended to fill
the belly but to elevate the spirit. Philo's explanation is related in
content to the rabbinic saying that one may not view the Torah 'as a
crown to honour oneself or a shovel with which to earn one's bread'.
Tora must be studied for its own sake (*m. Ab.* 4.5; *b. Suk.* 49b).

The allegory or spiritual explanation deserves separate attention. It
occurs as well in the New Testament, especially in the Gospel of John
(see Jn 6 about heavenly bread!) and in the Epistle to the Hebrews.
Many think that Philo, as well as John, relinquishes the literal significance of the text for the spiritual, and that this applies not only to
biblical personages and happenings, but in particular to the practical
commandments of the Torah. There is, however, an important passage
in which Philo contests exactly that point of view. It has to do with
Abraham, the 'archetype' of all believers, who upon God's command
departs for an unknown land of imperishable good, beauty and truth.
One of God's promises to him is that He will make his name great
(Gen. 12.2). But what does a name among men have to do with a true
spiritual purpose?

> According to me, it is like this. Just as it is praiseworthy to be good and
> noble, so likewise to have such a *reputation*. For although truth stands
> above reputation, blessedness comes from both... For there are those that
> view the *formulated laws* merely as *symbols of spiritual truths*, taking
> the latter seriously and neglecting the former... Thus they are as beings
> that are totally alone in the desert, as disembodied souls which know no
> city, village, or home, nor any human community; they despise what
> most people respect, and they try to approach truth in its nakedness...
> One must compare (the *commandments*) with the *body* and (their spir-
> itual *significance*) with the *soul*. Just as one must honour the body as the
> home of the soul, so must one pay attention to the formulated laws
> (*Migr. Abr.* 86-93).

The commandments help the believer find and keep his place within the community. True godliness cannot do without the commandments, if it is to avoid lapsing into a levitated idealism. This characteristically Jewish insight is expressed variously. There is a Jewish-Christian epistle in the New Testament, written in good Greek, which uses the image of body and soul to emphasize the importance of the commandments, only in an opposite application (Jas 2.26; see p. 351). To Hillel is ascribed the statement that it is a commandment to take care of the body, because it is the home of the soul (*Lev. R.* 34.4; pp. 777-78). Philo's principle of the irreducible literalness of the commandments corresponds to a maxim in the Babylonian Talmud: 'Scripture never departs from its literal meaning' (*b. Šab.* 63a). Finally, such a modern Jewish thinker as Abraham Joshua Heschel has pointed out the mutual connections between *halakah* and *aggadah*, between formulated commandments and their imaginative interpretation.

Philo and the rabbis arrive at related insights, but with different methods and goals. This raises the question as to how Alexandrian and Palestinian Jews judged each other's methods of interpretation. It is of importance first of all to realize that many in the Holy Land could manage in Greek. Furthermore, there was frequent correspondence with Jerusalem about matters of the law, which suggests that in Alexandria there were Jews who knew Hebrew or Aramaic. It was thus possible to make oneself understood in various manners. Philo's commentaries appear to be intended for an educated elite who could savour philosophic allusions, while most of the Alexandrian Jews were, no doubt, better served by a popular sermon like those produced by the rabbis. In this lies also a difference in intention. No matter how elaborate it can be, the rabbinic midrash continues to maintain contact with the people. Finally, we must avoid schematizing the differences between the rabbis and the Greek-speaking Jews. As we saw, certain rabbis had a predilection for Greek. Even more eloquent is the fact that an allegoric exegetical method is ascribed to Yohanan ben Zakkai (*t. B. Qam.* 7.2-9). Although Philo's philosophical interests place a stamp of elitism on his interpretations, his general attitude towards the Scriptures must have been neither strange nor uncongenial, at least to some rabbis.

The Law

Jewish law is a topic of endless paper warfare and numerous misunderstandings. Theological discussions on the law have been held since

Luther, but they revolve around Paul, to whom we turn in a separate chapter. At this point, the issue is the significance of the law within the context of Judaism itself, particularly in antiquity.

Rabbinic literature uses a particular term for the law's commandments: *halakah*. This concept is of vital importance to understanding Judaism, especially given the Christian tendency to spiritualize and depreciate the concrete commandments. The Jewish term itself is apparently not of Hebrew origin but must have derived from the Aramaic *halka* (Ezra 4.13), the Akkadian *ilku*, or the Iranian *harkara*, coming from the administrative context of the Persian or Babylonian Empire, whence its original meaning: '(taxation) rule'. In the Middle Ages the still popular etymology arose which derives it from the Hebrew verb *halak*, 'to go, to walk'. Thus the explanation of 'halakah' as 'the way in which one should go' is inspiring but historically incorrect. The word has not yet been found in the texts from Qumran. Perhaps it was avoided there because it did not fit in with the preferred biblical Hebrew. In modern Jewish usage, the word is used in the singular to indicate the whole of Jewish laws and commandments: 'the halakah'. In this sense 'the halakah' corresponds to what we thus far have called 'the Jewish law'. Halakah must be distinguished, however, from ethics, that is, contemplation *about* action: halakah is the detailed formulation about *how* to act.

To speak of the significance of the law or halakah in Judaism means in the first place to emphasize the importance of the Scriptures. Indeed, besides containing the narrative teachings about creation and primaeval times and the emergence of Israel, the Torah is the *legal code* of the Jewish people. Even though later many details and sometimes whole topics have been added, the Jewish law is unshakably anchored in the Torah. Already in the narrative beginning of the Torah, commandments are woven subtly into the story. The tale with which it all began, the work of creation in seven days, expresses the special significance of the Shabbat. The first explicit commandment is the circumcision of Abraham and his male descendants (Gen. 17), the next occurring commandments have to do with Passover (Exod. 11–12), and thereafter Israel is instructed how to keep the Shabbat (Exod. 16)—all before the revelation at Sinai. In other words, already previous to Sinai the emergence of the people is 'marked' by three customs that distinguish them internally and externally: *circumcision, Passover* and *Shabbat*. Undeniably, the climax is the revelation itself, in which Israel receives the Ten Words with the conditions of the covenant: God has rescued Israel, Israel keeps God's commandments. Besides this, there are large legal portions in Exodus, Leviticus, Numbers and Deuteronomy. That Christians usually skip over these is understandable, but this does not diminish their value to Jews. In later books of the Old Testament, the importance of the law is no longer a point of discussion, and 'the book of the law of Moses' has become the foundation of Jewish national existence (Ezra 7.6; Neh. 8.1).

This brings us to a second aspect of the law. If the commandments are to be viewed for a moment non-religiously, they are nothing other than the customs and practices of the Jewish people. Within the international contexts of the Persian, Hellenistic or Roman Empires, having such an ethnically delimited tradition was not unusual in itself. Customs like circumcision or keeping the Shabbat attracted attention, just as did, at least for the Greeks and Romans, the fact that Jews did not portray their God. The faithfulness with which they kept their 'ancestral customs', however, confirmed a generally appreciated moral value of that day and was by and large admired. An echo of this can be heard in the emphasis that Paul placed upon his upbringing in the 'ancestral tradition' (Gal. 1.14; Acts 22.3). The Greek word for the Torah was then, logically, *nomos*, the constitution of the 'people of the Jews', the *ethnos tōn Ioudaiōn*. This is the word 'law' that in the New Testament is the focus of discussion. This ethnic connotation of the 'law' was not an innovation of the Hellenistic period. The Torah began to function as the officially recognized foundation of the Jewish people within the framework of the Persian Empire. The precursor to the Greek *nomos* was the Iranian–Aramaic word *dat* (Ezra 7.26), and it has remained in Jewish usage, as can be seen in the Modern Hebrew *dati*, 'one who keeps the Jewish law'.

A third aspect is thus brought forward. The commandments are not only the characteristic customs and practices of the Jews, but they also determine Jewish identity, both internally and externally. Through the law, the lifestyle of individuals and of the community is structured and characterized as being Jewish. In regard to antiquity, what has been said about the relationship between religion and society must be kept in mind. Every crossroads, each fountain, every government building was 'marked' by some religious motif or another. Even the most commonplace matters had a religious significance. This was equally true of the Jews: everything they did was for themselves and their surroundings recognizably Jewish through the 'marking' effect of the commandments of the law, expressed not only in what one ate and drank, but, for example, also in clothing. Just as in olden days a Phrygian was recognizable by his soft, conical cap, immortalized by 'Marianne' of the French Revolution, so also the Jews had their characteristic attire (Josephus, *Ant.* 18.61).

A fourth aspect stands somewhat in contrast to the surrounding cultures. Jewish 'customs and practices' were not left to chance and mood, but were consciously and purposefully formulated in detail. While the basis was available for everyone to read—the Holy Scriptures, the Jewish 'constitution'—alongside it there were a multitude of post-biblical rules and regulations that were transmitted primarily orally. There are indications that the custom of the Essenes and the Sadducees to fix their interpretations of the law in writing was not generally shared. The majority of Jews of that time felt closer to the Pharisees and kept to the system of unwritten customs and practices as thought through and formulated by the Pharisaic movement. Their oral law tradition allowed for flexibility and multiformity, which was a thorn in the flesh to the more rigid Essenes. The Pharisaic movement also had differences in lifestyles, and accordingly divergent legal traditions. Their pluriformity offered the most room for the lifestyle of the majority of the people who did not join any movement.

A fifth aspect is that the commandments marked the whole of life, from the cradle to the grave, from morning to evening, for the individual and for society. This need not evoke a nightmarish image of suffocation. In such an environment, life can be just as natural as breathing, in spite of the inevitable presence of overly pious souls and formalistic quibblers. Furthermore, one should not exaggerate the number of commandments. Two-thirds of the commandments of the Torah are relevant only to the sanctuary and the priests, with which the average Jew did not often come in contact, a situation that eventually became permanent due to the destruction of the temple. There remained thus but a small portion of the Torah commandents that were generally applicable. Nonetheless, with their specifications and additions, they give the impression of embracing all of life. This notion was expressed in the number of commandments, 613, of which, however, the intention is often misunderstood. The number expresses not so much a quantitative *amount*, as a qualitative *unity*: '365 prohibitions, corresponding to the days of the year, and 248 positive commandments, corresponding to the number of members of the human body' (*b. Mak.* 23b). In other words, all of life and the whole of the body are involved, as the Torah says: 'You shall love the Lord your God with all your heart, with all your soul and will all your might' (Deut. 6.5). Total consecration to the Torah is also expressed in seeking the 'joy of the commandments' in each religious act (cf. *b. Šab.* 30b).

The fact that the commandments encompass all of life is also expressed in the scope of the *Mishnah*. This central summary of rabbinic halakah comprises the following six divisions:

(1)   *Seeds*: about the offerings which are set apart from the harvest, with an introductory treatise on prayer, *Berakot*.
(2)   *Times*: concerning Shabbat and festive times.
(3)   *Women*: on marriage and private law.
(4)   *Lawsuits*: mainly about civil and penal law.
(5)   *Holy things*: concerning everything having to do with the offerings.
(6)   *Purifications*: on the system of laws of cleanliness.

This list of contents is only global. Each of the 63 tractates of which the 6 divisions are comprised contains subjects not covered in the given title, due to the fact that the Mishnah is the result not of systematic codification, but of an organic process of selection, arrangement, and reformulation. In many treatises there are passages containing a principle of arrangement that is older and often even less systematic than the final formulation. Although the Mishnah summarizes only the Pharisaic–rabbinic legal tradition on the basis of the final Hillelite version, its comprehensiveness is representative for the place of the law in the life of Jews in antiquity.

A stifling effect can be produced when the efforts to maintain the tradition clash with changing circumstances. This is an unavoidable drawback of any system of life and law thats is expressly formulated and thus fixated. Such a system can never function without clarification in the form of additional details, adjustments, expansions or, in exceptional cases, abolishment of rules handed down. During the first century in particular, this process was in progress in regard to the laws from the Old Testament, which dated from centuries earlier and from an entirely different social situation. In this the Pharisees had the most flexible attitude. They declared the execution of the rebellious son to be a dead letter of the law; that of the transgressor of the Shabbat was limited to an almost impossible occurrence (Deut. 21.21; Num. 15.35; see p. 413). Here as elsewhere, the Pharisaic schools placed different accents: where the Shammaites tended to adhere to tradition, the Hillelites exhibited a logical realism. A measure is even ascribed to Hillel that abolished the literal validity of the biblical commandment. Changed economic circumstances had caused the regulation of remitting all debts in the Seventh Year (Deut. 15) to have precisely the opposite effect: no one wanted to lend money anymore. Hereupon, in order to restore its spirit, Hillel deactivated the letter of the law by means of a juridical fiction (the *prosbul*, *m. Šeb.* 10.3).

The law, the halakah, encompasses the whole of Jewish life and imparts to it structure and identity. Thus the sixth and final aspect is that study of the attitude taken towards the law, the halakah, renders significant information as to the place a person or a group occupies within Jewish society. In other words, the halakah is a social reference system, not only for those involved, but also for an external or later observer. Whereas ideas or motifs in the narrative interpretation of Scripture are difficult to localize or date, it is often much easier to do so with practical commandments. It is particularly in this area that the separate position of the Essenes becomes apparent, as does that of the Sadducees. The same principle applies to the Pharisees and rabbis: through one's interpretation of the law one can be recognized as a Shammaite or a Hillelite. Likewise, the practical interpretation of the law is determinant for the place of Jesus, Paul and other New Testament characters within the society of their time.

In view of the following chapters, we will now concentrate on several concrete parts of ancient Jewish law.

Shabbat
The observance of Shabbat is one area that evidences remarkable development and where differences between the movements clearly come to the fore.

In rabbinic literature an important rule is that the preservation of human life has precedence over the Shabbat. From other sources, which in this case are relatively extensive, it appears that this rule goes back to several centuries BCE. The decision to maintain this basic principle is specifically dated during the Maccabaean War, 167–164 BCE (1 Macc. 2.41). Interestingly, the discussion of the rule in rabbinic literature also reports a situation of war. In the Mishnah we find the general rule that one should not march out armed on the Shabbat (*m. Šab.* 6.2, 3). The Tosefta makes allowances for exceptions to this:

> When non-Jews advance upon Jewish cities, one marches against them with weapons and violates the Shabbat. When? If their approach means mortal danger... (*t. 'Erub.* 3.5).

This rule was written down approximately mid third century CE, but it is strongly reminiscent of the decision of the Maccabeans. That this opinion was generally held in the first century CE is apparent from the report of Josephus that the population of Jerusalem took up weapons when the Roman troups approached, although this fell on an exceptionally important Shabbat (*War* 2.517). It can be concluded with reasonable certainty that this particular rabbinic tradition dates from the Maccabaean period and codifies what had become a commonly shared notion.

Apparently, it was in this way that the Pharisaic–rabbinic principle emerged which later was called *piqquah nefesh*, 'care for life', which has precedence over the Shabbat. It is expressed in one case as follows:

> On the Shabbat one must take precautionary measures in life-threatening cases, the more carefully, the better, and without permission from the authorities. ... If someone has fallen in a well and is unable to come out, then one should break the wall open, descend and bring him up... One heats water for a sick person on the Shabbat, both for caring and for healing... Rabbi Yossi said: From which verse of Scripture do we know that the care for life is more important than the Shabbat?... (*t. Šab.* 15.11-16).

Here follows a series of midrashim that motivate the principle of 'care for life' from the Scriptures. Each time the limits are indicated. In the case of an ailment that was *not* life threatening, restrictive regulations were in force such as the prohibition to prepare a medicine on the Shabbat (*t. Šab.* 12.9-14). One of the supporting midrashim cited in a related passage merits our attention:

> R. Shimon ben Menasia says: See, it says: 'And observe the Shabbat for it is holy *for you*' (Exod. 31.14)—the Shabbat has been given to you, and not you to the Shabbat (*Mek., ki tisa* 1, p. 341).

R. Shimon ben Menasia (end second century CE) belonged to a pious group in the tradition of Hillel. A similar saying has been passed down from Jesus (see p. 153).

Concerning the Shabbat there is a clearly observable difference in accent between the Shammaites and the Hillelites. Using again the distinction made by R. Shimon ben Menasia: the Shammaites tended to hold on to the older tradition in which the Shabbat was pre-eminent, while the Hillelites emphasized respect for persons (*m. Šab.* 1.5-8). It appears, therefore, to be contradictory that R. Eliezer, who is known as a Shammaite, approves of carrying a sword on the Shabbat without there being direct mortal danger. In this case, the Shammaite respect of the Shabbat apparently gave way to their religio-national passion. The Hillelite objection with an appeal to the Scriptures is eloquent: 'It is written: "They shall forge their swords into ploughshares" ' (*m. Šab.* 6.4; Isa. 2.4; cf. pp. 64-65).

The fact that the ideas of the *Essenes* were much stricter than those of the Pharisees seems to be because they adhered to old traditions even more strongly than did the Shammaites. According to the *Damascus Document*, on the Shabbat one could bring cattle 2000 cubits outside of the place of dwelling to let them graze, but if an animal were to fall into a well, one may not 'raise it up'. If a person were to fall into water or some other dangerous place, one was not allowed to use a rope, a ladder, or other instruments for the rescue (CD 11.5-6, 13, 16-17). In another, recently published Essenic writing a less strict position is taken, which demonstrates that even the Essenes did not think uniformly in this matter (4Q265, *Serekh Damascus* frg 2, 1.5-7). As we have seen, the Pharisaic–rabbinic tradition resolutely chose another course in this matter. The calf in the well could be brought fodder 'so that it not die'; in order to rescue a person, one could go further and break down the well (*t. Šab.* 14.3; 15.13). It is important, furthermore, that the mentioned texts from the Damascus Rule belong to a collection of laws about various subjects that in form is strongly related to rabbinic legal literature (CD 9–14). The writing dates from the second century BCE and can be considered to be the oldest written collection of halakah.

The *Sadducees* placed the Shabbat rules strictly above those of a festival if this were to coincide with Shabbat. Hence their view that the Feast of Weeks (Pentecost, *Shavuot*) must always be celebrated on Sunday (see above p. 80). Essenes and Sadducees evidently both adhered to old ritual traditions and resisted the development of flexibility, such as that documented during the Maccabaean revolt, which apparently had the decided support of the Pharisees.

The result is a range of opinions, from the more conservative strict-

ness of the Essenes and Sadducees, through the moderately conservative Shammaites, and on to the flexible attitude of the Hillelites.

Purity Regulations
To understand the issue of purity, the significance of the temple must be
taken as point of departure. Even though the average Jew did not have
much to do with it, the temple ritual occupied a prominent portion of
Jewish law during the first century. In spite of reservations concerning
the high priestly families, the Pharisees still considered the temple to be
the focal point of Jewish existence. To this extent, the temple did have a
certain influence upon daily life, and that was true also for Jews in the
Diaspora. Philo tells of a pilgrimage to the Holy City, and from other
sources we understand that ten thousands of pilgrims went up annually,
many being from foreign countries (Philo, *On Providence* 2.64; Josephus, *War* 6.423-25; *t. Pisha* 4.14). Usually the three pilgrims' feasts
were celebrated in one's home town, but for purification after birth or
after the healing of leprosy, as well as for the fulfilment of a personal
pledge, an offering had to be brought to the temple. These occasions
were 'saved up', just as the money that was set aside for offerings. Once
in so many years one then went to the Holy City to celebrate, undoubtedly often choosing one of the pilgrims' feasts for the occasion. Such
an offering feast was then festive indeed. In antiquity, while one rarely
ate meat, those making the offering were allowed to consume the larger
portion of the Passover or peace offering that they had brought along.

This brings us to the *purity regulations*. Pilgrims often went up as a
group to Jerusalem, and to that end trained themselves in keeping the
rules of purity that were observed in and around the temple. A whole
system was involved that one could not easily master without concentrated training. A collection of such pilgrims' rules from the time of the
temple appear to form the core of the Mishnah tractate called *Ḥagigah*,
'Feast Times' (*m. Ḥag.* 2.5–3.6). The main principles of the system
were laid down in the Old Testament (Lev. 12–15), but this was later
expanded extensively. Just as in other areas, this development resulted
in a strong divergency of opinions, to which we will return later.

In the modern world, such matters can count little on being compre-
hended; it is, therefore, worthwhile to delve into the content of the
issue. It is true, however, that with the destruction of the temple, the
system of purification lost its basis and most of the rules have fallen

into disuse. Only a few rules that were not directly connected to the temple have remained in use in some other context.

The rules of purity can be understood as a structuring system that gives meaning through its own, non-rational logic. The basic principle is the antithesis between life and death concentrated around the offering. Everything having to do with the offering and the sanctuary belongs to the sphere of life and should be separated from the sphere of death outside. The contrast is expressed in the terms holy and unholy, pure and impure, and is further articulated in a concentric, hierarchic structure. Contact with something impure makes one unholy and that means being unfit for participation in the offering ritual. In order to be able to take part in the ritual, one must consciously train oneself in keeping the body in an uncontaminated state acquired through the relevant purity ritual.

As mentioned, the 'logic' of the system is not rational. The animal that is killed within the ritual counts as holy and must be treated in purity, but an animal that dies outside of this ritual is viewed as impure and unholy. Slaughtering for non-ritual purposes forms a neutral intermediate category: such meat is not holy and one does not, strictly speaking, have to treat it according to the rules of purity. On the other hand, it is kept separate from the flesh of animals that died a natural death or were killed in another manner, and requires separate stipulations, such as the 'pouring out' of the blood (see Deut. 15.20-25). These rules for 'normal' meat are still valid and are called, not without being paradoxical, 'ritual slaughter' (*šᵉḥiṭṭâ*).

In regard to the rules of purity, not only does the attitude of the soul count, but explicitly the disposition or indisposition of the body. It is necessary to enter into some detail here, keeping in mind that 'impure' is a priestly, technical term that does not coincide with 'filthy' or 'foul'. The strongest source of impurity is a human corpse. Persons and objects that touch it become a source of impurity. Discharges from the body, such as sperm and menstrual blood, are also a source of impurity, although ordinary urine and faeces are not. Leprosy is another source of impurity, as well as all dead animals that have not been ritually slaughtered.

The system consists of a concentric hierarchy expressed in two ways: in gradations of impurity and in levels of holiness (*m. Ḥag.* 2.7–3.6; *m. Kel.* 1). One who has been in contact with a source of impurity becomes impure and also transmits a derived impurity, thus yielding three degrees of impurity. Beside this, ascending levels of holiness can be achieved: first, the 'normal' gift for the priest (t^erûmâ), thereafter all sorts of offerings (*qodeš*), and finally the special 'sin offering' (*haṭṭā't*, see Num. 19). For each sort and degree of impurity and level of holiness there is a corresponding purification procedure, in which one bathes himself and observes one or more days of waiting. Contamination by a dead person was the most extreme type of defilement and required a waiting period of seven days, plus the sprinkling with the water of purification from the 'sin offering' and a ritual bath (Num. 19.11-12).

A classical problem is the group for whom the rules of purity were intended. Many biblical laws can be read as being valid only for those directly involved with the sanctuary and the offerings (see Lev. 15.31). Other laws clearly apply to the everyday life of the Israelites (Lev. 12.2; 13.46; 18.19). This means that in the various texts of the Old Testament there is no consistent boundary between the 'holy' and the 'profane'. According to one passage, the whole nation is called to be a holy congregation of priests (cf. Exod. 19.6). However that might have worked out in practice, in postexilic Judaism there was ambivalence and disagreement: the tendency to limit the validity of the purity regulations to the immediate range of the temple and the offerings did not dovetail with the flourishing concept that holiness was for the whole of Israel.

This difference was particularly true of a branch of the pilgrims' rules which deserves special attention: the purification of hands. Within the system this is a light impurity, from which one cleanses oneself by rinsing the hands. In the first century there was no consensus about the basis of this custom. A separate impurity of the hands does not occur in the writings of Qumran and there are well-founded reasons to assume that the Sadducees did not acknowledge it either. It was a characteristic Pharisaic custom, both according to the New Testament and according to the Talmud: 'Hillel and Shammai decreed the impurity of the hands' (*y. Šab.* 1.3d; Mk 7; see also pp. 157-58).

As is common with religious practices, this custom must have had a complex origin. There is a general connection to the widely spread custom in antiquity of washing the hands in running water or in the sea before prayer, as can be found already with Homer (*Odyssey* 2.261; 12.336). A more specific background probably lay in the training of pilgrims. Washing the hands before an ordinary meal is mentioned first in the collection of pilgrims' rules (*m. Ḥag.* 2.5). This simple gesture was evidently seen as an instructive religious exercise for all pilgrims. Certain Pharisees, however, observed it also apart from the pilgrimage. They considered themselves as 'pilgrims for life' and thus purified their hands each time before eating. In Jesus' time this must have been a fairly new custom that was not observed by all Pharisees. It is possible that it was practised especially in the context of the Pharisaic 'fellowships' (see p. 53).

The differences in opinion concerning the rules of purity involved as well an intermediate category between pure and impure that apparently had arisen from experience and involved waiting for sunset after the purifying bath in order to be completely pure (the *tebul yom*, see Lev. 15.5). This is comparable to the cleansing of hands as a separate category and was incorporated into the Pharisaic system in this manner. The Sadducees and the Essenes, however, did not seem to acknowledge this category either. In general, they thought less 'logically', but more literally and materially about purity and impurity. This difference was also reflected on a smaller scale within the Pharisaic movement. The Hillelites took the intention of the person more into account and therefore put more emphasis on the *significance* of the system of purity, while the Shammaites thought more in material and practical physical terms. In contrast to what one might expect, however, the Hillelite rationality in this area led to a stricter standpoint that that of the Shammaites.

The Essenes from Qumran employed their own system of rules of purity with characteristic rigour. They considered the commandment to be in a state of purity to be valid at all times. Just as in the Pharisaic fellowships, but much more strictly, they prepared themselves for every ordinary meal and the accompanying prayers as priests in the temple would do. Because they apparently did not acknowledge impurity of the hands as a separate category, they had to immerse themselves before every meal. This system, which contained an explicit gradation of purity of food and drink, also regulated the admittance to and the internal hierarchy of the sect.

A final relevant aspect relates to the geographic range of the purity regulations. In the first century, these were in principle only applicable within the Holy Land. For other countries, a principal and general decree of impurity was valid. This innovation in comparison to the Old Testament is ascribed to Shemaya and Avtalyon, leaders of the Pharisees from approximately two generations BCE (*y. Šab.* 1.3d). It was probably formulated because the dominant practice of idolatry or 'foreign cult' in other territories came to be associated with impurity, thus making all these areas impure, and it made the rules of purity inapplicable in the Diaspora. Further, Jews who came from the Diaspora had to purify themselves before taking part in the temple worship: they were counted to be impure as though they had touched a dead person, which demanded a purifying period of seven days. An example of this can be observed in relation to Paul (Acts 21.23-27).

Dietary Rules
Among New Testament interpreters a persistent confusion reigns on the topic of dietary regulations. This is particularly true concerning the explanation of Jesus' criticism of the Pharisaic commandment to wash one's hands (Mk 7.15) and concerning Peter's reluctance to be a guest of a non-Jew (Acts 10.28; 11.3). Ever since antiquity (see p. 261) exegetes have assumed that the latter issue had to do with forbidden food, thus misjudging an important distinction in the Jewish law. On the one hand, there is the 'impurity' of food, such as pork or eel, which are forbidden at all times (Lev. 11; Deut. 14.3-21). On the other hand, there is incidental impurity which can be transmitted to permitted food. The latter, a part of the system of rules of purity just discussed, is related to the temple ritual.

Somewhat confusingly, the Old Testament uses the same word, *tāmē'*, 'impure', for both categories. Nonetheless, two different systems are involved: dietary regulations and purity regulations. These two have a different status in the halakah, the Jewish law. The dietary rules are universally valid, for everyone at all times: they are clearly fixed in the Bible and have been expanded but little thereafter. The rules of purity, however, were valid particularly in the vicinity of the temple and in a limited manner also in normal life; these were expanded considerably after the Old Testament. Concerning the expansion of the rules of purity, the opinions diverged significantly among the various movements, including the Shammaites and the Hillelites.

The dietary regulations, which are primarily biblical, gave little occasion for discussion. One of the few expansions, which also led to a difference in opinion, was the prohibition to combine meat and milk. This was a generalization of the biblical prohibition to 'seethe a kid in its mother's milk' (Exod. 23.19). Although everyone agreed that this combination remained prohibited, there was room left for disagreement on fowl and milk products. The Shammaites thought that these could not be eaten together but could be served together, while the Hillelites —here as exception being stricter—held that they may not even be served together (*m. Ḥul.* 8.1). A basic biblical dietary regulation is the prohibition to eat blood and, therefore, also to eat meat that has not been slaughtered properly (Gen. 9.6; Deut. 12.23-24).

There was no debate on such biblical principles. While Jesus declares the cleansing of hands to be secondary to the biblical commandment of honouring one's parents, he would hardly do so in regard to the basically biblical rules for meat and drink (see pp. 157-58). It is also inconceivable that Peter waived the biblical dietary regulations in Caesarea: had he done so, the law-abiding brothers in Jerusalem would never have accepted him thereafter (pp. 231-32).

It must have been primarily other matters that played a role in the problems related to Jews and non-Jews or Jewish and non-Jewish followers of Jesus eating together. This topic will be pursued further later on in this chapter.

Divorce

The topic of divorce is of importance to the present discussion for two reasons. First, it was a significant source of strife in Judaism during the first century and we are, probably for that reason, well-informed about it. Secondly, it assumes an important place in early Christian writings as well. Together with reasons that will be clarified later, this topic in particular enables us to determine quite exactly the position of Jesus and his followers in the Judaism of their time.

The figure of John the Baptist offers an intriguing starting point. In all events, this sober penance preacher, introduced in the Gospels as the forerunner of Jesus, stood entirely within Judaism (cf. Lk. 16.16). There are two reports of his imprisonment by Herod Antipas; one is from Mark:

> He then, Herod, sent people and had him caught and chained in prison because of Herodias, the wife of Philip, his brother, for he had married her. For John used to say to Herod: It is not allowed for you to have the wife of your brother (Mk 6.17-18).

The report of Josephus is more complicated. Antipas proposed to Herodias and she accepted, after which both divorced their partners and married one another. In the meantime, John's summons to a God-fearing life received so much popular support that Antipas had him executed. An ensuing military defeat by his ex-wife was seen by the people as God's punishment (*Ant.* 18.109-19). Josephus is somewhat vague but does suggest that the critique on the royal marriage was the immediate cause of the execution. Among other things, Antipas transgressed the prohibition to marry one's sister-in-law (Lev. 18.16), while according to Jewish law Herodias had no right to initiate divorce procedures (see pp. 258-59). More specifically, Josephus reports that she despised the ancestral laws by remarrying while leaving her husband *'when he was still alive'* (*Ant.* 18.136).

Concerning the latter matter, Josephus himself differed with John the Baptist. In his autobiography he relates that he divorced his wife 'because in her behaviour she could not meet with approval', after which he remarried (*Life* 426). Such a discrete formulation can of course veil all kinds of misery, but in any case the author in principle saw no objection to divorce and remarriage. Even more clearly he states elsewhere in a commentary on the biblical laws that one could divorce 'for all sorts of reasons' (*Ant.* 4.253). This same specification is given by Philo of Alexandria in a commentary on the law (*Special Laws* 3.30). Apparently this was an accepted notion among prominent Jews in the first century CE. The undaunted preacher of penance did not agree. He was, as Jesus said, not 'a reed shaken by the wind' but steadfast as an oak that does not survive the violence of a storm unscathed (Lk. 7.24; see p. 142). The strict conviction of John is essential to what follows.

Valid grounds for divorce were a source of contention within the Pharisaic movement as well. Shammaites and Hillelites accepted the principle of divorce, which after all was assumed in the Torah, but disagreed as to the grounds for it. Disagreement focused on a text from the Torah (the patriarchal formulation is left for what it is):

> When a man acquires a woman and takes her in possession, and if she
> thereafter finds no grace in his eyes because he finds with her a matter of
> shame, and he writes her a declaration of divorce, puts this in her hand
> and sends her away from his house, and if she then... (Deut. 24.1-2)

In what follows, a further complication is mentioned that is not important here. The contested point concerned what constituted valid grounds for divorce, or, in other words, what was meant by a 'matter of shame'. The Shammaites placed the emphasis on the 'shame' and interpreted it as adultery or some other sexual misbehaviour. The Hillelites, on the contrary, emphasized the word 'matter': according to them *any matter* could serve as a valid reason when divorce seems inevitable (*m. Giṭ.* 9.10). It appears that the opinions of Josephus and Philo correspond to those of the Hillelites: divorce is allowed 'for all sorts of reasons'. A further look at the text teaches that this is also the intention of the Torah: the expression 'a matter of shame' is used in an earlier chapter in a clearly non-sexual context (Deut. 23.15[14]).

True to character, the Essenes had an extremely strict view in this area as well. They acknowledged no divorce at all, that is to say, they prohibited remarriage as long as the (former) partner lived. Among other things, they based this on the verse from the Torah that forbids the king 'to take many wives' (Deut. 17.17), to which they ascribed a broad implication:

> 'And you shall take not woman besides her sister...during her lifetime' (Lev. 18.18). And he shall take not woman besides her, for she alone shall be with him all the days of her life, but if she die he may marry another (*Temple Scroll*, 11QT 57.17-19).

The expression 'but if she die he may marry another' makes the intention clear: only when she dies may he remarry—divorce does not exist. This position is significant to our further argumentation. A passage from another Essene writing offers additional arguments. The writers accuse certain opponents:

> They take two women during their life, while the basis of creation is: 'Male and female did He create them' (Gen. 1.27); and they that went into the ark, 'came two and two in the ark' (Gen. 7.9); and about the Monarch it is written: 'And he shall not take many women' (Deut. 17.17). But David had not read the sealed book of law in the ark of the covenant, for it was not opened in Israel since the day that Eleazar died... (*Damascus Document*, CD 4.19–5.4)

The rule for the king, which David transgressed 'unknowingly', is here assumed to be applicable to others. Elements that will contribute to our further discussion include: the argument that the first created humans formed a single pair and the thought that later generations did not interpret the Torah according to its true intention.

Surveying the whole, we see a broad spectrum of positions. The Essenes totally rejected divorce and remarriage during the lifetime of the partner. The Shammaites allowed divorce but only in the case of adultery. At the other end were the Hillelites, as well as certain prominent Jews, such as Plato and Josephus, who accepted the dissolution of the marriage bond 'on all kinds of grounds'. John the Baptist, with whom we began, appears to have had affinity with the Essenes. In any case, he did not accept Herodias's divorce and considered her marriage to Antipas to be a double trespass. In the following chapter we shall see that a radical 'Essene' standpoint was adhered to by one who was at one time John's follower: Jesus.

Jews and Non-Jews

The attention given to living according to the law should not lead us to forget that Jewish existence in antiquity was determined for a large part by the relationship with non-Jews. This was not less true in the Holy Land than in the Diaspora. One could say that the relationship to other peoples forms a fundamental facet of what is designated as 'Jewish identity'. In itself this is not unique of Jews alone. A duality between the general and the particular lies at the basis of all human identity. We are ourselves in relation to others, and within the context of the closest affinity the most salient differences become apparent. The human spirit is binary and operates with polarities: yes and no, good and evil, inside and outside, familiar and strange. Nuances emerge from subtle gradations of correspondence and distinction.

Jewish Specificity and Universal Humanity

In Scripture itself that which is universally human is constantly placed alongside that which is uniquely Israelite. The Torah, the holy book of the Jews, does not start with the calling of Israel but with humanity as such, *humankind created in God's image* (Gen. 1.26-27). The list of 70 peoples, which stand for all of humankind, begins by repeating: 'Adam, human, begat (his third son) after his likeness and in his image...' (Gen. 5.3). This is reiterated a third time in the covenant with Noah, which forms the basis for renewed humanity after the flood: 'He who sheds the blood of man, by man shall his blood be shed, *for in the image of God did He make man*' (Gen. 9.6). In this manner, the history of the patriarchs and of the people of Israel, with as climax the giving of the law at Sinai, is placed—thrice emphasized—within the framework of the alliance to all of humankind.

This approach continues throughout the whole of the Hebrew Scriptures. The exclusive revelation of the law to Israel (Exod. 19–20) contrasts with the way in which Moses, one chapter previously, allows himself to be advised in jurisprudence and management by his non-Israelite father-in-law, Jethro. In yet another preceding chapter, there is an enigmatic story about the never-ending strife with Amalek, later understood as the proverbial arch-enemy, bent on destroying Israel. Further, the fear for the survival of person and possessions appears in the Torah back to back with openness and inquisitiveness towards the outside world. The same is true of later books: alongside the book of Ezra, which describes the recreation of the Jewish nation after exile, there is the universalist prophecy of Jonah in which Nineveh is presented to Israel as exemplary.

Within the Phaisaic–rabbinic movement as well there was a more universal pursuit beside a more particularistic one. The followers of Hillel emphasized the more universal aspects. His own statement that caring for one's body is a token of honouring God's image has been cited above. In another tradition, Hillel teaches a non-Jew what the essence of the Torah is, namely, the commandment to love one's neighbour, in the form of the Golden Rule: 'What you dislike, do not do that to another' (*b. Šab.* 31a). More than a century after Hillel, R. Akiva combines that which is universally human with the particularity of Israel. He taught in the humane manner of Hillel, was greatly influential in collecting and reformulating the Pharisaic–rabbinic tradition, and died a martyr in the second revolt against Rome (135 CE). Together this made him a figure of legendary significance for rabbinic Judaism. Of him it is written:

> 'You shall love your neighbour as yourself'—R. Akiva says: this is a fundamental principle of the Torah (*Sifra, qedoshim* 4.89b).

> R. Akiva taught: He who sheds blood, (the Scriptures) reckon it to him as though he has diminished the image (of God). Why? 'He who sheds the blood of man, by man shall his blood be shed', for 'in the image of God did He make man' (*Gen. R.* 34.4; p. 326; cf. Gen. 9.6).

This emphasis on loving the neighbour as the 'summary of the law' is obviously highly significant for our understanding of the New Testament.

Another attitude, with more emphasis on the specifically Jewish aspect, was championed by the Shammaites. As already mentioned, their position had the upper hand among the Pharisees before the war against Rome and even gained in influence towards the end (see pp. 64-65). In general, times of threat compel an emphasis on distinctive traits and on the differences with the enemy, while quieter times allow more charitable attitudes to flourish. Such feelings are not necessarily caused by the external circumstances: they are always present, openly or latently, but they flare up or ebb away, dependent on the circumstances.

That the more closed Shammaitic position undoubtedly had ancient roots becomes even more plausible when taking the attitude of the Essenes into consideration as it appears in the Qumran writings. Non-Jews never play a positive role in these writings, but occur primarily as foreign intruders who will be mercilessly vanquished in the final battle (1QM 14.4-5). They are evidently viewed as being nothing more than idolaters and godless, with whom contact, including economic relations, is strictly limited for fear of the contamination of idolatry (1QpHab 13.1-4; CD 12.8-11). Again we find that the Essenes maintained a more rigorous form of the motifs found among the Shammaites as well.

From the Torah texts given below, it is apparent that the openness of the Hillelites also has ancient roots. Furthermore, it is justified to relate this openness to their observable sensitivity towards the general Hellenistic manner of thought. Hillel's emphasis upon loving one's neighbour and upon caring for the body have already been mentioned. Another example is Yohanan ben Zakkai's allegoric Scripture interpretation (see p. 86). Such open-mindedness is naturally to be expected to a even greater degree of Diaspora Jews, of which Philo of Alexandria is a proverbial example. This is, however, not the only conceivable attitude present among the Jews of the Diaspora. The history of the North African revolt shows that under extreme circumstances the Hellenistic Jews were also capable of armed resistance (see pp. 36-38).

The shift from a Shammaite to a Hillelite majority after 70 CE is understandable due to the greater losses among the nationalistic Shammaites. Why they were dominant before the war is not exactly known. The deepest promptings of religious, cultural and national feeling of identity often elude assessment. It is, however, probable that the rising tide of anti-Roman sentiment before the war was an important contributing factor.

Speaking in terms of the subtle theology of the book of Deuteronomy, an additional aspect can be noted. The most characteristic trait of Israel does not, in the deepest sense, originate in themselves, but is bestowed on them by God's calling and purpose:

> Not because you are more numerous than all peoples did the Lord delight in you and choose you, for you are the smallest of all peoples, but because the Lord loved you and because He kept His oath which He had sworn to your fathers (Deut. 7.7-8; cf. 9.5).

Once present, however, the calling and the commission contained in it determine Israel's manner of life and its destiny. In a related passage in Exodus we read:

> I have carried you on eagle's wings and have brought you to Me; therefore, if you truly listen to My voice and keep My covenant, then you, out of all peoples, will be to Me a costly possession—for the whole earth is Mine—and you shall be a kingdom of priests to Me, a holy people (Exod. 19.4-6).

The final purpose of Israel, the 'invisible' core of its identity, lies in the covenant with God. All the characteristic traits, humanly speaking, are derivatives of this, as the stamp left on human existence by the divine signet. Jewish liturgy, Jewish rituals and customs, writings and traditions, community life, cultures and languages, the Jewish destiny, the inscrutable envy of the nations—this all is but a particular combination of traits that other peoples also have. Humanly speaking, the Jews are a people as other peoples. The true 'uniqueness' does not originate in themselves, but in what Scripture recognizes as the divine calling, which surpasses other peoples and even Israel itself.

As with all communities, the most characteristic trait of Israel, humanly speaking, is most demonstrably apparent in liturgy and ritual. At liturgic moments, such as the recitation of the Shema, the community, and the individual within the community, recognizes itself, as the fathers of old, to be rescued at the Reed Sea, chosen as God's people at Sinai, equipped for its destiny by the commandments of the law of the covenant. In Deuteronomistic terms, keeping the commandments is Israel's human answer to God's undeserved love, an answer that can be purified into an unselfish, reciprocal love. Jewish rituals and Jewish liturgy are in themselves in no sense superior to those of other peoples. The distinctiveness lies in the specific combination: *the uniqueness of Judaism lies not so much in its content as its form.*

This religious philosophic reflection also explains the fact that in antiquity two apparently contradictory aspects could go hand in hand in the attitude of many Jews towards the non-Jewish world. Opposite to their relative openness towards the many human aspects of relationships with the non-Jews there was the strict avoidance of all forms of idolatry. Many Greek-speaking Jews, as well as Pharisees and rabbis, and especially the Hillelites, valued good relations with non-Jews. Attention must now be given to the attitude towards idolatry.

Idol Worshippers, God-Fearers and Proselytes

The whole concept of 'idolatry' is only understandable in terms of the biblical-Jewish tradition, which is also normative for Christianity. This becomes clear in the Graeco-Jewish term *eidōlolatria,* 'idolatry, image worship', and even more explicitly in the Hebrew designation, *'abōdâ zārâ,* 'alien cult'. Fundamental to this is the exclusive attitude that conflicts with the general idea that all forms of worship essentially have the same goals in mind and are thus capable of flexible, reciprocal 'hospitality'. According to this general concept, a Syrian, Greek or Egyptian could participate in the local ritual anywhere he went, without being bothered by the fact that the gods were called by other names. On this point, the Jews remained spiritual outsiders, children of 'Abraham the sojourner' (Gen. 14.13 LXX). Their attitude of non-collaboration with any forms of idolatry, including that of the cult of the emperor, was readily perceived by others as a lack of loyalty. To an even greater extent, this was true later of the non-Jewish Christians, who had to distinguish themselves from the surrounding environment.

The Jew bore this stigma with pride and in general earned the respect of others. Their worship service was admired by many as being a strange but ancient and elevated tradition. With an emphasis that is understandable from the intention of his work, Josephus supplies a list of official declarations in which the Jewish communities were granted exemption from taxes, services or other civic duties that clashed with the practice of their religion (*Ant.* 14.185-267). Outbursts of enmity against the Jews as in Alexandria (see pp. 37-38) should be seen as exceptional. In terms of the Roman regime, Judaism was a *religio licita,* 'a recognized religion'. From this position, many Jews both in the Diaspora and in the Holy Land could allow themselves to have a fairly tolerant attitude towards the non-Jews.

In contrast, where local or central governments for some reason or another obligated the Jews to participate in the 'alien cults', they resisted, going as far as martyrdom or armed revolt. A prime example of this is the Maccabaean revolt, launched by the priestly family of the Hasmonaeans, also called the Maccabaeans, against the Graeco-Syriac king Antiochus Epiphanes, and still commemorated at the Feast of Hanukka. The revolt led to a full war of independence in which— unique in Jewish history—the neighbouring Idumaeans were violently forced to convert to Judaism (Josephus, *Ant.* 13.257-58). The destruction of heathen temples was greeted with elation, because these were perceived as a violation of the holiness of the country. An echo of this can be heard in the blessing that one said when seeing the ruins of a heathen temple (*m. Ber.* 9.1). This 'zealotic', religio-national motivation must have played a great role in the revolts against Rome in 66, 115 and 132 CE as well.

It was stated above that Jewish identity is made up of the duality of that which is individual and that which is universal. More explicitly, Jewish identity circles around two poles: *exclusiveness and tolerance*. In regard to 'alien worship', Jewish identity is exclusive: it avoids every contact with idolatry and its attributes. When no idolatry is involved, however, Jewish identity is capable of remarkable tolerance. R. Yohanan (mid third century) even went as far as stating that non-Jews in their own countries were not idolaters, because 'they possess the tradition of their fathers' (*b. Ḥul.* 13b).

Total avoidance of contact with idolatry entailed in principle for the Jews a taboo on pagan feast days, temples, offerings, and all ingredients and attributes connected with these, as can be read in the Mishnah (*m. 'Abod. Zar.* 1–5). Wine, meat and other ingredients known to be used in cultic ritual were forbidden by definition when of non-Jewish origin. When, however, it was clear that the element had no pagan ritual function, one was allowed to use it, according to the Pharisaic–rabbinic point of view. The decision about this was made on the basis of generally recognizable, external details. For example, damage to the nose or ear of human images on jewellery or utensils made these unfit for ritual use, so that the Jews could without further ado assume that non-Jews did not ascribe religious significance to them. The location and function of an object could also provide information as to its possible cultic function. A tale is told of a heathen philosopher who encountered Rabban Gamliel (end of first century) in a Roman bathhouse and asked him how he viewed the statue of Aphrodite standing there. The statue apparently caused no problem because its ornamental and non-cultic function were clearly recognizable (*m. 'Abod. Zar.* 3.4). In other words, Jews were trained to read the significance of certain things to non-Jews from the use made of them.

There were also philosophically inclined non-Jews who were critical of the worship of images and other material expressions of idolatry. The imageless worship of Judaism was often attractive to them as being more pure. Something of this nature can be heard in the question of the philosopher in the bathhouse. Herein lay part of the appeal of Judaism

for ethically inclined non-Jews, to which was added the moral selectivity of the Jews, who, just like the Christians after them, condemned
the shedding of blood at gladiator games and all kinds of sexual licentiousness. Jews of the line of Hillel could get on well with such ethically inclined non-Jews. R. Yoshua, one of the spokesmen of the
Hillelites (approximately 90 CE), is quoted as speaking of the 'righteous
among the nations, who have a part in the world to come' (*t. Sanh.*
13.2). With this he apparently referred to the non-Jews who withheld
themselves from idolatry, shedding of blood, and sexual offences, the
three central commandments that no Jew may ever transgress, that is,
universally valid commandments (*b. Sanh.* 74a). They were later called
the *Noachic commandments*, commandments for 'the children of Noah'
(cf. Gen. 9). Various traditions and opinions existed, according to
which the universal commandments counted four, six, seven, or more
(cf. *t. 'Abod. Zar.* 8.4).

In this connection, the so-called *God-fearers* must be mentioned. We
encounter them in the New Testament, for example, the centurion from
Capernaum, who had helped to build the local synagogue, and his
colleague from Caesarea whose name and unit are even known:
'Cornelius, the centurion of the so-called Italian Company, devout *and
God fearing*' (Lk. 7.5; Acts 10.2; see pp. 203-205). The Pharisaic–
rabbinic tradition mentions *yir'ê šāmayim*, 'they who fear Heaven', and
as non-Jews these are consistently differentiated from proselytes. The
claim that this is only a theoretical or 'theological' category has been
made untenable once and for all by a recently published Greek
inscription coming from Aphrodisias in Asia Minor and dating from the
third century. The inscription contains a list of members of a synagogue
in which, besides a series of Jews, a considerable number of God-
fearers are enumerated. These are non-Jews who turned away from
idolatry and felt drawn to the teachings of Judaism, without, however,
totally converting to Judaism. They were not treated as 'servants of
idols', but could join in the celebration of the synagogue services, at
least during the major feasts, and formed as such a circle of sympathizers around the synagogue. There were many such people in Antioch
according to Josephus (*War* 7.45), and it is not coincidental that
Christianity first spread among non-Jews in this area (Acts 11.20-26).

Besides the God-fearers there were also *proselytes*, that is, non-Jews
who fully converted to Judaism. Men had to be circumcised, take a
purifying bath and bring an offering; for women only the purifying bath

and offering were necessary. According to rabbinic thought, in practically everything proselytes are equal to born Jews, and their children are totally equal. It is said of various leading Pharisees that they descended from proselytes (for example, Shemaya and Avtalyon, *b. Sanh.* 96b). According to estimates, proselytes in the Graeco-Roman period must have formed a substantial portion of the Jewish people, and they were in general well accepted. In this again the school of Hillel exhibited the most tolerance towards non-Jews. A less accepting attitude was demonstrably present among the Shammaites. A series of stories has been preserved about non-Jews with questions about the Torah who were dismissed by Shammai but were received with warmth and humour by Hillel (*b. Šab.* 31a). The Essenes must to have been very rejecting of proselytes.

The non-Jews with whom a Jew could be confronted fell thus into three categories: idolaters, non-Jews of indeterminable background and God-fearers. Proselytes counted as Jews. The same distinctions were applied to objects and food products of non-Jews: consecrated to the gods, indeterminable or non-consecrated. On the basis of such divisions, all sorts of practical rules obtained in social traffic. In particular the Pharisaic–rabbinic tradition was characterized by a level-headed attitude: *idolatry is not in the things themselves but in people's minds.* Actual idolatry was taken seriously indeed, but non-Jews and their goods were treated with common sense, thus making it possible to maintain good relations with non-Jewish neighbours, fellow citizens, and business relations.

In contrast to what is often thought, it was not unusual for Jews and non-Jews to visit one another socially and partake of refreshments together. For practical problems, practical solutions were sought in line with the basic distinctions mentioned. A non-Jewish host could procure Jewish wine (*m. 'Abod. Zar.* 5.4-5), and the Jewish guest was not obligated actually to partake of all of the refreshments provided. Where people are prepared to live with such small inconveniences, nothing need stand in the way of a good relationship. Little matters become a problem between people only when outward or inward tensions charge them with extra significance. Something of this nature occurred on the eve of the first war against Rome when, under pressure from the Shammaites, the oil, bread, cheese and other products of the non-Jews were declared to be strictly forbidden (see p. 65). A number of these decrees were later migitated in practice.

In such matters there was considerable diversity of opinion. It is to be expected that here again the Essenes were the most repudiating of traffic with non-Jews, while the Hillelites were the most liberal. A story is told of R. Meir, a rabbi in the line of Hillel, mid second century, who was a guest of an affluent but uncouth non-Jew in his city. When his lordship missed a certain type of nut on his richly laden marble tripod, he smashed the costly piece of furniture, and, R. Meir continued, 'Then I applied to him the verse: '[The righteous eat to satisfy their souls, but] the belly of the godless shall suffer want'' (Prov. 13.25; *Pesiqta* 6, p. 115). R. Meir understood the art of self-control through wisdom, and could thus be at ease as the guest of a non-Jew. A strict, renouncing attitude is also present in later rabbinic traditions. According to R. Shimon ben Elazar, *nota bene* a disciple of R. Meir, Jews outside of the Holy Land are never safeguarded against idolatry. According to him, when they are guests of non-Jews, they have compromised themselves ahead of time even if they partake only of their own food and drink from their own utensils (*t. 'Abod. Zar.* 4.6). We see, thus, that both extremes of Jewish identity—exclusiveness and tolerance—are operative within the same rabbinic context.

'Jews' and 'Israel'

The bipolar identity of the Jews in antiquity had yet another remarkable aspect: they were designated by two names that were interchanged according to the situation: 'Jews' and 'Israel'. This double appellation plays an important role in the New Testament. The phenomenon still exists today, but has undergone many complications in the course of time.

Put simply, the phenomenon has to do with the context in which the Jews are seen. When viewed in the perspective of the biblical story, as the redeemed people that received the Torah, the designation 'Israel' is used. This is naturally the case for prayers in which they address their Creator. As long as only Jews are involved, this label is further found in the midrash or Scripture interpretation, in laws and commentaries, and in stories. In all of these situations, Jews are seen within an intra-Jewish setting and are indicated as 'Israel'. When non-Jews are involved as well, either as acting persons in laws, commentaries or stories or as direct partners in communication, the designation 'Jews' is used both by non-Jews and by Jews themselves. In other words, *'Jews' is the name used in interaction with non-Jews, 'Israel' indicates an intra-Jewish context*. This phenomenon operates in all relevant languages—Hebrew, Aramaic, Greek and Latin.

Thus we find in our sources that Jews pray to the God of 'Israel' and for the deliverance of 'Israel'; but the non-Jew rejoices over the incorruptible behaviour of a Jew and praises 'the God of the Jews'. Furthermore, in conversation with fellow Jews, Jews speak of themselves as 'Israel', but when a Jew is asked by a non-Jew concerning his background, he says, 'I am a Jew'. This socio-linguistic mechanism functions in a most refined manner, by which the designation 'Israel' sometimes assumes a sublime aspect through its association with the covenant and the worship service, while in antiquity 'Jew' was not negative but politically neutral.

The duality of the designations 'Israel' and 'Jews' has existed throughout the ages, but not always in the same manner. There are considerable shifts between consecutive periods: (1) the Old Testament period, (2) the Graeco-Roman period, (3) the Christian Middle Ages and (4) the modern era. We are particularly concerned with the Graeco-Roman period in which the New Testament emerged; however, the other periods cannot be left out of consideration. Our Bible translations confront us with modern usage; on the other hand, the concepts and traditions from the Middle Ages still have their effect, and in order to understand the usage in the New Testament, we must first consider the Old. Hence the four periods cannot be completely isolated, but they should be distinguished.

(1) According to the *Old Testament* the name 'Israel' was first given to the patriarch Jacob (Gen. 32.28). Thereafter it is used for the 12 tribes that issued from him, in the typically Hebrew expression 'the children of Israel'. At the end of the tenth century BCE the kingdom of David and Solomon fell apart (1 Kgs 12). The southern kingdom is called 'Judah' after the largest of the two southern tribes, the other one being Benjamin. The name 'Israel' now acquires a more limited, political significance as the designation of the northern kingdom comprising the other tribes. The book of Kings speaks thereafter consistently of 'the kings of Israel' in contradistinction to 'the kings of Judah'. This situation terminated when two centuries later Assyia 'took *Israel* into exile' (2 Kgs 17.6). It was to be an exile without restoration. Since that time 'the ten tribes of Israel' continue to exist only in legend (cf. pp. 371-72). Life went on in Judah, however. It is said of Hezekiah that he trust in 'the God of Israel'—the ancient name that evidently had

continued to be used as the indication of the covenant people (2 Kgs 18.5). Exile ensued there as well, but this time with a subsequent restoration, and thus Ezra in his chronicle of rebuilding the nation could speak of 'the children of Israel who returned from exile' (Ezra 6.21).

The name 'Judah', originally the designation of a tribe and its tribal territory, had now also assumed a limited, political significance indicating the southern kingdom. Since the Assyrian crusades, the word *Yehudi*, 'Judaean' or 'subject of Judah', occurs as well in Assyrian sources, and there is mention of 'Judaean' as a language (2 Kgs 16.6; 18.26, 28). During the Persian domination, the name Judah, in Aramaic *Yehud*, referred to the small administrative territory around Jerusalem. The inhabitants are called *Yehudim*, which we must translate as 'Judaeans', though the same people could be called 'Israel' (Ezra 6.14, 21). This is an early form of the double designation.

(2) In the *Graeco-Roman period* the significance of the name *Yehudim* shifts. The 'Yehudim' live dispersed from Babylonia to Spain, from Alexandria to the Black Sea, in Galilee and Perea, without political or geographic connection to Judaea, the Jewish country and Roman administration unit *Judaea*, although *Yehudim* live there as well. The name has come to indicate an ethnic-religious group which anyone who performs the required rituals could join. The earliest testimory to such a formal joining as proselyte can be found in the book of Judith (14.10; third—second century BCE). From this point on, the Hebrew designation *Yehudi*—Aramaic *Yehudai*, Greek *Ioudaios* and Latin *Iudaeus*—can only be properly rendered as 'Jew'. The Greek standard expression *ethnos tōn Ioudaiōn,* 'people' or 'community of Jews' (e.g. Acts 10.22), hardly has geographic connotations, but is instead clearly a religious and ethnic indication.

The name 'Israel' also undergoes some change at this time. This designation has a remarkable characteristic that has to do with aspects of the Hebrew language. From ancient times *Yisrael* occurs only in the singular, and in the Old Testament it indicates either the patriarch Jacob or the people as a collective; for the plural, 'children of Israel' is employed. In the Hellenistic period, the Hebrew *Yisrael* came to signify an individual as well. Confusion could be avoided in Greek by forming the word *Israēlitēs*, from which 'Israelite' is derived. This term is used, among others, by Jews who address their own people: 'Men, Israelites...' (e.g. Acts 2.2).

Thus the prerequisites for the double appellation are created: 'Israel' is used in the intra-Jewish context, 'Jews' when a non-Jewish context is implied. This socio-linguistic rule functions consistently in all sorts of ancient Jewish literature, in Hebrew and Aramaic as well as in Greek and Latin. An example is offered by the book of Esther, which preserves the atmosphere of the Persian period but which underwent a final redaction in the Hellenistic period. In the Hebrew version, only the name 'Jews' is used (*Yehudim*, 48 times) and the name 'Israel' does not occur. This corresponds to the setting of the book: the Jews are presented in the context of the Persian Empire where they lived scattered over 'the 127 provinces' (Est. 8.9). There is not a single reference to the Jewish religion. The Greek translation preserved in the Septuagint supplements what was felt to be lacking: Esther is presented as a devout Jewish woman who keeps all the commandments and with her uncle Mordechai prays to God 'to save *Israel*'. It is striking how in all of these added intra-Jewish scenes, only the name 'Israel' is used.

In a later chapter we shall see that this double appellation occurs in the same manner in the various part of the New Testament. 'Israel' continues to be the intra-Jewish name for the covenant people, 'Jews' the designation used in interaction with non-Jews. In the epistles of Paul and the Acts of the Apostles, this interaction is a matter of course, for example, in the characteristic expression *Ioudaioi kai Hellēnes*, 'Jews and Greeks' (Acts 14.1; 18.4; Rom. 1.16; Gal. 3.28). It probably derives from the Graeco-Jewish usage as appears in an Aramaic analogy in the Babylonian and Palestinian Talmud: *Yehudai we-Aramai*, 'Jew and Aramean' (*y. Šab.* 4.2, 35b; *y. Sanh.* 3.6, 21b; *b. Šab.* 139a; *b. B. Bat.* 21a). Just like 'Greek', 'Aramean' represents here the non-Jew, and the use of the name 'Jew' unmistakably indicates interaction with non-Jews.

(3) A following radical change takes place with the *rise of Christianity* as a world religion. This shift is related to the duality of the relationship of Christians to Jews, about which we spoke in the introduction. On the one hand, except for the confession of Jesus as Messiah, the Christians shared the cornerstones of their religion with the Jews: liturgy, Holy Scriptures, Scripture interpretation, belief in the creation and in redemption, and ethical obligations. On the other hand, they had to distinguish themselves from the Jews in the conviction that redemption dawned in the crucified and risen Messiah, Jesus. Gradually the church came to see itself as the true Israel and appropriated, along with the assurance of salvation, the name of the covenant people. In this,

'Israel' acquired an exclusively spiritual significance (see p. 35, [417]). The Jews were no longer 'Israel', but were from then on what the designation in its ominous tones indicates: 'Jews'. From that moment on there was no longer a duality of equal but socially specific designations. 'Israel' had become the chosen people, 'the Jews' the rejected one. In a later chapter we return to the momentous question to what extent this is already visible in the New Testament.

In the meantime, a third designation of the Jews emerged that has not yet discussed: 'Hebrews'. In the Old Testament this designation has the connotation of a 'subservient foreigner', like the children of Israel were in Egypt (Exod. 1–2). Later the term acquires somewhat the same function as 'Jews', namely, as an indication of Jews in non-Jewish speech context (Jon. 1.9). From the time of the Roman emperors on, this designation was used with the connotation 'ancientness and eminence'. The negative colouring of the word 'Jews' strengthened this development. An example from the church father Eusebius is remarkable: he is full of praise about the patriarchs as 'Hebrews', in contrast to the 'Jews' and their Mosaic law (*Praep. ev.* 7.6-8). The term 'Hebrew' as the designation for Jews is permanently established in some languages (Italian: *ebreo*; Russian: *evreyski*).

In mediaeval Christian Europe, the Jews were the only more or less tolerated dissident group. They were alternately driven out and then again admitted, now in this country, then in another. This vacillating socio-political policy issued from the same fundamentally ambivalent attitude of the Christians towards their mother religion. 'Jew' became a term of abuse that was equal to murderer of God, servant of Satan, and extortioner, the latter as result of their success in one of the few occupations that was allowed them due to the fact that it was forbidden to Christians: banking. Viewing Jews as the servants of Satan indicates a spread of diabolization, which will be treated in the final chapter. The Jews were now the scapegoat for all shortages and accidents. Crusades and the plague were just so many catastrophes for the maligned folk. Improvement came only with the Reformation, not because Protestants were fonder of Jews, but because religious pluralism developed. Considering the history of the Middle Ages, it is understandable that many Jews in modern times feel attracted to liberal and revolutionary movements. Equal rights emerged when the political domination of the church was curtailed for good by the American, French and following revolutions.

(4) This brings us to the contradictions of *modern times*. Church and state were separated, religion has become a private matter, the nation an all-determinant value. Many Jews greeted this change as a liberation, but the problems did not remain in abeyance and neither were the Jews spared them. How could one at the same time be a Jew and a citizen in this situation? Some fled into an assimilated Reform Judaism, others retreated into a bastion of 'orthodoxy'—a new concept for Jews. Many succumbed to baptism as the 'ticket of admission' to Christian civilization, or disappeared through silent secularization. How did a respectable citizen and Christian view all these emancipated, assimilated, orthodox Israelite, or baptized Jews? Were they regular citizens, or in the end still...Jews? What was determinant in this, now that religion had become a private matter? Racism offered a solution with 'semitic' being the foreign element, an argument that sounded both modern and familiar. Another solution was offered by state socialism that dispensed with Jewish distinctiveness as a capitalist creation, but nonetheless could be manifestly anti-Jewish. The Jews found their own answer: Zionism, the Jewish national movement based on the same contradictory separation of church and state. All these alternatively clashing and converging movements led in the end to two occurrences that have determined the profile of the twentieth century: the mass murder of Jews and the birth of the State of Israel.

What has become of the two designations in this turbulent time? For some time, 'Jew' became a term that no one dared to use. 'Israelite' was rediscovered. Since the nineteenth century, this Greek designation for a member of the Old Testament covenant people can also indicate a member of the Israelite religion. Since the founding of the State of Israel, the name 'Israel' has again acquired a political connotation. We now speak of 'Israelis', who are not only Jewish, but also Arabic, Muslim or Christian. At the same time, Israel is the 'Jewish' state where every Jew is freely admitted, by virture of the declaration of independence. A question that has not been solved in this regard is, 'Who is a Jew?' For the first national language, the other name was chosen, 'Hebrew', or in Hebrew itself *Ivrit*.

Chapter 3

JESUS

Turning now to the New Testament, there would be many reasons for not beginning but ending with Jesus. What can be said about this puzzling and penetrating figure—let alone his significance for time and eternity—if the stories of the witnesses, the commentaries that have arisen around them, the intuitions of saints and sages from all ages are not first allowed to have their impact upon us?

Testimonies, commentaries, intuitions—all *about* Jesus, but what do we have *of him himself*? The present chapter, in contrast to those following, is not about written texts by one or more authors and redactors. It concerns someone whose teachings and life's example were preserved in oral traditions committed to writing only after one or two generations. With the successive attempts at writing down the 'gospel', the design and message became progressively better thought through. What was won on clarity, however, was lost in proximity to the times and environment of Jesus himself. Many exegetes, therefore, consider it futile to inquire after the 'historical Jesus', and devote their attention rather to the final text of the Gospels.

Nonetheless, undeniably Jesus stands at the beginning. From all the testimonies an unmistakable personality emerges whose teachings and life's story in one way or another have always continued to appeal to us. He left us no writings, but his voice was incorporated in what his followers passed on. This 'living voice' is what we have *of him*. Therefore we begin at that beginning, with the consciousness that he who wants to say 'alpha' here, of necessity must also say 'omega'. Theologically speaking, we cannot begin at the beginning without some prolegomena about the problem of the historical Jesus. There is no objection, however, if the reader chooses to skip over the following section.

The Historical Figure of Jesus

The Strangeness

Let us start close to home. To what extent can a person ever be adequately described? Does not every one have a personal, irreducible secret that is never captured completely in terms of biography, psychology or sociology? On the other hand, how can we divorce someone's personality from the role and significance that she or he has for others? The more important someone is considered to be, the more this holds true: the person is ascribed special significance by investing in him or her something of oneself. The inscrutable secret of such a life lies then in the inpenetrable interior—the doubts, griefs or joys that are of no concern to the clamouring crowd. The popular curiosity about the private life of well-known persons is often an injustice to their real significance and is therefore petty, disrespectful and misleading. Recent Jesus films make that more than clear.

It is more fitting to allow oneself to be *amazed* by the uncommon significance that an apparently familiar person can have. Astonishment involves being open for the mystery, for the enigma that time and again reveals that a person is different from what one thought. It means welcoming that which is strange in another as something novel with a message, something that can effectuate changes. This does not happen of its own accord, for people tend to cling to the familiar and to resist what is strange.

An account from the Gospels places this vividly before us. At the beginning of his public ministry, when returning to the village where he had grown up, Jesus visited the synagogue and began to speak of things unheard of. The amazement of the village dwellers is imaginable:

> And many that heard him were perplexed and said: Where does he get this from? and what is that wisdom that has been granted to him, and all the miracles which his hands perform? Is this not the carpenter, the son of Maria and the brother of Jacob, Yosi, Judah, and Simon? And are his sisters not among us? And they were offended in him. And Jesus said unto them: A prophet is nowhere without respect except in his home town and among his relatives and in his own house. And he could do no miracles there… And he was amazed at their unbelief (Mk 6.2-6; cf. Lk. 4.22; Jn 6.42).

Certain details of the report suggest a connection with the direct environment of Jesus, for example, the names, including their form. *Maria* and *Yosi* represent the Galilean pronunciation of the biblical names Miriam and Joseph. The same is true of Jesus' own name. The Old Testament *Yehoshua* or *Yeshua* was pronounced in Galilee as *Yeshu*, from whence the Greek *Iēsous* and the Latin *Iesus*. The language of this account also reveals characteristic elements. The continually repeated 'and' at the beginning of the sentences and the expression 'nowhere... except' suggests there having been an Aramaic or Hebrew original. The word translated 'miracle' is more related to the Hebrew *gᵉbûrâ*, 'power of God', than to the Greek *dunamis*, 'dynamic', 'potential'. Jesus is thus portrayed here in his rural Galilean–Jewish surroundings.

Let us not, however, confine ourselves to the trivial, as did his fellow villagers. To call him 'Jesus of Nazareth' does have a biblical precedent (Acts 10.38), but it can obliterate the specific. Jesus' reaction exposes the mistakenness of his fellow villagers and offers a glimpse of his secret. That he was 'amazed at their unbelief' is striking, but understandable; he had evidently expected a different reaction. What did he mean, however, with the saying about a prophet not being 'without respect except in his home town and among his relatives and in his own house'? At first sight this appears to be an adage that expresses the necessary distance between an unusual person and his 'familiar' surroundings; however, more is involved.

The saying about a prophet and his home town occurs elsewhere, but not in this three-partite form (cf. Mt. 13.57; Lk. 4.24; Jn 4.44). In this form, there is a conspicuous parallel to God's commission to Abraham: 'Go out from your *country*, your *kinship*, and your *father's house*, to a land that I shall show you' (Gen. 12.1). Such implicit biblical allusions can be observed in many statements of Jesus and also occur in the Jewish literature of his day. Through this reference, which can go back to some tradition or another, Jesus apparently identified himself with the patriarch who, as spiritually homeless, had to break the bonds with kin and country in order to follow his destiny. The same insight is worded more sharply in several sayings of Jesus to his disciples: 'He that does the will of God is my brother, my sister, and my mother' (Mk 3.35); 'He who loves his father or mother more than me is not worthy of me' (Mt. 10.37; cf. Lk. 14.26!).

The account of Jesus and his home town shows something of the mystery and unexpectedness that was part of his essence as historical figure.

Theology and History

Even when, humanly speaking, beginning 'close to home' we can only do justice to a personage like Jesus when we take into account the enigma that surrounds him. This can, however, give rise to an exactly opposite misunderstanding. Christian tradition has taught that he should be seen as being *absolutely novel*, as the unique *Son of God*, who descended from heaven and who surpasses all things human. In this way, all bonds with his family, folk, culture and religion become irrelevant and even distract from the essence. Does not Paul say that 'even if we have known Christ after the flesh, we know him thus no longer' (2 Cor. 5.16)? According to a widespread interpretation, this means that after Easter the earthly Jesus is of no more significance, and only the heavenly Christ is to be taken into account. From Paul's viewpoint this is erroneous, for he emphasized, for example, in the midst of a strongly theological passage that Jesus, just like other Jews, was 'born of a woman, born under the law' (Gal. 4.4).

The difficulty here has to do with having to think both theologically and historically, a problem we mentioned in the introduction and which here is focused upon the 'historical Jesus'. Not by coincidence, this was the central theological issue during the nineteenth century when historical criticism arose and the Bible, too, came to be treated according to the methods of modern historical research. Attempt no longer was made to interpret biblical persons and movements within a confessional or dogmatic framework, but from their human, historical context. This produced a whole series of biographies of Jesus that exhausted themselves, for example, in psychological descriptions of his 'religious genius'. Later it became apparent that this approach was based more on sympathetic imagination than on studying the sources. The first phase of the 'quest of the historical Jesus' ran aground.

The question then became, Are the available sources actually suitable to base a biography on? Are the Gospels not pre-eminently *confessional writings*, which do not share our historical interest? The pendulum swung in the opposite direction, and diligence was applied to the heavenly Christ as depicted in the earliest Christian confession. With an appeal to the text of Paul just cited, it was claimed that theology only has to do with the 'kerygmatic' Christ. This shifting back and forth from a so-called purely historical to a purely theological approach is still going on. Preference is still being voiced for the 'real historical Jesus', which the Christian theology should keep its hands off, as well as for the opposite, namely, that the 'so-called historical Jesus' is no concern of Christian theology. What significance, however, can Jesus have for us if denuded of his human existence? Equally, what does that existence have to say if its meaning for later generations is not taken into account? The mingling of theology and history proved to be a deceptive path, but an absolute divorce of the two offers no solution either.

Christianity and Judaism

The two opposite approaches mentioned above had an element in common: the New Testament was read in isolation from its direct historical surroundings—Judaism of the first century. The so-called 'historical Jesus' was captured in a bloodless and artificial character, and the 'kerygmatic Christ' remained a kind of Hellenistic demigod. A change came when the Jewish apocalyptic writings were rediscovered and read alongside the Gospels. Images such as the 'son of man', the resurrection of the dead and the last judgment, that play such an important role in the teachings of Jesus were encountered in these. Through this it became possible to understand both the teachings *of* Jesus and the preaching *about* him from the perspective of his own time. In the meantime, interest in the figure of Jesus also arose within the circles of Jewish historical scholarship, and the affinity between his teachings and that of the Talmud was discovered. These remained, however, marginal to the two mainstreams of theological scholarship—the historical and the confessional. One wonders whether this had some relation to traditional Christian disinclination towards Judaism.

A comparison with the *premodern period* can be instructive. In that era, when the relationship between Judaism and Christianity was not as yet viewed within a historical perspective, both traditions of belief were perceived as timeless, closed, mutually exclusive theological systems. The emergence of Christianity was, thus, not seen as a process of growth from Judaism, but as a *creatio ex nihilo*, a creation out of nothing, which came into being in one fell swoop through the preaching of Jesus. This approach still exists in what was just called the 'purely theological' point of departure. Nascent historical criticism had as its goal the investigation of the rise of Christianity within the framework of the historical circumstances, free from confessional standpoints. It is curious indeed that in this hardly any attention was paid to the Judaism of that day. This is even more peculiar given the flourishing interest of

Christian exegetes of the *premodern* period for rabbinic literature. It appears, therefore, plausible that the unhistorical model of the watershed between Judaism and Christianity had unconsciously continued to exist in the minds of historical-critical researchers. Both approaches thus operate on the basis of a radical separation: in the confessional point of view, Jesus is exalted above *all* history; the historical-critical approach sees him as free from the *Jewish* world of faith. The result is that neither approach perceives Jesus within his own historical context.

In this book, it is assumed that it is indeed possible to discover traces of the historical figure of Jesus, namely, within the context of the Judaism of his day. In this we find ourselves in the vicinity of what is called 'the third quest of the historical Jesus'. A second phase, beginning in the fifties, sought to break through the separation between historiography and theology. Presently interest in the Jewish context occupies centre stage, particularly due to renewed interest in the Dead Sea Scrolls.

We suspect, however, that it is precisely Jesus' *theological significance* that becomes clearer within his Jewish context. This is equally valid in relation to his contemporary meaning, in so far as that must always be tested and corrected by the significance given him by his first followers, that is, by the earliest forms of Christology. Who Jesus was, how he viewed himself, and what significance he was later accorded by his followers—this all is best explained within the context of the Judaism of his day, by which we mean all of the material and spiritual aspects of Jewish life. In the first place, this involves the Scriptures as the theological frame of reference within which all aspects of life are endowed their meaning. To this must be added the liturgy, the interpretation of Scripture, the concepts of faith, the practical customs and rules of living—the whole framework within which for his disciples the life of Jesus took shape and within which they later observed it in its exalted significance. Even the theological importance of Jesus must be approached primarily historically, namely, through the meaning that he was given within the context of the Scriptures and the Jewish world of belief.

Certain delineations are advisable in this regard. It is not our intention to exalt Judaism into a magic potion for all of Christianity's ills. A single and univalent Judaism does not exist, and certainly did not in Jesus' time. Besides the mystery of his own personality, there is every reason to assume that he received his education from a quite

distinct tradition within Judaism. It is also not our intention to exclude
the broader Graeco-Roman context of the Judaism of that day. The
world in which Jesus lived was determined by the cultural effects of
Hellenism and by the politico-military power of the Romans. Reverting
to the image of a concentric system, the outer, most general sphere of
influence is that of the Graeco-Roman world, within this lies that of
variegated Judaism, and the inner circle is the specific environment of
Jesus himself. This is clearly exemplified in the messianic significance
that was given to Jesus. It is plausible that his disciples tied in to his
own enigmatic statements pointing in that direction; however, their later
confession must be viewed within the broader context of Jewish
religious thought, within which a 'messianic significance' possessed a
myriad of other aspects. For the average Greek, in contrast, this
confession must have had associations with mythical demigods of yore,
and for Roman rulers it must have contained political overtones. All of
these inferences and connotations indisputably play a role, but not all
have the same order of precedence.

The Nature of the Gospels
A final complication in the description of the historical figure of Jesus
has already been mentioned—the nature of the sources. The Gospels
are a witness in the double meaning of the word: they not only tell
about what Jesus taught and did, but also confess his significance. Each
report has the aim of testifying as well and in that sense the Gospels
cannot be approached as being purely historical.

   This does not imply, however, that the Gospels contain no information that is historiographically significant. That Jesus died as 'King of
the Jews' on a Roman cross is indisputable, including the fact that this
took place 'under Pontius Pilate', as stipulated even in the creed. The
various spheres of connotation in which this title was understood have
been mentioned. Furthermore, it is clear that Jesus travelled about as a
preacher, performed many healings and paid particular attention to the
socially rejected, such as whores, tax collectors, the needy and the
chronically ill. Stories of miraculous healings and suchlike may have
both a historical core and a legendary encasement. The question is how
one evaluates legends. A nuanced approach to what has been ascribed
to him as teachings is also necessary. On the one hand, we can assume
that his disciples transmitted his sayings, parables and instructions as
faithfully as possible. On the other hand, it is quite probable that what

was passed down was influenced by later developments. That this transmission must have been a multifaceted development is proven by the totally distinct tint of the Gospel of John.

How can the Gospels be useful in describing the historical figure of Jesus? In the first place, we must keep in mind the mentioned complications: the personal, human secret of the figure of Jesus, the interlocking of historical and theological significance, the interpretative context of Judaism of that day in all of its aspects, including the Old Testament, and the creedal quality of the Gospels.

A more specific prerequisite is that we take the literary singularity of the Gospels into account. They represent a separate literary form hallmarked by collective authorship. They are tradition literature comprising community texts: for several generations the Gospel material was passed on and reworked. A distinction must be made in this between the redaction of written texts and the oral transmission and processing. On these points, a comparison of the Gospels with rabbinic literature can be fruitful: there, too, we find the written fixation of oral traditions in different 'collections'. The same small unit could be encountered in various forms in diverse contexts. The challenge is to do justice both to the intention of the redactor of the collection and to that of the 'author(s)' of the oral tradition.

The first necessity is, therefore, to be alert to the individual character of each Gospel. What specific style and vocabulary are employed, what intention of the evangelist is observable in the structure of his text? This is, however, not sufficient. The 'text-immanent' approach advocated by some who study only the text in its final form is useful but in isolation leads to an ahistorical one-sidedness. An inquiry into the historical circumstances under which the evangelist created his final text must not be omitted. One highly important aspect is his relationship to Judaism. The Gospels are texts of communities whose relationship to Judaism underwent changes during the very time in which the Gospels came into being. That is, awareness of the possible stages of development, and, thus, of the successive layers of the Gospels in their present form, is needed. The final text of the Gospels could be called their youngest or *surface level*.

A *second, older level* underneath this is formed by the written or oral traditions from which the composers of one particular Gospel must have drawn. To approach this level, comparison with the other Gospels is useful, so that shared primal elements become apparent. The first three

Gospels give the most opportunity for such a comparison and are for this reason called the 'synoptic' Gospels, from *synopsis*, 'viewing together'. Because it has very much a quality of its own, the fourth Gospel can at times through comparison bring important primal elements to light.

Beneath these we can assume another *third, oldest level*, namely, the oral form in which Jesus' words and deeds were deposited by his disciples. Just as in rabbinic literature, it is often not possible to distinguish between a formulation which derives from a disciple and one which derives from his teacher, or perhaps from his teacher's teacher. Instead of 'Jesus' own words' we will, therefore, rather speak of the layer of the milieu of Jesus, which can be assumed in small units in the text of the Gospels, such as a saying found in widely differing contexts, for example, in all four Gospels. Here again a comparison with rabbinic literature can be enlightening. On a far greater scale, it is possible to find there ancient elements that, via sundry stages of oral transmission, have ended up in a much later, written context.

This division into three levels is schematic. In reality things will have often been much more complex and diverse intermediate phases must be assumed. Furthermore, even the first, youngest or surface level often exhibits traces of being reworked by successive 'evangelists' and later copyists. This terminology will not be employed strictly but often more globally, speaking in the plural of 'older' and 'younger' layers. Sometimes, on the other hand, there is occasion to distinguish four layers explicitly. In all events, the intention is not to render a rigorous text-archaeological description. It is to offer a hypothetical model, a reading help that serves to sharpen our perceptivity. In individual cases this can be further elaborated to achieve a more precise dating and historical description by comparison with external sources.

With these reservations in mind, the successive text layers of the Gospels will be taken into account. The chapters about the Gospels according to Luke, Mark, Matthew and John concentrate, of course, on the surface layer, the final texts of the evangelists. In the chapter on Paul, several traditions about Jesus that refer to the level of oral tradition are discussed. The present chapter is about Jesus himself, that is, our attention is focused on isolated sayings and reports of the oldest level, the layer of the environment of Jesus. In doing so it is, of course, never possible to bypass the process of transmission and reworking of the material.

The question concerning the literary relationships between the Gospels is not a main issue in this book. We assume the accepted hypothesis that Mark represents the oldest written fixation of the gospel tradition. This 'primal Gospel' must thereafter have been taken as a point of departure by Matthew and Luke, who furthermore each added an amount of material from other sources, especially sayings by Jesus himself. To the extent that this additional material in Matthew and Luke exhibits strong affinity, one can presume a second written source, further unknown to us. Thus one speaks of the two-source hypothesis: besides from Mark, Matthew and Luke must have drawn from the sayings source designated as *Q*. For our method of reading, this means that Mark (or an earlier form thereof) and *Q* belonged to the middle layer of Matthew and Luke. Finally, John reflects a development of the gospel tradition of its own, which has only incidental overlap with the synoptic Gospels. Its singularity lies in the completely different significance that is ascribed to Jesus' life and teachings, and in the fact that the Gospel has preserved unique traditions about the life of Jesus. The latter are relevant to the present chapter.

With all these complications and prerequisites in mind, let us now with quasi-simplicity begin at the beginning...

The Mission of Jesus

All reports relate that at some point Jesus began to appear in public. According to the first three Gospels this took place directly after his baptism by John the Baptist and his temptation in the wilderness; shortly thereafter he called his first disciples (Mk 1.9-20). His ministry itself involved travelling about *preaching and healing*: 'And he came throughout all Galilee, preaching in their synagogues and casting out demons' (Mk 1.39). In the fourth Gospel, the story is slightly different. The baptism by John is mentioned merely in passing, followed first by the calling of the disciples and only after that by the first public appearance (Jn 1.29-51). This Gospel relates only occasionally a 'sign' that Jesus performed, and focuses all attention on his preaching, rendered in long, contemplative addresses. Nonetheless, here as well the work of healing is apparently assumed to be present (Jn 2.23; 11.47; 20.30). According to all witnesses, therefore, preaching and healing are the main components of Jesus' ministry. This appears to belong to the oldest layer of tradition: a preacher and healer with a remarkable awareness of his calling appears on the scene.

The First Appearance

After the onset, each evangelist goes his own way. Mark tells about Jesus' visit to Capernaum and the miraculous healing there. John places the wedding of Cana with the 'first sign' here, and thereafter a trip to Jerusalem with the cleansing of the temple. In Matthew the Sermon on the Mount is presented, a long summary of Jesus' teachings, and Luke relates the story of the preaching in the synagogue of Nazareth.

We could say that after Jesus' initial appearance each evangelist continues with what to him appears to be exemplary of Jesus' ministry. Turning the water into wine in Cana symbolizes his mysterious spiritual authority to a relatively closed group, after which this is made public through the cleansing of the temple (Jn 2.1-22). In this it appears that the significance of his ministry is of more importance than the ministry itself. In Mark to a certain extent we find the reverse. After the preaching in the synagogue of Capernaum, we hear of the amazement of the listeners concerning 'his teaching with authority' (Mk 1.21-22), while we are told nothing of the content of the preaching. After the ensuing expulsion of the demon, the observers are even more astounded: 'a new teaching with authority' (v. 27). Here again the content of Jesus' message is not reported and all emphasis is on his work of healing. Nonetheless, both John and Mark, each in his own way, draw attention to the *mysterious authority* of Jesus.

In Luke and Matthew the spotlight is turned in another direction. More than in Mark, the content of Jesus' preaching is in focus, without shifting the work of healing into the background, as in John. Both elements of Jesus' work are evidently intimately connected. Luke begins with a different, more extensive report on Jesus' preaching in the synagogue of Nazareth than that found in Mark, cited at the beginning of the chapter:

> And a scroll was given to him of the prophet Isaiah, and when he had opened the scroll, he found the place where it is written: 'The Spirit of the Lord is upon me because He has anointed me, to bring a gospel to the poor has He sent me, to preach liberation to the imprisoned and the opening of eyes to the blind' (Isa. 61.1f.). And he closed the scroll, gave it to the servant and sat down. And all eyes in the synagogue were fixed upon him. Then he began to speak: Today is this Scripture fulfilled in your ears… (Lk. 4.17-21).

The intention is clear: Jesus is aware of being sent with a 'gospel', good news, for the poor, the bound and the ill. In this consciousness of being called, he is inspired by the prophetic writings, and he propagates this in what he preaches. The assembled fellow villagers react first with surprise and then with irritation. They go so far as wanting to throw him off a cliff, but with mysterious power he walks through their midst and disappears.

This extensive report has been read as a composition of Luke. This need not be incorrect if one keeps in mind that at the same time the evangelist appears to incorporate specific traditions rooted in the Judaism of that day. In the direct context of the portion that Jesus read are the words that the prophet is sent 'to comfort all those that mourn' (Isa. 61.3). It is logical that this well-known passage indirectly echoed along with that which was read. In antiquity, certainly in the case of a well-known text, one did not bother to reiterate the entire citation.

These same words about comfort for those that mourn are in the *beatitudes* with which Jesus begins his preaching in Matthew, and therewith his public ministry:

> And when he saw the multitude he climbed up a mountain. And he sat down, and his disciples gathered themselves around him. And he opened his mouth and taught them with these words:
> Blessed are the poor of the Spirit, for theirs is the Kingdom of Heaven;
> blessed are those who mourn, for they shall be comforted;
> blessed are the meek, for they shall inherit the earth (Mt. 5.1-5; cf. Lk. 6.20-21).

Further study reveals that the beginning of the beatitudes harbours even more allusions to the passage in Isaiah. This comes to light when the Hebrew text is consulted, including the end of the previous chapter in Isaiah, which is the more fitting because our chapter divisions did not exist in antiquity. In Hebrew there is an aspect that cannot be expressed easily in translation, namely, the similarity between the *aniyim*, 'poor', and the *anawim*, 'meek'. The resemblance is strengthened by the fact that the distinction between the *wav* (w) and the *yod* (y) in handwritten Hebrew is often vague. Thus the 'poor of the Spirit' correspond to the 'poor' to whom the gospel is preached, and these are again closely related to the 'meek' who shall inherit the 'land' or the 'earth' (Isa. 60.21; cf. Ps. 37). The existence of these links is supported by the expression 'meek of the Spirit' in an eschatologically tinted text from Qumran (' *ᵃnawê ha-rûaḥ, War Scroll*, 1QM 14.7). Thus the beginning of the beatitudes spells out in so many words what is said in Isaiah: 'to the poor the gospel is preached'.

In summary, while John and Mark each in their own manner describe the first appearance of Jesus as a manifestation of his mysterious spiritual authority, Luke and Matthew place it against the background of the prophecy of salvation in Isaiah 60–61. Both aspects appear to belong to the historical figure of Jesus.

The Gospel

The word 'gospel', used several times in the rendering of the Isaiah text, has a primordial connection there that now deserves further attention. The Greek *eu-aggelion* meant originally 'good news' or 'reward for good news', which also could include an offering to the deity to whom the good news is attributed. The characteristic Christian usage derives, however, from the *future aspect* that the word was given in the Greek–Jewish translation of Isaiah and other prophetic texts. This is also true of the related verb *euaggelizomai*, 'to proclaim salvation', in which the future purport well expresses the prophetic intention.

This verb, 'evangelize', is used particularly by Paul and Luke, usually in the sense of 'proclaiming the message of salvation of (or about) Jesus', but also with the wider scope of 'proclaiming messianic salvation' (Lk. 1.19; 2.10; 3.18). The noun 'gospel' is used especially by Paul, for example, in the expression '*my* gospel', that is, his manner of proclaiming to the non-Jews (Rom. 2.16; 16.25). This terminology is unmistakably more centred on the significance of the person of Jesus; nonetheless, the broader connotation of salvation continues to be present, as when Paul frequently speaks of 'the *gospel of God*' (Rom. 1.1; 15.16; 2 Cor. 11.7; 1 Thess. 2.2, 8, 9).

There are no direct indications that Jesus himself used the noun 'gospel' (in Hebrew *b^esōrâ*); however, the nature of his ministry as ascribed to him by the sources unmistakably recalls the same passage in Isaiah and the verb used there—'evangelize', 'proclaim salvation'. To that extent it is relevant that Mark does not only relate the word 'gospel' to him (cf. 1.1), but even places it in his mouth, precisely at his first appearance:

> After John (the Baptist) was imprisoned Jesus came to Galilee and *proclaimed the gospel of God* with the words: 'The time is fulfilled and the Kingdom of God is nearby, repent and *believe the gospel*' (Mk 1.14-15).

The intended message is that the gospel that Jesus proclaimed entailed the coming of the Kingdom of God. This becomes explicit in the somewhat more concise version of Matthew, although the word 'gospel' does not occur: 'From that time one Jesus began to *preach* with the words: Repent, for the Kingdom of Heaven is nearby' (Mt. 4.17). 'Heaven' is here a veiled designation for God, frequently employed by Matthew and also often occurring in rabbinic literature.

According to the testimony of Mark and Matthew, Jesus began his intriguing appearance by proclaiming the 'gospel that the Kingdom of God is nearby'. Perhaps we may go a step further. The key word from Isaiah 60–61, 'evangelizing' or 'proclaiming salvation', is central at the beginning of the beatitudes. Matthew places these at the opening of Jesus' first long address. In his rendition, the 'gospel' of Jesus consists of bringing the good news to the 'poor of the Spirit', that 'theirs is the Kingdom of Heaven', and to 'those that mourn', that 'they shall be comforted'. In this the same basic tradition is present that we also observed in Luke, namely, that the preaching with which Jesus begins in Nazareth is nothing other than 'bringing good news to the poor'. To that extent we can speak of 'the gospel of Jesus'.

Jesus and John the Baptist
In the quote from Mark above, Jesus' first public appearance is presented as occurring after John the Baptist was imprisoned. This seems to suggest not only a fortuitous temporal link but also a necessary connection, as though Jesus carried on the work of the Baptist. A relation between the two preachers is made more plausible by a series of accounts scattered throughout the four Gospels that appear to represent an early tradition stratum:

(a)   Jesus submits himself to the 'baptism of repentance' of John, a fact that the fourth Gospel seems to obscure (Jn 1.32).
(b)   According to Matthew, Jesus appears on stage with the message of the Baptist: 'Repent, for the Kingdom of Heaven is near' (Mt. 3.2; 4.17).
(c)   According to a Johannine tradition, Jesus himself also baptized (Jn 3.22-24; 4.1-2; see pp. 307-308).
(d)   There were mutual contacts between Jesus, John and their disciples (Mk 2.18; Jn 1.35-41).
(e)   Two of John's disciples left their master to follow Jesus, and the brother of one of them was Peter, Jesus' most prominent disciple (Jn 1.37, 40).
(f)   John's disciples came to tell Jesus about their master's death (Mt. 14.12).

(g) Jesus sent his disciples out with the same message that he and John had initiated (Mt. 10.7, see below).

(h) Disciples of both of them went forth to preach as far as in the Diaspora (Acts 19.3).

(i) Jesus saw the Baptist as his prophetic precursor (Mt. 11.10; 17.13).

(j) Matthew and Luke relate an account in which Jesus, in answer to the Baptist, summarizes his work by an allusion to the words of Isaiah 61. Because of the literal correspondences between the two versions, it is presumed that behind this report lies the sayings source *Q*:

> And John, who in prison had heard of the activities of Jesus, told him through his disciples: Are you the one who is to come, or do we expect another? And Jesus gave him as answer: Go back and report to John what you have heard and seen. The blind can see again and the lame walk, the lepers are cleansed and the deaf can hear, also *the dead are raised to life* and *the gospel is preached to the poor*. And blessed is he that is not offended in me (Mt. 11.2-6; Lk. 7.18-23).

It is not coincidental that 'evangelizing', the bringing of the 'gospel' or good tidings from Isaiah 61, receives the emphasis at the end. Further study would reveal that this portion contains many other allusions to Scripture passages.

The cumulation of connections between the ministry of Jesus and that of the Baptist raises the question whether Jesus was perhaps more than an arbitrary person being baptized by John. Was he perhaps his disciple for a while? Such a connection between the two becomes historically plausible by a comparison with a number of strikingly related texts from Qumran. One of these is a hymn in which the ministry of a messianic figure is described by means of allusions to the same text from Isaiah 61:

> [The Hea]ven and the earth shall listen to His Anointed
> (...) And His Spirit shall blow upon the humble
> (...) He shall honour the faithful
> upon the throne of the Kingship for ever,
> setting prisoners free, giving sight to the blind (...)
> (...) He shall heal heavily wounded,
> and *revive the dead*,
> *preach salvation to the meek* (...) (4Q521 frg 2, 2.1-12).

It is particularly remarkable that the reviving of the dead, which does not occur in Isaiah 61, is inserted before the preaching of good tidings to the meek, just as in the Gospel account, near the end of the listing of messianic activities. These specific correspondences make it plausible that Jesus' answer to the Baptist and this Essene hymn on the Messiah draw from the same tradition. It consisted of reading texts from Isaiah and other Scripture portions together and interpreting them in a messianic manner.

A motif of separate interest is that of the *desert*. Ever since Exodus, the desert has been the place of contemplation, liberation and revelation. It occurs in this way in Isaiah as well and from there the motif plays its role in the Qumran Scrolls and in the New Testament. The desert was in general a favourite location for messianic movements (Acts 21.38). The appearance of John is depicted in the words of another well-known text from Isaiah: 'A voice of one calling: '*In the wilderness prepare the way of the Lord*, make straight the paths'...' (Isa. 40.3; Mk 1.3). This same text was also readily quoted in Qumran and applied to the desert community itself. Of importance is the fact that the 'preparation of the way' was explained as the 'study of the Torah', *midraš ha-tōrâ* (1QS 8.14; cf. 9.19-20). In this light, Jesus' temptation in the wilderness and his repeated returning to desert-like places to pray has uncommon significance (Mk 1.12-13, 35, 45; Jn 10.40-41).

Did John, the 'one who prepared the way in the wilderness', in his own manner also teach the 'study of the Torah', and was Jesus a participant in this? The Lukan account is eloquent in this regard, for when the penitent multitude, tax collectors and soldiers asked the Baptist, 'What must we do?' he gave them instructions (Lk. 3.10-14). A theme that comes to mind is the exceptional prohibition of divorce that John shared not only with Qumran but also with Jesus; to this we will return later.

A final element that apparently likewise belonged to the desert is the baptism of repentance and forgiveness of sins that John preached (Mk 1.4; Lk. 3.3; Acts 13.24; Jn 3.22-24). Here again a comparison with Qumran would seem in place, for the Essene baptism had the aspect of conversion and cleansing through the Spirit (1QS 3.4-11; 4.21). The differences may, of course, not be forgotten, such as the extensive and stringent Essene rules of purity (pp. 48, 97). John, and certainly Jesus, were anything but members of the Qumran community.

In summary, with his 'gospel' Jesus linked up with the preaching of

John the Baptist. In this he seemed to continue a messianic-prophetic tradition that had also inspired the Essenes. Perhaps Jesus came forth from the movement of John, and was for a time his disciple and partner in the 'study of the Torah'. In the end he submitted to the baptism of conversion and was tested in the wilderness. Thereafter he began his own public ministry with the same motto as his teacher. This ministry attracted attention by its enigmatic authority. Jesus viewed his work as the beginning of the fulfilment of God's promises of salvation, while John, though the greatest of prophets, was yet 'the smallest in the King-dom of Heaven' (see pp. 138-39). What distinguished Jesus is precisely what the evangelists noted as the essence of his ministry: his work of liberation and healing (Mt. 11.5; Jn 10.40-41) and his teachings (Mk 1.22). *The gospel of Jesus was a strikingly new sound within an existing movement.*

The Mission

According to all the evangelists, from the beginning Jesus manifested a mysterious certainty concerning what he had come to do. He knew that he had been sent by God. This, too, reflects an element from the passage in Isaiah: '...in order to bring the gospel to the poor *has He sent me.*'

The word 'send' (*šalaḥ*) has acquired a specific significance in post-biblical Hebrew: the sending of a delegate with a clearly specified assignment. Such an 'emissary' (*šālîaḥ*) operates in the name of and on the authority of his commissioner. In a proverb-like phrasing from rab-binic legislation, this is called: 'Someone's agent (literally: sent one) is as himself' (*m. Ber.* 5.5). This means not only that a fault of the envoy is imputed to the sender, but also that the reception that he receives counts as though it were accorded to his sender. For this concept, the Greek-speaking Jews used primarily the verb *apo-stellein*, 'to send out', and the noun *apostolos*, from this the Christian 'apostle' has been derived. It is possible that the expression in Isaiah was understood with that specific, postbiblical significance.

The fact that Jesus knew himself to be 'sent' is said emphatically in certain characteristic statements. To the Greek woman who approached him in the region of Tyre and Sidon, before healing her daughter, he said, '*I am sent only* to the lost sheep of the house of Israel' (Mt. 15.24). This reservation towards non-Jews is unusual, even within Matthew, and gives the report an authentic ring. In another formulation, it is said,

'I must preach the Kingdom of God also in other cities, *for thereto am I sent*' (Lk. 4.43). Jesus was aware of being commissioned with a 'mission' that specifically entailed that which we found to be the essence of his work: bearing witness to the proximity of the Kingdom of God.

In this connection, a series of isolated sayings deserve our attention. They are proverbial in form, which makes them difficult to ascribe to some specific person. On the other hand, they manifest exceptional variation and are widespread, even being found in the Gospel of John (to be further discussed in Chapter 7). This fact points to the oldest layer of tradition, an assumption confirmed by the analogy with the just-mentioned ancient Jewish principle of the representation of the sender by the agent. The proverbial nature means that even if these maxims were not coined by Jesus, they could have been used by him, perhaps in accordance with a tradition passed on to him. In any case we find ourselves here in the environment of Jesus himself.

> He who receives you, receives me, and he who receives me, receives the One who sent me (Mt. 10.40).
>
> He who receives one whom I have sent out, receives me, and he who receives me, receives the One who sent me (Jn 13.20).
>
> He who listens to you, listens to me, and he who rejects you, rejects me, and he who rejects me, rejects the One who sent me (Lk. 10.16).
>
> He who believes in me, believes not in me but in the One who sent me, and he who sees me, sees the One who sent me (Jn 12.44-45).
>
> He who receives such a child in my name, receives me (Mt. 18.5).
>
> He who receives this child in my name, receives me, and he who receives me, receives the One who sent me (Lk. 9.48).
>
> A disciple is not above his teacher (Lk. 6.40).
>
> A disciple is not above his teacher, nor a servant above his master (Mt. 10.24).
>
> A servant is not more than his master, nor an 'apostle' than his 'sender' (Jn 13.16).

The correspondence with the ancient Jewish concept of 'agency' gives rise to the assumption that Jesus delegated his disciples to do his work in his name. That is precisely what we find in the context in which the first saying is transmitted, namely, the account that is known as the dispatch of the apostles. In the version of Matthew and Luke, Jesus sends them forth not only to do his work of healing but also to spread his message: 'Go forth and proclaim: the Kingdom of Heaven has come close by; heal the weak, arouse the dead, cleanse the lepers, cast out the demons' (Mt. 10.7; cf. Lk. 9.2; 10.9). It also is clear in the formulation that the person of Jesus is represented by the disciples whom he sends forth: his followers were to do the work of healing and liberation 'in his name' (Lk. 10.17; Mk 9.39; cf. Mt. 7.22). As true delegates, they were invested with his authority over demons (Mk 6.7; Mt. 10.1; Lk. 9.1). Finally, the designation 'apostle' expresses fully that Jesus delegated his disciples. Authorized 'apostles' in the Jewish context were sent forth two by two, as witnesses who support one another—Jesus and his followers do the same (Mk 6.7, see below; Acts 11.30; 15.25).

The accounts of the ordaining and commissioning of the 'apostles' are scattered throughout Mark. In conclusion, we will view these now together and italicize the discussed expressions.

> And he appointed twelve (...), in order that they would keep him company, and in order that he could *send them forth to preach* and to have *authority* to cast out demons. Thus he appointed the twelve, and he gave Simon the name Peter... (Mk 3.14).

> And he called the twelve to himself, and began *to send them forth two by two*, and he gave them *authority* over impure spirits... And they went forth and *proclaimed* that they should repent, and they cast out many demons and they anointed many sick ones with oil and healed them (Mk 6.7, 12-13).

> And the *apostles* gathered themselves to Jesus, and they told him everything that they had done and taught (Mk 6.30).

We notice in passing that the apostles also taught, which was yet another aspect of Jesus' work according to Matthew (Mt. 4.23; 9.35). In addition, Simon received from Jesus another name as apostle. In summary, the 'apostles' that Jesus 'sends forth' do his work 'in his name' and in this way carry on his own 'mission'.

'I am come to...'

Jesus had an intense awareness of being sent. This is unequivocally worded in a number of sayings ascribed to him containing the expression that he is 'come', or, more precisely, 'I am not come to...but to...'. In these statements Jesus summarizes the aim of his 'coming'.

> I am not come to call the righteous but sinners (Mk 2.17; Mt. 9.13; Lk. 5.32).

> Do not think that I am come to annul the law or the prophets. I am not come to annul but to fulfil (Mt. 5.17).

> Do not think that I am come to cast peace upon the earth. I am not come
> to cast peace but the sword (Mt. 10.34).

In all instances, the saying involved is of such an unusual nature that it
does not readily bring the usage of a later congregation to mind. We
could question whether the introduction to the second and third saying,
'Do not think that I am come...' was not added by tradition. On the
other hand, it is not barred that two sayings of the same teacher begin
with the same formula. In all events, three aspects of Jesus' mission are
placed in the light of the dawning of the time of salvation or the end
time: his solidarity with the morally outcast, his paradoxical attitude
towards the law and the sharply divergent reactions to his work that he
foresees. We will pursue the matter of the law in the next section;
something must be said here about the other two elements, beginning
with the last one.

The saying about the sword is passed on in a context that deals with
the rift within a family caused by following Jesus (Mt. 10.34-39). This
is clearly connected with the adage about the prophet who is not
respected in his own home town. In the same context, a quote from the
prophet Micah follows about the enmity between household members
in connection with the end time (Mt. 10.35; Mic. 7.6). The context of
the end time becomes explicit in a most remarkable passage in Luke
that shows clear connections with the saying about the sword:

> Fire I have come to cast upon the earth, and what can I desire, if it is
> already ignited? With a baptism I must be baptized, and how it oppresses
> me until it be past. Do you think I am come to cast peace upon the earth?
> Surely not, I say to you, but contention (Lk. 12.49-51).

'Fire' is an unmistakable symbol of the end time. Jesus sees himself as
a sort of nominal figure in the dramatic culmination of final events,
which he himself cannot control and which will engulf him as well. In
another unusual statement, Jesus links his lot to the end time and says,
'But whoever has a purse, he must take it...and buy a sword' (Lk.
22.37; cf. 10.4). This set of sayings makes it clear that the aim of Jesus'
coming is to be placed within the perspective of the end time.

The statement that Jesus 'is not come to call the righteous but
sinners' does not directly have to do with the imminent end of the
world and the termination of his acitivities, but with an aspect of his
ministry itself, and it is in another way just as pressing and 'eschatological'. The indications that he was aware of being especially called

to share his 'gospel' with the morally outcast are numerous, wide-spread, and evidently considered to be characteristic of Jesus' ministry. His entering into the house of Levi-Matthew called forth the question, 'Why does your teacher eat with tax collectors and sinners?' (Mt. 9.11; Mk 2.16). The answer was explicit: 'I am not come to call righteous but sinners.' When he went to Zacchaeus, we read, 'And all who saw it murmured because he associated with a sinner' (Lk. 19.7). The woman who sprinkled Jesus' feet with tears of repentance makes the host think, 'If this man were a prophet, he would have known what kind of woman it is who touches him, for she is a sinner' (Lk. 7.39). Likewise, in the story of the adulterous woman, which some manuscripts transmit in the Gospel of John, Jesus says to the accusers, 'He who is without sin must throw the first stone' (Jn 8.7). This all does not mean that Jesus trivializes sin, but rather that he is attuned to the hidden longing for a turn-about. This is one of the central aspects of his mission.

How central the place of repentance and forgiveness is assumed to be for Jesus' message is apparent also from the place these concepts occupy in the best-known words transmitted from him—the Lord's Prayer (cf. p. 388). In the version of Matthew it is supplied with a special commentary:

> '...And forgive us our debts, as we also forgive our debtors...' For if you forgive other people their transgressions, your heavenly Father will also forgive you, but if you do not forgive other people, your Father will also not forgive you your transgressions (Mt. 6.12-15).

Living on the basis of repentance means that we, with the turn of phrase characteristic of Jesus, as children of the heavenly Father forgive our fellow humans and assume their hidden wish for a turn-about. In this Jesus incorporated a thought of the mildly pious Ben Sira: 'Forgive the sins of your neighbour so that when you pray your transgressions will be forgiven' (Sir. 28.2; cf. also Mt. 5.23-24). In a related context Jesus uses a saying that is also known in the Mishnah and apparently is quite ancient: 'With the measure with which you measure it shall be measured unto you' (Mt. 7.2; *m. Soṭ.* 1.7).

In certain other sayings, the goal of Jesus' coming is summarized in combination with the enigmatic expression 'son of man'. The phrase comes from the image in ancient Jewish writings of a heavenly redeemer who at the end of time shall come upon the clouds to assume sovereignty (Dan. 7.13). According to tradition, Jesus himself also spoke of that figure (Mt. 24.30; 26.64). Furthermore, he used that designation to indicate the ultimate nature of his mission:

> *The Son of Man is come* to seek and to save that which was lost (Lk. 19.9-10).

> *The Son of Man is not come* to be served, but to serve and to give his life a ransom for many (Mk 10.45; Mt. 20.28).

The first saying occurs in the story of the tax collector, Zacchaeus, who gave half of his ill-earned gain to the poor and compensated fourfold those he had disadvantaged. There is a clear connection with the earlier cited saying about the 'calling of sinners'. Conversion and forgiveness belong to the urgent ultimate goal of Jesus' coming.

In regard to the second saying, it is difficult to preclude the possibility of adaption to a later tradition. The immediate context is, however, characterized by a number of highly remarkable sayings. When Jesus' disciples James and John, the sons of Zebedee, ask him if they may sit on his right hand and on his left hand 'in his glory', he answers:

> You do not know what you ask. Can you drink the cup that I drink, or be baptized with the baptism with which I am baptized?... To sit on my right hand or my left hand is not mine to give away, but to him for whom it is prepared... He that will be great among you let him be your servant, and he that will be first among you, let him be the slave of all. For the Son of Man is not come to be served, but to serve... (Mk 10.35-45; cf. Mt. 20.20-28)

We recognize the infrequent expression of the 'baptism', which, like the 'sitting at the right hand and left hand', is linked with the 'fire' of the end time (Lk. 12.50). That it is not up to Jesus to designate those who are to sit at his right hand and left hand can hardly be considered an addition by a later tradition, thus making the authenticity plausible, which is probably also true of the saying that Jesus saw himself as the Son of Man who is servant of all. Whether this also applies to the part about 'a ransom for many' will need to be taken up later.

Finally, let us consider briefly another expression of Jesus' extraordinary awareness of a mission, namely, the vocative, 'Father', in several of his prayers that have been transmitted (cf. also pp. 309-10):

> I praise you, Father, Lord of heaven and earth,
> for You have hidden this from the wise and understanding

but have revealed it to the simple,
Yes, Father, thus was the desire before your countenance... (Mt. 11.25;
Lk. 10.21).

Abba—that is, Father—everything is possible for You
Make this cup to pass from me
But not what I desire, but You (Mk 14.36).

Now is my soul shocked, and what must I say?
Father, save me from this hour—
but to this end am I come.
Father, glorify Your name! (Jn 12.27-28).

Father, Your name be sanctified
Your kingdom come... (Lk. 11.2).

The simple, intense form of address, 'Father', expresses a consciousness of a great closeness and familiarity with God. In Mark, the Aramaic form *Abba* is explicitly passed on as well. According to statements
by Paul, this was also used in the prayers of non-Jewish believers
(Rom. 8.15; Gal. 4.6). That this leads us indirectly back to Jesus' own
surroundings, probably to Jesus himself, becomes even more probable
given the fact that such intimate forms of communion with God were
customary among the ancient Hasidim. There is a story from the first
century BCE about Honi, 'the Circle Drawer', who, because of his
powerful prayer, saw himself as being 'at home' with his heavenly
Father and for this, just like Jesus, was viewed with suspicion by the
Pharisaic leadership (*m. Ta'an.* 3.8; Josephus, *Ant.* 14.22). There is
literal witness to this form of address, 'Father', in a rabbinic writing
that also is related to the ancient Hasidic circles (*S. El. R.* 19, pp. 111-
12).

That Which Is New
That the 'gospel' of Jesus was a remarkable new element within an
existent movement needs to be pursued further. While he took over the
torch from John the Baptist, our sources also point out differences
between them. Although in this it is apparently necessary to reckon with
a later rivalry between the disciples of the two preachers (Jn 3.25-36;
5.33-36; 10.41; Acts 18.25; 19.3), there are indications that Jesus himself was also aware of an essential difference with John:

Jesus began to speak to the crowd about John: What did you go to the
desert to see? A reed shaken by the wind?... No! What did you go to
see? A prophet? Yes, I tell you, more than a prophet... Amen, I say to

you: Of those born of women, there is none arisen that is greater than John the Baptist; but the smallest in the Kingdom of Heaven is greater than he (Mt. 11.7-11; Lk. 7.24-28).

In spite of all his appreciation of John, Jesus hardly sees the Baptist as being a part of the dawning Kingdom of Heaven. The directly preceding portion with Jesus' answer to John's question about whether he was the one 'that it is come' has been quoted above. This whole passage can be seen as related to the sayings source *Q*, as well as to the mentioned tradition in Qumran (see p. 130).

In what then follows, another exquisite saying about John is quoted. This appears to be closely linked to a report, passed on elsewhere, in which Jesus likewise distinguished the ministry of the Baptist from that which is new in his own coming:

> With what shall I compare this generation? It is like children in the market place who call to one another: We played the flute for you but you have not danced; we lamented but you did not grieve. For John came, who did not drink and eat, and you say: he has a demon. The son of man came, who drinks and eats, and you say: see a guzzler, a wine bibber, a friend of tax collectors and sinners! (Mt. 11.16-19).

> I am not come to call the righteous but sinners!... And they came and asked him: Why do the disciples of John and the disciples of the Pharisees fast, but your disciples do not fast? And Jesus said to them: The children of the wedding cannot fast as long as the bridegroom is with them... No one sets an unshrunk piece of cloth in an old (woollen) cloth, otherwise it will shrink over the whole surface [...] and a worse tear will come. And no one puts new wine in old skins, otherwise the wine will make the skins burst and the wine and the skins will be lost... (Mk 2.17-22).

In contrast to John, Jesus does not appear as an ascete (cf. Mk 1.6), neither does he avoid the company of 'tax collectors and sinners'. This is a remarkable combination if we realize that both characteristics are placed in the context of the coming Kingdom. Jesus is aware of a mission to 'call sinners', namely, *to repentance*, and the joy of being together with his disciples is borne by the quiet realization that he himself is the bridegroom. The reference here is, of course, to the bridegroom from the Song of Songs, the song of love and longing that of old has been read as an allegory of the relationship between Israel as the bride and her Redeemer. The same surprising combination of repentance and joyfulness is present in Jesus' statement about fasting: 'But you, when you fast, anoint your head and wash your face, so that your fasting is not exhibited to people but to your Father in secret' (Mt. 6.17-18). In the consciousness that he himself plays a role in the imminent redemption, Jesus is aware of being on another plane than John. This unusual combination of humaneness, awareness of a calling and a future expectation are the irreducible trademark of the personality of Jesus.

Jesus does not hesitate to emphasize that which is new in his mission, that which breaks through the old framework. In doing so, he delineates himself not only from John with whom he otherwise had so much in common. Earlier in this chapter his statement was quoted that 'a prophet is not without honour except in his own home town'. The following sayings can be added to this:

> And when he was travelling, someone said to him: I will follow you wherever you go. But Jesus said to him: Foxes have holes and the birds of the heaven have nests, but the son of man has no place to lay his head to rest.
> And he said to another: Follow me. This one said: Lord, allow me first to return and bury my father. And he said to him: Let the dead bury the dead, but you, go hence, proclaim the Kingdom of God.
> And yet another spoke: I will follow you, Lord, but allow me first to instruct my servants. But Jesus said to him: No one who puts his hand to the plow and looks back to what lies behind him is fit for the Kingdom of God (Lk. 9.57-62).

As we shall see, the saying about the foxes and the birds has international connections. Furthermore, the radical rejection of all community responsibilities shows affinity to the roaming wisdom preachers, which, in the Hellentistic world, were associated with Cynic philosophy. This, too, is an aspect of the complex figure of Jesus.

That which was 'new' in Jesus' message, however, has yet another dimension. On certain points of the Jewish law, he took a radical standpoint closer to that of the Essenes than to that of the Pharisees, as will be discussed later: the 'overabundant righteouness' that he demanded of his followers sounds extreme (Mt. 5.20; see Chapter 6). In this respect Jesus had an eccentric position within Jewish society. The expressiveness of the words 'new' and 'old' is by nature often equivocal, certainly in the context of social relations. Is the radical demand of the Old Testament prophets to return to the covenant 'new' or actually 'old'? In all events, Jesus' radical standpoints were out of the ordinary, and in an unusual manner he combined these with great humaneness.

Later interpreters within the church have strongly emphasized that which was new in Jesus' message, in particular contrasting it to the 'people of the old covenant'. The gospel was played out against the law, the 'New' Testament against the 'Old'. All such thoughts were foreign to Jesus. His conception of that which is new—the incompatible—had to do with the Kingdom that was near by. He did not turn against the law, but against the 'lack of faith' and the 'sluggishness' of 'this generation' (Mk 8.38; 9.19; Lk. 24.11). In relation to law and tradition, Jesus was sometimes radical, then again mild, but never totally rejecting. His attitude is expressed in the saying about the Pharisaic commandment concerning the tithing of culinary herbs in contrast to the 'most weighty matters of the law': 'One should do this, but not neglect the other' (more on this later). In this another aspect of Jesus' personality comes to the fore, namely, his affinity to the Pharisees.

The Preaching
To do any kind of justice to the puzzling figure of 'the historical Jesus', we must not neglect his preaching. Its humane traits link him to the ones who, unjustly, are often viewed as his chief enemies, namely, the Pharisees.

A primary place must be allotted to the parables and proverbs that were ascribed to him and in which he excelled. The proverb is a genre of popular literature related to the fables and fairy tales of all peoples. As to form and themes, however, the parable is typical of Pharisaic–rabbinic Judaism. It is a dramatic mini-story with a schematic plot and a metaphoric intention, which not infrequently is hinted at through biblical allusions. In rabbinic literature there are thousands of parables, about 'a king of flesh and blood' and his son, his servants or subjects, about a master and his wife, and so forth. Outside of the rabbinic writings, the only place where parables with this form and these themes occur is the New Testament, that is, in the preaching of Jesus as contained in the synoptic Gospels.

The parable's childlike and disarming charm can speak candidly to the heart. Parables are ageless and for all ages, except for those not yet capable of thinking figuratively. The parable speaks to the adult who has retained or regained the receptivity of a child. As for many rabbis, for Jesus this was apparently an important component of his preaching. He knew how to deposit the quintessence of his message in it. The return of the prodigal son and the contrast with the obedient son, the mercifulness of the Samaritan in contrast to the priest and the Levite, the callousness of the servant to whom so much had been forgiven, the care of the shepherd for his one lost sheep—so many images, meta-phors of God's love for mankind as Jesus conceived and proclaimed it. The profundity and novelty of these parables again show the stamp of an original personality. There is no reason for insurmountable doubts that this was the carpenter from Nazareth, the preacher of whom it was said that 'all the people hung on his words' (Lk. 19.48).

Parables are related to the 'international' folk literature of antiquity. The connection is even more direct in the fable-like parables ascribed to Jesus. Fables are often about animals with human characteristics, such as industrious ants and a 'playful' cricket, the sly fox, the mean wolf and unsuspecting sheep. In antiquity an extensive collection of fables was ascribed to the Phrygian slave Aesop (sixth century BCE). They were known of old in east and west, and traces of them can be found both in the Talmud and in the New Testament. The industriousness of ants was proverbial already in the Old Testament (Prov. 6.6-8; cf. 1 Kgs 4.33). It is told that R. Meir (second half second century) knew three hundred fables about foxes, of which, unfortunately, few have been preserved (*b. Sanh.* 38b-39a). There is a fable-like parable about 'the fox and the fish' ascribed to his teacher R. Akiva (*b. Ber.* 61b).

This affinity with the international folk literature lends human colour to Jesus' preaching, like when he called Herod, the tetrarch, a 'fox' (Lk. 13.32), or his prophetic progatonist, John the Baptist, not a 'reed bent by the wind', but—as the perceptive listener will understand—a tree which is uprooted by the storm (Lk. 7.24; Mt. 1.7). The latter is an unmistakable allusion to the fable of the reed and the olive tree known from the collection of Aesop (no. 239). Similarly, the adage of Jesus, 'Foxes have a hole and the birds of heaven a nest, but the son of man has no place...' (Lk. 9.58; Mt. 8.20). But what cause is there for worry?

> Observe the birds of heaven—they sow not nor reap, neither gather they in barns, and your heavenly Father feeds them!... Learn from the lilies of the field, how they grow: they toil not nor spin and I tell you that even Salomon in all his glory was not clothed as one of these! (Mt. 6.26-29; Lk. 12.24-27)

In like manner, Jesus sends his disciples into the world: 'See, I send you as sheep in the midst of wolves; be therefore shrewd as snakes and innocent as doves...' (Mt. 10.16; Lk. 10.3).

These fable-like proverbs are similar in content to those of the 'Cyn-ics', wandering teachers in the Hellenistic world. Comparable traces of an international, 'Hellenistically' tinted thinking also occur in rabbinic literature, thus showing that such elements could be assimilated into authentic Jewish contexts without difficulty. Incidentally, these proverbs of Jesus occur only in Luke and Matthew, with a high degree of literal correspondence, and are, therefore, one of the most convincing indications of the existence of the sayings source *Q*.

An essential part of Jesus' ministry as preacher consists in his playful weaving of scriptural allusions into his sayings and parables. We have seen how in the accounts of the beginning of his public ministry the text of Isaiah 60–61 is inferred in many ways. As with his parables and sayings, one must listen with a certain amount of imagination, which can be aroused best by an awareness of the manner in which biblical quotes and references play a role in rabbinic literature.

Thus it is possible in the case of the parable of the merciful Samaritan (Lk. 10.30-36) to recall the text that plays a role in another statement of Jesus: 'I desire mercy, *not sacrifice*', the latter being that which so preoccupied the priest and the Levite (Hos. 6.6; Mt. 9.13; 12.7). The parable occurs in the context of a conversation about the 'great commandment' also found in Mark, in which context a short paraphrase of the Scripture quote in fact is given: 'Loving the neighbour as oneself has greater value than offerings' (Mk 12.33). The necessity of this approach to Jesus' statements and stories becomes even more convincing when we consider the absurd hour of the bridegroom's arrival in the parable of the ten maidens: 'at midnight' (Mt. 25.6). What bridegroom comes at midnight to fetch his bride? If, however, we assume that the bridegroom is the one who brings redemption—here again the Song of Songs plays a role!—then it would be natural to associate this with the deliverance from Egypt at midnight (Exod. 11.4; 12.29). The plausibility of the connection between the Song of Songs, Passover and Exodus is confirmed by their association with one another in later rabbinic writings.

Jesus' preaching has a surprising and liberating quality that seems to contrast with the deep earnestness and piety that he also displays, but which evidently likewise reflect his trust in God's goodness. When, after one of the announcements of his coming suffering and death, the disciples begin to discuss who will be their leader, he places a child in their midst, puts his arm around it, and says, 'He who receives one of such children in my name, receives me...' (Mk 9.31-37). Jesus' recognition of the despised tax collector Zacchaeus's longing for a total about-turn is equally emancipating (Lk. 19.5). His attitude is similar towards the woman who, wordlessly weeping, anoints his feet, a woman branded as sinful by those who are present (Lk. 7.36-50). Jesus allows himself to be surprised, like when he noted the faith of the centurion in Capernaum or of the Greek woman in the region of Tyre (Lk. 7.2-10; Mk 7.27-30). All these accounts give the impression of an independent and creative personality.

The aspect of surprise and liberation can be rendered as being Jesus' humour. The short Zacchaeus in his sycamore tree is somehow irresistibly amusing, which Jesus recognizes just as unerringly as the earnestness hidden beneath the surface. Taking a child as an example for the aspiring disciples also shows his characteristic humour. A suggestion of a reciprocal sense of humour is present in the dialogue with the Greek woman ('the crumbs for the puppies', Mk 7.28) and with the servant of the centurion (the soldiers who at command come, go and take action, Lk. 7.8). Humour binds people together ingenuously before God's presence.

In this all, a deep love for humankind is expressed. One of the characteristics of the amazing figure of Jesus is that he—a pious individual who isolated himself in the wilderness to pray—loved sinners. He forgave the woman who anointed his feet the sins for which she was known, 'because she has loved much' (Lk. 7.47-48). Only when we allow the shockingly double meaning of this expression to sink in can we see the pure love of Jesus for this woman who at the deepest level was seeking God's presence. In the same manner, Jesus looks upon the man who, imprisoned in his own riches, was searching for the Kingdom, 'and he began to love him' (Mk 10.21). Jesus' preaching is permeated with what he saw as God's boundless, humour-saturated love for people:

> I say to you, love your enemies…so that you might be the children
> of your heavenly Father, for He lets his sun shine on the good and the
> evil and makes it rain upon both the righteous and the unrighteous
> (Mt. 5.44-45).

Jesus and the Law

Jesus' statement has been quoted that he 'came not to annul the law and the prophets but to fulfil them' (Mt. 5.17). Christians have always been amazed and irritated by these words. Marcion, a theologian from the second century who rejected both the Old and a large portion of the

New Testament as being too Jewish, was of the opinion that Jesus only could have said the opposite: that he had not come to fulfil the law but to annul it. Likewise, Rudolf Bultmann, one of the most influential exegetes of the twentieth century, thought that the statement could not possibly have been made by Jesus but that it had been ascribed to him by Judaizing Christians. Both of these theologians assumed that Jesus fundamentally rejected the Jewish law. For lack of further information, we cannot determine whether this single statement originated from Jesus or not, but we can verify to what extent it is consistent with the figure of Jesus presented in the totality of our source material.

That Which Is Most Important in the Law

A characteristic aspect of Jesus' attitude towards the Jewish law is ascribed to him in a number of interrelated stories concerned with the essence of the law. Christian exegetes have read in these that, in comparison to its essence, the 'letter' of the law was of little significance to Jesus. That the opposite is more likely true becomes apparent from a comparison with related rabbinical traditions.

> And while he was on the road, someone walked up to him and fell on his knees and asked: Good master, what must I do to inherit eternal life? But Jesus said to him: Why do you call me good? No one is good except God alone! You know the commandments: 'Thou shalt not kill, thou shalt not commit adultery, thou shalt not steal, thou shalt not bear false witness, thou shalt not rob, honour thy father and thy mother'. But he said to him: Master, all these have I done from my youth on. Jesus looked at him, and began to love him and said to him: You lack one thing; go, sell all that you have and give it to the poor and you shall have treasure in heaven, and come here, follow me. But he became dejected at that statement and went away sadly, for he had many possessions (Mk 10.17-22; Lk. 18.18-23; cf. Mt. 19.16-22).

The authenticity of the situation as related is suggested by Jesus' unpretentiousnesss, which is characteristically 'corrected' in Matthew: 'Why do you ask me concerning that which is good?' (Mt. 19.17). In all events, Jesus, too, agrees with the fact that, in order to 'inherit eternal life' as a Jew, one must keep the law, here summarized in a selection of the Ten Commandments. The point is that he demands more. Total consecration is involved, or, biblically phrased, consecration 'with heart and soul'. Perhaps indeed the text from the Torah plays a role: 'Thou shalt love the Lord thy God with all thy heart, all thy soul, and all thy potential' (Deut. 6.4). This verse was important in general, but the

assumption that it is alluded to is supported by the interpretation of
R. Eliezer (end of first century). He shared various insights with Jesus,
including that concerning the matter of possessions, which is here under
discussion. In the verse both 'with all thy soul' and 'with all thy potential' are mentioned, 'because there are those that are more attached to
their bodies than to their possessions…and those that are more attached
to their possessions than to their bodies' (*Sifre Deut.* 32, p. 55). 'Possessions' is in Hebrew *mammon*, and this brings to mind Jesus' statement that one must choose, that one 'cannot serve God and mammon'
(Mt. 6.24). As in the case of the rich man, possessions can compete
with our love for God.

Comparable issues are at stake in the story of the summary of the
law, in which the same verse from Deuteronomy is explicitly quoted.
Here again there is a close affinity to rabbinic tradition.

> And one of (the Pharisees), a law teacher, asked (Jesus), in order to test
> him: Master, what is the greatest commandment of the law? And he said
> to him: 'Thou shalt love the Lord thy God with all thy heart and with all
> thy soul and with all thy mind'—that is the greatest and first command-
> ment. And the second, equal to it, is: 'Thou shalt love thy neighbour as
> thyself' (Lev. 19.18). On these two commandment depend all of the law
> and the prophets (Mt. 22.35-40; cf. Mk 12.28-34; Lk. 10.25-28).

For R. Akiva, a leading rabbi from around the beginning of the second
century, the love of one's fellow-man counted as 'the great summary of
the Torah' (*Sifra, qedoshim* 89b). Jesus' insistence upon the love for
God first and then for the fellow-man undoubtedly places his own
accent, but remains within the same sphere. This becomes apparent
from the fact that the double commandment of love, love for God and
for one's fellow-man, is also preserved in rabbinic literature (*Sefer
Pitron Torah*, pp. 79-80).

A third motif in this connection is the Golden Rule, which has been
ascribed both to Jesus and to Hillel (end of first century BCE) as the
'ethical summary' of the law. Jesus' phrasing is positive: 'do unto others
what you would that they do unto you', Hillel's is negative: 'what you
find to be odious, do not to others' (Mt. 7.12; *b. Šab.* 31a). A small
difference in accent is to be noted; however, both expressions share an
echo of the biblical commandment to 'love your neighbour as yourself'.
The other one is just like you are—treat her or him then as you yourself
would like to be treated.

For Hillel, Akiva, and other rabbis, such a summarization of the law did not mean at all that keeping the 'ordinary' commandments had become superfluous. The same can be assumed of Jesus. He was concerned with something that surpassed the law, something 'more than the usual', as expressed in the following saying:

> Woe to you, scribes and Pharisees, hypocrites, for you give tithes of mint, dill, and cummin, but you neglect the weightiest aspect of the law: judgment, mercy, and faithfulness (cf. Mic. 6.8); one should do these but not leave the other undone (Mt. 23.23).

The fact that this saying occurs in a simpler form in Luke (11.42) makes the doubt concerning the authenticity of the saying non-compelling, in spite of the recognizable stylizing hand of the Matthaean evangelist. The details as well suggest a real discussion with the Pharisees (see further pp. 273-74). It is conceded to them that a 'light' commandment, like giving a tithe of garden herbs, should be observed; however, the 'weightiest' aspect of the law lies elsewhere: in the unconditional devotion to God and one's fellow-man.

In a comparable manner, within a clearly redactional framework, Matthew transmits how in the elementary commandments Jesus hears an augmented application, which penetrates to the depths of the human heart. Just as in the story of the rich young man, these elementary commandments comprise the second half of the Ten Commandments.

> You have heard that it was said to the ancient ones: 'You shall not kill', and he who kills must come before judgment. But I say to you that whoever lives in anger towards his brother must stand before judgment, and whoever says to his brother *raka*, 'rubbish' must appear before the Sanhedrin, and whoever says 'fool' must face the Gehenna of fire...
> You have heard that it was said: 'You shall not commit adultery'. But I say to you that anyone who looks at a women to lust after her has already committed adultery with her in his heart (Mt. 5.21-22, 27-28).

Rather than annulling the literal significance of the elementary commandments, Jesus makes them transparent down to the 'small' commandments that, as it were, are written along with them. One can wound another with words in such a way that it amounts to psychological murder; a man can strip a woman naked with his eyes. For both of the 'small commandments' there are parallels in rabbinic literature that confirm the probability of a relationship (cf. also pp. 285-86). With the rabbis as well it is naturally not the intention that the 'small' commandments annul the 'great', as though 'do not be wrathful, do not gaze lustfully' would imply that killing and adultery are of no consequence. Even the terminology itself of 'small' or 'light' commandments occurs in rabbinic literature. The 'weightiest' of the law lies precisely the 'small' things that are hidden within the 'great' commandments: the love towards one's neighbour.

We can now reconsider the remarkable saying with which this section began. It occurs directly preceding the portion just quoted:

> Do not think that I have come to annul the law or the prophets; I am not come to annul them, but to fulfil them. Amen, I say to you indeed, before heaven and earth pass away not one dot or curl of the law will pass away until everything shall be fulfilled. Whoever, therefore, shall annul one of these smallest of commandments and shall teach people thus, he shall be called the smallest in the Kingdom of Heaven; but he who does them and teaches them shall be called great in the Kingdom of Heaven. For I say unto you: unless your righteousness exceed that of the scribes and the Pharisees, you shall surely not enter the Kingdom of Heaven (Mt. 5.17-20).

Here again, the stylizing hand of the evangelist is recognizable, as in the expression 'scribes and Pharisees', to which we shall give more attention in Chapter 6. It is, therefore, improbable that Jesus spoke in this form. The tenor, however, the importance attached to even the 'smallest' or the 'lightest' commandments invisibly written along with the others, and the struggle for a total, unlimited consecration corresponds to his preaching about the law as has come to the fore in the sayings studied above. In light of the imminent Kingdom, Jesus was aware of being 'sent' 'to bring the gospel to the poor' and to summon to conversion, *'today'*, now 'this Scripture is *fulfilled* in your hearing', now 'I must come to your house'… The possibility is not barred that indeed the saying is based on a tradition of Jesus' very words.

The Specific Commandments
The previous section dealt with that which is 'most important'—the aim or significance of the law. The discussion of the specific commandments, the practical rules about which, according to the tradition, Jesus also expressed himself, is of a different order. Here, we become entangled in heated discussions. In particular in the area of Shabbat and laws of purity, conflict over the Jewish law is inevitable. More than elsewhere, it is expedient to keep the notion of the layers in the Gospel tradition in mind. The development of the relationship between Jews and Christians makes it plausible that especially the later layers of the

Gospels exhibit an aggravation of the conflicts. On the other hand, it is unreasonable to assume that the oldest layer, that of the milieu of Jesus himself, should be completely free of such tensions. Time and again it is relevant to determine precisely which persons and institutions are involved in the tensions and conflicts.

In the preceding chapter we have seen that in Jesus' time there were essential differences of opinion concerning certain areas of the law. Regarding both purity and Shabbat, the Essenes adhered strictly to a radical and apparently older legal tradition. As far as we know, the Sadducees were conservative on both points as well. The Pharisees, however, accepted changes in the customs of the people and adapted the law accordingly. In this the school of Shammai was somewhat more conservative than that of Hillel, although the final result is not always directly derivable from this difference. Thus the Hillelites were milder than the Shammaites concerning Shabbat, while, due to their logical reasoning, they were sometimes stricter in the laws of purity. These two movements do not exhaust the diversity within Judaism. In between the two groups, pious individuals must have each exhibited their own variety.

Especially in the area of the practice of the law, the uniqueness of the figure of Jesus can be clearly outlined. The *halakah*, the law in its practical aspects, functioned as a system of social reference (see p. 91). We shall now read the Gospels in their layeredness from the perspective of the development of the Jewish law. Although our attention is primarily focussed on the context of Jesus himself, we must not cherish the illusion that we can observe this in isolation, for the influence of tradition and of the evangelist must always be taken into account.

Divorce

We begin not with Shabbat and purity, but with the question of divorce, an issue of great importance in early Judaism, concerning which divergent standpoints were taken. The Essenes were strict in their thinking on the matter and rejected divorce categorically, among other arguments, with an appeal to the story of creation. The Pharisees accepted divorce in principle, but disagreed as to the valid grounds for it (pp. 100-101). To judge from the sources, Jesus' followers adhered nearly unanimously to the strictest standpoint on this issue. The topic is, therefore, fitting as an opener on two accounts: in the Gospels the issue is not tainted by conflict over Jewish law, while the well-documented diversity in Judaism of that time allows us to define Jesus' position quite well.

Jesus' point of view was the occasion for the following passage in Mark:

> And Pharisees asked him whether a man is allowed to send away his wife, for they wanted to test him. And he answered: What has Moses commanded you? They said: Moses has instructed 'to write a letter of divorce and to send away' (Deut. 24.1). But Jesus said to them: Because of the hardness of your hearts has he written down that commandment for you. But from the beginning of creation 'he created them male and female' (Gen. 1.27); 'therefore shall a man leave his father and his mother [and adhere to his wife], and they shall become one flesh' (Gen. 2.24)—so that they are no longer two but one flesh. What God has paired together, mankind may not separate (Mk 10.2-9).

According to this report, Jesus rejected the principle of divorce. Marriage lasts for life: as long as the partner lives, one is not free to remarry. In content this is in complete accord with the Essenes, and in his argumentation as well Jesus conforms to the Essenes. Both reached beyond the accepted Old Testament legislation back to the more radical intention of the Torah as they understood it from Genesis. It is important that John the Baptist, whom we can assume to have been Jesus' teacher, was of the same opinion. These connections lend the report in Mark an authentic tone. The Pharisees who came to test Jesus evidently wanted to determine where he stood. Possibly they suspected him of having an Essene point of view.

The continuation of the story cannot be authentic in its present form:

> And when they were in the house the disciples asked him about this again. And he said to them: Everyone who sends away his wife and marries another commits adultery with her, and if she sends her husband away and marries another, she commits adultery (Mk 10.1-12).

The woman's initiative in the last sentence does not tally with the Jewish law of that time, where the woman was not an acting party. According to Hellenistic law, the woman could initiate a divorce, especially if she was well-to-do. The latter portion of the citation is, therefore, apparently an accommodation to the situation of non-Jews. A comparable adjustment can be found in Paul's writings (1 Cor. 7.10; p. 197, cf. pp. 100, 258-59). A layer of Mark that addresses itself to the non-Jewish believers manifests itself here.

It is worthy of note that in this form adapted to non-Jews, there is no trace of tension concerning the Jewish law. This corroborates our assumption that divorce was not an issue of conflict between Christians and Jews. On the other hand, when questioned by the Pharisees, Jesus appears to have a Essene standpoint concerning marriage. This controversy signifies that already the oldest layer of the Gospel tradition contained tension concerning the law, in this case between Jesus and the Pharisees about the validity of divorce. Nonetheless, such tensions did not develop into a conflict between Christians and Jews.

The wording of the rule in Luke, however, which is transmitted in the midst of a series of unconnected maxims without further narrative embedding, is compatible with ancient Jewish legislation:

> Everyone who sends away his wife and marries another commits adultery; and whoever marries a woman sent away by her husband commits adultery (Lk. 16.18).

The first part of the rule formally denies the principle of divorce. Even though a man has dismissed his wife, apparently with a letter of divorce, the wedlock continues to be valid as long as she lives, and to remarry is to commit adultery. As clarification, the second part adds the standpoint of the woman: if she has been dismissed, she still may not remarry. In this more authentic Lukan form, the rule agrees completely with Jesus' fundamental rejection of divorce in the story in Mark. Apart from the adaptation already mentioned, the authenticity of the rule is confirmed by Paul (1 Cor. 7.10-11, 39-40). We will discuss the Gospel of Matthew at a later point because it contains a development which complicates the issue (see pp. 286-87).

In summary, a comparison of how a commandment is practically interpreted appears to be an effective means of localizing people and movements within ancient Jewish society. Concerning divorce, Jesus, like John the Baptist, agreed with the Essenes and was stricter than the most stringent Pharisee. This contrasts with indications elsewhere that Jesus distinguished himself from the Essenes and in some regards thought more akin to the Pharisees. Such confirms our assumption that Jesus like John should be localized somewhere between the Essenes and the Pharisees. Later followers of Jesus strictly kept the commandment of their master. The adaptation to the situation of non-Jews that can be found with Mark and Paul proves that this was equally true of the non-Jewish Christians. The issue of divorce gave no occasion for conflict with the Jews: on this point, the Christians were stricter than most Jews.

Shabbat

The Shabbat is a living reality to Jews, wherever on earth they might live. The Bible teaches us that Israel began to keep the Shabbat in the desert before the revelation at Sinai and the building of the sanctuary (Exod. 16). As Abraham Joshua Heschel so aptly has stated: for Israel the Shabbat is 'a sanctuary in time'. Nonetheless, in antiquity there were significant differences in opinion concerning details, as we have seen in the previous chapter. The following account about Jesus can be seen in this light:

> It happened once that he was walking through a grain field on the Shabbat, and his disciples plucked and ate the grain by rubbing it in their hands. And certain Pharisees said: why do you do that which is not permitted on the Shabbat? (Lk. 6.1-2).

It is certainly possible that Jesus, who maintained such a distinct position on divorce, was further questioned by the Pharisees on the matter of Shabbat. If we are to read this report as belonging to the oldest layer of the Gospel tradition, we could assume a conflict between Jesus and the Pharisees here. This, too, is historically plausible. In his answer, Jesus referred to the freedom taken by David and his men by eating the priests' shewbread (1 Sam. 21.1-6), and he concludes with the saying: 'The son of man is lord of the Shabbat' (Lk. 6.5). What is the significance of the freedom of this 'son of David'?

The possibility that Jesus bluntly ignored the Shabbat can be excluded. As depicted by the synoptic tradition, even the 'light commandments' carried weight for Jesus and Moses' rule of divorce was only a concession. How much more should he not be devoted to the commandment of the seventh day, which God himself held in honour 'from the beginning' (Gen. 2.1-3)? On this matter, the Gospel of John takes a radically different standpoint that will be discussed elsewhere (Chapter 7). The question here is whether the account can be authentic in its quoted form.

Rabbinic literature can assist us in grasping what possibly was at stake here. The rubbing of grain was a well-known problem in early rabbinic halakha:

> On the Shabbat, he who rubs, blows (the chaff) away while he lets (the grains) fall from the one hand to the other, but does not (let them fall) into a basket or a dish (*t. Šab.* 14.16; *t. Yom tov* 1.20-22).

There was perhaps also a standpoint that one was allowed to pluck ears in small amounts. The latter is, namely, reported in a related context concerning herbs (*b. Šab.* 128a, R. Yehuda). The point of contention between Jesus and the Pharisees, therefore, can be either the rubbing of the ears or the plucking. In Luke it is called 'plucking *and* rubbing', in the other synoptic Gospels only 'plucking' (Mk 2.23; Mt. 12.1). There are also two versions of the story with only 'rubbing': the Arabic translation of the *Diatessaron*, a harmony of the four Gospels from the second century, and a tenth-century Arabic text that quotes an older Jewish-Christian source. These would suggest an original version with only 'rubbing'. We would then have a so-called conflation in Luke, an expansion based on the version with 'rubbing' to which 'plucking' has been added. The matter can be left undecided. Whether it was originally rubbing or plucking, in both interpretations Jesus moved within a certain legal tradition, and the discussion with the Pharisees was not about *whether* the Shabbat was to be respected but about a detail of *how* this should be done.

In Mark, the story has a remarkable finale: 'And he said to them: *the Shabbat was made for man and not man for the Shabbat*; therefore the son of man is lord even of the Shabbat' (Mk 2.27-28). The somewhat proverbial character of the part in italics is confirmed by the fact that the saying is transmitted in a slightly different version in rabbinic literature, where it is ascribed to R. Shimon ben Menasia (p. 92). Such congruency between the New Testament and rabbinic literature is unusual. Even more striking is the fact that in both cases the saying serves the same purpose: to underpin the 'human purpose' of the Shabbat. Mark in its final form does not manifest any special sympathy for Judaism (see Chapter 6). The connection with the rabbinic saying testifies, therefore, to an older layer, perhaps that of Jesus' own environment. Jesus was probably questioned by the Pharisees concerning his divergent outlook on Shabbat, and he motivated this then or at another occasion with the saying about humankind and Shabbat. The arcane allusions to the 'son of man' and the 'son of David' reflect Jesus' characteristic awareness of having a mission (cf. p. 164).

Of crucial importance are the healings on Shabbat, not only because of their significance to Jesus' mission, but also because of their function in the various Gospels, which is not always the same in the successive layers, and certainly not in John. We restrict ourselves again to the synoptic Gospels and direct our attention particularly to the oldest layers.

First, a survey of the reports would be useful. Taking the parallels between the synoptic Gospels into account, five stories are involved, in this discussion indicated by numbers. Mark opens Jesus' ministry with the exorcism of the evil spirit in the synagogue of Capernaum (no. 1) and proceeds with the healing of Simon's mother-in-law (no. 2). Both accounts are also in Luke (Mk 1.21-31; Lk. 4.31-39). These are followed in Mark by the healing of the man with a withered hand (no. 3), which is also found in Matthew and Luke (Mk 3.1-6; Mt. 12.9-14; Lk. 6.6-11). Luke then relates the healing of a woman with a 'spirit of weakness' and of the man with 'dropsy' (nos. 4 and 5; Lk. 13.10-17; 14.1-6). Summarizing, in Mark we find nos. 1, 2 and 3, in Matthew only no. 3 and in Luke all five stories.

Two aspects of these accounts are important to us. First, the *action* undertaken by Jesus is reported. In two healings, he only gives a command (nrs. 1 and 3). In the case of Simon's mother-in-law (no. 2), according to Mark Jesus takes her hand and in Luke he only speaks. In the other cases, he either lays his hand upon the sick one (no. 4) or grasps the sick person (no. 5). Not one of the synoptic accounts reports that Jesus prepares a medicine: he does not execute a single 'work' that is forbidden on the Shabbat, as that was later summarized in a rabbinic formulation (*m. Šab.* 7.2). Healing, however, entails a change in circumstances and the issue is how this is viewed.

A second aspect is the *argumentation* used in the accompanying discussions, which is present with nos. 3, 4 and 5. Number 3, also found in Luke, occurs in Mark and Matthew at a strategic moment in the story and has a catastrophic effect (Mk 3.6; Mt. 12.14). The confrontation is also the sharpest there and centres around the question, 'May a person do good or evil on the Shabbat? save a soul or destroy it?' (Lk. 6.9; Mk 3.4; Mt. 12.12). The Pharisees present observe Jesus closely, apparently being of the opinion that to 'do good' and 'save' entails a change in circumstances that is inappropriate on the Shabbat.

In Matthew's version, Jesus cites an halakhic argumentation that is also known to us from ancient Jewish literature (cf. pp. 92-93). If someone's sheep

> falls into a well on the Shabbat, shall he not grasp it and raise it up? How much more does a person surpass an animal? Therefore it is permitted to do good on the Shabbat (Mt. 12.11-12).

With the last healing in Luke (no. 5) Jesus brings forward this same argumentation: 'If someone's donkey or ox fall into a well, shall he not immediately pull it out on the Shabbat?' (Lk. 14.5; cf. p. 220). In case no. 4, Jesus also presents a similar argument: 'Does not each of you untie his ox or donkey from the manger and lead him away to drink? And this is a daughter of Abraham...' (Lk. 13.15-16).

We mentioned earlier that the Pharisaic–rabbinic principle of the care for life surpassing the keeping of the Shabbat apparently was supported by broad layers of the populace (see pp. 91-93.). Unmistakably this is implied in the question around which the discussion turns: 'May one save or *kill* on the Shabbat?' (see Mk 3.4). This question now becomes more understandable, for no one is, of course, planning to kill a sick person. The 'killing' would, however, occur should nothing be done. According to the Pharisaic standpoint, one is obliged instead to take action in order to 'save'. All things considered, this is a rhetorical exaggeration because in none of the reported cases was there a life-threatening situation.

The halakhic argument, which bears scrutiny, is that of the preservation of the life of cattle and, therefore, also of humankind. Such an argument *a minori ad majus*, in Hebrew *kal wa-homer*, 'from light to heavy', is a standard form of argumentation in halakah, and occurs in the New Testament as well in various applications (1 Cor. 9.8-10; Mt. 6.28-30). Jesus' argumentation assumes that his discussion partners agree with 'raising' an animal that has fallen in a well, or with 'untying' an animal and allowing it to drink. Luke reports that in all cases Jesus' questioners indeed have nothing to say against Jesus' argumentation and silently accede (Lk. 6.11; 13.17; 14.6). In contrast, according to Mark and Matthew their reaction in case no. 3 is murderous (see further pp. 259, 272). Within the halakhic context, this reaction can hardly be called forth by a violation of the Shabbat and must reflect a later situation—or a later layer of the Gospel. In contrast to the Old Testament and the conservative, strict book of Jubilees, even Essene legislation explicitly rejected the death sentence for unintentional violations of the Shabbat (Num. 15.32; *Jub.* 2.25-27; 50.8; CD 12.3-4). This must be even more true of the far milder Pharisaic–rabbinic tradition. Luke's version fits better with the discussions in the time of Jesus and the Pharisees, and probably reflects the oldest layer of tradition.

A comparison of the content with ancient Jewish sources confirms this conclusion. The reluctant agreement of the Pharisees corresponds to the striking affinity of Jesus' argumentation with the principles of Pharisaic–rabbinic tradition. We have seen in the previous chapter that their tradition explictly allowed one to bring food and drink to an animal that had fallen into a well, and thus to 'save' it. If a person had fallen into a well, one was permitted to try to save them on the Shabbat, just as one could warm up water for a sick person if there were the slightest chance of a threat to life. In these matters, the Essenes were stricter. According to one text, they explicitly prohibited 'raising up' an animal that had fallen into a well, precisely the expression used in Matthew (Mt. 12.11). According to another passage, one was allowed to 'untie' animals and bring them to a place to fodder. These similarities support the impression that the Shabbat stories in Luke reflect the oldest layer of tradition, at least as far as the content is concerned. Jesus apparently distanced himself from the strict Essenic halakha and challenged the Pharisees to do likewise—a challenge which they could, of course, not refuse.

In his mildness towards the keeping of Shabbat, Jesus went further than the more conservative Pharisees wished to do. This is in stark contrast to the issue of divorce, on which he shared the Essene standpoint and was stricter than the most conservative Pharisee.

Purity

The third area of Jesus' practice of the law that we will discuss is that of purity. The system of ritual purification and cleansing has been treated in the previous chapter. A separate portion of this system has also been discussed, namely, cleanliness of the hands, which was characteristic of the Pharisees' system of purification. In principle, it was only applicable to pilgrims on the way to or in the temple, but there were also Pharisees who practised it in daily life as well.

This information enables us to position the account of Jesus' discussion about the laws of cleanliness, for which we will follow the version from Matthew. In the latest layer, Mark exhibits complication that can better be treated in Chapter 6. The 'evangelist' in Matthew has also set his mark on the story, of course, but it requires a less disruptive explication at this point.

> Then there came Pharisees and scribes from Jerusalem to Jesus and said: Why do your disciples transgress the tradition of the Ancients? For they do not wash their hands when they eat bread.
> But he answered them: Why do you yourselves transgress the commandment of God through your tradition? For God has said: 'Honour your father and your mother' (Exod. 20.12), and, 'He that curses his father or his mother shall be put to death' (Exod. 21.17). But you say: Whoever says to his father or mother: 'That what you could have had

from me is a gift for the temple', does not have to honour his father.
Thus you cause God's word to be inoperative through your tradition.
...And he called the multitude to him and said to them: Hear and
understand! Not what goes into the mouth makes a person unclean, but
that which goes out of the mouth, that makes a person unclean... Everything that goes into the mouth stays in the stomach and is disposed of in
the privy, but what goes out of the mouth comes forth from the heart and
that makes a person unclean. For from the heart come forth evil thoughts,
thoughts of murder, adultery, theft, false witness, slander. These make a
person unclean, but to eat with unwashed hands does not make a person
unclean (Mt. 15.1-20; cf. Mk 7.1-23).

The debate between Jesus and the Pharisees is about the authority of
the 'tradition of the Ancients', a Pharisaic expression for the commandment to cleanse the hands. Jesus' disciples do not observe this, and, in
answer to the criticism of the Pharisees, Jesus poses an argument on
principles. According to Jesus, obedience to the Scriptures has precedence over the tradition of the Pharisees. In their manner of reasoning,
it is indeed even possible to disannul the basic commandment to honour
one's father and mother. In conclusion, Jesus summarizes his answer in
the saying that only that which goes out of the mouth defiles a person.
This saying, too, involves the authority of the Pharisaic tradition, as
becomes clear through further study of rabbinic literature, by which
also Jesus' position in regard to the Pharisaic movement is given more
relief.

In rabbinic literature, the commandment concerning the 'cleanliness
of hands' is explicitly considered to be a postbiblical institution. It is
described as one of the 'words of the scribes' with the implication of its
being less authoritative (*m. Yad.* 3.2). In the previous chapter we have
seen that its use must have been fairly recent in Jesus' time. The story
just cited is, therefore, in general historically plausible. Jesus,
apparently sharing the viewpoint of many of his contemporaries, did
not accept the general obligation of the cleanliness of hands.

Jesus' defence is based upon the authority of the biblical commandment to honour one's father and mother, another portion of the law that
also was contested in ancient Jewish literature. According to general
opinion, the biblical commandment entailed that children were obligated to sustain their parents materially. One must, however, be realistic
in one's conception of this, and take into consideration, for example, an
unlimited demand on the part of the parents. One way to escape this
was to arrange a pledge in order not to have to give material advantage

to another, in this case to the parents. The pledge cited in the Gospel account, 'that what you could have had from me is a gift for the temple', agrees literally with the cited formulation in the Mishnah (*m. Ned.* 8.7; 1.2; Mk 7.11). Jesus apparently did not accept the validity of such a fictitious pledge. Besides his preference for the written Torah, this also has to do with his general rejection of oaths and vows (Mt. 5.33-37). On this point he again exhibits a stricter concept of the law. The Essenes strictly forbade all pledges that went against the Scriptures (CD 16.8-9). The opinion of the conservative Shammaite R. Eliezer has been preserved, stating that a pledge can be annulled for the benefit of 'honouring one's father and mother' (*m. Ned.* 9.1). This corresponds exactly to the attitude of Jesus, who on this point evidently protested against the juridical pliancy of the Hillelites.

In the third part of the account, Jesus returns to the matter of the cleanliness of hands by broadening the discussion to rules of cleanliness in general. The phrase 'nothing which enters the mouth makes a person unclean' makes a clear halakhic point. He rejects the principle that food or drink that is touched by an unclean person should acquire a derived impurity, which in turn can be passed on to the one who consumes it. This part of the system of rules of purity was in Jesus' time not yet generally accepted, not even among the Pharisees. In terms of the system, it was of the same limited importance as the uncleanliness of hands (*m. Zab.* 5.12). The Essenes and the Sadducees probably rejected these two principles (p. 97), and this standpoint was apparently shared by Jesus as well. In his own particular way, he related it subsequently to 'the most weighty of the law' (Mt. 23.23) by insisting upon the cleansing of the heart. In this, the repeated emphasis upon the second table of the Ten Commandments is remarkable (cf. Mk 10.19). The account is rounded off by a repetition of the opening theme—the cleanliness of the hands; this can be ascribed to the evangelist.

The account fits into the stage of development of the law in the first century, such as it also is presented in ancient Jewish literature. It is, therefore, likely that the basic elements are authentic and belong the the oldest layer of the Gospel tradition. The distance Jesus took to the 'tradition of the Ancients' is easily understood, not only because of his use of the term, but also because of the stand he takes. He rejects three innovations of the Pharisees: the instruction, advocated by some, to cleanse hands before regular consuming of food; the Hillelite custom of making pledges that invalidate a biblical commandment, at least the commandment to honour one's parents; and the derived uncleanliness that can be transmitted through food or drink. The traditional Christian explanation that Jesus put his own authority above that of the Torah is, therefore, erroneous. His objection to the disputed practice of making pledges is precisely that it invalidated the biblical commandment. In a radical manner reminiscent of the Essenes, Jesus adheres to the written Torah and refuses a number of Pharisaic elements.

When we survey Jesus' attitude towards the law on the points discussed, it becomes apparent that this does not coincide with one of the known movements. He is Essene in his radical rejection of divorce, conservative Pharisaic in his viewpoint on pledges that were to get around 'honouring' one's parents, mildly Pharisaic in his conception of the Shabbat, and in his conservative attitude towards laws of purity he again reminds one of the Essenes and the Sadducees. Jesus was not at home anywhere, except perhaps in the proximity of the 'nonconformistic companionship' of pious individuals.

The Non-Jews

Within the context of the New Testament as a whole, the question of Jesus' own position regarding non-Jews is an interesting one. The diverse Jewish factions showed considerable differences on this matter. Should Jesus' attitude on this point as well turn out to be somewhere between that of the Essenes and the Pharisees, then he would maintain moderate to considerable distance to non-Jews. That seems indeed approximately to have been the case, but there are surprises.

Within the first generations of his followers, powerful shifts must have taken place on this point as well. The so-called 'missionary dispatch' at the end of Matthew is well known, in which the Risen One commissions his disciples, 'Go forth, make all peoples to be my disciples…and teach them to keep all what I have charged you' (Mt. 28.19). Because of the contrast with a number of other passages in Matthew, this appears to belong to the last stage of development of the Gospel (see further Chapter 6). In other Gospels there are also traces of a later development (Lk. 24.47; Jn 10.16; 11.52). This reveals undoubtedly that all the Gospels acquired their final form in congregations in which non-Jews were prominent.

In the synoptic tradition, and especially in Matthew, another line is

visible that seems to bring us in the vicinity of Jesus himself. Remarkably, the first of these two texts, which we have already considered in
another connection, also occurs in the context of an account of the
disciples being sent out:

> These twelve did Jesus send out with the following assignment: Turn not
> aside on a road of non-Jews, and do not enter a Samaritan village, but go
> rather to the lost sheep of the house of Israel (Mt. 10.5-6).

> Amen, I say to you, you shall not have travelled around all the cities of
> Israel before the son of man comes (Mt. 10.23).

> I have been sent only to the lost sheep of the house of Israel (Mt. 15.24).

According to this tradition, in his own understanding of it, Jesus' commission and that of his disciples was limited to the Jews. The metaphor
of the sheep appears to belong to the oldest tradition, and occurs also in
the introduction to the dispatching of the disciples, although there in the
third person: 'And when he saw the multitude he was moved with compassion for them, for they were harassed and dismayed as sheep without
a shepherd' (Mt. 9.36). In the Old Testament, the expression 'as sheep
without a shepherd' had a proverbial connection with the king, who, as
in other ancient eastern cultures, liked to be seen as a shepherd of his
people (Num. 27.17; 1 Kgs 22.17). Jesus evidently had appropriated
this image, which also appears in the parable of the lost sheep (Lk.
15.3-7; Mt. 18.12-14) and the Johannine saying, 'I am the good
shepherd' (Jn 10.11, 14). The 'sheep' to which Jesus felt himself to be
sent were in the first place the Jews.

The same is confirmed by a number of sayings scattered throughout
the Gospels that express reservation towards non-Jews. Such is difficult
to imagine as part of the last redactional layer.

> Do not worry, saying: 'what shall we eat?' or 'what shall we drink?' or
> what shall we put on? *for all these things do the non-Jews pursue* (Mt.
> 6.32; Lk. 12.30).

> If you only greet your brothers, what is special about that? *Do not the
> non-Jews also the same?* (Mt. 5.47).

> When you pray, do not be verbose *like the non-Jews*, who think that
> because of a flood of words they shall be heard (Mt. 6.7).

This type of statement is imaginable in the older layer of Matthew. A
related saying, however, carries the clear mark of the congregation after
Jesus:

> If your brother sins, go to him and reprove him... But if he does not
> listen, report it to the church. And if he does not listen even to the
> church, let him then be to you as a non-Jew and a tax collector (Mt.
> 18.17).

The word that is here rendered as 'church' is derived from the Greek
Old Testament (p. 24). This is a trace of the 'Jewish church' in which
the Gospel of Matthew partially acquired its present form.

One could, then, assume that also the earlier quoted statements could
have been inspired by this Matthaean church. That is, however, neither
cogent nor probable because related traces are encountered in the other
Gospels. The statement of Jesus in the conversation with the Samaritan
woman is remarkable in this connection: 'You worship what you do not
know; we worship what we know, for salvation is from the Jews'
(Jn 4.22). This statement is quite striking in relation to the Jews within
the framework of this Gospel, but is even more so in relation to the
disparagement of the Samaritans. It concurs with the commission to
'not turn aside on the road of non-Jews, nor enter a Samaritan village'.

The clearest affirmation of Jesus' reticence towards non-Jews can be
found in two accounts in which it appears that, in spite of his reserve,
he could allow himself to be surprised; we mentioned this already in
connection with his loving humour. The first has to do with the Roman
centurion in Capernaum whose slave was seriously ill (Lk. 7.2-10; for
Mt. 8.5-13 see Chapter 6). The centurion had a good rapport with the
local Jews, respected their customs, and can be described as 'God-fearing' (see p. 108). The 'elders of the Jews' whom he dispatches to Jesus
relate, 'He loves our people and has had our synagogue built.' Out of
respect for the Jewish law, he asked Jesus not to come into his home,
but 'speak only one word and my slave shall be healed'. He emphasizes
this with the illustration of the obedience that his soldiers owe him. If
we recall the reputation of the discipline of the Roman army, Jesus'
surprise comes across even more vividly:

> When Jesus heard this, he was surprised, and turned towards the multi-
> tude which followed him and said: I say unto you, even in Israel have I
> not found such faith.

The use of the term 'Israel' implies that his audience consisted of Jews
(see pp. 112-13) with whom he shared his surprise at the faith of this
non-Jewish military man.

The other story is that of the Greek woman who approaches Jesus in
the region of Tyre because of her daughter, who was possessed by

'impure spirits'. She found her way to Jesus, although he 'wanted to know no one' in that region and had retreated into a house. His answer to her plea is equally reserved, but here again he allows himself to be surprised:

> He said to her: Let the children be fed first, for it is not fitting to take the children's bread and throw it to the puppies. But she replied: Lord! Even the puppies under the table eat the crumbs which the little children drop. Then he said to her: Go home now because of these words, for the demon has departed from your daughter (Mk 7.27-30).

The use of the diminutive, first by Jesus and then by the woman ('little children', 'little dogs'), has an endearing effect, but should not make us ignore the embarrassing designation of the non-Jews as dogs. That mistake is made when the story is read as though Jesus crossed over the boundary between Jews and non-Jews here in a significant manner, as seems to be suggested by the context in Mark (see pp. 261-62). In the parallel story in Matthew, however, Jesus says explicitly that he has been sent to 'the lost sheep of the house of Israel'. One could reason that the Matthaean evangelist supplemented the story with this remark, but the opposite is just as probable, namely, that the redactor of Mark omitted this sentence in view of his non-Jewish readers. In all events, Jesus' initial derogatory attitude towards the Greek woman in the story has the quality of being original.

Jesus' ensuing surprise is equally authentic. Precisely here, at the boundaries of his world, he exhibits openness for the unexpected, for the hidden turn for the better. We noted this as well in the story of Zacchaeus, and, significantly, there again it had to do with an outcast, a tax collector. The later church hailed Jesus' joy about the faith of the non-Jews, but unfortunately was less enthusiastic about his dedication to Israel...

Passover in Jerusalem

A large portion of the Gospels is dedicated to Jesus' final days in Jerusalem. In Mark and John, this takes up about a half of the Gospel (Mk 11–16; Jn 11–21), showing the importance of the passion story. For that very reason, however, not only is it laden with all of Christianity's belief, but it is also supplied with all sorts of later explanation and elaboration. It is extremely difficult here to distinguish between what is an eye-witness report and what is a later supplementation. With regard to the passages about the significance of Jesus' sufferings, it is even commonly accepted among exegetes to ascribe everything to a later congregation. On the other hand, no single fact of his existence is so unquestionably certain as his fatal conflict with the temple authorities and his crucifixion by the Romans. At the end of this chapter we will, therefore, address the question of what the tradition possibly has preserved of Jesus' own view on this 'crucial' moment in his life.

To begin with, we must recall the extraordinary consciousness of being commissioned with which he began. He was convinced that he was 'sent' with a unique message regarding the coming of the Kingdom of God; he could proclaim that the words of the prophets were 'today fulfilled in your ears'. With this outlook, it is conceivable that Jesus saw the opposition on the part of the Jerusalem authorities also in the perspective of the coming Kingdom.

At his triumphal entrance into Jerusalem tension already hangs in the air. The throng cheers and sees his behaviour in a messianic light. The sympathy of the people is noteworthy in the Gospels, precisely because of the later tensions with the Jews (Mk 11.8-10; Mt. 21.8-9; Lk. 19.37-38; Jn 12.13-15). Equally remarkable is the cleansing of the temple square with which Jesus proceeds directly after his arrival. In John, where this report is placed at the beginning of the Gospel, the detail is added that Jesus made a 'whip of cords' and attacked the merchants with it (Jn 2.15), a vehemence which could hardly have been thought up by a later evangelist. As commentary, a quote is added: 'The zeal for your house has consumed me' (Ps. 69.10; Jn 2.17). Is this merely asking for trouble? In any case, Jesus shows himself in what follows to be extremely explosive towards the temple leaders.

The temple leadership is presented in the persons of the upper priests and scribes (Mk 11.18), who then decide to deliver Jesus to the Romans to be executed (Mk 15.1). When they ask Jesus who has given him the authority for his actions, he reciprocates with a question concerning the mandate of John the Baptist, to which they dare not give an answer (Mk 11.27-33). In the parable of the rebellious tenants of the vineyard, which he proceeds to tell, according to Mark and Luke with an eye on the temple authorities, he gives them notice in so many words of their loss of power over the temple (Mk 12.1-2; see p. 225). The prediction of the destruction of the temple (Mk 13.1-2) must also be seen in that light. The upper priests, who were closely connected to the Sadducees, enjoyed little respect at that time (see pp. 55-56). Jesus calls their temple a 'den of thieves' (Mk 11.17; Jer. 7.11) and forecasts their dismissal and the destruction of their 'inheritance'. A comparable prophecy is not known from Essene sources, but the Qumran scrolls contain sharp denunciations of the temple government in Jerusalem. Such criticism can also be found in other ancient Jewish writings, including predictions of destruction. In this again Jesus' affinity to radical pious Jewish circles becomes apparent. Upon his arrival in Jerusalem, he appears intentionally to enter into conflict with the temple authorities.

The next question is what significance Jesus attached to the conflict, and likewise to the violence that he could expect as a result. In the first place, his counter-question concerning John the Baptist implies a messianic self-confidence in this conflict. This becomes even more explicit in the same context by his posing the question to the authorities concerning the son of David, who is simultaneously his Lord. In this he apparently alludes to his own authority as son of David and, thus, as legitimate aspirant to the leadership over the people (Mk 12.35-37). A second aspect has to do with messianic suffering. In the synoptic Gospels thrice an account is given in which Jesus foresees the inevitable suffering and death of the 'son of man' (see Mk 8.31; 9.30; 10.32). In these it is hardly possible to distinguish between original material and later clarification and supplementation by his followers. The case is different perhaps in the words that we cited earlier: 'The son of man is not come to be served but to serve and to give his life as a ransom for many' (Mk 10.45; Mt. 20.28).

This leads us back to the final days in Jerusalem, in particular to the *last supper*. The accounts contain an unquestioned indication that Jesus foresaw his death, and likewise his resurrection. After the blessing over the cup he says, 'Amen, I say unto you, I shall no more drink of the fruit of the vine until the day that I shall drink it anew in the Kingdom of God' (Mk 14.25; Mt. 26.29; Lk. 22.18). This can hardly be other than authentic, given the fact that Jesus is speaking of his resurrection on the last day. That the last day had not yet dawned on that particular Easter morning was, of course, not unknown to his first followers, and, therefore, it is extremely improbable that they themselves would have placed this saying in Jesus' mouth. He foresaw, thus, his death, and it can hardly be otherwise than that this was related to the opposition of the temple leadership. He apparently also saw his death and resurrection, just as his ministry as such, as an essential event in the light of the coming Kingdom. This invites us to consider whether the words about the blood that was 'shed for many' (Mk 14.24) were not spoken by Jesus himself.

A few words about the belief in the resurrection from the dead are fitting here. This belief occurs only on the outer margins of the Old Testament (Isa. 26.19; Dan. 12.2), but had become widespread in the Judaism of Jesus' time. There were, however, exceptions, such as, in particular, the Sadducees. To this witnesses the well-known discussion between the Sadducees and Jesus, who, in his own way, proves that the resurrection of the dead is indeed consistent with the Scriptures (Mk 12.18-27). The Talmud as well contains such a discussion between Gamaliel the Elder and what apparently are Sadducees (*b. Sanh.* 90a). Gamaliel, the Pharisee leader, is also mentioned in the New Testament (Acts 5.23; 22.3). The belief in the resurrection of the dead, which to the present day figures in Jewish prayers, was an important tenet of the Pharisees; the New Testament is a prominent source of information on this point (Acts 23.6-8). Jesus shared fully in this belief; even stronger, he lived on the basis of this belief and saw even his own dying in the perspective of the dawning of the Kingdom. The Christian confession of the resurrection of the dead, first of the Messiah and thereafter of all believers, is a direct continuation of Jesus' own belief.

Furthermore, we must point to two portions from the Torah which, according to ancient custom, were read on Passover. The calendar of the Essenes, to which I referred in the preceding chapter, bears a relation to this. This calendar is emphatically commented on in the book of *Jubilees*, which dates from at least the second century BCE (see pp. 80-81). In this same document the near-offering of Isaac falls on the *exact calendar date* of Passover (*Jub.* 17.1; cf. Gen. 22). According to this calendar, on Passover not only the Passover lamb of Exodus 12 is involved, but also the ram that Abraham offered in Isaac's stead (Gen. 22.13). In rabbinic tradition, the identification of both Torah portions has been preserved as well. In one tradition, the blood of the Passover lamb is equated to the blood of Isaac (*Mek. bo* 7, *pishka* 11, p. 39). This identification was adopted by Christians and applied to the death of Jesus. According to a tradition that dates at least from the second century, the two passages from Genesis and Exodus were read at the ancient Christian remembrance of Jesus' death and resurrection on Easter (Melito of Sardes, *Concerning Easter*). The oldest witness to this Christian application is the exclamation by Paul: 'For our Passover lamb has been slain, Christ!' (1 Cor. 5.7). There are indications that

Jesus at least on this occasion followed some form of the Essene calendar (see pp. 277-79). Then, in his milieu as well, Exodus 12 could have been read together with Genesis 22. The identification of Jesus' dying with the blood of the Passover lamb and the blood of Isaac evidently goes back to the direct environment of Jesus.

For yet another element of importance we return once more to Jesus' counter-question to the upper priests at the temple square whether 'the baptism of John was from Heaven or from mankind'. They did not dare to give a negative answer 'for all considered John truly to be a prophet' (Mk 11.32). It must, however, have been known to all that the Baptist had been executed because he had not kept silent before King Herod (Mk 6.18). The multiple thrust of Jesus' question contained thus also the vivid awareness that prophets are persecuted and killed. This is also an important aspect of Jesus' parable of the tenants of the vineyard that ensues. The theme of the murder of prophets, a well-known tradition in the Judaism of that time, occurs quite widespread in early Christianity (*The Lives of the Prophets*; Jas 5.10-11; Heb. 11.37), and also plays a role elsewhere in Jesus' teachings (Mt. 5.10-11; 23.37-39; Lk. 13.34-35).

All these elements open the possibility that Jesus himself saw his own imminent death depicted in the ram that Abraham offered for his *only beloved son* (Gen. 22.2) and in the Passover lamb that *averted the death threat* for Israel in the night of the exodus. The connection appears to be confirmed by the divine utterance that according to the synoptic tradition was heard both at Jesus' baptism and at the transfiguration on the mount: 'This is my son whom I love...' (Mk 1.11; 9.7). It is difficult to conceive that a later congregation ascribed the vision at the baptism to her master. It is more probable that it originated from Jesus' direct surroundings. In the midst of all these connections the authenticity of the saying about the son of man who 'is come to give his life a ransom for many' becomes more plausible (see p. 137).

We can thus picture how, on the evening before he was taken captive, the evening in which the offering of Isaac and the liberation of Israel were remembered, each in his own circle of intimates, Jesus passed the cup around and spoke the words, '*This is my blood* [of the covenant] which is *shed for many*' (Mk 14.24). The words between square brackets occur in the manuscripts in sundry variations and are even completely lacking in a Latin manuscript from the fifth century, thus diminishing the likelihood of them being original. Probably it was in the liturgical tradition of his followers that the motif of the (new) covenant was added to the texture of the references of which Jesus' words are composed here. From this usage it could have easily been added to the text of Mark. That must have occurred quite early, for we find it in our most ancient account, that of Paul.

As witnesses of the resurrection, Jesus' followers continued his mission: his gospel of the coming Kingdom for the poor, his teachings, his work of healing. He left no literary corpus behind. His spoken and lived teachings were, however, embodied in the oral tradition of his apostles, from which later written 'Gospels' were composed for fellow-believers far away. An exceptional trace of this oral tradition is found in the Epistle of Paul to Corinth. It is the only passage in which Paul more or less literally quotes the teachings of Jesus and therefore it is also the oldest documentation of the words of this enigmatic figure:

> For I have received from the Lord, that which I also have passed on to you, namely that the Lord [Jesus] in the night in which he was betrayed took bread, said the blessing, and broke it and said: this is my body for you, do this in my remembrance; and thus also the cup after the meal, by which he spoke: this is the cup of the new covenant in my blood, do this, as often as you drink, in remembrance of me. For as often as you eat this bread and drink this cup, you proclaim the Lord's death, until he comes (1 Cor. 11.23-26).

Chapter 4

PAUL

The preceding chapter was about the figure of Jesus as initially embodied in the oral transmission of his disciples. From this point on our attention will be directed to authors, namely, persons who committed their own thoughts to writing. Partially the same documents are involved: the Gospels not only give an impression of Jesus' teachings and life but also show the stamp of the evangelist. There are also other types of documents to be treated: the Acts of the Apostles, the many epistles, and a Revelation. The authors of these writings would, if asked, say that they did nothing other than testify concerning the story of Jesus. It was also to that purpose that their writings were read, preserved and finally collected—brought together as one literary corpus that witnesses to the one Lord and teacher.

The order in which we will consider this collection departs from the traditional canon, for we will begin with the letters of Paul. There are various reasons for this. First, Paul's writings are the oldest of the New Testament, dating from the forties and fifties, approximately one generation earlier than the other writings. Secondly, due to their early dating, we can assume that in these the process of estrangement between Christians and Jews that we later observe was as yet in an initial phase. Thirdly, the book of Acts, which in the canon precedes the epistles and also gives information about Paul, was written in a later context and, according to many, gives a distorted picture of Paul.

The Jewish Apostle to the Nations and his Epistles

There is yet a fourth reason for beginning with Paul, and it brings us right to the heart of the matter. According to a dominant interpretation, Paul championed the rift between Christianity and Judaism, though according to others, this is entirely inaccurate. Thus, besides the early date of his writings, the interpretation of Paul is strategic to the main theme of this book. If we are able correctly to determine his position regarding Judaism and burgeoning Christianity, we will have acquired an Archimedian point, a trustworthy basis for the reinterpretation of the other New Testament writings.

To read Paul as unadulteratedly as possible, one must begin with his own epistles. Here again the circuit, called by exegetes the hermeneutic circle, is unavoidable. His letters can only be understood well if there is a clear picture of his situation, but insight into his situation is to be had primarily from his epistles... This closed circle can be broken open to the extent that external sources are available, but that is where the discussion begins. There are, of course, sources of general interest about his world, such as Graeco-Jewish Diaspora literature and a number of Greek and Roman writings. Progressively it has become more acceptable to glean specific information about Paul's background from the Hebrew sources of his time: first, those from Qumran, because of their certain dating, and, thereafter, early traditions that can be traced in rabbinic literature. The extent to which Acts can be used for information about Paul remains disputable. In this chapter we will only refer to it for confirmation when it accords with information within Paul's letters. The road to improved insights lies initially via Paul's own epistles.

Concerning the epistles themselves, in contrast to the Gospels, there are many passages of a reasoned, theological nature. This has led to misunderstandings. The epistles have been read from purely theological interest as scattered chapters of dogmatics. More recently, a more adequate presupposition has been made, namely, that they are real letters, each written with its own, concrete immediate cause. Each letter, including the 'theological' passages, must therefore be interpreted as far as possible in the light of that which induced its writing, before looking at the links in content to other epistles. By the way, in all of his epistles, Paul addresses himself to non-Jewish believers, including those in Rome (1 Cor. 12.2; Gal. 4.8; Col. 2.11; 1 Thess. 1.9; cf. pp. 185-86).

As far as dating goes, most of the epistles of Paul derive from a limited number of years in the later part of his career. Those to Corinth, Rome, Philippi, Colossus, and probably also Galatia, must have all been written in the first part of the fifties; the First Epistle to Thessalonica appears to be a year or so older. It is questioned whether perhaps the Second Epistle to Thessalonica and the Epistle to Ephesus were written by a colleague of Paul; for the First Epistle to Timothy and the Epistle to Titus this is practically certain. One does well to recall that in antiquity in general, one dictated one's letters. Every educated person could read, but writing was for clerks. In the unquestioned letters of Paul there are passages where he corrects himself during the dictation (1 Cor. 1.14-16) or where the writer makes himself known (Rom. 16.22). Often Paul closed the letter in his 'own hand' (1 Cor. 16.21; Gal. 6.1; Col. 4.18; 2 Thess. 3.17; Phlm. 19). The epistles to Ephesus, Timothy and Titus could thus very well be Pauline in a derived sense: written by a colleague commissioned by Paul. These 'deutero-Pauline' epistles will be discussed at the end of the following chapter.

An appropriate starting point for a 'restored portrait' of Paul is his well-known designation of himself as 'the apostle to the nations' or *apostle of the non-Jews*. One often is not aware of the context in which this occurs, namely, in a passage in which he emphasizes the enduring calling of Israel (Rom. 11.13). His 'gospel for the non-Jews', as he calls it elsewhere, stands apparently in a direct and positive relationship to the calling of the Jewish people.

This initial surmise leads us at once into conflict with the mentioned prevailing interpretation that Paul had principally and exemplarily broken with Judaism. This reading, accepted by church fathers and reformers, acquired a particular intensification in modern historical criticism. Because of his assumed breach with Judaism, Paul was understood to have drawn inspiration primarily from Greek thinking and Hellenistic religiosity, thus being radically opposite to Peter and James, the leaders of the Jewish church in Jerusalem for whom the law retained its validity. Paul would have liberated the gospel from the constraints of the Jewish law and have cleared the way for Christianity as a universal religion. For a long time this view seemed to be so convincing that it was adhered to by Christian and Jewish scholars alike, who, however, deduced opposite conclusions from it. According to the Christians, Paul carried out the actual intention of Jesus and thus became the second and true founder of Christianity. From a Jewish viewpoint, he was the great spoiler who had dissociated Christianity from Jesus' teachings and faithfulness to the law. These contradictory assessments of Paul are still widespread among Christians and Jews. They both go back to one and the same presupposition: *Paul's radical break with the Jewish law and with the teachings of Jesus and his Jewish followers.*

During the past decennia, there have been changes in these view-points. A growing number of researchers have begun to wonder whether the Jewish apostle to the nations did not indeed implement Jewish methods of Scripture interpretation, and whether it is reasonable to assume that he had radically rejected the Jewish law and turned away from the teachings of Jesus. It has begun to dawn that the use of the Greek language in letters and in daily life does not necessarily exclude participation in a Jewish lifestyle. In general, a better understanding has developed of the situation of such Jews as Philo of Alexandria, who in many aspects adapted to their Greek-speaking environment, but nonetheless continued to attend the synagogue and maintain their own customs. Could not something similar have been the case with Paul, who in his writings exhibits considerably fewer traces of Hellenization than Philo does? We have come to realize that Hellenism was not in the least an unequivocal phenomenon, and that Jewish Hellenism had its own individual nature. These altered insights have led to renewed research into ancient Jewish sources and into Paul's own epistles.

The fact of the matter is that in his preserved epistles Paul empha-sizes his Jewish origins various times, although there appears to be a heated debate on its significance:

> Are they Hebrews? So am I! Are they Israelites? So am I! Are they seed of Abraham? So am I! Are they servants of Christ? I speak but in the man-ner of a fool: I even more! More difficulties, more imprisonments, many more blows, more than once unto death. From the Jews I have received five times forty-minus-one blows with a stick… (2 Cor. 11.22-24).

> I speak the truth in Christ and lie not, for my conscience also testifies to this in the Holy Spirit, that I carry great sorrow and incessant grief in my heart. For I would almost pray to be banned from Christ myself for the sake of my brothers, my fellow citizens after the flesh, who are after all Israelites, to whom belongs the sonship, the glory, the covenants, the lawgiving, the worship and the promises, of whom are the patriarchs and from whom the Christ came in the flesh—He who is God above all be praised until eternity! Amen (Rom. 9.1-5).

The second quote in particular makes clear that Paul does not view his Jewish descent as being negative, as something to which he had bidden a permanent farewell. The election of Israel remains valid and he proudly appeals to his origins. His life has, however, taken a turn that has brought him into profound conflict with most other Jews. He belongs to a faction that is rejected by them, sometimes with violence, but he in turn is convinced that *they* are the ones who are wrong. Due to the turn-about in his life, he, together with his Jewish and non-Jewish associates, belongs to the spearhead of a new humanity to which 'all Israel' will some day belong (Rom. 11.26).

This depiction is confirmed by Acts. In the speeches there placed in his mouth, Paul says that he hails from Tarsus in Asia Minor, but grew up in Jerusalem; that he is a Pharisee who, just as the other Pharisees, believes in the resurrection of the dead; and that he was taught the law in the school of Gamaliel (Acts 22.3; 23.6). The radical change is also reported that transformed him from a vehement opponent of the Jesus movement to a passionate adherent. Likewise it is emphasized that he and his Jewish associates remained faithful to Judaism, even though other Jews opposed them fiercely as heretics (Acts 21–23).

In other words, Paul and those with him differed profoundly with the rest of the Jews over the question of what 'true Judaism' was. This was not at all unusual in his time. In particular the Essenes saw themselves, together with their specific conception of the law, as a messianic vanguard, and the rest of Israel as blinded. Something of the sort, though less extreme, can be imagined of the Jews who confessed Jesus to be the Messiah. In response to his preaching, and after the shocking circumstances of his death and resurrection, they formed a separate community that lived in the expectation of his imminent return and the consequent commencement of the restoration of Israel (cf. Mt. 19.28). In this context we can certainly understand a remarkable passage by Paul:

> Not he who is externally so is a Jew, nor what is external in the flesh is circumcision, but he who is a Jew in that which is hidden, and a circumcision of the heart, in the Spirit and not the letter: whose praise is not from men but from God.—What then is the advantage of the Jew, or what is the use of circumcision? Much, in every respect! Above all, the words of God were entrusted to them... (Rom. 2.28–3.2).

The final sentence recalls the words quoted from Rom. 9.1-5; it is clear that Paul is not arguing here for a radical spiritualization or an actual abolition of circumcision. He is opposing another front, a radical 'reification', namely, the notion that the bare fact of circumcision would determine someone's destination as a Jew and achieve his justification before God. He is not arguing *for* a purely spiritual circumcision, but *against* a purely literal one, one that is only external. In this he does nothing other than apply the theme of the 'uncircumcised of heart' known from the Torah and the prophets (e.g. Lev. 26.41; Jer. 4.4), and his intention is, just as in those passages, that only he who is also a Jew in his inner being and is circumcised in his heart can reflect the purpose of Israel. Most of Paul's Jewish contemporaries will have agreed with him, even if they held other opinions about what that concretely entailed. A similar positive appeal to the designation 'Jew' occurs in rabbinic sources (*b. Meg.* 13a; *Targ. Ps.-Jon.* on Gen. 49.8).

We must now confront a passage from Paul's oldest preserved letter whose purport is determinant for our main theme. To the church at Thessalonica, who evidently had just endured much opposition, he writes:

> You have become imitators, brothers, of the churches of God which are in Judaea in Christ Jesus, for you have experienced the same from your fellow citizens as they have from the Jews—who have even killed the Lord Jesus and the prophets and have persecuted us, and do not please God but thwart all people, by preventing us from speaking to all nations so that they might be saved, in order to thus steadily bring their sins to fullness; 'and the wrath of God has come over them to the end' (1 Thess. 2.14-16).

This is the sharpest statement that Paul makes about his fellow Jews. Is he not downright anti-Jewish here? Particularly the second part rolls on as a cumulation of intemperate accusations following the actual provocation, namely, the violent opposition of the Greeks in Thessalonica and that of the Jews in Judaea.

It is striking that Paul here appears to have entirely forgotten what he underscores elsewhere, namely, that he himself once was one of the most vehement persecutors of the churches in Judaea! There are scholars who therefore consider these verses, or a part of them, to be a later addition to the text. There is some support for this to be found in the fact that traditional manners of expression appear to be used. The theme of the persecution of prophets, amply present in ancient Jewish literature and in the New Testament (see p. 166), is related to the end time and that fits well with this epistle, which from start to finish is about oppression and the imminent end time. The very last part of the citation, placed between quotation marks, occurs also in an originally Jewish writing transmitted and reworked by the church, namely, the *Testament of Levi* 6.11. On the other hand, the expression that the Jews 'thwart all people' occurs in various forms in several Roman writings, with a clearly anti-Jewish intent. Among the manuscripts of the New

Testament, there is an Old Latin manuscript in which the final sentence is lacking; there is no further support for the presumption that this is a later addition.

It is, therefore, advisable to be cautious and read this as an authentic statement of Paul, except perhaps for the final part. We must then presume that he uses existent polemic expressions in an attempt to encourage the church of Thessalonica: they are being persecuted just as the prophets who spoke in Jesus' name had been. Paul places himself in the position of the persecuted Jewish minority, and here again a comparison with the members of the Qumran sect and their hostile language can be enlightening. Like the latter, Paul does not here necessarily intend a general rejection of the Jews, but could be expressing a strongly deviating standpoint, condemned by the majority, concerning the interpretation of Judaism.

An explanation is still needed for Paul's silence about his earlier persecution of the church, which so conspicuously contrasts with his later epistles and with Acts. Was there perhaps an inner development after the writing of 1 Thessalonians, a later softening of his standpoint concerning the Jews? An objection to this is that Paul's relation to the church in Jerusalem worsened particularly in the later period of his work (see below), and it is difficult to imagine how that would coincide with a more lenient attitude towards other Jews. A possible inner development would more likely have turned in the opposite direction: from initial sympathy to later reservations. Nor are there many further indications of a later leniency in Paul's thinking regarding the Jewish law. On these points the totality of his epistles gives us the impression of a flexible, sometimes almost contradictory manner of expression, based upon one and the same basic attitude towards the law and the Jews. We should therefore consider external causes. Paul must have written this earliest preserved letter under exceptional circumstances, and we could perhaps suspect a connection with reports over tumultuous happenings among the Jews in Palestine and Asia Minor in the forties. It could even be that the uproar was in part directed against the new faith, and that Paul and the church in Judaea in that situation felt the sympathy of the persecuted minority. In this connection, it is significant that the passages on the persecution of the prophets occur in Matthew and James, two documents that have a common affinity with the church in Judaea, as well as in the account of the stoning of Stephen in Acts, which stems from the same tradition.

Opposite to the hostile passage in 1 Thessalonians 2 there are, thus, the passionately solicitous words in Romans 9—two extremes by one and the same author within a time span of less than ten years. Between these extremes lie the remarks in 2 Corinthians 11, where Paul continues to cling to the importance of his Jewish descent, though with pain. Surveying all of this, it appears that, in spite of all opposition, Paul perpetually viewed himself as a Jew, even after beginning to propagate his 'gospel for the non-Jews'. In order to test this presupposition further, we must discuss the significance of the great change in his life.

A question which we here merely pose in passing is whether Paul remained a Jew even after his conversion. The only passage where he goes into this matter, 1 Cor. 9.19-23, is so loaded with interpretational difficulties that we must first study what is written elsewhere in his epistles.

Paul's Conversion

When designating the turn-about in Paul's life as a conversion, one must be careful to avoid a misunderstanding. Awareness of the significance of a couple of biblical expressions is imperative. For two centuries now, 'conversion' has acquired a reduced connotation, namely, that of changing religions or churches. In reference to Paul, such was absolutely out of the question. The reduction of the meaning of this word was accompanied by a narrowing of the significance of another concept directly related to it—*missions* or *apostolate* (see pp. 132-34). Jesus was aware of being 'sent' to Israel, that is, he came to convey a message. His message was—and here the connection between the two concepts becomes apparent—'*Convert* your way of life, for the Kingdom of Heaven is at hand.' In this, the original, broader significance of both words is clear. Jesus did not mean that the Jews were to change religions, but that they were to practise their present religion in a manner more true. In the Bible, 'conversion' is not so much assuming a different doctrine, as reversing an attitude, a re-evaluation of oneself in order to come to a better, more genuine way of life.

This significance is also present with Paul, and this is important when we speak of his own 'conversion'. In the quote above about the meaning of circumcision, he says that it is about the 'circumcision of the heart', and about 'being a Jew *in that which is hidden*'. It cannot be coincidental that Jesus uses exactly the same expression when proclaiming to his fellow Jews that when they fast, pray and give alms they must serve God as a 'Father who sees *what is hidden*' (Mt. 6). In any case it testifies to a certain continuity between the message of Paul and that which has been passed on about Jesus. This is confirmed by the fact that the words 'conversion' and 'to convert' do not belong to Paul's vocabulary proper, but appear to be derived from the Jewish–Christian tradition. He does not employ them often, but when he does it is consistently with the same tenor of self-re-examination, of changing one's life (2 Cor. 12.21; Rom. 2.4; 2 Cor. 7.9-10).

Jesus sends disciples forth to carry on his work, and that is why they are called *apostles*, envoys, emissaries (see p. 132). Paul also presents himself as such in the opening lines of his epistles, although he was not a direct disciple of Jesus: 'Paul...a called apostle of Christ Jesus' (1 Cor. 1.1; Rom. 1.1). It is striking that he calls himself a 'called' apostle. Both in everyday Greek of that time and in biblical Hebrew, the word 'to call' means 'to invite' and especially '*to call to* a function or office'. Paul is convinced that he is called to be an apostle of Jesus Christ, or, in other words, he considers himself to be appointed to that by God. This conviction came to him during the great change in his life, which is therefore often indicated as his 'calling', in order to avoid misunderstandings connected with 'conversion'.

All of these elements play a part in the important passage in which Paul himself relates his 'conversion':

> You have heard of my conduct at that time in Judaism, how I persecuted and destroyed God's church beyond measure, and in Judaism went further than many contemporaries among my people, so zealous was I for the tradition of my forefathers. But when it pleased Him who had set me apart as from my mother's womb, in his grace to reveal to me his son so that I should proclaim him among the nations, I immediately did not seek support from flesh and blood... (Gal. 1.13-16)

The first element demanding attention is the frank remorse with which he speaks about his former conduct. He had been zealous, literally a *zealot*, and had violently pursued Jesus' followers as a threat to the Jewish law. He has, however, resolutely turned away from that 'zealotic' manner of conduct. Yet it is possible to read this in such a way that he continued to see himself as a Jew even after his about-face. He condemns his own conduct of that time 'in Judaism' and not Judaism itself. He now follows a different conduct 'in Judaism', because he sees the confession of Jesus as Messiah as the fulfilment of Judaism. We

have seen above how he—even in his last letter—continues to emphasize his Jewish identity.

The following passage indicates more vividly the contrast between
the two phases of his life:

> If another thinks that he can trust in his own flesh, I even more: circum-
> cised on the eighth day, of the people of Israel, of the tribe of Benjamin;
> a Hebrew among the Hebrews, concerning the law a Pharisee, concern-
> ing zeal a persecutor of the church, concerning the righteousness which
> is of the law impeccable! But all that was gain to me, I have come to see
> as loss for the sake of Christ... (Phil. 3.4-6).

The two halves of Paul's life contrast sharply with one other. His pride
over his former 'zealotism' is striking. If this were intended to be sarcastic, we must understand it in connection with the scathing outburst
from which the quote is taken. His opponents apparently boast themselves in their own Jewishness as Christians, thereby relegating the
non-Jewish Christians to an inferior position. Paul always protested
against such, and it is not by chance that we here hear an echo of his
characteristic conception of justification by faith. Nonetheless, even this
outburst is not so much a condemnation of Judaism as of his own
earlier 'zealotism' and that of his present opponents. The turn-about in
his life was a 'conversion' in the sense of a turning *away from* the
wrong manner of life *towards* his calling in the service of Jesus. We
return to the passage from Galatians and pause at other important
elements contained in it:

> But when it pleased Him who had set me apart as from my mother's
> womb in his grace to reveal to me his son so that I should proclaim him
> among the nations, I immediately did not seek support from flesh and
> blood.

Paul's conversion was not only a turning away from his 'zealotism', but
also a calling to be a proclaimer of Christ. This contains a clear reference to the prophetic calling of Jeremiah:

> And the word of the Lord came to me: 'Before I formed you in the belly,
> I knew you, before you appeared out of the womb, I have set you apart;
> to be a prophet for the nations have I appointed you' (Jer. 1.4-5; cf. Isa.
> 49.1).

In hindsight, just like Jeremiah, Paul sees himself as predestined from
his youth by divine providence for his task. From the beginning, this
calling was to preach Christ among the nations, or, in his own, later

words, to be an *apostle of the nations* (Rom. 11.13; see p. 211). This calling, he assures us, was by divine intervention. Even when still in the full concord with the apostles in Jerusalem he went out to the nations, he sought no support from 'flesh and blood'. This is a reference to the clash with the Jerusalem apostles, which will be discussed later.

In summary, Paul, predestined as 'called apostle of Jesus Christ', at the right moment turned himself away from his zealotic-Jewish opposition of the church and became an 'apostle of the nations'. As such, he has, however, not written off Judaism, but pleads, particularly with his non-Jewish readership, for the enduring calling of Israel. If this be so, it should not be surprising that Paul applies elements of the Jewish law in total seriousness.

Again we must interrupt our line of argumentation for a passage that is at odds with it, according to the traditional interpretation of Paul. The Second Epistle to the Corinthians is characterized by sharp polemics with other Jewish 'apostles', who apparently appropriate Paul's absence to bring a 'different gospel' (2 Cor. 11.4-5, 22). In this context, the notorious disgression about the 'covering upon the reading of the old covenant' occurs (2 Cor. 3.14). The image employed is that of Moses, who, when descending from Sinai, put a covering over his countenance because the Israelites could not bear to look upon the reflection of the encounter with God (Exod. 34.29-35). The 'covering' upon the Torah of which Paul speaks is 'only done away with in Christ'. In contrast to 'the old covenant', Paul even speaks here of 'a new convenant, not of the letter, but of the Spirit, for the letter kills, but the Spirit animates' (2 Cor. 3.6, 8).

Does this imply that at his conversion Paul turned away from the law of Moses? The incorrectness of this interpretation is apparent from the fact that the shroud that disappears in Christ impedes the proper understanding of *Moses* (vv. 15-16)! Indeed, it is of great significance that the Qumran sect applied the expression 'a new covenant' from Jer. 31.31 to itself, whereby the validity of 'Moses', of course, remained intact (CD 8.21; 19.23-24; 20.12). By analogy, Paul's speaking of 'a new covenant' by no means necessarily signifies the invalidation of the Torah and the commandments. For him, there was no absolute antithesis between the law and the Spirit (see Rom. 8.2).

Finally, we cast once more a sidelong glance at the book of Acts because it confirms our interpretation of Paul. Thrice the story of his conversion is related, each time in a slightly different manner, but each time it is about a 'conversion' in the sense of an about-turn and a calling (Acts 9; 22; 26). It happened on the way to Damascus, we are told here, where Paul was travelling with the authorization of the high priest to combat the congregation of Jesus. In broad daylight he is caught unawares by a revelation of the Risen One, after which he cannot see for three days, until 'the scales fall from his eyes' (Acts 9.18). He then gets up, is baptized and begins to 'proclaim Jesus the son of God' (v. 20). From zealotic persecutor of the congregation of Jesus, in one fell swoop he is 'converted' to being a witness proclaiming the same. In this as well a turning away from Judaism as such is not involved.

The Gospel for the Non-Jews

Returning now to the content of the preaching to which Paul was called at his conversion, once again we shall see how his work among the non-Jews is based upon the continued significance of Israel and the Jewish law.

In Galatians Paul tells about an 'apostolic division of labour' that was decided upon in Jerusalem. This took place during a meeting with Barnabas and the apostles, where Paul told about his work and which, according to his statement, occurred about 17 years after his conversion, thus, at the end of the forties CE (Gal. 1.18; 2.1). A literal translation sounds rather crude but it is better for a good understanding of the issues involved:

> When they saw that to me was entrusted the gospel of the foreskin, just as to Peter that of the circumcision—after all He who had given Peter power for the apostolate to the circumcision had also given me power for that to the nations—and when they had come to know of the gifts of grace given to me, James and Cephas and John, who were considered to be pillars, gave me and Barnabas the right hand (as a sign) of mutuality: we to the nations, and they to the circumcision! Only we must continue to remember the poor, and precisely to that end have I exerted myself (Gal. 2.7-10).

A few details: Cephas is Peter. Both names mean 'rock', *kifa* in Aramaic and *petra* in Greek, the apostolic name of Jesus' disciple Simon (Jn 1.40-42). 'Apostolate' (*apostolē*), employed in the already described sense of being sent out on a mission, is here a synonym of 'evangel', indicating not so much the content of the proclamation as the proclaiming itself. The 'foreskin' represents the uncircumcised, that is, the non-Jews or the nations, just as the 'circumcision' is a designation of the Jews. Paul uses these two words unabashedly, just as his contemporaries do, and we would do well to get used to it. Metonymy, indicating the whole by means of an aspect or part, was a favourite means of expression in antiquity.

The indicated division entailed that Peter and the others were responsible for 'the apostolate to the Jews' and Paul and Barnabas for 'the gospel to the non-Jews'. From the immediate sequel it becomes apparent that this agreement failed, with as result a harsh clash between Paul and the Jerusalem apostles. Nonetheless, Paul's report about the division of tasks is extremely revealing about his attitude towards Judaism. He writes several years after the conflict, when the tensions had mounted to a high level, and this lends more authenticity to his report over his agreement with the apostles. We can assume that they indeed had confidence in his 'gospel for the non-Jews', did not see it as threatening for their own 'apostolate to the Jews', and were sufficiently convinced of his loyalty to Judaism and the law. As stated earlier, not only was Paul's 'gospel for the nations' closely connected to the enduring calling of Israel, but it also assumes respect for the Jewish law.

The latter is made explicit in Paul's rule of thumb, which occurs in most of his epistles. The clearest is a passage in 1 Corinthians. In a chapter on practical questions concerning marriage and celibacy, Paul uses a comparison to illustrate that it does not matter whether someone is married or not. The comparison, however, makes use of a motif from an entirely different context, namely, that of the relationship between Jews and non-Jews within the churches:

> Everyone, each as the Lord has endowed him, each as God has called him, so must he walk. For thus I prescribe in all churches. Is someone called as circumcised, he should not allow it to be stretched back; is someone called 'in the foreskin', he should not let himself be circumcised. For circumcision means nothing and the foreskin means nothing, but 'keeping God's commandments'. Each should remain in the calling in which he was called (1 Cor. 7.17-20).

Again, a few details must be clarified first. 'Circumcision' and 'foreskin' again stand for Jews and non-Jews, as is clear here in the expression 'so must he walk': it concerns two manners of life. The 'stretching back' of the foreskin is a historic reality: in antiquity some Jews felt themselves so attracted to the Hellenistic culture and so desired to participate in gymnastics (literally: 'naked exercise') that they let the circumcision be made undone to all appearances. For those faithful to the circumcision, this was equal to 'desecration of the covenant (of circumcision)' (1 Macc. 1.15; *t. Šab.* 15.9). The verb that Paul uses here for 'stretching back' (*epispasthai*) is rare in this context, but gives an exact rendering of the Hebrew term (*limsôk*). The expression 'keeping God's commandments', finally, derives from the wisdom tradition, in particular from the verse, 'In all that you do be true to your soul, for that is the keeping of the commandments' (Sir. 32.23). Paul means that each must do what for him or her is essential.

Paul assumes that there are two possibilities: one is called by God as a Jew, or one is called as a non-Jew. What then does the gospel concretely mean for these two groups? This was apparently not a theoretical question, but a constant part of Paul's teaching: '...for thus I prescribe in all churches.' This was, so to say, Paul's apostolic rule of thumb: 'Each should remain in the calling in which he was called...as God has called him, so should he live.' One who as a Jew came to believe in Jesus should remain a Jew, and a non-Jew should continue to live as a non-Jew; for to live as a Jew or as a non-Jew is not significant, but only whether one lives truly according to one's own destination.

The rule of thumb just indicated stands central in the epistle in which Paul pleads the most passionately for the freedom of the non-Jews to believe in Christ as non-Jews—the Epistle to the Galatians. As many as three times the rule is cited, each time with different wording. The latter is characteristic of Paul: he varies the text and seldom quotes literally.

> For you are all children of God through faith in Jesus Christ. After all inasmuch as you have been baptized in Christ, you have donned Christ, no longer Jew or Greek, no longer slave or freeman, no longer 'male and female'. For you all are one in Christ Jesus (Gal 3.26-28; cf. Gen. 1.27).

> For in Christ Jesus is neither circumcision nor foreskin of value, but faith which expresses itself in love (Gal. 5.6).

> For neither circumcision nor foreskin means anything, but 'a new creation'. And to all who keep that rule, peace be to them and mercy, and to the Israel of God (Gal. 6.15-16).

The explicit mention of a rule (*kanōn*) in the last passage is intriguing. This must refer to the preceding, and there is much to be said for the assumption that indeed the third citing of Paul's rule of thumb is intended, which would then render yet another explicit reference to it. A 'new creation' is here printed as a quote. The same expression is used by Paul in a well-known verse: 'Therefore, if any one be in Christ, he is a new creation; old things are passed away, see, that which is new has come into being' (2 Cor. 5.17). The expression occurs also in rabbinic literature as a designation of the person who is 'renewed' in repentance before God (*Lev. R.* 29.12, p. 686). An echo can be heard in this of the 'new heavens and the new earth' of Isaiah (65.17).

In the first quote, another aspect is expressed: the rule had its natural application at baptism, the ritual of incorporation into the church of Christ. By 'donning Christ' one becomes part of a greater whole in which the distinction between Jew and Greek, slave and free, 'male and female' becomes insignificant. Incidentally, the exact phrase 'male and female' implies a reference to the creation of humanity as 'male and female' (Gen. 1.17). Thus, Paul's apostolic rule of thumb is presented here alongside a summary of his view of the church, his *ecclesiology*, in which baptism and the Eucharist, or the Lord's Supper, are included.

In the first quote a characteristic expression is used: *Jew and Greek*, meaning, of course, Jew and non-Jew. In the various phrasings of Paul's basic rule, this pair is parallel to *circumcision and foreskin*. It occurs also in the Epistle to the Romans. 'Jews and Greeks' is a variation on the Old Testament theme of 'Israel and the nations'. Given the synonymous 'Jews and Arameans' in rabbinic literature (see p. 113), it is probably correct to assume that it derives from Hellenistic–Jewish usage.

The cited texts have always been recognized as being characteristic of Paul's gospel. There has been less understanding for how Paul intended his rule in actual practice as regards the Jews. In fact, this is usually read one-sidedly with the non-Jews in mind, as though it stated only 'for circumcision means nothing'. This is conceivable in a non-Jewish church feeling the necessity of reacting against the Jews, but it does not do justice to Paul, who likewise states, 'foreskin, being uncircumcised, being a non-Jew means nothing'. The rule was just as much against Jewish Christians who made being a Jew a prerequisite, as against non-Jews who wanted to ban the practical aspects of Jewish life from the church. The undeniable connection with the explicit consequence of the rule in 1 Cor. 7.17-20 makes it clear that Paul's 'gospel for non-Jews' assumed that Jews and non-Jews respect each other's way of life and remain faithful to their own lifestyle. This did not mean, by the way, that the non-Jews had no rules to abide by, as we shall see.

Thus an answer is provided to the question posed at the beginning, Did Paul live as a Jew after his conversion? Given his basic principle, the answer must probably be affirmative. How could he argue with the non-Jews for respect for the Jewish way of life if he himself as a Jew did not adhere to Jewish rules for living? The confidence that the Jerusalem apostles placed in his work, according to his own statement, forces this conclusion upon us. How could they have trusted him in his attitude towards the practising Jew if he himself did not keep the law?

The logic of Paul's own statements presupposes that he maintained a Jewish lifestyle. The unique but complex passage in which Paul speaks of his own Jewishness in connection with his preaching can now be interpreted better:

> While I am free towards all persons, I have made myself of service to all, so that I might win as many as possible. Thus for the Jews, I am born as a Jew so that I might win the Jews; for them that are under the law, as being under the law, although not being myself under the law; for them that are without law, as being without law, although not without law before God but law-abiding before Christ, so that I might win those that are without law; I am for the weak as one born weak, so that I might win the weak. I have become all things to all men that I might by any means save some (1 Cor. 9.19-22).

The rendering 'born as a Jew' dovetails with a related passage where Paul says that Jesus is 'born of a woman, born under the law, so that he might ransom those that are under the law' (Gal. 4.4). The point is thus not an external adaptation to, but an internal and unconditional acceptance of Judaism by both Jesus and Paul. That Paul himself is not 'under the law' is expressed elsewhere indirectly: 'For you are not under the law but under grace' (Rom. 6.14-15). We will return in the following section to the precise meaning of this, but here it is sufficient to establish that he did not see himself as being under the law. On the other hand, he is also not without the law, but 'law-abiding before Christ'. The latter is a compact and brilliant, characteristically Pauline expression. It contains the aspect of being 'in the law', in Greek literally 'law-abiding' (*ennomos*), but then 'before Christ', that is, in view of Christ or as a member of his one church of Jews and non-Jews. The 'weakness', finally, that Paul reports is perhaps the physical ailment to which he alludes elsewhere (2 Cor. 12.7-9; cf. Gal. 4.14). The nature of this ailment is not known.

In short, Paul was open to anyone who was willing to listen to the gospel. Because of his respect for their style of life, Paul could relate to both Jew and Greek; this respect he also requested reciprocally. The above excludes that he totally abandoned his Jewish lifestyle when he moved in non-Jewish circles. At most he will have adapted himself within the limits of what he regarded to be permissible, a practical matter to which we will return. The following passage is not only related in content but also indicates how profoundly this attitude was intended, and how far removed it was from opportunism:

> Be without offence both to the Jews as to the Greeks and to the church of God, as I also in all things do please all, by not seeking my own interests but those of the congregation, so that they might find salvation. Be followers of me as I also am of Christ (1 Cor. 10.21–11.1).

Justification of Jew and Greek

For traditional Protestant theology, the 'justification by faith, without the law' is the core of Paul's thinking and of all of biblical theology. The importance of this theme for Paul is undeniable, and the Protestant's emphasis on this matter is justifiable. The question is, however, whether by making it the crux of a theological system one does not go too far. Is justification such a central theme in the various epistles? To start with, each letter of Paul should be read as a one-off writing induced by a specific situation. One who wishes to maintain the doctrine of justification as the kernel of Pauline theology can, just as the Reformers, appeal to only two letters of Paul—Romans and Galatians. In the other epistles, this theme is marginal or missing.

Study of the key words involved yields more precision. Within the whole of the New Testament, the words *justification* and *justifying* occur by far the most frequently in the Epistle to the Romans, with Galatians as a good second. This is even more true of the word *law*, somewhat less true of the word *faith*. In no other of Paul's letters is there such a frequent use of these three words occurring together. In the epistles to Corinth, Colosse and Thessalonica there are problems about the interpretation of the law or of certain legal practices, but judging from the vocabulary, the characteristic theme of 'justification without the law' is lacking. Only Philippians contains a short passage on this theme with the terms 'justification' and 'faith', which we already cited (Phil. 3.2-14). The question is why does Paul place justification by faith central in Romans and Galatians, while in his other letters the theme is peripheral or absent?

In order to answer this question we must look at the particular occasion of the writing of the two epistles. In style, Galatians differs greatly from Romans. At the beginning and the end, the vehemence is remarkable with which Paul accuses the Galatians, whose church he had founded, that they have departed from his gospel for 'another gospel' preached by people 'who want to coerce you to let yourselves be circumcised' (Gal. 1.6; 6.12). In this both the occasion and the intention of the writing are immediately clear. Written in his own hand, the closure in which he summarizes the essence of the letter and repeats his rule of thumb for the third time (6.15), speaks volumes. The Galatians had evidently been approached by preachers who maintained that they must be circumcised in order fully to belong to Christ. We will later go into the precise circumstances (pp. 202-208). Forcing the law upon the non-Jewish believers was a total denial of Paul's 'gospel for the non-Jews', which explains the fervour of this epistle.

In constrast, the letter to the church in Rome is characterized by great equilibrium, while the concrete occasion of the writing is difficult to fathom. Paul did not found this church and had not even visited it, as is apparent from his wish finally to come to Rome (Rom. 1.13; 15.22). Nonetheless, this church was not totally unknown to him. He sends greetings to Priscilla and Aquila, Jewish fellow-believers in Rome with whom he had worked closely earlier (Rom. 16.4; 1 Cor. 16.19; Acts 18.2). While this long epistle has a high level of theological content, its tone is not distant but personal, sometimes even almost dramatic. This is particularly so in the remarkable chapters on the enduring calling of Israel, in which the non-Jews are addressed directly (Rom. 9–11; 11.13). At the beginning the theme of the epistle is formally announced in the motto 'The gospel...for everyone that believes, *for the Jew first but also for the Greek*' (1.16-17). This expression recurs (2.9-10) and sounds like the theme of the entire epistle, but it is unique in Paul's letters. The explicit order is striking: 'the Jew first'.

With this motto as leitmotif we can oversee the epistle as a whole. *Both Greeks and Jews* have sinned before God (Rom. 1–3), but *both* are justified by faith just as Abraham was (ch. 4) and renewed as Adam was (ch. 5). No one is free from the fight against sin under the law (chs. 6–7), but *all* are God's children in Christ (ch. 8). What is the situation of Paul's *fellow Jews who do not believe in Jesus*? A remnant is saved, and *in the end 'all Israel shall be saved'* (chs. 9–11). In the meantime, live respecting God and loving your neighbour, submit yourselves to the government and love one another (chs. 12–13). As to the 'weak in faith', *who do not eat and drink everything and who set apart certain days*, accept them hospitably as Christ has accepted you, so that *'the circumcision'* and *'the nations'* praise God unanimously (chs. 14–15). Finally, there are greetings to *fellow Jews* (16.4, 7, 11, 21). In short, the epistle addresses the non-Jews in the church in Rome, instructs them concerning the one way of salvation through Christ for Jew and Greek, but in this points out to them the enduring precedence of the Jews in the history of God's salvation and urges them to accept hospitably the Jewish brothers and sisters.

The question remains as to what the problem was with the 'acceptation' of the Jewish Christians in the mid fifties in the church of Rome. A plausible explanation is based on the banishment of the Jews or of the Jewish Christians from Rome about five years previously, perhaps because of the commotion among the Roman Jews concerning the new teaching. We are told more about this in connection with Priscilla and Aquila (Acts 18.2). Due to the fact that the decree of banishment lost its power, the Jewish Christians were probably able to return several years later, but they met with resistance from the non-Jewish believers, who had continued to gather together in home congregations (cf. Rom. 16.5). This will have been one of the earliest examples of Gentile-Christian opposition to Jewish Christians, and it is therefore significant to our topic. In any case we can imagine how Paul exhorted the non-Jews to a hospitable 'acceptation' of the Jewish fellow-believers, and to unpretentiousness towards the Jews in general: 'Be not high-minded, but be respectful!' (Rom. 11.20).

Both in Galatians and Romans we can relate the theme of justification to the occasion of the writing of the epistle—the relation between Jews and non-Jews in respect to the Jewish law. The other epistles, where justification is not the theme, have different immediate causes. 1 Corinthians is entirely concerning the internal affairs of the church there, 2 Corinthians is about Paul's authority as an apostle in competition with others, Philippians centres around Paul's imprisonment, Colossians contests false teachers, 1 and 2 Thessalonians are about future expectations, and Philemon about the slave Onesimus. The theme of justification is, therefore, for specific reasons present in Romans and Galatians and must not be viewed as the systematic core of Paul's doctrine.

Furthermore, the unfolding of the theme does not have the form of systematic theology. Both in Romans and Galatians it assumes the form of an exegetical excursion on the biblical figure of Abraham. One should be aware that the patriarchs, in particular Abraham, play a proto-typical role in ancient Jewish literature as a whole. Abraham is taken as the first to renounce idolatry and superstition and to believe in God, and therefore he has become the forefather not only of all Israelites, but also of all who join Judaism as proselytes to the present day. In the second place, Paul's manner of thinking reminds one of ancient rabbinic Scripture interpretation in which elements of the biblical story and of later legends are imaginatively intertwined. Paul applies the traditional motif, however, to a new situation, that is, that of one messianic community of faith in which Jews and non-Jews participate 'without distinction', respecting each other's manner of life. In this way he arrives at a brilliant innovation, namely, Abraham as prototype of both circumcised and uncircumcised believers. The point of departure is the text to which also various Jewish texts attach the laudation of faith: 'Abraham believed in God, and that was accounted to him as justification' (Gen. 15.6).

In Romans, Paul emphasizes that these words occur at a moment in the Bible story when Abraham was as yet uncircumcised; circumcision followed later (Gen. 17). Thus he could become the 'father of believers' of both groups:

> 'Faith was accounted to Abraham as justification'—but how was it accounted to him? when he was 'in the circumcision' or 'in the foreskin'? Not in the circumcision, but in the foreskin! And he received the sign of circumcision as the seal of the justification by faith that he already had 'in the foreskin'. Thus he could become the father of all who believe in the manner of 'the foreskin' and justification could be accounted unto them; and the father of 'the circumcision' not only for those who are 'from the circumcision' but also those who remain in the line of the 'foreskin faith' of Abraham, our father (Rom. 4.9-12).

We see how the words 'faith', 'justification' and 'accounted to', familiar to us as key words of Protestant dogmatics, are creatively derived from the Bible story and applied to the distinct circumstances of Jewish and non-Jewish believers. Furthermore, there is a clear connection to the basic principle of there being 'no distinction between Jew and Greek'. Reasons are also given for the fact that this rule of thumb does not mean that there are no more differences. There are distinctions, but nonetheless there is 'no differentiation'. We recall the 'rule' in 1 Cor. 7.18: 'Is someone called as circumcised, he should not allow it to be stretched back; is someone called "in the foreskin", he should not let himself be circumcised.'

In Galatians, Paul brings another element of the story of Abraham to the fore. Here again he goes about it almost playfully, while addressing himself to the specific occasion of the epistle. In this there is affinity with ancient Jewish literature, where the diversified interpretation of Bible texts corresponds to a variety of exegetical situations. Again the point of departure is Gen. 15.6, but now used to defend the freedom of the non-Jewish Christians. In order to do this, Paul emphasizes only the uncircumcised state of Abraham, the believer:

> Like Abraham: 'He believed in God, and that was accounted unto him as justification'. Consequently you know that those that are 'of faith' are the children of Abraham. And the Scriptures, foreseeing that God justifies the nations through faith, announce ahead of time to Abraham: 'In you shall all the nations be blessed' (Gen. 12.3; 18.18). Thus all those that are 'of faith' are blessed in union with Abraham, the faithful (Gal. 3.6-8).

It is remarkable that Paul skips over, as it were, the circumcision episode and takes his point of departure directly from the inclusive promise to Abraham. The reason is to be sought again in the occasion of the writing of Galatians: 'God justifies the nations through faith.' On the other hand, this one-sided emphasis on Abraham's uncircumcised state is not to be divorced from the basic principle cited at the end of the chapter and thereafter twice more: 'There is neither Jew nor Greek any more...for you all are one in Christ Jesus.' Here he 'proves' his rule of thumb by use of the figure of Abraham, as is clear in that which directly follows this text: '...and if you be Christ's, then you are Abraham's seed, heirs according to the promise' (Gal. 3.28-29).

The theme of justification is dynamically unfolded in two different but related situations by use of the story of Abraham. The terminology as well is taken from the story as needed: justification, faith, accounting, circumcision, foreskin, nations... A formal description, therefore, would be: the justification motif is primarily an *exegesis* of the prototypical story of Abraham and only thereafter a *theological* theme.

We must now delve more deeply into the different functions of the theme in the two epistles. Galatians resolutely and one-sidedly resists the forced circumcision of non-Jewish Christians, that is, their incorporation into Judaism, because 'God justifies the nations through faith' (Gal. 3.8). On the other hand, Romans argues for accepting Jewish fellow-believers because 'there is no difference between Jew and

Greek, all...are justified freely' (Rom. 10.10-12; 3.21-22). The theme functions, thus, in diametrically opposed situations: in Galatians to defend the non-Jewish believers, and in Romans to defend the Jewish believers. How can this be explained? Not by taking 'justification by faith' as the core of Paul's thinking, for that is not supported by the other epistles. There must be a specific reason that has as much to do with the freedom of the non-Jewish believers in Galatia as with that of the Jews in Rome. The motif of justification has to do with Paul's 'gospel for the non-Jews', that is, the basic principle that in Christ there is 'no difference between Jew and Greek'. A functional description of this would be: the theme of justification through faith accounts *theologically* for the *diversity* in form of the one faith in Jesus Christ.

That this all undeniably is related to the law becomes explicit in the immediately subsequent portions of the passages cited earlier:

> For all who are of the works of the law are under a curse, for it is written: 'Cursed is everyone who does not abide by what in written in this book, by doing it' (Deut. 27.26). That, however, no one is justified before God by the law is clear, for 'The just shall live by faith' (Hab. 2.4) (Gal. 3.10-11).

> For the promise that they are 'heirs of the world' does not come to Abraham or to his descent through the law, but through justification by faith... Therefore is the promise through faith, in order that it might correspond to grace, so that it thus might be trustworthy for all of his seed, not only for those who are of the law, but also for those who through faith are of Abraham, the father of us all, as it is written: 'I have appointed you to be a father of many nations' (Gen. 17.5) (Rom. 4.13-17).

We first note the wording. 'Works of the law' in the first quote is a wooden translation of an equally awkward Greek expression whose Hebrew background is now known. In several texts from Qumran, the expression *maase Torah* occurs, which means approximately 'commandments of Jewish law' (4QMMT 113; 4Q174 [flor] 1.7). We will return to the theme of the 'curse of the law' in Galatians; here Paul says in any case that keeping the law in itself does not lead to justification, for '*through faith* the just shall live'. In rabbinic literature as well as in the Qumran scrolls, the importance of faith is connected to the verse in Habakkuk, as well as to Gen. 15.6. In Romans this quote occurs already in the opening lines (1.17). Finally, Romans emphasizes here again the duality: *not only* those who are of the law, *but also* those who are through faith alone.

The pivot here is the significance of the law. The motif of justification in Galatians and Romans makes clear that God accepts Jews and Greeks on the basis of faith in Jesus, not on the basis of observing the law. If the latter were true, only Jews could be saved, a concept that Paul opposes with all his might in Galatians. The promise was valid 'first for the Jew but also for the Greek', not 'especially for the Greek', as some in Rome apparently thought. Here again Paul does not write off the law but indicates its rightful place. This becomes more than clear from a series of emphatically positive statements about the law (Rom. 7.7, 12, 14; 9.5; 13.8-10; Gal. 5.3, 13-14, 23; see also pp. 349-50). The law itself is not the watershed, for 'in Christ there is no difference'. One can thus also be blessed 'in the law'. What is decisive is the one faith in Jesus, to which Jews and non-Jews each must give expression corresponding to their 'calling'. A second functional description would therefore be: the motif of justification entails a *relativizing of the Jewish law as the exclusive way of salvation.*

This external or social aspect of the theme of justification concerns the problem of the law in the relation between Jews and non-Jews. There is also an inner aspect that we shall cover in the following section. Such a relativization of the significance of the law was not exceptional in Judaism of that day, even though this particular one is unique in its kind. The Hillelite Pharisees, in contrast to the Shammaites and certainly to the Essenes, were familiar with the thought of the 'just from among the nations' (see p. 108). For them as well, the keeping of the law was thus not an exclusive prerequisite for salvation. At this level, the law is neither less nor more than the lifestyle of the Jews, just as other people also had their own cultural traditions. This is also the scope of the Greek word for 'law' which Paul uses, *nomos*, 'constitution' or 'custom' (see p. 88). When he says that salvation is not obtained by observing the law, this means in the first place nothing other than that the non-Jews can be included as well.

Justification of the Sinner

Having considered the external aspect of justification, we turn now to the inner aspect, the aspect that traditional Protestant theology rightfully emphasizes, although unjustly systemizing it as the centre of theology. In doing so, the important external aspect has been neglected—the function of justification in relation to Jews and non-Jews.

The internal aspect represents the very depths of the doctrine of justification. Several of its attributes were brought forward in the last quotations. In Gal. 3.10-13 Paul argues that keeping the law is sanctioned
by a curse, while in the ensuing chapters the aspect of slavery under the
law is emphasized. In Rom. 4.15 he mentions the wrath and the transgression incurred by keeping the law, a theme that in the following
chapters is elaborated by means of the concepts of sin and death. There
is a difference in tone in the two epistles. In Romans Paul speaks about
the law more from the inside, including himself in the discussion. This
undoubtedly has to do with the intended identification of the reader
with the position of the Jewish Christians. In Galatians he speaks only
from the outside, placing himself in the position of the non-Jewish
Galatians, reminding them that they are already justified without the
law.

Paul does not consider the law itself to be a curse—on the contrary,
as is apparent from the fact that he bases his argument explicitly on
three texts from the Torah. We have also pointed out a series of
emphatically positive statements about the law. In using the sombre
terminology of sin, death, curse and slavery, his intention is quite
another, namely, the depth of justification: *the reception of the law
entails not only a privilege, but also a profound testing.* Paul develops
this viewpoint exemplarily in Romans 6 and 7, where it is more than
clear that this has to do with the inner aspect. It is a quasi-
autobiographic outpouring of the soul—'wretched person that I am!'
(Rom. 7.24)—who as slave of sin, law and death reaches out for God's
merciful justification.

Because the law is an inescapable trial, one would only reach out to
the law when prepared for great self-sacrifice, never for one's own
benefit. According to Paul, this is the reason why Jews cannot boast of
the law and why non-Jews should not think they will be benefited by it.
This manner of viewing the law, which was certainly not shared by all
Jews in anquity, can be considered as a personalization and radicalization of the prophetic vision of Israel as a people with a high calling.
The result is a specific, rather pessimistic view of humanity, outlined
earlier in certain psalms and expressed extensively in the Thanksgiving
Psalms from Qumran. The messages of both John the Baptist and Jesus
contain an echo of this, as do such writings of the pious Jewish circles
as the *Testaments of the Twelve Patriarchs* and the *Derek-Erets* literature (see pp. 63-64).

An important expression of this occurs in a psalm verse quoted in different variations in the hymns of Qumran:

> *Enter not into judgment with your servant,*
> *for before your presence no living being is justified* (Ps. 143.2).

> What is the one formed from clay, that he should magnify the wonders?
> For he is in sin from his mother's womb, and to his hoary head guilty of disobedience.
> And I know that humanity has no righteousness, nor the child of man flawlessness of walk (1QH 4.29-31).
> But I knew that there was hope in your loving kindness, and expectation in your great power.
> For no one is justified in your judgment, nor can he get off free in your lawsuit (1QH 9.14-15).
> Only in your loving kindness is a man justified, and in your great mercy... (1QH 13.16-17).
> And I knew that a man is not justified without you... (1QH 16.11).

We should recall that the Qumran sect exhibited extreme conscientiousness in following the law. Here, the awareness of human sinfulness was not an argument against the law—on the contrary. The same is true for the preaching of John the Baptist and of Jesus. This makes Paul's positive statements about the law even more eloquent.

This same verse from the Psalms functions as an axis of Paul's theme of justification in both Romans and Galatians:

> So that the whole world is worthy of punishment before God, therefore, that by the works of the law 'no flesh is justified before his presence', for through the law is knowledge of sin (Rom. 3.19, 20).

> We, who are Jews by birth and not sinners from the nations, knowing that 'a man is not justified' through the works of the law except with faith in Jesus Christ, we, too, have put our faith in Christ Jesus. (Gal. 2.16)

It is striking that in both passages Paul speaks from a Jewish point of view, as he elsewhere makes explicit: it is for the Jew that the law effectuates the 'knowledge of sin' (Rom. 2.12-29; Gal. 3.19-24; Rom. 9.31-32; 7.7-13). This is, therefore, an intra-Jewish reasoning that by no means contradicts the law but rather reflects the depth of the testing by the law. At the same time, this ordeal is a privilege, from which Paul will not absolve himself: 'What is the advantage of the Jew, or what is the use of circumcision? Much, in every respect, first, that to them were entrusted the words of God!' (Rom. 3.1-2; cf. 9.1-5; see p. 171).

It is also interesting *how* Paul cites the psalm verse. Not only does he, following the context, add the 'works of the law', the term we also know from Qumran, but furthermore he paraphrases twice differently. This appears to be a free use of tradition. Significantly, however, these paraphrases recall the varied quoting of the psalm verse in the Essene hymns. Both form and content—the sinfulness of humankind contrasting with God's holy law—suggest a certain affinity with the Essene world of thought.

Thus, we must conclude that Paul does not simply quote Ps. 143.2, but that he quotes from an existent, flexible tradition of interpretation that gauges the ordeal of the law from the inside. The correspondence to Essene thinking is evident but may not be interpreted as being identical with or dependent on it. A link can sooner be presumed with the milieu of Jesus and perhaps more indirectly with that of John the Baptist. In Jesus' preaching, a Pharisee who self-satisfiedly boasted of keeping of the law is further removed from the Kingdom of Heaven than a contrite tax collector who is prepared to change his life:

> I say unto you that this one went home *justified*, in contrast to the other, for everyone who elevates himself shall be humbled, but he who humbles himself shall be elevated (Lk. 18.10-14).

In summary, the theme of justification in Romans and Galatians assumes the form of an exegesis of the story of Abraham: it functions as a clarification of the Jewish and non-Jewish form of believing in Jesus and relativizes the law as the exclusive way of salvation. This is the *external*, social aspect. The *inner*, anthropological aspect is the consciousness that 'no flesh shall be justified before His presence' and that the law is a formidable testing for Israel. This aspect exhibits affinity with an Essene outlook and with Jesus' preaching. Viewed thus, it is plausible that Paul has adopted the train of thought on the inner aspect from the apostolic tradition or from another specific tradition. The external aspect, however, is to be found in its characteristic form only with Paul, in the two passages that principally defend his view of the church of Jews and non-Jews. This is probably an innovation of Paul himself—a brilliant ecclesiologic application of the time-honoured theme of justification.

The Law and the Teachings of Jesus

A reader who has come thus far in general consent will have said farewell to the notion that Paul principally and radically broke with the Jewish law and with the teachings of Jesus and his Jewish followers. Paul did not break with the law but viewed it no longer as the universal way of salvation. For Jewish followers of Jesus the calling to live according to the law remained valid, and the one who took this calling truly seriously in Paul's sense could not possibly assert that a Pharisee was closer to the Kingdom than a contrite tax collector. This of necessity implies two things: for all his emphasis upon the 'justification without the law', Paul does ascribe practical significance to the law, and shows affinity with the teachings of Jesus. There is an epistle that indirectly but extensively provides information on both issues—the First Epistle to the Corinthians.

Among Paul's letters, 1 Corinthians is remarkable. In the first place, it contains no treatise on justification and on the significance of the law, as is apparent from the words used: 'law', 'justification' and 'works' occur but not in the specific significance of the theme of Abraham in Romans and Galatians. 'Justification' occurs twice in connection with baptism and sanctification, with the significance 'making righteous' (1 Cor. 1.30; 6.11). Once Paul speaks of his 'justification' in a strictly future sense, on the basis of his conduct: he *shall* be justified on the basis of his actual 'work' as an apostle (4.4). Even more remarkable is his positive appeal to the law. The 'law (of Moses)' is quoted explicitly several times in support of practical instructions (see below). Furthermore, the story from the Torah about Israel in the wilderness is read as having 'occurred for our example', also with clearly practical implications (10.1-14).

The Paul that speaks here is so different from the 'traditional' Paul that some interpreters ascribe this epistle to a completely different period in his thinking. Yet it cannot be maintained that the problem of the law and justification did not exist for Paul when he wrote this letter, as is shown by the cited passage about 'remaining in the calling in which each is called' (7.17-20). This incidental reference is used as illustration in a context that deals with totally different matters, thus confirming that Paul's thinking concerning the law was here the same as in Galatians and Romans, although in this epistle he did not have cause to go into the matter extensively. The same is true of two other passages (1 Cor. 9.19-23; 15.54-57). It is, therefore, not possible to ascribe this epistle to an 'earlier, Jewish Paul'. 1 Corinthians confirms our assumption that Paul maintained the positive, practical value of the law, while developing his argument on justification without the law in so far as that was necessary.

The second striking aspect of 1 Corinthians is the abundance of *practical instructions*, apparent already in the wording with which several new sections begin: 'Now concerning the things over which you have written me' (7.1); 'Now concerning virgins' (7.25); 'Now concerning the offerings to idols' (8.1); 'Now concerning the gifts of the spirit' (12.1); 'Now concerning the collection' (16.1). One by one, the writer deals with a number of practical questions. The phrasing 'now concerning...' (*peri de...*) occurs also in the *Didache* and appears to be specific to nomographic or legal texts (see p. 387).

From 7.1, 'the things over which you have written me', it is furthermore apparent that Paul is answering a letter from Corinth in which the issues mentioned were raised. One of the reasons for writing was, thus, to deal with these written questions. It could be that the lost letter from Corinth requested further clarification concerning an earlier letter of Paul's, in which he had set forth the main features of the same practical questions, for 1 Cor. 5.9 mentions in passing an earlier letter: 'I wrote you already in my letter...', and the intended meaning is about the same subject. This letter has not been preserved either. In what we call the Second Epistle to Corinth, Paul mentions yet another letter to that city, which does not concur with 1 Corinthians and with which we therefore are unfamiliar as well (2 Cor. 2.4, 9). From this it appears in any case that 1 Corinthians should be read as a part of an ongoing correspondence in which practical questions were raised and answered. It should be recalled that the church in Corinth was founded by Paul himself and in a certain sense was 'his own' church (see 1 Cor. 2.1; 3.6; 4.14; Acts 18).

The exchange was both by letter and orally: Paul gives attention to problems in Corinth of which he had heard by word of mouth. He had heard from the 'people of Chloe' (1.11) of the dissension in the Corinthian church, to which the first four chapters are devoted. Perhaps these were also the ones who had brought the letter with questions from Corinth. Furthermore, the long, next-to-last chapter goes into a matter evidently communicated by word of mouth: '...How can some then say that there is no resurrection of the dead?' (15.12). One gets the same impression from the introductory wording of two of the practical questions that concern us here (5.1; 11.2-3).

In short, in the extensive centre portion of 1 Corinthians, Paul treats a number of practical matters in the life of 'his' church, issues that had come to his attention either by letter or by word of mouth. These concern, consecutively, a case of sexual misconduct (5.1–6.20), the question of celibacy for the sake of 'the things of the Lord' (7.1-40), food dedicated to idols (8.1–11.1), traditions concerning the liturgy (11.2-34), and the requirement of order in the worship service (12.1–14.40). While by nature this series of practical questions is partially a product of its own time, it grants us precious information about life in one of the earliest churches in Greece and its relationship to the 'apostle of the non-Jews'.

A third aspect of 1 Corinthians is related to that just mentioned. Especially in his answers to all those practical questions, Paul explicitly indicates his *sources of authority* and several times differentiates clearly between the various sources. One of these has already been mentioned, namely, the law (9.8; 14.21, 34) or 'the law of Moses' (9.9). Although the appeal to the Scriptures is quite normal, as it is in other epistles, this explicit use of the law as a source of authority for practical instructions is remarkable. Another authority to which Paul twice specifically appeals is 'the customs of the churches of God' (11.16), respectively, the manner of conduct 'as in all churches' (14.34). This gives the impression that the authority of churches had been established some time previously (see below). There are two more sources of authority mentioned by Paul that will be reviewed directly. We can already conclude that in this epistle not only does Paul deliberately deal with practical questions that were posed to him in writing or otherwise, but he bases his answers upon formal sources of authority, thus lending to 1 Corinthians an official, apostolic character.

The fourth in this ascendent series of characteristic features is the explicit and official manner in which Paul appeals four times to *the authority of Jesus* for his instructions. In a number of cases, he does so while clearly distinguishing his own authority as apostle. This brings the number of explicit sources of authority to four: the law, the customs of the churches of God, his own authority as an apostle and the teachings of Jesus. Particularly in 1 Corinthians 7 Paul distinguishes between his own authority and that of Jesus. In that chapter he devotes attention to the question posed from Corinth on whether it is allowed for the sake of the 'things of the Lord' to live in celibacy, whether by not remarrying, or by divorcing, or by not marrying at all. One should conceive of these questions being quite concrete in a community in which there were 'not many prominent ones' (1.26), but a mixture of slaves and freemen, Jews and Greeks, men and women (7.18-22; 11.3-16). In particular, Paul mentions those whose marriage to a non-believing Jew or Greek formed a hindrance to their own life as a believer (7.12-16).

The interesting fact presents itself that this urban, socially hybrid group of followers of Jesus poses questions to its apostle that the teacher from Nazareth himself could not possibly have foreseen. Paul is, therefore, all the more explicit in matters of which Jesus had spoken:

> *I say* to the unmarried: it is good if they remain as I also am...
> And the married *I command—not I but the Lord*: the woman may not depart from her husband, and if she has departed she must remain unmarried or reconcile herself to her husband, and the man may not send away his wife.
> And to the rest *I say, not the Lord*: if a brother has an unbelieving wife, and she consents to remain with him, he may not dismiss her; and if a woman has an unbelieving husband, and he consents to remain with her, she may not dismiss the husband... But if the unbeliever wants to depart, let him depart; in such a case the brother or sister is not bound. (...)
> And concerning the virgins, *I have no commandment from the Lord, but I give my own opinion...* The unmarried concerns himself with the things of the Lord...but he that is married is concerned about the things of the world... (1 Cor. 7.8-33).

In this forthright casuistic chapter, case by case the apostle distinguishes the authority of 'the Lord' from his own authority. Where there is no tradition, he must rely on his own authority for an answer: in the cases of the mixed marriages, the unmarried and the 'virgins'. There is a general commandment from 'the Lord' for those married. They may at most live separately, but not divorce, let alone remarry. We see that 'the Lord' is a designation for Jesus, and his 'commandment' is the prohibition of divorce known from the synoptic tradition, adapted to the Hellenistic legal situation that prevailed in Corinth (see pp. 99-100, 258-59).

In 1 Corinthians there are two more commandments that Paul explicitly ascribes to 'the Lord': concerning the sustenance of the apostles (9.14) and the order of elements of the Eucharist (11.23-25). Here again there are convincing similarities to Jesus' teachings as we know them from the synoptic Gospels (Mt. 10.9-10; Mk 14.22-25). We should probably add the commandment that women keep silent during the worship service (1 Cor. 14.37). Though this is not documented in the Gospels, the fact that Paul so earnestly ascribes this teaching to Jesus as well lays the burden of the proof upon the interpreter who contests its authenticity.

We thus arrive at some momentous conclusions. In giving practical instructions, four times over Paul appeals explicitly to the teachings of Jesus, three of which are demonstrably in accordance with the Gospel tradition. The precise distinction that he makes with his own authority makes it clear that Paul accorded the highest authority to the teachings of Jesus. This gainsays the second presumption upon which for a long time modern exegesis has based its interpretation of Paul. Although he relativizes the law as a means of justification before God, Paul does not discard it, but continues to attach practical importance to the Jewish law and in this ascribes the highest authority to the legal instructions of Jesus.

Another conclusion touches on Paul's relation to Judaism. We saw in the previous chapters that Jesus' prohibition of divorce is stricter than the position of the Pharisees and in fact concurs with that of the Essenes (see also pp. 100-102). It is this 'commandment of the Lord' that is explicitly cited by Paul, an ex-Pharisee who formerly must have adhered to either of the Pharisaic positions. On this point Paul must have abandoned his Pharisaic tradition for a greater authority: the teachings of Jesus. His departure from the Pharisaic tradition was, however, not in the least a break with the Jewish law. In this case it even entailed transferring to a much *stricter* notion. The importance of this should not be underestimated. In Chapter 2 (p. 91) it was stated how the halakah forms a framework for Jewish life and provides at the same time a social system of reference. We have also seen how pronouncedly this worked out in antiquity in the matter of marriage and divorce. Paul's identification with Jesus' strict view of marriage gives us highly specific information about his position within Judaism.

Paul's place within Judaism can be even more exactly defined if we consider the instruction that he cites at the end of the same chapter. The quote is presented as an accepted, authoritative rule, noticeably differing with his own opinion, which he gives thereafter:

> The woman is bound as long as her husband lives. But if the man dies she is free to marry with whom she will, provided that it be in the Lord.—Although she is to be considered more fortunate if she remain as she is, *in my opinion* (1 Cor. 7.39-40).

The traditional nature of this rule is apparent from the way in which Paul cites it elsewhere (Rom. 7.2). It is a rule from the apostolic tradition, as is attested by the expression 'provided that it be in the Lord', that is, provided that it be within the community of Jesus. That the tradition goes back to Jesus is to be deduced from the hereby presumed prohibition of divorce 'as long as the husband lives'.

Furthermore, it can be demonstrated that three formal elements in this rule are related to Jewish legal tradition in the first century. The prohibition of divorce is known to us from Qumran. Besides divorce, death of the partner as a formal conclusion of the marriage bond with all of its implications is found in the Mishnah: 'The woman...acquires her freedom by two means:...through a letter of divorce and through the death of her husband' (*m. Qid.* 1.1). Even the wording 'she is free to marry with whom she will' accords with rabbinic law, in which a restriction like 'provided that it be in the Lord' is recognizable as an older stratum (*m. Giṭ.* 9.1-3). Paul evidently quotes an ancient Jewish rule of law that derives from the apostolic tradition and goes back to the authority of Jesus. In other words, Paul *cites the Jewish-Christian apostolic tradition of halakah.*

A separate issue is the manner in which Paul quotes the words of Jesus. Of the three references that we can check there is only one that corresponds at all literally to the Gospel tradition known to us—the words of the last supper (1 Cor. 11.23-25; cf. Mk 14.22-24, etc.). In the other two cases he gives a summary of the content (1 Cor. 7.10-11; cf. Lk. 16.18; 1 Cor. 9.14; cf. Mt. 10.10). To this could be added a list of possible, vague allusions to statements of Jesus, but the situation has been interpreted as a lack of interest on Paul's part in the words of Jesus. The example of divorce teaches otherwise. A more plausible explanation takes into account the phenomenon of oral transmission. In Paul's day there were as yet no written Gospels and everyone quoted by memory. In so far as the apostolic-Christian milieu was related to the Pharisees, it will at first not have been the intention to write down Jesus' words (cf. pp. 66-67). In this regard, it is significant that at the end of the first century, when there were written Gospels for some time already, there remained a preference for the 'living voice', the oral transmission of Jesus' words (see p. 256). Perhaps Paul, the ex-Pharisee, preferred not to write down Jesus' words. For some reason or another, he apparently made an exception for the tradition of the Lord's Supper.

Explicitly addressed to non-Jewish believers (cf. 1 Cor. 12.2), this epistle raises the question whether, according to Paul, the Jewish law was after all still valid for non-Jews. Paul considered a limited number of universal commandments to be effectual for non-Jews, that is, he shares the concept of what later came to be called the Noachic commandments, of which the core is formed by the prohibition of idolatry, sexual misbehaviour and the shedding of blood (see p. 108). It is precisely this core that occurs in 1 Corinthians: idolatry in chs. 8–10, sexual misbehaviour in chs. 5–7, and the shedding of blood may be counted to be implied in the 'catalogue of sins' in 1 Cor. 6.10 (cf. Rom. 1.29-31).

The regulations for the liturgy and the worship service (1 Cor. 11–14) were also apparently valid for all believers, according to Paul. That this is not self-evident is apparent from the prescription that women be silent and wear a head covering during the worship service. Paul prescribes this for the Corinthian women with an appeal to the custom in all churches (1 Cor. 11.16; 14.34). As was said, this creates the impression of churches that had already existed for some time. That these could have been the 'Jewish churches' in Judaea and Galilee is confirmed by the fact that their 'customs' in all aspects correspond to the general Jewish customs of that time (cf. p. 74). A universal obligation to worship God in the appropriate manner is not a part of the 'Noachic commandments' in rabbinic tradition. We find only the prohibition of cursing his name (b. Sanh. 56a-57b). Within the framework of the Jewish law we must therefore understand the instructions for liturgy and worship service as cited by Paul to be a special obligation for 'God-fearing' non-Jews.

The prohibition of idolatry deserves more attention here. Paul devotes three chapters to this topic, apparently again in response to a written question: 'Now concerning offerings to idols...' (1 Cor. 8.1). He begins with a general explanation of the significance of idolatry: although actually a fiction because idols do not really exist, idolatry still forms a real problem. Many have the principle of idol worship in their minds even after their conversion; therefore, others should be careful in their presence and if necessary deny themselves certain things. In the ensuing chapter, this readiness to self-renunciation for the sake of others is expanded upon using Paul's own example. The chapter after that follows with a condemnation of idolatry on principle, using the story of the Israelites in the wilderness that has been told 'for our example' (1 Cor.

10.1-22; cf. Exod. 32; Num. 25). Finally, Paul gives a direct rule, by which he apparently arrives at the actual query of the Corinthians:

> Everything that is for sale in the market, eat that without making inquiries because of the awareness... If a non-believer invites you...eat everything that he sets before you without making inquiries because of the awareness. But if someone says: this is consecrated food, then do not eat it for the sake of the one who gives the warning... *I mean not your own awareness but that of the other* (1 Cor. 10.25-29).

As long as there is no one around for whom the worship is a reality, the non-Jew is free to partake, whether the food has been consecrated or not, for idols do not exist. If, however, someone explicitly says that it has been consecrated, one may *not* eat of it because that would strengthen the thought of idol worship in his mind. To indicate this 'thought in the mind', Paul uses the word *suneidēsis*, which literally means 'knowing along with', from whence consciousness, self-awareness, or (moral) conscience. Modern translations render this usually as 'conscience', but that leads the reader on to a wrong track. Paul makes it expressly clear after all that this concerns the *other one* and thus not his moral conscience, but his intention or *awareness* regarding idolatry. The principle that idolatry is a reality only in people's minds, and that one should therefore be careful in their presence, is a guiding principle in the legislation in this area within rabbinic literature (p. 107). It appears that Paul here applies this Pharisaic principle.

It is even plausible that Paul is the author of this regulation. It applies to the situation of non-Jews that is not covered in the teachings of Jesus and is hardly imaginable in the teachings of his direct disciples. For Jews it would not have been an issue: they would not have bought wine, meat and other usual ingredients of the pagan cults from a non-Jewish supplier. What should non-Jewish believers, however, do when invited by non-believing relatives or friends? Paul's rule assumes being able to depend on the fact that their own awareness was free from idolatry and that they were known for this. The possible consecration of food to idols would therefore have no effect on them. In fact, through their 'unbelief' in idols, they would desecrate the offering. Such appears from somewhat later reports according to which Jews and Christians were accused of *a-theotēs*, god-lessness, because they did not participate in the general worship. For this reason Paul suggested that non-Jewish believers not make inquiries. To eat in the presence of someone who expressly points out the actual consecration, however, would suggest participation in idolatry. Paul's condemnation of idolatry in principle on the basis of the biblical story is clear enough on this point. He agreed in this with later Christian witnesses who would rather die than worship idols or the emperor (see pp. 373-74).

In short, we see how, when answering the practical questions of the church at Corinth, Paul followed the apostolic legal tradition in which the teachings of Jesus had the highest authority. This legal tradition is to be situated somewhere between that of the Essenes and that of the Pharisees. In the context of his 'gospel for non-Jews', Paul considered only a few universal commandments to be obligatory for non-Jewish believers, while abiding by the law as a whole remained the calling of Jews. His standpoint concerning the universal commandments was moderate. In this he differed from some Jewish fellow-believers, for example, in the circle of James. The following section deals with this matter.

The Clash with Jerusalem

We spoke earlier about the agreement that Paul reports as having been made with the apostles in Jerusalem (Gal. 2.1-10). The accord, which must have been reached approximately at the end of the forties and which concerned a division of labour between 'the apostolate to the circumcision' and 'that to the nations', was based upon mutual trust. Directly thereafter, however, Paul relates a clash with Peter and other Jews in Antioch (Gal. 2.11-14), through which a rift between Jews and non-Jews was created and little mutual trust was left. The circumstances of this conflict can help us to understand it somewhat.

The epistle in which Paul relates these matters is a passionate appeal to non-Jewish Galatians to keep believing in Jesus 'without the works of the law'. There are apparently great tensions in Galatia, and it is logical that in this epistle the reports about the happenings in Jerusalem and Antioch are coloured by these. The account of the clash in Antioch flows directly into the vehement main portion of the epistle. On the other hand, the report of the meeting in Jerusalem contrasts with these later tensions to such an extent that it leaves a historically trustworthy impression. The contrast between the two causes one to wonder whether the clash in Antioch did not mark the beginning of an enduring worsening of the relationship between Paul and 'Jerusalem'.

Previously, things had apparently been otherwise. What do we know about this from Paul himself? A year or more before the agreement in Jerusalem, Paul wrote the first epistle known to us, the Epistle to the Thessalonians. This was shortly after the nascent church in Thessalonica had met with heavy opposition. Paul's spirited outburst against the unbelieving Jews there was related to the persecution of the church in Judaea that had taken place some time earlier. The remarkable silence concerning his own past as persecutor of the church has already been explained on the basis of the mutual sympathy then present between him and the church in Judaea—fellow-believers within a climate of persecution. We could assume that the meeting in Jerusalem several years later took place in such an atmosphere of rapport. Could there be more involved here than a common lot?

In the first chapter of Galatians, Paul provides relatively extensive accounts about his previous life, but these are inextricably related to the enormous tensions that had led to the writing of the epistle. From the first verse on he does nothing but declare his independence of 'Jerusalem' (Gal. 1.1); his gospel 'is not of man, for I have not received it or learned it from a human, but through the revelation of Jesus Christ' (1.11-12). To the verses about his conversion which we have cited, he adds: '...directly, I sought no support from flesh and blood, neither did I go up to Jerusalem to those who were apostle before me...' (1.16-17). The report of the agreement in Jerusalem in Gal. 2 also serves as proof of his independence of the apostles and of the authenticity of his gospel. This does not weaken our conclusion concerning the trustworthiness of the announcement itself. The same is true of his account of an earlier visit to Jerusalem not long after his conversion:

> Then three years later I went up to Jerusalem to confer with Cephas, and
> I saw no other apostle except James the brother of the Lord, and what I
> write to you, see, before God's presence: I lie not! (1.18-19).

The tensions between Paul and his readers and the conflict concerning his gospel are tangible. Precisely for this reason the statement about his voluntary visit to Peter is intriguing.

Within the whole of this epistle, which is laden with the conflict in Antioch and Galatia, these positively contrasting reports reflect an open relationship with Jerusalem in the preceding years. Why was that visit to Peter in particular? The explanation that Paul received from him the tradition of the words and deeds of Jesus cannot be proven, but should also not be rejected out of hand. The discussion of 1 Corinthians has taught us that in one way or another Paul was familiar with this tradition and that he ascribed to it the highest authority. The wording with which he introduces one of the Jesus traditions is relevant in this connection: 'For I have received from the Lord, that which I also have delivered unto you, that the Lord Jesus in the night in which he was betrayed...' (1 Cor. 11.23). 'The Lord' means 'Jesus' here, just as in the phrase already cited, 'James, the brother of the Lord'. This is evidently the manner of speech of Jesus' direct followers. We see how, just as in rabbinic tradition, the reception and transmission of the words of the Lord was an intentional act invested with authority. Paul has 'received' the tradition from Jesus, via Peter or another direct follower of the Lord. This confirms that in earlier years he indeed did have a relationship of trust with 'Jerusalem'.

The next question is why actually the meeting in Jerusalem took place. Paul relates at once as well that he—with Barnabas by the way— travelled to Jerusalem 'in response to a revelation' (Gal. 2.1). This does not exclude other immediate causes, and in what follows he tells that he presented his gospel to the apostles 'to see whether or not he was running without sense' (2.2). There was evidently reason enough for such a conversation, and the trouble that Paul takes to prove his own independence indicates that it was important to himself as well. Two things are apparent: Paul attached importance to the opinion of the apostles, and his preaching had become a matter of discussion.

Indeed he then mentions 'false brothers who had intruded in order to observe our freedom' (2.4). The issue at stake was whether Titus, one of Paul's companions who was a 'Greek', should be circumcised, as the 'false brothers' apparently demanded. A nearly insoluble text-critical problem makes it difficult to decide whether Paul did or did not have him circumcised, but in any case the apostles did not coerce him (2.3, 5). We observe that the legitimacy of Paul's 'gospel for the non-Jews' was contested by certain other Jewish Christians. Their demand that non-Jews like Titus be circumcised was rejected by Paul as a violation of the 'freedom' of the non-Jew to believe without following the law. The other apostles supported him in this.

At this point, again a glance at the Acts of the Apostles is warranted. Acts reports a meeting of Paul and Barnabas with the apostles in Jerusalem that revolved around the question of whether the non-Jewish believer should be circumcised, as a number of 'Pharisees who had come to believe' demanded (Acts 15; see p. 233). The correspondence to Paul's account is evident, and the dating accords approximately as well. In addition, there are a number of discrepancies about which we will speak in the following chapter. We note now that Acts confirms the main features of Paul's report, and we conclude that, during the first half of his ministry, Paul was in good standing with 'Jerusalem'. At the end of the forties, however, resistance to his 'apostolate to the non-Jews' mounted; the agreement in Jerusalem was an attempt to avert these. The breakdown was not long in coming, as the following relates:

> When Cephas, however, arrived in Antioch, I resisted him personally, because he stood condemned. For before certain people of James came, he was accustomed to eat with non-Jews, but when they came, he withdrew and kept himself separate for fear of those 'from the circumcision'. And the other Jews followed him in this attitude, so that even Barnabas was dragged along with their attitude. But when I saw that they did not act coherently in regard to the truth of the gospel, I spoke to Cephas in the presence of all: 'If you as Jew can live according to the customs of the nations and not Jewishly, how can you force the non-Jews to live Jewishly?' (Gal. 2.11-14).

The final sentence is the beginning of a speech directed to Peter–Cephas, which imperceptibly flows over into the main portion of the epistle where Paul summarizes his argument concerning justification without the law. As noted earlier, the theme of justification is for Paul the 'theological explication' of his basic principle that non-Jews as well as Jews should continue to live as they are accustomed to.

What, however, is the significance of the sentence that Peter first 'could live according to the customs of the nations and not Jewishly'? The issue involved eating with non-Jews, otherwise the Jerusalemites would not have stopped doing so. Paul's protest against this has been viewed by interpreters of all ages as proof that Paul had set aside the dietary laws for the sake of fellowship with the non-Jews. Peter would have initially done so as well, and this is incorrectly brought into relationship with Peter's dream in Acts 10. In the following chapter we will see that this interpretation is totally at odds with the intention of Acts; furthermore, Paul's 'gospel for the non-Jews' was based upon respect for the Jews and their law, which would exclude dispensing with the Mosaic dietary laws.

According to another interpretation, Paul wanted to abolish the laws of purity. For this, reference is made to the chapter in Romans where Paul defends the table fellowship of Jews and non-Jews:

I know and I am convinced in the Lord Jesus that nothing in itself is
unclean, except for the one who considers it to be unclean: for him it is
unclean. For if your brother is offended by food, you are not walking
according to love. Do not by your food destroy the one for whom Christ
died... Everything is pure, but it is evil for the one who eats in a pro-
vocative manner (Rom. 14.14, 20).

Here again it is not clear from the context precisely which customs are
involved. That is not really of consequence, for Paul's appeal in this
chapter, as in the epistle as a whole, is for the acceptance of the Jewish
believers with their customs. His argumentation amounts to a rational-
theological interpretation of ritual customs: something is not unclean *of
itself*, but impurity is *ascribed* to it. In other words, purity or impurity is
not a physical circumstance, but a metaphorical *significance*. Paul does
not here reject the purity laws or the dietary regulations, but actually
creates room for them. This discussion, however, cannot hinge on the
laws of purity in themselves, which, as we have already seen, were not
applicable outside of the Holy Land (pp. 97-98).

The discussion must have been about some other point unrelated to
the dietary or purification laws. James's followers considered it forbidden, Paul did not, and Peter and Barnabas were indecisive. It had to
do with *the lifestyle of the non-Jews*, for Paul accuses Peter and the
Jerusalemites of 'forcing them to live Jewishly', and the matter manifested itself at the table.

Two possibilities remain. Either the non-Jews ate certain victuals and
the Jerusalemites did not want to be present at table with such, or the
Jerusalemites thought that they could not eat in the company of non-
Jews at all. The first possibility would entail that the non-Jews ate, for
example, shellfish, shrimp or cheese, which were not allowed to the
Jews. The accounts of rabbis who attended a festive meal of non-Jews
show, however, that this would not necessarily create a problem (see
p. 110). This was apparently also the situation in Antioch, because
Barnabas, Peter, Paul and the other Antiochian Jews initially sat at table
with non-Jews without a problem. Those who protested were, therefore,
especially sensitive or concerned. It is not probable that the issue was
the fare about which it was uncertain whether or not it had been consecrated to idols. The non-Jews would certainly have known that this was
a sensitive issue in the Jewish law, and would thus have been disre-
garding all respect for this sensitivity. Such would have been adverse to
the Jerusalem agreement as we have interpreted it.

The other possibility is the more likely: the Jerusalemites in Antioch apparently thought that they *could not eat with non-Jews at all*. We have already seen that such an over-sensitivity has been expressed in rabbinic literature (see p. 110). The Jerusalemites apparently feared that they could never be certain that non-Jews were completely free from association with idolatry as long as they did not actually live according to the Jewish way of life. Paul sensed this to be a fatal infringement of the agreement in Jerusalem. Did not his non-Jewish followers respect the 'calling' of their Jewish brothers and sisters? Were they not themselves fully fledged children of Abraham, the father of all who truly believe in the Most High? And had not James and the others confirmed this with a brotherly handshake? Paul's stance is hard to confute.

We must, however, also listen to the other side. In Jerusalem, then still together with James and the other apostles, Peter had evidently opposed the demand of the 'false brothers' that the non-Jewish believers be circumcised. In Antioch, however, he allows himself, together with the other Jews and 'even Barnabas', to be persuaded by the people of James of an attitude that amounted to what he had once been against. Realizing that they certainly would not have been persuaded lightly, one wonders what has brought them to change their minds?

Apparently, within a few years' time a tide had arisen that could not be reversed. The meeting in Jerusalem took place at the end of the forties, the Epistle to Galatia was probably written several years later, and the conflict in Antioch lay in between. The group that in Jerusalem could be outvoted by the apostles had brought James around several years later and had even succeeded in getting Peter, Barnabas and other Jews to accede. Those who a couple of years later in Galatia 'preached the circumcision'—the occasion of Paul's epistle—could perhaps be seen in this same light. Similar indications appear in other epistles of Paul (2 Cor. 10–12; Phil. 3; Col. 2). What Paul writes to the Romans while he is travelling to Jerusalem with a collection for the poor also gives the impression of a change in climate. He hopes that he 'will be saved from the unbelievers in Judaea' and that his 'service to Jerusalem will be favourably received by the saints' (Rom. 15.30-31). This reflects an apostle who has become isolated between the closing ranks of the Jerusalem brothers and the camp of the intolerant non-Jews in Rome.

At this point it is justified to consult Acts. We are told that after his return to the Holy City, Paul was taken prisoner at the instigation of the fanatic Jews from Asia Minor, because he was said to be 'teaching against the people, the law, and the (holy) Place' (Acts 21.27-28)— apparently to be an intentional initiative against Paul and his work (cf. 20.18-19). On the other hand, there was also great unrest concerning Paul among the Jewish followers of Jesus. He was said to teach 'apostasy from Moses', so that the believing Jews 'no longer circumcised their children and no longer lived according to custom' (21.21). It is imaginable that the protest movement of Asia Minor Jews pressured the Jewish Christians into a more scrupulous position regarding the non-Jewish believers and their apostle. Perhaps his imprisonment brought the growing mutual mistrust to an acme, and he could do little to prevent further escalation during the four years of his imprisonment in Caesarea and Rome, from approximately 57 to 61 (Acts 24.27; 28.30). According to reports from the ancient church, he was executed in Rome shortly thereafter, when commotion concerning the new faith had led to a crisis there as well.

In Judaea, Asia Minor and Rome, Paul's 'gospel for the non-Jews' had come under duress not only from the Jews in general, but also from within the Christian movement itself. James and his cohorts could not withstand this. The depth of Paul's isolation echoes in the Second Epistle to Timothy, which presents itself as having been written during his imprisonment in Rome, and which as a whole makes a fairly authentic impression: 'You know this, though, that all in Asia Minor have turned themselves away from me' (2 Tim. 1.15, 17). Fortunately that was not true everywhere, as we shall see in the following chapter when we discuss the letters which Paul's co-labourers wrote in his name, but the rift between the 'churches of the non-Jews' and the Jewish churches eventually proved to be irreparable.

The Irrevocable Calling of Israel

Particularly against the background of the breach between Paul and the apostles in Jerusalem, the epistle that he wrote to Rome some years later is a striking document. We have seen that the Jewish Christians at that time probably had difficulties in returning to the church in Rome. The question at stake was the right of existence of a specifically Jewish group among the followers of Jesus. Indirectly linked to this is the existence of the *Jewish people as such*. Both issues, essential to the theme of this book, are treated in Romans 9–11 in relationship to one other. It is, however, not correct to see these chapters as a sort of diversion within a line of reasoning concerning some other issues. From our survey of its contents (p. 185), it is apparent that the whole of Romans is about the relationship between Jewish and non-Jewish believers, and that within this chs. 9–11 are concerned with a concentrated consideration of the position of Jews who do not believe in Jesus.

The passage opens with the verses in which Paul first expresses his 'great grief' about the chasm that separates him from his unbelieving fellow Jews, and then sums up the 'privileges' of the Jews in general (Rom. 9.1-5; see p. 171). In this, everything is actually already said. While the apostle grieves about the sometimes violent unbelief of most of his 'kinsmen after the flesh', he counts them, nonetheless, among the nation that once stood before Sinai as a congregation and there received the 'sonship', 'the glory, the covenants, the law giving, the worship service, and the promises', who are the physical relatives of 'the patriarchs' and of 'the Christ'. The intention of the enumeration is apparently that the validity of all these 'privileges' is undiminished, just as the 'advantage of the circumcision' in Rom. 3.1-2. How can these two viewpoints be coalesced? The whole passage circles around this question.

The image of *Sinai* surfaces several more times. This can hardly be coincidental. 'Sinai' represents covenant and disobedience, the tablets of stone and the golden calf—images that Paul apparently has in mind as he writes about the destiny of his people. He opens by stating that he 'would rather be banned from Christ himself for the sake of his brothers' (Rom. 9.3). One cannot help but be reminded of Moses' prayer following God's wrath towards the people: 'Forgive them their sins—but if not, blot me out of the book which You write' (Exod. 32.33). The beginning of the same chapter in Exodus could perhaps play a role as well. God had threatened earlier to blot out the people and to make Moses, the only faithful one left, into a great nation (v. 10), a threat that Moses warded off by appealing to God's covenant with Abraham, Isaac and Jacob. Thereafter we read, 'And God regretted the evil which He had wanted to do to his people' (vv. 13-14). In this dramatic wording, it is apparent that God's gracious faithfulness to his people is founded upon his irrevocable pledge to the patriarchs. This theme obtained a central place in Jewish exegesis and liturgy, probably already in Paul's day, and in our passage it is evoked by the mention of 'the patriarchs' (Rom. 9.3).

When in the sequel Paul speaks about God's freedom to choose his own elect, he emphasizes this by a sentence from the same story in

Exodus: 'For He says to Moses: I will be merciful to whom I will be merciful and show compassion to whom I will show compassion' (Rom. 9.15; Exod. 33.19). Within the book of Exodus as a whole, these words have their own particular place in the progression from the revelation in the burning bush to the unveiling of God's merciful name after the episode of the golden calf (Exod. 3.6-15; 6.2-3; 33.18–34.10). While Paul also cites multiple other texts, it is as though the scene of the nation before Sinai lies at the very basis of his exposition.

It is, then, not surprising that a bit further on Moses' counterpart appears on stage: Elijah. Elijah climbed the same mount, now called Horeb, but in contrast to Moses he pointed out the sins of the people with the words, 'Your prophets have they slain, your altars have they torn down, and I, I alone, remain' (1 Kgs 19.10; Rom. 11.3). The story of this prophet, who in his righteous zeal assumes exactly the opposite position to Moses, contains undeniable irony (1 Kgs 19.9-19). Paul echoes this: 'But what does the divine word say? "There are seven thousand men remaining for Me, all of whom have not bent their knees to Baal"...' (Rom. 11.4; 1 Kgs 19.14). Confronted with Israel's failure, Paul does not choose a position *opposite to* the people as Elijah did: like Moses, he *vouches* for the people, prepared to offer himself. This obvious contrast between the 'righteous' Elijah and an ideal prophet like Moses occurs also in rabbinic literature (*Mek. bo* p. 4).

In this tenor, Paul now develops the theme of Israel's disobedience: 'For not all who are from Israel, *are* Israel as well; not because they are of the seed of Abraham are all also (actually) his children' (9.6-7). The motif has played earlier, but it is now placed centrally: real circumcision of the heart (see pp. 172-73). The sect from Qumran had its own outlook on this, but so did, for example, John the Baptist. In his upbraiding of the unrepentant he says, 'Do not think that you can say: we have Abraham as father, for I say to you that God is able to raise up children for Abraham from these stones' (Mt. 3.9). For Paul it is beyond doubt: true worship of God lies for Israel in faith in Jesus, which does not exclude but include the keeping of the law. Jews who oppose this are like misshapen clay figures that the potter must remodel (Rom. 9.20-23), or a useless olive branch that the cultivator must prune away (11.17-24). 'They have a zeal for God, but without insight' (10.2), 'they are hardened, as it is written: "...Their eyes are darkened, so that they might not see" ' (Rom. 11.9; Ps. 69.24).

In the end, however, the hardening is only 'partial' and 'all Israel shall be saved' (11.25-26). The sub-theme here is the about-turn of Israel as a resurrection from the dead. Just as God 'is able to raise up children for Abraham from these stones', Paul states concerning the severed branches that 'God is able to graft them again' and he calls the return of Israel 'life from the dead' (Rom. 11.23, 15). Paul spoke earlier in the same manner about Abraham who became 'father of us all' 'because he believed in God who makes the dead to live and who calls into being that which is not...as it is said "so shall your seed be"' (Rom. 4.17-18; Gen. 15.5; cf. Heb. 11.19). Echoing in this one can hear the vision of dead bones that the Spirit revives to new life and to return to the land (Ezek. 37).

Alongside Israel's temporary disobedience, a second main theme plays in these chapters: *the influx of the nations*. The epistle as a whole is to a large extent an appeal to the non-Jews hospitably to 'receive' the Jewish brothers and sisters. In his contemplation of the temporary hardening and the eventual salvation of Israel, Paul can therefore not neglect the position of the non-Jews in the history of salvation. This is given particular attention in Rom. 11, through the well-known image of the olive tree:

> I speak to you, non-Jews! insofar as I am the apostle of the non-Jews...
> If several branches have been pruned away, and you, wild olive branch, have been grafted in between them and have been given a share of the moisturizing root of the olive, boast not then over against the other branches. If you will boast—you do not bear the root, but the root you. Think not too highly of yourself, but fear! for if God did not spare the natural branches, he shall also not spare you (Rom. 11.13-21).

In other words, the issue of Israel's sins is between Israel and God alone. Non-Jews are not to meddle in this, but to take heed of their own behaviour. Should they not heartily welcome their Jewish brothers and sisters, then they will have forfeited all right to say anything...

The addressed non-Jews are admonished, as it were, to be silent and respectful witnesses of the judgment scene between God and his covenant people. This insight can clarify the remarkable fact that Paul in these three chapters continually uses the covenant name 'Israel' (11 times; cf. pp. 110-11). In the rest of Romans he does not use it at all and in his other epistles only sporadically, which is quite consistent since all of his epistles are directed to non-Jews. The use of 'Israel' in these three chapters forms a remarkable contrast and places the readers as it were in the inner Jewish situation of the covenant people at Sinai. The two exceptions occur precisely where the relationship of 'Jew and Greek' is touched upon (Rom. 10.12; 9.24).

With this the theme of *the relationship of Jews and non-Jews within the church* is brought forward, giving occasion to reiterate the motif of justification, although it has already been treated thoroughly in this epistle (Rom. 4–8). It is in this context that Paul's statement about Christ being the 'end of the law' occurs. This well-known expression must be understood within the prevailing tone of the whole passage:

> They (the Jews) have a zeal for God, but without insight. For not knowing of God's justification and searching to establish their own justification, they have not submitted themselves to God's justification. For Christ is the end of the law to the justification of everyone that believes (Rom. 10.2-4).

Having understood the purport of the epistle, the expression of Christ being the 'end of the law' in any case does not signify that Israel's right of existence and that of its law are defunct. Greek *telos* means both 'end' and 'goal', and both meanings play a role. For Jewish believers, the law is not an end in itself, but is focussed upon Christ. That is why he is its *goal*: observing the law in itself will never justify them. On the other hand, non-Jews are justified *without* the law, namely, in Christ, who is the *end* of the law as universal prerequisite for salvation. Thus, 'there is no distinction between Jew and Greek, for he is Lord for all' (10.12). This final phrase is an echo of Paul's practical rule of thumb: while Jews observe the law and non-Jews do not, both are reckoned to be righteous only in Christ.

Two theological lines are intertwined in this portion, and if we are to follow the intention of the apostle, these two must be both distinguished and held together. On the one hand he assumes the enduring calling of Israel and accentuates this with the exclamation, 'The gifts of grace and the calling of God are irrevocable' (11.29). On the other hand, he sees salvation as being only through faith in Christ: 'For if you confess with your mouth that Christ is Lord and believe in your heart that God has raised him from the dead, you shall be saved' (10.9). Next to the lasting calling 'in Moses' there is one 'in Christ': the question is, again, how the two accommodate one other. The paradox is strengthened again by the fact that for Paul here, too, the covenant with the 'fathers' plays a role: the Jews are, it is true, 'as far as the gospel goes enemies for your sake, but as far as the election is concerned *beloved, for the sake of the fathers*' (11.28), for 'theirs are the covenants...theirs are the fathers' (9.4).

The word 'election' is fairly infrequent within the New Testament. While Paul uses it here for Israel (also in Rom. 9.11; 11.5, 7), elsewhere he and others use it for the 'election' of Christians (1 Thess. 1.4; Acts 9.15; 2 Pet. 1.10). We could narrow down our statement concerning the two lines and say that *two elections are intertwined* in this passage—that of *Israel* and that of *the church of Christ*. Again the question is, How is this contradistinction to be resolved? Modern theologians would possibly register this as a contradiction, but Paul takes it as an enigma of history.

When approaching this mystery, Paul's style rises to an elevated tone. First, in solemn phrasing, he makes his readers participants in a *mystery*:

> I would not that you were ignorant, brothers, of this mystery, so that you might not be wise in your own eyes: a partial hardening has come over Israel, until the fullness of the nations has arrived, and thus shall all Israel be saved... (Rom. 11.25-26).

By 'mystery' (see also 1 Cor. 15.51), Paul means an apocalyptic mystery concerning the coming course of events; in this he is still addressing the non-Jews. With this revelation he wants to guard them from the misunderstanding in which they are liable to lapse. The influx of non-Jews into the church does *not* signify that the history of the Jewish people is terminated. One could view this unexpected course of history as a strange and temporary 'changing of the guard'. Paul expands somewhat on the topic. Just as the disobedience of the Jews appears to have the effect of an influx of non-Jews, in turn this influx must herald the salvation of all Israel.

The expression *all Israel* derives from the language of liturgy and prophecy (*T. Benj.* 10.11; *m. Sanh.* 10.1). The expression gives extra accent to the elevated tone of the finale. Thus Paul concludes his discussion of the puzzling coexistence of Israel and the church in the single history of salvation with a biblically inspired hymn of praise to God's miraculous wisdom:

> O the depth of the riches and of the wisdom and knowledge of God... For who has known the mind of the Lord, or who has been his counsellor? [Isa. 40.13]...For from Him and through Him and to Him are all things; to Him be the glory in all ages. Amen (Rom. 11.33-36).

Chapter 5

LUKE AND ACTS

Continuing our deviation from the canonical order of the New Testament, from Paul we progress to Luke and Acts. The order of treatment is not due to chronology, for both writings are probably somewhat younger than the Gospels of Mark and Matthew, but is related to our main theme. In comparison to Mark, and especially to Matthew, Luke and Acts show a remarkably positive attitude towards Judaism. The question of the how and why for this needs to be dealt with thoroughly, and that is facilitated by studying Luke and Acts first. The difference with Matthew and Mark gives further reason to treat Luke and Acts in direct connection to Paul. Besides, it is highly elucidating to view Luke together with Acts.

Coherence, Theme and Goal

Although from an early stage the Gospel of Luke and the Acts of the Apostles must have circulated separately, there is reason to view them as parts of a diptych that belong together. The links between the books comprise both formal aspects (style and structure) and content (subject matter, rhetorical purport), even to such an extent that they seem to share one and the same author. One of the areas where that is expressed clearly is precisely in the relationship to the Jews and the Jewish law—one of our main themes. Therefore Luke–Acts, as the diptych is often called, is highly important to our investigation.

The connection is formally expressed in the two preambles in which the author presents the books to the reader, following the custom of Hellenistic historians. In this it is undeniably clear that one author is involved, offering not only a brilliant sample of his stylistic aptitude in Greek, but also declaring how conscientiously he had undertaken the task that he had set for himself:

After many already have ventured to compose a written account of the facts which have been accomplished among us—according to that which has been delivered to us by those who from the beginning were eye witnesses and ministers of the Word—have I also decided, after having verified everything closely from the beginning, to write this down in an orderly manner for you, most excellent Theophilus, so that you can realize the trustworthiness of the things in which you have been instructed (Lk. 1.1-4).

The former book have I made concerning all things, O Theophilus, that Jesus began to do and to teach until the day that he gave his instructions through the Holy Spirit to the apostles which he had chosen, and he was taken up (Acts 1.1-2).

The Theophilus to whom the books are dedicated, and who perhaps also financed the hand-written publication, is further unknown. The form of address is that of an administrative dignitary, roughly equivalent to 'your excellency' (Acts 26.25, see p. 216). Apparently, this esteemed individual had become involved with the gospel and the author saw occasion to provide him with trustworthy and stylistically sound information. Hence this diptych, the first part of which explicitly refers back to Gospels written earlier. The second part, Acts, must also rely on earlier sources, but these are unknown to us.

The two preambles draw attention to the person of the author, who further remains anonymous. According to old church tradition, he was Luke, the physician mentioned by Paul in Col. 4.14 as a co-worker. Though this is not impossible, it is equally uncertain. Where this author is mentioned, we will refer to him as 'Luke'. The Gospel itself will be indicated as Luke, without quotation marks.

In both works, 'Luke' exhibits a varied use of language that betrays a socially sensitive awareness of style. Besides in the preface to his illustrious reader, he uses cultured Greek, for example, in his rendering of Paul's oration to the philosophers in Athens, a theme that then, too, must have been of interest to the educated reader (Acts 17.16-34). Directly following the preface, on the other hand, the reader finds himself in the midst of the stories of the births of John the Baptist and of Jesus (Lk. 1–2), in which the author uses both the motifs and the Hebrew-influenced style of the Greek Bible, while his own stylistic refinement continues to be actively present. The same is true of the stories of the resurrection and the ascension (Lk. 24; Acts 1). In general, there appears to be a strong influence of the Septuagint on the style of 'Luke'. A third type of style is the succinct simplicity of the tradition of the words and deeds of Jesus, in which, by the way, the author subtly corrects the Hebraizing translation Greek of his sources, particularly in the narrative portions. The many speeches held in Acts probably also reflect a certain style, namely, that of the discourses in synagogues and related locations. 'Luke' uses all of these styles to address and inform his highly honoured reader.

If we survey the diptych as a whole, the attention given to the role of the non-Jews is conspicuous. Particularly in Acts 10–15, the 'God-fearers' are central (cf. p. 108). The conversion of Cornelius, the God-fearing centurion from Caesarea, functions as a turning point in the spreading of the gospel. This episode introduces us to another characteristic of 'Luke': the use of corresponding pairs. The counterpart of Cornelius is the anonymous centurion of Capernaum, who was in good standing with the Jews and had financed the building of their synagogue (Lk. 7.5). This connection lends extra significance to Jesus' statement that he 'did not find such faith even in Israel' (Lk. 7.9).

Both centurions become involved with the gospel through a synagogue, and this, too, is a motif in the diptych. Both Jesus and Paul begin their preaching time and again in synagogues, even though the opposition of the Jews at times assumed violent proportions (Lk. 4.29; Acts 14.19). Progressively, more Jews and in particular God-fearers give ear to the message and the gospel expands from the midst of the synagogue, as it were. The clash with the Jewish leaders, which also occurs in 'Luke's' writing and is particularly sharp in the temple surroundings, gives extra relief to the more positive role of the synagogue (Lk. 20–22; Acts 4–5; 21–23). There is also a third centurion—the one in command at the crucifixion of Jesus. He occurs in Mark and Matthew as well, but in Luke he gives a remarkably positive testimony concerning Jesus: 'Truly, this man was righteous' (Lk. 23.47). The positive role of the Roman military must have appealed to Theophilus as well.

Finally, attention is given to the Roman government. Jesus' coming is placed within the framework of the regimes of the emperors Augustus and Tiberius (Lk. 2.1; 3.1), and his execution occurs under the authority of the military governor Pontius Pilate and viceroy Herod Antipas (Lk. 22–23; cf. 3.1). In Acts, due to his work, Paul is confronted with the proconsuls Sergius Paulus of Cyprus, Gallio of Achaia, and the 'excellencies' Felix and Festus, successors of Pilate in Judaea

(Acts 13.7; 17–18; 23.26; 26.25). Meanwhile, the name of Emperor Claudius is mentioned (18.2), and, finally, Paul is transported to Rome to stand trial before the emperor, that is to say, Claudius' successor, Nero. It is made clear to the reader that not only Jesus was unjustly charged, but also Paul, which is stated in so many words by the Roman governors (Lk. 23.14-22; Acts 18.14-15; 25.25; 26.32). The names of Pontius Pilate and Lucius Junius Gallio have been recovered from inscriptions, so that modern historians as well have solid ground under their feet in these events...

With great care, the author describes the history of the gospel from the birth of John, the prophetic precursor, via the preaching of Jesus and his disciples in Galilee and Judaea, on through the preaching of Paul in Asia Minor, Greece and Rome. He places this history explicitly within the framework of the Roman Empire, shows how Roman authorities as well become involved in this, and indicates how the gospel progressively spreads via the surroundings of the synagogue. Thus the excellent Theophilus can read with confidence that, in spite of all allegations, the growth of the Word of God is the work of God himself, who in the face of the Roman potentates causes it to take root and blossom among the Jews and all peoples. This survey provides a preliminary insight into the aim of this double volume, to which we will return repeatedly in the course of our discussion.

The Positive Significance of the Law

Within the framework of Luke and Acts just sketched, the theme of the significance of the law is conspicuously present, spanning the entirety from the birth stories at the beginning of the Gospel to the conflicts around Paul at the end of Acts. Besides the moderately positive appraisal of the Roman rulers, the author makes it clear that, in spite of continual conflict with the Jewish leaders, Jesus, his disciples, and Paul have not violated the law but have observed it with conviction.

A great emphasis on the Jewish law is first present in the two opening chapters of Luke, which diverge strongly in form and content from the other Gospels, so that this emphasis is characteristic of Luke. Themes from the Torah play an important role, in particular motifs from the story of the birth of the prophet Samuel at the beginning of 1 Samuel. Zachariah and Elisabeth, the parents of John the Baptist, are depicted following the model of Elkanah and Hannah, the parents of Samuel;

Mary's hymn of praise is clearly inspired by Hannah's hymn of praise; the devout, aged Simeon, who takes the child Jesus in his arms during his presentation in the temple, is an 'improved edition' of the elderly priest Eli.

Thus while biblical elements are employed, these are 'improved' upon in accordance with the ideals of postbiblical Jewish piety. Zachariah and Elisabeth are not only both descendants of Aaron, but they also 'walked blameless in all the commandments and institutions of the Lord' (Lk. 1.6). As a perfectly natural consequence, they circumcise their child on the eighth day and give him the name John (Lk. 1.59-60). The aged Simeon is said to be 'righteous and devout', and Anna, the prophetess, having remained unmarried as widow, is said to 'not cease worshipping in the temple with fasting and prayer day and night' (Lk. 2.25, 37)—likewise allusions to the postexilic Jewish ideal of piety.

The author describes the law-abiding natures of Joseph and Mary even more emphatically. Their child is, of course, also circumcised on the eighth day, but more is involved. When the period of purification 'according to the law of Moses' is past, Jesus is brought to Jerusalem to be 'sanctified' as firstborn, 'as it is written in the law of the Lord'. Accompanying this dedication a thank-offering is brought, again 'according to what is said in the law of the Lord' (Lk. 2.22-24; cf. Lev. 12.3-8; Exod. 13.2, 12). The thrice-repeated, explicit reference to the law within this short passage is intentional and eloquent. After they have 'accomplished everything according to the law of the Lord', Joseph and Mary return to Nazareth (2.39). According to 'Luke', this is not the only time that Joseph and Mary made the pilgrimage to Jerusalem, for they went up for the Passover feast annually (2.41). From other sources it appears that this could not have been said about the majority of Jews in the Holy Land, and it therefore indicates special devoutness. The intention is clear: Jesus is raised in a pious Jewish environment.

One aspect that deserves separate attention is the significance of prophecy within these circles. Elisabeth, Zachariah, and Simeon each in turn speak full of the Holy Spirit, and Anna is called a 'prophetess' (Lk. 1.41, 67; 2.26, 36). The hymn of praise that Mary declaims when she meets Elisabeth also appears to be intended as Spirit-filled (1.46-55). The hymn is modelled after Hannah's song (1 Sam. 2.1-10), and it is not coincidental that Hannah's song in the rabbinic paraphrase of the Bible, the Targum, is rendered as a prophetic hymn of praise to the glorious future of Israel, in which her son Samuel would have the role of deliverer. Hannah's husband is here called a 'disciple of the prophets' (*Targ. 1 Sam.* 1.1; 2.1-6). Their pious Jewish milieu is depicted as true to the law and the prophets—the same atmosphere found in the birth stories in Luke.

One could question whether 'Luke' places this explicit accent only to emphasize the correspondence with the Greek Bible and the Jewish tradition, in accordance with the intention of his writings, or whether he incorporated actual traditions from the milieu of the 'holy family'. The latter is the more probable, if only because of his expressed claim of trustworthiness in the introduction to the Gospel. This it is not to say that these traditions could be taken integrally as 'historical' in the modern sense of the word, since the 'pious ideal' undeniably plays a role in shaping the stories. Nonetheless, there are elements that are difficult to imagine as purely pious fiction, such as, for example, the detailed mention of the descent of the prophetess Anna, 'a daughter of Phanuel, from the tribe of Asher', and the information that Zachariah belonged 'to the course of priests of Abijah' (Lk. 2.36; 1.5). Given the fact that in that time lists of descendants of priestly families existed, and given the recently found sarcophagus with the inscription 'House of David', there is even reason to take the Davidic descent of Joseph seriously (Lk. 2.4; 3.31; cf. pp. 339, 388). There is apparently here an inextricable intertwining of pious ideals and devout reality.

This brings us to Jesus' own faithfulness to the law. The story about his surprising wisdom as a 12-year-old conversing with 'the teachers' in Jerusalem belongs to the legendary childhood stories (Lk. 2.47). Besides conveying the unusual giftedness of the child, the devoutness of his Jewish environment is emphasized again. More characteristic for the figure of Jesus himself is the determined manner in which in the final phase of his ministry he 'set his face to go to Jerusalem' for the Passover feast—the reason why the Samaritans, who did not worship in Jerusalem, did not want to accept him (Lk. 9.51-53). Jesus' faithfulness to the law does not limit itself, however, to a simple, practical following of its ordinances, but expresses itself even more—paradoxically, one could say—in the stories of healings on Shabbat.

The details of these stories in Luke are not only relevant to the historical figure of Jesus, as we argued in Chapter 3, but also reveal the particular interest of the author. 'Luke' presents five such stories, while Mark has three and Matthew only one (see pp. 153-54). Second, in the last two stories 'Luke' uses an analogy about rescuing animals on Shabbat, which was convincing for the Pharisees and which occurs once in Matthew. Third, 'Luke' describes the reaction of the Pharisees invariably as confusion and amazement, while their reaction in Mark and Matthew is rendered as the historically improbable resolve to liquidate Jesus. The author makes us understand that Jesus, the gifted child of yore, was completely at home in the argumentation of the scribes, and in that field enjoyed the benefit of the doubt with more mildly tempered Pharisees.

The last two stories, which occur only in Luke, give us information even about Jesus' own attitude towards the Jewish law. In one story, Jesus quotes that one could 'unbind' his ox or his donkey on Shabbat and bring it to a place to drink (Lk. 13.15), which was a generally accepted rule, even for the Essenes. The embarrassed silence of the opponents is eloquent, revealing also the attitude of the evangelist. In the other story, Jesus reasons that one could 'pull his donkey or ox' out of a well on Shabbat (Lk. 14.5). (Some modern translations follow the senseless manuscript version 'his *son* or his ox', which disrupts the whole argument 'from light to heavy' and is easy to be explained as a reading error, while the other reading is well testified.) Pulling up an animal is not, however, in keeping with the Jewish law, not even in the opinion of the later rabbis (cf. p. 93). On the other hand, in Matthew Jesus uses the exact halakhic expression that the animal may be *raised up* (Mt. 12.11). In comparison to this, 'Luke' betrays a lack of practical knowledge of the Jewish law, in striking contrast to his otherwise so sympathetic attitude towards Jewry. *The author of Luke and Acts apparently did not have Pharisaic schooling and was probably not a Jew himself.*

Another example of Jesus' faithfulness to the law can be found in the incident of the centurion of Capernaum (Lk. 7.1-10; cf. p. 161), which occurs with a different emphasis in Matthew (8.5-13; see pp. 282-83). In both cases, the man said to Jesus that he should not come 'under his roof', which Jesus indeed did not do. This is not mere politeness. Within the framework of the diptych, this centurion has his pendant in Acts, and there it is apparent that a problem of the Jewish law is involved. Both in Luke 7 and in Acts 10 the centurion is said to be known to the Jews as philanthropic and a God-fearer, an accent indicating sympathy towards the Jewish law that is missed in Matthew. Parallel to Acts 10 (see pp. 231-32), the evangelist shows that Jesus himself also kept to the rule that one should avoid the house of a non-Jew in order not to contaminate oneself.

Our insight into this passage would be benefited by acquaintance with the rule which is linked with the ancient notion that everything having to do with idolatry—and thus everything that is non-Jewish—is impure. The expression 'to come under my roof' confirms that this notion plays a role here. According to the strict interpretation, contamination of the same order as that produced by a dead person is involved, contamination that was therefore also carried over within a covered space (cf. Num. 19.14). The specific term that the ancient halakah used to refer to this is important to us, namely, 'hooding-over, awning' ('*āhîl*). The centurion meant, thus, that Jesus should not come inside and contaminate himself, but should avoid the 'awning'. It is noteworthy that the initiative for this comes explicitly from the centurion. The philo-Semitic portrait that 'Luke' gives of him is hereby strengthened. This God-fearer could apparently feel comfortable with this type of custom of his Jewish friends! Jesus' surprised exclamation that he had not found faith like that of the centurion 'even in Israel' gives the story an authentic ring. Again we see how the purpose of the evangelist coincides with giving historically relevant information.

The description of being God-fearing and faithful to the law is applied not only to Jesus himself and the milieu of his family, but also to his disciples and the first community of believers. This becomes particularly clear within the framework of the diptych, an extended perspective that, of course, is lacking in the other Gospels. Thus women who had followed Jesus from Galilee and wanted to embalm him after his death wait 'according to the commandment' until the Shabbat is past—an accent that only occurs in Luke (23.56; cf. 8.1-3). After Jesus' resurrection the congregation is also presented in this manner. The new community of followers came into being in Jerusalem during the celebration of the Feast of Weeks or 'Pentecost' (see p. 79). Besides attending their own meetings, the members continue to faithfully participate in the daily prayers in the temple (Acts 2.46; 3.1). Further on in Acts as well, the congregation in Jerusalem is characterized by its exceptional faithfulness to the Jewish law.

Great emphasis is placed on Paul's faithfulness to the law. This must have to do with the aim of 'Luke's' work as a whole. Both as unconverted and as apostle at the height of his career, Paul is characterized thus. His pre-Christian background is mentioned several times. As a young man, he attended and assented to the stoning of Stephen, who was lynched as a false prophet by zealots. Thereafter Paul himself takes violent action against the followers of Jesus, both in Jerusalem and in Damascus, and that with the full consent of the high priest (Acts 7.58–8.3; 9.1-2). He, too, was thus depicted as a 'zealot', who in particular strove against the (presumed) enemies of the law within his own circle. This is stated in so many words in Paul's speech to the Jews 'in the Hebrew language', Hebrew or Aramaic:

> I am a Jew, born in Tarsus in Cilicia, brought up in this city, at the feet of Gamaliel trained according to the scrupulousness of the law of the forefathers, a zealous one for God like you all are today... (Acts 22.3).

whereupon the story of his persecution of the church and his conversion follows. The mention of Gamaliel is not by accident, as will become apparent.

The author places equal emphasis on Paul's faithfulness to the law after his conversion, namely, in two actions full of fundamental significance. In the first place, he lets Timothy, who had a Jewish mother and a Greek father, be circumcised, 'because of the Jews in those places, for everyone knew that his father was a Greek' (Acts 16.1-4). What does this mean? Does Paul under pressure conform himself to the Jews? This is out of the question, because one chapter earlier the author tells us that in Jerusalem it had just been decided that non-Jewish believers in Christ do not have to be circumcised, and Paul could hardly have assumed a stricter attitude in this than the other apostles. The point is, thus, that Paul viewed Timothy as a Jew because of his Jewish mother, and therefore had him circumcised. This concurs with the rabbinic interpretation, by which a person who has a Jewish mother is considered to be a Jew (cf. *m. Bikk.* 1.4-5). It lends significance to the statement that Paul did this 'because of the local Jews': non-Jews who believe in Jesus do not have to be circumcised, but for believing Jews it is a natural step to be circumcised and Paul agreed with this.

The second principal example of Paul's faithfulness to the law occurs after his return from his third journey and exhibits a clear stylistic connection with the first example. James and the elders welcome him and listen with joy to his stories about the preaching among the non-Jews. They then point out the tensions with the other Jewish believers:

> You are aware, brother, that several thousands of Jews belong to the believers, and that they are all zealous for the law. Now it has been told them that to all Jews in the diaspora you teach defection from Moses, by

saying that they must not have their children circumcised nor keep
themselves to the customs (Acts 21.20-21).

It is then suggested that Paul join four men who had to 'sanctify
themselves' in order to be able to bring the prescribed offerings in the
temple for the fulfilment of a pledge. Apparently pilgrims from foreign
countries, who had to go through a purification procedure of seven
days, were involved (see pp. 97-98). The intention in regard to Paul was
that 'all shall see that what is said about you is not the case, and that
you yourself also are devoted to keeping the law' (21.24). Paul agrees
to the suggestion, but James's plan is thwarted. In what follows, Jews
from Asia Minor, probably from the same zealous circles that had dis-
credited him, succeed in having Paul imprisoned. With this began a
long series of court sessions that probably took up the last years of
Paul's life.

According to our author Paul stood trial while being totally innocent.
This is summarized succinctly during the examination before Festus:
'Paul defended himself in this manner: I have offended neither the
Jewish law, nor the temple, nor the emperor' (Acts 25.8). Theophilus
can be assured: the gospel is not against the Jewish law, nor against the
Jewish temple and its authorities, nor against the Roman government,
but is in all respects an honourable creed. A legitimate question is
whether this concurs with what Paul himself thought; we return to this
in a later section.

The Positive Portrayal of the Pharisees

From the particular interest of 'Luke' sketched above, one striking and
for us significant fact becomes easily comprehensible: the positive picture that this author draws of the Pharisees in comparison to what the
other evangelists do. Even more so than in the preceding, it is repeatedly observable that the image he portrays has a high level of authenticity.

Exemplary of this is the event reported only by this author: 'In that
time some Pharisees came and said to (Jesus): depart from here, for
Herod wants to kill you' (Lk. 13.31). While in this Gospel, as we shall
see, the Pharisees are not at all involved in Jesus' trial and execution,
here they even want to save his life! This Pharisaic sympathy is even
more remarkable because Jesus, several verses further on, comes home
for a Shabbat meal with 'one of the leaders of the Pharisees', at which
'they kept an eye on him' (14.1). Then ensues the healing of the man

with dropsy already discussed, where Jesus uses the argument that one is allowed to save even an animal on the Shabbat. Precisely because they 'kept an eye on him', the conclusion resounds emphatically: 'they could say nothing against it' (14.6). In other words, in spite of their reservations Jesus is above reproach in their opinion.

The Pharisees in the story of 'Luke' are portrayed as having mixed feelings about Jesus. They do not fundamentally reject him, but neither do they trust him completely. Jesus' reserved attitude towards them corresponds to this: he agrees with them on the essentials, but has serious criticism on details. Thus he reprimands them for their tendency to assume the place of honour at a meal: 'When you are invited, go recline at the lowliest place' (14.10). A comparison with rabbinic sources is of interest here. The godly modesty that Jesus teaches resembles the devout tendency in the writings denoted as *Derek-Erets* literature and that of the pious individuals mentioned in the rabbinic writings. The latter are viewed with the same reserve by the Pharisees and rabbis as Jesus is. They are suspiciously observed, but usually there is nothing essential for which they can be reproved (see pp. 60, 138). These correspondences give a convincing degree of authenticity to 'Luke's' description of the relationship between Jesus and the Pharisees.

Acts confirms these observations. When 'the high priest and all with him, that is the party of the Sadducees', take Peter and Jesus' other apostles captive and want to try them because of their preaching, protest comes from the Pharisees:

> But a Pharisee in the council named Gamaliel, a teacher of the law, held in honour by all the people, stood up and said... Keep your hands off of these men and let them go; for if this council or this work be of men, it will fall apart; but if it be of God, you will not be able to make it fall apart without becoming adversaries of God (Acts. 5.33-39).

This same Gamaliel is also mentioned as Paul's teacher (Acts 22.3): not only is he known in the Talmud as a leader of the school of Hillel, but he is also the only Pharisaic leader to be mentioned by name in the New Testament. The repeated mention of the man in Acts cannot be other than intentional. Comparison with rabbinic literature confirms the impression that the words that the author ascribes to Gamaliel are based on tradition (see pp. 419-22). The account is sympathetic towards the Pharisees and appears to be plausible.

Further, it is important to emphasize that in 'Luke's' writings, Jesus and his apostles did not clash with the Pharisees, but with the Sadducees, the powerful minority party of prominent priests. The same constellation appears when Paul is taken captive in the temple at the instigation of the 'zealous ones', but now the distinction between the factions receives extra emphasis. In his plea before the Council, he says:

> 'Men, brothers, I am a Pharisee and a son of Pharisees, concerning the hope and the resurrection of the dead am I judged.' When he said this, dissension arose between the Pharisees and the Sadducees and split the meeting apart. For the Sadducces say that there is no resurrection, nor angel or spirit, while the Pharisees subscribe to both. A great tumult arose and several scribes of the party of the Pharisees stood up and argued vehemently: 'We find no evil in this man; what then if an angel has spoken to him?' (Acts 23.6-9).

In the light of the preceding, it is of decisive significance that in the diptych the Pharisees have no responsibility for the condemnation of Jesus. In contrast to Matthew, they are mentioned nowhere in connection to the happenings in Jerusalem, with one revealing exception. When Jesus enters the city upon the donkey's colt and the multitude ecstatically hail him as 'the king who comes in the name of the Lord', 'certain of the Pharisees among the multitude' say to him, 'Master, rebuke your disciples' (Lk. 19.39). They express their concern about this excitement, which, just as in Lk. 13.31, sounds like regard for Jesus' safety. The real conflict is with 'the eminent priests and the scribes and the prominent among the people' (Lk. 20.1).

This image is further confirmed by inspecting several discussions Jesus has with Jewish leaders, and by comparing these with Mark and Matthew. A couple of days after Jesus' triumphal entry into Jerusalem he has a series of exchanges with the temple administrators, in which, among other things, he tells the parable of the vineyard and the disobedient tenants. The conclusion of the parable is that the owner ejects the tenants from the vineyard. In reaction 'the scribes and eminent priests attempted to lay hands on him…for they understood that he had spoken this parable with them in view' (Lk. 20.9-19). In Mark the situation is not much different, although directly thereafter 'several Pharisees and Herodians' are sent to Jesus with a trick question (Mk 12.12-13). In Matthew, however, we read, 'And when the eminent priests *and the Pharisees* had heard his parable, they understood that he had spoken it in view of them' (Mt. 21.45).

The disparity with Mark and Matthew at the beginning of the Gospel is even more striking in the story where Jesus heals the man with a withered hand in the synagogue in the presence of several Pharisees. In Mark the story ends, 'And the Pharisees went directly outside with the Herodians and held counsel concerning him in order to *kill* him' (Mk 3.6). In Matthew likewise, 'And the Pharisees went outside and held counsel concerning him in order to *kill* him' (Mt. 12.14). In Luke, however, we read, 'And (the scribes and the Pharisees) were completely perplexed and spoke with one another about *what they could do to him*' (Lk. 6.11). This version accords with the impression that 'Luke' had already given about the reciprocal reservations that Jesus and the Pharisees had for one another, and it sounds more authentic. At that moment in the Gospel, indeed, no mortal conflict is present, but the question is *where were they to place Jesus?* According to this author, the fatal conflict of Jesus and his apostles was not with the Pharisees but with the leadership of the temple predisposed towards the Sadducees.

A final point of comparison can be found in that which has been transmitted of Jesus' condemnatory speech to the Jewish leaders, which has been processed in Luke and Matthew in vastly divergent manners. In Luke the setting is at a meal to which Jesus has been invited by a Pharisee (Lk. 11.37). This is a noteworthy occurrence that is related only by this author and which in his Gospel does not stand alone (see also Lk. 7.36; 14.1). The personal interaction of Jesus with the Pharisees underscores the positive basis of their otherwise reserved relationship. In the story in question, 'the Pharisee was amazed that Jesus had not first bathed himself before the meal' (Lk. 11.38). Jesus answers with three reproaches to the Pharisees, the last one reinforced with 'woe to you': they 'cleanse the outside of the cup and the saucer', while on the inside they 'overflow with plundering and evil'; they 'tithe mint and rue and all herbs', while they 'neglect judgment and the love of God'; and they 'love the places of honour in the synagogues and the greetings on the market place', while they 'are like invisible tombs' that make someone imperceptibly impure (Lk. 11.39-44). Rabbinic literature confirms that such subtleties in the area of purity and tithing were characteristic of Pharisaic tradition. The objection against pedantic piety can be related to the tradition that condemned the tendency to superficial piety within the Pharisaic movement (p. 53).

A 'scholar of the law' now involves himself in the conversation and says to Jesus, 'Master, if you say this you affront us as well' (Lk. 11.45). Jesus' answer is now a threefold 'woe': those learned in the law lay heavy burdens on the people that they themselves 'do not even touch with a finger', they build beautiful monuments for the prophets that their own precedessors have killed, and they appropriate for themselves the 'key of knowledge', while they 'themselves also do not enter' (Lk. 11.43-44). It ends in a conflict and Jesus departs. The 'scribes and Pharisees' begin to attack him vehemently about all kinds of matters and try to trip him up on a word (Lk. 11.53-54). While it is not precisely clear what the relation of these 'scholars of the law' is to the Pharisees, Jesus' reproaches to them are noticeably more serious. The clear distinction between the two groups is important to us.

This is, namely, where Luke characteristically differs from Matthew. All reproaches of the Pharisees and those 'learned in the law' are bundled together in Matthew in one long discourse against 'the scribes and Pharisees' (Mt. 23). Moreover, it is placed in the antagonistic atmosphere of the temple square in Jerusalem, a scene that in Luke, as already said, is completely devoid of Pharisees. In Luke we do find a warning to the 'scribes' at this point:

> they love to walk in long garments, and they love the greetings in the markets and the places of honour in the synagogue and at the meal; they eat up the houses of widows and articulate long prayers for a pretence (Lk. 20.46-47).

Part of the same reproach occurs in Lk. 11.43, there directed against the Pharisees, thus giving the impression that the author processes different parallel traditions. The sympathetic portrait that he continues to give of the Pharisees is therefore the more remarkable.

Yet this is not the whole story. In four passages in Luke the generalized category of 'scribes and Pharisees' is mentioned. In Lk. 5.17 it is still about 'Pharisees and those learned in the law' who are present in the house where Jesus forgives a paralyzed person his sins and later heals him. However, it is '*the* scribes and *the* Pharisees' who take offence at Jesus' behaviour (5.21). This accent is even more striking because Mark and Matthew only speak of 'several scribes' in the parallel to the latter passage (Mk 2.6; Mt. 9.3). Nonetheless, 'Luke' states, 'the scribes and the Pharisees kept an eye on Jesus', where Mark writes '*they* kept an eye on him', evidently referring to the earlier mentioned 'Pharisees' (Lk. 6.7; Mk 3.2; 2.24). Finally, only in Luke do we find that 'the scribes and the Pharisees' kept an eye on Jesus after a clash and that 'the Pharisees and the scribes grumbled' because he ate with sinners (Lk. 11.53-54; 15.2).

As we shall see in the following chapter, the use of the generalizing category 'scribes and Pharisees' is characteristic of the Gospel of Matthew. That is not to say that 'Luke' had Matthew in front of him. With his emphasis on the Pharisaic tolerance towards Jesus and his apostles elsewhere, the Lukan evangelist gives the impression that here he processes sources reflecting a somewhat different attitude towards the Pharisees. Some confirmation for this can be found in the occurrence of the same combination in the Gospel fragment on the 'adulterous woman', which most manuscripts place somewhere in John, but some in Luke (see pp. 272-73).

We now return to the Pharisee Gamaliel. According to 'Luke', not only were he and other Pharisees reservedly positive towards Jesus' apostles, but he himself was also held in honour by all of the people (Acts 5.39). This concurs with the witness of Josephus that the Pharisees enjoyed the sympathy of the people (see p. 58). On the other hand it is important what 'Luke' says about the attitude of the people towards Jesus in Jerusalem. According to the synoptic Gospels, the interest of the people prevented the temple leaders from doing anything against Jesus (Mk 12.12; Mt. 21.46; Lk. 20.21). Mark reports as well that 'the great multitude heard him gladly' (Mk 12.38). The Lukan evangelist goes further. The temple leaders were unable to do anything 'because all the people hung on his lips'. Furthermore, he says that 'all the people came to him in the temple early in the morning to hear him' (Lk. 19.48; 21.37-38). When Jesus is led away, 'Luke' relates that 'a great mass of people followed, as well as women who smote themselves on the breast and lamented over him' (Lk. 23.27).

The author of the Lukan diptych informs us about the sympathy of the people for Jesus, the positive reciprocal reservedness of Jesus and the Pharisees, and the sympathy among the people for the Pharisees. This mutual sympathy is given relief by their antipathy for the Sadducees, attested to not only by 'Luke', but also by Josephus and rabbinic sources. From this we can understand the remarkable announcement in Acts that a number 'of the party of the Pharisees had become believers' (Acts 15.5; cf. 11.2; 21.20). This Lukan report is confirmed by an unexpected source: the Gospel of John. There it is related that the Pharisaic leader, Nicodemus, together with the Councillor Joseph of Arimathea took care of Jesus' burial (Jn 19.38-42; cf. 3.1). The sympathetic image of the Pharisees that our author provides appears to be little distorted.

Jewish and Non-Jewish Christians

The explicit attention that the author gives to 'God-fearing' non-Jews such as Cornelius and his anonymous collegue from Capernaum, has already been pointed out. Cornelius's conversion with Peter present (Acts 10) functions as a turning point in the story of Acts, a watershed confirmed in principle by the meeting in Jerusalem precipitated by Paul's preaching among the non-Jews (Acts 15). Together these two episodes offer the essential overview of the blueprint of Acts as a whole.

This plan is summarized in a statement at the beginning of Acts that picks up a thread from the end of the Gospel, where Jesus had said to his apostles that the preaching would go forth 'to all peoples; beginning at Jerusalem you are witnesses of it' (Lk. 24.47-48). In Acts Jesus says, 'You shall be my witnesses in Jerusalem and in all of Judaea and Samaria, and unto the uttermost part of the earth' (Acts 1.8). This sequence, *Jerusalem—Judaea and Samaria—the ends of the earth*, contains the 'blueprint' of the spread of the gospel and with it the layout of the book of Acts. In working this out, the author's preference for the use of pairs is recognizable, now involving the apostles Peter and Paul. The first 12 chapters are dominated by the preaching in Jerusalem, Judaea and Samaria, Phoenicia, Cyprus and Antioch, in which *Peter* plays the main role, with the *conversion of Cornelius* as revelatory episode. In the rest of Acts, the spotlight is on the preaching of *Paul* in Asia Minor, Greece and eventually Rome, with in the midst the *meeting in Jerusalem* as fundamentally significant moment.

The leitmotif is, therefore, the preaching of the gospel among all peoples, 'going out from Jerusalem'. For Paul, this is worked out in a pattern of conduct that appears to deflect from the position he himself assumes. He calls himself explicitly the 'apostle of the nations' and addresses all of his epistles to non-Jews (p. 169). His preaching in Acts, however, always begins in the synagogue, including his first preaching directly following his conversion in Damascus (Acts 9). In Cyprus, Asia Minor and Greece, Paul constantly starts his preaching on Shabbat in the synagogue (Acts 13; 17–19). The reaction of the Jews is negative or disunified, except in a few exceptions (17.11). Why would the author so consistently maintain this pattern? The answer lies most likely in the main thrust of his story: the spread of the gospel is to proceed *from Jerusalem to the nations*. The negative reaction of most Jews forces Paul to turn to the non-Jews, as he twice expressly states (Acts 13.46;

18.6). In other words, his work among the nations does not reflect a fundamental rejection of the Jews, but lay in their lack of response. The legitimacy of the preaching among the nations is hereby supported, so that one principal aim of this diptych is attained.

The author makes this abundantly clear in the decisive final chapter. After his arrival in Rome, Paul engages in earnest deliberations with the Jewish leaders about the nature of his preaching. 'Some were convinced over what we discussed, but others remained unbelieving, and in this discord they departed hence' (Acts 28.24-25). In this context Paul quotes the well-known text about being 'hearing-deaf' (Isa. 6.9-10). The final words of the apostle are, 'Know then that this salvation of God is sent to the nations, whosoever will hear it' (Acts 28.28). Some interpreters see in these words the clinching of the rejection of the Jews. That does not accord, however, with what Paul says when he meets the Roman Jews. He relates that he must appeal the indictment by his fellow-citizens in Jerusalem to the emperor, 'but not thus, that I would charge my people of anything' (Acts 28.19). Furthermore, the conversation in Rome has an open end, thus granting the same to the relationship to the Jews within the diptych. The Jewish leaders are divided, 'and in this discord they departed hence'. In short, the author is not out to have Jews rejected: the relationship to the Jews remains unresolved. The concern of the author is that the preaching to the nations is shown to be a legitimate continuation of the preaching among Jews.

Of great significance in this connection is the term that the author consistently uses for non-Jews appearing in and around the synagogue: *God-fearers*. We have already seen that this was a real and more or less recognized category (pp. 107-108), reflecting not only the 'theological intentions of Luke', but also the actual relationships between Jews and non-Jews in the first century. 'God-fearers' sympathized with Judaism, believed in God, and partook in the synagogue services and celebrations without formally joining Judaism. Illustrative of this is the emphasis with which Cornelius is designated as 'a God-fearing and righteous man who was well-known among the whole Jewish people' and 'who gave much alms to the people and regularly prayed to God' (Acts 10.22, 2). This term and a synonymn—'worshipper (of God)'—are used henceforth by the author whenever Paul turns to the non-Jews in the context of a synagogue.

There is yet another appellation of historical significance employed with a certain emphasis: *Christians*. After briefly relating how Paul and

Barnabas were accommodated for a year by the church in Antioch while they taught, the author announces: '...and in Antioch the disciples were called Christians for the first time' (Acts 11.26). He uses the word a second time as a general designation in a statement of King Agrippa (Acts 26.28). Paul does not use the term himself in the epistles that have been preserved, but speaks only of 'believers', Jewish or non-Jewish followers of Jesus. It is striking that the author never puts that word in Paul's mouth, a clear example of his method of consistently employing a style and language that belong to an earlier situation. The name occurs once more in the New Testament (1 Pet. 4.16) and the report about the origin of the name being in Antioch is confirmed by other sources (see p. 250).

We pause now at the episode involving Cornelius. His conversion is, as already said, a turning point in Acts, but it does not come totally unexpectedly. Peter and other apostles had already previously brought the message to the Samaritans (Acts 8.4-25). The Samaritans, who incidentally still exist as a community, lived at that time according to religious customs that in many ways were related to those of the Jews. A next step is the conversion of the Ethiopian eunuch through the efforts of Philip, who was specially called to do so by an angel (Acts 8.26-40). As an intermezzo with far-reaching consequences, the author relates the conversion of Paul, and then returns to Peter. A brief mention of the conversions of Jews in Lydda and Joppa (Lod and Jaffo) indicates what Peter's 'normal' work was (Acts 9.32-43). The reader is prepared in this manner for the miraculous events relating to Cornelius.

The initiative for the conversion of Cornelius again comes from God, this time through a dramatic vision (Acts 10). Peter sees a sheet let down from heaven by the four corners with all kinds of animals, and he hears a voice saying to 'slaughter and eat'. He protests that as a Jew he is not allowed to eat unclean animals, whereupon the message is repeated twice. When the vision is over, he is invited to accompany several men whom Cornelius had sent in the meantime, likewise on the basis of a vision. Peter goes along and enters the house of Cornelius, the story of whose conversion follows.

What does the author intend by Peter's vision? Ever since the church fathers, the opinion has been propagated that Peter must literally dare to eat the unclean animals because the law of Moses was cancelled. We saw in the previous chapter that this is often seen in relation to the attitude of Peter in the conflict with Paul in Antioch (Gal. 2.11-13; see

p. 177). Such is, however, completely contrary to the message that the author of the diptych presents in so many details. His emphasis upon the significance of the Mosaic law entails also that the dietary laws, which are firmly anchored in the Bible and have retained their validity for every Jew, remain effectual (see pp. 98-99). Nowhere is it indicated in what follows that at Cornelius's house Peter ate things prohibited by Jewish law. On the contrary, just like the centurion of Capernaum (Lk. 7.6), Cornelius himself is full of understanding for the Jewish customs. The author indicates his intentions clearly in the words that Peter speaks when he enters Cornelius's home: 'You are familiar with the fact that it is unlawful for a Jew to have close contact with a stranger or to enter his home; but God has taught me to call no person unholy or unclean' (Acts 10.28-29). The sheet in the vision contains not only unclean animals, but 'all sorts', that is, also clean animals. Together with the 'four corners', which probably represent the four quarters of the earth, the vision proclaims that not only the Jews, but also the nations are called. In short, here again 'from Jerusalem to the ends of the earth'.

Meanwhile it is clear from the story that Peter overstepped an actually perceived boundary related to the Jewish law: 'When Peter went up to Jerusalem, those of the circumcision began to discuss with him because he had entered and eaten with uncircumcised people' (Acts 11.2-3). What is this about, if the author in his whole work seeks to foster sympathy for the Mosaic law? All in all, he localizes the problem in the 'entering and eating', in other words, in eating at the home of a non-Jew. It must, thus, have to do with the impurity that was attributed to all that was related to idolatry and was transmitted by an 'awning' (see p. 221). At the same time, the implication is that the prohibition to contaminate oneself was in effect in everyday life, even apart from the temple worship. Again we must take into account not only the interests of the author but also the actual circumstances in the first century. The rules involved were of postbiblical origin and were contested at that time. In rabbinic literature, alongside the more scrupulous attitude, there is a tolerant attitude according to which a Jew could be the guest of non-Jews (see p. 110). According to 'Luke', Peter initially shared the more cautious standpoint, as did the believers 'from the circumcision' in Jerusalem and—not to be forgotten—*Jesus himself* in Capernaum. The case of Cornelius, however, made the hospitality of non-Jews acceptable. Thus the tolerant standpoint prevailed among the Jewish followers of Jesus.

Tolerance is, of course, not without limits, and the question thus arose, *Which rules are to be applied to non-Jewish believers*? A decision on this is taken at the meeting in Jerusalem (Acts 15). Meanwhile, Paul has appeared on the scene with his remarkable success among the non-Jews, and thereby the question becomes acute. According to 'Luke', this took place precisely in Antioch, where Paul and Barnabas had just returned from their first great missionary journey: 'And there came several from Judaea who taught the brothers: if you do not let yourselves be circumcised according to the custom of Moses, you can not be saved' (Acts 15.1). The question could not be resolved and it was decided to send Paul and Barnabas with several others to 'the apostles and elders' in Jerusalem. When they reported about the influx of non-Jews, it was again stated, now more explictly by 'believers who were from the movement of the Pharisees', that they 'must circumcise the non-Jews and instruct them to keep the law of Moses' (15.5). The contrast with the tendency of the author to present the Pharisees in a positive light makes this account the more credible.

What follows does not concur with what we read in Paul's own writings; we will return to this later on. It shows us more clearly the intention of the author. Paul gives only a brief report of his work and holds his peace. The main spokesmen are Peter and James. Peter refers, of course, to the precedent of Cornelius, but his phrasing is remarkable: 'we believing Jews should not impose on the neck of the non-Jews the yoke which neither we nor our forefathers could bear', for 'we are saved in the same manner as they' (Acts 15.10-11). Just as in the earlier case in Antioch, we are reminded directly of Paul's own account (Gal. 2), about which more will be said later. That the decisive speech here is held by Paul's apparent opponent in his epistle to Galatia, James, is striking indeed. After several apt quotations from the prophets, he formulates a rule that is put in a letter to be sent around and that is accorded a key significance in the rest of Acts. The non-Jewish believers are not to be burdened with the whole law of Moses, 'but they are to abstain from that tainted by idols, from sexual misbehaviour, from what was suffocated and from blood' (Acts 15.19-20; cf. 15.29; 21.25). The assembly agrees to this and puts it officially in writing 'to the brothers among the non-Jews who live in Syria and Cilicia'—that is, the regions to the south and west of Antioch.

There is much to be said about the four precepts themselves. It is important at this point that the 'abstinence from things tainted by idols' was apparently already practised by God-fearers, such as Cornelius. Peter would otherwise not have been able to enter his place at all. Abstinence from idolatry is one of the universal commandments comparable to the later 'Noachic commandments' from rabbinic literature (see pp. 107-108). The apostles thus formally ratify the status of non-Jewish followers of Jesus as 'believing God-fearers'. These are to keep a limited number of universal commandments, while their Jewish brothers and sisters must observe additionally the rest of the law. The respective responsibilities of Jewish and non-Jewish Christians is thus clearly demarcated and, thereby, their relationship to each other. Particularly the latter is nicely put by James at the end of his oration: 'For Moses has since time unknown in every city (those) who preach him by reading him aloud every Shabbat in the synagoge' (Acts 15.21).

This so-called Apostolic Decree is of central significance in the diptych as a whole. The author tells how Paul with Barnabas and two others are sent as representatives to take the letter to Antioch. Once there, Paul puts the decree immediately into practice by having Timothy circumcised, who was Jewish through his mother and thus actually bound to the whole law (Acts 16.1-4). Several chapters further on, when his imprisonment is announced in dramatic farewell scenes in Ephesus and Caesarea, Paul participates voluntarily in a purification ceremony in the temple. This takes place again at the suggestion of James, in order to gainsay the rumour that Paul teaches the Jewish believers in the Diaspora defection from the law, with an explicit appeal to the Apostolic Decree (21.21, 25).

With this presentation the author gives the reader a double message. On the one hand, he emphasizes that the Jerusalem apostles continue to stand fully behind Paul's work among the non-Jews, as long as these are prepared to keep the universal commandments. On the other hand, Paul's dedication to that work does not entail that he as a Jew is unfaithful to the law. Again we recognize the motto on the diptych: 'To the nations, beginning at Jerusalem.'

Luke's Image of Paul

The question can no longer to be avoided—a classical question of historical criticism, To what extent does the image that the author gives of Paul agree with his own writings? The answer presumes a historical-critical approach in which the distinct literary intentions of Paul and of the Lukan author are interpreted within a single historical framework. Acts is written from the perspective of a later situation, and many scholars are of the opinion that its irenic attitude towards the Jews and the Jewish church in Jerusalem diverges strongly from that of Paul himself. This provides yet another reason for beginning with Paul's own epistles in our description of him, and only incidentally consulting Acts for support. Furthermore, there are indeed some striking differences between Acts and Paul, to which we will now give attention.

From the above and from the preceding chapter, one important conclusion can be drawn: there is fundamental agreement between Paul and the Lukan author concerning the importance of the Jewish law. Both emphasize its enduring validity for Jews and Jewish followers of Jesus, while for the non-Jewish believers only a number of universal commandments apply. In our chapter on Paul we found it credible that in his own conduct he respected the Jewish law. This accords with the two occurrences that are described with a certain emphasis in Acts: the circumcision of Timothy and Paul's participation in the temple ritual (Acts 15–16; 21).

The question of the dependability of our author now becomes acute. His emphasis on the two examples of Paul's faithfulness to the law makes it indeed impossible to distinguish between actual facts and a general bias in his writings. The matter is different with those happenings reported without obvious emphasis. After his stay in Corinth, Paul boards a ship to Asia Minor accompanied by his Jewish fellow-Christians Priscilla (Prisca) and Aquila, 'after he had his hair cut in (the harbour city) Cenchreae, *for he had a vow*' (Acts 18.18), an abbreviated reference to the ceremonial vow of abstinence during which one was not allowed to cut one's hair (Num. 6). The account in Acts agrees here surprisingly well with what Paul himself relates about Prisca, Aquila and Apollos (1 Cor. 1–3; 16), thus again confirming its trustworthiness. Other details that in passing betray Paul's faithfulness to the law are the mention of 'the days of unleavened bread' during which Paul and the narrator ('we') wait before boarding a ship from Philippi to Troas, as well as Paul's wish to celebrate the following 'fiftieth day' in Jerusalem (Acts 20.6, 16). The latter is confirmed by a comparable wish that Paul himself expressed in relation to Ephesus (1 Cor. 16.8).

On the other hand, what Paul himself writes here is not elevated above all 'historical criticism'. It is even probable that, in the heat of the discussion, he distorted events somewhat. Besides Galatians 1–2, one could bring up the outburst against certain Jewish-Christian opponents in Phil. 3.2-3: 'Beware of dogs, beware of evildoers, beware of self-mutilation...' (*katatomē*, 'cutting off', instead of *peritomē*, 'circumcision'), indicating a fierce conflict. Under such circumstances one could hardly expect a level-headed rendering of the facts.

A difference between Paul and the Lukan author that has already been mentioned lies in the manner in which Paul went about his preaching. According to the division of labour that he himself reported (Gal. 2), he was responsible for the 'apostolate to the nations', and this is borne out by the fact that in his epistles he explicitly addresses himself to non-Jews (p. 169). In Acts, however, everywhere he goes he begins his preaching *in the synagogue*, and he is explicitly introduced as the witness to the nations *and Israel* (Acts 9.15). The division of labour was made at the assembly of the apostles in Jerusalem (Gal. 2). If this is the same meeting as that reported in Acts 15, which we will go into in more detail later, the account that follows makes it clear how the author understood the outcome. Paul begins, as always, in the local synagogue: 'They arrived in Thessalonica where there was a synagogue of the Jews; and as was his custom Paul came to them and discussed the Scriptures during three Shabbats...' (Acts 17.1-2). In a later chapter as well it appears that the custom to go pray in the synagogue was for Paul a natural occasion to propagate his message. The Lukan author appears, thus, to interpret the division quite differently than did Paul himself.

This difference can be related to the author's purpose of emphasizing the continuity of the movement 'from Jerusalem to the nations'. More could, however, be said. In Acts 16, he relates how Paul, after his arrival in Philippi, first went to the 'place of prayer', which must refer to a synagogue. The Greek word used is *proseuchē*, which primarily means only 'prayer' but which was also used to indicate a synagogue. The report occurs in one of the three portions of Acts that are written in the 'we' form (the others are Acts 20–21 and 27–28). If the author himself is not speaking here, then he follows an eyewitness. According to another report, Paul and Barnabas began their first missionary journey from Antioch through to Cyprus 'to preach the word of God in the synagogues of the Jews' (Acts 13.5). This apparently old and authentic tradition implies that Paul and Barnabas at that time operated as an Antiochian Jewish apostolic duo. Even if we must identify Paul's reported method of working as a conscious accent of the author, to all appearances this concurs with a faithful rendering of the facts. His unmistakable historiographic talent is here revealed: the art of respectfully fitting observed facts into a meaningful presentation.

The next question is whether the impression that we get from Paul's epistles tallies completely. Did he indeed turn exclusively or primarily to non-Jews? Is it not probable that he had *not* abandoned his custom of going to the synagogue one Shabbat, and that in these visits he did not keep his compelling message to himself? Confirmation of this can be found in his own allusion to clashes with synagogue rulers (2 Cor. 11.24-25; cf. 2 Tim. 3.11). The fact that in the epistles that have been preserved he kept himself so strictly to the designation of responsibilities agreed upon may be due to circumstances. The epistles are all written at a time when the tension with Jerusalem increased under the influence of the competing 'apostolate of the circumcision'. His freedom of movement was therefore considerably decreased. On the other hand, the division of labour was a global demarcation that he did not take too strictly, as appears from passages that speak of his longing to make his fellow Jews 'jealous' and to 'win' them for Christ (Rom. 11.14; 1 Cor. 9.20), as well as from his explicit motto 'the gospel...for all who believe, for the Jew first but also for the Greek' (Rom. 1.16). This confirms that, although not entirely free of a particular slant, the rendering of the Lukan author is reasonably trustworthy and that Paul, under the pressure of circumstances, did not always give a balanced picture.

Nonetheless the impression remains that Paul and 'Luke' assess the difficult relationship to the Jews and the Jewish Christians differently. Paul, who becomes vehemently polemical when driven into a corner (Galatians), can yet plea for mutual acceptance (Romans) with equal passion. 'Luke', however, describes the conflicts of Paul and his opponents in a matter-of-fact manner against a background of continuity between the Church and Judaism—and that approximately one generation after Paul, when the relationship to Jewish churches and to Jews in general had not become easier. Already in Paul's day, repercussions of the increasing tension are observable, as is apparent in the non-Lukan Gospels. What makes 'Luke' so tranquil and balanced? We are faced with an enigma.

A second prominent difference between Paul and 'Luke' has played a crucial role in historical criticism from the very beginning, and has to do with the *proceedings of the 'apostles' council' in Jerusalem*. According to Paul, apart from a private meeting with Peter and James several years after his conversion (Gal. 1.18-19), there was also the official meeting in Jerusalem during which he and Barnabas presented his gospel to the other apostles and where it was decided to demarcate the two apostolates (Gal. 2.1-10). The reported insistence of several 'false brothers' to have Titus circumcised (v. 4) confirms the fact that the assembly discussed the notion that non-Jewish believers should be circumcised and keep the law. The other apostles did not succumb to the pressure and the assembly went no further than a designation of responsibilities: 'Those who were held in esteem did not impose upon me anything more...only that we should remember the poor' (Gal. 2.6, 10).

'Luke' as well relates first a brief visit to Jerusalem shortly after Paul's conversion, where Paul together with Barnabas delivered funds raised in Antioch (Acts 12.25; 11.30). The larger assembly takes place years later. During Paul's and Barnabas's stay in Antioch (Acts 14.26), 'some' from Judaea come who say that the non-Jews must be circumcised in order to be saved. Paul and his companion resist this, after which the Antiochian church delegates them to discuss this issue in Jerusalem (15.1-2). After Paul had told of his work, again 'Pharisees who had come to believe' want to prescribe circumcision for non-Jews. Much discussion came of this, but through the mediation of Peter, Paul and Barnabas continue to be listened to sympathetically.

Thus far the two accounts concur. We must thus assume that Paul does not mention the Judaeans who come to Antioch to pressure for circumcision *before* the meeting in Jerusalem, and that 'Luke' is silent about the clash between Peter in Antioch *thereafter*. This can be explained by the particular individual penchant: Paul harps on the support from Jerusalem, 'Luke' emphasizes the unanimity of the apostles.

After this, however, 'Luke' relates the decision that the apostles put in a letter to Antioch and surrounding regions, according to which the non-Jews were to abstain not only from idol offerings and sexual immorality, but also from 'what is strangled' and from 'blood'. The latter are two dietary laws that entail that non-Jews as well were allowed to eat only meat of slaughtered animals from which the blood had been properly drained (cf. pp. 95, 99). Furthermore, precisely Paul and Barnabas are the ones delegated by the apostles to relay the decision to Antioch (Acts 15.22-31). When after all this Paul has Timothy circumcised, it appears as though the author consciously 'corrects' what Paul himself relates about Titus in Gal. 2.4-5! Finally, the decision of the apostles later on in Acts has the important function of underscoring the unanimity about Paul's apostolate and his faithfulness to the law (Acts 21.21-26).

On the other hand, nowhere does Paul report a unanimous and authoritative decision of the apostles. Such dietary rules are not even compatible with what he writes on similar topics. The most explicit is in 1 Cor. 10.25-27 where the only restriction he imposes is that non-Jewish believers may not eat meat that explicitly counts as having been consecrated to gods. It is inconceivable that Paul would subscribe to a commandment of kosher meat for non-Jews, let alone that he would propagate it. The account in Acts can in no wise be correct here, and we even get the impression that the author was not familiar with Paul's epistles. In any case one wonders what caused this breakdown in his otherwise so trustworthy manner of working.

It is logical to presume that 'Luke's' point of departure was a later situation. Thus, following an explanation current at that time, he has confused the meeting in Jerusalem with a later assembly where the regulations were settled on. This decision would have taken place without Paul, after the clash in Antioch, as a clear rejection of his standpoint—reason enough for Paul not to mention it. This hypothesis, however, has no direct support in the text and there are several objections to it. The relationships after the clash were not such that the standpoint of Paul is openly condemned by the other apostles. He still is given hospitality in Antioch and, conversely, Peter visits Paul's 'own' church in Corinth (Acts 18.22-23; 1 Cor. 9.6). Paul also continues to exert himself for the collection to benefit those in Jerusalem and to plead for loyalty towards the Jewish brothers and sisters (1 Cor. 16.1-3; Rom. 9–11). Furthermore, it is difficult to imagine that the otherwise so careful 'Luke', even with his particular bias, would have switched the reports about these two quite distinct meetings.

Another solution equates the two collections, the one of which Paul speaks (Gal. 2.20; 1 Cor. 16) and the one in Acts (Acts 11.29; 12.25). In this way the Jerusalem meeting of Gal. 2.1-10 would coincide with the earlier one in Acts 11. The place of Acts 15 then becomes a problem. It would be a later official assembly where Paul also was present but about which he was silent. Then, however, Paul's 'other' first visit of Gal. 1.18 is left dangling. A third alternative is that Paul himself confused matters and that the meeting in Jerusalem (Gal. 2.1-10; Acts 15.2) actually took place *after* the conflict in Antioch (Gal. 2.11-14;

Acts 15.2!). Nonetheless, the contrast between both *renderings* of the decision of the Jerusalem meeting remains unresolved.

The simplest soultion is to assume that both sources refer to the same private meeting in Jerusalem as well as to the second public one in which the apostolate to the nations was discussed. The deficiency of Paul's report and the silence of 'Luke' about the clash in Antioch are easier to explain than drastic changes in sequence. Concerning the suppression by 'Luke', a comparison with Josephus is fitting, for he relates almost nothing about the Christians while indirectly it is apparent that he does know about them (see p. 58). We must also assume that the account of 'Luke' as we know it reflects a later situation, and in particularly takes into account the fact that the relationships among Jews, non-Jews, and Jewish Christians had hardened as time progressed. It is advisable to take Paul himself as point of departure.

We begin with the emphasis which Paul lays upon his recognition by the other apostles, particularly in his letter to the Galatians in which he energetically defends his apostolate. The recognition by the other apostles necessitated that they trusted his attitude towards the law and the non-Jews. An important correspondence with the Lukan writings lies in the relationship of authority in which Paul places himself in regard to the Jerusalem apostles. In the same epistle Paul quotes thrice his basic principle of the relationship of Jews and non-Jews (Gal. 3.28; 5.6; 6.15). The third time he even speaks of a 'rule' (*kanôn*, Gal. 6.16). A comparable explicit designation, this time without polemic emphasis, occurs in 1 Cor. 7.17-19, where he introduces the same rule of thumb with the words: 'This is what I prescribe in all churches...' That is to say, Paul himself wields a fixed and as such known rule for the practical relationship of Jews and non-Jews. Precisely in the epistle in which he defends his apostolate by an appeal to the apostles in Jerusalem, he cites that rule three times.

Proceeding from the data in Paul's writings, the agreement in Jerusalem must have contained not only the recognition of his apostolate to the non-Jews but also explicitly his apostolic basic principle: 'everyone should remain in the calling to which he is called'—the circumcised observe the law, the uncircumcised do not. All are required to 'keep God's commandments' (1 Cor. 7.19), which for non-Jews included that they were to abstain from *sexual misbehaviour* and from *idolatrous offerings* (1 Cor. 6–7; 8–10). In terms of the story of Acts, the Jerusalem apostles in the presence of and with the approval of Paul must then have come to the conclusion that non-Jews must abstain from idol offerings and sexual misconduct. These are two of the three universal commandments that later formed the core of what is called the 'Noachic commandments' (see pp. 108, 200), and indeed they are the first two elements of the apostolic decision 'to abstain from *idol offerings*, from *sexual misbehaviour...*' (Acts 15.20, 29).

What remains is the complication created by the dietary laws mentioned thereafter, '*that which is strangled and blood*'. This need not, however, be insurmountable. An unforced solution presents itself via a long known text-critical problem connected to this verse. Several ancient manuscripts and Latin church fathers quote the decree of the apostle in the form of not four but *three* rules: 'To abstain from *offerings to idols, sexual misbehaviour, and blood*'. No dietary regulations are mentioned, and there is a clear connection to the fundamental form of the three universal commandments of Judaism of that time. On the basis of the origin of these manuscripts, scholars have spoken of the 'western text' of the decree of the apostles. It was assumed that this was a *later*, 'ethicizing' simplification of an originally four-part decree. Such a diminishing of the commandments is in general quite improbable, the more so given the increasing worsening of relations. For both reasons, an *expansion* at a later date is more probable. Paul's basic principle is then the form in which he applies the decree of the apostles, and his practical instructions in 1 Corinthians show what was concretely involved.

Is it also possible to explain why the decree was later made more stringent, undeniably against the spirit of Paul? Such a development is well imaginable in the hardening climate of the forties and fifties. Due to the course of events, in particular the growing enmity towards the Romans and the rise of the 'Zealots' as a political movement, the extremists in the Jewish churches caught the wind in their sails. In that situation it is conceivable that the church leadership in Jerusalem imposed the commandment of ritual slaughtering upon the non-Jewish brothers that excluded every heathen ritual of slaughter. There were even Old Testamental grounds for this (Gen. 9.1-6). In the end, this revision of the decision of the apostles must have been inserted into the text of Acts, certainly when the writing came to be recognized as authoritative. In remote corners of the church worldwide, however, such as North Africa and Gaul, apparently 'Luke's' original version was preserved, the so-called 'western text'.

With this reconstruction we have rehabilitated the reputation of our author as historian; moreover, the reconstructed account accords with what we read in Paul's own writings. If this is acceptable, we are faced anew with the enigma of 'Luke'. The possible *secondary adaptation* of his text to a later hardening of standpoints would in itself accent the amazing level-headedness of his original text. He must have composed his diptych several decades after the Jewish war against Rome. As we can observe in the other Gospels, completed approximately at the same time or a little earlier, the situation had gravely worsened. The more stringent decree must then already have been in circulation and would not have been unknown to our author: he must have deliberately ignored it.

We could also read this with more suspicion. 'Luke' *himself* could have introduced the revision of the apostle's decree in a second edition of his work. Such holographical 're-editing' was not uncommon in antiquity. We would then have to assume that he succumbed to the pressure of circumstances and of the Jerusalem church leadership, and quietly adapted his text. We cannot completely bar this suspicion, but neither is it wholly justified, given 'Luke's' purposeful and conscientious method of working as chronicler of an eventful history.

It has been assumed that the entire work of 'Luke' is intended as an *apologia for Paul*, literally a defence address during a trial. This would explain why the chronicle ends with Paul's arrival in Rome: it would have been written while the legal proceedings were still in progress. Such would require a dating in the sixties, which, given the references to the outcome of the Jewish war against Rome in the Gospel, is difficult to accept. A dating in the eighties or nineties is much more plausible. What then was the purpose of the author, and why is he silent about the execution of Paul, as though covering up a painful episode? We recall the dedication to the 'excellent Theophilus', elsewhere a title of address for a Roman dignitary, as well as the emphasis with which 'Luke' places his whole work within the context of the Roman administration. With the attention given to the influx of non-Jews, his emphasis on Paul's consistent faithfulness to the law attracts notice. Without denying 'Luke's' conscientiousness, we still get the impression of a more general apologetic intention, which could perhaps be described as follows.

By the faithfulness to the law of Jesus and Paul, the two most important 'founders', the author demonstrates that the new faith is a sincere and *legitimate continuation of Judaism*. His balanced and courteous attitude towards the Roman government was intended evidently to remove any suspicion in that direction as well. His apologia was not intended for Paul himself, who was probably already executed under circumstances of which the author would rather not be reminded. His very first reader, the illustrious Theophilus, is already 'instructed' about 'the facts which were accomplished among us', but apparently is interested in a 'trustworthy' report.

This all fits well into the atmosphere of the eighties and nineties, when, on the one hand, the tension between Jews and Christians had increased enormously and, on the other hand, the regime of Emperor Domitian exhibited an unprecedented distrust towards Jews and Christians (cf. pp. 373-74). We have also made a link between these circumstances and the apologetic tendency of Flavius Josephus and his reserve towards Christianity. Thus a fundamental correspondence between the two writers becomes apparent. Both stand within the Hellenistic tradition of *'apologetic historiography'*, in which the originality and antiquity of one's own eastern culture and religion is rendered in Hellenistic terms (see p. 30). During the regime of Domitian this apologetic tendency acquired extra urgency. Josephus, therefore, eloquently describes the honourableness of Judaism, but does not mention the incriminating new sect. 'Luke', on the other hand, as spokesman of the new faith, emphasizes both its right of existence and its being the sincere, legitimate continuation of Judaism. The option chosen by others of exonerating Christianity by maligning Judaism is rejected by him.

With these factors in mind, before us rises an author who faces the tensions of his day with unusual serenity. He appears to have an unshakable trust in the single history of God's salvation for Jews and Greeks. As such we can envision him as a convinced and level-headed follower of Paul, who remained true to the vision of his teacher even in difficult times. It is not barred to think with a sharpened awareness of 'Luke, the beloved physician', who kept Paul company towards the end of his life, at times being his sole companion (Col. 4.14; Phlm. 24; 2 Tim. 4.11).

Luke's Gospel

After the preceding consideration of the Lukan oeuvre in relation to Paul, it is worthwhile to return to the Gospel. Our starting point is again the *foreword* with which the author announces and accounts for his project. In this he distances himself from his work in a manner that sets him off from the other evangelists. Announcing to the highly esteemed Theophilus a better description than those that preceded, he appeals to certain norms of historiography that have self-critical implications: he undertakes a deliberate synthesis of a number of critically selected and analyzed sources. Time and again we have observed that his historiography has a fairly high degree of plausibility. More in particular this is true of his approach as an evangelist. In the context of the present volume, the latter fact acquires a heightened significance.

On the basis of the large degree of correspondence in structure, narrative content and phrasing of the shared material, it is generally accepted that the design of the Gospel of Luke, just as Matthew, is based upon Mark. Both Luke and Matthew also insert material from other sources within the framework of Mark. 'Luke's' methodology distinguishes itself at once. Matthew not only interpolates material from elsewhere, but also rearranges numerous portions of Mark. 'Luke', however, maintains the sequence of Mark integrally, merely introducing large blocks of other material at two points (Lk. 6.20–8.3; 9.51–18.14). With this manner of working he cannot avoid giving an impression of eclecticism, but he apparent considered that acceptable in order to be able to maintain the integrity of his sources. His respect for his sources goes so far that he does not even smooth away obvious repetitions (for example, the repeated commissioning of the apostles, Lk. 9 and 10). As to provenance of material, the Gospel is an anthology, or, better, a polyptych with unconnected scenes from various sources.

The evangelist's manner of working can, of course, be checked in detail in the portions parallel to Mark, revealing how faithfully he follows his sources. His most important changes are improvements in the Greek style, the abbreviation of narrative sections, and the toning down of Mark's impassioned manner of expression. In so far as it is possible to check, 'Luke' usually copies the sayings of Jesus literally.

Within the two blocks of inserted material, 'Luke' incorporates more *unique narrative material* than Matthew does. The passages involved include the story of the dead boy from Nain (7.11-17), the anointing by the woman, the report about the women who followed Jesus (7.36–8.3), the Samaritan inn (9.51-56), the house of Mary and Martha (10.38-42), meaningless suffering (13.1-9), the ten lepers (17.1-19), and familiar parables such as the good Samaritan (10.29-37) and the prodigal son (15.11-32). Compared to the other Gospels, the evangelist betrays a certain alertness to the situation of women and of Samaritans. Totally unique to Luke, and thus drawn from further unknown sources, are, finally, the childhood and resurrection stories (Lk. 1–2; 24.13-53). The author had thus at his disposal ample sources besides Mark and the tradition of Jesus' words that he shares with Matthew.

Luke is for this reason extraordinarily significant for the study of the synoptic tradition. While his material is clearly related to what we find in Mark and Matthew, the material unique to him gives us information about an otherwise unknown and singular segment of the tradition. As appears from the listing above, this has partially to do with passages that could be counted as authentic and characteristic of the teachings of Jesus, thus exposing the poverty of our information. If this evangelist could select such material from one or more Gospels unknown to us, then the 'authentic' Gospel tradition was far more extensive than we could imagine on the basis of Mark and Matthew alone.

Not only as preserver of tradition, but also as author, the importance of this evangelist is not to be underestimated. Undoubtedly he wrote with a particular purpose in mind, one which we have attempted to describe in the preceding sections. One should not, however, exaggerate the degree of creative freedom that he took. Unless there are clear indications for doing so, one should not, for example, ascribe various scenes or statements to 'the theology of Luke'. As illustration we take the childhood and resurrection stories, which assume a special place within the whole of the Gospel. 'Historiography' in the strict sense of the word is not applicable here, a statement which at a closer look also holds true for further material which must be entitled 'legendary'. This illuminates a crucial aspect of the diptych: the author is a witness of the miraculous spread of the gospel through the world, which, of course, is at the same time the fulfilling of the Scriptures. 'Historiography' signifies here: writing the history of salvation, and is, therefore, also an interpretation of the Scriptures. It is especially in these passages that the stylistic talent of the author flourishes in the form of Septuagint Greek (see p. 215). The story of the birth of John the Baptist, for example, is written as a counterpart to that of Samuel, including characteristic stylistic details (Lk. 1; 1 Sam. 1). He does not, however, simply imitate the Septuagint: there are important details in the story, such as Elizabeth and Zachariah being prophets, that are only to be explained on the basis of the use of traditional sources (see pp. 218-19). The unforgettable story of those travelling to Emmaus (Lk. 24.13-35) is suffused with the atmosphere of early Christian tradition, in which the motif of the 'breaking of the bread' is eloquently effective. The same context of the liturgy and the history of salvation can be presumed in the story of the Feast of Pentecost (Acts 2). This subtle use of tradition is a characteristic trait of our evangelist.

Like every historiographer, 'Luke' also has his meta-historical assumptions and goals. As proposed earlier, writing history is the synthesizing of observed facts documented in sources into a meaningful whole. The assumptions referred to are contained within this 'meaning'. Without the ascription of significance there is no writing of history, but only a listing of words and occurrences. Historiography means reading a meaning into that which is experienced and committing this to an orderly account. The process involves making choices on the basis of cause and goal, effect and means, responsibility and guilt—and we could go on to speak biblically: suffering and death, promise and fulfilment, exile and redemption. It is not by coincidence that 'Luke's' Gospel, with its self-critical preface, evokes this type of reflection. Every writer of history does nothing other than *interpret* on the basis of extra-historical values and intuitions; this should be admitted and expressed in a foreword and an epilogue, or even in a 'proto-history' and 'post-history'. The difficulty is that the 'rational-objective', positivist historical science usually does not do so. The fact that 'Luke' does, does not make his writing of history inferior, but, in its *modesty*, even more soberly professional. The 'meta-history' of 'Luke's' stories of birth and resurrection reveal the goal, the motivation and hence the criteria of his historiography, thus making his judgments and interpretations verifiable and transparent. In this he has set an example for all time.

In this manner we are led back to the main motifs of the Lukan diptych discussed above: the positive significance of the law, the differentiated depiction of the Pharisees, and the respectful coexistence of Jews and non-Jews. These themes have special significance in the framework of his Gospel, certainly in comparison to the other Gospels. In contrast to the Gospel of Mark in its final form, Luke's attention for the situation of non-Jews does not entail indifference towards the Jews, let alone hostility towards them as in Matthew or John.

Gradually we begin to fathom why 'Luke's' rendering gives the impression of being so balanced and trustworthy. Not only was he literarily gifted and trained, but he could also apply these qualities subtly from his meta-historical point of departure—the vision of one history of salvation for Jews and non-Jews. This he had adopted from Paul, so we have come to suspect. His respect for the sources, including the more or less primitive, written and oral renditions of Jesus' teachings and life, is not only historically and literarily sophisticated, it is apparently also theologically motivated. We could even consider whether in his preface he means to say that he corrects earlier Gospels in their presentation not only in a general sense, but in particular on the point that occupies such a central place in his double work: *the relationship to the Jews and the Jewish law*.

A Pauline Canon

By departing from the canonical order in first treating Paul and thereafter Luke and Acts, a remarkable secondary effect has been achieved. We presumed that the positive attitude towards the Jews in the Lukan double oeuvre is not unrelated to his apparent spiritual affinity with Paul. This traditionally known fact acquires here new relevance. Because these two are the most productive of the New Testament writers, nearly half of the New Testament derives from authors who agree in their respect for Jews and Judaism.

To this we could add the letters written by close co-workers of Paul, the so-called deutero-Pauline epistles: Ephesians, First and Second Timothy and Titus. The First Epistle of Peter could also be reckoned with these, about which we will speak later. Together these encompass more than half of the New Testament; these mutually related writings could be called a *Pauline canon*.

The idea of a Pauline canon existed already in antiquity, but on a completely opposite basis. At the beginning of the second century CE, Marcion defended an exclusively Pauline canon. He accepted only Luke and the epistles of Paul, and even in these he made deletions. According to Marcion, the God of the Old Testament was not the same as the Father of Jesus. In this way he renounced not only the belief in a good creation, but the Old Testament as a whole, and he also rejected the Gospel of Matthew. For this reason he was condemned by the church in Rome (144 CE). In actual fact Marcion's exclusively Pauline canon was based upon a radical anti-Jewish reading of Paul and the Gospel of Luke.

This episode makes it clear that the Pauline canon was a historical reality. It is quite logical that Paul's letters were the first to be collected. Paul's exhortation that his epistles be read aloud in other churches (Col. 4.16) most likely led to the collection of copies of epistles that were considered important. The author of 2 Peter speaks of 'all of the epistles' of Paul, in which he incidentally read 'many incomprehensible things' (2 Pet. 3.15-16). The existence of a Pauline canon is difficult to imagine before the beginning of the second century. In the intervening years written Gospels had appeared on the scene, initially separately from each other. Marcion admitted only Luke and Paul's epistles into his canon. It is not probable that he was the first to lay this link. Because of the affinity of Paul and 'Luke' it is plausible that their writings circulated in the same surroundings. The deutero-Pauline epistles could also have been attached to these. There are examples of mutual influence between Lukan and Pauline texts (1 Cor. 11.24-25 and Lk. 22.19-20; Lk. 10.7 and 1 Tim. 5.18). Thus it is conceivable that in one or more places a 'Pauline collection' emerged. Possibly Marcion was not even so much an innovator as someone who radically held to an older Pauline collection. He read it in an anti-Jewish manner and dismissed everything that did not comply with this. Indirectly, this shows as well that the original 'Pauline canon' presupposed the reading of the Old Testament aloud.

Meanwhile, theologians like Marcion forced the church to form their own canon of writings. The Greek word *kanôn* means 'standard, criterion, rule'; we have encountered this in Paul's writings (Gal. 6.16). In early Christianity, the term was used to designate both the creed or 'rule of faith' and the 'standard' for the authoritative writings. At first there was no demand for such. Just as in Judaism, certain writings acquired authority of their own accord, first in restricted circles and gradually more generally. The same process had taken place with the Old Testament as well. The Septuagint as a collection contains more books than the Hebrew Bible, while originally this need not have indicated a difference in principle (see p. 61). Books acquire authority as a matter of course in the slowly changing practice of a reading community. Only when internal strife arises is one forced to draw a sharp demarcation in the formation of a 'canon'. This raises the question what the rejection of Marcion's 'Pauline' canon entailed for the interpretation of Paul and 'Luke' by the orthodox majority, a weighty question within the context of this book.

The answer is contradictory, and this contradiction will continue to occupy us. With his anti-Jewish reading of Paul and 'Luke', Marcion found himself in good company. He went only one radical step further by introducing an exclusive canon criterion. He was condemned because he rejected the Old Testament and certain apostolic writings that the majority accepted, but not because of his anti-Jewish reading of Paul and Luke, a position shared by many church leaders both before and after him.

A characteristic example is Ignatius, a bishop of Antioch who died as a martyr at the beginning of the second century. His letters to the Asia Minor churches, preserved as a monument to the courage of his faith, testify in a general sense to the heritage of Paul who indeed had accomplished much in Antioch and the surrounding regions. In his relationship towards Judaism, however, Ignatius deflects sharply from Paul:

> Do not go astray in heresies nor in the ancient tales which profit no one. For if we have been living thus far according to Judaism, then we confess not to have received grace. For the devout prophets lived according to Jesus Christ…no longer keeping the Shabbat, but living according to Lord's Day…let us, having become his disciples, learn to live according to Christianity… It is inappropriate to speak of Jesus Christ and to live Jewishly. For it is not so that Christianity believed with Judaism in view, but Judaism with Christianity in view… (*To the Magnesians* 8–10).

To 'live Jewishly' was a taboo for this bishop of a city where Jews and non-Jews traditionally had lived together. For him, Judaism was doomed to be assimilated into non-Jewish Christianity. His consciousness of Christian identity was thus based upon an antithesis with Judaism. Quite literally he placed 'Christianity' opposite to 'Judaism', *christianismos* over against *ioudaismos*. This is anti-Judaism in *optima forma*, and it had a future. The extremely influential works of Eusebius of Caesarea could be counted as representative here (beginning of fourth century). He writes from the same consciousness of identity, though not in the context of a half-tolerated church of martyrs, but from a majority religion supported by the emperor. His church history is an apologetic for Christianity based upon the demonstration of the historical failure of Judaism. The self-assurance with which he appeals to the apostle of the nations and his disciple, 'Luke', his model as historiographer, thus acquires an acrid flavour.

Bitter irony is also to be found in another aspect. There is some reason to assume that Luke as well had connections with Antioch. Not only is the Antiochian church the axis around which the whole book of Acts turns, but the author also has access to specific information concerning it. In addition, Eusebius preserves a tradition according to which Luke himself comes from Antioch (*Church History* 3.4.6). Among Luke's detailed pieces of information is the announcement that 'the disciples were first called Christians in Antioch' (Acts 11.26; see pp. 230-31). On the other hand, the noun 'Christianity' is used for the first time in the passage of the Antiochian bishop just quoted. Perhaps Luke even knew Ignatius. In that case, the church in Antioch, where from the beginning many non-Jews were members, must have undergone a split: on the one side, a group powerful enough to choose Ignatius as bishop and who read Paul in an anti-Jewish manner, and, on the other side, people like Luke, who, in spite of growing tensions, adhered to Paul's vision.

According to the account in Acts, Antioch was the mother city of the apostolate among the nations. Even if the author of this work himself did not hail from that city, it was the crossroads to regions beyond. This was the home base for Paul's missionary journeys; this is where the conflict with Peter about the status of the non-Jewish believers took place; this is where the breach between the Jewish churches and the churches of non-Jews began to take shape. The schism meant the demise of Paul's motto, *'first* for the Jew, but *also* for the Greek'. It would seem logical that the breach first began to be noticeable within the churches of Paul himself. The two important documents concerning his gospel for Jews *and* Greeks—Galatians and Romans—witness to this. Beginning in Antioch, Pauline 'Christianity', as it was called by then, must have split into an *anti-Jewish, Ignatian* wing and a wing that maintained the *Lukan interpretation of Paul.*

The *First Epistle of Peter* is interesting in this relation. While we can not verify whether the apostle thus named dictated this letter himself or not, various passages remind one strongly of Paul's line of reasoning. If we have understood Paul correctly in the previous chapter, this need not exclude a connection to Peter. The epistle was written and delivered by Silvanus, a name mentioned several times by Paul, and it is from 'Babylon', that is, Rome, addressed to churches in northern Asia Minor (1 Pet. 5.12-13; 1.1; see below). An interesting appellation is also 'Mark, my son' (5.13; see pp. 255-56). The text of the epistle itself provides no reason to doubt these identifications. At the end, the readers are encouraged to remain steadfast in suffering and persecution and in this to take 'Christ' as an example (3.18; 4.1, 13)—'Christ' without the definite article, as a proper name. Directly thereafter follows the name that is derived from the Antiochian designation for the believers, with an emphasis that gives the impression of it being a newly acquired distinction of honour: 'Let no one among you suffer as a murderer or a thief...but if it be *as a Christian*, he must not be ashamed, but glorify God *by that name*' (4.15-16). Given the opposition to Rome–Babylon, the epistle as well as the Revelation of John has been dated under the reign of Domitian (c. 95; see pp. 373-74), but a dating under Nero (beginning of the sixties) is not impossible either and concurs better with the facts mentioned earlier. The epistle is, by the way, strongly Old Testamental and Judaeo-Christian in its use of language. With reference to the split suggested above, 1 Peter should not be categorized as belonging to the Ignatian wing, but to the Lukan.

This occasions taking a closer look at the name '*Christian*'. According to Acts, it originated in Antioch (Acts 11.26). A confirmation of this is the earliest known use of the noun 'Christianity' by Ignatius, bishop of Antioch. Both sources are from the end of the first century. 1 Peter, with its apparently new use of 'the name Christian', can be several decades older. Silvanus, who sent the epistle from Rome, was in any case familiar with the use. Possibly he is, then, under an abbreviated form of his name, the same as Silas, who both in Paul's writings and in Acts is often mentioned together with Timothy and, according to Acts, stayed with Paul in Antioch (Acts 15; 17.14; 18.5; 2 Cor. 1.19; 1 Thess. 1.1; 2 Thess. 1.1). The use of the name in the *Didache* (12.4), a writing with a Jewish-Christian background also associated with Antioch, must stem from approximately the same time. The following picture is created: the name 'Christians' appears to have arisen in Antioch, outside of the influence of Paul but in circles with which he worked. In the last decades of the first century, the name became generally adopted among Christians and it could be used in an epistle from Rome to northern Asia Minor. Especially given the use in Acts and in the *Didache*, the name apparently applied originally to Jewish and non-Jewish believers together. For Ignatius, however, 'Christianism' is diametrically opposed to 'Judaism', in line with his anti-Jewish reading of Paul.

We turn now to the deutero-Pauline epistles. Judging from their vocabulary, these are apparently not composed by Paul but by his co-workers, perhaps on the basis of a brief assignment from the apostle himself. Our interest is primarily in their position in the presumed split within Pauline Christianity.

First, the so-called Epistle to Ephesus—'so-called', because textual problems in the superscription lead one to suspect that it originally was an unaddressed circular letter read aloud in various churches, perhaps by Tychicus who delivered it (Eph. 6.21). Significantly, the first, proclamatory half of the epistle is totally dedicated to the equivalent relationship of Jews and non-Jews within the churches. Although once in a while whole sentences appear to draw on Paul's letter to the Colossians, the style diverges occasionally from that of the apostle. The line of reasoning as a whole, however, is quite cognate. Speaking of the 'so-called foreskin' and the 'so-called circumcision' is not alien to Paul, nor that in Christ the law has been 'made ineffectual' (Eph. 2.11, 15; cf. pp. 172, 175-76, 212). The long benediction in the opening portion is noteworthy, and seems to derive largely from the particular usage of the Greek-speaking synagogue (Eph. 1.3-14). The well-known final portion about spiritual armour, in contrast, seems to be rather Essenic, but is also known from Paul (Eph. 6.10-17; Rom 13.12; cf. Isa. 59.17). There is every reason to reckon Ephesians to the 'Lukan' wing of Pauline Christianity.

1 Timothy is formulated in quite general terms and does not much resemble a real letter. The language deflects clearly from that of Paul. 'Paul' calls himself 'the teacher of non-Jews' (2.7), after which follow several instructions concerning the worship service, in particular in regard to women, and this brings to mind the Jewish-Christian 'customs' in 1 Cor. 11 and 14 (see p. 200). Another passage is clearly related to what Paul writes about preachers who may 'live off the gospel', with a reference to the 'threshing ox' (1 Tim. 5.18; see 1 Cor. 9.8-9; Deut. 25.4). It is remarkable, however, that the saying of Jesus about livelihood that follows is quoted, in the version of 'Luke', as though it is Holy Writ (1 Tim. 5.18; Lk. 10.7). This deviates entirely from the parallel passage in Paul and it is difficult to conceive of as being his, in so far as he must have been familiar with the oral transmission of postbiblical teachings (see p. 199). Various things suggest that it must have been written in the entourage of Paul by one not familiar with Jewish customs. That is, however, not sufficient basis for classifying it with the anti-Jewish wing of Pauline Christianity.

2 Timothy is a real epistle and in its structure shows affinity with Paul's own epistles. Many details betray precise knowledge concerning the circumstances of Timothy and Paul. Typically Jewish-Christian are the mention of Paul's devout forefathers (2 Tim. 1.3), the emphasis on Jesus' Davidic descent (2.8; cf. Rom 1.3), and the comparison of certain false teachers with legendary opponents of Moses (2 Tim. 3.8). The request of Paul to Timothy to take along the books that he had left in Troas, 'especially the (costly) parchments' (2 Tim. 4.13), is touching. This can hardly have been made up. There is actually nothing that would prevent us from assuming that this letter was dictated by Paul himself in Rome (1.17) and addressed to his Jewish disciple and co-worker Timothy. If it is to be classified, it definitely belongs in the Lukan camp.

The situation is quite different with the *Epistle to Titus*. Titus is the name of Paul's companion who as non-Jew figured at the council of the apostles in Jerusalem (see p. 204). The one thus addressed in this epistle receives a number of instructions for church order, for the benefit of the church on Crete (Tit. 1.5), which are reminiscent of 1 Timothy in style and content. Conspicuous among these is the rhetoric against the 'undisciplined chatterboxes...especially those of the circumcision':

> Reject them resolutely, so that they might become sound in the faith, and attach no value to Jewish tales and commandments of men who stray away from the truth. To the pure all things are pure; to those however who are tainted and unbelieving nothing is pure, but their mind and con-sciousness are tainted (Tit. 1.10-15).

This outburst against certain Jewish-Christian opponents reminds one of Colossians, Philippians and Galatians, but evokes an anti-Jewish reading to an even greater extent. Unmistakably directed against the Jewish law is the saying, 'To the pure all things are pure.' This appears to be a radical flattening out of Paul's subtle statement, 'Nothing is impure in itself, but it is impure for the one who views it as impure' (Rom. 14.14; p. 206). While Paul means that Jewish 'sensitivity' deserves respect, here such sensitivities are condemned in general as Jewish fairy-tales. The epistle is thus marked as anti-Jewish and belonging to the Ignatian camp. There are even literal correspondences between the 'Jewish tales' and the 'old tales' in the above quote from Ignatius. If Paul did indeed commission the letter himself, then in any case the writer has made his intention much more radical. If such be the case, the Ignatian interpretation would have taken root even among Paul's own co-workers.

The conclusion is that the First Epistle of Peter and most of the deutero-Pauline epistles follow the Lukan line. In the major part of the Pauline collection—the crystallized core that came to constitute more than half of the New Testament—Christianity is not contrasted with Judaism. The Epistle to Titus, however, documents the early presence of the Ignatian, anti-Jewish interpretation within that milieu. We return thus to the intuition expressed at the beginning of Chapter 4 that the interpretation of Paul is the Archimedian point for the reinterpretation of the New Testament as a whole. The 'Pauline canon' here redis-covered places the reader for the choice of how he will read Paul: Ignatian or Lukan, anti-Jewishly demarcating oneself, or in respect and sympathy for the Jews and the Jewish law.

Chapter 6

MARK AND MATTHEW

Although Mark is presumably the oldest written Gospel, we have post-poned discussing this document until this point. The theme of the present volume is not the literary-historical connections between the Gospels, but their relationship to Judaism. Within that approach, it is more fitting to have considered Paul first and then Luke and Acts. Matthew, with its close affinity to Mark, will be treated here as well. The individual character of the two Gospels comes out better by a comparison with one another. Because of the clear relatedness, analo-gies between them and the third 'synoptic' Gospel, Luke, will also be repeatedly indicated.

An historical-literary approach will again be employed. We will read the development of the Gospels in relation to the earliest history of Christians and Jews, and vice versa. Attention will once more be given to partially the same material as in Chapter 3, but this time with a focus not on the figure of Jesus, but on the evangelists and their final texts.

Mark: The First Written Gospel?

Eusebius, the ever-resourceful historiographer of the church, quotes a report about the origin of the Gospels transmitted by Bishop Papias, who in turn says to have received it from 'the elder, John'. Papias flour-ished during the first half of the second century, so that this John must be from the end of the first century. According to this tradition, the Gospel of Mark was the first written record of the words and deeds of Jesus. Previous to this, and also long afterwards, Jesus' words and deeds were passed on orally by the apostles and their successors. Papias relates as well how that took place in the case of Peter, and how Mark, his interpreter, compiled a first Gospel from his words:

> This, too, did the elder [John] say: Mark, who had been the interpreter of
> Peter, wrote down carefully everything that he could remember of what
> the Lord had said and done, but not in sequence. For he had not heard
> and followed the Lord himself, but, as I have said, Peter, later; and the
> latter adjusted his teachings according to the need, without, however,
> presenting an orderly whole of the words of the Lord. Therefore Mark
> has not acted wrongly by writing down certain things as he remembered
> them (Eusebius, *Church History* 3.39.15).

According to another tradition that Eusebius cites, Mark set himself to writing at the insistence of the Christians in Rome for whom 'the unwritten instruction of the gospel of God' that Peter had entrusted to them did not suffice (2.15.2). 'Mark' is probably 'John surnamed Mark', Barnabas's nephew and temporarily Paul's co-worker (Col. 4.10; Acts 12.12; 15.38-39; 1 Pet. 5.13).

Viewed within the broader context, these traditions have a certain degree of plausibility. Of interest is the detail concerning the manner in which Peter instructed: in his teachings he cited the words and deeds of Jesus in a constantly varying sequence. Papias relates as well that in his day, at the end of the first century, preference was given to the 'living voice' rather than to written gospel texts (Eusebius, *Church History* 3.39.4), reminiscent of the oral manner of instruction reflected in rabbinic literature. Indications of an oral treatment of the words of Jesus occur also in the writings of the ex-Pharisee, Paul (see p. 193). The intermediation of an interpreter was an important element of oral rabbinic instruction in the synagogue and the house of study (see pp. 40, 78). The origin of rabbinic literature is therefore instructive in relation to for the emergence of the Gospels, in the first place, of Mark.

The collections that rabbinic literature comprises are the written record of instruction that for a long time had been orally reproduced and passed on. The fluidity and vicissitude of this oral tradition is apparent time and again when certain textual units occur in various collections in divergent forms. The different portions of rabbinic tradition were, incidentally, not all fluid and variable to the same degree. The Mishnah is the result of a process of several generations of intentional redaction, for which the written record was probably only a final step. Such a purposeful recording had to do with the central authority ascribed to this collection, and this did not apply to the narrative midrash. By analogy, the multiformity of the gospel tradition can as well be seen as the deposit of a flexible oral tradition.

The fact remains that there is no direct confirmation that the Gospel known to us descends directly from the Mark mentioned by Papias; nonetheless, this Gospel does have traits that bring Papias's account to mind. Compared to Matthew and Luke, Mark is characterized by greater drama and expansiveness in the description of Jesus' miraculous ministry. Furthermore, his Greek is somewhat careless and at times exhibits clear traces of being a rough translation from Aramaic or Hebrew. It cannot be said that the Gospel has a distinct structure, except for the obvious ascent to Jerusalem in the second half of the Gospel. Compared to the other two synoptic Gospels, Mark resembles most an improvised written report. If to this is added the consensus of scholars that some form of Mark lies at the basis of both Matthew and Luke, then it is reasonable to view this Gospel as the first written record of the oral gospel tradition. In what follows, the Gospel known to us will be simply designated as 'Mark'.

A different matter is the fact that the extant text of Mark shows traces of repeated editing, for example, a passage in which information has been inserted concerning Jewish customs for the readers who are not familiar with Judaism (Mk 7.3-4). In the ensuing centuries, the text continued to be revised. If this indeed is the oldest written Gospel, the form known to us is not the original one and probably also not the one that Matthew and Luke had in front of them. A Gospel, even the 'oldest', is first and foremost a community text, and carries the traces of an eventful history that stretches over various generations and divergent milieus.

Mark and Judaism

In the textual texture of Mark there are traces both of the Jewish background and of estrangement from it. To a large extent, the Jewish background was exposed in Chapter 3, where we focussed on the historical figure of Jesus and his milieu. We now direct our attention to the text of Mark as it lies before us. Its individual characteristics appear, however, even more clearly if we keep in mind the contrast between the final text and its preliminary stages.

A good example is offered by the statement of Jesus: 'The Shabbat has come about for man, and not man for the Shabbat, therefore the son of man is Lord also of the Shabbat' (Mk 2.27-28). The first part is found only in Mark, the sequel occurs also in Matthew and Luke: 'The son of man is Lord of the Shabbat' (Mt. 12.8; Lk. 6.5). The latter has a christological tone in comparison to which the first part is a general maxim. Possibly Matthew and Luke left this part out because the dignity ascribed to man might diminish the uniqueness of the son of man. If so, on the basis of its development the saying would belong to the oldest layer of tradition, that is, the milieu of Jesus. This is indirectly confirmed by a corresponding saying that in rabbinic literature is ascribed to R. Shimon ben Menasia (pp. 92, 153). The parallelism in wording and background could counterbalance the fact that this saying was only written down a century or two later, and thus witness to the presence of the earliest transmission from the milieu of Jesus in the final text of the evangelist.

In surveying the final text of Mark, in contrast to the other Gospels, surprisingly enough Judaism and the Jewish law hardly appear to constitute a theme. Luke emphasizes the positive importance of the law, while in John, as we will observe, the opposite is true, and Matthew gives a divided image. In Mark the issue is neutral, with the exception of two trenchant passages on the Shabbat and the laws of purity, portions of halakah that characteristically distinguish Jews from non-Jews. Without undue emphasis, a third important item of the law—divorce—reveals the main interest of the Gospel as a whole: the situation of non-Jews. This leads to a far-reaching conclusion in connection with what was stated above: if Mark indeed represents the first written Gospel, this writing down of the Gospel tradition was apparently undertaken for the sake of non-Jewish believers.

The matter of divorce was an area of Jewish lawgiving that was not a point of Christian polemics. On the contrary, Jesus' standpoint, which became normative within the apostolic tradition, lines up with the strictest position of his day (Chapters 2 and 3). For this reason it is a good aspect to begin with.

According to Jesus' position, which he shared with John the Baptist and the Essenes, the marriage bond remains as long as both partners live, and he who marries a divorced woman commits adultery. This phrasing is based on Jewish law, where the man is the acting party. Hellenistic law, which was current in the early Roman Empire, recognized an informal marriage that became effective without ceremony by living together and that could be broken by either partner, that is, by the woman as well, by departing. In well-to-do circles women took the initiative to dissolve even formally contracted marriages (see pp. 100, 150-51). This Hellenistic juridical situation is presumed in the phrasing that Mark gives to Jesus' prohibition of divorce: 'He who sends away his wife and marries another commits adultery with her, and *she, too, if she sends away her husband* and marries another, commits adultery' (Mk 10.12). The adaptation to the situation of non-Jews corresponds to that of Paul (1 Cor. 7.10-11; see p. 197), but is stated more emphatically and more generally. In neither case is there an anti-Jewish implication. The adjustment does not need to have been made very late, considering that Paul himself also wrote comparably at the beginning of the fifties. Likewise, a non-Jewish target group could be assumed already in the preliminary oral stages of the Gospel.

Concerning the Shabbat, the situation is different. In the synoptic accounts of healing, in the opinion of the Pharisees Jesus performed no deeds that were in conflict with the Shabbat (see pp. 153-56, 219-20). According to Luke, they consequently reacted only with surprise and bewilderment. If there would have been a transgression of the law in the opinion of some, then this was not considered a capital offence, not even in Essene tradition. The conclusion of Jesus' discussions on the Shabbat in Mark must therefore reflect a very specific later situation: 'And...the Pharisees directly held a meeting about him with the Herodians in order to kill him' (Mk 3.6). Where does this fierce anti-Pharisaic shift come from? Though a non-Jewish milieu comes to mind, such an environment need not necessarily result in an anti-Pharisaic attitude, as we have learned from the example of the prohibition to divorce. This final statement, however, accentuates the conflict, as though in a healing on the Shabbat the Pharisees anticipate the deadly animosity in Jerusalem. It implies a milieu in intense conflict with the Pharisaic leaders. Further, it is remarkable that the Pharisees do not play such a hostile role in Mark's passion story. The ending of this story of healing is the most hostile passage towards the Jews in Mark.

The account of the washing of hands before regular meals (Mk 7.1-23) is also complicated. The general obligation to wash one's hands, as well as the notion that food can be impure in a derived sense, was maintained in Jesus' day by certain Pharisees with whom he apparently did not agree (see pp. 96-97, 156-59). The following two digressions in the account by Mark witness both to a non-Jewish context and to a conflict with Jews or Jewish leaders:

> And when (the Pharisees) saw that some of his disciples ate their bread with unclean, that is unwashed hands—for the Pharisees and all Jews do not eat unless they have washed their hands at the fist, holding fast to the

> tradition of the elders, and also from the market, unless they have immersed, they do not eat, and many other things there are which they hold from tradition, immersing of cups, and jugs, and kettles [and beds] —and the Pharisees ask him...
>
> And...his disciples asked him...And he said to them... Do you not know that nothing which enters a man from the outside can make him unclean? For it goes not to his heart but to his stomach and it comes out on the privy, making all foods clean (Mk 7.2-5, 17-19).

The digression on the Jewish customs of cleanliness in the first fragment is not only conspicuously extensive but is also rather awkward. The expression which is here translated 'at the fist' is hardly comprehensible in Greek. Furthermore, the mention of the 'tradition of the elders' lacks subtlety in its anticipation of v. 5. The 'immersion' in relation to 'the market' is far from clear. Does it mean that the persons immersed themselves, which was the custom only of extremely devout ones, or that the utensils or foodstuff bought at the market were immersed? In the parallel passage in Matthew (15.2-3), the entire portion is lacking. All evidence points to this being an insertion into an older account, intended to instruct the non-Jewish reader about these unfamiliar customs. It is, however, in no wise anti-Jewish.

In the second fragment, Jesus clarifies the saying about 'what comes from outside the person'. The greatest difficulty lies in the phrase translated as 'making all foods clean' (*katharizōn*). Modern translations here follow the older manuscripts, which as a rule have the better text, and read '*thus he declared all foods to be clean*'. That would seem to mean that Jesus did away with the dietary laws, a biblical cornerstone of Jewish law observance (see pp. 98-99). If this is the correct reading, Jesus is here portrayed as being anti-Jewish.

In itself, it is difficult enough to conceive of Jesus dispensing with the dietary regulations. More specifically, this is not to be reconciled with his reproach, n.b. in the very same account, that the Pharisees on the authority of their tradition did away with the biblical commandment (Mk 7.13; see p. 157-58). The grammatical construction in the indicated text version is also rather strained. There is, however, a somewhat different text in most of the later manuscripts that amounts to the rendering that the natural process of digestion 'makes all foods clean' (*katharizon*). This concurs with Jesus' earlier described position, namely, a rejection of the Pharisaic principle of the derived impurity of food (p. 158). The manuscripts with this version are in general less authoritative, but they do counterbalance the contradictory content of the other version.

It is equally difficult to conceive of the text being altered later to correct the contradiction with the biblical dietary laws. The opposite is more logical, and besides historically plausible. The influential church father Origen (third century) says in his commentary on the parallel passage in Matthew that Jesus teaches us that the Mosaic dietary laws from Leviticus and Deuteronomy are not meant literally, as claimed by the Jews and Ebionites (a Jewish-Christian group, see p. 280). The statement that 'not what goes into the mouth makes a person unclean' is after all elucidated by Jesus in Mark with the words '*while he made all foods clean*'. For the spiritualizing of the dietary laws, Origen appeals to the Epistle to Titus: 'To the pure all things are pure, but to the impure and unbelieving nothing is pure' (Tit. 1.15; Origen, *Commentary on Matthew* 11.12). In the preceding chapter we related this passage to the Ignatian, anti-Jewish interpretation of Paul (see p. 253). We observe now that this interpretation was a criterion for the Gospels as well. Origen was familiar with the 'anti-Mosaic' version of Mark, so that the adjustment must date from before his time.

Through these examples we can observe in the history of Mark an increasing distance from Judaism, which could signify various things. The account containing the discussion on divorce, Shabbat and laws of cleanliness could have been adjusted where necessary for the non-Jewish audience without implying anti-Jewish sentiment, as is apparent in the case of divorce. The explanation about the Jewish purification customs need not be read anti-Jewishly either. Shabbat and purity, however, were loaded issues in the relationship between Jews and non-Jews, and in these passages more was involved. A dismissal of the dietary laws on principle was read into Jesus' statement about cleanliness, and the discussion about the Shabbat received an inexplicably fierce anti-Pharisaic intensity. In the final phase of the text, a church is speaking that undergirds its non-Jewish lifestyle on the basis of principle by reading a general rejection of the law into the discussions about its details. At that point, *the contrast with Judaism* had become the dominant criterion.

If our interpretation of Mark were to be based upon this criterion, then the process of becoming more radical could derive its logic from the broader context of the passage. A progressive movement from the first to the second miraculous feeding of the multitudes is observable, in

which the theme is consistently that of *bread* (Mk 6.30–8.21). Following the first feeding of the multitude, there is a discussion about washing hands before 'eating bread'. Thereafter comes the conversation with
the Greek woman with the mention of 'the little children's crumbs of
bread' (7.24-30). After the healing of her child, the second feeding
takes place and Jesus warns against the 'leaven of the Pharisees' (7.31–
8.21). In this manner, on the basis of doing away with the biblical
dietary laws, the criticism of the Pharisaic tradition would clear the way
for the non-Jewish woman.

We could, however, also read this sequence in another manner (cf.
also pp. 161-62) by not following the criterion of contrast to Judaism
and taking into account the successive phases of the text. Jesus' clash
with certain Pharisaic standpoints can be left as it is, as well as his
surprise at the perserverance of the faith of the Greek woman, without
casting doubt on his faithfulness to the Torah. The passage about
Jewish purification customs and about 'making all foods clean' does not
force an anti-Jewish reading either. An unmistakable anti-Pharisaic and
anti-Jewish intent arose only with the accentuation of the discussion on
the Shabbat and with the version 'thus he made all foods clean'. If
we isolate those adjustments, we can read the Gospel of Mark as it
apparently was from the beginning: a moving, popular description of
'the gospel of Jesus' for non-Jewish believers.

The Gospel of Mark has always stood in the shadow of its more
subtle synoptic brothers, yet it deserves our sympathy and attention
because of its unpretentious rendering of the deeds and words of Jesus.
The lack of schematic arrangement, the irregularity of the Greek, and
the literary unevenness are all part of the bargain. The lack of polish is
unprompted and transparent and makes the testimony of the Gospel
more true to life, thus strengthening the probability of the assumption
that Mark reflects the first attempt at a written Gospel.

A serious problem is formed by the anti-Jewish alterations in the text.
This brings to mind the split that, in the previous chapter, we presumed
to have taken place within Pauline Christianity. It could be that this
correspondence is not coincidental. If Mark originally was intended for
non-Jewish Christians, then a relation to the Pauline churches is natural.
The traditional ascription of the Gospel to Mark, the co-worker of Paul
and Peter, points indeed in the direction of this milieu. The effect of
these speculations is in any case that the present text of Mark presents
us with a choice. Are we going to read anti-Jewishly, as did the writer

of the Epistle to Titus, as did bishop Ignatius, and as later Origen did? Or are we to take distance from the anti-Jewish editing of the Gospel and to read on the basis of the vision of Paul and Luke, with respect and sympathy for the Jews and their law?

Matthew's Revision of Mark

Reading Matthew and Mark together compels one to recognize a close literary relationship. The only question can be that of precedence. The church father Augustine maintained that Mark was a kind of excerpt of Matthew that omitted much of Jesus' teachings and embellished the stories of the miracles, thus pointing out two prominent differences between the two Gospels. The consensus in historical criticism assumes the opposite, namely, that Matthew, like Luke, is based on Mark. The classic proof of this is that in their main outlines both Gospels do not concur with one another in deviating from the sequence in Mark. The extra teaching material in Matthew, which partially is parallel to Luke, must in that case stem from another source. Even then there remains much to be explained, such as the 'minor agreements' where Matthew and Luke together diverge from the phrasing in Mark. Finally, the mutual influence did not end after the 'synoptic Gospels' had come into being, and the final text of Mark, for example, was in turn influenced by Matthew and Luke. We shall not linger at the many refinements of the theory, but merely repeat that the Gospels were community texts with a complicated and continuously interwoven history.

If once settled that Matthew qua material and structure is based upon Mark, then the way is free to observe Matthew's own creation, here again speaking quasi-naively of Matthew without quotation marks. Lacking further confirmation, we must leave the ascription to 'Matthew, the tax collector' (Mt. 9.9; 10.3) for what it is: a later legend. In reality here again it is not a matter of one author, but a lengthy process of redaction. Besides the basic text of Mark, apparently other written texts were used as well as oral traditions, and this process must have extended over several generations and milieus.

In the first place, it is indisputable that the structure of Matthew purposefully digresses from that of Mark. At strategic points in the Gospel, five lengthy orations of Jesus are inserted: the Sermon on the Mount (Mt. 5–7), the address at the commissioning of the apostles (ch. 10), the speech of the parables (ch. 13), the discourse about sin and forgiveness (ch. 18), and the double oration against the scribes and about the last things (chs. 23–25). These all end with a formula like 'and it happened when Jesus had ended these words...' (Mt. 7.28; 11.1; 13.53; 19.1; 26.1). In contrast to the imposing healer he is in Mark, Jesus is here portrayed as a 'teacher with authority' (Mt. 7.29). Many of these words of Jesus correspond to those in Luke, with characteristic differences: Matthew has less of a tendency to succinctness and allows for more Semitic-sounding figurative language and terms.

This brings us to a second characteristic. In the five orations, Jesus comes to the fore not only as a 'teacher with authority' but as a Jewish teacher. Besides numerous Semitic-sounding terms, the Sermon on the Mount contains the most conspicuous expression of Jesus' explicit faithfulness to the Torah. Numerous correspondences with rabbinic literature can be pointed out, as is also the case with the address at the dispatching of the disciples and the speech of parables. The passage on forgiveness resembles non-Pharisaic forms of Judaism, in particular the Essene writings, while the discourse on the last things sounds more Pharisaic–rabbinic. Characteristic of Matthew is the Jewish–scribal emphasis, introduced perhaps during the first editing of the basic text of Mark. An eloquent example is the designation 'Father in the heavens', in which the plural 'heavens' reminds one of a translation of the Hebrew *šāmayîm*. This expression does indeed occur frequently in rabbinic literature; it is found but once in Mark (11.25), never in Luke or John—but 11 times in Matthew.

A third characteristic of Matthew's redaction of Mark is that the material is reorganized according to content. As in much ancient literature, the result is not a completely rigorous division. Nonetheless, there is a great difference with Mark, and, therefore, also with Luke, because the latter leaves the sequence of Mark much more intact. After the first great oration, the Sermon on the Mount (chs. 5–6), Matthew groups together (chs. 8–9) a number of healings and miracles that are scattered throughout Mark. Thereupon follows the commissioning of the apostles (Mt. 10), a chapter over the particular nature of Jesus' work in relationship to John the Baptist (ch. 11), a clash with the Pharisees (ch. 12) and a series of parables (ch. 13). This order appears to reflect a deliberate plan. If we view the beatitudes as a summary of Jesus' gospel of the coming Kingdom, then chs. 5–9 as a whole function as an elaboration of the three elements of Jesus' work summarized in Mt. 4.23: *preaching* (5.1-16), *teaching* (5.17–7.28) and *healing* (8, 9). The commissioning of the apostles is an expansion of that same work (cf. 9.35). To the extent that authentic traits of Jesus' work occur, Matthew moves within the framework of the Jewish-Christian tradition.

A fourth characteristic is formed by the so-called 'fulfilment texts'. Scattered throughout the entire Gospel are such expressions as, 'This all happened so that it would be accomplished what was spoken by the prophet' (Mt. 1.22), and each time an extensive quotation from the prophets or the Psalms follows. Although this phenomenon is also present in the other Gospels, in Matthew it is given special emphasis. Consistently, the quote from the prophets enables the evangelist to provide a commentary on his own account. In doing so he clearly chooses a position outside of his story and steps somewhat to the fore. The choice of position diverges strongly from the customary hidden-ness of the evangelist behind his text. A ripened stage of development of the text is hereby suggested, a suggestion that becomes stronger if note is taken of the content. The quotes from the prophets are intended to undergird the Messianic confession of Jesus' followers. The com-mentary thus assumes polemic aspect: Jesus' being Messiah must evi-dently be 'proven' in the face of internal or external contestation. Are we to envision a conflict with other Jews and with Pharisaic leaders?

The latter is clearly the context of the fifth characteristic, the caustic polemics against the 'scribes and Pharisees', which contrasts with both Mark and Luke and will be further elaborated in the following section. A polemic with the Pharisees is certainly imaginable within a Jewish environment and is, for example, to be compared with the writings from Qumran.

A sixth and final characteristic of Matthew, however, betrays a dif-ferent tendency. Alongside clear Jewish and Jewish-Christian accents in this Gospel there is a surprising turning towards the non-Jews and a turning away from the Jews, even with a marked anti-Jewish accent. The effect is a confusing contradictoriness. It is difficult to imagine that these divergent accents arose simultaneously. A remarkable shift must have taken place in the last stage of development.

A provisionary picture of the stages of development of the Gospel can now be sketched. The evangelist found a starting point in Mark's summary of Jesus' activities. We do not know precisely what form this had, but in any case a period of oral transmission must have preceded it. If we are to call the original oral tradition the *first* stage, then the proto-Mark unknown to us represents the *second* stage. The Matthaean evangelist then went to work, inserting long portions of Jesus' teachings drawn from the tradition of Jesus' words and added in accordance with the structure that he now introduced. Thus the *third*, characteristic layer of the Gospel emerged. In the meantime, circumstances had changed. The 'Jewish church' in which the Gospel was transmitted had come into open conflict with the Pharisees. This is also reflected in the third layer. During the *fourth* and final stage, the Gospel ended up in a non-Jewish church and the interests of the non-Jews were emphasized to the detriment of the Jews. More about this will be said later.

In this regard, the references of the church fathers to the 'Hebrew Gospels' or 'the Gospel of the Hebrews', which were held in honour among Jewish Christians, apparently in divergent versions, are significant. The term 'Hebrew' could refer to the fact that the Gospel involved belonged to the Jewish Christians, without excluding the possibility of an Aramaic or Greek text. Another report of interest is given by Papias, who was quoted earlier, namely, that Matthew had written his Gospel in Hebrew (Eusebius, *Church History* 3.24.6; 3.39.16). We know none of these texts and are unable to judge what they had in common. Further, there are quite confused reports that the 'Hebrew Gospel' somewhat corresponded to Matthew (Epiphanius, *Panarion* 28.5.1; 30.12.7; 30.13.2; cf. Jerome, *Commentary on Matthew* 12.13). These reports suggest that there was a Gospel written in Hebrew or Aramaic that was related to Matthew in one way or another.

The Gospel of Matthew known to us, however, is based upon Mark or a proto-form of Mark, and that was in all probability a Greek text. This limits the possibilities of the relationship of the Matthew text known to us to a 'Hebrew proto-Matthew'. One possibility is that Mark was first translated back into Hebrew or Aramaic, that then the characteristic Matthaean material was inserted, and that this 'Hebrew Matthew' was subsequently translated again into Greek. So much translation back and forth is, however, unlikely, and, besides, the literal correspondences between the present Mark and Matthew indicate the contrary. The possibility remains that the 'Hebrew Matthew' circulated in Greek or was translated into Greek, and was as such integrated into the 'primal Mark', thus resulting in the basic form of the present Gospel of Matthew.

The 'Hebrew Matthew' of the church fathers cannot therefore be more than the source of the typically Matthaean material known to us, which in particular comprises Jesus' teachings and besides partially corresponds to Luke. In terms of our model of development, the third layer of Matthew would be based upon Mark and the Matthaean primal source translated into Greek. The Semitic characteristics of the final text of Matthew are well conceivable as being derived from this Greek Matthaean primal source. The bitter conflict with 'scribes and Pharisees' is also not difficult to imagine. A Jewish-Christian context in fierce contention with the Pharisees is suggested hereby. The turning away from the Jews must indeed be ascribed to the fourth and final phase of the Gospel.

Jesus' Enemies in Mark and Matthew

Our next theme is relevant to all of the Gospels, but provides extra relief to the comparison of Mark and Matthew. The question of who are indicated as the mortal enemies of Jesus, and whether this designation is differentiated or general in nature, is an effective touchstone for the attitude of the Gospels towards the Jews. Dependent on the exacerbation of the relationship, the image of the other group becomes more antagonistic. On the other hand, not all debates need lead to enmity, nor does all enmity of necessity end in violence. Jesus' discussions with the Pharisees are not infrequently open and even friendly, as we noticed in the Gospel of Luke (Lk. 7.36-50; 14.1-6). In this regard Matthew, in comparison to Mark, shows a clear generalizing tendency, a propensity towards lumping together all of the different opponents of Jesus.

An evaluation of this requires insight into the diverse factions of Jewish society of that day, in particular into the institutions and functions having to do with the temple. A discussion of the Pharisees and Sadducees was given in Chapter 1. Concerning the *Pharisees* it can be added that, as a social movement, they apparently cannot be identified completely with the teachers of the law and the scribes, who will be discussed below and who can be viewed as the actual predecessors of the 'rabbis' or masters. It could be that the Pharisaic movement to a great extent was determined by the 'fellowships' mentioned in Chapter 1, whose goal was the communal practice of the law and the celebration of Shabbat and festivals. The movement appeared to have had a political dimension as an opposition party to the Sadducees (cf. Josephus, *War* 1.107-12). The relation between such aspects remains unclear due to the nature and deficiency of our sources.

Scribes

This term is an indication not of a movement but of a *function*. The Greek word *grammateus* has the general significance 'clerk' and usually means 'secretary' or 'administrator'. Thus in Acts 19.35, the *grammateus* of Ephesus is mentioned, from the context evidently the secretary or mayor of the city. A *grammateus*, an 'administrator', functioned also as an adjunct of the temple commander in Jerusalem (Josephus, *Ant.* 20.208-209; see p. 269). The function *grammateus* also occurs in inscriptions from synagogues, where it apparently again means something like clerk or administrator. This functional aspect must be understood as present in the habitual translation 'scribe', which we shall use in what follows.

The Hebrew equivalent is *sōpēr*, which occurs already in the Old Testament. Thus we find a 'scribe of the king' (2 Kgs 12.11), Baruch the 'scribe' of the prophet Jeremiah (Jer. 36.32), and Ezra the priest and 'scribe in matters of the commandments of the Lord' at the Persian court (Ezra 7.11). This ancient administrative function seems to offer an explanation for the rabbinic designation of *soferim* for certain leaders from ancient times. In rabbinic usage, with reference to contemporaries, the word does not signify 'teacher of the law', but actually 'scribe' or 'teacher'.

The restricted technical significance of *grammateus* becomes even more clear in Acts 23.9 where 'certain scribes of the party of the Pharisees' are in opposition to the Sadducees. Somewhat the same happens in Mk 2.16, which speaks of 'the scribes of the Pharisees' (cf. Lk. 5.30). One may presume apparently that there were also 'scribes' of the Sadducees. The regular appearance of 'chief priests and scribes' (see p. 271) together seems to support this surmise.

In the New Testament 'scribes' evidently also have to do with the Scriptures. Compare the question of Jesus, 'How can the *scribes* say that the Christ is a son of David?' (Mk 12.35; cf. 12.28, 32). Jesus warns as well for the 'scribes' who are fond of their own honour but do not pursue righteousness heartily (Mk 12.38). In contrast to the 'scribes', as the Gospel tradition relates, Jesus taught 'with authority' (Mk 1.11; Mt. 7.29). Matthew also tells of a 'scribe (*grammateus*) who had become a disciple of the Kingdom of Heaven' (Mt. 13.52).

A related Greek term, *nomikos*, 'scholar of the law', occurring particularly in Luke, often instead of the *grammateus* of Mark and Matthew (Mt. 22.35; Lk. 7.30; 10.25; 11.45-46, 52-53; 14.3), also indicates some sort of functionary. A third term is used only in Luke: *nomodidaskalos*, literally 'law teacher'. In Lk. 5.17 'Pharisees and law scholars' are mentioned, and in Acts 5.34 we encounter the familiar 'Pharisee from the Sanhedrin called Gamaliel, a scholar of the law, honoured among all the people'. It is clear that 'Pharisee' and 'scholar of the law' do not coincide, although both are applicable to Gamaliel.

Chief Priests
This term is vague and flexible. The singular indicates the functioning high priest, in Greek *archiereus*, of which there was, of course, but one. He performed the most holy transactions in the worship service and was likewise head of the Council. The plural, *archiereis*, usually translated 'chief priests', were apparently the still-living predecessors of the high priest as well as their immediate family, in other words, the priestly aristocracy. These were also usually members of the Council and formed the core of the small but powerful 'party of the Sadducees' (Acts 23.6).

In the previous chapter we saw that, according to Luke and Acts, which within the New Testament give the most exact information, these were the sworn enemies of Jesus and the apostles. The apostles were made prisoners by 'the priests and the temple magistrate and the Sadducees', or more in particular by 'their administrators, elders, and scribes…and Annas the high priest, Caiaphas, John, Alexander, and all who were of the high priestly lineage' (Acts 4.1, 5-6). A chapter further on it is 'the high priest and all of his, that is the party (*hairesis*) of the Sadducees', or 'the temple magistrate and the chief priests' (Acts 5.17, 24).

The 'temple magistrate' (*stratēgos tou hierou*), whose eminent, well-described function is also known from Josephus and the Mishnah, was the right-hand man of the high priest and had command over the temple guards. In the Mishnah he is designated by the old Babylonian administrative term *segen*, 'overseer' (Ezra 9.2), or *s⁼gan ha-kōh⁼nîm*, 'overseer of the priests', and he appears sometimes to have been an adherent of the Pharisees (*m. Yom.* 4.1; *m. Pes.* 1.6). A Zealot-minded holder of this office gave the actual thrust to the revolt against Rome in 66 CE (Josephus, *War* 2.409-10). His adjunct, a *grammateus* or 'administrator', has already been mentioned. The temple guards, called *stratēgoi*, 'head men', maintained order in and around the temple, and they are the ones who went out against Jesus 'with swords and sticks', together with the 'chief priests' and the 'elders' (Lk. 22.4, 52).

The Elders and the Council

The Greek *presbuteroi*, 'elders', is the consistent translation of the Hebrew *z^{e}kēnîm*, literally 'bearded ones'. This pre-eminently patriarchal term signifies in the Old Testament not only the hair that clothes the face, but also the authority vested in a person. Whether all 'elders' in the Graeco-Roman period still wore beards is questionable. In any case, it is certain that they were members of the highest administrative and judicial organ as prominent non-priests, and that they were not all aloof aristocrats. 'Joseph of Arimathea, a prominent member of the Council who himself also expected the Kingdom of God' requested the body of Jesus from Pilate, wound it in linen and buried it (Mk 15.43-46). According to a tradition in the Gospel of John, he did this together with Nicodemus, a Pharisee and probably also member of the Council (Jn 19.39; 3.1). Yet a third Pharisaic Councillor did not maintain an attitude of rejection toward Jesus and his followers—Gamaliel the Elder (Acts 5.34).

There are various theories about the nature and function of the Council. The difficulty again is that the sources use several terms, each with its own fluidity. Thus there is the Greek appellation *gerousia*, 'council of elders', *boulē*, 'council', and *sunhedrion*, 'court session', alongside the Hebrew *k^{e}nesset ha-gedōlâ*, 'large assembly', *sanhedrin*, 'court session' (from the Greek), and *bêt dîn ha-gādôl*, 'higher court of justice'. In all events, the highest administrative and judicial organ is indicated, which must have existed from the time of the Persian regime onwards. Its jurisdiction and composition changed, as well as its designations, which often occurred simultaneously. What is certain is that the high priest had a leading role and was assisted by the priestly elite of the Sadducean 'party'. Besides these, well-to-do and educated non-priests were members of the Council, whose membership comprised in part those of the Pharisaic 'party' or those connected to it as scholars of the law.

The highest Council gathered in the temple. In rabbinic tradition, it was counted as the highest institution of appeal and the place 'from which halakah spread over Israel' (*t. Ḥag.* 2.9; cf. *m. Pe'ah* 2.6). Both Josephus and rabbinic tradition report that the Sadducees were cruel in jurisprudence and could occasionally impose this tendency against the will of the Pharisees. Disconnected to this was the offering ritual in the temple, where the high priest and his cohorts played a central role as well, but where they were forced to follow the Pharisaic support of the people's customs (see pp. 56, 81).

A much-discussed question is whether or not Jesus did have a legal trial before the Council. An insurmountable problem appears to be that both the assumed evening and morning sittings directly after Jesus' last supper fell on the evening before and the first day of Passover (Mk 14.12, 17, 54-55; 15.1). Rabbinic tradition, which probably continues the Pharisaic position respected in the temple, demands, however, that trial be held during daylight and never on a feast day (*m. Sanh.* 4.1). The strength of this argument is reinforced by the fact that the Sadducees, with whom the high priest and his associates usually were connected, probably adhered strongly to the holiness of the Shabbat (see pp. 80-81). Connected to this is another problem, namely, whether Jesus' last supper fell *upon* Passover, as the synoptic tradition reports, or *before* Passover, according to John. A real solution, which allows for the different juridical procedures, presents itself in the then prevailing differences in the dating of the feasts and in particular of Passover (see further pp. 310-12).

Jesus' Enemies in Mark
In Luke's passion story the Pharisees do not occur, except where they voice their concern about the Messianic enthusiasm of the people at Jesus' entry into Jerusalem (Lk. 19.39). In the passion story of Mark as well, the Pharisees appear only once on the scene and then in a subordinate role. 'Certain Pharisees' with 'Herodians' are sent to Jesus with the question about paying taxes to the emperor (Mk 12.13). The responsible ones offstage are the 'chief priests, scribes, and elders' (11.27).

These 'chief priests, scribes, and elders' are consistently indicated as the actual mortal enemies of Jesus in the passion story of Mark (11.18, 27; 14–15; cf. 8.31; 10.33). Just as in Luke, the high priest and the other members of the priestly aristocracy, assisted by the 'scribes', prominent non-priestly members of the Council, and the temple magistrate and his men are the ones who capture Jesus, put him on trial, and turn him over to Pilate for execution. No Pharisees are involved.

This invites a look back to the two specifically anti-Pharisaic passages already discussed. As Jesus' partners in the dialogue concerning washing hands, Mark mentions 'the Pharisees and certain scribes from Jerusalem' (7.1). This appears to involve the *local* Pharisees, besides scribes or scholars of the law from the capital. The outcome of this discussion about a characteristically Pharisaic theme is not mentioned, but no mortal enmity is reported. Doubt thus increases concerning the originality of the text version according to which Jesus declared 'all foods to be clean'.

This doubt makes the passage in which 'the Pharisees and Herodians' plan to kill Jesus after a discussion over plucking grain on Shabbat even more exceptional (Mk 3.6; see p. 259). The context of ancient Jewish law in general makes this an improbable reaction. Within the whole Gospel, including the passion story, the verse gives the most antagonistic portrayal of the Pharisees, and therefore seems the more to be a later insertion into the text of Mark. One could even consider whether this happened under the influence of Matthew (Mt. 12.14).

Jesus' Enemies in Matthew

For purposes of comparison, we now lay the text of Matthew, as it were, over the text of Mark and observe where the two coincide and where they deviate. This will, of course, not reveal the suggested possible cases of later influencing of Mark by Matthew.

In Matthew's passion story again the sworn enemies of Jesus are as a rule the 'chief priests', sometimes complemented with the 'scribes' and 'elders'. They approach him after the cleansing of the temple and inquire concerning his authority (Mt. 21.15, 23); they decide to put him to death, in consultation with Judas they let him be captured, pass judgment in the Council and mock him before the execution (26.3, 47, 57; 27.1, 41). On all of these points, Matthew corresponds with Mark and —not insignificantly—also with Luke.

We observed how in Mk 7.1 'the Pharisees and certain scribes' approach Jesus with the question about washing hands. Mt. 15.1 abbreviates this to 'Pharisees and scribes', which in a later manuscript is changed to 'scribes and Pharisees'. The latter is an adjustment to the hostile standard combination that occurs often in Matthew, never in Mark and only four times in Luke. We have noted that a certain tension is apparent here with the sympathy which 'Luke' otherwise exhibits towards the Pharisees and scholars of the law, and we assumed that he was dependent on a different source at that point (see pp. 227-28).

The combination occurs also in Jn 8.3, a gripping tale in which 'the scribes and Pharisees' bring a woman caught in adultery to Jesus and he forgives her sins. The language is non-Johannine, and only in later manuscripts is that passage inserted into John at various places. Several later copyists included it in Luke, probably due to its affinity to that Gospel (cf. Lk. 7.36-50). It is apparently a fragment from a text that came into being independently from the Gospels known to us. Papias (see pp. 255-56) refers to such a story as belonging to 'the Hebrew Gospel' (Eusebius, *Church History* 3.39.17). We can merely admit how inadequate our information is.

The significance of the expression 'scribes and Pharisees' in Matthew becomes clear through bitter polemics against them in two strategic passages. In both cases it is in an address of Jesus, that is, in material that Matthew inserted into the story of Mark. In the programme-like opening section of the Sermon on the Mount, which deals with the interpretation and keeping of the Law, Jesus says, 'If your righteousness is not abundant, more than the scribes and Pharisees, you shall not enter into the Kingdom of Heaven' (Mt. 5.20). Thereafter follow the so-called 'antitheses', in which Jesus presents his own Torah interpretation as opposed to that of the other authorities (see pp. 285-86).

A head-on collision occurs during the long arraignment against 'the scribes and Pharisees' at the temple square (Mt. 23). Like the Sermon on the Mount, this is a characteristically Matthaean element of composition. The speech replaces two short warnings against the rich scribes in Mark and Luke (Mk 12.38-44; Lk. 20.45–21.4). Matthew adds 'Pharisees' and expands the indictment to a whole chapter, in which material found scattered throughout Luke is included (see p. 227). Eight times the combination resounds in this chapter, after the first time repeatedly being introduced by the threatening 'Woe to you', and given extra emphasis by the label 'hypocrites' (more on this later): 'Woe to you, scribes and Pharisees, hypocrites…!' Only in Matthew does the typically anti-Pharisee reproach occur that in order to exhibit their piety they 'make their phylacteries broad and the tassels large' (Mt. 23.5), evidently referring to the commemorative tassels (*şişit*) on the corners of the garment (Num. 15.38-39). The conclusion that this is an anti-Pharisaic chapter is inescapable: we have here to do with an evangelist whose congregation lives in open conflict with the Pharisaic leaders. This will be filled in later with further data.

For a clear understanding of the historical development, it must be stated that this chapter nonetheless contains material that testifies to an actual discussion with the Pharisees concerning specific issues (cf. also pp. 147-48):

> The scribes and Pharisees have set themselves upon the seat of Moses. All that they say to you, do and keep, but do not do their works, for they say but do not do.

> Woe to you, scribes and Pharisees, hypocrites, for you tithe mint, dill, and cummin, but you neglect the weightiest of the law: judgment, mercy, and faithfulness. This one should do, but not neglect the other (Mt. 23.2-3, 23).

Rendering tithes of herbs such as mint, dill and cummin was a typically Pharisaic refinement of the biblical commandments. Jesus does not reject this Pharisaic 'extra' but notes it as something that should be done as well. The emphasis, however, is upon the 'weightiest of the law', the fear of God and love for the fellow-man, in which the 'scribes and Pharisees' are deficient. The same position is expressed by Jesus at the beginning: the commandments of the scribes and Pharisees should be followed, but not their manner of living. The 'seat of Moses' appears to be more than an apt figure of speech. A teacher sat down to give instruction, as is reported of Jesus (Mt. 5.1-2; Lk. 4.20-21) and is also known from rabbinic literature, where the 'seat of Moses' is assumed to be an item familiar to the audience (*Pes. K.* 1.7, p. 12). There are indeed synagogues excavated with a beautifully decorated chair found in a central position, apparently the place of honour for the Scripture scholar or teacher.

Such points of contact with the Pharisaic–rabbinic tradition lend a measure of precision to the anti-Pharisaic polemics in this chapter. At this level, the text is apparently occupied with a real but harsh debate with the Pharisaic tradition. Even though the hand of the evangelist is clearly recognizable in the stereotype 'scribes and Pharisees, hypocrites', an echo is heard of the discussions that in the milieu of Jesus must have taken place with the Pharisees, or perhaps an echo of Jesus' own words. The latter possibility is supported by the fact that the saying in response to the tithes, 'this one should do and not neglect the other', also occurs in Luke (11.42).

That the milieu of Jesus and his disciples was on a tense footing with the Pharisees can be deduced as well from the stereotype label 'hypocrite'. This word occurs scattered throughout the synoptic Gospels (Mt. 7.5 = Lk. 6.42; Mt. 15.7 = Mk 7.6; Mt. 22.18; Lk. 12.56; 13.15) and is in itself not characteristic of Matthew alone. What is Matthaean is the threefold repetition of the term in the passage about giving alms, praying and fasting (Mt. 6.2, 5, 16). In contrast to the 'hypocrites' who do these good works in public, Jesus emphasizes piety towards 'your Father who sees in what is hidden'. Even stronger is the sevenfold, stereotypical polemic use of the word in Matthew 23, which gives the impression that the Pharisees are depicted as 'hypocrites' by a group that interprets piety more radically. A historical backdrop for this impression is provided by an analogous use of 'hypocrites' in the *Didache*, a text related to Matthew, which apparently reacts against the Pharisaic tradition (see p. 388). Comparable tones can be expected to come from the context of Qumran, where the term 'slippery interpreters' is found, apparently polemically intended against the Pharisees (see pp. 49, 81).

Thus there are at least two levels of the text and as many stages of development of the community of Jesus and his followers: the discussion of Jesus with the Pharisees about, for example, the tithing of herbs and the weightiest issues of the law, and the polemic of the evangelist whose community was in a general conflict with the Pharisaic leaders and their tradition. The contrast with the Gospel of Mark is clear, where the relationship to the Pharisees and the Jews is neutral, except for the additions mentioned. We have traced the polemics with the 'scribes and Pharisees' back to a Matthaean primal source, which besides Mark formed a basis for the third layer of Matthew.

The radicalization of the relationship to Judaism in Matthew's congregation and the development of his text proceeded further. Greater tension with the Jews is reflected in the combination of 'Pharisees and Sadducees', a polemic combination found only in Matthew (Mt. 3.7; 16.1, 6, 11-12). How great the distance towards Judaism at this point becomes apparent if one realizes that, according to other sources, Pharisees and Sadducees were each other's fundamental opponents. That this is a typical Matthaean adjustment can be observed in the request for a sign by 'Pharisees and Sadducees'. In Mark only 'Pharisees' are mentioned, while in Luke no one is called by name (Mt. 16.1; Mk 8.11; Lk. 11.29). In Matthew itself a parallel to this statement occurs as well, a so-called doublet, in which 'scribes and Pharisees' are mentioned (Mt. 12.38; the 'scribes' are even missing in one important manuscript).

The development appears to progress even further when in Matthew's story of the passion twice the 'chief priests and Pharisees' cooperate against Jesus and his disciples. After the first clash with the 'chief priests and scribes', Jesus tells the parable of the rebellious tenants from whom eventually the vineyard is taken away. In Mark and Luke it is clearly directed against the same opponents, with the intention that these will lose their power over the temple (see pp. 163-64). In Matthew, however, we read, 'When the chief priests and Pharisees heard this, they understood that the parable was directed against them' (Mt. 21.45). This is made even more pointed in Matthew by the fact that at the end of the parable the vineyard is given to 'another people' (more about this later). The monstrous alliance of 'chief priests and Pharisees' comes into action again to request of Pilate that a watch be set by the tomb (Mt. 27.62). In the presentation of Matthew, the Pharisees have become the confederates of Jesus' mortal enemies: a great distance has developed to the original Gospel tradition, as well as to the Gospels of Mark and Luke. Interestingly, the combination of 'chief priests and Pharisees' is also found in John (11.57; 18.3). In all cases, the context is that of a police or a judicial action. This recalls the situation during the war against Rome, concerning which Josephus, too, reports this exceptional alliance.

More clarity about the background of the growing distance vis-à-vis the original gospel tradition is given by a detail in the address against the scribes and Pharisees. Jesus reproaches them because they like *'to be called rabbi* by the people', and to his disciples he then continues, 'but you shall not let yourselves be called rabbi, for there is one who is your teacher, and you are all brothers' (Mt. 23.7-8). This reproach occurs only in Matthew, and it is logical to think of the institution of 'rabbi' as a standard title for an ordained scholar of the law (see pp. 36, 49). To call Jesus 'rabbi', as is sometimes done nowadays, is doubly inaccurate, in spite of all good intentions. In the first place, this designation did not exist as a fixed title in his day, and, secondly, it is characteristic of the rabbinic–Pharisaic milieu to which he did not belong. To that extent, the Matthaean evangelist was completely correct in supplying his 'added clarification' concerning the term!

We have seen that Mark's Gospel is addressed largely to non-Jewish Christians and reflects no particular difficulties in the relationship to Judaism, except in the additions concerning Shabbat and purity. On the contrary, Matthew is characterized by sharp polemics against the Jewish leaders, directed primarily against the 'scribes and Pharisees', and in a later development apparently also against 'Pharisees and Sadducees'. Finally, the Pharisees are made to be accomplices of the chief priests in their fatal struggle against Jesus.

Jews and Israel

The manner in which the designations 'Jews' and 'Israel' are used is an important issue for all portions of the New Testament, and is one of the means by which a speaker or writer expresses his attitude towards the Jews (see pp. 110-15). In our treatment of Paul and Luke there was, however, no occasion to discuss this problem because their use of the two appellations concurs with their largely positive attitude towards the Jews. In the comparison of Mark and Matthew, several interesting shifts are observable. The matter will prove to have real urgency in the Gospel of John.

In ancient Jewish literature, in distinct situations the two names were used as designations for the same group. Within a wholly Jewish context, such as in prayers, in the law or in certain stories, the name 'Israel' is used to indicate the Jews. When a non-Jewish context is implied, however, the external designation 'Jews' is employed. A text with only the designation 'Israel' transfers the reader, as it were, to a Jewish point of view, while a text with the name 'Jews' views the same from an external perspective. The latter need in no way imply a negative attitude towards the Jews; the reader is merely placed at a non-Jewish vantage point. Such a switch can occur incidentally as well in a brief conversation with a non-Jew within a story otherwise situated within a Jewish context, or vice versa. When, however, from an external perspective, the term 'Jews' is used, and at the same time a negative role is assigned to them, the text or passage must be labelled as anti-Jewish.

This pattern holds true in ancient literature both Jewish and Christian. The synoptic Gospels are in fact a suitable example for demonstrating the principle. In *Mark* the name 'Jews' is used five times in ch. 15 where Jesus is in the hands of the Roman military. Each time it concerns a passage in which Romans speak or write, for example, the inscription on the the cross: 'And the inscription with the accusation was written above: "The king of the *Jews*"' (Mk 15.26). Likewise the soldiers mock him with the words 'Hail, king of the *Jews*' (v. 18). When the chief priests and scribes deride him on the cross, however, the text is, 'The Anointed, the king of *Israel*, may he now come off of the cross...' (v. 32). This last example is thus a fragment where Jews, speaking among themselves, use 'Israel' even though it involves *hatred*.

The opposite occurs in the introduction of the discussion about washing hands. While Jesus is being interrogated by 'the Pharisees and some scribes', the evangelist interrupts the story to explain to the non-Jewish reader that 'the Pharisees and all *Jews* do not eat unless they have washed the hands at the fist' (Mk 7.3). This merely reflects a non-Jewish speech context and need not be read in an anti-Jewish manner. In connection with this verse, the non-Jewish context is confirmed by the text fragment about the 'purification of all foods' (v. 19). When we read there 'thus all foods *become* pure', the explanation about the purification rituals appears to be only an external Jewish text fragment within the story. When, however, we read 'thus *he declared* all foods to be pure', the external Jewish fragment in v. 3 acquires an anti-Jewish implication: the dietary regulations are declared then to be outmoded and the 'Jews' who continue to propagate them are ascribed a negative role.

Turning to *Matthew*, a notable difference with Mark is that the name 'Israel' is used much more often, each time in material lacking in Mark. Thus the angel in Egypt says to Joseph, Mary's husband, in a dream, 'Arise…go to the land of Israel; and he arose…and went to the land of Israel' (Mt. 2.20-21). The 'land of Israel', *Erets Yisrael*, is in rabbinic literature the normal Jewish designation for the Holy Land, and suggests thus a intra-Jewish context. Likewise, Jesus commissions his disciples: 'Go rather to the lost sheep of the house of *Israel*,' as he himself was 'only sent to the lost sheep of the house of *Israel*' (10.23; 15.24). In a remarkable text Jesus says further that the apostles 'in the Regeneration…shall sit upon twelve thrones and judge the twelve tribes of Israel' (19.28). In Matthew as well the chief priests, scribes and elders are heard mocking Jesus: 'The king of Israel is he? let him now descend from the cross…' (27.42). The name 'Jews', which occurs relatively little in Matthew, is spoken naturally by the Roman military: 'king of the *Jews*' (27.11, 29, 37). Once as well it is the wise men from the Orient who ask Herod, 'Where is the newborn king of the Jews?' (2.2).

One passage in Matthew remains in which the name 'Jews' occurs. It is addressed directly to the reader, as a commentary within the text, and follows the report in which 'the chief priests and Pharisees' request Pilate to set a watch by the tomb (27.62-66). When amidst apocalyptic phenomena Jesus is resurrected, the guards report the tomb to be empty, whereupon the chief priests bribe them to say that the disciples had stolen the body away. The text then comments, 'And this story is spread among Jews up to the present day' (28.15). The entire account, not in the least because of the improbable combination of chief priests and Pharisees, can be classified as a polemic legend. That this story indeed circulated among the Jews is in no wise impossible; however, the fact remains that this fragment not only creates a non-Jewish speech context, but it also ascribes a negative role to the Jews. It is a forthright anti-Jewish passage that appears to belong to a late stage of the text.

A comparison of Matthew and Mark again reveals a pattern of correspondences and differences. There is correspondence in the interchange of the use of 'Jews' by the Romans and 'Israel' by the chief priests in the scene at the cross. A clear difference is that Matthew contains more passages with the name 'Israel'. This material could be considered as having derived from the intra-Jewish 'Matthaean primal source', which, alongside Mark, lay at the basis of the third text layer. Compared at this level, Mark lends itself even more to being read as a Gospel intended for non-Jewish Christians, while Matthew adds to the basic scheme of Mark much explanation that draws on a Jewish context.

Finally, both Gospels contain a passage providing commentary to the name 'Jews', however, each with a different effect. The explanation about the purifying customs of 'all the Jews' can be read as neutral information. The commentary on the false rumour 'spread among Jews' contains, however, an unmistakably negative message. The final text stage of Matthew testifies to estrangement from the Jews; in combination with the conspicuous amount of Jewish-Christian material that it contains, the text confronts us with a curious contradictoriness.

Matthew, the Jews and the Non-Jews

The use of the appellations 'Jews' and 'Israel' is not the only means of expressing the attitude towards the Jews. In this section, other distinguishing characteristics will be presented. The antilogy of Matthew on this point will become even clearer. More than ever it can be helpful to read the present text of the Gospel as a result of successive redactional stages.

The third layer of Matthew has been depicted above as a reworking of the basic text of Mark complemented with material from the originally Hebrew Matthaean primal source. The striking intra-Jewish statements that Matthew transmits from Jesus and that we reviewed in Chapter 3 fit into that context:

> If you only greet your brothers, what is special about that? Do not *the non-Jews* also the same? (Mt. 5.47).
> When you pray, do not be verbose like *the non-Jews* (Mt. 6.7).
>
> Do not worry, saying: 'what shall we eat?'...for all these things do *the non-Jews* pursue (Mt. 6.32; Lk. 12.30).

> These twelve did Jesus send out with the following commission: Turn
> not aside on a road of *the non-Jews*, and do not go to a Samaritan village,
> but go rather to the lost sheep of *the house of Israel* (Mt. 10.5-6).

> I am only sent to the lost sheep of *the house of Israel* (Mt. 15.24).

> If your brother sins, go to him and reprove him... But if he does not
> listen, report it to the church. And if he does not listen even to the
> church, let him then be to you as *a non-Jew* and a tax collector (Mt.
> 18.17).

In Chapter 3 it was suggested that the reserve towards non-Jews
ascribed to Jesus was plausible, considering his surprise at the unexpected faith of the centurion in Capernaum and of the Syro-Pheonician
woman. This does not, however, mean that all of these statements were
recorded verbatim. Particularly in the last quotation where the 'church'
is mentioned, it is clear that at least the retouching pen of the evangelist
intervened. The elements from the oldest layer or from the direct milieu
of Jesus present here are embedded in the Matthaean primal source
(layer 2) or in the first reworking of the text of Mark (layer 3). Apparently following in the footsteps of Jesus, this Jewish church was not
very welcoming towards non-Jews.

These types of statements bothered the church fathers. According to
Origen, Jesus could not have meant literally that he was only sent to the
'lost sheep of the house of Israel'; Origen makes this clear in a mocking
outburst against the Ebionites, a Jewish-Christian group of his day (cf.
also pp. 345-46):

> We do not understand this as do the poor in comprehension, the Ebion-
> ites, so called because of their poverty of comprehension—for with the
> Hebrews, *ebion* means 'poor'—as though we must presume that the
> Christ by preference dwelled among the Israelites according to the flesh,
> seeing that 'not the children according to the flesh are children of God'
> (*De principiis* 4.3.8; cf. Rom. 9.8)

Origen's derision, which as a Hebraist he based upon the correct significance of the word *'ebyôn*, 'poor one', became commonplace among
the church fathers. His appeal to Paul contains a polemic polarization in
his intention that not all 'Israelites' are automatically guaranteed to be
children of God. To us it is striking, on the other hand, that Jesus 'by
preference dwelled among the Israelites according to the flesh', but that
he let himself be surprised by outsiders. It is important to note that the
Ebionites appear to share the more restrictive attitude of the Matthaean
primal source, and this suggests polemics between Jewish and non-

Jewish Christians, in which Jesus' message must perforce have become incomprehensible.

This brings us to a practically opposite characteristic of Matthew: the fundamental turning to the non-Jews, which must belong to the final stage of development of the text. The commission to go 'to all peoples', ascribed to the Risen One, is indeed difficult to harmonize with his prohibition to go 'on a road of the non-Jews' or 'to a village of the Samaritans' (Mt. 28.19; 10.5). Both the book of Acts (Peter's dream, Acts 10–11!) and Paul's letters testify furthermore to a certain disinclination of the church in Jerusalem to initiate and carry on the turning to the nations. An unequivocal commandment of Jesus in that direction would have made such hesitancy untenable. Therefore a Matthaean 'Judaizing' of Jesus' statements is not plausible, as has been presumed, but rather the opposite, namely, the adaptation of the gospel tradition to the turning towards the nations. The Gospel of Matthew appears to document this.

Thus it is surprising to read, directly after the prohibition to go to the non-Jews: 'Before rulers and kings shall you be brought for my sake, for a witness to them and *to all nations*' (Mt. 10.18), and further: 'This gospel of the Kingdom shall be proclaimed in the whole inhabited world *to all peoples*, and then shall the end come' (Mt. 24.14). Particularly in the first statement 'all nations' comes somewhat awkwardly in second position, giving the impression of being a revised text. The most explicit turning to the nations is, of course, the universal missionary commission at the end, which is in such remarkable contrast to the dispatching of the disciples to the 'sheep of the house of Israel' in ch. 10: 'Go forth, make all peoples into disciples…and teach them to maintain all that I have charged you' (Mt. 28.19).

This turning to the nations must reflect a later stage in the history of the text. The adaptations can, however, often be slight and can be understood as a continuation of older themes. The fact that Jesus' statement that 'first the gospel must be proclaimed to all peoples' also occurs in Mark (13.10) is not in itself conclusive. The so-called 'synoptic apocalypse', which is found both in Mark 13 and in Matthew 24 as a whole, carries traces of being a later revision, and in the case in point such a suspicion is unavoidable. A text such as the following contains even more convincing proof that older themes from prophetic texts echo in this:

> And then shall all tribes of the earth mourn and they shall see the Son of
> man coming upon the clouds of heavens…and his angels…shall gather

the chosen from the four corners of the earth (Mt. 24.30-31; see Dan. 7.13-14; Zech. 2.10).

A different issue is what the turning to the nations must have meant for the position of the Jews. Here again, certainly after what we have just seen, Matthew appears to be a document with an eventful history. First, there is the conclusion of the parable of the vineyard that Jesus tells at the temple square; we must now cite it in full:

> Therefore I say to you that the Kingdom of God shall be taken away from you and given to a people that bears the fruit thereof... When the chief priests and Pharisees heard this, they understood that he had directed his parable against them (Mt. 21.43, 45).

It is important to repeat that the phrase about the 'taking away of the Kingdom of God' occurs neither in Mark nor in Luke and must be an addition of the Matthaean evangelist. Secondly, it is remarkable that he speaks here of the 'Kingdom of God' instead of the Semiticizing 'Kingdom of the Heavens' that is otherwise characteristic of this Gospel. Thirdly, the improbable combination 'chief priests and Pharisees' occurs here, which has already been discussed. Finally, mention is made of 'another people' (*ethnos*), which appears to imply a breach with the Jewish people. This all unmistakably reflects a late stage of revision of the text, in which the estrangement from the Jews had become a fact. For the community of Matthew, the conflict of Jesus with the temple administrators had expanded into a clash with the Jewish leaders and their people.

The same appears to be the case in the Matthaean version of the story of the centurion at Capernaum. Initially the last part follows the parallel version in Luke (cf. pp. 161, 220-21), but then the paths part:

> When Jesus heard this he was surprised and said to those that followed him: Amen, I say to you, with no one in Israel have I found such a faith! But I say to you that many shall come from east and west and shall recline with Abraham, Isaac, and Jacob in the Kingdom of the Heavens, but the children of the Kingdom shall be thrown out... (Mt. 8.10-12).

The closing sentence occurs also in Luke in another form at a completely different place (Lk. 13.28-29), but there it has a more general purport and lacks the expression the 'children of the Kingdom'. The Matthaean evangelist draws a sharp contrast between the unbelief of Israel, apparently intended by the 'children of the Kingdom', and the believers that come from east and west—referring apparently to the nations. Here again the text seems to be from the last stage of revision.

At last, we must discuss the notorious text from the scene of Pilate and the Jewish leaders. Rather than the rebel Barabbas, Pilate wanted to release Jesus, in whom he sees no danger. When the 'chief priests and elders' and the mob instigated by them continue to shout for Barabbas, Pilate washes his hands demonstratively:

> I am innocent of the blood of this one [Jesus]. And the whole people answered and said: *His blood be upon us and upon our children!* (Mt. 27.24-25).

The details of the innocent blood and the washing of hands occur only in Matthew. We must question what could be intended at the different levels of the text. The association with the appeasement ritual prescribed in the Old Testament in cases where someone is found murdered by an unknown party has been pointed out. In such a case the elders must wash their hands over an animal of sacrifice and state that they and their community have not shed the blood of this unfortunate one (Deut. 21.6-8). This connection is not very realistic as background for the gesture of a Roman military man, but it could certainly offer an interpretation of the happening to readers well-versed in the Bible.

A more direct correspondence is to be found between the cries of the mob in Matthew and the words of the high priest addressed to Jesus' apostles in Acts:

> Have I not strictly commanded you not to teach in his name? and behold, you have filled Jerusalem with your teachings, and you continue to try to bring down the blood of this man upon us! (Acts 5.28).

We could suspect there being a common tradition behind this, because in both cases it involves the reaction from the same quarters: the chief priests and their 'mob' (cf. Mt. 27.20). Observed at this level, the passage means that Pilate rejects the responsibility for Jesus' death, while the chief priests and their cohorts stand behind it with conviction. Up to this point, the passage in Matthew does not deflect from Mark and Luke, where the chief priests and scribes count as Jesus' mortal enemies.

In Matthew, however, something else happens. We have already seen that in the various revisions successively the chief priests, Pharisees and Sadducees are made responsible, and that finally the whole people is expelled from the 'vineyard' of the 'kingdom'. It therefore appears not to be coincidental that in this fragment the ominous exclamation is not made by 'the whole multitude', which is mentioned in v. 20, but by 'the whole people (*laos*)'. Just as in Mt. 21.43, where the synonym *ethnos* is used, this is not an indifferent term but evokes the Old Testamental covenant people. This is a subtle difference and it is easy to reconstruct the preceding links of the portentous statement. Nonetheless, the broader context makes the conclusion inevitable that this passage in Matthew makes the whole Jewish people responsible for Jesus' death. The historical inaccuracy has not prevented it from having a great effect on history. From the fourth century onwards, the passage has been used in the polemics against the Jews.

We are thus left with the paradoxical conclusion that Matthew with its strong Jewish-Christian colouring simultaneously contains a turning towards the non-Jews with an anti-Jewish tenor.

The Jewish Law in Matthew

In conclusion, we come to a topic of supreme importance within the context of this book: the place of the Jewish law in the first Gospel. The enigma so characteristic of Matthew again confronts us. How can one and the same document maintain both the rejection of the Jews and the inviolability of the Jewish law? It seems logical that the latter can be ascribed to the strong Jewish-Christian deposit present in the Matthaean primal source. Yet this is at most half of the explanation. How could a community have read this Gospel with its strong accentuation of the Jewish law, while recognizing itself as a non-Jewish church in the 'other people who will bring forth the fruits of the Kingdom', and while the 'children of the Kingdom are cast out'?

Attempts to remedy the contradiction have not been lacking. In Chapter 3 mention was made of discerning outsiders in antiquity as well as hypercritical scholars in modern times who have suggested corrections for one of the central texts involved:

> Do not think that I have come to annul the law or the prophets; I am not come to annul them, but to fulfil them... Before the heavens and the earth pass away not one jot or crotchet of the law will pass away... Whoever, therefore, shall annul one of these smallest of commandments and shall teach people thus, he shall be called the smallest...but he who does and teaches them shall be called great... Unless your righteousness is not abundant, more than the scribes and the Pharisees... (Mt. 5.17-20).

The typically Matthaean polemics against the superficial piety of the 'scribes and Pharisees' is recognizable. Polemics is a negative sign of affinity, and the latter betrays itself in the characteristically Pharisaic notions that this passage also contains. Jesus admits here to a more radical version of the Pharisaic observance of the law. The stunning fact that all this is present in the final text requires further discussion.

The polemic affinity with the Pharisees is expressed in the technical terminology. In rabbinic literature as well the 'jot and the crotchet'— the smallest letter *yod* and the small curls that decorate the letters—are proverbial for the great significance of small details. With ironic exaggeration it is said of R. Akiva that 'from every crotchet (of the *yod*) he shall derive heaps of halakhot' (*b. Men.* 29b). Similarly, the text goes on to speak of the 'smallest' commandments, a term that, just as 'the weightiest of the law' (Mt. 23.23), is related to rabbinic usage.

'Annulling' a text from Scripture is also a rabbinic term, indicating that someone goes too far in interpreting a text and thereby actually decommissions it. The antonym is 'confirming', as can be observed by a well-known ex-Pharisee: 'Do we annul the law by (our emphasis upon) faith? Certainly not! Rather we confirm the law,' after which he proceeds to substantiate his argumentation with the biblical example of Abraham (Rom. 3.31). It is not insignificant that our passage speaks of *fulfilling* and not of 'confirming'; we return to this later. What follows makes clear, however, that here, too, the issue is whether or not one 'annuls' the law by his interpretation of it: 'He who annuls one of the smallest commandments and teaches people to do so, shall be called the smallest...but he who keeps and teaches them shall be called great...' Jesus is on Pharisaic turf and uses the appropriate terminology.

Before we proceed, we draw attention to the fact that the continuation of the Sermon on the Mount works out the just-articulated principle further. In the so-called antitheses, five or six times Jesus points to the interpretation of a biblical commandment with the introductory words 'you have heard that it has been said...', and then advances his own interpretation in contrast to it: '...but I say to you...' To the extent that antitheses are present, these are not directed against the Torah. Jesus accuses the Pharisees of taking away the force of the Torah's intention by means of their interpretation (Mt. 15.3-6). He pursues the radical intention of the Scriptures. The issue is not just the literal 'do not kill', but also mental murder; not only the literal 'do not commit adultery', but also the behaviour that leads up to it (5.21, 27). To 'take an oath falsely' is rightly prohibited, but it is better not to take an oath at all. 'An eye for an eye, a tooth for a tooth' suggests proportional restitution, but you should not ask for restitution at all; 'love for one's neighbour' that excludes the 'enemy' is not real love (5.33, 38, 43; see pp. 147-48).

Here again the phraseology is related to rabbinic literature. In form, the recurring 'you have heard...but I say unto you...' resembles the terminology used in a discussion in which the rabbis reject an incorrect interpretation and introduce the correct one. In content, the teachings of Jesus show affinity with the manner of thinking of pious individuals (see p. 60).

In order to grasp the import of the text as a whole, we must think at several levels at once. Contentwise, this interpretation of the law concurs with what we can recover of Jesus' own awareness of a calling and his specific piety, that is, the first layer. To this must be added the layer of the evangelist (layer 3) and his Jewish-Matthaean primal source (layer 2), in which an accentuated polemics with the Pharisaic leaders is voiced. The hand of the evangelist is in any case recognizable in the stereotype 'scribes and Pharisees' with which we are also now familiar from Matthew 23. It is not possible to determine whether the characteristic Pharisaic terminology found only in Matthew derives from Jesus himself or is inserted by the evangelist. The fact that he was capable of intervening in the content of Jesus' teachings on the law will be demonstrated below. There is, however, no rational argument conceivable why Jesus himself could not have used this phraseology in his discussions with the Pharisees. The writings from Qumran also contain expressions related to those of the rabbis. It is not possible to say more than this with certainty. A fourth level is not visible here—that of the non-Jewish congregation in which the Gospel received its final form. How 'not annulling a jot and a crotchet' and the 'smallest commandments' would have been understood in that congregation remains an even greater puzzle...

A clear but rather unexpected indication of the position of the Jewish-Christian evangelist is offered by the topic of divorce. This controversial and, therefore, richly documented theme in early Judaism provides the opportunity of determining Jesus' own position quite exactly (see pp. 149-51, where our sources were Mark, Luke and Paul). Matthew follows a divergent course that now deserves attention. Jesus' rule is most succinctly worded in Luke: 'Everyone who dismisses his wife and marries another commits adultery; and he who marries her that is dismissed commits adultery' (Lk. 16.18). In short, divorce does not exist, for remarriage after divorce is impossible. This notion, reminiscent of the Essenes, undergoes a conspicuous softening in Matthew. The topic was apparently so important that the evangelist incorporates it twice, once among the 'antitheses' of the Sermon on the Mount and a second time in the discussion with the Pharisees on divorce:

> It has been said: 'He that sends away his wife, must give her a letter of divorce.' But I say unto you that whoever sends away his wife *for a reason other than unchastity* makes her into an adulteress, indeed he who marries one who has been sent away commits adultery (Mt. 5.31-32).

> But I say to you that he that sends his wife away—*except for unchastity*—and marries another commits adultery (Mt. 19.9).

It is noteworthy that the conversation with the Pharisees, which in Mark is coherent with the ensuing prohibition of divorce (Mk 10.2-12), in Matthew has been given a different structure and is also expressed in different terms. The question of the Pharisees is no longer 'whether a person is allowed to send his wife away', but, 'Is a person allowed *for every reason* to send his wife away?' (Mk 10.2; Mt. 19.3). As appeared from our survey in Chapter 3, the question amounts to asking whether Jesus is in agreement with the standpoint of the Hillelites that divorce could be based 'on every ground'. Equally surprising is the fact that the answer is in conformity with the Shammaite standpoint: marriage can only be disbanded for unchastity or sexual licence. In other words, in Matthew Jesus chooses sides in an intra-Pharisaic discussion.

The unequivocal witness of Mark, Luke and Paul lend a great historical probability to Jesus' Essene-like prohibition of divorce. Just as clearly, Matthew's Gospel speaks in the name of a congregation that, on this point, identified itself with the Shammaites, in clear divergence from its master. This contrasts conspicuously with Paul, who apparently had abandoned his previous Pharisaic standpoint and had assumed the stricter rule of 'the Lord'. At this level, which we must designate as the second or third layer of the Gospel, the text of Matthew has, thus, a Pharisaic–Shammaite appearance. Due to this, the Matthaean affinity with Pharisaic terminology, as, for example, in the Sermon on the Mount, is even more remarkable. Another interesting point of comparison is offered by the *Didache*, a text related to Matthew (see p. 352). We conclude that in general among Jesus' followers there must have been diverse opinions concerning such an important issue as divorce.

Matthew defies, however, all simple explications. On the matter of Shabbat, there is a detail that suggests a much stricter interpretation of the law than was conceivable even for the Shammaite Pharisees. In his eschatological address, Jesus advises his followers to flee immediately to the mountains in the face of the imminent persecution, and then proceeds: 'Pray that you flight be not in winter and not on the Shabbat' (Mt. 24.20). It would thus be forbidden to flee on Shabbat in order to save one's life. As we have seen, this notion was abandoned by the majority of Jews since the Maccabaean War, and certainly by the Pharisees (see pp. 91-93). On this exceptional issue, Matthew's Gospel presents itself as extremely radical and rather Essene. The whole appears rather incoherent.

On the matter of cleanliness, there are no complications in Matthew. The dubious text fragment from Mark about the 'cleansing of all victuals' does not occur here. Jesus merely rejects the specifically Pharisaic washing of hands before ordinary meals (Mt. 15.1-20; see Mk 7.19, pp. 259-60).

The anti-Pharisaic standpoint of the Gospel in its second and third layer has already been underscored. Both the stereotype contrast to the 'scribes and Pharisees' and the prohibition to allow oneself to be called 'rabbi' point to this.

The Gospel itself offers no indications of a more specific identification of the Jewish-Christian milieu in which it must have received its basic form (see further Chapters 8 and 9). There appears on some points to have been a greater affinity with the Pharisees than Jesus himself showed, while on the other hand the breach with the Pharisees and rabbis from a later time is unmistakable. The holiness of the Torah and its commandments are beyond dispute. The enigma of how this was reconciled with the turning towards the nations and the rejection of the Jewish people, which we observed in the fourth layer, remains unexplained.

Once this has been stated, in conclusion another aspect deserves our attention. Thrice in Matthew, Jesus makes a fundamental statement that involves not only 'the law', but 'the law and the prophets':

> Do not think that I have come to disband the law and the prophets... (Mt. 5.17).

> All that you want people to do to you, do that likewise to them, for that is the law and the prophets (Mt. 7.12).

> 'You shall love the Lord your God with all your heart...'—that is the great and first commandment. And the second is equal to it: 'You shall love your neighbour as yourself.' On these two commandments hang all of the law and the prophets (Mt. 22.40).

All things considered, in these statements 'the prophets' are superfluous in relation to the content. Besides in the material directly following the first passage, the issue is 'a jot or crotchet of the law' and 'the smallest commandments of the law'. In the 'antitheses' in the rest of the fifth chapter of Matthew as well, only quotes from the law of Moses are treated (Mt. 5.20-48). Likewise, the second and third passages are about the love for God and for the neighbour, which are couched in the commandments of the Torah (Deut. 6.5; Lev. 19.18). Thus 'the prophets' appear to be an addition, undoubtedly due to particular interests. In the fourth passage, the mention of 'the prophets' is even more remarkable. After an obscure sentence about the 'violent breakthrough' or the Kingdom of the Heavens 'being overpowered…since the days of John the Baptist', Jesus says, 'For all the prophets and the law prophesied up to John' (Mt. 11.13). These words occur as an isolated saying in Luke, there phrased as, 'The law and the prophets are until John…' (Lk. 16.16). The reversed order in Matthew betrays special emphasis on the prophets.

The significance of this emphasis in Matthew requires explanation. The quotes from the prophets occur in prominent places scattered throughout the Gospel and are meant to demonstrate that Jesus brought the fulfilling of the prophetic promises. Such quotes also occur in the other Gospels, but neither so frequently nor so emphatically. We have raised the question whether this should be seen in relation to the 'Matthaean-Jewish congregation' and its conflict with the Pharisaic and rabbinic leaders. As we have observed, this congregation put great emphasis on the holiness of the Torah, and it is difficult to grasp why it would inappropriately add 'the prophets' to statements about the fundamental validity of the law. Should we here see a final stage of redaction when the Gospel was adopted by a non-Jewish church, for whom the prophets were of more importance than the law, just as for the later church? Would this then be the background of Jesus' statement that he was not come to disband 'the law *and the prophets*' but '*to fulfil* them'?

The proposal would at last throw some light on the enigma of the incorporation of the Jewish law material in the anti-Jewish revision that comprises the fourth layer. The non-Jewish church of the last stage of Matthew would have, as it were, read over the legal aspect and have placed all emphasis on the prophets. That was, after all, also the 'recipe' by which the later non-Jewish majority church appropriated the Old Testament.

In the final chapter we will return to the history of the redaction of Matthew in comparison to Mark, viewed within the whole of the New Testament.

Chapter 7

JOHN

Johannine literature, that is, the Gospel and the three epistles 'of John', belongs to the youngest writings of the New Testament, having acquired a definitive form perhaps in the nineties of the first century. These writings, with their own peculiar world of concepts, exhibit great mutual affinity, while being strongly distinctive to the rest of the New Testament writings. One of the most salient points of difference has to do with the relationship to the Jews.

The Gospel and the epistles are traditionally ascribed to one and the same John. Though this is not impossible, it remains unresolved who that is. According to their headings, the second and third epistles are written by 'the elder'. Only a few late manuscripts add a name in the inscription: 'John (the apostle)'. In two papyri from as early as the third century, the Gospel carries the inscription 'according to John', in agreement with the conviction, which circulated since mid second century, that the writer was John the apostle, one of the two sons of Zebedee. If this were the same as the 'elder' who wrote the epistles, it would seem logical to think of the 'elder John' whom Papias had known (cf. pp. 255-56). Eusebius, however, pointed out already that the identification of the 'elder' and the 'evangelist' is incorrect (*Church History* 3.39.5). The argumentation for the apostolic authorship is equally unconvincing. The idea arose when the preference of the Gnostics for the Gospel brought it into discredit. There is, thus, little ground for definite conclusions.

Such unanswered questions are raised by the text itself, apparently intentionally. Mysteriousness is one of the distinguishing traits that must be accepted if we are to understand the intention of the fourth Gospel.

The Peculiar World of the Gospel of John

Together with the epistles, the Gospel of John creates a world of its own, and is as such one of the great puzzles of the New Testament. Apart from the authorship, there are numerous questions. In what actual circumstances are we to conceive of this 'world'? What is its relationship to the synoptic tradition and to the teachings of Jesus? What was the relationship between the distinct community that speaks from these documents and the other followers of Jesus, Jews and non-Jews? What relationship did it have to Jews in general? These questions can only be partially and hypothetically answered because there is so little external information. There is no other way than to read and reread as conscientiously as possible, and then to draw level-headed conclusions. More than in the preceding chapters, therefore, the first half of this one is taken up with introductory questions and textual studies. Curiously, besides the purely technical introductory questions, approaching the text in this manner proves to be the natural way of gaining access to it, for the mysterious universe of John differs entirely from everything we read elsewhere in the New Testament.

The Mysterious Author

Among the four Gospels, only the last two have an author who presents himself, although not by name. We have considered how conscientiously and transparently the author at the beginning of the third Gospel accounts for his motives and manner of working (pp. 214-15). The remarks of the author in the fourth Gospel have an entirely different function and significance.

These remarks occur in two places: at the end of both the final and the penultimate chapters. This in itself is remarkable: both chapters present themselves as final chapters, which indicates that the second is a later addition:

> Many other signs now has Jesus done before his disciples, which are not written in this book. But these are written that you might believe that Jesus is the Christ, the son of God, and that believing you might have life in his name (Jn 20.30-31).

> And there are yet many other things which Jesus has done which, if they were written down piece by piece—then the whole world, I would think, could not contain the written texts (Jn 21.25).

Besides the animated and crooked syntax of the second quote, the use of the first person attracts attention. A final redactor is speaking, supplying his commentary to the preceding Gospel as a whole. He should thus be distinguished from the evangelist, at least from the evangelist at an earlier stage. Both the complexity of the situation and the openheartedness concerning it are characteristic of John. The first quote relates something about the goal and manner of working in the preceding chapters: they describe signs that are to arouse and strengthen the faith of Jesus' followers. We will return later to these key words. First another question, Why did the final redactor find it necessary to add a complete chapter?

The events of the added final chapter take place at the Sea of Tiberias. In a first scene, the Risen One joins his disciples and the miraculous catch of fish occurs; in this Peter plays the main role. During the second scene, Jesus invites Peter thrice over to confirm that he loves him, and predicts that he will die a martyr. The final scene then follows with enigmatic but apparently significant announcements about the Gospel as a whole:

> When Peter turned he saw *the disciple following whom Jesus loved*, and who had lain at his breast at the meal... Peter now said to Jesus: Lord, and he? Jesus said to him: If I want him to remain until I come, what is that to you?... Thus the rumour spread among the brothers that this disciple would not die... *This is the disciple who testifies of these things and who has written them down*, and we know that his testimony is true. And there are yet many other things which Jesus has done... (Jn 21.20-25).

The 'meal' refers to the memorable scene at the last supper, in which this disciple, 'whom Jesus loved', and who reclined at his right side, at a sign from Peter asked who it was that would betray him (Jn 13.23-25). It is remarkable that the disciple apparently here, too, is closer to Jesus than Peter, but is never called by name. This pattern is repeated in the intervening chapters: in the courtyard of the high priest, at the cross, and after the resurrection (Jn 18; 19; 20). Though never mentioned by name, time and again the 'other disciple' outruns Peter. The baffled reader cannot help but ask, Who is this other disciple?

One could recall the scene of the disciples' calling, in which Andrew, the brother of Peter, together with a second, unnamed disciple 'transfers' from following John the Baptist to Jesus (1.40). According to the other Gospels, the brothers John and James, sons of Zebedee, were indeed the partners of the fishermen Simon Peter and Andrew (see especially Lk. 5.10). One of them could then be the nameless disciple who first was a follower of John the Baptist. The problem is, however, that in the final chapter, besides a number of named disciples, not only 'the sons of Zebedee' but also explicitly 'two of (Jesus') other disciples' are mentioned—again a significant reference in which no names are given (21.2). The track dies out, apparently intentionally. The intriguing question about who the disciple was 'whom Jesus loved' can only be answered *by the initiated*. We are left with the impression of a group that for unknown reasons reacted against Peter, and perhaps also against his surroundings.

The Asides
One of the many paradoxes of the fourth Gospel is that the writer, in spite of his obscurity, is emphatically present, or is made present by the final redactor. This phenomenon is observable throughout the whole of the Gospel, including in the two extensive quotes above. A convincing example is the second chapter, in which the discussion with the Jews triggered by the temple cleansing ends:

> The Jews said: Forty-six years was this temple in building, and you will make it rise up again in three days?
> *He spoke however of the temple of his body.*
> *Now when he was resurrected from the dead, his disciples remembered that he had said this, and they believed in the Scripture and in the word that Jesus had spoken.*
> And as long as he remained in Jerusalem at Passover, at the feast, many placed faith in his name because they saw the signs which he did.
> *But Jesus himself placed no trust in them because he knew all, and since he did not need that anyone testified concerning man, for he knew what is in man* (2.20-25).

In this one passage three separate 'asides' occur, italicized for clarity. These typically Johannine asides have various functions: they explain Jesus' true purpose, they contrast this to the lack of understanding of both his opponents and his disciples, and they fill in what happened after the resurrection. Somewhat earlier in the same chapter there is a fourth, more general function, namely, to interpret that which is narrated: 'This Jesus did as first of the signs in Cana in Galilee, and he revealed his glory, and his disciples believed in him' (2.11). We will return shortly to the 'signs' and the 'belief'.

The theme of the disciples' lack of understanding occurs in the other Gospels as well. Twice Mark relates that the disciples did not understand what Jesus meant with the announcement of his death and resurrection. Their powers of comprehension failed, as it were, and 'they were afraid to ask him further' (Mk 9.10, 32). This apparent breakdown is smoothed away in Matthew, which is typical of that Gospel. Luke maintains it, however, and elaborates on it somewhat (Lk. 9.45; 18.34), apparently in connection with the incomprehension of those on the Emmaus road and others after the resurrection, as well as the lack of understanding of Joseph and Mary for their 12-year-old son (Lk. 24.35, 45; 2.50). Luke thus writes from a certain distance to the event, but keeps it to a passing, neutral mention. In the Johannine asides, the theme receives noticeable emphasis:

> His disciples did not understand this, but when Jesus was glorified, then they remembered that this had been written about him and that they had done this with him (12.16).

The interpretation of that which has been told is more emphatic in John than in the other Gospels:

> This Jesus did as first of the signs... This was again a second sign which Jesus did... (2.11; 4.54).

> He spoke, however, about Judas the son of Simon Iscariot, for he was going to betray him, one of the twelve (6.71; cf. 6.64; 13.11, 28-29).

Furthermore, there is a greater temporal distance from that which is narrated, and the interpretation has an outspoken theological purport:

> This [Caiaphas] said not of himself, but as high priest of that year he prophesied that Jesus would die for the people—and not for the people alone, but also so that he should gather the scattered children of God together. Now from that day on they deliberated to kill him (11.51-53; cf. 18.14).

> This he spoke about the Spirit which they who believed in him should receive, for the Spirit was not yet because Jesus was not yet glorified (7.39).

The first quote reveals to the reader the actual significance of the words of the high priest, which the man himself did not realize. The second one seeks to grant us insight even into the deepest motives of Jesus himself. Particularly in such asides the daring presence of this evangelist comes to the fore:

> And before the feast of Passover Jesus, knowing that his hour had come
> that he should pass from this world to the Father, having loved his own
> in this world, he loved them to the end (13.1).

Thus the fourth evangelist chooses a vantage point superior to that of Jesus' bystanders and disciples. The author presumes a great proximity to Jesus, practically even the ability of speaking in his name. The same vantage point is expressed in Jesus' long exposition at the last supper (chs. 13–16), and particularly in the long prayer in the first person (ch. 17). Again the 'disciple whom Jesus loved' comes to mind. Is he not the mysterious figure who is so close to Jesus that he can relate the deepest intention of his behaviour?

Simultaneously, the asides of the evangelist imply, nonetheless, a clear distance in time to that which is related. The impression of an extensive, late redaction is unmistakable, confirmed as well by other literary details, including the addition of the final chapter. The final redaction stage must have been much more drastic than in the case of the synoptic Gospels, with the result that John appears to be more of a unity. Nonetheless, we shall see that this Gospel contains as well ancient layers with authentic Jewish-Christian traditions.

The Vocabulary and World View
The presentation in this section is valid for both the Gospel and the Epistles of John: they have the same peculiar worldview, which is expressed in a distinct and rather limited vocabulary. This could bear a relationship to the emphatic myteriousness regarding the author. Both aspects portray a fairly closed world. Peculiar to Johannine language is the use of a limited number of key words in continuously varying combinations, giving a cyclic or spiral impression, and perhaps reflecting a special style of preaching. (Owing to the numerous references, in this section passages from the Gospel of John are indicated merely by chapter and verse numbers in italics.)

To Love / to Hate. The important place which the disciple 'whom Jesus loved' takes in the Gospel has already been indicated, as well as the emphasis with which the Risen One asked Peter whether he 'truly loved' him. The verb 'to love' (Greek: *agapan* or *philein*) occurs with striking frequency in the Johannine writings. Four relations are involved: the love between God and humankind (e.g. *3.16*; 1 Jn 4.10), between God and the Son (*3.35*; *5.20*; *14.31*), between the believers and the Son

(*13.1*; *14.15*), and among the believers (1 Jn 4.7; 2 Jn 5). Additionally, the close connections between all of these love relationships is characteristic:

> A new commandment I give unto you, that you love one another; as I have loved you, that you might also love one another. In this shall all men know that you are my disciples, if you have love one for the other (*13.34-35*; cf. 1 Jn 2.7-8).

The 'new commandment' refers possibly to the washing of feet at the beginning of the last supper earlier in the chapter. Apparently, an interpretation of the double love command, carried to an extreme, is involved:

> If anyone says that he loves God and hates his brother, he is a liar. For he who loves not his brother, whom he has seen, can not love God, whom he has not seen. And this command we have from him, that he who will love God must also love his brother (1 Jn 4.20-21).

In a typically Johannine manner, the fact that this mutual love is the one and only 'commandment' is repeated in continuous variation. The opposite is the verb 'to hate', which occurs far less frequently, but still more often than in other New Testament writings. In contrast to the love for one another there is, in particular, the hate for 'the world' (*7.7*; *15.18-19*; *17.14*; 1 Jn 3.13). Thus a community is portrayed that cultivates love among themselves, in particular at the communal meals, but which feels hatred for the outside world. Hate towards the outside world played a distinct role in Qumran, about which we will speak later.

The World / I, You. A typically Johanine key word is indeed 'world', *kosmos*, often with the negative connotation of 'outside world'. The following fragment is characteristic (note also the use of the word 'to love'):

> Love not the world, neither the things that are in the world. If any one love the world, the love of the Father is not in him. For all that is in the world, the lust of the flesh and the lust of the eyes and the pride of life, is not of the Father but is of the world. And the world passes away and the lusts thereof, but he that does the will of God abides until eternity (1 Jn 2.15-17).

In the Johannine writings, the word *kosmos* occurs much more frequently than in the synoptic Gospels. Furthermore, the 'world' is made an independent, almost personified, timeless opponent of God and his witnesses. Only sporadically is 'this world' spoken of in the manner of the Jewish apocalypses, that is, this world that passes away (*8.23*; *12.25*; *18.36*), concentrated in 'the ruler of this world' (*12.31*; *16.11*). Then again there is the timeless expression that Jesus 'passed from this world to the Father' (*13.1*). Opposite to the timeless, independent 'world' is the congregation, but, in the first place, Jesus himself ('hate', 'love'!):

> If the world hates you, know that they have hated me before you. If you were from the world, the world would have loved its own. Because you are not from the world, but I have chosen you out of the world, therefore the world hates you (*15.18-19*).

The contrast is not symmetric. We read as well:

> Behold, the lamb of God, that takes away the sins *of the world*! (*1.29*).

> For God so loved *the world*, that he gave his only begotten son, that whosoever believes in him shall not perish but have everlasting life (*3.16*; cf. *12.47*).

In other places, however, the salvation of the believers is contrasted to 'the world' (*17.9*; 1 Jn 4.9). Characteristic of the Gospel of John is the use made of the emphatic, in Greek non-essential, personal pronouns 'I' and 'you'. 'I' is used primarily by Jesus and usually in a polemic manner (ch. *8*). Particularly in chs. *13–16*, in the setting of the last supper, Jesus' followers stand together with him opposite to the world: 'You are clean...' (*13.10*; *15.3*).

Light / Darkness. This pair of concepts is a widespread means of expressing a cosmic dualism. It is found with characteristic frequency in the Johannine writings, and that has given scholars reason to search for its spiritual background. Quite correctly, the writings of Qumran have been singled out. Earlier (p. 48) a passage was cited in which love towards the 'children of light' is contrasted with hate for the 'children of darkness'. 'Children of light' occur also in the New Testament, including once in John (see below; also 1 Thess. 5.5; Eph. 5.8). 'Children of darkness' does not occur, but 'the child of destruction' (*17.12*; 2 Thess. 2.3) and 'a child of the devil' (Acts 13.10) do. In all of these cases, the phrasing 'child of...' is typically Semitic and means 'subject of...'. The dualism in John is less explicit than in Qumran, but much

298 _'If this be from Heaven...'_

stronger than elsewhere in the New Testament. The correspondence with Qumran regarding the 'love of the brother' is striking:

> He who says that he is in the light and hates his brother is in darkness until now. He who loves his brother remains in the light, and there is no offence in him. But he that hates his brother is in darkness and walks in darkness, and he knows not where he goes, for the darkness has blinded his eyes (1 Jn 2.9-11).

The following passages show that the dualism of light and darkness, just as the contrast to the 'world', is concentrated in the person of Jesus in the Gospel. Further, there appear to be links in content between the Gospel and the epistles, although not necessarily the same author is implied:

> I am the light of the world. He that follows me shall not walk in darkness but shall have the light of life (8.12; cf. 9.5; 12.46).

> Yet a little while is the light among you. Walk as long as you have the light, so that the darkness does not overtake you. For he that walks in darkness does not know where he goes. As long as you have the light, you must trust in the light, so that you will be children of light (12.35-36).

How different is this from the climate of the synoptic tradition in which Jesus addresses his disciples as 'the light of the world' and summons them to let their good works shine before people (Mt. 5.14-16; see further pp. 292-93).

Truth / Lie. Just as with 'love' and 'hate', 'light' and 'darkness' here again there is a somewhat lopsided dualism. The words 'truth', 'true' and 'truly' occur frequently, certainly in comparison to the other New Testament writings, while 'lie' and 'liar' occur less often. 1 John 4.20 has already been quoted: 'If anyone says that he loves God and hates his brother, he is a liar.' An explicit passage occurs in a dispute with the Jews, where we will pause in another connection:

> You are from the father-devil and want to do the lusts of your father. He is a murderer from the beginning, and he does not stand in the truth because there is no truth in him. When he speaks lies, he speaks from his own, for his father is a liar as well (8.44).

The polemic tenor of the words 'truth' and 'lie' appears also in the following reference, where it is about the sharp contrast between one's own congregation and 'the others':

> Beloved…try the spirits whether they be from God, for many lying prophets have come into the world… You are from God, little children, and you have conquered them, for he that is with you is greater than he that is in the world. They are from the world, therefore they speak from the world and the world listens to them. We are from God, he that knows God listens to us, he that is not from God listens not to us. From this we know the spirit of truth and the spirit of deception (1 Jn 4.1-6).

There is here also a Christ-centred intensification, for example, in the well-known verse, 'I am the way, the truth and the life' (14.6). Apocalyptic language involving the 'spirits of truth and of deceit' are found throughout the Qumran writings (e.g. 1QS 3.18-19).

The words discussed here primarily concern the manner in which the Johannine community viewed itself and the outside world, and that is, of course, but one aspect. There is also a whole series of key words that define the distinguishing traits of Johannine theology, to which we will return in the section about the christological allegory.

The Structure: Feasts and Signs

An obvious difference between John and the synoptic Gospels has to do with composition. In contrast to the first three Gospels, the cleansing of the temple occurs, for example, at the beginning of Jesus' ministry. Two aspects should be noted: the progress of Jesus' public ministry and the structure of the story. These do not coincide, for the arrangement of the story has apparently undergone its own development.

In the Gospel of John, a whole series of Jewish feasts are mentioned where Jesus is present, mostly in Jerusalem:

2.13   'And the *Passover* of the Jews was nigh, and Jesus went up to Jerusalem'—after which follows the cleansing of the temple (see also 2.23; 4.45).

5.1   'Hereafter there was *a feast* of the Jews and Jesus went up to Jerusalem'—the healing of the lame man at Bethesda, dispute with the Jews.

6.4   'And *Passover* was nigh, the feast of the Jews,' in Galilee (6.1) —follows the miraculous feeding and the dispute about 'bread from heaven'.

7.2   'And the feast of the Jews was nigh, the *Feast of Booths*,' Jesus, too, went up to Jerusalem (v. 10); on 'the last day of the feast' (7.37) Jesus speaks about 'living water'.

10.22 'Then there was (the feast of) *Rededication* in Jerusalem, it was winter, and Jesus walked in the temple in Solomon's colonnade' —a dispute ensues because 'Jesus makes himself God' (v. 33).

> 11.55 'And the *Passover* of the Jews was nigh, and many went up
> to Jerusalem.' Jesus, too, makes his entry from neighbouring
> Bethany (11.12-15), has his last supper (13.1), is taken captive
> and dies on the eve of the feast (18.28, 39; 19.14).

Three Passovers are involved, and in between another unnamed feast, a
Feast of Booths, and a Feast of Rededication (see about feasts, p. 79).
In the synoptic Gospels the last two feasts are not even mentioned, and
but one Passover is spoken of. Where does this Johannine emphasis
upon Jewish feasts come from?

An attractive explanation is that the pattern of the *Jewish festival
calendar* underlies the fourth Gospel as a whole. The mention of the
three Passovers would then, for example, reflect a triannual cycle of
Torah reading in the congregation of the evangelist (see p. 78). Traces
of this would be discernible around the feasts. Indeed echoes of Passover resound in the story of the miraculous feeding and the discussion
that follows it: *manna*, 'bread from heaven', and the 'murmuring' of the
Jews and the disciples (Jn 6.31, 41, 61). Furthermore, by 'the last day of
the Feast (of Booths)', on which Jesus spoke about the 'living water', is
meant the joyous feast of the pouring of water that was celebrated in the
temple at that time (*m. Sukkah* 4.9). On the other hand, the Gospel of
John as a whole evidences great aversion towards Jewish ritual. To the
extent that there indeed is an interest in the feasts, this must have
belonged to an early stage in the development of the Gospel.

Another explanation would be that the Gospel of John draws from
a further unknown source, a 'Gospel of Signs', in which Jesus was
present at all of these feasts. The feasts should, then, be read not in the
perspective of the composition of the Gospel, but in the context of the
progress of Jesus' actual public ministry. A difficulty is then to clarify
why there is no trace of these accounts in the other Gospels. The two
explanations need not exclude each other. It could be that Jesus indeed
attended all those feasts, but that in Johannine circles there was particular interest for this information, thus explaining also their absence in
the other Gospels.

We return to the structure. If a division is made between John 12 and
13, an interesting dichotomy is produced. The first portion comprises
Jesus' public ministry up to and including the resurrection of Lazarus
and the triumphal entry into Jerusalem; the second half contains the
occurrences of the last days, the last supper, suffering, death and resurrection. Both parts end, thus, with the motif of dying and resurrection,

so that John 11–12 forms the first climax of the Gospel. The first half is marked by public polemics with opponents, the second by his teaching the disciples in the seclusion of the last supper. After the opening chapter, the first part begins with a powerful scene in public in the temple; it also closes with the same. In contrast, in the second half Jesus remains inactive towards the outside world.

With this structure in mind, a place can be given to another important element of John, namely, the *signs* performed by Jesus, which play a role only in the first half. The miracle in Cana 'was the first of the signs which Jesus did', and 'many believed in his name when they saw the signs which he did' in the temple. The healing of the son of the courtier in Capernaum was 'again a second sign that Jesus did' (2.11, 23; 4.54). The allusion to the importance of the signs continues throughout the first half, but the numbering is discontinued (6.2, 14-15; 9.16; 11.47; 12.37). A passage towards the end of the first half, about the glorious entry into Jerusalem, is most emphatic:

> Thus the multitude testified which was with him when he called Lazarus out of the grave and raised him up from the dead. And for this reason also the multitude came to meet him because they had heard that he had performed a sign. Now the Pharisees said to themselves: You see that you accomplish nothing. Behold, the whole world has gone after him! (12.17-19).

One of the explanations for this explicit emphasis on the 'signs' is again that it is a stylistic device of the evangelist for structuring the material. The series of signs, culminating in the resurrection of Lazarus, gives rhythm to the first half of the story and is a basic pattern for the whole Gospel, as the 'first ending' makes clear: the signs serve to arouse and strengthen the faith of the reader (20.30-31). The emphatic use of the word 'sign' for relatively few stories of healings and miracles is a distinguishing Johannine trait. This structuring element must have functioned primarily in a preliminary stage of the present Gospel, because the counting of the signs ceases after the second one, while on the other hand other miracles had already taken place (2.23). Furthermore, after the closing chapter about the significance of the signs, another entire chapter is added. This all has served to underpin the unprovable but illuminating theory that there must have been a 'Gospel of Signs' that was incorporated into the present Gospel.

Such considerations indicate in any case that the fourth Gospel has undergone a radical redactional process. Besides a new final chapter there must have been at least one other chapter inserted, as can be deduced from the fact that the story in ch. 4 ends in Galilee, ch. 5 transfers the story to Jerusalem, while ch. 6 continues in Galilee as though there had been no change in location. Ch. 5 about the unnamed feast in Jerusalem must, thus, have been inserted. Finally, ch. 2 shows signs of being heavily reworked, among other things in the high concentration of asides (see 2.11, 17, 21, 22, 24-25). It could even be assumed that the whole second chapter was inserted at this place at a later stage of redaction.

The Christological Allegory

John distinguishes itself from the synoptic Gospels not only in vocabulary but also by a totally unique, theologically tinted style.

An initial assessment is negative. It is striking that the *parables*, so characteristic of the teachings of Jesus in the synoptic Gospels, are completely lacking in John. Considering the fact that outside of the New Testament parables occur only in rabbinic literature, this difference speaks volumes. With regard to this characteristic portion of Jesus' teachings, the affinity with the Pharisaic–rabbinic milieu that we encountered in the synoptic Gospels is lacking in John.

Instead of the parables, the Johannine Jesus utters characteristic contemplative, figurative language. These metaphors concur with the parables in the pedagogic use they make of well-known images, but they differ strongly in the manner of doing so. Like a fable, a parable consists of a brief tale in which the intention can be summarized in a moral. The Johannine figures of speech, however, provide the intention of the imagery in direct speech. The following is a salient example:

> I am the good shepherd. The good shepherd lays down his life for his sheep. He who works as hireling and not as shepherd—whose own sheep they are not—sees the wolf coming, leaves the sheep behind, and flees, so that the wolf grabs them and mauls them. For he is a hireling and the sheep do not matter deeply to him. I am the good shepherd and I know my own... (Jn 10.11-14).

The details give rise to the suspicion that a real parable lies at the basis, which has been reworked into an extended metaphor in the first person: 'I am the good shepherd...' That would mean that the explicitly Johan nine figures of speech represent a reworking of parables whose traces are still observable.

Although explicit interpretations, such as that of the good shepherd, form a consistent part of Johannine imagery, that is not to say that they are directly understandable. On the contrary, the *incomprehension of the listeners* is a main them of the Gospel, and the tension between these two motifs is one of the distinguishing features of John. When Jesus speaks to Nicodemus about being born again, *nota bene* as a prerequisite for seeing the Kingdom of God, the latter takes this literally: 'A grown person can not crawl back into his mother's womb, can he?' (3.4). As explanation, Jesus speaks of 'the wind blowing where it chooses' and of the snake that was 'raised' in the desert—earthly images by which, however, heavenly matters are intended (3.12). The same occurs when Jesus begins to speak about water with the Samaritan woman. He is indeed thirsty, but he refers to 'living water', which he himself gives, 'a fount of water welling up unto eternal life' (4.10, 14). In a later 'aside' the image of water is further specified as 'the Spirit' (7.38-39). At the feeding of the multitude, Jesus does not mean 'food that perishes but…that which remains until eternal life, …the true bread from heaven' (6.27, 32). Towards the end of the ensuing conversation, he speaks of 'chewing' his flesh and drinking his blood, which even the disciples themselves consider to be a 'hard saying'. In reaction, apparently as basis behind this whole imagery, we read, 'It is the Spirit that makes alive, the flesh serves no purpose' (6.63). Constantly, something else than the obvious, literal sense is involved.

There is thus every reason to qualify Johannine imagery as intentional 'allegory'. This Hellenistic term means literally 'to intend something else', something other than, for example, the literal significance of the rough stories of gods in Homer or the 'primitive' passages in the Old Testament. We encountered this phenomenon earlier with Philo, precisely with the example of the 'bread from heaven' (see pp. 84-85). The Johannine saying that 'the Spirit makes alive, while the flesh serves no purpose' is unmistakable allegory. There is even a certain affinity to Paul, who says concerning the real significance of the Scriptures, 'The letter kills, but the Spirit makes alive' (2 Cor. 3.6; see p. 178), and who explicitly uses the term 'allegorizing' (Gal. 4.24-26, Sarah and Hagar as symbols of the heavenly and earthly Jerusalem, see p. 367).

It is not without significance that the lack of comprehension concerning the intended spiritual rebirth comes from Nicodemus, who is addressed by Jesus as a 'teacher of Israel' (Jn 3.10). Hereby it must be noted that the expression 'being born again' is ambiguous in Greek: *anōthen gennasthai* also means 'being born *from on high*'. Besides not understanding Jesus' spiritual intention, Nicodemus does not grasp the Greek play on words. The tension here between explicit metaphor and incomprehension borders on sarcasm. We can conclude that the text about the conversation with Nicodemus was formulated in a Greek milieu, in which one apparently resisted 'teachers of Israel' and in which allegory was a favourite method of expression.

The matter is, however, more complex. The play on words between 'wind' and 'Spirit' does work via the Greek *pneuma*, which has both significances, but it is best explained from the Aramaic and Hebrew *ruah* (Gen. 1.2). Here again we have a trace of a narrative parable, interrupted by 'you know not...' (Jn 3.8). Finally, the expression 'living waters' (Jn 4.11; 7.38) is originally Semitic. These three facts point to an older, Semitic layer under the Greek surface text of the Gospel, recalling the transition from speaking in parables to thinking in allegories, which we began to presume in the above.

In all events, in the extant text level, allegoric thinking dominates and is a general characteristic of the Gospel. Thus all the 'signs' in John receive a spiritual, heavenly significance. The changing of water into wine at Cana and the resurrection of Lazarus are pre-eminently 'signs', in both cases the emphasis being clearly not upon the miracle but upon the significance thereof. In this, the true sense of the typically Johannine term 'sign' reveals itself. Reciprocally, this must be related to the lack of miracle stories like those in the synoptic Gospels. The reviving of the dead youth is here called a 'sign', as is the miraculous multiplication of bread (Jn 4.54; cf. Lk. 7.1-17; Jn 6.26). It is specifically in this context that Jesus enunciates the words charged with significance, 'It is the Spirit that makes alive, the flesh serves no purpose.' In other words, the point is no longer to understand the things which Jesus does in a fleshly manner, but spiritually, as signs.

The most characteristic application of the Johannine allegory involves the figure of Jesus, or what we could call the *christological allegory*. At the same time, this is one of the most prominent differences with the synoptic Gospels. In the latter, Jesus can forbid making known his messianic glory and reject the form of address 'good Master' (Mk 5.43; 8.30; 10.17). He indicates his awareness of his messiahship only indirectly and warns against those that assert 'I am the one' (Mk

13.6, but cf. 14.62). In John, however, he declares openly, in a mounting series of statements, in direct speech, in the first person, not veiled by narrative form or proverb:

> I am the bread of life... (6.35, 41, 48, 51)
> I am the light of the world... (8.12; 9.5)
> I am the door of the sheep... (10.7, 9)
> I am the good shepherd... (10.11, 14)
> I am the resurrection and the life... (11.25)
> I am the way, the truth and the life... (14.6)
> I am the true vine... (15.1)

Keeping in mind the exclusive standpoint which the evangelist seeks in 'the disciple whom Jesus loved', and the asides in which he reveals the deeper sense of that which is told and the true intention of Jesus, it appears that *the Johannine evangelist writes, as it were, in the name of Jesus himself.*

In addition, the christological allegory and the Johannine imagery in general are drawn out in long discourses as a rule. This often occurs within the framework of a conversation, such as that about heavenly bread or the light of the world. At the last supper, Jesus holds practically one long monologue. It is this discursive and allegorical nature that lends to the Johannine style such a typically reflective, 'theological' character, here again in sharp contrast to the synoptic Gospels.

In exemplary fashion, the christological-allegorizing aspect of the Gospel is expressed in the so-called *prologue*, Jn 1.1-18. It is a type of hymnic composition of themes from the whole Gospel and gives the impression of being a later completion. Quite distinctive is the occurrence of a conspicuous key word that in this sense does not occur further in John nor in the New Testament: *logos*, 'word'. This is a preeminently Hellenistic term with roots both in Greek philosophy and in biblical usage, and is perhaps for this reason a favourite word of Philo of Alexandria, as well as of Greek church fathers such as Origen and Eusebius. Using such terms as 'beginning', 'word', 'God', 'light' and 'world', the hymnic prologue is clearly a variation on the beginning of the creation story (Gen. 1.1-5; cf. Prov. 8.22-23). At the same time, everything concentrates upon the word, the Son or Christ, and we can rightly speak of a 'cosmic-christological hymn'. Two passages about the precursor, John the Baptist, are worked into this, and form a direct connection to the actual introduction to the Gospel. We shall now allow this majestic, ever mysterious hymn to speak for itself, and in doing so render several peculiar Greek expressions and textual variants:

> In the beginning was the Word, and the Word was with God, and God was the Word. This one was in the beginning with God.
> Everything became through him, and outside of him nothing became. What became through him was life, and the life was the light [of humankind]. And the light shines in darkness, and the darkness has not grasped onto it.
> There came a man, sent from God, named John...
> And thus the true light, which lightens every person, was coming into the world...
> And the word became flesh and dwelled among us, and we beheld his glory, the glory as of the firstborn of the Father, full of grace and truth. John testifies about him...
> For the law was given through Moses, grace and truth have come into being through Jesus Christ. God—no one has ever seen; an only begotten God, which is on the bosom of the Father, he has explained him (Jn 1.1-18).

A Peculiar Jewish-Christian Tradition

The fourth Gospel is a complex whole, and includes unique accounts of Jesus and his disciples that not infrequently appear to go back to authentic tradition. These must belong to an older layer of the Gospel that represents another Jewish-Christian milieu than that of the synoptic tradition.

The attention given to the feasts provides interesting *chronological information*, according to which Jesus would have travelled to Jerusalem twice for Passover, and have celebrated the same feast once in Galilee. That would mean that his public ministry lasted minimally two and a half years, much longer than the year or half a year that we can deduce from the synoptics. Further, he would have gone up to Jerusalem at least four times—for the first and last Passover, the unnamed feast, and the Feast of Booths (Jn 5; 7). From this last feast on, he would have stayed on at least two months in the Holy City, that is, up to and including the Feast of Rededication (see 10.40-41). Thus a substantial portion of Jesus' public ministry would have taken place in Jerusalem itself. On the other hand, Mark and the other Gospels report but one Passover, and Jesus' ministry appears to have lasted a half a year or at most a year, and his stay in Jerusalem one or several weeks. Although the latter is the accepted version, it appears to be rather short for the amount of reports about his work. The accounts of Jesus' many discussions at the temple square and of his continual teaching of the people also seem to imply a stay of months rather than weeks (Mk 12.38; Lk. 19.48; 21.37). The synoptic chronology appears to have been abbreviated, while the Johannine seems more plausible.

A number of detailed *geographic specifications* are also characteristic of John. The healing of the lame man on the Shabbat is introduced as follows: 'There is in Jerusalem near the Sheep Gate a water bath which in Hebrew is called Bethzatha and has five colonnades' (Jn 5.2). The exact name is contested already in the ancient manuscripts, which indicates an archaic tradition. Other forms of the name are: Bethesda (known from the traditional translations), as well as Bedsaida, Bethsaidan and Belzetha. Comparably 'precise' and therefore contested in the manuscripts is the report that John the Baptist first baptized in Bethania, also called Bethabara, or, geographically more plausible, Betharaba, in other words, Beth-Arava (1.28). Later it is said that John baptized 'at Ainon near Salem' (3.23). Related to this are the unique reports about Jesus' work of baptism. In the same connection (cf. 4.1-3), we are informed about his conversation with a woman in the Samaritan city Sychar (or Sichar, also called, but less likely, Sichem), 'close to the land that Jacob gave to his son Joseph; Jacob's well was there' (4.5-6). The authenticity of this account appears to be contradicted by the Matthaean prohibition 'to enter a city of the Samaritans' (Mt. 10.5). Nonetheless, in Matthew as well Jesus becomes involved in a conversation with a woman on non-Jewish soil (Mt. 15.22; cf. pp. 162, 280). Furthermore, the well is situated outside of town (Jn 4.28) and the evangelist does not say that Jesus entered the town.

The fourth Gospel provides unique information about the relationship to *John the Baptist*. We are told that two disciples of John transferred to Jesus, which assumes a fairly close relationship between the two teachers (Jn 1.35-41). We are told that Jesus and his disciples baptized 'in the region of Judaea', apparently not far from the locations where John baptized (3.22-26; 4.1-2; 1.28; 10.40). The statement that occurs in all of the Gospels that John said that after him someone would come 'who will baptize with the Holy Ghost (and fire)' is hereby cast in an unusual light (Mk 1.8; Mt. 3.11; Lk. 3.16; Jn 1.26, 33). An actual baptism with water can be included in this. Precisely that could be implied in the story that immediately, and apparently purposely, precedes the accounts of Jesus' work of baptism, namely, the conversation with Nicodemus: 'If someone is not born of water and Spirit, he can not enter the kingdom of God' (Jn 3.5). Alongside this close affinity there are also traces of a certain rivalry between Jesus' disciples and those of John (Jn 10.41, cf. 5.36; see also pp. 132, 139-40).

Directly after the report of the 'transfer' of two disciples, remarkable things are reported about two other *disciples of John*. One of them, who is not mentioned in the other Gospels, is explicitly introduced later: 'Nathanael, from Cana in Galilee' (Jn 21.2).

> The following day he decided to go to Galilee and he found Philip. And Jesus said to him: Follow me. Philip came from Bethsaida, the city of Andrew and Peter. Then Philip found Nathanael and said to him: The one of whom Moses in the law and also the prophets wrote have we found, Jesus the son of Joseph from Nazareth... Jesus saw Nathanael coming to him and said about him: See, in truth an Israelite in whom is no guile... Then Nathanael answered him: Rabbi, you are the Son of God, you are the King of Israel (Jn. 1.43-49).

The account derives apparently from the same tradition as the one directly preceding it. There, too, Jesus is addressed as 'Rabbi', not in the meaning of the title 'rabbi' but literally 'my master' (see pp. 51-52). This significance is supplied here in so many words: 'Rabbi, which translated is to say "master"...' (1.38). This Hebrew form of address occurs also elsewhere in the New Testament, but most frequently in the first half of John (also 3.2, 26; 4.31; 6.25; 9.2; 11.8). As to Christology or the theological valuation of Jesus, the statements of Philip and Nathanael sound plainly archaic. We find ourselves apparently again in an older segment of the Johannine tradition.

The accounts concerning *Nicodemus*, which occur only in this Gospel, can also be seen in this light. He is 'one of the Pharisees' (3.1) who came to talk with Jesus by night, as one of the 'many' in Jerusalem who 'had come to believe in him' (2.23). The conversation has the same characteristics as the rest of the Gospel and has not escaped the pen of the redactor. The possibly Semitic origin of the saying about the wind and the Spirit has already been discussed (p. 304). Confirmation of our surmise of a special tradition can be gathered by taking the reports about Nicodemus together. As a Pharisee with an open attitude, his role is somewhat comparable to that of Gamaliel in Acts (Acts 5.34). When the leaders are divided about the messianic significance of Jesus' ministry, Nicodemus defends him: 'Our law does not judge someone, does it, unless he has first been heard and one knows what he does?' (7.51). In spite of sarcastic reactions, he later again shows his allegiance by bringing the enormous amount of 100 pounds balm of myrrh and aloes for Jesus' burial, again an exclusively Johannine report (19.39). This positive attitude towards a Jewish leader contrasts with the message of the Gospel as a whole and points to an underlying tradition.

An even more prominent figure, not mentioned elsewhere, is *Lazarus* from Bethany near Jerusalem, a brother of Mary and Martha who occur in Luke as well (10.38-39). Lazarus' resurrection from the dead is the last and greatest of Jesus' 'signs'. The possibility has been touched upon that the story belongs to the older layers of John as part of a former 'Gospel of Signs' (p. 268). The repeated mention of many Jews from the milieu of Mary, Martha and Lazarus who, just as Nicodemus and many others in Jerusalem itself, sympathized with Jesus also appears to be ancient (11.19, 31, 36, 45; 12.9-19). Again, the positive Jewish interest in Jesus is at odds with the Gospel as a whole.

Belonging to the old Jewish-Christian tradition in John as well are certain concepts and arguments used. The connection between the saying that the 'wind blows where it will' and baptism (Jn 3.8) has been suggested above. The 'blowing' of the Spirit over the water is reminiscent, of course, of the story of creation and, on the other hand, there is the synoptic account that when Jesus was baptized the Spirit descended upon him 'as a dove' (Mk 1.10). These links are strengthened by a comparison with two ancient Jewish texts. In a Qumran fragment a rare Hebrew verb *rāhap*, 'flutter', used in Gen. 1.2 for the wind over the surface of the waters, is applied to the Spirit resting upon the meek (4Q521 frg 2, 2.6; see pp. 130-31). In a rabbinic tradition the 'Spirit' that 'flutters' over the primal flood is compared to a dove who flutters coolness to her young (*b. Ḥag.* 16a). Such connections are apparently inexplicitly presumed in the saying in Jn 3.8.

At the end of the section on the Shabbat (see p. 318), another example of a Jewish-Christian tradition will be discussed, involving an argument for healing on the Shabbat that accords with a rabbinic midrash. As an exception, the Johannine tradition here confirms the synoptic depiction of Jesus' familiarity with the Pharisaic–rabbinic manner of thinking.

The striking emphasis on the *exclusive relationship of Jesus to God* as 'son' of the 'father' appears also to have come forth from a particular type of Jewish-Christian tradition. Though the complexity of this case exceeds that of all other instances, it appears at the same time to be an enlargement of an element from the primal tradition. Earlier we noted that Jesus expressed his strong sense of being sent in the introductory word of prayer, 'Father', chiefly preserved in the synoptic tradition (see pp. 137-38), but also occurring in the Johannine tradition (Jn 12.27-28; 11.41; 17.1, 5, 11), thus being a basic element in the earliest Christian tradition. Jesus' strong awareness of being 'son' of his 'heavenly Father', which in the synoptic Gospels plays a role somewhat behind the scenes (cf. Mt. 11.25-27), appears to be drawn to the footlights in the Johannine tradition, in accordance with the tendency of the evangelist to identify himself with Jesus and to speak for him.

The Date of Passover
Another characteristic of the fourth Gospel rooted in a Jewish-Christian tradition involves the question of the calendar, already touched upon several times, and, connected to this, the date of the Passover and Jesus' last supper (see pp. 79-81, 165-66).

According to the synoptic tradition this meal was held on the evening before the first day of Passover (Mk 14.12). Apparently his interrogation, condemnation and execution occurred later on the same day; this was on Friday (Mk 15.42; Lk. 23.54; Jn 19.31). As we have already discussed (p. 271), the Sanhedrin could not possibly have had a session on Passover. The synoptic calculation of time is here internally contradictory. This is not the case in John: Jesus' last supper, trial and execution all take place *before* Passover; the priests celebrate Passover the directly following day (Jn 13.1; 18.28; 19.14). The last supper is then not a Passover meal, and the well-known introductory words, which at least according to one version contain an explicit reference to Passover (Lk. 21.15), are lacking. Apart from that, the Gospels contain reports about various questionings—in front of the high priest, Pilate, Herod Antipas and again Pilate. It is difficult to conceive of this all happening in one day. A difference is expressed as well at the anointing in Bethany. According to the synoptic chronology, this occurred *two* days before Passover (Mk 14.2-3; Mt. 26.2, 6), while according to John it was *six* days before Passover (Jn 12.1, 3). The literal correspondences between the two versions—remarkable in themselves—suggest one and the same event.

For these issues, the French scholar, Annie Jaubert, has suggested a solution both astute and simple. Divergent Jewish calendars of that day are assumed and the one occurrence that is unambiguously dated in both traditions is taken as a point of departure, namely, the anointing in Bethany.

According to the Johannine narrative, the anointing took place six days before Passover, and Jesus died on the Friday afternoon before the beginning of Passover. Counting back six days, the anointing would have taken place on Sunday evening. Somewhere in between Jesus' last supper took place, with only the indication that it was 'before the feast of Passover' (Jn 13.1). According to the synoptic tradition, on the contrary, the anointing occurred two days before Passover Eve, the evening in which the last supper took place. If this is the same anointing, as suggested by the Gospel of John, and this also took place on Sunday, then a different dating of Passover is implied, namely, two days after Sunday evening, that is, Tuesday evening. Following Jewish custom, the preceding evening is counted along with the following day. In Johannine tradition Passover occurred on the Friday evening and Saturday, but on Tuesday evening and Wednesday according to the synoptic calculation of time. The usual conception that the last supper took place on Thursday evening, which seems to come from simply reading John and the synoptics together, cannot be harmonized with this. It could not be preceded by the same anointing, because this would then have occurred on Tuesday evening according to the synoptic narrative, but on Friday according to the Johannine tradition.

John reckons as the priests in the temple did, and that must have been according to the Pharisaic calendar (18.28; 19.14). A surprising confirmation of this can be found in a report in the Talmud, in which as a matter of course the Pharisaic calendar is assumed, but which is lacking in traditional Talmud editions due to Christian censorship: 'On the evening before the Shabbat, on the evening before Passover, they hung up Jesus the Nazorean (*Yeshu ha-noṣri*)' (*b. Sanh.* 43a-b, Florence ms.). The synoptic accounts appear thus to follow a divergent calendar.

The result of this reconstruction is that there were three days between Jesus' last supper and his execution. Both the synoptics and John appear, however, to suggest that this was but one space of 24 hours. We have already assumed (pp. 306-307) that the chronology of Mark has been abbreviated, and his description of these eventful days will form no exception. In Mark, for example, we read nothing about the interrogation before Herod Antipas, of which Luke does tell (23.6-11) and which hardly could have been construed. John also does not provide a coalescent account. He is silent concerning the interrogations not only before Herod Antipas but also before the Sanhedrin, both quite time-consuming occurrences. We are confronted with a characteristic of ancient historiography that even the conscientious historian Luke exhibits: instead of a continuous stream of events that modern historians strive after, only representative episodes are described. The unconventional assumption that Jesus' captivity lasted three nights and days solves the question of all those interrogations as well. With the intermediate space of three days, it is conceivable how he successively was brought before the high priests, the Sanhedrin, Pilate, Herod Antipas, and again Pilate, subsequently was flogged and crucified, and eventually, in contrast to the two criminals who came straight from prison, died of exhaustion on the cross.

Jaubert found the clincher of her solution in ancient ecclesiastical traditions according to which Jesus' last supper occurred on *Tuesday* evening. That is not an arbitrary calendar day, but is the evening before the fourth day of the week on which Passover should fall according to the Essene calendar (see p. 80). The surprising result is that Jesus and his disciples, at least in that year, celebrated Passover according to a calendar that diverged from the Pharisaic and was somewhat akin to the Essene. In the following chapter we will discuss the *Didache* where another more or less Essene feature will be encountered in a Jewish-Christian calendar.

There appears to have been surprising diversity within nascent Jewish Christianity. The early Johannine tradition was one of the variants, which on the exceptional issue of the feast calendar appears to be closer to the Pharisees than the synoptic tradition and Jesus himself. The question had great consequences in the early church: still at the end of the second century many Asia Minor churches celebrated Passover on the rabbinic–Pharisaic date, with an appeal to 'John', the beloved disciple of Jesus! They were contested by the bishop of Rome and his cohorts, who based themselves upon the 'apostolic tradition', apparently derived from the synoptic Gospels (Eusebius, *Church History* 5.23–25).

The Johannine Milieu

The preceding elicits a preliminary survey of the differences between the Johannine milieu, that of the synoptic Gospels, and that of Jesus himself.

The Gospel itself provides certain indications about its milieu. It evokes a closed, dualistic thought world, from which an isolated community speaks, a community that viewed itself as sharply contrasting to the hostile outside world. Added to this is the mysterious 'disciple whom Jesus loved'. According to the final redactor, this was the author of the Gospel; he must have had an important position in the Johannine community. The 'evangelist' writes from the viewpoint of this disciple on the bosom of Jesus and thus practically speaking for Jesus himself. This is also expressed in the commentarial asides and in the phrasing of Jesus' words. Finally, there is the covert but consistent rivalry between the mysterious disciple and Peter. The Johannine tradition represents a group that reacted against 'the world', identified itself closely with Jesus through the person of its leader, and disputed the authority of Peter.

We can supplement these impressions from other sources. In most New Testament writings, Peter has the position of the most prominent disciple, the 'rock' upon which Jesus built his church (Gal. 1.18; 2.7-8, cf. p. 179; Mk 3.16; Acts 1.15; 2.14; Mt. 16.18). In other words, there were broad, non-homogeneous circles within which not only Paul's epistles, Luke and Acts belonged, as well as the first epistle 'of Peter', but also the Gospels of Mark and Matthew. The anti-Petrine attitude of John appears to be a tradition that 'from the beginning' chose the position of a dissident minority.

External sources can substantiate this impression. The Qumran texts, with their largely dualistic and dissident terminology, also lend themselves to being read as the reflection of a persecuted community of chosen ones in the midst of an evil world. Analogous to this, the presence of dualistic terminology and the absence of parables in John imply a fairly great distance to the Pharisaic–rabbinic environment. In that regard, the Johannine community appears to be more 'Essene' and less 'Pharisaic' than the broader early Christian circles in which Peter was revered. Due to the fragmentary and biased character of our sources, however, it is difficult to know in which proportions these correspondences and differences should be seen. In all events, the fact that calculations were made according to the Pharisaic calendar excludes an Essene identification of the Johannine tradition.

The last trace may be followed perhaps a bit further. The Gospel follows the calendar that was adhered to in the temple at the instigation of the Pharisees. Through the mysterious disciple, it seeks to bring the reader close to the bosom of Jesus. At a dramatic moment, the reader is informed that this disciple was 'an acquaintance of the high priest' (Jn 18.15-16). This is the more intriguing due to the exceptional attention that the evangelist gives to the happenings in and around Jerusalem and his familiarity with the prominent Nicodemus (Jn 2–3; 11–12; cf. 7.25). Was the mysterious disciple perhaps affiliated with the Sadducees, who we imagine primarily to reside in Jerusalem and who had to subordinate their own opinions on temple ritual and calendar to that of the Pharisees? The unpopularity of the Sadducees could give the Johannine mysteriousness extra relief.

The Gospel's affinities to Greek elements could confirm these conjectures further. The allegory, the Greek play on words in the conversation with Nicodemus, and key concepts like *kosmos* and *logos* point to a Hellenistic-Jewish context. The timeless nature of the Johannine conception of the world points in the same direction; Philo's work also employs a timeless, non-eschatological world image. We know that some of the high priestly families that formed the core of the Sadducees since Herod the Great came from Alexandria (Josephus, *Ant.* 15.320-22). Because the Sadducean high priests were forced to follow the popular Pharisaic temple ritual, the confluence of Hellenistic–Sadducean affinity and fidelity to Pharisaic rules is conceivable. Such groups as the Therapeuts (see pp. 48-49) have taught us further that in and around Alexandria groups could flourish that lived in seclusion and practised an introverted Torah mysticism. Some combination of these elements could have been the cradle of Johannine thinking. It is not possible to be more specific. We know as yet painfully little about the Sadducees, and the mysteriousness of the fourth Gospel remains inexorable.

The obvious differences with the synoptic-Pauline circles imply as well a clear distance to Jesus' milieu. The question is how this developed. It appears to be a tradition that from the beginning assumed an excentric position in regard to the other disciples of Jesus. Nonetheless, there were connections, such as the correspondences prove. The term 'a peculiar Jewish-Christian tradition' summarizes the presence of affinity and differences. The disparities appear to have increased, as is well imaginable in the climate of growing social unrest after mid first century, when, for example, the tension between the Pauline churches and the churches of Judaea also mounted. The war and the destruction of Jerusalem will not have diminished the difficulties.

Shabbat (Sabbath)

Theoretically it would be more logical to discuss the law first and then the Shabbat, for the Shabbat is but one commandment of the law. In the fourth Gospel, however, the order is reversed, and the great discussions about the law arise as a result of the two concrete clashes about Shabbat. Because of this, more than in the other Gospels, these discussions acquire a dimension of being a matter of principle. On the other hand, there is no trace of the synoptic discussion about purity and divorce, nor of Jesus' scattered remarks concerning other practical commandments. We can surmise that the evangelist or final redactor had the choice from a variety of material, but apparently had reasons for incorporating only these two stories.

Both accounts begin with a healing and, like all happenings in John, are charged with significance. Furthermore, they occur in Jerusalem at a strategic moment, as becomes apparent from the structure of the Gospel. After the beginning of his public ministry in Cana, Jesus goes to Jerusalem, cleanses the temple, performs other signs (ch. 2), and holds a conversation with Nicodemus, after which there are reports concerning his work of baptizing and that of John (ch. 3). On the return trip to Galilee, the conversation with the Samaritan woman follows plus another healing (ch. 4). When Jesus again goes to Jerusalem for a feast, the first healing on the Shabbat takes place, and the first public dispute with the Jews issues from it (ch. 5). Back in Galilee, the miraculous feeding of the multitude takes place and the ensuing exposition on spiritual bread (ch. 6). Jesus then goes for a third and final time to Jerusalem. The primary phase of this stay consists of long and vehement disputes with the Jews with reference to the Feast of Booths (chs. 7–8), the second healing on the Shabbat (chs. 9–10), and finally the Feast of Rededication (end of ch. 10). The resurrection of Lazarus (chs. 11–12) follows as a pause before the final phase of Jesus' ministry (last supper and suffering). The healings on the Shabbat mark important moments in the escalating conflict between Jesus and the Jews in Jerusalem.

The first healing on the Shabbat concerns the paralyzed at 'Bethzatha', a place-name discussed above. Jesus heals the paralytic by merely saying, 'Stand up, take up your mattress (*krabbaton*) and walk' (5.8), which indeed happens. This is a second exceptional case of literal correspondence with the synoptic Gospels. The link is with Mark, in particular with the healing of the paralytic let down through the roof (Mk 2.11; cf. Mt. 9.6; Lk. 5.24). The literal parallel creates the impression of purposeful composition. The quite straightforward story of healing is followed by the true essence: the discussion with the Jews, introduced by a redactional aside: 'Now that day was the Shabbat' (5.9). This comment suddenly places the account in strong contrast to the synoptic story where the Shabbat is not at all involved. In the intention of the evangelist, Jesus not only heals the man, but also orders him to carry his mattress on the Shabbat.

The same stage setting frames the other story (ch. 9). Jesus heals the man born blind by making a paste of spittle and smearing this on the man's eyes. This 'remedy' was not unknown in antiquity and has a clearly suggestive, not to say magic power. However that may be, Jesus prepares a remedy for healing. The actual healing occurs when the man washes himself in the pool of Siloam. After one scene with his neighbours, he is brought to 'the Pharisees'. Here, too, an explicative aside follows that leaves nothing to guesswork in its terminological precision: 'It was, namely, Shabbat on the day that Jesus had made the paste and had opened his eyes' (9.14). The author–redactor assumes apparently that the reader is aware that making a remedial substance on the Shabbat was prohibited when life was not endangered. Even the later, mild rabbinic legislation allows this only in cases of a direct threat to life (see p. 92).

We must draw attention for a moment to the fact that we here are observing only one aspect of these stories, namely, the attitude towards the Jewish law. Besides this, the characteristic Johannine profundity is not lacking. Once there is clarity on the matter that concerns us in this book, other issues can be fully pursued. We could even imagine that the problematic theme of the law was added extraneously or at a later stage, while the deeper message of the story continues to sound unspoiled throughout. On that deeper level the turning point in the first story is reached when the lame man says that he has no one to throw him into the water as the first one, to which Jesus replies by simply commanding him to stand up with his mattress and to go hence: Jesus' commanding faith gives him the courage to believe. In the other story, the disciples inquire concerning who had sinned, the blind man or his parents, for blindness is a punishment from God. Jesus turns it upside down. It is not due to some sin or another, but 'that the works of God be revealed in him' (9.3). The theme of the interwovenness with the parents and relatives continues when first they and then the Pharisees question how the healing came about. By then the man can see and he can stand on his own two feet as a witness to the 'prophet' (9.17).

We return to the theme of Shabbat that is awarded the most attention by the evangelist. When he relates that Jesus makes a remedial medicine and tells someone to carry a mattress on Shabbat, he is working conscientiously and he makes that clear as well. In both stories, Jesus explains his behaviour by referring to the necessity of *working*, and the intention is: also on Shabbat. 'Work' is a comprehensive concept in the Torah that touches the core of the Shabbat commandment. We cite the Greek text that appears to be presumed in our passage: 'Six days shall you *work* (Greek: *ergai*) and do all your *works* (*erga*), but the seventh day rest' (Exod. 20.9). In the discussion after the first healing, Jesus uses precisely this verb: 'My Father *works* up to today and I, too, *work*' (5.16-17). Because of the links in Scripture, one cannot fail to be reminded of the story of creation, where the same words are used: 'And God completed on the sixth day his *works* (*erga*) which He had made, and He rested upon the seventh day from all his *works* which he had made' (Gen. 2.2 LXX; the 'sixth' day is not important to us here). With this allusion, the evangelist appears to imply that the seventh day of 'rest' mentioned in Genesis is applicable only to the coming age, and that the Creator himself works up to the present—on the Shabbat. With the second healing, the theme of 'work', by now familiar to the reader, functions introductorily: 'We must *work* the *works* of my Sender while it is day' (9.4). The doubled contruction in Greek (*erga, ergazesthai*) directly recalls the Greek of Exod. 20.9.

The conclusion seems unavoidable: in this account of the Johannine evangelist, Jesus tramples the Shabbat underfoot, with an intentional purposefulness that contrasts strangely with the other Gospels. Furthermore, the evangelist expresses this intention in an 'aside', following the statement of Jesus already cited:

> And therefore the Jews took action against Jesus because he did such things on the Shabbat. But Jesus answered them: My Father works up until now, and I, too, work. Because of this the Jews sought the more to *kill* him, because he not only *annulled the Shabbat*, but also called God his own Father and *made himself equal to God* (Jn 5.16-18).

Several expressions require clarification. The 'annulling' of a commandment or law is a Jewish technical term that means 'invalidate by means of a particular interpretation'. This term occurs in Matthew, where Jesus expresses his fundamentally positive attitude towards the law as follows: 'Do not think that I am come to annul the law…' (Mt. 5.17; see pp. 284-85). In John, the exact opposite is stated in regard to the Shabbat. The evangelist explains the hatred of the Jews for Jesus from the fact that he declared the Shabbat invalid—a fact undisputed and apparently supported by the evangelist. Then there is the accusation that Jesus 'made himself equal to God'. This recurs later in the Gospel (10.33; 19.7) and is related to the elevated christological statements in the prologue as well (1.1, 18), which make it more poignant. It could even be that the links with the prologue include the 'works' mentioned here, in other words, that he, who is the Word through which everything came into being, is also 'working' today as God himself works up to the present. It seems, furthermore, to signify that the evangelist undergirds the annulment of the Shabbat christologically. We will return to this later.

In all events it is clear that, according to the fourth Gospel, Jesus deliberately and knowingly transgresses the Shabbat. Such a message is heard nowhere else in the New Testament, not even in Mark and Matthew, for there the clashes with the law are by far not as pronounced and they seem to belong to the last redactional phase. The fact that the voice of the evangelist dominates as in no other Gospel has far-reaching effects here. We must also assume that he expresses the sentiments of his community, who apparently thought that the Shabbat was annulled on principle. Because this is the only practical commandment that is brought to discussion, it appears to give an exemplary judgment on the Jewish law. In the following section, this impression is confirmed by the place and significance explicitly awarded to the law in the Gospel.

Nonetheless, something completely different is also said about the Shabbat. In a discussion with the Jews about the law, Jesus refers back to his first healing on the Shabbat and quotes the following argument:

> If a person receives circumcision (even) on the Shabbat, in order that the law of Moses not be annulled, how can you be angry at me because I have made a whole person healthy on the Shabbat? (Jn 7.23).

Again the technical term 'annul' is used, here with reference to the law as a whole. In the context of the discussion about the 'care for life' that has precedence over the Shabbat (see pp. 92-93), R. Eliezer (end first century) brings forward the following argument:

> For the benefit of the circumcision (on the eighth day of life), the Shabbat is set aside.... From this follows an argument from light to heavy. Just as for the sake of one of his parts the Shabbat is set aside, it is logical that the Shabbat be set aside for the sake of the person as a whole (*t. Šab.* 15.16).

The striking correspondence of this rabbinic passage with the reasoning in John 7 yields its explanation as well. Circumcision, which involves one small part of the body, has precedence over the Shabbat and is always performed on the eighth day—how much more then the saving of a whole life?

The conclusion is that this argument of Jesus must represent a Jewish-Christian layer in the Gospel. In that environment, circumcision evidently was an accepted point of departure, which implied keeping all of the law. The principle that circumcision supersedes the Shabbat was not contradictory to this, just as it was not for R. Eliezer and his colleagues. Furthermore, we have seen in Chapter 3 (pp. 154-55) that in the synoptic Gospels Jesus also used argumentation that was related to the Pharisaic–rabbinic tradition. It is, therefore, in no way excluded that this Jewish-Christian tradition in John goes back to Jesus himself or his direct environment.

We are confronted with a sharp contradiction within the fourth Gospel in its present form. While the Johannine primal tradition assumes the keeping of the Shabbat, the evangelist or final redactor considers it to be 'annulled' on principle.

Jesus, Moses and the Law

In the preceding material the question arose of a possible relationship between the prologue of the Gospel and the argument that Jesus made himself equal to God by appealing to him in connection to a transgression of the Shabbat. The staggering probability of this link increases if we reconsider the end of the prologue, where, in the midst of all the other ponderous words, a fundamental statement concerning the law occurs:

> The law was given through Moses; grace and truth have come into being through Jesus Christ. God—no one has ever seen; the only begotten God, who is in the bosom of the Father, he has declared him (Jn 1.17-18).

This is not, however, unambiguous. That Jesus should surpass Moses is hardly surprising in this Gospel. The question whether he is 'more than our father Jacob' is affirmatively implied, and to the question, 'You are not more than our father Abraham, are you?' he replies, 'Before Abraham was, *I am*' (4.12; 8.53, 58). More specifically we are reminded how Moses, with whom God spoke 'face to face as one speaks with a friend', received in answer to his request to be able to *see* God: 'A human shall not see My face and live' (Exod. 33.12, 20). Jesus was thus 'more than Moses'. The pressing question is, however, do Moses and

Jesus complement each other, as the synoptic tradition proposes in the
story of the transfiguration (Mk 9.4), or do the law of Moses and
salvation through Jesus exclude one another?

To answer this question it is again necessary to distinguish between
the Gospel in its final form and the layers of which it seems to be built
up. In the relationship between Moses and Jesus, both an answer of
complementarity and one of reciprocal exclusion are found. It is difficult to see how these two notions could exist side by side in one community, but it is not difficult to conceive of them as reflecting two
different stages of development. A stage at which it appears that Moses
and Jesus supplement each other is, thus, distinguishable as well.

The complementary answer in unabridged form is present in the story
of the calling of Philip and Nathanael, which for other reasons we have
ascribed to the earliest, Jewish-Christian stage. Philip comes elated to
Nathanael and calls out, 'He of whom in the law Moses has written and
the prophets, him have we found: Jesus, the son of Joseph from Nazareth!' (Jn 1.45). Complementarity can be read as well in the plea of
Nicodemus, when he says to his colleagues who sneer about 'the throng
who do not know the law', 'Our law does not condemn someone without first hearing him, does it?' (7.49, 51). Loyalty to Jesus is supported
by an appeal to the law.

Although formally the same position is maintained, a different tone is
audible in the following words of Jesus, spoken to the Jews after the
first healing on the Shabbat:

> Do not think that I will accuse you before the Father. There is someone
> who accuses you: Moses, upon whom you have placed your hope. If you
> had believed in Moses, you would have believed in me, for he wrote of
> me. If you do not believe in *his written letters*, how shall you believe in
> my spoken words? (Jn 5.45-46).

Although this piece of polemics appeals to the authority of Moses, it is
chock-full of tensions. Were the opponents correct in putting their hope
in Moses or not? If Jesus supersedes Moses to such a degree, what is
the value of an appeal to his writings? This does not take away the fact
that the statement about the 'written letters' and the 'spoken words'
(*grammata, rhēmata*) evidences spiritual power and, furthermore,
contains a clear echo of the paradox between written and oral Torah.

Ambivalence is also present in the argument for healing on the Shabbat in analogy with circumcision. This argument, which *n.b.* is related
to the midrash of R. Eliezer, serves as a defence of healing the man

whom Jesus allowed to carry off his mattress on the Shabbat! The internal tension increases when Jesus, on the one hand, relativizes the importance of Moses and, on the other hand, says that Moses had given the law and the circumcision 'to you', by which he appears to exclude himself:

> Has Moses not given you the law? And none of you does the law: why do you seek to kill me?... I have done one work and you are all surprised! For this reason Moses has given you the circumcision—not that it derives from Moses but from the patriarchs—and you circumcise someone on the Shabbat. If a person is circumcised on the Shabbat, so that the law of Moses not be annulled, do you become angry at me because I have made a whole person healthy on the Shabbat?! (Jn 7.23).

It appears that, from the perspective of the Gospel, the appeal to Moses and the law belongs to the past and functions only polemically. This concurs with our hypothesis on the layeredness of the Gospel. The analogy of circumcision and the healing on the Shabbat, which early in the Johannine tradition was still based on the confirmation of the law's authority, in a later phase received a polemic function on the basis of the invalidation of that authority. The matter is complicated in that the earlier stage continues to resonate—although that is, of course, the only way in which we could continue to hear both stages. Being not only complex, but also painfully contradictory in its expression, the polemics even acquire a certain sarcasm. The same can be observed in the following fragments (the portions between brackets are lacking in some manuscripts):

> Jesus spoke again to them: I am the light of the world... Then the Pharisees said to him: you testify concerning yourself, your testimony is not true. Jesus answered and said to them...I stand not alone, but I and he that sent me, the Father, and in *your law* it is written that the testimony of two people is true. (Jn 8.12-17; cf. Deut. 17.6).

> The Jews answered him: not because of a good deed do we want to stone you but because of blasphemy, for you make yourself as human to be God. Jesus answered them: is it not written in [*your*] law: 'I have spoken: You are gods'? (Ps. 82.6). If he called them gods [...] and that [word of Scripture] can not be annulled...do you say then 'you blaspheme' because I say that I am God's son? (Jn 10.33-36).

Within the framework of the Gospel as a whole, the reference here is to the prologue (the light, the word as God). In the meantime, the two healings on the Shabbat have taken place, in which Jesus clearly and consciously transgressed generally accepted Jewish customs. It is now obvious that the evangelist indeed suggests that he did this in the consciousness of being God's son. By this the ambiguous relationship between the law of Moses and the grace and truth in Jesus Christ present in the prologue is reduced to a reciprocal exclusion. Sarcasm is expressed in Jesus' appeal to the same law as *your* law.

On other grounds, it was concluded that the Gospel of John speaks for a community that was opposed to the 'synoptic' and Pauline circles where Peter was taken to be the most prominent apostle. To this can be added the radical contrast between law and gospel observable in the final text of the Gospel. In the time during which this was taking shape, the Jewish law had apparently acquired a highly negative significance in the Johannine milieu. In this milieu dominated by dualism, the words that Jesus speaks in the intimacy of the last supper aquire an ambiguous and sarcastic tone:

> If I had not done works which no one else had done, they would have no sin. Now, however, they have seen these, but have hated both me and my Father. But (this is) so that the word might be fulfilled that is written in *their law*: 'They have hated me without a cause' (Jn 15.25; Ps. 35.19).

Jews and Israel

The social function of the double designation 'Jews' and 'Israel' has already been discussed (see pp. 110-15, 277-79). This phenomenon is of exceptional significance in the fourth Gospel. Within the totally unique thought world of the Johannine milieu, not only the Jewish law but also the name 'Jews' receives a negative connotation. This has strong social implications, from which far-reaching conclusions follow for the Gospel as a whole. As explanation, again the hypothesis of the layeredness of the Gospels is opportune, the more so since several glaring contradictions can be clarified by it.

Because the Gospel of John strongly diverges from the other New Testament writings, we begin with a survey of the latter. In the synoptic Gospels the name 'Jews' occurs relatively infrequently (16 times); the name 'Israel' occurs more frequently (26 times). With the exception of two occurrences, these all function within the narrative following the double Jewish usage: 'Jews' in a conversation with non-Jews, 'Israel' in intra-Jewish situations. This points undoubtedly to continuity with the apostolic tradition of the words and deeds of Jesus. The two exceptions involve passages in Mark and Matthew which, as an 'aside' of the evangelist, fall outside of the story. Here the author places himself in the non-Jewish standpoint, apparently to address non-Jewish readers: 'the Jews' have all sorts of cleansing customs (Mk 7.3), and 'Jews' spread the rumour that Jesus' body had been stolen by his disciples (Mt. 28.15). From the passage in Mark, we surmised that this usage need not function anti-Jewishly; it is possible thus to express merely a non-Jewish speech situation. In contrast, the same usage in the passage in Matthew has acquired an unmistakably anti-Jewish function, apparently in a situation of enmity with the Jews. The difference lies not in the expression or speech situation itself, but in the role that the Jews are given in that context.

This conclusion is confirmed in the Acts of the Apostles and the epistles of Paul. In contrast to the synoptic Gospels, these writings are primarily drafted in a mixed, and thus not intra-Jewish communication situation. There are, therefore, many more occurrences of 'Jews' (79 times in Acts, 29 times in Paul) and fewer of 'Israel(ites)' (20 and 18 times, respectively). Nowhere does the name 'Jews' have a compelling anti-Jewish significance, although it sounds quite bitter in 1 Thess. 2.14. In Acts, 'Israel' does occur in intra-Jewish speech situations within the narrative. In Paul's correspondence the use of 'Israel' involves references to biblical Israel or to the synagogue of his day. To this belong several remarkable cases in which God-fearers, or non-Jewish believers who are apparently reckoned as such, are counted as being constitutive of the intra-Jewish conversational situation (Acts 10.36; 13.16-24; Rom. 9–11).

The Gospel of John contrasts strikingly with all of these writings. A great difference with the synoptic Gospels lies in the numerous occurrences of the name 'Jews': 71 times (or 70: 'Jew' in 3.25 is text-critically debatable). Non-Jewish speech situations are thus frequently implied. A second remarkable difference is that this usually does not happen in exceptional situations within the story, but involves the framework of the narrative itself. A comparison with Acts is instructive. There 'Jews' occurs also more than 70 times, especially from ch. 13 on when Paul begins to operate in non-Jewish contexts, but also already in the story following Pentecost. Both Acts and John are thus conceived of as being within a non-Jewish or at least a mixed speech situation. Though this is quite logical for Acts, which as a whole unfolds in a mixed situation, it is not for John. The conversations that Jesus holds with his friends and opponents can hardly be conceived of other than being intra-Jewish, as is confirmed in the synoptic Gospels. Nonetheless, the fourth Gospel indicates the persons Jesus was speaking to continuously as 'Jews'. This yields the first general conclusion: *the fourth Gospel views the Jewish people to whom Jesus speaks from the outside.*

An anti-Jewish function of the designation 'Jews' need not hereby be implied. Indeed we do find about ten times that the evangelist clarifies matters for his readers by telling about 'Passover' and other Jewish feasts (Jn 2.13; 5.1; 6.4; 7.2; 11.55; 19.42), about Jewish customs (2.6; 4.9; 19.40) or about a Jewish leader (3.10). The designation functions totally neutrally, but clearly in a non-Jewish speech situation. Remarkably enough, this occurs also in the story of Lazarus where repeatedly the sympathy of the 'Jews' for Jesus is reported (11.19, 31, 33, 36, 45; 12.9, 11). One can say the same of 'the Jews which had come to believe in him' (8.31; cf. the same expression in Acts 15.5; 21.20, 25). The second conclusion is thus: *the fourth Gospel views Jesus' Jewish associates also from the outside.*

It will not be surprising now that Jesus' opponents are also viewed from the outside and designated as 'Jews'. What is striking is that Jesus himself also denotes them thus from within the seclusion of the circle of disciples:

> Little children, yet a little while am I with you. You shall look for me, and *as I said to the Jews*: where I go, you can not come, and now I say it to you (Jn 13.33).

It can hardly be otherwise than that this is the evangelist projecting his own speech situation in relationship to the Jews back on to Jesus' situation. Confirmation is found in the indication of 'fear for the Jews' as the reason that people in Jerusalem did not dare to show their sympathy for Jesus (7.13; 19.38; 20.19). This becomes explicit in the 'aside' of the evangelist after the evasive answer that the parents of the healed blind man gave to 'the Jews':

> This his parents said because they feared the Jews. For *the Jews had already agreed* that if anyone should confess him as Christ, he would be banned from the synagogue (Jn 9.22).

The Gospel in its present form presumes a situation in which Jewish believers in Jesus are excluded from the synagogue, or, as our passage states, *apo-sunagōgos*, 'banned-out-of-the-synagogue'. Such a situation probably began to take shape only towards the end of the first century (see p. 66). The evangelist, however, projects it back into his story, and even into the words of Jesus, with all consequential contradictions:

> Likewise even many of their leaders believed, but because of the Pharisees they did not confess this in order not to be banned-out-of-the-synagoge, for they loved the honour of man more than the honour of God (Jn 12.42-43).

> *They shall make you banned-out-of-the-synagogue.* But the hour comes that everyone who kills you shall think that he does God a favour (Jn 16.2).

The third conclusion to be drawn is: *the fourth Gospel phrases Jesus' story from the situation of a total break with the Jews.*

The Gospel portrays the evangelist and his congregation as being outside of Judaism, after a fatal breach with the Jewish leaders. This concurs with the closed character of the Johannine thought world and the reaction against the 'synoptic' and Pauline circles in which the primacy of Peter held sway. Because of the indications of a peculiar primal Johannine tradition within early Jewish Christianity, these closed and reactionary aspects must originally have been independent of the break with Judaism. One of the most cutting passages in the Gospel confirms this, namely, Jesus' conversation with the 'Jews who had come to believe in him':

> *Now Jesus said to the Jews who had come to believe in him*: if you remain in my word, you shall truly be my disciples...and the truth shall set you free. They said to him: We are Abraham's seed and have never been slaves to another; how can you say, 'You shall be free'?... Then Jesus said to them: If you be children of Abraham, do then the works of Abraham; but now you seek to kill me... You do the works of your father. They said to him... One Father we have, God. Jesus said to them: You are from the father-devil and desire to do the lusts of your father. He is a murderer of men from the beginning and in the truth does he not stand... When he speaks a lie, he speaks it of his own, for a liar is his father as well (Jn 8.31-45).

'Father-devil' is a rendering of a strange Greek construction that perhaps is derived awkwardly and literally from Hebrew or Aramaic, where it could involve the construction 'Father of devils'. It is unclear which situation the evangelist has in mind when he charges the Jews who believe in Jesus of being accomplices to the murder of Jesus or his followers. In any case extreme enmity between the Johannine community and certain Jewish Christians is expressed. Who they are is not said, but they apparently maintained contact with the synagogue. It is perhaps not too far afield to think of the Jerusalem congregation around James, with whom the Pharisees sympathized when he was executed by the high priest (see p. 58). The fourth general conclusion is: *the fourth gospel appears to speak from a total breach with the Jewish church in Jerusalem.*

It should now be specified that in about half of the cases in John, the 'Jews' are identical to the Jewish opponents of Jesus and his own. This begins as early as the ministry of his predecessor, John the Baptist, when '*the Jews* sent from Jerusalem priests and Levites to interrogate him' (1.19). The remarkableness of this sentence comes out if 'the Jews' is replaced by 'they': the sentence remains totally understandable and within the framework of the story there is no need to mention 'the Jews' by name. The necessity arises apparently from the situation of the evangelist or redactor. He relates his Gospel from the perspective of an unbridgeable gap with the Jews and Judaism, which induces him to summarize the opponents of Jesus as 'the Jews'.

Because within the account more differentiated designations for Jesus' opponents were left untouched, contrasts arise in which the evangelist can be seen at work. Thus 'the Jews who came to believe in him' are suddenly designated as 'the Jews' (8.48, 52, 57). Further, hostile Jewish leaders who are first identified as 'the chief priests and Pharisees', in later references are abbreviated to 'the Jews' (11.47 and 18.14; 18.3 and 18.12). It is characteristic as well how Jesus' words cited above, 'as I said to the Jews', refer to a statement made to 'the (chief priests and) Pharisees' (7.33; 13.33). Thus it is 'the Jews' who confront Jesus critically from the beginning of his ministry (2.18, 20), who persecute him and want to kill him (5.16, 18; 7.1; 10.31; 11.8), and who by stubborn perserverance finally succeed in having him executed by Pilate (chs. 18–19).

In the previous chapter (see pp. 275-76) we asserted that the Gospel of Matthew has a tendency to generalize in the designation of Jesus' enemies. While Mark differentiates between scribes, chief priests, Sadducees and Pharisees, Matthew lumps them together, especially the 'scribes and Pharisees'. This is even more striking in comparison to Luke who has preserved the diversity present in Mark. In contrast, in John we encounter a more extreme form of the tendency towards generalization. There is little distinction left between the various groups.

Even the combination 'chief priests and Pharisees' is perceptibly generalized to 'the Jews', the same hostile category under which all types of Jewish followers of Jesus fall. The fifth conclusion is, therefore: *the fourth Gospel expresses itself in terms of enmity towards the Jews.*

This is a shocking conclusion, and many commentators have sought an escape by looking for explanations as to whom then John could have intended by 'the Jews'. Declaring it to be a designation for the spiritual leaders of the people who were antagonistic towards Jesus only makes things worse because then the word 'Jew' would have become shorthand for 'enemy of Christ'. Moreover, this explanation does not tally with the texts. 'Jewish' feasts are not feasts of the spiritual leaders, nor is Jesus buried by Joseph and Nicodemus according to the rites of those leaders. Another explanation would have it that the Greek *Ioudaios* means 'Judaean', as it did in the pre-exilic period (see pp. 90-91). Besides thus making the text of the Gospel of John a remarkable exception in the Graeco-Roman world, this explanation does not hold true within the Gospel itself. In Galilee people keep the cleansing rituals of 'the Jews' (Cana, 2.6) as well as their Passover (6.4). Jesus as well and his brothers from Nazareth and Philip of Bethsaida in Galilee celebrate the Feast of Booths and the Passover of 'the Jews' (7.2, 10; 12.21). Yet another contradiction in this is that 'the Jews' are at the same time Jesus' enemies; we will pursue this further below. Explaining the word as 'Judaeans' does not work in any case. In the fourth Gospel, no other significance is intended with 'the Jews', whether favourably or unfavourably, than what is designated in the ancient expression 'the people' or 'the nation of the Jews' (*ethnos tōn Ioudaiōn*).

In this matter there are crass contradictions within the fourth Gospel. How could Jesus and his associates keep the feasts and customs of 'the Jews' if they were their enemies? How can 'Jews who had come to believe in him' suddenly, apparently because of their opposition, flatly be called 'Jews', enemies of Jesus who descend from the 'father-devil'? The most confusing are the passages in which the Samaritan woman addresses Jesus as 'Jew' and he admits, without further ado, to belonging to the people and the community of faith of 'the Jews':

> The Samaritan woman said to him: How can *you who are a Jew* ask water to drink from me, who am a Samaritan woman?... Jesus said to her: Believe me, woman, an hour comes in which you shall worship the Father neither on this mountain nor in Jerusalem. You worship what you do not know; we worship what we know, *for salvation is from the Jews* (Jn 4.9, 22).

The simplest explanation is that this is an ancient text fragment within the Gospel. That Jesus indicates himself as being a Jew, and lets himself be so designated, concurs totally with the effect of the double Jewish self-designation: 'Israel' in the intra-Jewish context, but 'Jew' in a mixed speech situation. Although related in many respects, Samaritans were not the same as Jews. In other words, these are fragments of the Johannine primal source in which the Jewish self-designation is used in a mixed speech situation.

It would be logical to view the contradictory evaluation of 'the Jews' as a product of the history of the Johannine community. To this must now be added the five striking instances of 'Israel'. They all occur in intra-Jewish speech within the story: John the Baptist to other Jews (1.31), Jesus to Nathanael and vice versa (1.47, 49), Jesus to Nicodemus (3.10) and the Jerusalemites to Jesus (12.13). Just as in the synoptic tradition, Nathanael and other Jews call Jesus 'king of Israel', while Pilate asks him, 'Are you the king of the Jews?' (18.33). The whole exchange between Jesus and Pilate can be read as a mixed speech situation within the narrative ('Jews' in 18.35-36, 39; 19.3, 19, 21) and could belong to the Jewish-Christian phase, but is in fact not distinguishable from the non-Jewish speech situation of the Gospel as a whole. The Lazarus cycle (Jn 11–12), however, contrasts clearly with the rest of the Gospel by the positive function of the name 'Jews'. This concurs with earlier conjectures about the antiquity of this portion (see p. 309).

The strongest contrast is that between Jesus' words to the Samaritan woman—'salvation is from the Jews' (4.22)—and those to 'the Jews who had come to believe in Jesus'—'You are of the father-devil' (8.44). The latter can belong only to a later stage. As a final general conclusion, we therefore posit: *the fourth Gospel exhibits a development from an intra-Jewish discussion to anti-Jewish polemics.*

The Johannine Milieu and the Jews

In keeping with the preceding, the fourth Gospel can be read as reflecting a development within a community where major shifts must have taken place. We have voiced the suspicion that from the beginning it was quite an exclusive group, characterized by strong dualistic thinking and, in distinction to the apostolic–synoptic tradition, by the keeping of the Pharisaic calendar. Somewhat isolated from Jesus' other Jewish followers and perhaps somewhere in the Diaspora (Egypt?), this group originally operated, nonetheless, within the framework of Judaism.

At a second stage, the isolation must have turned into a breach. In this, reservations towards the community of Peter will have hardened to a literal diabolizing of other Jewish Christians. This was not unusual in dualistically thinking Jewish circles and it also dovetails completely with the Johannine image of the world (more concerning this in Chapter 9). Whether the breach occurred before or after the fall of Jerusalem is not clear. Because it is probable that the last stage of the Gospel also took about a generation, the breach will have come before the destruction, for the Gospel dates from the end of the first century at the latest. Perhaps the second phase of the history of the community began in the fifties and sixties.

The transition to the third phase is the most difficult to understand. From the massive enmity towards 'the Jews' that must have arisen at this stage, we get the impression of a community that came to be in a completely non-Jewish context. For an explanation we cannot depend on indications of a predominance of intolerant non-Jews, as in the Pauline churches. Not that the non-Jews are totally lacking in the Gospel: there are 'Greeks' who want to see Jesus (12.20), apparently meaning non-Jews, God-fearing pilgrims at the Passover in Jerusalem, and the mention of 'other sheep, not of this fold', by which non-Jewish Christians could be intended (10.16; cf. 11.52). These are, however, rather marginal passages in the Gospel as a whole. In the final chapter we will return to this difficult episode and attempt to clarify the third phase of the Gospel within a broader context.

The Johannine epistles have not been discussed as yet. They offer us some further illumination. In their vocabulary and worldview, they concur largely with the fourth Gospel, especially in the dualistic combination of love for the brothers and hate for the opponents (see pp. 295-96). This does not necessarily imply that they were also written by the same individual as was the Gospel, but certainly within the same group or tradition, and at approximately the same time, that is, about two to three generations after Jesus. The common vocabulary and conceptual world appear also to imply the same distance to the 'synoptic' and Pauline circles.

Of particular interest to us is the third epistle of John, the shortest document in the New Testament (235 words). For a Johannine writing, it is relatively rich in historical data, of which we quote the most salient:

> The elder to the beloved Gaius, whom I love in truth... Beloved, trustworthy do you act in all your efforts for the brothers, and that while they are strangers... For they are come for the sake of the name, without taking anything from the heathen. We ought to greet such people, so that we become colleagues in truth. I have written something for the church, but the imperious Diotrefes will not receive us... Concerning Demetrius, there is testimony from all and from truth itself (3 Jn 1, 5-9, 12).

We are already sufficiently familiar with the Johannine preference for the words 'to love' and 'truth'. Together they make up five per cent of this small epistle. The three Graeco-Latin names give us unfortunately little foothold. The praised function of Demetrius is not clear, but that of Diotrefes is: he is the leader of 'the church' and a rival of the author, 'the elder'. Gaius, on the other hand, stands on the side of the elder and receives his people. Precisely what the conflict was about remains likewise unclear. It could have been doctrinal or disciplinary or both. In the first case, that which the elder had 'written for the church' could have been a sort of treatise. It is tempting to think in this connection of the first epistle of John, which is not a letter but a treatise against apostate forms of thinking and living, but there is no concrete basis for this assumption.

In any case we read here of a split in the Johannine community, and that is an important fact. Upon further consideration, it fits well with the separatist manner of thinking characteristic of this literature. It could also be brought into relation to the repeated redactions of the Gospel and the contrast between the various layers. On the other hand, in spite of closely associated terminology, there are clear doctrinal differences between the Gospel of John and the first epistle. The Johannine tradition, which possibly from the start very much followed its own course, appears thus already within several generations to have produced repeated schisms. Thus the transition from the intra-Jewish stage to the anti-Jewish stage of the Gospel becomes somewhat more conceivable. In such an exclusively dualistic manner of thinking, each difference of opinion can lead to a split, and social tensions, such as those between Jews and non-Jews, could catastrophically turn into total enmity. Such could indeed have taken place in the confusion during or following the war against Rome.

Of particular importance to us is that in the Johannine epistles the appellation 'Jews', so frequent in the Gospel, is totally lacking. This points to a homogeneous speech situation. It could be either a fully intra-Jewish or a completely non-Jewish setting. There are, however, two reasons for caution. The texts concerned are small or very small, so that the chance of occurrence is limited. Furthermore, the texts function within a group which has closed its ranks to the outside world, so that the use of the name 'Jews', that indicates the involvement of Jews in a non-Jewish context, is not really to be expected.

The mention of 'heathen' in the third epistle of John is, therefore, the more striking (v. 7). This quite rare adjective (*ethnikoi*) is usually read as a contrast to the Johannine Christians. One wonders whether that is correct. Non-Christian authors from that time, among whom are Philo and Josephus, use the word the most frequently in the sense of 'popular, of the people, national'. That does not exclude a significance such as 'belonging to the non-Christian people' in 3 John 7. The other occurrences of the word in the New Testament are, however, specifically intra-Jewish. It is used thrice in Matthew, and then in a sharper, more disparaging tone than the usual *ethnê*, whose usual meaning is 'nations, peoples' and which we have consistently translated as 'non-Jewish'. The specific word can there be rendered better as 'heathen'. According to the Matthaean Jesus, 'heathen' greet only their brothers, are verbose in prayer, and are morally at the level of tax collectors (Mt. 5.47; 6.7; 18.17; see pp. 279-80). Even Paul uses the word once in order to make a clear distinction between 'heathen' and 'Jewish' life (Gal. 2.14), though apparently rather ironically. From the designation 'heathen' in 3 John 7, the text could appear, therefore, to be speaking from a Jewish point of view.

If this were correct, then the third epistle of John was composed in a Jewish-Christian context. The absence of the name 'Jews' in the three epistles would then indicate that the 'elder', who likewise signed for the second epistle (2 Jn 1) and perhaps also wrote the first one, was in a homogeneous Jewish-Christian speech situation. The difference vis-à-vis the fourth Gospel with its anti-Jewish framework could hardly be greater. It would also mean that the three epistles are still within the Jewish bedding of the Johannine tradition, while the Gospel had broken away from that. This need not be in conflict with the usual assumption that the epistles were written after the Gospel. Within the Johannine tradition as well, a Jewish-Christian movement could have continued to exist, in spite of and beyond the catastrophic break between 'Christians' and 'Jews' reflected in the fourth Gospel.

The latter possibility seems to be confirmed by a manuscript fragment known as the *Papyrus Egerton 2*, dated at the beginning of the third century, whose text itself could have originated about a half a century earlier in Egypt. It not only concerns passages from an otherwise unknown Gospel, but it combines elements known from the Johannine and the synoptic traditions. It has to do with a discussion with 'scholars of the law' and an account of a healing in which Jesus repeatedly is addressed as 'teacher' and, in spite of bitter clashes with the Jewish leaders, appears himself to adhere to the stipulations of the law. Although there is no dependency on the Johannine writings known to us, the affinity with them is clearly greater than with the synoptic Gospels. An independent reworking of Gospel material in a Jewish–Johannine milieu is hereby suggested.

Chapter 8

LETTERS OF THE JEWISH CHURCHES

After all that had to be said about the Gospels, it is regrettable that the 'Hebrew Gospels' of which the church fathers testify are no longer available, except for a few quoted snippets (see p. 267). We do not know how the words of Jesus were transmitted in Hebrew or Aramaic, nor how the Jews in Galilee spoke about him. There is only the echo of the gospel in its non-Jewish version, the most pure being in Luke's version, where the boundary between Jew and non-Jew is treated in such a matter-of-fact manner.

The Hebrew Gospels and other Jewish-Christian writings disappeared from history along with the groups in which they were written and cherished. Before long, these communities were overshadowed and banned by the non-Jewish majority churches, and their writings were counted as curious but closed documents. This situation became normative under the orthodox imperial church (fourth century), in which climate eventually the Jewish churches completely disappeared.

In this light, several half-forgotten writings in the New Testament acquire primary significance. The epistles of Jude and James, the Epistle to the Hebrews and the Revelation of John probably all originated among Jewish followers of Jesus, so that the New Testament itself provides us with several documents concerning how Jesus was spoken of in Jewish circles. To this can be added yet another, non-canonized writing from the same time, the *Didache*. Sometimes we are richer than we think…

'Jewish Churches' and Other Terminology

We cannot proceed without first some clarification of terms. Such is possible only if we become aware of the extent to which our words, concepts and terminology are determined by our own or inherited experiences and memories. Christians and Jews, whether practising and believing or not, are all raised with the idea of two mutually exclusive religious systems. One is either a Jew or a follower of Jesus, and between these two positions there are no connections. Nor is this merely a mental concept, but an experience carved in the communal memory through generations of misunderstanding and fear, denial and persecution.

To deny the experience does not make it go away, but only impairs getting to know ourselves and the other one better. If we accept the reality of this experience, however, our vision is freed to distinguish between the Middle Ages, during which Christianity and Judaism formed two closed blocks, and the initial period, in which the boundaries between them were vague and fluid. The initial period is in focus here, the time in which there were many types of Jewish followers of Jesus, partially tolerated, partially thwarted by the believing non-Jews, or non-Jewish Christians. We are dealing with the Jewish followers of Jesus in antiquity and their writings.

The next question is to what extent we can speak here of Jewish documents. A general answer is difficult to give. Is literature 'Jewish' when it is about Jews or a Jewish topic, or when it is written by Jews? What exactly are 'Jewish topics'? Who precisely is to be designated as 'Jewish'?

For the past century or two, this last question in particular has become complicated and emotionally charged. From time immemorial, two prerequisites were valid: a Jewish lifestyle and a family tie with the Jewish community. In modern times, however, these two elements often do not coincide, and that complicates the issue. Matters become even more intricate when a Jew embraces another religion. Thus, for example, becoming a Christian is reason enough for an Israeli court to disown one as a Jew. Here the implication of the modern nation state and the privatization of religion make themselves felt. By allowing oneself to be baptized as a Christian, one chooses individually for another religious affiliation and cuts ties with Jews and Judaism. This is usually also the implication of missions to the Jews, which are quite active in Israel. It is difficult to defend an alternative judgment on such conversions as long as churches and missions continue to see themselves exclusively as the True Israel.

To a certain extent this was less intricate in antiquity. To be a Jew was to live as a Jew, although that certainly did not imply uniformity (see Chapters 1 and 2). Whatever form of Judaism one adhered to, one celebrated the Shabbat and feast days, circumcised one's sons, refrained from certain foods and products, married within Jewish circles, and was in all these points recognizably Jewish. According to the testimony of no one less than the church fathers, this was also true of the various Jewish-Christian groups, and precisely for that reason these were counted as *Jewish* and not as heretics or apostates in general.

Thus we speak here of 'Jewish churches' in antiquity; these were mentioned at the end of the introduction. The ones involved are followers of Jesus who, like Jesus himself and his first disciples, lived within Judaism. In this, their standpoints concerning the law, their relationship to non-Jewish believers, and their Christology could be extremely divergent. During the generation of Paul and James, Christians worked on the basis of a compromise between Jewish and non-Jewish believers; as a result, coexistence of Jews and non-Jews was also possible within the church. This enabled the name 'Christians' to be used in Antioch as a designation that originally included both groups (see pp. 230-31, 250). At the same time, Paul could speak of 'churches of non-Jews' (Rom. 16.4) with mainly non-Jewish members. In this a distinction is implied with the churches under Peter's authority, which will have comprised mainly Jewish members (Gal. 2.7-9). Later the compromise ran aground and the Jewish and non-Jewish churches went their separate ways, with the consequences already mentioned.

Returning now to the 'Jewish-Christian writings', the question about what can be called 'Jewish' is different when applied to books than when applied to people. A clear criterion would appear to be the author himself, in particular his position towards Jews and Judaism. In accordance with the circumstances in antiquity, a writing is 'Jewish' when the author has a Jewish lifestyle and Jewish affiliation. In spite of all their sympathy for Jews and Judaism, the writings of Luke, apparently a non-Jew, can, therefore, hardly be called Jewish. On the other hand, Paul's epistles, given his polemics against 'unbelieving' Jews and Judaizing missionaries, are seldom read as being Jewish. If our conclusion, however, is valid that he remained faithful to the law and the calling of Israel, it is not clear why he should not count as a Jewish author. The Gospel of John, in contrast, is continually about the 'Jews' and certainly has a Jewish background, but due to its strong antagonism towards the Jews and the law, it should not be called Jewish but anti-Jewish.

The great significance of the writings now to be discussed becomes apparent. They are Jewish in that their authors speak from a specifically Jewish-Christian milieu and identify themselves observably with it. With this knowledge, we now turn to the letters of the Jewish churches in the New Testament.

Jude

The 25 verses comprising the Epistle of Jude are perhaps the most neglected of the whole New Testament. Although this small document did not incite theological opposition, it remained largely outside of exegetical spotlights. Viewed within a Jewish framework, it can yield several surprises.

In the introduction, the author calls himself 'Jude, the brother of James'. Traditionally this is understood to be 'Jude of James', a disciple of Jesus (Lk. 6.15; Acts 1.13). That designation, however, should be read as 'son of James', and to which James it refers is totally unknown. The fact that the brother of our author is indicated by his name alone singles him out as being a person of some importance. The most probable candidate is the eldest of Jesus' brothers (Mk 6.3), whom Paul calls 'James, the brother of the Lord' (Gal. 1.19) and whom Paul as well as Luke consider to be the leader of the church in Jerusalem (Gal. 2.9; Acts 12.17; 15.13). James must have come to believe in Jesus only later and was not one of his apostles (1 Cor. 15.7; Jn 7.5). The pretension of 'Jude' is apparently that he was Jesus' less-known brother whom we know from Mark as 'Judas', though the Greek there reflects the more Semitic form *Iouda* or, indeed, 'Jude' (Mk 6.3).

Most scholars take this dubbing to be a pseudonym, among other things because the Greek of the epistle is not at all of a poor quality, which would be hard to imagine of a brother of Jesus. More recently, however, the authenticity has been defended with a whole series of new arguments.

Jewish-Christian Apocalyptics
Following the introduction and greeting, the aim of the epistle is explained:

> Beloved...I felt the need to write you with the admonition to remain steadfast in the faith once committed to the saints. For some people have penetrated, who are already long condemned to judgment, godless ones who turn the grace of God into lasciviousness and deny our one Ruler and Lord, Jesus Christ (Jude 3-4)

Different personages involved deserve attention. 'Beloved' is a common form of address for fellow-Christians, and 'saints' as an honorary indication of the congregation derives from the hymnic–apocalyptic language of Jews and Jewish Christians. The 'godless' are naturally their antagonists, also known from the Psalms. A dualistic and apocalyptic tone is set, also expressed in 'condemned to judgment' (cf. Heb. 12.22, see below). The christological title 'Ruler' (*despotēs*) is striking. In the New Testament this is used further only in 2 Pet. 2.1, a passage that appears to be influenced by Jude. It occurs also as a liturgical form of address for God and derives from the Septuagint (Lk. 2.29; Acts 4.24; Rev. 6.10; *Did.* 10.3).

Besides the opening lines, greeting and introduction (Jude 1-4), and farewell formula (vv. 24-25), the relevant main portion of the letter consists of a type of exegetical admonition (vv. 5-23). In four 'rounds', the godless are identified with the proverbial sinners in history, each time through an important identification formula.

In the first round (vv. 5-7), the bad examples are cited of the Israelites in the wilderness, the fallen angels (Gen. 6.1-4), and the inhabitants of Sodom and Gomorrah. The writer then identifies his godless opponents with the formula: '*Even so these…these however…*' (vv. 8-10). For further support he points in v. 9 to the modesty of the archangel Michael in his conflict with the devil over the body of Moses. In another form, this motif is known from the apocalyptic *Testament of Moses*.

In the second exegetical round, for the sake of brevity the names of the biblical rebels Cain, Balaam and Korah are evoked, followed by the identification, '*These are* the blot of your love meals…' (vv. 11-13).

The third round is interesting because, instead of the Old Testament, an apocryphal text is quoted. The identification of the contemporary opponents is the more powerful due to the repeated 'godless', as is announced already in the introduction:

> *And concerning these* Enoch, the seventh from Adam, prophesied, saying: See the Lord comes with his holy ten thousands, to speak judgment over all, and to punish all souls for all their works of godlessness which they committed in godlessness and over all the hard things which they as godless sinners spoke against Him. *These are the murmurers…* (Jude 14-16).

The quotation is from the Jewish apocalypse of Enoch, apparently in written form. The passage corresponds with the first Book of Enoch known to us (1.9). The wordy expression 'works of godlessness committed in godlessness' has a Semitic structure. The Greek of Jude is here apparently closer to the original Hebrew or Aramaic than the text known to us. At Qumran, indeed several Aramaic fragments of Enoch were found, but this text is not among them. This quote from Enoch is the only time in the New Testament that a non-canonical, Jewish writing is quoted expressly. Its content underscores once more the apocalyptic focus of Jude. The quote is placed in a central position and was apparently considered by the writer to be important.

Announcing the final admonition, the fourth round begins with the words 'But you, beloved...'; the two portions overlap each other. Once more the quote is from a post-Old Testamental source, this time a word 'of the apostles of our Lord Jesus Christ', that is, a Christian prophecy: 'At the end of time there will be mockers...' (vv. 17-18). Here again an identification follows: '*These are* the creators of schisms...'

The importance of the terminology—'these are...'; 'even so these...' —which identifies contemporary godless ones with their notorious examples is apparent from the occurrence of related expressions in the Qumran scrolls, where likewise contemporary enemies were identified by using biblical examples: '*And these are* they of whom it is written in the book of Ezekiel the prophet... *These are*...' (4Q174 [flor] 1.16-17). In the positive sense such identifications can also be found both in Qumran and in the New Testament: '*This is* the one of whom was spoken by Isaiah the Prophet...' (Mt. 3.3; cf. also Gal. 4.24; 2 Tim. 3.8).

At work here is the simultaneous interpretation of the Scriptures and of contemporary history, characteristic of the prophetic–apocalyptic view of history practised by the Qumran community and the earliest Christians, and occurring in rabbinic literature as well. Another Palestinian-Jewish phenomenon is the importance attached to Enoch, a book also readily perused at Qumran.

We pause now at the eschatologically charged Christology, contained not only in the opening lines but also in the conclusion:

> To Him who is able to keep you without stumbling and to present you spotless with jubilation before his glory, to the One God our Saviour, be, through Jesus Christ our Lord, glory, greatness, power, and might for all eternity and now also and in the ages of ages! Amen (Jude 24-25).

This is apparently a formulation from the liturgy, in which the members of the church are seen in the salutary light of the end times. The ranking order between God, called the 'One' and 'Saviour', and Christ, through whom God is glorified, is striking. This christological order of rank is, however, also observable in Paul's writings, and has the same eschatological slant (1 Cor. 15.23-28; Rom. 8.31-38). It is remarkable that in the church of Jude, which we apparently must localize somewhere in the Holy Land, a Christology akin to Paul's could flourish. Reciprocally, this means that we should perceive Pauline Christology in a more eschatological and 'Jewish' manner than is customarily done.

A Relative of Jesus?
The probability of a Palestinian-Jewish background is sufficient occasion to take seriously the author's identification of himself as being the brother of James and Jesus. Richard Bauckham, whose inquiry we follow here, found an unexpected point of departure: the indication of Enoch as being 'the seventh from Adam' (Jude 14).

This designation of Enoch can naturally be seen as implied in the story of Genesis (5.1-18); however, the explicit emphasis with which it appears in the apocalypse of Enoch (*1 En.* 93.3, cf. 60.8) is a different matter. Thus we read of a series of seven times seven generations, of which the first 'generation week' is crowned by Enoch, the righteous, and the seventh by 'the righteous chosen ones of the eternal planting of righteousness' (*1 En.* 93.3, 10; cf. Isa. 60.21). The apocalypse of Enoch is, however, a complex document. A second list of generations occurs, based on a counting of ten 'generation weeks'. The final judgment and the renewal of heaven and earth take place at the end of the tenth group of sevens (*1 En.* 91.12-16). Due to redactional alterations it is not clear whether these 70 generations include Enoch's own 'week' or begin after him. Elsewhere, however, we read of 'seventy generations' *after* Enoch until the day of judgment (*1 En.* 10.12). The Enoch literature contains in any case a tradition of *77 generations* from Adam to the last day.

This counting recurs in a surprising place, namely, in the genealogy of Jesus in Luke (Lk. 3.23-38). If one reckons back via Enoch as the seventh, Abraham as the twenty-first, David as the thirty-fifth, and Joseph, the 'supposed father' of Jesus (v. 23), as the seventy-sixth, one ends up with Jesus being the seventy-seventh from Adam. The Davidic lineage is hereby also confirmed.

These multiple correspondences lead to various conclusions. We see once more to what extent 'Luke', even in the 'legendary' opening portion of his Gospel, incorporates traditions (see p. 219), in this case those imprinted by Palestinian–Jewish Enoch motifs. Furthermore, this tradition has the effect of 'grafting' the family tree of Jesus into the line of Enoch, so that he appears as the seventy-seventh generation, during which creation will be renewed. Given the fact that 'Luke' himself wrote approximately two generations later, he must have derived this tradition from 'authoritative' Jewish-Christian circles.

The Epistle of Jude has a double interface with this ancient tradition: the line of Enoch, and the relation with Jesus' brother, James. It is, therefore, well possible that in the opinion of the author, who thought strongly apocalyptically and 'Enochically', Jesus, the 'only Ruler and Lord', was the seventieth from Enoch and the seventy-seventh from Adam. It is conceivable that such an Enochic genealogy was cultivated by Jesus' own family members. Thereby, the statement of the writer that he was a brother of James, and thus also of Jesus, sheds much of its incredibility. In its unembellished state, it acquires even a certain degree of probability.

Conclusion
The Epistle of Jude derives from a Jewish church, probably connected to the family circle of Jesus, and possibly written by his own brother Iouda. In this milieu, where great importance was attached to apocalyptic books, such as Enoch, writing reasonable Greek formed no obstacle. Apart from the eschatological Christology, the epistle contains no themes of orthodox theological relevance. The incorporation into the orthodox canon should possibly be attributed to the presumed family relationship to Jesus.

James

That the Epistle of James has had more difficulties being accepted by the orthodox mainstream than its younger brother Jude seems to be related to certain striking characteristics: a scarcity of clear christological formulations, a consistent emphasis on obedience to the law, and an explicit plea for 'justification by works' and 'not by faith alone'.

The latter is like a kick in the Pauline shins of Protestant doctrine. Luther called it a 'straw letter', 'concocted by some Jew or another'. Perhaps this referred to the random manner in which one subject follows another, which was taken to be a 'Jewish' manner of reasoning. In any case, the emphasis on the law is a recognizably Jewish position. Nonetheless, Luther, like all great spirits, was more versatile than his followers and valued the Epistle of James because of its earnestness concerning the obedience of faith. For Luther as well, 'faith without works is dead'.

Thus we arrive at our theme. The Epistle of James, a Jewish-Christian document with a 'low Christology', places great emphasis on the law and opposes a one-sided accent on faith. Before proceeding further, a few things must be said about the epistle itself.

An 'Epistle' of James?

The opening lines of the writing are those of an epistle: 'James, the servant of God and of the Lord Jesus Christ, to the twelve tribes in the Diaspora: greetings!' Besides this highly vague address, there is nothing in James that resembles a letter. It is a treatise on general themes that apparently for the occasion was provided with the opening lines of an epistle, and it is at most an open letter or 'encyclical' epistle. For this reason, in later manuscripts James is correctly counted as the first 'catholic (general) epistle'.

Who are, however, the addressees, 'the twelve tribes in the dispersion'? Since, after going into Assyrian exile, the 'ten tribes' of the Northern Kingdom disappeared from history (see pp. 111-12), the designation must be figurative. It turns out that a widely ramified tradition lies behind this, on which we will expand when discussing the Revelation of John (see pp. 371-72). The expression is an apocalyptic metaphor for the chosen remnant of Israel. Given the content of the 'epistle' as well, it is logical that 'James' here indeed intended the Jewish Christians of the Diaspora. We return to this at the end of this discussion.

In itself, the writing is difficult to place. Its Greek belongs to the best of the New Testament. In contrast, it entirely lacks an orderly composition, at least in comparison to an author like Paul, who, alongside vivid variation, always follows a clear rhetorical line, even in highly emotional epistles. In James, unrelated pieces of advice, extending over several verses, are strung together. The content exhibits an unmistakable affinity to the spirit of moderation and righteousness known from the ancient wisdom tradition. There are also striking points of contact with the synoptic tradition, in particular with the Sermon on the Mount. Along with a number of other elements, this all points to a Jewish or, more correctly, Jewish-Christian background. As to form and content, this writing is somewhat comparable to the pious tractates known as the *Derekh-Erets* literature (see pp. 63-64).

Who then is this 'James'? As established in regard to the Epistle of Jude, it is logical that the singular designation refers to 'James, the brother of the Lord', the leader of the Jewish church in Jerusalem. The canonization of the dogmatically rather 'problematic' writing must have been based upon that assumption. Most modern exegetes, however, cannot conceive of how such excellent Greek could have come from the village school of Nazareth. Further, the discussion of the theme 'faith and works' would testify to such a temporal distance from Paul that the authorship of Jesus' brother James would be practically excluded, for he was killed at the beginning of the sixties (Josephus, *Ant.* 20.200).

We shall see, however, that the contrast to Paul should not be exaggerated. As to the language, we have already seen that the author of the Epistle of Jude, apparently from a Palestinian–Jewish milieu and perhaps being James's own brother Jude, was also capable of casting his apocalyptically tinted message in good Greek. The assistance of a Greek-speaking 'amanuensis', or secretary, which was possible to procure even in Nazareth, is not excluded. Finally, Acts reports that the Jerusalem church under the leadership of James sent an official circular letter to the churches of Antioch and surrounding regions (Acts 15.13-29). A qualified Greek-speaking secretary would certainly have been hired for the occasion. Something similar is by all means conceivable for this 'catholic letter'.

A Jewish-Christian Document
It is remarkable that, besides the opening lines, the tractate 'of James' contains but one passage with a clear Christian reference, and this, too, is in its Christology most restrained: 'My brothers, preserve the faith of our Lord Jesus Christ—in glory—but not with respect of persons' (Jas 2.1). An admonition to equality within the church follows, about which we will expand later. What the 'faith of Jesus Christ' involves is not stated in so many words, but the end of this admonition makes it clear that when the readers divide the seats in the church with respect of persons, they 'blaspheme the splendid name which has been called out over you' (2.7). This is, therefore, about humility and justice according to the example of Jesus, in particular during the gatherings in his name.

The Christology of 'James' contrasts soberly with that of Jude, and certainly with that of Paul. It is uncertain what type of conclusions can be drawn from this. Of importance, on the one hand, is the unaccepting reaction of Jesus when someone called him 'Good master': 'No one is good except God alone!' (Mk 10.18). It could be that James shared in this christological or 'messianologic' reservation. Nonetheless, we are told that also in his congregation 'the splendid name' of Jesus Christ was 'called out', 'in glory' at that—a Semitizing manner of expressing Jesus' eschatological exaltation. Furthermore, most of the admonitions in this treatise are conceivable as being directly derived from Jewish tradition. This possibility is proven by the *Didache*, a Jewish-Christian writing whose composers, without mentionable Christianizing, were able to incorporate a traditional Jewish source (see below).

A cautious conclusion is that 'James' saw no occasion to provide the admonitions in his tractate with a Christian stamp. The one exception that we mentioned is explainable: it concerns the ethical implication of the liturgical use of the name of Jesus Christ. This, too, suggests affinity to Jewish pious literature.

There is another portion in the New Testament writings that is eligible for comparison with Jewish pious literature, namely, the Sermon on the Mount. The following points of contact with James are highly interesting:

> From the same mouth come forth blessing and cursing!?...This, my brothers, should not be so... Can a fig tree, my brothers, bring forth olives, or a vine figs? (Jas 3.10-12).
> One does not pick grapes from thornbushes, or figs from thistles, does one? So every good tree produces beautiful fruit, but the rotten tree produces bad fruit (Mt. 7.16-17).

> He who speaks evil of his brother or judges his brother, speaks evil of the law and judges the law... One is there who gives the law and judges, who is capable of saving and allowing to perish, and who are you, that you judge your neighbour? (Jas 4.11-12).
> Judge not, that you be not judged. For with the judgment with which you judge, you shall be judged, and with the measure by which you measure you shall be measured (Mt. 7.2-3).

> Come on then, you rich ones... Your riches are rotten, for your clothing has become food for moths, your gold and silver is mildewed and mold has become your witness and shall also corrode your flesh as fire. You have gathered treasures yet in the last days... (Jas 5.1-3).

Gather no treasures for yourselves upon the earth, where moths and mould make them unpresentable and where thieves break in and steal... (Mt. 6.19-20).

Above all, my brothers, swear not, neither by heaven nor by the earth nor by any other oath. Let your yes be 'yes' and your no 'no', so that you do not come under condemnation (Jas 5.12).

I say to you, swear not at all, neither by heaven because that is the throne of God, nor by the earth because this is the footstool for his feet, nor by Jerusalem because it is the city of the great king... Let your word be 'yes, yes', 'no, no', because everything that exceeds this is of evil (Mt. 5.33-37).

Of primary importance is the fact that all of these passages have also more or less direct parallels in rabbinic literature. Two outstanding examples: 'With the measure by which you measure you will be measured' occurs in the Mishnah, and 'gathering treasures in heaven' occurs in an old midrash on Deut. 28.12 (*t. Pe'ah* 4.18; *Sifre Deut.* 40, p. 83; see also above pp. 145-46). Secondly, these are minor elements that surface isolatedly in James's reasoning. It does not appear that 'James' is quoting from the Matthew known to us.

If we keep the correspondences in content and form with rabbinic literature in mind, it would seem that the relative parallelism between these passages in James and the Sermon on the Mount do not go back to different reworkings of a written source, but to a flexible oral tradition. James's treatise and the Sermon on the Mount seem to form two elaborations of one and the same Jewish-Christian tradition of teachings.

Of incalculable significance is the fact that this conclusion converges with our earlier suspicions that a primal Matthaean source translated from Hebrew or Aramaic must have been processed into the third layer of Matthew (see pp. 266-67). The isolated, but unmistakable correspondences between the Sermon on the Mount and the Epistle of James point to a shared, original oral tradition of teachings, which as far as we can judge coincides with the specific Matthaean material. The author of the Epistle of James evidently employs the same Gospel tradition that was available to the first redactor of Matthew in his Matthaean primal source.

Another element shared by James with the synoptic tradition relates to the 'gospel of the poor'. For this we return to the appeal for equal treatment. After the opening already quoted, we read:

> If a gold-ringed man in splendid garments enters your meeting, and a poor man in rags comes in, and you then take notice of the one with splendid garments and say: Sit in this lovely seat! but to the poor man you say: Go stand over there, or: Sit below at my feet—do you not discriminate among yourselves, and are you not judges with bad motives? Listen, my beloved brothers: Has not God chosen the poor of the world to be rich in faith and as heirs of the Kingdom that he has promised to those who love Him? (Jas 2.2-5).

The theme recurs in the case of the field labourers who wait for their pay in vain, so that their cries rise 'to the ears of the Lord of hosts'; the outburst against the mildewed riches of the landlords has already been quoted (Jas 5.1-5). This manner of thinking also occurs in various forms in the synoptic tradition, such as the outburst of Jesus:

> Beware of the scribes who love going around in long mantles, greetings in the squares, seats of honour in the meetings, and seats of honour at meals, who eat up the houses of widows and pray with expansive verbosity; they shall receive a heavier condemnation (Mk 12.38-40; Lk. 20.46-47; cf. Lk. 11.43; Mt. 23.6-7).

A biblical text on which this is based makes the connection to James clear:

> Woe those who string house to house and add field to field so that there is no place left [for the neighbour] and you alone live upon the land: in the ears of the Lord of hosts (this is heard)! (Isa. 5.9; the additions in the Septuagint are in square brackets).

Common to all of these passages is the condemnation of riches derived from the gathering of real estate in combination with outward piety.

This throws new light on the well-known beginning of Jesus' beatitudes: 'Blessed are the poor of the Spirit, for theirs is the Kingdom of Heaven...blessed the meek, for they shall inherit the land' (Mt. 5.3, 5). Elsewhere we have already discussed the biblical and Jewish backgrounds of these texts, as well as the relation between 'poor' and 'meek' (see p. 127). It should be added that the first beatitude in Luke is simply 'Blessed are the poor' (Lk. 6.20). Completely in concurrence with Psalm 37, which also echoes here, those 'poor' and 'meek' are impoverished upon the *land* that they have been promised to inherit. This is now the 'good news' for the 'poor' (Isa. 61.3). An ancient Palestinian-Jewish agrarian piety seems to be reflected, whose roots can be traced through to the biblical prophets and which is also recognizable in Essene piety. In the Qumran community one could call oneself 'poor of the Spirit', and our translation of Jesus' beatitude is based precisely on that parallel (see p. 127). It is not without significance that Paul as well could designate the beneficiaries of his collection for the churches in Judaea simply as 'the poor' (Gal. 2.10; Rom. 15.26). That this tradition carried on for centuries longer is demonstrated by the name of the Jewish-Christian group from the time of Origen, the Ebionites, which is nothing other than the Hebrew word for 'poor', *ebyonim* (see p. 280).

There is yet another common Jewish element shared by the Sermon on the Mount and James's treatise that I have saved for the last because of its exceptionality. In the summons to equal treatment at gatherings, a striking Greek word is used: 'A gold-ringed man enters your *synagogue*...' The same word occurs in a closely related statement of Jesus about the scholars of the law: 'The scribes love seats of honour in the *synagogues*' (Jas 2.2; Mk 12.39). Jesus is not, of course, speaking of 'Christian' synagogues, but James is. This is the only time that the word is thus used, though this possibly has to do with the fragmentary preservation of ancient Jewish-Christian literature. Precisely for this reason, the exception is eloquent.

The Importance of the Law
With the absence of Gospels in their original Jewish form and the general scarcity of ancient Jewish-Christian literature, James' words about the law are significant. Before discussing the aspect that has occupied Christian exegetes the most—the relation to Paul—we will attempt to allow this Jewish-Christian tractate to speak for itself concerning the importance of the law and the commandments.

Amidst the short admonitory passages, there are three in which keeping the law is emphasized, plus a fourth one about works and faith that we will discuss later. This recurrence within an 'unorganized' whole indicates fulfilling the law to be a main theme. The law is denoted as 'the perfect law of freedom' (1.25), 'the law of freedom' (2.12) and 'the royal law' (2.8). Doing the law is concisely emphasized in the expressions 'doers of the law' (4.11), 'transgressors of the law' (2.11), 'doers of the word' (1.22-23) and 'doers of the (good) work' (1.25).

Usually unable to explain how freedom could be related to the law, exegetes have concluded that something more universal than the Jewish law must have been involved. The same connection, however, occurs in a midrash about the tables of stone:

> R. Yoshua ben Levi said… 'The tables were the work of God and the
> writing was the writing of God, carved (*harut*) upon the tables' (Exod.
> 32.16)—do not read *harut*, 'carved', but *herut*, 'freedom': Only he who
> makes the words of the Tora stand is free (*m. Ab.* 6.2, text according to
> *Midrash haGadol Exodus* 32.16, p. 668).

R. Yoshua ben Levi taught mid third century, but a parallel tradition
of a century earlier already presumes the core of this midrash (*Tanh. ki
tisa* 16.122a). It is thus plausible that at the beginning of the second
century the correspondence between the Hebrew words for 'carved' and
'freedom' was already being played on, and, not impossibly, that this
play on words could have been part of the spiritual accoutrements of the
author. Nonetheless, we shall see that the expression also contains a
universal aspect.

With this in mind, let us listen to the first three passages in which the
law is spoken of:

> (1) Be *doers of the word* and not hearers only, who deceive themselves.
> For if someone is a hearer of the word but no doer, he resembles a man
> who wants to view in a mirror the face with which he grew up: he views
> himself, goes away, and forgets immediately how he looked. But he who
> bends over *the perfect law of freedom* and remains with it, not as a hearer
> of forgetfulness but as a *doer of the work*, he shall be blessed in his
> doing (Jas 1.22-25).

Three of the key concepts occur here. The intriguing image of the man
in the mirror reminds one of Greek wisdom traditions. 'Know yourself'
is the motto that is said to have been above the gateway of the oracle
temple in the Greek Delphi. The thought that one remains true to oneself by fulfilling the divine law resembles the Stoic manner of thought.
Thus, international notions of wisdom are fitted into the typically
Jewish emphasis upon keeping the Torah. In this James's treatise is
related to rabbinic literature that also adopted Hellenistic, in particular
Stoic, themes of wisdom.

> (2) If, however, you fulfill the *royal law* according to the Scriptural word
> 'Love your neighbour as yourself', you do well. But if you want to show
> respect of persons, you bring about sin and you are *declared by the law
> to be guilty as transgressors*. For *he who keeps the whole law, but
> stumbles in one (commandment), becomes guilty of all*. For he who said:
> 'You shall not commit adultery,' also said: 'You shall not kill.' If you,
> then, do not commit adultery but do murder, you have become a
> *transgressor of the law*. Speak thus and act thus as though you will be

judged by *the law of freedom.* For the judgment is unmerciful for him
who does no mercy; mercy boasts against judgment (Jas 2.8-13).

The remarkable rule, 'he who keeps the whole law...', will occupy us
later. Again we find a resemblance to the Stoic tradition, in particular in
the rule, 'speak and act as though you shall be judged by the law of
freedom'. This introduces us to the other, 'Hellenistic' side of the
expression 'the law of freedom'. The statement of Yoshua ben Levi that
'only he who makes the words of the Tora stand is free', is also related
to the popular Stoic theme that life according to 'the law of nature'
grants inner freedom. This was apparently completely conceivable
within Judaism. The rabbis as well as Philo viewed the Torah simultaneously as being the universal basis of creation and the exclusive
constitution of Israel.

> (3) Speak no evil of each other, brothers. He who speaks evil of his broth-
> er or judges his brother, speaks evil of the law and judges the law; and if
> you judge the law, you are no *doer of the law* but a judger. There is one
> who gives the law and judges, who is able to save and to make perish,
> and who are you then, that you judge your neighbour? (Jas 4.11-12).

The climate of wisdom literature is again noticeable. The affinity with
the synoptic tradition, which receives ample attention in Paul's writings, has already been pointed out. The concise Jewish expressions,
such as 'doing' and 'transgressing the law', in the admonitions of
'James' are combined with international wisdom motifs. The law is
central, both in the universal perspective and in the Jewish-Christian
point of view.

Faith and Works: James and Paul

There is a fourth passage on the importance of the law, which addresses
itself explicitly against certain Pauline ideas. A fragment: 'A person is
justified by words and *not by faith alone*' (Jas 2.24). This contrast
between two writings of the New Testament canon can place Christian
exegetes in a delicate predicament. Protestant exegetes solve it by
saying that 'James' is not addressing Paul himself, but his one-sided
followers. It is in itself odd that only when confronted with James does
an awareness of this multifaceted aspect of Paul manifests itself. Paul
did indeed emphasize 'works', the law retains a relative validity for
him, and obedience is required of believers (2 Cor. 9.8; Rom. 7.12; Gal.
5.13). One should recall that 'justification by faith' assumes a central
place in only two of Paul's epistles (see pp. 184-85).

Further, it is demonstrable that Paul and 'James' share certain basic assumptions concerning the law. Through these, it is possible to trace better what the outspoken differences in accent between the two signify. In James there are three parallels with Paul's writings in content and sometimes even in vocabulary, all three in the passages discussed above about one of James' main themes, the law. These parallels will be treated one by one.

> (a) Be *doers of* the word and not hearers only, who deceive themselves...
> But he who bends over the perfect *law* of freedom and remains with it, not as a *hearer of* forgetfulness but as a *doer of* the work, he shall be blessed in his doing (Jas 1.22-25; cf. 4.11).

> For not the *hearers of the law* are justified before God, but the *doers of the law* shall be justified (Rom. 2.13).

This last passage in Paul's letter to the Romans has surprised some exegetes. An interesting suggestion is that he here reproduces a traditional piece of Hellenistic-Jewish preaching. Indeed, in this chapter the apostle addresses himself to unbelieving *Jews*, while the preceding is against unbelieving non-Jews. *Within that context*, he can thus employ terminology that could appear to be borrowed straight from 'James'. In both cases, a rather special Greek word is used for 'hearer', *akroatês*. One conclusion is that Paul customarily did not speak 'in that context', that is, to the unbelieving Jews, because he usually addressed himself to non-Jews. Another implication appears to be that James here addresses Jewish believers.

In any event, both use the term 'doers of the law' in a positive sense. The Hebrew background for this expression is confirmed on the basis of the Qumran scrolls (*'ôsê ha-tōrâ*, e.g. 1QpHab 7.11; 8.1; 12.4), related to the Pauline term 'works of the law', or 'commandments', which we also know from Qumran (*ma'asê tōrâ*, see p. 163). In his 'anti-Pauline' passage, James uses the shorter form 'works', also often encountered in Paul's own writings.

The second parallel:

> (b) For he who keeps the whole law, but stumbles in one (commandment), becomes guilty of all. For he who said: 'You shall not commit adultery,' also said: 'You shall not kill' (Jas 2.10).
> See, I, Paul, say to you: if you let yourselves be circumcised, Christ shall be pointless to you. Once more I affirm to each who lets himself be circumcised, that he is indebted to do with whole law (Gal. 5.2-3).

Here the contexts are clearly different. James argues for love of one's fellow-man as a commandment that must be kept: even though you might not be an adulterer, your lack of love towards your poor brother makes you a transgressor of the law. Paul is concerned with the right, nay, the duty, of the Galatians to remain faithful non-Jewish followers of the Jewish apostle of the nations; circumcision would for them destroy his pluriform gospel.

Both, however, use the rule that to take the commandments upon oneself entails that one keep the whole law, with literally the same Greek expression, *holon ton nomon*. It is not difficult to trace this back to the Hebrew expression, *kol ha-tōrâ kullâ*, or *kol dibrê tōrâ*, and indeed both versions occur in a rabbinic rule concerning conversion to Judaism: 'A proselyte who takes upon himself *the whole Torah except for one thing*, should not be accepted' (*Sifra, qedoshim* perek 8.91a; cf. *t. Dem.* 2.5).

Paul apparently uses an early form of this rule in support of his argument that circumcision would make the Galatians full proselytes and thus invalidate his 'gospel for the nations'. 'James' uses the rule (or a variation of it) in an opposite manner: if you have taken the commandments upon yourself, you may not transgress one of them—a rather strict standpoint. Elsewhere he admits in fact that 'we all stumble in many respects' (3.1). Is he appealing to his readers here on the basis of their Jewish-Christian calling?

The third parallel is of less direct importance to us:

> (c) There is one who gives the law and judges, who is able to save and to make perish, and who are you then, that you judge your neighbour? (Jas 4.11-12).

> But you, why then do you judge your brother?... For we all shall stand before the judgment seat of God (Rom. 14.10).

Within the loosely woven texture of James, his statement serves to underscore his summons against slander (4.11-12; cf. 3.1-11); it is not filled in further. The context for Paul is the tension about sharing meals together within the church in Rome, where Jews and non-Jews judged each other for their lifestyle. In James as well it appears to have to do with the pretence of being able to judge a brother on the basis of his keeping of the law (see Jas 4.11). If he indeed wrote to Jewish believers in the Diaspora, the reference would be to disagreement about the law among Jewish Christians in the Diaspora.

In summary, 'James' and Paul both speak from a common Jewish background in which 'doing the law' and 'works' are positive values, where while 'the whole law' is taken upon oneself, God is left to judge one's neighbour's faithfulness to the law.

What then is the significance of James' explicit contention against the Pauline motto of 'justification by faith without the works of the law'? Let us quote the fourth, anti-Pauline passage concerning the law:

> (4) Do you want to know, O vain person, that faith without works is empty? Abraham our father, was he not justified by works through the fact that he laid Isaac, his son, upon the altar? Do you see that his faith worked together with his works and that his faith was perfected by his works? And thus was the Scripture fulfilled that said, 'And Abraham believed God and it was counted to him as righteousness' (Gen. 15.6), and he was called a friend of God (Isa. 41.8). You see that a person is justified by works and not by faith alone. Likewise, was not Rahab the whore justified through the fact that she received the messengers and let them disappear by a different way? Thus it is that just as the body without the soul is dead, so is faith without works dead (Jas 2.20-26).

The intention is clear from the beginning and the end: faith without works is 'empty' and 'dead'. We proposed that Paul would have subscribed to this. Further, the example of Abraham is given. Though this theme was extremely widespread, including in the New Testament, the combination with 'faith and works' is hardly coincidental. 'James' must have had the specific message of Paul in mind; however, there is not a total contradiction. For Paul, Abraham's 'faith' entailed obedience and perserverance: he 'believed against hope upon hope' in God who brings the dead to life, without taking the 'deadness' of his body into consideration (Rom. 4.17-22). This accent remains in the background, in any case in Romans and Galatians, as comparison to a related passage in Hebrews makes clear (Heb. 11.8-18; see p. 355). This could be summarized as follows: there are shared basic assumptions, but the passage in James is at odds with Paul's 'gospel of the non-Jews'. The statement that 'a person is justified by works and not by faith alone' can not be interpreted otherwise. What is going on?

The argument that 'James' is not addressing Paul himself is not conclusive. Paul's epistles were probably only locally known in the first century. Even the author of Acts, the great advocate of the apostle to the nations, does not give the impression that he was well acquainted with them (see p. 239). On the other hand, Paul was thoroughly misunderstood. He himself complains about the unilateralization of his pluriform gospel, as though he would set the law aside 'so that grace might abound' (Rom. 3.8; 6.1). That is exactly what is reported in Acts, where the church in Jerusalem, under the leadership of James, says to Paul:

> (The believers among the Jews) hear concerning you the rumour that you *teach defection from Moses* to all Jews among the nations by saying that they should not circumcise their children nor live according to custom (Acts 21.21).

The question is whether 'James' believes these rumours about Paul or actually will contest them. On the basis of their common basic assumptions we can assume the latter. 'James' would then be admonishing his Jewish fellow-believers in the Diaspora not to judge their fellow-Jew, Paul, because of his pluriform conception of the law. The drastic statement that 'a person is justified *by works* and not by faith alone' would then be intended to challenge the unilateralizing misunderstanding of Paul, in the sense of 'this is what Paul intended with the example of Abraham'. Possibly, he did not know that Paul himself wrote something completely different. When read thus, 'James' exhibits an unintentional anti-Paulism.

On the other hand, perhaps we must assume the opposite: did James (this time without quotation marks) give ear to anti-Pauline extremists in the Jerusalem church? At the end of Chapter 4 we summed up the evidence that from the late forties there were great tensions and even a breach between Paul and the church in Jerusalem. 'People of James' came to Antioch and drove a wedge between Jewish and non-Jewish Christians, thus frustrating the pluriformity of Paul's gospel (Gal. 2.11-14). On his way to Jerusalem with the collection, Paul himself expresses fear 'for the disobedient in Judaea' and the distrust in Jerusalem (Rom. 15.31). Is the Epistle of James with all its emphasis upon the 'doing of the law' and 'justification through works' a treatise from Jerusalem aimed against Paul and his 'churches of non-Jews'?

The answer is dependent upon which readers it was written for. If, besides Jewish, *also non-Jewish* members of the Diapora churches are addressed, then an anti-Pauline intention is inescapable: non-Jews are then also summoned to do 'works of the law'. If the addressees are, however, *only Jews*, then the author could have been contesting a radical misunderstanding of Paul, as though Paul had sought to dispense with the law for Jews as well. An indication of the latter possibility can be found in the address 'to the twelve tribes in the dispersion'. It is further confirmed by the similarity in terminology with the 'intra-Jewish Paul' in Rom. 2.13. The bitter irony of church history is that it was precisely the incorporation of this epistle into the orthodox non-Jewish canon that caused a compelling anti-Pauline reading.

Conclusion

The Epistle of James is an exhortatory treatise from a Jewish-Christian milieu which summons its readers to sympathy with that milieu. It exhibits affinity to pious Jewish writings in the peripheries of rabbinic tradition, emphasizes the importance of 'doing the law', and places an anti-Pauline sounding emphasis upon 'justification by works'. This could be intended as a summons to Jewish readers in particular not to think that Paul sought to abolish the law. The traditional ascribing of the epistle to Jesus' brother James can not be further supported, but there is also little against it. The tractate could have circulated already during Paul's lifetime.

Hebrews

Hebrews places us in a completely different cultural climate whose 'Jewish' character cannot easily be captured. After a high-christological prelude, the attention of the reader is drawn by the allegory of Jesus as heavenly high priest of true, spiritual worship. Whether one could call this Jewish depends, however, on one's image of Judaism in antiquity. An important gauge is provided by the writings of Philo of Alexandria. Because of his strong predisposition for allegory many consider him more Hellenistic than Jewish. When one realizes, however, that he visited the synagogue weekly and clearly rejected pagan customs, it becomes clear that his Hellenistic world of thought had an unmistakably Jewish infrastructure. One of the questions will therefore be how the writer of the Epistle to the Hebrews—however his thinking is to be characterized—stood in relation to the observance of the Jewish law.

Concerning Christology, it is necessary once more to realize that Judaism in antiquity accommodated diversity in thinking, such as that of the Essenes, of the Hillelites, and of thinkers like Philo. Jesus' own thinking cannot possibly be categorized as being 'average Jewish'. Furthermore, there are the mystical, not to say theosophic, speculations that in antiquity were practised by prominent rabbis (see pp. 67-68). Speaking of Jesus as being placed above the angels, as 'the radiance of God's glory and the imprint of his being' (Heb. 1.3-4), is not out of place in such a context and can at most be characterized as being 'heterodox Jewish'. In the introduction to this chapter, it was suggested that it is the manner of life more than the manner of thinking that makes one Jewish.

Little direct information is given about the author of Hebrews. On the basis of its language, Origen had already alleged that it could not have been Paul, in spite of the tradition that already then had ascribed it to him, for the Greek of Hebrews is the most cultured of the entire New Testament. On the other hand, in the closing portion with greetings, a certain Timothy is mentioned in whose company the author hopes to visit his readers (13.23). If this is the same one as Paul's co-worker (Rom. 16.21; 1 Cor. 4.17; 16.10), the author of Hebrews must also have belonged to Paul's entourage. He writes that he hopes to be returned soon to his readers and appears by this to allude to imprisonment (13.19). He sends greetings from 'those from Italy' (13.24), but it is unclear whether he is imprisoned there and his readers live elsewhere, or whether it is the other way around. That is the difficulty with other people's correspondence: so little is explained to outsiders... An attractive assumption is that of Luther, namely, that the author is Apollos, the Alexandrian-Jewish preacher who ministered in Corinth and Ephesus during Paul's day (see p. 235). That would fit with the character of the epistle and the loose association with Paul. There is no further data to go by. It will have to suffice that the writer of Hebrews was 'someone like Apollos'.

Besides its ending, Hebrews hardly has the character of a letter. It is more like an essay or a sermon written out, apparently sent to the readers with some personal communications added to it. For convenience's sake, however, we will continue to speak of an epistle.

Concerning the date, we largely must grope in the dark. The readers or hearers have become sluggish in listening while they actually should have been teachers (5.11-12). This moves us in any case to the second generation of Christians, about the second half of the first century. A further dating is dependent on whether the 'epistle' was written before or after the destruction of the temple, to which we will return later.

There are three main sections: (1) a eulogy on Christ as the Son *par excellence* and as heavenly high priest, ending with a summons to perseverance (1.1–6.20), (2) an elaboration of Christ's heavenly office as the high priest who himself brought the definitive offering (7.1–10.18), and (3) a further encouragment to perseverance (8.19 to the end).

Jewish-Christian Elements

Within the context of our investigation, a number of clearly Jewish elements must be discussed. The address 'To the Hebrews', which ever since the beginning of the fourth century occurs at the bottom of the 'epistle' (as was then the custom for a 'heading'), must have been added later on the basis of the content of the epistle—but not without reason. An indirect but fairly clear indication of the addressees can be found at the end of the second chapter, where we read that the Son became 'in all things equal' to the 'little children' given to him, 'the seed of Abraham', and, therefore, in the same manner he took on 'flesh and blood' in order as a 'faithful high priest' to propitiate for the 'sins of the people' (2.14-18). The latter, expansively treated image is viewed by the author totally within the context of the Jewish worship service. Thus at the beginning of the 'epistle' it appears that a Jewish audience is implied.

Some affinity to Paul is apparent: the readers are 'heirs of the promise' to Abraham (6.17; cf. Gal. 3.29; Rom. 9.8), and 'where a testament is, there must be the death of the testator' (9.16; cf. Gal. 4; 2 Cor. 3; Rom. 7). Chapter 11 is a eulogy on faith, one of Paul's central concepts: 'faith is the substance of things hoped for, the evidence of things not seen' (11.1; cf. Rom. 8.24); Noah is 'heir of the righteousness according to faith' (11.7; cf. Rom. 4.13). When the author, however, begins to relate what faith entails, another accent is heard: in particular obedience during testing is involved. For Abraham, for example, it meant that 'when he was called, obeyed and went to the place which he would inherit', and that he 'offered Isaac when he was tested' (11.8, 17). That this accent in Paul's writings is more in the background (p. 351) could have to do with a difference in the specific occasion of writing.

There is, however, more involved. Upon a closer look, in the laudation of the faith of all those witnesses, no Christian application or interpretation is added. Chapter 11 can be read without difficulty as a Hellenistic-Jewish eulogy on faith. What is said about the witnesses who were 'stoned' and 'sawn asunder' is also significant (11.37): it must be reminiscent of the legendary martyr's deaths of the prophets Jeremiah and Isaiah, related in the apocryphal Jewish writing, *The Lives of the Prophets*.

In an extension of this, ch. 12 presents Jesus as the 'leader and fulfiller of faith', the greatest witness of all, 'who for the joy that was set before him endured the cross, despising the shame, and is seated on the right side of the throne of God' (12.2). This sounds like the summary of an early Jewish-Christian confession of faith. A similar quotation occurs also at the end of the first main section, where the writer once more recalls the 'main issue of the Word of Christ' for his readers, the 'foundation' of faith: 'turning from dead works, belief in God, instruction on baptism and the laying on of hands, the resurrection of the dead and the eternal judgment' (6.1-2). On the basis of these passages, the writer can be characterized provisionally as having a 'Hellenistic-Jewish-Christian' type of thinking.

More Jewish and Jewish-Christian elements can be pointed out. The eulogy on faith forms the core of the third main section where perseverance is encouraged. At the beginning and end of this portion, persecutions that the readers have undergone appear to be alluded to (see especially 10.34). In that connection the writer cites the words of the prophet, also used by Paul, but here given a different accent: 'For yet a short, short time, then shall he who comes arrive and not tarry; and the righteous shall live by My faith...' (10.37-39; Hab. 2.3-6). The word for 'faith' (*pistis*) can be rendered better as 'faithfulness', and in that sense the quote is closer to the context in Habakkuk than Paul's use of it. 'My faith' can here, in accordance with the extant variants of the Greek text of Habakkuk, mean both God's trust and trust in God. In all events the writer remains in the prophetic-eschatologic line of encouraging faith in times of testing. Though not absent in Paul's writings, this element is here more emphatically in the foreground.

Markedly Jewish-Christian eschatology is perceptible at the end of the third main section as well, in one unrestrained breath:

> But you have come to Mount Zion and the city of the living God, the *heavenly Jerusalem*, and myriads of angels, to the ceremony and the gathering of the first-born who are registered in heaven, and to God, the Judge of all, and to the spirits of the perfect righteous, and to the mediator of the new covenant, Jesus, and to the blood of sprinkling that speaks better than that of Abel (Heb. 12.22-24).

The writer assumes a sharper tone than do other New Testament authors, by recalling that a believer who has become apostate cannot possibly turn back (10.26-31; 12.16-17). More emphasis is placed on the impossibility of a 'second conversion' in the admonitory end of the first main section. By means of allusions to Old Testament and Gospel passages, the author speaks of the apostates as being 'thorns and thistles' destined for 'burning' (Heb. 6.4-8; cf. Gen. 3.18; Mt. 3.10; 7.16; 13.7; Jas 1.11). A related motif occurs at the end of the third main section: ' "Let not a root of bitterness shoot up and incite turmoil", and by it many be defiled' (12.15). Incidentally, the author here quotes from a then current Greek translation of the Old Testament (Deut. 29.18), and clearly not from the Hebrew text known to us where 'a root which makes poison and bitterness shoot up' (Deut. 29.17) is mentioned.

We see that in this last passage, the author uses the Greek Bible, and this example could be supplemented by many others. If he does not hail from Alexandria, then it is from some other Hellenistic-Jewish milieu.

The Platonizing Allegory
The Jewish and Jewish-Christian elements that we brought forward because of their relative unfamiliarity occur particularly at the end of the first and third main sections. The 'epistle' is better known for its Platonizing allegoric tendencies, expressed primarily in the first and second main sections.

By 'Platonizing', we do not mean that the writer quotes Plato, but that concepts and thought patterns are used that were current among Hellenistic Jews and in which Plato's influence is unmistakable. Alongside these, other influences also play a role, primarily the Old Testament. The close interwovenness of 'Plato' and the Bible is apparent in the fact that in certain key passages the Septuagint translators chose Greek words that also fit into Plato's thinking. Particularly the passages where this overlap occurred attracted the Hellenistic-Jewish interpreters, of whom Philo of Alexandria is our best-known example.

An important Greek–Jewish text in this connection is the *Wisdom of Solomon*. Preserved in the Septuagint, this writing comprises a series of hymns on divine Wisdom, in which we read:

> She is the dew of God's power, and the radiation of the pure glory of the Almighty; therefore, nothing defiled coincides with her. For she is the *reflection* of the light which surpasses time, an unclouded *mirror* of God's energy, and the *likeness* of his *goodness* (Wis. 7.25-26).

The Platonizing key words have been italicized. In a clearly related manner, Hebrews opens with a song of praise to the Son, 'through whom God made the worlds'; again the Platonizing terminology is italicized: 'Who is the *reflection* of the glory and the *imprint* of his being, and who bears everything in the words of his power...' (Heb. 1.3).

Christ, the Son, is here identified with the divine Wisdom, and one could call this a Platonizing wisdom Christology.

Platonizing allegory plays a role in particular in the second main part, the exposition concerning the heavenly high priesthood of Christ. Jesus is our high priest, naturally not 'according to the order of Aaron' as a bodily descendant of Levi, for, after all, as son of David he is from the tribe of Judah (7.13-14). Besides, the Levitical high priests are mortal and must replace one another in hereditary succession. Jesus is 'high priest in eternity, according to the order of Melchizedek', that is, eschatologically and eternally perfect (7.15-28). In the Old Testament, Melchizedek is the mysterious priest of Salem who blesses Abraham (Gen. 14.18-20). The reference in Hebrews is, however, a citation of an equally enigmatic verse from the Psalms (Ps. 110.4; also quoted in Heb. 5.6; 6.20). These references have extraordinary significance since an eschatological application of the Melchizedek motif also occurs in a writing from Qumran (11Q *Melchizedek*). The intermingling of Platonizing and biblical eschatology will continue to intrigue us.

The Platonizing allegory culminates by indicating that Jesus' heavenly work of reconciliation is the true and hidden significance of the Levitical priestly service here upon earth:

> They perform their service as a *depiction* and *reflection* of the heavenly matters, as was announced to Moses when he set out to prepare the tent: 'For behold, He said, you shall make all things according to the *example* that was shown to you upon the mountain' (Heb. 8.5; Exod. 25.40).

Again, the Platonizing terms are italicized. One of them, 'example', *tupos*, occurs in the quote from Exodus, and is an important example of the overlap between 'Plato' and the Bible, pre-programmed as it were by the choice of words in the Septuagint. A related verse from the same chapter in Exodus echoes in this passage as well: 'And you shall make everything for me that I show you upon the mountain, the *model* of the tent and the *model* of all its utensils, so shall you make it' (Exod. 24.9). The word 'model' is the Greek *paradeigma*. Just as *tupos*, 'example', it stands for the Hebrew *tabnit*. In the verse from Hebrews, a related word is used, *hupodeigma*, which has been rendered here with 'depiction'. In this way, both verses from Exodus play a role in the allegory in Hebrew, through the two Platonizing key words.

A few more comments about this allegory are in order. The italicized words occur in particular in Plato's dialogue about the creation of the world, the *Timaeus*. This dialogue employs the image of a divine 'craftsman', the *dēmiourgos*, who first forms a mental concept of the work, which he thereafter implements. This image is used extensively by Philo of Alexandria, naturally simultaneously linking it with the biblical story of creation (Philo, *On the Creation of the World*). Reminiscences of the building of the tabernacle according to the model upon the mountain are used there as well, a theme that Philo elaborates on more thoroughly elsewhere. The key words we mentioned continually play a role. In Philo we encounter a comparison between the creation and the building of the tabernacle as well as an overlap of Plato and the Bible. Even aside from the preparatory work of the Septuagint translators, the naturalness of this partial coincidence cannot help but be striking. An interesting final note in this excursion is that the image of the Creator as an artisan with a plan, the Torah, also occurs in rabbinic midrash (*Gen. R.* 1.1 p. 2).

The differences between Hebrews and Philo must also be touched upon; these include not only the christological filling in but also the references to the biblical Prophets, from which Philo rarely quotes. The eschatological passage from Habakkuk has already been mentioned. The author of Hebrews also cites a text from Jeremiah directly after the allegory of the heavenly tabernacle, in which God's 'new covenant' with Israel is mentioned: 'not according to the covenant which I made with their fathers' (Heb. 8.8-9; Jer. 31.31-32). This has many implications. The author of Hebrews shows himself to be 'more Jewish' than Philo by his use of the Prophets. Furthermore, the concept of the 'new covenant' has a Jewish-apocalyptic background, occurring as such also in Qumran and in Paul's writings (see p. 178).

Finally, in the third main section of Hebrew, where the eschatological motifs dominate, a Platonizing passage occurs. In the eulogy on faith, it is said of Abraham that 'he expected a city with foundations, whose designer and builder (*technitēs kai dēmiourgos*) is God' (11.10). The second Greek key word has already been encountered. Again, various influences are intertwined: the apocalyptic image of the heavenly Jerusalem appears to be anchored in the biblical account of the model sanctuary upon the mountain and to be refined with key words from the Platonized story of creation.

The Practical Validity of the Law

As we have said, the attitude towards the practical commandments is a crucial issue in determining the 'Jewish calibre' of Hebrews. Several negative statements about the law occur:

> In speaking of a new (covenant) he (the Scripture) declared the first to be old, and what is old, ages as well, being close to demise (Heb. 8.13).

> The blood of bulls and goats is not capable of taking away sin. Therefore he says, coming to the world: 'Offerings and gifts You do not desire, You shall prepare me a body; in burnt offerings and sin offerings You do not delight' (Heb. 10.4-6); (quote from Ps. 40.7-9 according to some Greek version).

The quotes in the second statement are related to a verse that is cited in two sayings ascribed to Jesus: 'Mercy I desire, and not offerings' (Hos. 6.6; Mt. 9.13; 12.7). If these indeed derive from Jesus, this does not necessarily mean that he hereby rejected the temple worship, even though that was later asserted by Jewish Christians (see p. 379). Jesus' lesson on remorse and forgiveness as prerequisites for offerings teaches otherwise (Mt. 5.23-24). The same could be true in Hebrews 10. Could we presume something of the like in relation to the transient 'old covenant' alongside and simultaneous with the 'new' one effectuated in Christ?

In order to answer our question we return to the allegory of Jesus as heavenly high priest. In ch. 9 the author draws attention to how the sanctuary in the wilderness contained a first tent equipped with candlestick, table and shew bread, behind which was a second space, the Holy of Holies. Here such mysteries as the jar with manna, the heavenly bread, the tables of the covenant written by the finger of God and 'the Cherubim of (God's) glory which overshadowed the seat of atonement' were to be found. These attributes are established springboards for mystical speculation, which the author, however, does not wish to divulge: '...we can not now go more deeply into these.' The mysterious aspect possibly has to do with the fact that these were the elements that Moses was shown upon the mountain.

The high priest enters the Holy of Holies but once a year after having brought the necessary sacrifices—and at this point the author writes in the present tense apparently with the temple in Jerusalem in mind:

> With this the Holy Ghost makes it clear that the way to the Holiest is not revealed as long as the first tent still stands. And this is a symbol of the present time, according to which continually gifts and sacrifices are brought which can not perfect the offerer in his consciousness, because they only have to do with food and drink and various baptismal baths—ordinances of the flesh which are valid until the time of restoration (Heb. 9.8-10).

While the author is clear on the superbness of the worship of the 'new' covenant, he speaks of the 'old' as something that still continues and that is symbolized in the temple service in the present time. The work of Christ consists, then, not so much in disbanding the worship prescribed by the old covenant, but in fulfilling its true significance while 'the first tent still stands': 'through the better, more perfect tent which is not made by hands, that is, not of this creation', he has entered the Holiest and has brought redemption through his own blood (9.11-12; cf. p. 342). The 'ordinances of the flesh', of the contemporary temple, are 'valid until the times of restoration'.

The following two verses prove beyond a shadow of a doubt that the argumentation of the writer presumes the reality of the 'old' covenant:

> For if already the blood of goats and bulls and the sprinkling with the ashes of the heifer sanctify the defiled one unto purity of flesh, *how much more* then shall the blood of Christ…purge our consciousness from dead works to serve the living God (Heb. 9.13-14).

This type of 'argument from light to heavy' is characteristic of rabbinic exegesis, in which, of course, the appropriateness of the 'heavy' does not do away with the reality of the 'light'. An example of this can be found in the synoptic tradition: '*If* God…*thus* clothes the grass of the field, *how much more* then you, little of faith?' (Mt. 6.30). The same is true of the second example in Hebrews:

> If someone *has pushed aside the law of Moses*, he must without pity 'upon the word of two or three witnesses be put to death'; *how much heavier*, do you think, will the punishment be for him who tramples underfoot the Son of God? (Heb. 10.28-29).

Not only is the continuing reality of the 'light', that is, the 'ordinances of the flesh', presumed here, but this allegoric interpretation, like that of Philo, reckons on the ongoing, practical validity of the law, as we initially had supposed.

With this the intended effect of the Platonizing allegory is finally clear. The 'first tent', the earthly worship service that is performed 'in this creation', is merely an illustration of the 'heavenly example' which was shown to Moses. As the author himself says: 'The law contains a shadow of the good things to come, not the image of the matters themselves' (10.1; cf. 8.5). More precisely phrased: the worship service of the 'old covenant' is a secondary portrayal. The primary image is the high priestly service of Christ, who offers himself and thereby implements the 'new covenent'. Meanwhile, 'the first tent is still standing'. The 'new covenant', if we may thus accentuate it, is valid only in heaven, not yet upon earth. The 'good things', of which Christ is the direct image, are yet to come. In fact, the whole Platonizing allegory remains within the eschatological framework supposed in the original text from Jeremiah, which the author quotes word for word:

> See the days come...that I with the house of Israel...will make a new covenant, not as the covenant that I made with their fathers... For this is the covenant that I will make with the house of Israel after these days, says the Lord: that I shall place my laws in their thoughts and inscribe them in their hearts, and I shall be to them a God, and they to Me a people... (Jer. 31.31-34; Heb. 8.8-12; 10.16-17).

Conclusion

The so-called Epistle to the Hebrews combines Platonizing and apocalyptic patterns of thought, both of which enjoyed a wide recognition in the Judaism of that day, within a Christologic-allegorical interpretation of Scripture. The implementation of the law and the temple worship continue unimpeded, even after its real purpose had been fulfilled in Christ. Because the temple service is spoken of in the present tense, the document could date from before 70 CE. It appears to be a sermon written in eloquent Greek, addressed by a Jewish Christian, perhaps from Alexandria, to a Jewish-Christian audience.

The Revelation of John

The final book of the New Testament is in general neither known nor cherished. This could be due to its impenetrability both in form and content. The 'apocalyptic' visions of terror and the prophecies of salvation with which the writer intends to encourage his readers in a situation of persecution do not appeal to everyone's imagination. The document receives little attention from theologians of the established churches. It has more appeal in times of menace and war, respectively, in situations where Christians feel disowned by a majority church that has accommodated itself to the hostile world.

Whatever position one may assume in this, the Revelation of John belongs fully in the present chapter. In the first place, it is one of the most explicitly Jewish-Christian writings within the New Testament, as is apparent from the language, the images, and the message of the book, as well as from the many strong correspondences with Jewish writings and traditions of that day. In the second place, Revelation as a whole has the form of a letter. Following the heading there is a traditional letter opening ('John to the seven churches of Asia Minor', Rev. 1.4-6) and it ends with a greeting (22.21). This is underscored yet again by the admonitory and encouraging letters addressed to each of these same seven churches, all in the south-west of Asia Minor: Ephesus, Smyrna, Pergamum, Thyatira, Sardis, Philadephia and Laodicea (1.11; 2.1–3.22).

Nature and Composition

In the superscription, the word *apokalupsis*, 'revelation', occurs: 'Revelation of Jesus Christ, which God...communicated to his servant, John' (Rev. 1.1). This label became proverbial because biblical scholars began to use it for a so-called 'apocalyptic' literature with corresponding characteristics (see pp. 62-63), though such is rather arbitrary because Revelation does not share some of those characteristics. For example, an 'apocalypse' is supposed to be a pseudepigraphic work, written under a biblical name like Enoch or Ezra. Revelation, however, presents itself with the name of the mentioned author, John. Who exactly that was, incidentally, is unknown. The tradition that he was the apostle, the son of Zebedee, is certainly secondary and is also improbable. Furthermore, Revelation is extremely Christo-centric, intended to be an actual 'revelation of Jesus Christ'. Paul, too, speaks of the 'revelation of (God's) son' in connection to his calling (Gal. 1.16). In this usage, 'apocalypse' designates not a literary form, but an event: an appearance of Christ and the calling connected to that.

Theologically speaking, the Apocalypse is not a 'revelation' in the sense of an exact blueprint of the future, just as little as the biblical Prophets are. The emphasis upon 'the things which must happen quickly' (Rev. 1.1) should rather be related to Jesus' words about 'the son of man who must suffer much' (Mk 8.31), that is, the happenings that 'hang in the air' and that correspond to the words of 'Moses and the prophets' (Lk. 24.26-27). What is involved is being able to read the signs of the times—a biblically inspired interpretation of contemporary history. The abundance of biblical quotes and allusions is not only artful decoration, but a necessary part of this interpretation. The 'significance' is found in the coincidence of Scripture and event.

The inaccessibility of Revelation is caused, among other things, by what at first appears to be a tangled structure. It is necessary to dwell on this somewhat. Confusion is inevitable as long as one is looking for linear chronological order. The structure of the book follows its own logic, in which linear and cyclic movements go side by side. The church father Augustine observed that, while it appears that different happenings are described, at a closer look these turn out to be different renderings of the same happening (*The City of God* 20.17). This can be compared to the structure of a symphony, in which the richness of the main theme comes out in the various developments it is given and the combinations in which it appears, or like artful fireworks that strike up first here, then there, break out simultaneously, swell and silence to eventually discharge in a breath-taking grand finale.

The book comprises two main parts. After the superscription, the first part contains the vision of the calling of the visionary and the epistles to the seven churches (chs. 1–3); the second part is a complex and drawn-out vision of the cosmic last struggle between Christ and Satan and their respective faithful supporters (chs. 4–22). The two main parts are, however, closely linked, not in the least because the seven epistles themselves issue forth from a revelation of the heavenly Christ and are addressed 'to the angel' of each of the churches. The earthly existence of the churches is thereby in direct 'communication' with the cosmic occurrences in the second main part.

The second main part is complex and comprises three different elements: (1) static 'takes' of the heavenly reality, which alternate with (2) sevenfold sequences of the execution of judgment, and (3) dualistic scenes of the cosmic final battle. It is not coincidental that Revelation evokes film terminology: the visionary rendering of the fearful lot of the soul and of humanity in the universe has inspired countless writers from Dante onwards, as well as various filmmakers.

The continually recurring static images of heaven (1) show us the unthreatened celestial splendour of the Lamb and his chosen ones (chs. 4, 5, 7, 10, 11, 14, 15, 19, 20). These depictions are, however, constantly dissected by the other elements that dramatize the shocking life of the churches in the world (2, 3). In such a context, the striking hymnic–liturgic nature of the static elements is understandable. The incessant heavenly songs of praise, no doubt reminiscent of the liturgy of the churches in Asia Minor, grant the composition its cyclic aspect: the reader begins with and returns continually to the victory of the Lamb. In this, too, the unity of the book becomes apparent: the epistles to the seven churches all end with an invocation to continue on in this victory.

The most spectacular elements are (2) the three sequences of seven seals, seven trumpets, and seven vials, which chant the jolting but inevitable progression to the final judgment. Confusion is created by the dynamic application of this element. The sequences overlap and are disrupted. The first and second sequences (6.1–8.5; 8.6–11.19) are interrupted close to the end by a heavenly scene (1). The suspense hereby created is strengthened by the more ponderous onset of the numbers five and six in each sequence. The two series are interconnected by the fact that the seven trumpets issue forth from the seventh seal (8.1-5). This gives a 'two-stage' effect that reminds one of fireworks. The second and third sequences are coupled as well. The heavenly temple from which the angels of the third series step forward opens briefly at the end of the second series (11.19; 15.5). Furthermore, the three series are related and progress partially parallel, as Augustine indicated: the sun is darkened during the sixth seal, the fourth trumpet, and the fourth vial; water turns to blood at trumpets two and three and vials two and three. These motifs have, naturally, their background in the 'apocalyptic' images of the exodus from Egypt and the coming Day of the Lord (Exod. 7.20-21; 10.22-23; Joel 2.30-31).

The third element (3) comprises dualistic scenes of the cosmic final battle and provides a framework for the third sequence. First, a heavenly woman and her child, assisted by angel hosts, wage war against a dragon and his cohorts, a blasphemous beast in two consecutive forms of appearance (Rev. 12–13). Parallel to this, after the seven vials, follows the fall of 'the great Babylon, mother of whores' who is seated upon a beast (chs. 17–18), with in contrast the glorification of 'the bride, the wife of the Lamb', the heavenly Jerusalem (chs. 21–22). The parallelism between the two double scenes, indicating simultaneity, becomes apparent from the fact that both are shown to the visionary by an angel from the last sequence (17.1; 21.9), and that the beasts in both scenes have seven heads and ten horns (13.1; 17.3). A ten-horned beast occurs in Daniel 7 as well: there it has four heads and stands for the invincible kingdom of Alexander the Great and his four successors.

Numbers play a prominent role. The number seven in particular attracts attention, occurring 55 times in Revelation, as compared to 40 times elsewhere in the New Testament. Seven is also a main element in the apocalyptic calendar (see pp. 80-81, 62). Numerical symbolism or *gematria* acquired its own place in rabbinic literature, whereby the influence of the Pythagorean thinking certainly played a part. Furthermore, in Qumran many traces are found of mystical, astrological and calendric calculations. An important number in Revelations is 144,000, the number of the sealed ones, 12,000 from each of the 12 tribes, of which we will speak later. Finally, there is the forever fascinating 'number of the beast: 666' (13.18), which must indicate the numerical value of a name, for in Greek and Hebrew, letters were used as numbers as well. The candidate best fitting the number appears to be 'Emperor Nero' (in Hebrew, *Nērôn Qēsār*).

In this way the identity of the opponents is made clear. The seven-headed beast and the whore of Babylon depict blasphemous Rome, worthy successors of Alexander's world empire: the seven heads are the hills upon which the city is built (Rev. 17.9). The heavenly Jerusalem is naturally the *mētropolis*, mother city of God's people. Who is meant: Israel, the church, or both? This touches on the key question of this book: what attitude does the author have towards his Jewish environment? In order to determine this, insight into the Jewish-Christian background and historical situation of the book is required.

Jewish Background: The Heavenly Jerusalem

Two external characteristics of the Jewish background of this book merit attention first. The Greek of Revelation is a topic in itself, containing more Hebraisms than any other New Testament or Greek–Jewish writing. The cases where a Greek word can only be understood from the biblical meaning of the Hebrew equivalent are arresting. In Rev. 10.1 we read, 'His *feet* were as pillars of fire,' where the connotation 'legs' of the Hebrew *raglayim*, 'feet', is more fitting. In Rev. 3.8 the literal Greek equivalent of the Hebrew *nātan*, 'to give', is used: 'I have *given* a door in front of you,' while the connotation 'to place' must have been intended: 'I have *placed* a door.' In short, while the author writes in Greek, he seems to think in Hebrew. Though it is conceivable that he conciously Hebraizes in order to give his Greek a 'biblical' sound, he also clearly makes a few mistakes in Greek grammar, so that the assumption of Hebrew or Aramaic as his mother tongue seems to be warranted. This would point to a Jewish background.

The same conclusion arises from the manner in which the author uses biblical and Jewish prophetic themes. The biblical subject matter is self-evident. The throne with the four beasts and the scroll (Ezek. 1–2; cf. Isa. 6), the beast and the final judgment (Dan. 7), the apocalyptic plagues and the final battle (Exod. 6–10; Ezek. 38–39; Joel 1–2), the vision of the new temple (Ezek. 40–48)—these are the daily fare of the seer. Besides this, nearly each verse contains an allusion to the Old Testament, and a commentator rightly observed that as long as this is not found, the verse is not interpreted (R. Kraft). That is, however, but the half. At least as important are the post-Old Testament, Jewish motifs and traditions of interpretation used in Revelation. This alone, however, is not a sufficient answer to the question as to the attitude towards the Jewish background. We have seen how Matthew and John fit Jewish and Jewish-Christian material into an anti-Jewish frame of thought. It is necessary, therefore, critically to observe how the author of Revelation goes to work.

A good touchstone, in more than one connotation, is offered by the image of the heavenly Jerusalem, with which Revelation closes as a truly grand finale. In order to appreciate this properly, it is necessary to observe how it occurs in other sources. The image is new in relation to the Old Testament, although it is closely related to the vision of the new temple in Ezekiel 40–48. The author has used it already in the letter to Philadelphia, in a manner that gives the impression that he is applying a known tradition (Rev. 3.12), which is confirmed by its widespread occurrences in early Christian and ancient Jewish writings. We will pursue these in order to achieve a further sharpening of our key question, *What is the relation of this heavenly Jerusalem to the earthly one?*

In the New Testament, the image occurs more than once. Besides in Revelation, '*heavenly* Jerusalem' occurs literally in Hebrews (11.10; 12.22-25; pp. 356, 359). We concluded there that the author of that epistle, with all its spiritualization, was speaking about the temple worship in Jerusalem in the present tense, and that he considered this to be enduring, though subordinate in importance. The same is true of Paul, who uses the image in a polemic passage about the two women in Abraham's life, Hagar and Sarah:

> Hagar…is to be equated with the present Jerusalem, for it is in slavery with her children. But the *Jerusalem from on high* is free—that is our mother. For it is written: 'Rejoice, barren one who bore not…for many are the children of the desolate, more than of her who has a husband' (Gal. 4.24-27; Isa. 54.1).

Many exegetes read this as a 'radical allegory' that cancels the literal sense, and with it the promises to Sarah. In Chapters 4 and 5, however, we concluded that, in spite of his sharp conflict with certain Jewish and Jewish-Christian circles, the law and the temple most certainly retained their validity for Paul. Meanwhile, the quotation from Isaiah 54 is brilliant because not only is the contrast between Hagar and Sarah reflected, but also between the heavenly city and its foundations; we return to this later. The motif of the heavenly Jerusalem was apparently fairly widespread in the earliest Christian sources.

The extensive diffusion of this allegory within Judaism need cause no surprise. Three different categories provide examples: rabbinic literature, Qumran and the apocryphal writings. Beginning with the last-mentioned category, *4 Ezra* is in theme closely related to the Revelation of John, although less concentrated and vivid in style. Mid second century, this Jewish apocalypse must have been provided with two Christian opening chapters and a Christian closing chapter, while the Jewish middle portion was written 30 years after the destruction of the temple (*4 Ezra* 3–15; see 3.1). The book makes use of ancient motifs: the seer observes a grieving woman, a symbol of the desolate city already known from Lamentations and the Prophets (*4 Ezra* 9.38–10.24; Isa. 54.1!). The next moment, however, she changes into 'a *built city*, a place with extensive *foundations*' (10.27). This image of the rebuilt city is revealed to the seer in the same desolate field (9.24)—it is, therefore, a vision of the heavenly Jerusalem. The expressions 'built city' and 'extensive foundations' will be clarified later.

Of importance to the basic inquiry of this book is the fact that the Christian portion of *4 Ezra* unmistakably contains a disinheriting of the Jews, precisely on the basis of the destruction of their city (1.33–2.14; 2.33-48). In its final Christian form, the book plays the heavenly Jerusalem off against the destroyed, Jewish Jerusalem. Images are used that are related to the Revelation of John, including the multitude that no one can count (*4 Ezra* 1.42; Rev. 7.9). Of interest is, of course, whether the disinheriting is John's intention as well. In all events this is not the case with the original Jewish Ezra apocalypse, which counts on the preservation of Israel through the remnant that repents and keeps the commandments (7.45; 12.46-48; 14.34). The result of the Christian reworking is a double estrangement: not only does the heavenly Jerusalem become exclusively Christian in contrast to Judaism, but also Ezra's words of comfort to those grieving for Jerusalem are annexed.

In rabbinic literature, the insoluble bond between the heavenly and the earthly Jerusalem is emphasized. Three portions of Scripture are involved, first a Psalm:

> Thus spoke R. Yohanan (±250): The Holy One, praised be He, said: I shall not enter the Jerusalem on high until I have entered the Jerusalem below.—Is there then a Jerusalem on high? Yes, for it is written: 'Jerusalem, built as a city where everything unites together' (Ps. 122.3) (*b. Ta'an.* 5a; *Midr. Pss.* 122.4)

The Psalm is read eschatologically, so that 'built' means 'rebuilt'. This is, incidentally, the background of the wish that one customarily says to one another in the State of Israel at the end of the Seder meal: 'Next year in the *built* Jerusalem!' Hereby the explanation of the first peculiar expression from *4 Ezra* is provided, 'a *built* city'. The words 'the Jerusalem from on high' are also important. This is the exact expression used by Paul, who possibly is thinking here more from the Hebrew than the author of Hebrews does: the expression, 'the *heavenly* Jerusalem' sounds good only in Greek.

We remain with the reciprocity of the earthly and the heavenly Jerusalem. This concerns, of course, Jerusalem as the Holy City, that is, as the city of the temple, thus lending the image of the heavenly Jerusalem a deep, mystical sense. Was the temple worship not always about an encounter with the living God? Can the building with its furniture and ritual ever be more than a symbol of what in fact is invisible and undepictable? Has rabbinic Judaism, in spite of the grief over the destruction of the temple, not been able to turn over a new leaf in the consciousness that the temple worship was not indispensable? (see story about Yohanan ben Zakkai, p. 73). Similarly, R. Yohanan, a century and a half after the destruction, did not presume the temple, but the city in his argumentation. Just as clear, however, the intended significance is that the heavenly Jerusalem is not perfected as long as the earthly Jerusalem is not redeemed. Precisely the Jewish bond with the earthly city in its unredeemed state makes the image of the heavenly Jerusalem a touchstone for our inquiry.

The second main portion of Scripture on this theme in rabbinic literature is the triumphant conclusion of the song of Moses by the Reed Sea:

> You bring them and You plant them upon the mountain of Your inheritance, a design for Your dwelling which You have made, LORD, a sanctuary of the Lord that Your hands have designed—the LORD is king for ever and always (Exod. 15.17-18).

The Hebrew is very concise and not without ambiguities for later readers. It was humanly fallible Israel that was led to this dwelling—but how could this then be 'a sanctuary of the Lord' made by '*his own hands*'? Is this about two different temples?

In a discussion about the orientation towards the holy place during prayer, use is made of this ambiguity. According to R. Hiya the Elder (beginning third century), one must direct one's heart to the Holy of Holies 'on high', according to Shimon ben Halafta to that 'below'.

> Then spoke R. Pinhas: I combine your two opinions. It must be in the direction of the Holy of Holies *on high*, for that is directed towards the Holy of Holies *below*, as it is written: 'A design for your dwelling which You have made LORD'—[do not read *mākôn*, 'design', but *mᵉkuwwān*, 'directed'] directed towards Your dwelling: that is the temple below! (*Shir. R.* 4.11; cf. *Tanḥ. wayakel* 7.130b)

It is indeed about two temples, but the Holy of Holies 'on high' and that 'below' are orientated towards one another and presume each other. During the worship service below, one is to direct one's heart towards the unseen heavenly sanctuary. This was true both when the temple was still standing and after its destruction.

We follow a tangent for a moment. The mentioned Bible text seems to form part of the background of an important expression in the New Testament that we encountered already: '...through the more important and more perfect tabernacle, *not made with hands*...Christ has entered into the Holiest' (Heb. 9.11)—the author apparently has in mind the 'sanctuary that *Your hands* have designed'! The same expression occurs in Paul's and Luke's writings (2 Cor. 5.3; Acts 7.47-50; 17.23-25), and perhaps even in Jesus' mouth, if he indeed said that within three days he would build '*another temple, not made with hands*' (Mk 14.58). In Hebrews there is yet another Old Testament passage involving the idea of the heavenly sanctuary, namely, the 'heavenly model' of the earthly sanctuary that Moses was shown on the mountain with God (see p. 358). In this connection one can also bring to mind the sevenfold candlestick (Rev. 1.12; Exod. 25.31; cf. also Rev. 11.4; Zech. 4.2-3).

The third main Scripture portion on this theme provides an element not present in the previous ones:

> Rejoice, barren one, who did not bear, break forth in joy...for many children does the abandoned one have, more than the one who has a lord... See I: with glistening ore I lay your stones, I found you upon sapphire, your pinnacles I make of rubies and your gates of carbuncles, and all of your boundaries of precious stones. And all your sons shall be taught of the Lord, great of peace your sons (Isa. 54.1, 11-13).

We see in passing that this text, of which Paul quoted the beginining, appears to reflect the heavenly Jerusalem, and it could hardly be otherwise than that the apostle had that in mind. Our concern here is with an element that was thus far missing: the foundations of the heavenly city. We can now completely understand the striking phrase from *4 Ezra* 10.27: 'a *built* city with extensive *foundations*', as well as the expression from Heb. 11.10, 'a city with *foundations*'. Incidentally, in a well-known rabbinic midrash the end of the same passage plays a role. Placing it in a broader connection, it is clear that the midrash is about the value of learning as the foundation of the mother city of peace:

> The disciples of the wise increase peace upon earth, for it is said, 'And all your sons are taught of the Lord, great of peace your sons' (Isa. 54.13)—do not read *banayikh*, 'your sons', but *bonayikh*, 'your builders' (*b. Ber.* 64a).

Finally, we come to the texts from Qumran, in which the same portions of Scripture play a role. In particular here, as in the cited midrash, the third portion of Scripture is applied both to the heavenly Jerusalem and to their own community:

> 'Your foundations upon sapphires'—[*its interpretation*:] They shall found the Council of the Community, the priests and the people (…) 'Your pinnacles I make of rubies'—*its interpretation*: the twelve main priests with the judgment of the Ummim and the Tummim (…) 'And a[ll your boundaries of precious stones']—*its interpretation*: the heads of the tribes of Israel in the la[st da]ys […] (4Q164).

The link to the priests and the Council is naturally that they are the ones who will instruct the 'sons'. Another fragment teaches us that it is about the 12 gates with the names of the 12 tribes of Israel: 'The gate of Shimon...the gate of Joseph... All buildings in it are of sapphires and rubies, and all windows of gold...' (4Q554 frg 1, 1.13–2.10; frg 2, 2.15).

The mention of the 12 tribes derives from Ezekiel as well (48.30-35), but is noteworthy, nonetheless. While in Ezekiel's time there could still have been hope for the return of the ten tribes of the Northern Kingdom, several centuries later it was clear that they had been lost in their exile. Their return will then belong to the unheard-of miracles of the last day. In this manner, the 12 tribes appear as well in the earliest Christian writings, beginning with Revelation: 'The number of the sealed ones: 144,000 sealed from each tribe of the sons of Israel: from the tribe of Judah 12,000 sealed ones...' (Rev. 7.4-8; cf. 14.1-5). The 12 tribes also occur in the opening lines of the Epistle of James (see

p. 341). Finally, they are mentioned in a peculiar saying of Jesus where he says that his apostles 'in the regeneration', that is, at the last day, 'shall sit upon twelve thrones to judge the twelve tribes of Israel' (Mt. 19.28; cf. Lk. 22.30).

Here in passing we find yet another linking text. The thrones, the judging and the tribes come from the psalm about the rebuilt Jerusalem: 'For thereunto *the tribes* went up...there are seated the *thrones* of *judgment*' (Ps. 122.4-5). The connection is made explicit in a midrash related to the rabbinic discussion about the direction of prayer:

> R. Aha said: Jerusalem will only be rebuilt thanks to the tribes, for it is said: 'Jerusalem the built one...', and what is written thereafter? 'For thereunto the tribes went up' (*Tanhuma Buber, wayišlah* 21, 87b).

Taking the second Scripture portion, the Song of Moses, as point of departure, another Qumran fragment describes how the future, eternal temple was conceived of:

> 'A sanctuary for the Lord that Your hands have designed; the LORD is king for ever and always' (Exod. 15.17-18)—That is the sanctuary into which eternally no Ammonite or Moabite shall enter, no bastard and no stranger or sojourner forever... He said also that they must build Him a human sanctuary in which works of the law would be offered before his presence as incense (4Q174 [flor] 1.3-7).

The 'human sanctuary' applies apparently to the community that performs a 'spiritual worship' with their works of the law. This use of terms reminds one of Paul (Rom. 12.1-2; 1 Cor. 3.16; 2 Cor. 6.16), although Paul allots quite a different place to the 'works of the law'. The contrast with the 'sanctuary for the Lord' not made with hands is thus even more significant in the Qumran fragment.

The members of the Qumran community did not participate in the worship service in Jerusalem, not because they rejected the temple worship as such, but because according to them incorrect rules were maintained there. All of the texts seem to indicate the building of the perfect 'sanctuary of the Lord' in the earthly Jerusalem.

Along these circuitous routes we finally arrive at the summit from which we can view the breath-taking final scene of Revelations; the biblical allusions already mentioned are italicized:

> And one of the seven angels...took me in the spirit to a great and high mountain. And he showed me the holy city, Jerusalem, descending from heaven from God: she had the glory of God, her glittering was like the *most precious of stones*, like crystalline *jasper*; she had a great and high

rampart, she had *twelve gates* and upon the gates twelve angels and names written, which were the names of the *twelve tribes* of the sons of Israel...and the rampart of the city had twelve *foundations* and on these the twelve names of the twelve apostles of the Lamb... And I saw no temple within her, for the Lord God, the Almighty, is her temple, and the Lamb. And the city had no need of the *sun* nor of the *moon* to shine upon her, for the glory of God *lightened* her, and the candelabrum was the Lamb (Rev. 21.9-23).

We remain with the question with which we began, If the city descending from heaven contains no temple, what then is the relationship to the earthly Jerusalem? The answer to this will be sought in the light of the historical situation.

Historical Situation: The Earthly Jerusalem
The seven churches of Asia Minor to whom John writes are under persecution. He writes them as their 'brother and companion in the persecution...and in the perseverance of Jesus' (1.9), with the aim of exhorting the churches to this same steadfastness.

These circumstances are confirmed by external sources. At the beginning of the second century, the Roman governor of north-west Asia Minor, Pliny the Younger, sent a letter to Emperor Trajan asking what was to be done with the Christians reported for not participating in the cult of the emperor. Some cases date 'even from twenty years ago', apparently during the regime of Domitian (81–96). Indeed we know that during the final years of his regime Emperor Domitian demanded participation in the imperial cult and had himself called *dominus et deus*, 'Lord and God'. Yet this did not involve a systematic persecution of Christians, but rather incidental confrontations, perhaps often related to local irritation with the Christians. Pliny relates further that many had renounced their faith by offering wine and incense to the emperor at the insistence of the interrogators, but that some persevered. Their error, he writes, not without irony, consisted of:

> They were accustomed to gather before dawn and to say a hymn to Christ as though he were a god, and that they obliged themselves by oath to perpetrate no single wrong-doing, but to commit neither thievery, nor robbery, nor adultery, nor to renounce the faith, nor to deny a possession entrusted to them if it were demanded (Pliny the Younger, *Epistulae* 10.96).

Christians lived virtuously, they were honest and they worshipped Christ in their songs of praise in the morning. We are reminded of the liturgy in Asia Minor. From other sources it appears that Domitian's distrust was also towards the Jews and God-fearers. This even cost his own cousin his life, because of the accusation of 'atheism' customarily attached to this, that is, refusal to participate in the imperial cult.

The 'beast from the pit' which persecutes those faithful to the Lamb (Rev. 13) must, therefore, refer to Domitian. What is the relation to the 'number of the beast' (13.18), which indeed refers to Nero? During the final year of Nero's government (54–68), an initial, incidental persecution of Christians occurred in Rome, apparently at the instigation of the emperor. According to a report (Tacitus, *Annals* 15.44) the occasion was a fire instigated by the emperor himself, but according to other accounts it was merely his proverbial cruelty, perhaps activated by aversion to Christians among the populace. However that may be, in later Christian sources Nero and Domitian are together counted as the arch enemies of Christianity. This could explain why in Revelation 13, a beast appears twice (13.11-12), apparently an echo of the legend of *Nero redivivus*, 'Nero reborn', which circulated at that time in the east.

The Revelation of John contains certain facts that fill in further details. The letters to the churches of Pergamum and Thyatira are against people there that taught that one 'may eat *idolatrous offerings* and *commit harlotry*' (2.14, 20). They are later designated as 'Balaam' and 'Jezebel', two non-Israelites who, by their sinister influences, brought Israel to idolatry and sexual misconduct (Num. 22–25; 1 Kgs 16.31; 21.25-26). In the area of sexual relations, John was apparently stricter than these opponents; exactly what this is about is not elucidated in the text. The matter is different with the eating of idolatrous offerings. Its prohibition was one of the fundamentals of early Christian tradition (Acts 15.20, 29; *Did.* 6.3). For the sake of the non-Jewish Christians, however, Paul had given a further stipulation that some Jewish Christians probably thought to be too supple (see pp. 200-202). This opinion will certainly have been widespread in both churches, for Paul had a close relationship with at least two other of these seven churches, Laodicea and Ephesus, and had even lived in Ephesus for two years (Col. 2.1; 4.13-16; 1 Cor. 16.8; Acts 19.10). It appears that the seer John on this point adhered to a more radical, anti-Pauline standpoint.

Another explanation, namely, that John's opponents were libertines who did not respect any prohibitions, is less probable. The situation is one of persecution and the vital point was whether one remained faithful to the basic premises and abstained from idolatry. These basic premises are explicitly summarized in a few general condemnations of *idolatry, shedding of blood* and *sexual misconduct* (Rev. 9.20-21; 21.8; 2.15; see p. 108). On the other hand, the denunciation of opponents, who were conformed to the world, as biblical villains occurs in the Epistle of Jude as well (Balaam, see p. 337), and in Qumran (Ephraim and Manasseh). The fact that non-Israelite 'villains' are mentioned makes it even more probable that the opponents sympathized with the Pauline 'gospel for the nations'. The Jewish-Christian profile of Revelation is thus given a sharper profile.

The emphasis upon 'works' as a touchstone of faith in the face of persecution sounds non-Pauline, but rather exclusively Jewish-Christian. At the final judgment, the dead will be judged according to their works (20.12-13; cf. 14.13; 22.12). This is particularly true of the church of Thyatira (2.23), to whom Christ also says that the essence is to 'keep my works to the end' (2.26). Likewise, he says in the laudatory opening of most of the letters, 'I know your works' (2.2, 19; 3.1, 8, 15). An un-Pauline emphasis upon works is given also in the Epistle of James (see pp. 351-53), and there clearly the commandments are intended. The same can be found in Revelations: faithful are they 'who keep God's commandments and have the testimony of Jesus' (12.17; 14.12). Such an emphasis on the commandments occurs also in the Jewish portion of *4 Ezra* (7.45-46). In short, a certain non-Pauline or anti-Pauline attitude is outlined here, which Revelation more or less appears to share with the epistles of James and Jude.

Another, equally significant demarcation is made in the letters to the churches. The church in Smyrna is slandered by 'them that say that they are Jews but are not, but are of the synagogue of Satan; fear not what you will suffer: behold, the devil shall throw some of you in prison' (2.9-10). The suggestion is that this church in a precarious situation is opposed by local Jews. The same is explicitly testified to more than a half century later in the Martyrdom of Polycarp, bishop of Smyrna; there, too, the life-and-death question was whether one worshipped the emperor or God. This appears to imply that the Jews involved were more prone towards compromise with the Roman government than were those who were kindred spirits with John. Similar to this, though somewhat different, were matters in Philadelphia:

> Behold, I shall give from the synagogue of Satan, from those that say that they are Jews and are not but lie—behold, I shall cause that they

shall come and kneel before your feet and know that I love you, because
you have kept my word of perseverance... (3.9).

Alongside Jews more prone to compromise, there were apparently in
Philadelphia also those who were impressed by Christian steadfastness.
Jewish circles thus display disunity concerning the policy towards the
pretentious emperor. Such differences in the Jewish attitude towards
external relations was not unusual (see pp. 65-66, 109-110).

Another important factor must have been the competition present
between Jews and Christians, certainly in Asia Minor. Paul writes as
well concerning Asia Minor Jewish opposition to Christianity (pp. 207-
208), in which a difference in the legal position of Christians and Jews
also played a role. Josephus quotes official documents from earlier
times in which the position of the Jews was laid down in Laodicea,
Pergamum, Sardis and Ephesus (*Ant.* 14.21, 237, 259, 262). These are
the four most important of John's seven cities, and in Smyrna and
Philadelphia the rights of the Jews will not have been much different.
Apart from that, the war in Judaea placed stress on the situation of all
Jews of that time. Nonetheless, the position of the Christians was probably much less certain. Non-Jewish Christians estranged themselves
from their own milieu, and that must have also influenced the position
of their Jewish fellow-believers. In contrast to Judaism (see p. 106),
Christianity never became a 'recognized religion' for the emperor. Only
under the patronage of Constantine (313 CE) were the roles reversed.
Such tensions usually become acute in times of crisis, and local
collaboration of Jews against the Christians is conceivable, however
unpleasant that may sound.

Thus gradually the contours of the Jewish-Christian position of John
and his associates become clear. Under the capriciousness of Domitian's regime, they assumed a more intransigent position than certain
fellow-Christians, who possibly belonged to the Pauline wing. They felt
more affinity with radically minded Jews, and in any case condemned
the synagogues in Smyrna and Philadelphia because of their laxness
and their enmity towards persecuted Christians.

This puts us in a position to assess the purport of the two uncompromising qualifications that John employs: 'The synagogue of Satan,
of them that say that they are Jews but are not.' The two pretensions of
these Jews are mockingly rejected by John: they form a synagogue, but
it is of Satan; they call themselves Jews, but they are not. The label
'Jew' has, thus, a positive connotation for John, a value dishonoured by

the Jews of Smyrna and Philadelphia. A similar appeal to the name 'Jew' can be found in Paul's writings and in rabbinic literature (see pp. 172-73). The distorted explanation that John turned against non-Jewish Christians who call themselves 'Jews' is thus disposed of. Satan figures in other letters as well: he 'thrones' in Sardis, where a certain Agrippa was killed as a witness of Christ, and in Thyatira he makes the followers of 'Jezebel' to know his 'depths' (2.13, 24). 'Satan' is thus embodied in the persecuting Roman government, and in one way or another 'Jezebel' is associated with it. Elsewhere, 'Satan' is none other than 'the great dragon, the old snake, also called Devil', whose seven heads and ten horns recur in the 'beast' (12.3, 9; 13.1), in other words, in the dominion of Rome. The term 'synagogue of Satan' signifies in any case that John views these Jewish opponents absolutely as being in 'the other camp', that is, they are *diabolized*, a phenomenon that will occupy us in the final chapter. The Jewish-Christian profile of Revelation becomes progressively sharper due to all this.

It is now time to return to our earlier question, What is John's attitude towards the earthly Jerusalem, now that the heavenly Jerusalem apparently contains no temple? A useful lead is the manner in which he speaks about this old temple city.

During the intermezzo that interrupts the seven trumpets, the seer is assigned to take the measurements of 'the temple of God and the altar and those that kneel there' (Rev. 11.1). The measuring of the sanctuary is again derived from Ezekiel (40.3); it recurs, remarkably enough, later in relation to the heavenly Jerusalem (Rev. 21.15). Here it concerns the earthly city and its unfortunate lot, as appears from what follows:

> But leave out the outermost court and measure it not, for it is delivered to the nations, and they shall trample the holy city, two and forty months long (11.2).

John's words are again saturated with biblical allusions, specifically Isaiah (63.18, the trampling of the sanctuary) and Daniel (7.25, three and a half 'times'). Meanwhile, he speaks here of the 'holy city', a designation reserved elsewhere for the heavenly Jerusalem (Rev. 21.2, 10). That the reference is to the earthly Jerusalem becomes clearer when in what follows the two unnamed witnesses of Jesus perish in 'the great city, which is called spiritually Sodom and Egypt, where also the Lord was crucified' (11.8). The designation of a desolate Jerusalem as 'Sodom' comes from Isaiah (1.9-10), the proverbial use of 'Egypt' from Deuteronomy (17.16). Further, the designation 'great city', which elsewhere refers to Babylon–Rome (18.10, etc.) catches the attention. Not only the heavenly, but in another manner also the earthly Jerusalem is a counterpart of Rome.

In the following intermezzo as well, the nations appear, now in sanguinary images of the final judgment derived from the Prophets, including the passage from Isaiah just mentioned (Isa. 63.1-6; Joel 4.9-13). 'Someone like a son of man' comes upon a cloud and 'mows down the earth' with a sickle, after which an angel with a sickle 'reaps the vineyard of the earth' and treads the bloody winepress 'outside the city' (Rev. 14.14-20). The location is again Jerusalem. The designation of Jerusalem in the final intermezzo is striking indeed. After the end of the thousand-year kingdom, the nations will surround 'the *army camp of the saints* and the beloved city' (20.9). The designation 'army camp' is derived from the camp of the Israelites in the wilderness with the tabernacle in their midst, and stands thus for the temple city. The eschatologic application is strongly reminiscent, however, of the Qumran writings in which all of Jerusalem, that is, the earthly, is subjected to the holiness norms of the biblical 'army camp', such as the demand that latrines be made outside of the 'city of the temple' (11QT 46.13-14; Deut. 23.10-14). Finally, here more than anywhere else, John's appreciation of the earthly Jerusalem comes to the fore in the simple words, 'the beloved city'.

The surprising outcome of our survey is that the earthly Jerusalem itself appears in two forms, namely, as the city where Jesus and his witnesses are killed, as 'Sodom and Egypt', but at the same time as 'beloved' and 'holy', the 'city of God' that in the end will triumph over the godless 'great city' Rome. There is a clear contrast to the Christian reworking of *4 Ezra*, in which the destruction of Jerusalem is presented as the underscoring of the disinheriting of the Jews (p. 368). The conclusion is that the heavenly Jerusalem in the Revelation of John coincides with the earthly Jerusalem in her future glory.

According to the final vision, there will be no temple in it, for 'God is her temple and the Lamb' (Rev. 21.22). Remarkably, however, John unequivocally speaks in earlier passages about 'the temple in heaven' (7.15; 11.19; 15.5). There are two possibilities. Either the final vision reflects a later revision of Revelation by the seer himself or a redactor, or the seer is, with his non-linear logic, insensitive to such contradictions and in the end presents a specific vision of faith. The second explanation is to be preferred, precisely because it is more difficult to conceive of by modern readers and because in this way the text is treated more economically. The passages about the heavenly temple should then be seen as fragments of a widespread tradition that were left unadapted by the author.

For a clarification of John's concept, we must first realize that the new Jerusalem also needed no sun or moon because God and the Lamb lighted it (22.23). The absence of the temple fits, thus, completely into the transcendant–eschatological frame of the new creation (Rev. 21.1; Isa. 60.19; 65.17). Further, we can point to a remarkable expression in Ezekiel, the book that so inspired John. Here again we must not be shocked by contradictions: in the new Jerusalem of Ezekiel, the temple is central! In the passage concerned, the godless inhabitants of Jerusalem say to the Judaean exiles, 'Stay far away from the Lord, to us has this been given, the land as possession!' to which the divine statement was, 'Yes, I have brought them far away among the nations, ...but *I was to them a little as a sanctuary* in the lands where they ended up' (Ezek. 11.15-16). A passage in the Talmud takes this expression up in order to compensate for the absence of the temple: ' "I was to them a little as a sanctuary"—These are the synagogues and houses of study in Babel' (*b. Meg.* 29a). In his own manner, John could have meant that the presence of God and the Lamb replaces the temple in the new Jerusalem.

Apparently, those in the Jewish-Christian milieu of John foresaw no temple in the rebuilt Jerusalem. Somewhat the same is told of the Ebionites (cf. p. 280). According to their 'Hebrew Gospel', Jesus had spoken against the bringing of offerings, by which the temple became superfluous (Epiphanius, *Panarion* 30.16.5; cf. p. 266). Radical criticism of the temple as such can also be heard in Stephen's appeal, which ended in the statement that God 'does not live in that which is made by hands' (Acts 7.48). Further, it is important that in Revelation, alongside God, the Lamb also takes the place of the temple. Perhaps this should be read in view of the crucifixion of Jesus as the ultimate sacrifice, in accordance with both Hebrews and the oldest gospel tradition (see pp. 165-66). The special point of John and his milieu is that this ultimate 'sacrifice' makes all others superfluous. This could betray a certain aversion to bloody sacrifices, which certainly was not unusual in antiquity. The destruction of the temple could have strengthened this motif more; something of the sort has already been suggested in connection to Yohanan ben Zakkai (see p. 73).

The Christo-centric accent of the final vision must be accepted as part of the Jewish-Christian profile of Revelation: in all 'heavenly intermezzos' the glorification of the Lamb is central. Nonetheless, the Lamb, that is, Christ, remains subordinate to God (Rev. 5.13; 7.10; 19.6-7). This disposition, which would be branded as 'subordinatianism' by later orthodoxy, is also present in Paul's writings and in the Epistle of Jude (see p. 304) and can be reckoned as being typical for the majority of the churches in the apostolic era.

Conclusion

The Revelation of John documents an extremely strict Jewish-Christian milieu in which any compromise with the emperor cult was rejected. Those with a suppler attitude were sharply condemned: Jews as 'the synagogue of Satan', non-Jewish Christians as 'Balaam' and 'Jezebel'. In the midst of apocalyptic contractions, the seer depicts the earthly Jerusalem alternately as the unredeemed city and as the 'holy' or 'beloved' city 'of God'. In the final vision, this flows over in the image of the heavenly Jerusalem descending upon earth. In the final unity between the earthly and the heavenly Jerusalem, Revelation remains Jewish. The absence of the temple must be taken as characteristic of this Jewish-Christian milieu, and should be distinguished from the later, general Christian opinion that the destruction of Jerusalem was punishment for repudiating Jesus and seal of the disinheriting of the Jews.

Appendix: The Didache

An Unusual Document

In the nineteenth century a Greek manuscript from 1056 was discovered, which, besides a number of known early Christian works, contained a document with the double title: 'Instruction of the Twelve Apostles; Instruction of the Lord by the Twelve Apostles to the Nations'. In this an extremely ancient writing was regained that had enjoyed quite extensive authority in the early church, but was up to then only known by name.

In form it is not a letter but a sort of church order, a document of regulations, written in simple, often Semitizing Greek. It opens with an admonitory introduction designated as 'the Two Ways'. A series of regulations on food, baptism, fasting, prayer, the Eucharist and hospitality towards prophets and ordinary believers follows. It ends with an eschatological admonition.

The *Didache* is of utmost importance to us, allowing us a look into the earliest stage of Christian literature, where the boundaries with ancient Jewish literature were as yet completely fluid, in a milieu open to believing non-Jews. The points of contact with the Gospel of Matthew are telling, while there are also traces of a tradition previous to the Gospels known to us. Finally, the writing offers a unique example of Jewish-Christian *halakah* that was apparently natural in this milieu. From this there are interesting conclusions to be drawn about the connections between the milieu of this document and that of the Jewish-Christian writings of the New Testament. For all of these reasons it deserves the place of honour of a special appendix to this chapter.

There are literary-critical grounds for dating the first 13 chapters of the *Didache* before the written fixation of the Gospel of Matthew, and the whole towards the end of the first century. Because of the implied frequent association of Jews and non-Jews and on the basis of certain geographic indications, the place of origin is thought to be Syria, perhaps Antioch. Its frequent mention by the church fathers suggests that the writing originally enjoyed some authority. With the formalization process of the canon in the fourth century, it ended up on the peripheries and eventually disappeared from view.

The name *Didache*, 'Instruction', is noteworthy. The church fathers speak of 'the Instruction (*Didache*) of the twelve apostles'. It is thus named in the first, shorter title that we cited. The more extensive second title is rather an indication of the actual content: 'Instruction of the Lord by the twelve apostles *to the nations*'. Interestingly, non-Jewish believers are here explicitly involved in a recognizably Jewish-Christian tradition.

The 'instruction of the apostles' was a household word already in the New Testament. In Acts the tradition is quoted that the first congregation 'persevered in *the instruction of the apostles*' (Acts 2.42). Consistently, instruction, alongside preaching and healing, is an important activity of the apostles (Acts 4.2, 18; 5.21, 25, 42). This is the threefold summary of the mission of Jesus and his representatives (pp. 133-34). Undoubtedly, the instruction of the apostles contained the transmitted words of Jesus, the earliest stage of the Gospel tradition. How much of this is still to be detected in the *Didache* is difficult to ascertain, but without a doubt it would be less than in the Gospels. Certain customs having to do with baptism, fasting, prayer, table prayers and the community fund could be related to the milieu of Jesus and his disciples. It is equally certain that various elements have been added and made more detailed according to the needs of later situations.

The 'Two Ways'

The first part of the *Didache* is a tractate about 'Two Ways', comprising four chapters about 'the way of life' and a fifth about 'the way of death'. It begins as follows:

> Two ways there are, one of life and one of death, and there is a great difference between the two ways. Now the way of life is this: first, you shall love the God who has made you; second, your neighbour as yourself. And everything that you do not want to happen to you, do that also not to another. The instruction of these words is... (*Did.* 1.1-3).

Hereafter first there is what is called the 'gospel interpolation' (insertion), comprising ancient material from the gospel tradition that will occupy our attention later. Then follows a listing of commandments and exhortations. The beginning of this portion and the beginning of the 'way of death' are given here:

> You shall not murder, you shall not commit adultery, you shall not violate boys, you shall not commit harlotry, you shall not steal, you shall not exercise magic, you shall not prepare magic potions, you shall not murder a child by abandoning it nor kill that which has been conceived... (*Did.* 2.2).

> The way of death is this: first of all, it is evil and full of cursing: murders, adulteries, lusts, harlotries, thieveries, idolatries, magic tricks, magic potions, robberies... (*Did.* 5.1).

The fact that the way of life is also expressed in prohibitions is both remarkable and stylistically weak. The lists form an elaboration of the so-called 'second table' of the Ten Commandments, with important additions, such as magic and sorcery, artificial abortion and child abandonment. The latter was widespread in the Greek world, most frequently applying to girls and occurring the most often during the oft-occurring shortages of grain.

The opening of the 'way of life' contains two elements that are known from Jesus' teachings as well: the double love commandment and the Golden Rule. This is the notion of the 'summary of the law' that occurs in the New Testament and in the Hillelite tradition (see pp. 146-47). Related to this is the genre of summarizing lists of commandments, of which the opening lines of the way of life and of the way of death are examples. It entails a flexible, widely ramified tradition, a version of which is also ascribed to Jesus: 'You shall not kill, you shall not commit adultery, you shall not steal, you shall not bear false witness, you shall not rob, honour your father and your mother' (Mk 10.19). The flexibility is apparent in the fact that the final commandment of the 'first table' is added to the 'second table'. Paul's epistles also contain examples of this (1 Cor. 5.10; 6.9-10; Gal. 5.14-26), as do diverse Greek-Jewish writings.

An extraordinary aspect is the duality of the way of life and the way of death, again having sundry variants. The words of Jesus are transmitted to us as follows:

> Enter through the narrow gate! For wide is the gate and broad is the way that leads to corruption, and many are they that enter therein. How narrow is the gate and confined is the way that leads to life, and few there be that find it! (Mt. 7.13-14).

The same is expressed in the parable of the house upon the sand and the one upon the rock (Mt. 7.24-27). Related matters are encountered in rabbinic literature, for example, when R. Yohanan ben Zakkai asks his disciples 'which is the good way that a person should adhere to' and which the evil one 'from which he should keep far away' (*m. Ab.* 2.9).

The choice between life and death, between blessing and cursing is present already in the Old Testament (Deut. 11.26-28; 27–30; Jer. 21.8; Ps. 1), but it does not include the application in an individual and a cosmological sense. In Paul's writings, for example, there is a more apocalyptic phrasing of 'the fruits of the flesh' in contrast to 'the fruits of the Spirit' (Gal. 5.19-26). The apocalyptic tone is much stronger in a parallel of the Two Ways occurring at the end of the so-called *Letter of Barnabas*:

> Two ways there are of instruction *and power*, the way of *light* and that of *darkness*. And there is a great difference between the two ways: over the one *God's light-bringing angels* are appointed, and over the other *the angels of Satan*; the One is Lord from eternity and unto eternity, and the other *the ruler of the present time of lawlessness* (*Barn.* 18.1-2).

This is a straightforward example of apocalyptic dualism, according to which earthly life is a battlefield of the armies of light and of darkness. The epitome in this area, however, is the 'treatise of the two spirits' in the *Community Rule* from Qumran (1QS 3.13–4.46), wherein all of human life seems to be determined by the influence of the Angel of Light and the Angel of Darkness:

> In the hand of *the Prince of Light* is the *sovereignty* over all sons of
> righteousness, so that they go in the ways of *light*; but in the hand of the
> *Angel of Darkness* is all the *sovereignty* over the sons of evil, so that they
> go in the ways of *darkness*. And through the Angel of Darkness comes
> the digression of all the sons of righteousness, all their sins, their
> transgressions... (1QS 3.20-22; cf. 4.2-14)

In the midst of this gamut of variants, the tractate of the Two Ways in
the *Didache* emerges as non-dualistic and non-apocalyptic, and is as
such more or less kindred to the phrasing of Jesus and of Yohanan ben
Zakkai.

We progress a step further. If one reads the treatise of the Two Ways
in the *Didache* in its entirety, not a single typically Christian expression
is encountered in it. This has led to the theory that it was originally
a devout Jewish tractate, incorporated at an early stage. Decisive
evidence for this was found in the existence of texts that contain no
more than a variation of the same treatise of Two Ways, such as the
parallel in the *Letter of Barnabas*. The first composers of the *Didache*
were evidently in a milieu where no boundary was felt between
'Jewish' and 'Christian' literature. This environment appears to have
been not far removed from that of the early rabbis and close to that of
Jesus. In other words, as one of the consequences of its being incorporated into the Jewish-Christian *Didache*, this tractate of Two Ways
itself grants us a glance into the environment of Jesus and his disciples.

The 'Gospel'

The *Didache* enables us to trace further contours of the image that we
have of the earliest 'gospel'. In Chapter 3 (pp. 128-29) we spoke ten-
tatively of the 'gospel' of Jesus in the sense of the liberating message
with which he came. Precisely that wording occurs in a passage in the
Didache, which discloses a link in content as well: 'Pray not as the
hypocrites, but *as the Lord in his gospel commanded*: "Thus shall you
pray: Our Father in heaven..."' (*Did.* 8.2). More will be said later about
the prayer, but here we point out that the preaching of 'the Lord', that
is, Jesus, is called 'gospel'. This 'gospel', however, was broader than
the message of Jesus himself. We read elsewhere, 'Concerning the
apostles and prophets: act according to the commandment of the gospel' (*Did.* 11.3). The lines following presume a network of (Jewish-)
Christian churches and testify, thus, to circumstances after Jesus. In this

milieu, evidently 'the gospel of Jesus' was seen as a part of a more extensive movement. Our earlier conjecture of the existence of a sort of preaching movement that showed some affinity with the Essenes and from which the preaching of John the Baptist and of Jesus originated (see pp. 130-31) appears to be corroborated.

The *Didache*'s text has undergone reworking at various stages, which is quite logical for a community text such as 'a church order'. The whole within which the treatise of Two Ways is incorporated represents a second stage in which perhaps what 'the Lord in his gospel has said', or, as we find elsewhere, 'about this the Lord has said...' (*Did*. 9.5) was still thus spoken of. There are, however, indications that later redactors had a more clearly defined gospel before them. The penultimate chapter states, 'Correct each other not in wrath, but in peace, *as you have it in the gospel*...your prayers and alms and all deeds must you perform *as you have it in the gospel of our Lord*' (15.3-4). This is somewhat repetitive of material in ch. 8 where rules are already given for prayer. The passage appears to belong to a later stage of redaction in which fixed and perhaps already written gospels were available; another example will be given.

The question now is which 'Gospel' these later redactors of the *Didache* had before them (or perhaps in their oral memory). In the Gospels known to us, there is but one passage on rules governing church life, namely, the text on the procedures for reprimand within the congregation found in Matthew (18.15-17), but it provides no concrete correspondences to go on. Matthew also includes a passage about prayers and alms, but again with little to go by (6.1-15). Within the same passage, unmistakable conformity to Matthew is present in the use of the word 'hypocrites' for certain opponents; to this we will return later. Literal equivalence occurs in the sentence, 'Give that which is holy not to the dogs' (*Did*. 9.5; Mt. 7.6); we will return to this later as well. A more convincing proof of the connection to this Gospel is the practically literal text of the Lord's Prayer of Matthew's version occurring in the passage on prayer that I already cited (*Did*. 8.2; see below). A final parallel teaches us more about the exact relationship to Matthew:

> Every prophet that speaks in the Spirit, you shall not test or judge him; for every sin shall be forgiven, but this sin shall not be forgiven (*Did*. 11.7).

> Every sin and blasphemy shall be forgiven to humans, but the blasphemy of the Spirit shall not be forgiven (Mt. 12.31).

The context of this undeniably identical element differs significantly: while Matthew is concerned with slandering Jesus, the Didache is about the slander...of other prophets. The divergent applications of the same tradition points to a flexible and perhaps yet oral stage of transmission.

There appears, thus, to be an unequivocal connection between the *Didache* and Matthew, but it is just as clear that this could not possibly involve the final text of the Gospel. As in the case of James, it is natural to think of the original Hebrew or Aramaic Matthaean primal source that was incorporated into the Gospel in the third layer.

In a certain sense, this possibility is confirmed by the gospel interpolation, which is lacking in parallel texts containing only the Two Ways. The insertion into the Jewish treatise was probably made during the first Christian reworking. I cite a portion:

> Bless those who curse you and pray for your enemies, and fast for your persecutors; for what kind of grace is it if you love those who love you? Do not the non-Jews do the same? You, however, love your haters, and you shall have no enemy. Refrain from fleshly and bodily passions. If someone gives you a blow on the right cheek, turn also the other one to him, and you shall be perfect... (*Did.* 2.3-4).

Careful comparison shows that both the wording and the order of these known admonitions deviate from what we read in the existing Gospels (Lk. 6.27-36; Mt. 5.38-48). Furthermore, the *Didache* version contains elements that are lacking in the Gospels, such as fasting for the persecutors and the passage 'love your haters, and you shall have no enemy; refrain from fleshly and bodily passions'. The interpolation must go back to an independent form of the synoptic tradition, apparently inserted into the Jewish tractate of the Two Ways in a Jewish-Christian milieu at a time in which it was possible to treat the gospel material freely.

Taking note of this casual relationship to the Gospel of Matthew known to us, everything points to the fact that in any event the first main portion of the *Didache* (chs. 1–13) must have taken shape before the extant Matthew acquired authority, or at least outside of its formative milieu. That means that the first portion of the *Didache* belongs to the most ancient of Christian documents. The repeated editing in the final chapters (14–16) indicates a dating of the whole towards the end of the first century.

Jewish-Christian Halakah

We now will review briefly the subjects for which the *Didache* gives regulations. The focus will be on the Jewish elements, especially noting information to be gleaned from them about the specific Jewish-Christian milieu of the *Didache*.

To begin with, the formulation that introduces a number of the subjects is of general significance: 'Now concerning...' (*peri de...*). This phrasing occurs also in 1 Corinthians, again involving a series of practical rules (see p. 195). It can be found in older Greek literature as well, but apparently enjoys a certain preference in Greek-Jewish texts that give regulations. A Hebrew parallel to this formulation has come to light in the halakhic letter from Qumran (*we-'al...*, 4QMMT, *passim*).

> (1) Now concerning food. As much as you can, bear it. But keep yourself far from idol sacrifices, for that is worshipping dead gods (*Did.* 6.3).

The prohibition of idol sacrifices was general in the early church and is repeatedly prescribed in the New Testament (see pp. 200, 233, 374). It is interesting here that this is a minimum demand, which leaves open the possibility of taking more commandments upon onself. That this entails Jewish commandments (apparently dietary rules) appears from the affinity of the 'honouring of dead gods' with the biblical–rabbinic term 'offerings to the dead' (*m. Ab.* 3.3; Ps. 106.28).

> (2) Now concerning baptism. Thus shall you baptize: after you have first said all these things, baptize in the name of the Father and the Son and the Holy Spirit, in living water, and if it can not be in cold, then in warm (water). And if you have neither of the two, pour then thrice water over the head... (*Did.* 7.1-3).

'Thrice pouring', with the threefold formulation: are we here not confronted with the *liturgical* origin of the dogma of the Trinity (David Flusser)? In any event, in this Jewish-Christian milieu there was no difficulty with a 'liturgical Trinity'. The rules concerning water are significant as well. In rabbinic literature, related series of prescriptions occur in relation to the ritual bath: the best is 'living' (running) water, preferably cold, otherwise warm, and in extreme cases one may pour (*m. Miq.* 1; *b. Ḥul.* 106a). The *Didache* here gives a Jewish-Christian baptism halakah. Associating this with the baptismal practice of John the Baptist and his former disciple, Jesus, is certainly not barred (see pp. 130-31, 307-308).

> (3) Your fasting must not coincide with the hypocrites. Now they fast
> upon the second and the fifth day after the Shabbat; you, however, must
> fast upon the fourth and the Preparation (day).
> And pray not as the hypocrites, but as the Lord commanded in his
> gospel: 'Thus shall you pray: Our Father in heaven, sanctified be Your
> name...' Thrice daily shall you thus pray (*Did.* 8.1-3).

The term 'hypocrites' here is the same term used in Matthew, where it
is clear that it refers to the Pharisees. Corresponding to the above are
rabbinic regulations according to which Monday and Thursday are set
aside as days of fasting and one must say 'Eighteen Berakot' thrice
daily (*t. Ta'an.* 2.4; see p. 76). The *Didache* replaces the Pharisaic
prayer with that of Jesus. Given the pluriformity of practice during the
first century, it could be that this was even Jesus' intention. The preference for Wednesday and Friday concurs with the Essene solar calendar,
to which we already related the divergent date of Passover in the synoptic Gospels (see pp. 80-81, 310-12). This is a strong indication that the
early Jewish-Christian milieu, as well as that of Jesus himself, followed
a non-Pharisaic, somewhat Essene calendar of feasts.

> (4) Now concerning the Eucharist (thanksgiving). Thus shall you give
> thanks. First over the cup: We give thanks to you, our Father, because of
> the holy vine of David your servant, whom you have made known to us
> through Jesus, your servant. To you be the glory in all ages. And over the
> bread: We give thanks to you, our Father...And no one may eat or drink
> of your Thanksgiving except those baptized upon the name of the Lord.
> Now the Lord has said about this: 'Give not the holy to the dogs' (*Did.*
> 9.1-5).

The natural identification of Jesus as descendant of David is striking
(cf. p. 339). The 'quote' from Mt. 7.6 is intriguing: its significance is
clear here, while in Matthew it stands in enigmatic isolation. Is the
composer of the *Didache* giving an interpretation himself, or is he quoting an ancient interpretation of the saying? Concerning the Eucharist or
Thanksgiving, the order involved is first wine, then bread. That is the
opposite to the general Christian custom, which is found not only in
Mark and in the tradition of the Lord's Supper in Paul's writings, but
also in Matthew: first bread, then wine (Mk 14.22-25; Mt. 26.26-29;
1 Cor. 11.23-25).

A difference within the Judaism of that day corresponds to this. In
rabbinic tradition, and probably also with the Pharisees, God is blessed
at the beginning of the festive meal first over the cup, then over the
bread. The order bread–wine is found, however, at Qumran (1QS 6.5-6;

1QSa 2.19-20). Within earliest Christianity, thus, the same divergence can be traced (cf. the 'Pharisaic' order in 1 Cor. 10.16, and a mixed version in Lk. 22.17-20). The implication seems to be that Jesus and his disciples kept the Essene custom, while the Jewish-Christian community of the *Didache*, among others, behaved 'Pharisaic'.

> (5) Now concerning the apostles and prophets. According to the order of the gospel, thus shall you act. Every apostle who comes to you, he shall remain but one day. And if it be necessary, also the second. But if he remains three, he is a false prophet...
> Every one who comes in the name of the Lord must be received; thereafter you must test him and get to know him... He may remain only two or three days with you, if it is necessary. And if he will establish himself as craftsman, let him work and eat... (*Did*. 11.4-5; 12.1-3).

The passage deals with the hospitality that each church offered from community funds. The New Testament also treats this issue, as well as the obligation for the able-bodied to work for their own sustenance (1 Thess. 4.9-12; 2 Thess. 3.6-13). According to rabbinic tradition, each Jewish community was to have a poor fund, but he that was able was to work for his bread. We could also think of the much more encompassing communality of goods, such as found among the Essenes and in the first church, and possibly also in the group of disciples around Jesus (see p. 48; Acts 4.32–5.11; Jn 13.29).

> (6) Each day of the Lord you must congregate, break bread, and give thanks, after you have confessed your transgressions, so that your offering be pure... (*Did*. 14.1).

Once again we observe that the *Didache* is layered. The Eucharist had already been discussed in *Did*. 9–11; now a further stipulation follows, which undoubtedly indicates a later development of the text. Those of this community congregated on Sunday for the Lord's Supper. This does not necessarily mean that the Jewish members did not observe the Shabbat. The preference for Sunday, Wednesday and Friday was characteristic of the Essene calendar, as we have already seen, and the *Didache* prescribes fasting on Wednesday and Friday. Sunday is, of course, celebrated as the day of the Resurrection, but, perhaps not by coincidence, it corresponds as well to the solar calendar. The possibility that the Christian celebration of Sunday derived from this separate stream of Jewish tradition can not be excluded.

In each of the rules cited, there are Jewish elements: regulations concerning food, baptism, fasting upon Wednesday and Friday, praying three times a day, the festive meal, the community fund and the gathering on Sunday. These elements are, however, just as the treatise about the Two Ways, completely and totally absorbed into this 'Christian' rule governing church life. This is a Jewish-Christian legal tradition, or, in other words, a form of early Jewish-Christian halakah.

Conclusion: the Didache *and the Jewish-Christian Milieus*
Alongside the devout ethical treatise of the Two Ways, the *Didache* contains a series of legislative Jewish elements that makes it an important document of early Jewish-Christian halakah. Because the opinions in the halakah offer significant indications as to one's place in Jewish society (see p. 91), the halakah in the *Didache* can be taken as a source of information concerning the earliest Jewish-Christian milieus.

A Jewish-Christian legal tradition is also found in Paul's writings (see pp. 197-98), but has a different interpretation. A significant distinction has to do with food. It is difficult to image that Paul would say to his spiritual children, 'As much as you can, bear that' (*Did.* 6.3), which means that the *Didache* was also less supple in regards to what had possibly been offered to idols. This yields an initial demarcation. It is true that the *Didache* community was open to non-Jewish believers, but it encouraged them, in contrast to Pauline tradition, to conduct themselves as much as possible according to the Jewish law.

Clear points of correspondence are present between the *Didache* and Matthew, such as the text of the Lord's Prayer, the saying about giving 'the holy to the dogs' and the opposition to the Pharisees as hypocrites. The version of the saying about blasphemy of the Spirit makes it clear that the relationship involves an earlier form of the tradition incorporated into Matthew. There is also a difference in the order of wine and bread for the Eucharist: the *Didache* follows the Pharisaic custom, Matthew the Essene, thus indicating independence with regard to the tradition of Matthew. The anti-Pauline accent of the *Didache* is not dissimilar to the closedness towards non-Jews in earlier stages of Matthew. An important distinction to the final text of Matthew is that there is no trace of a turning away from the Jews, thus limiting the relationship to the earlier phases of Matthew, and we suggest, once again, a connection to the primal source of Matthew.

There are no direct points of contact between the Epistle of James and the *Didache*. We can only conclude that there was a relationship through the common bond with the tradition behind Matthew. In James this is particularly related to the Sermon on the Mount. Here again, not the final text of Matthew is involved, but possibly the gospel tradition which we suppose to be present in the Matthaean primal source. James places an explicit anti-Pauline accent that again reminds one of the earlier stages of Matthew.

The Revelation of John appears likewise to have a strained relationship with the Pauline tradition in relationship to non-Jews. The protest against so-called Jews who in fact are the 'synagogue of Satan' appears to be prompted by a much more rejecting attitude towards the Roman government than most other Jews had. In the strict rejection of eating of idolatrous sacrifices and in the importance that prophets have in the church there is affinity with the *Didache*.

The Epistles of Jude and to the Hebrews give neither halakhic nor other clues as to their specific Jewish-Christian milieu. In general cultural background, Jude is more or less related to James and the Didache, and Hebrews to Paul.

Surveying the whole, early Jewish-Christian milieus exhibit a diversified panorama. Striking, though understandable, is the shared distance to the Pauline tradition. The *Didache*, James, Revelation, as well as an earlier form of Matthew all draw a clearer boundary with regard to non-Jews and non-Jewish churches. This will be related both to internal differences of opinion and to the growing external tensions between the Jewish churches in Jerusalem and Judaea and the Pauline churches of non-Jews. On the other hand, in these Jewish-Christian documents, there is no trace of turning away from the Jews such as is to be read in the final text of Matthew.

Chapter 9

THE NEW TESTAMENT AND THE JEWS

In this final chapter we bring the strands together and see what patterns emerge. Our interest lies primarily in the position of the various New Testament writings with regard to Jews and Judaism. This means that at the same time we must inquire concerning the relationship to Judaism of the environments in which these writings originated. In this we must keep in mind the insight from Chapter 6 that the Gospels are community texts and that they carry the traces of the history of their contexts.

We shall see that the Gospel of John is conspicuous in its explicit opposition to, not to say hatred of, the Jews. In order to try to fathom this, we will first dedicate a section to the phenomenon of hatred as it manifests itself here. We will then take a tour of the different early Christian milieus with their traditions and texts. Thereafter we will delve into the question of how a Christian within the practice of Scripture reading in the church can handle the painful fact of the 'biblical' hate for the Jews. We will conclude with some thoughts on the church as an open community characterized by its reading of the Scriptures.

The results of the previous chapters are presumed here, and for the sake of readability only a few explicit references will be given.

Hate and Diabolizing

Most Christians dislike the word 'hate', and in this at least they are faithful disciples of their Master, who taught, '*Love your enemies*, do good to them that hate you' (Lk. 6.27). One could wonder who he intended by 'enemies'. His own treatment of temple leaders and money changers was far from benign, and his message of recrimination against the 'hypocritical scribes and Pharisees' has no doubt an authentic kernel (Mt. 22–23). Possibly he did not mean enemies of the community against whom any right-thinking person would take action, but personal antagonists in the sense of the opponent with whom one is to make amends 'while you are yet under way' (Mt. 5.25). It could also be that the extreme demand to 'love your enemy' was motivated by protest against the 'holy hate' propagated by the Essenes. Jesus' pure love for 'tax collectors and sinners' points in that direction (see pp. 135-36, 144). However that may be, his rejection of hate for the opponent was unique in the context of the Judaism of his day. We can recognize in it the realization that *each* person is a child of light and a bearer of God's image.

On the other hand, indignation at injustice is a wholesome and indispensible emotion of which the 'consuming zeal' of Jesus' action against the temple commerce (see pp. 163-64) is a good example. This may not be forgotten amidst the emphasis on his gospel of liberating love. The question is, however, whether this righteous anger should result in a hatred towards 'God's enemies'. Jesus appears to reject this, explaining that God 'sends rain on the just *and the unjust*' (Mt. 5.45), which confirms the anti-Essene purport of his position.

A different tenor can be heard in the Psalms: 'Do I not, O Lord, *hate them that hate you*?...I hate them with perfect hatred' (Ps. 139.21-22). This attitude is encountered in an extremely radical form in the opening sentences of the Rule of Qumran, where the assignment of the community is 'to love all the children of light...and *to hate all the children of darkness*' (1QS 1.9-10). A cosmic–moral dualism resounds here that has by now become familiar to us in a different form from the Johannine milieu. A sharp echo can be heard in the Apocalypse, where the heavenly Christ praises the church of Ephesus because they 'hate the works of the Nicolaitans, which I also hate' (Rev. 2.6). Although the hatred is directed not to the Nicolaitans but to their works, this still diverges significantly from the teaching of Jesus in the synoptic tradition.

Within dualistic–apocalyptic thinking, hostility towards God's enemies has a natural place. In the younger parts of the Old Testament and in post-biblical writings, the words 'Hate' and 'Enmity' are even used as two of the names of the angel of evil, that is, the personified antagonism towards God. The names are derived from the two related Hebrew verbs *sātan*, 'to hate', and *sātam*, 'to treat with enmity'. The one name in Hebrew is *Mastema*, 'Enmity' (*Jub.* 10.8; CD 16.5; cf. Hos. 9.7-8; 1QS 3.23). The more familiar appellation is *Satan*, 'Prosecutor' (Zech. 3.1; Job 1–2). This latter designation is rendered in Greek as *diabolos*, 'prosecutor', from whence our word 'devil' is derived. In apocalyptic literature, Satan reigns over the enemies of God, who, within this dual-istic frame of reference, most likely correspond to the enemies of the writer and his milieu.

Characteristic of the apocalyptic manner of thinking is, therefore, that the godless opponents were *diabolized* or represented as satanic. An exceptionally intemperate form of this is reflected in the abhorence of the community of Qumran for 'the children of darkness', who were said to be 'under the domination of the Prince of Darkness' (1QS 1.10; 3.21). Within the New Testament, this phenomenon also occurs. In Revela-tions we find a remarkable outburst against 'them that say they are Jews, and are not, but are *the synagogue of Satan*' (Rev. 2.9; 3.9). It is important here that, just as in the Qumran scrolls and in the pseude-pigraphic texts, the reference is to Jews being thus judged by fellow-Jews, in this case by a Jewish-Christian author. It is of crucial signifi-cance that the appeal made to the designation 'Jew' is a positive one. The cases mentioned thus far relate to an *internal Jewish diabolization of opponents*. Pharisees, too, expressed themselves at times in this man-ner, as in the story where they accused Jesus of casting out demons 'by Beelzebub the prince of devils' (Mt. 12.24). Beelzebub is yet another name for the prince of darkness. In the Johannine epistles opponents are diabolized as well: 'He who sins is *of the devil*, for the devil has sinned from the beginning... Every one that hates his brother is a murderer...' (1 Jn 3.8, 15). These letters appear to assume a Jewish-Christian audi-ence, so that this polemic can be read as an internal Jewish affair.

As with the Qumran scrolls and other apocalyptic writings, it is not correct to label such *intra-Jewish* diabolization of opponents as anti-Judaism or anti-Semitism. The Qumran community continued to see itself as a part of Israel and persisted in the expectation of salvation for 'the whole community of Israel', even though the latter was regarded as being temporarily blinded (1QSa; CD 16.2-3). The situation shifts when the diabolization motif is brought to bear in the field of tension between Jewish and non-Jewish Christians. We will return to this in the follow-ing section.

Early Christian Milieus in Relation to Judaism

On the basis of the preceding chapters, we now take a tour past the following early Christian contexts and traditions or writings: (1) Jesus and his words that were passed on; (2) the Jewish churches and their writings; (3) the Pauline tradition, the Lukan writings, and the non-Jewish churches; (4) the Johannine tradition with its Jewish and non-Jewish phases; and (5) the Gospels of Mark and Matthew, which cannot be immediately placed in a specific context. For the sake of completeness, we also look at (6) the Gnostic Gospels. At each point we will pose questions concerning the relationship of these various elements to Jews and Judaism.

Jesus and the Gospel Tradition

Three phases are distinguishable: the environment in which Jesus himself was formed, the context that he and his disciples created together, and the milieu in which his words were formulated and handed down. The three phases are continuous but do not coincide for two reasons: Jesus followed an independent track with respect to his teachers, and the process of transmitting his words fanned out into various traditions. This phenomenon is characteristic of truly great figures: they stand head and shoulders above their contemporaries, forge a new unity out of divergent tendencies and traditions, and must resign themselves to the fact that their followers will each work out but a single aspect of their legacy.

Another reason why it is imperative to discuss the contexts relating to Jesus is that often it cannot be determined whether a certain statement comes from himself, from his disciples, or from his teachers. The same margin of uncertainty is applicable to rabbinic literature and can no doubt be ascribed to the process of oral transmission.

Concerning the *environment in which Jesus was formed*, the only direct information comes to us through John the Baptist, 'the voice crying in the wilderness'. Together with a series of other facts, this citation from Isaiah 40, also used in Qumran, has led us to the assumption that John headed a movement of penance and Torah study in which Jesus also participated for a time, but from which he finally separated himself in order to go his own way. This movement was located literally in the desert, like the sect of Qumran, though this fact in itself need not indicate that John or Jesus belonged to the Essenes. Jesus' ironic critique of deep-rooted antagonism towards enemies and total rejection of Mammon shows clearly that he distances himself from such a movement. Before he began his public ministry, he must have absorbed other influences. His obvious knowledge of halakhic discussions about the Shabbat, the parables, the Golden Rule, the double commandment of

love and other elements point to an intimate acquaintance with the
Pharisaic tradition. A number of elements indicate more specifically an
affinity with pious individuals marginal to the Pharisaic movement. The
environment in which Jesus was formed includes, thus, the teachings of
the Pharisees, ancient Hasidic circles, and the preaching movement of
John the Baptist.

In a more direct sense, Jesus formed his own milieu in *the community
of his disciples*. Here his independent performance revealed itself, as he
himself was well aware. He spoke of his work as the initiation of
something new and called himself the 'bridegroom' and the 'son of
man'. He viewed his disciples as being a special community, as 'the
light of the world', the vanguard of the Kingdom, and he sent them out
to proclaim his message and to continue his work. Just as is known of
Pharisaic leaders, his disciples associated daily with him. They apparently had a communal housekeeping, with Judas as treasurer. In this
daily companionship, instruction took place. Just as in Pharisaic milieus
it is probable that here as well the oral arranging, preserving, and
transmitting of Jesus' words took place. This is where the various influences that he had absorbed in himself must have come together. The
course of this process must, however, have been dependent on the
aptitude and development of each follower, on what was retained of the
words of the Master, and on the manner in which this was preserved by
the follower. The divergencies in the gospel tradition could have had
their beginnings as early as at this point.

Particularly by comparison to the halakah, the Jewish legal tradition,
it becomes possible to specify Jesus' independent position within the
Judaism of his day. His attitude towards divorce is Essene, while his
ideas on Shabbat were mild Pharisaic, and concerning the rules of purity
he was more conservative Pharisaic. The order of bread before wine at
the meal and the probable date of his last Passover meal point again to
affinity with the Essenes. On these points, Jesus apparently took a more
or less independent position within the broader context of his day.

With the handing down and further working out of the gospel tradition *after Easter* we arrive at the third phase of Jesus' environment. In
this phase, the different forms of the gospel tradition must have been
given their definite form. We observed the Johannine tradition as being
divergent; in language and thought world it suggests a minority group.
Through the disciples, who then functioned as apostles or ambassadors,
the mainstream has become known to us in the Gospels of Mark,

Matthew and Luke, in other words, in the *synoptic tradition*. The authority of this form of the tradition is apparent from a number of direct, authoritative references by Paul, from the Matthaean affinity of the Epistle of James and of the *Didache*, and from the 'Gospel interpolation' in the latter writing. The embryonic setting of this tradition must have been the Jewish churches in Judaea and Galilee, which, under apostolic authority, cultivated the oral tradition, but before long it included the churches of non-Jews as well, to which the gospel was brought by Paul, Peter and other apostles. The following phase began with the *commitment to writing* of the gospel tradition. If our conclusion (Chapter 6) is correct that this was done initially for the sake of the non-Jewish Christians, then this phase falls outside of Jesus' milieu in the broadest sense.

The Jewish Churches and their Writings
Diverging from the order of the preceding chapters, we let the discussion of the Jewish churches and their earliest writings follow upon that of Jesus' milieu because we can assume a direct continuity between if not identity of the two. In this, the Epistle to the Hebrews with its Platonizing manner of thinking is excluded, even though traces of Jewish-Christian eschatology do indicate affinity with the churches in the Holy Land. The Revelation of John likewise has a somewhat distinct nature. The Epistles of Jude and James and the *Didache*, however, testify to a Jewish-Christian context familiar with the Pharisaic and apocalyptic manner of thinking, where Jesus' gospel in oral form must have continued to be transmitted. Although the spoken languages were probably primarily Hebrew and Aramaic, Greek must also have been spoken, given the good quality of the Greek in James and Jude. It is not impossible that the translation of the gospel tradition into Greek was begun in such an environment.

The *Jewish-Christian phase of Matthew*, known especially from the Sermon on the Mount and other characteristic portions of Matthaean teaching, can be included in this milieu. This material is clearly related to a number of short, proverb-like statements in the Epistle of James and to certain essential elements in the *Didache*. The unmistakable but incidental character of this relationship indicates more than anything else a shared oral tradition. It is plausible that this is indeed a reflection of the continuation of the tradition of Jesus' teaching within its own environment. In this context, the teaching of the 'two ways' was a

favourite genre, of which we have at least two different elaborations—
at the beginning of the *Didache* (*Did.* 1–5) and at the end of the Sermon
on the Mount (Mt. 7.12-27).

The relation between the Enoch tradition in the Epistle of Jude and
the undoubtedly traditional Enoch genealogy of Jesus in Luke indicate
an interesting aspect. Here again it is not a matter of dependency but of
variant processings of the same material. This tradition evidently also
originated in a Palestinian Jewish-Christian context and had a direct
relation to the entourage of Jesus.

Halakhic data can be of assistance in arriving at a further determination of position. If it is assumed that the synoptic tradition proceeded
from the context of Jewish churches, then the specific accents of the
Didache and of the Jewish-Christian phase of Matthew can be conceived of within this framework. Though related to this milieu and
particularly to Matthew, the *Didache* diverges from the synoptic tradition in its order wine–bread, while it adds a quasi-Essene feature in
specifying fasting on Wednesday and on Friday. Matthew diverges
from Jesus' teaching in allowing divorce in the case of adultery, and
apparently also in his striking prohibition to preserve life by fleeing on
the Shabbat. While we can speak of a Jewish-Christian context in which
the synoptic tradition arose, this contained specific, small variations.

The *Didache* takes non-Jewish believers into account and summons
them in particular to observe as many commandments as possible, an
attitude that could have been shared by Jewish-Christian churches. In
any case it accords with the anti-Pauline emphasis of James on justification 'not by faith alone' but by works. Although this environment
was open to non-Jews, they were evidently stimulated in a Judaizing
direction.

In comparison to this group of documents, the Revelation of John
gives the impression of being somewhat exceptional. The type of echoes
from the gospel tradition that we find in James and the *Didache* are
lacking. The introduction of the heavenly Jesus speaking in the first
person to the seven churches of Asia Minor, together with the elaborate
apocalyptic vision that follows, suggest a different spiritual climate than
that of James, Jude, the *Didache* and the Jewish-Christian phase of
Matthew. Revelation does share, however, the anti-Pauline accent that
we also detected in the other writings.

The Epistle to the Hebrews has been ascribed to a preacher who felt
at home both with a Platonizing–allegorical and with an apocalytic way

of thinking. He might have been educated in Alexandia, but in any case sent greetings to those 'from Italy', and he moved within the Diaspora milieus. Hebrews can be read as a document from a Hellenistic-Jewish Diaspora church that was in contact with the churches of the Holy Land and their apocalyptic traditions.

The Churches of Non-Jews: Pauline and Lukan Writings

Paul portrayed the church as a body in which Jewish and non-Jewish believers differ but are equivalent members. This pluralistic view was based on a relationship of mutual respect, expressed in Paul's basic rule: Jewish and non-Jewish believers respect each other's differences in dealing with the law.

Paul's relationship to the gospel tradition indicates a fundamentally positive attitude towards the church in Jerusalem. Our conclusion was that he based his practical teachings not only on the Jewish law, but also on the apostolic legal tradition which goes back to Jesus' teachings: he explicitly refers to the teaching of 'the Lord' four times. Given the fact that Paul was familiar with the gospel tradition and the fact that Paul's citations are usually not literal but are paraphrases or allusions, it is plausible that Paul had this information in oral form and, as a former Pharisee, preferred not to write it down. The introductory words of the Lord's Supper appear to form an exception to this, for he literally cites certain portions (1 Cor. 11.23-25). Paul's knowledge of the gospel tradition could be related to his announcement that several years after his conversion he spent two weeks in Jerusalem with Peter to 'become acquainted' with him or to 'inquire of' him (Gal. 1.18).

However, the concord with Jerusalem came under pressure, traces of which are discernible in Paul's own epistles. In Galatia missionaries circulated who forced non-Jews to *Judaize*, while non-Jewish believers in Rome protested about *Jewish customs*. The conflicts are also reported in Acts, in this case primarily from Jewish-Christian circles. From the end of the forties onwards, tensions escalated to such a degree that Paul became isolated between the polarized Jewish and non-Jewish churches, as is reflected in the attitude of the Jewish-Christian writings towards non-Jewish believers.

From both sides, Paul was now understood in a biased manner. The Epistle of James takes issue with the standpoint that one is justified 'by faith *alone*', an oversimplification of Paul's position that apparently was shared by both supporters and opponents, as can be deduced from

Paul's own writings. Furthermore, it is probable that the mounting conflict drove Jewish and non-Jewish believers apart, so that there were progressively fewer Jewish Christians among Paul's followers. The explicitness of James's opposition suggests estrangement. On the other hand, the Epistle of Titus, written 'in the name of Paul', objects to the dietary and purity laws in a manner that sounds far more radical than what Paul himself wrote on this topic. These two epistles exemplify the isolation of Paul's position.

In contrast, Luke in his Gospel and his history of the apostles rendered the Pauline tradition in accordance with the original. In comparison to the progessive isolation of Paul, this appears to be a minority position, which is even more remarkable if we may assume that Luke had ties with the church of Antioch whose bishop Ignatius several years later was to write that *Christian belief* and *Jewish lifestyle* cannot go together. The Pauline tradition suffered a split into what we described as a Lukan position, which maintained Paul's pluriform vision, and an Ignatian camp, which interpreted the apostle's message in a biasedly anti-Jewish manner. The latter position eventually gained the upper hand in the orthodox, anti-Jewish position of the church fathers. Nonetheless, as we shall see, the vision of Paul persisted even in their days.

Within Ignatian Paulinism we are confronted for the first time with massive opposition to Jews and Judaism, that is, with anti-Judaism. In itself, this is not yet hatred of the Jews. It could have been an aversion to the Jewish-Christian dietary customs and suchlike. Though this is not in the least a praiseworthy attitude, it is as yet not hatred. It could also have been a reaction to the rigid position taken by Judaizing Jewish-Christians, certainly if this intolerance was accompanied by agression. With the growing gulf between the Jewish and non-Jewish churches during the last quarter of the first century, a reciprocal antipathy was but to be expected. Due to the attitude of open competition that developed between the churches and the synagogues half way through the second century, the antagonism becomes even more probable. Though, as the Lukan tradition reminds us, this polarization was not inevitable, a breeding ground was created for the development of hatred for the Jews. We will pursue this further in the following section.

A growing number of writings were read and preserved in the Pauline milieu: in the first place the epistles of and 'in the name of' Paul, then the Gospel of Luke and the Acts of the Apostles, and perhaps the First Epistle of Peter. Lacking only the Johannine writings, the Gospels of

Mark and Matthew, and the epistles of the Jewish churches, this early Pauline canon must have contained most of the elements of the later New Testament.

The Johannine Tradition and Writings

At the beginning of this chapter while speaking of the tendency to diabolize opponents, mention was made that this is to be found in the Johannine epistles. The Johannine Gospel is also not free from this predisposition. Jesus is reported as saying 'to the Jews who believed in him…*you are from the father-devil* and desire to do the lusts of your father; he is a murderer of men from the beginning' (Jn 8.31, 44). The affinity with the First Epistle of John is clear: 'He who sins is *of the devil*, because *from the beginning* the devil sins… Every one who hates his brother is a *murderer* of men…' (1 Jn 3.8, 15). The epistle can be read as part of a correspondence of Johannine Jewish Christians, of which the existence appears to be confirmed indirectly by a papyrus fragment (*Egerton 2*). Even so, a significant difference remains: while none of the Johannine epistles is directed against Jewish Christians or 'the Jews', the Gospel in its entirety addresses itself against *the Jews* as such. In the cited passage, furthermore, it explicitly speaks out against *Jewish Christians*, who in one breath are designated, with clear dissociation, as 'the Jews' (Jn 8.48).

In particular the latter is determinant. It is not improbable that already in the Jewish-Christian phase of the Gospel of John, as well as in the Revelation of John, certain Jewish-Christian opponents were viewed as cohorts of the devil. With some caution we made mention of the underlying criticism of Peter. The Gospel of John in its final form reflects a milieu that had come entirely free of Judaism, so that the intra-Jewish diabolization in this final phase is transferred to 'the Jews' in general. This must have been done by a redactor who placed himself outside of the context of Judaism.

In Chapter 7 we reached the conclusion that the Gospel of John conceives of Jews in terms of enmity and that the term anti-Judaism was applicable. It now appears that we must go further. In the mentioned chapter from the Gospel, the Jewish Christians, together with 'the Jews', are seen as children of the devil, who is the angel of Hate and Enmity. Nowhere is it explicitly said that 'the Jews' are hated or should be hated; only in Revelation is there a commandment to hate (Rev. 2.6). Nonetheless, the Gospel leads up to this by diabolizing the

Jews. Put provocatively, *John 8 is the classical starting point for Christian hatred for the Jews*. The unmistakable rift between this position and Jesus' commission not to hate the enemy but to love him should be noted anew.

Johannine rudiments of hatred towards the Jews comprise two elements: the apocalyptic–Jewish motif of diabolizing the enemy and the effect of an anti-Jewish context. A difference with the Ignatian wing of Paulism becomes apparent here. The anti-Judaism of the Ignatian wing was explained as an aversion arising from the social tensions between Jewish and non-Jewish Christians. What was not present, at least not initially, was the diabolization motif, and that is why one cannot call the Ignatian position actual hatred towards the Jews. It is not difficult to imagine how, by the addition of the diabolization component, the breeding ground for anti-Judaism present there could produce a powerful hatred for the Jews.

Further contemplation of the enigmatic adoption of the Johannine Gospel by a non-Jewish milieu is required. In Chapter 7 we noted that the problematic relations between Jews and non-Jews, of which we hear so much in the Pauline tradition, are a marginal theme in John. The reason for the adoption of the Johannine Gospel can, therefore, not be the attention it gives to the position of non-Jews. Nonetheless, there must have been some reason for the attraction of the non-Jews to this serene, closed and dualistic Gospel. A comparison with Gnosticism can elucidate this, though it is not fully explained thereby.

The name *Gnosticism* is derived from the Greek word *gnōsis*, 'knowledge', an important concept both in general religious usage and in the Jewish and Christian language of faith. Since the first or second centuries CE there were small Christian groups who claimed to possess exclusive knowledge concerning the heavenly origin of and divine salvation for humans; in doing so they reacted against church authority. This exclusive knowledge was couched in a dualistic manner of thinking that included a rejection of creation as being basically good, of the Old Testament, and, therefore, also of Judaism. Since the discovery in 1946 of the bundle of Gnostic writings near the Egyptian Nag Hammadi, we can trace in detail how various sorts of Jewish and, in particular, apocalyptic motifs were incorporated into a more or less Christian, anti-Jewish whole. Within the context of a dualistic world concept, anti-Judaism acquired cosmic dimensions and one can rightly speak here of hatred for the Jews. Further, two non-Christian Gnostic movements, the

Manichaeans and the *Mandaeans*, who arose in the third and fourth centuries CE in Syria and West Persia, are of importance. These non-Jewish movements also adopted Jewish or Jewish-Christian rituals and apocalyptic motifs. Apparently, in the south and east of the former Persian, Graeco-Roman world, there were milieus that eagerly incorporated apocalyptic motifs from Judaism.

By analogy it is possible to visualize the transition to the non-Jewish phase of the Gospel of John. Belonging to a fairly exclusive Jewish-Christian faction, this writing must have attracted certain non-Jews, perhaps in Egypt or Syria. The strained relations with other Jewish Christians and with the rest of the Jews did not create a problem for them. After members of the Johannine community were expelled from the synagogue, the break with Judaism was probably complete, certainly in so far as the rest of the community by then comprised non-Jews. Just as in the Ignatian–Pauline churches, a massive anti-Judaism must have been generated. In this case, however, the Johannine–Jewish-Christian diabolizing of opponents was added and applied to Jews in general. Analogically to the Gnostic groupings, the Johannine tradition developed a *cosmic–dualistic anti-Judaism*; in other words, given the Gospel's account of the passion of Christ, there was a *christologically motivated hatred of the Jews*.

The comparison with Gnosticism is not intended to indicate that the Gospel of John itself should be labelled as Gnostic. On the contrary, John contains clearly anti-Gnostic accents: the creation by the Word, the incarnation of the Word, and the fact that Jesus physically died on the cross (Jn 1.1-3, 14; 19.34-35). To ascribe to the body such an important role within the history of salvation was repellent to Gnostics. Nonetheless, the Gospel shares aspects with Gnosticism: the dualism of divine light and a dark world, the emphasis upon the heavenly origin of the Son of God, and the estrangement from Jews. Little is known with certainty about the Gnostic movement within the first century when this Gospel was taking shape. The simplest hypothesis is that the Gospel of John contains important ingredients of the later Gnosticism but that more radical interpretations of these are rejected.

How the Johannine history thus described fits into the early history of the church is an intriguing question. Two main streams have been distinguished: the Jewish churches and the Pauline 'churches of non-Jews'. The uneasy relationship between the Johannine community and Peter and the other apostles could have resulted in a schism somewhere around the fifties or the sixties of the first century CE. There is no trace of any contact or affinity with Pauline congregations. The 'Johannites' must have lived in isolation at first, but from the non-Jewish phase onwards, this must have changed. During the important conflict at the end of the second century over the date of Easter, the Gospel of John was apparently the mainstay of the Asia Minor churches. According to data from the church fathers, the Gospel of John circulated in the familiar constellation of the 'four Gospels' already half a century earlier. This means that meanwhile a wide circle of non-Jewish churches allowed the virulent Johannine anti-Judaism a place in their canon of Gospel writings.

The history of the Gospel of John is paradoxical. During the second century it appears to have held a great attraction for Gnostic groups, which caused many western Christians to distrust it. Nonetheless, it had already grown to be highly valued by many orthodox Christians. So it was that the prominent theologian Origen undertook his comprehensive commentary on John in order to protect it from being appropriated by the Gnostics. Brought up in Alexandria, Origen felt primarily attracted by the christological allegory of John and was evidently not disturbed by the closed world image that so appealed to the Gnostics. The same was true of the orthodox theologians' preference for John in the christological discussions of the fourth century. Curiously enough, this was the same century in which orthodox Christianity consolidated its position of power against the Jews. The paradox is that this Gospel continued to fascinate both Gnostic heretics and their orthodox opponents. Could this be related to the fact that both of these parties shared with the late-Johannine milieu one explicit interest: *the adoption of Jewish motifs within an anti-Jewish framework*?

Mark and Matthew

At first sight these two Gospels do not belong to the contexts and traditions discussed thus far. Both seem to have undergone an anti-Jewish revision in the last phase, Matthew more so than Mark. Nonetheless, both contain the transmitted form of Jesus' words that was also incorporated by Luke and reflected in Paul, James and the *Didache*, that is, the *synoptic tradition* that was preserved by Jesus' apostles.

The Gospel of *Mark* appears from its very conception to have been intended for a non-Jewish church, and that tenor was strengthened by successive revisions. Except for the Shabbat and the cleansing of hands, subjects which for non-Jews could have had a 'negative interest', questions of the Jewish law are given little attention. The formulation of the prohibition of divorce is intended for the non-Jewish situation. The explanatory insertion about the Jewish purifying customs (Mk 7.3-4) betrays a non-Jewish context. Perhaps the anti-Jewish formulation of the Pharisaic reaction to Jesus' healing on the Shabbat (Mk 3.6) was an addition by a later revisor, and perhaps an even later revision is represented in the textual variant 'he made all food pure' (Mk 7.19).

Except for such retouches, there is *no trace* of motivated hatred towards the Jews as there is in the Gospel of John, although there is estrangement, at most aversion. Nothing impedes viewing Mark as having been written for some non-Jewish church, such as the one in Rome, as tradition has it. There are neither direct points of contact with the Pauline tradition, nor prominent differences. The fact, however, that 'Luke' took the Gospel of Mark as a point of departure implies a relationship: Mark circulated in Pauline milieus. In that case, the incidental anti-Judaism would be in keeping with the Ignatian wing in divided Paulinism.

The indications that Mark, intended for non-Jews, was indeed the first written Gospel invites a digression on the *commitment to writing* of the gospel tradition. The whole phenomenon of the writing down of the gospel tradition appears originally to have been intended for non-Jews. It is revealing that of the four times that Paul quoted an authoritative word of Jesus, three of these are in the form of a paraphrase. As already mentioned, this could have been related to the Pharisaic reluctance to write down post-biblical teachings. Another relevant fact is that the post-New Testamental Christian writings, the so-called Apostolic Fathers, do not quote the canonical Gospels literally, in spite of their probable familiarity with one or more of these. Apparently, for a long time the Apostolic Fathers adhered to the oral gospel tradition, and this custom seems to derive from the Jewish context of early Christianity.

Adherence to oral tradition does not imply that Jewish-Christian circles were unable to compose a Gospel. Reports of 'Hebrew' Gospels indicate that the Jewish Christians resorted to this option after confrontation with the Gospels known to us. It is even probable that the Jewish Christians originally wrote the 'Hebrew' Gospels in order to rectify certain accents rejected by them, although little can be said about this as long as only loose fragments are available. It is also conceivable that those of the Johannine-Jewish circle decided to write a Gospel on their own initiative. The existence of pseudepigraphic literature proves that in the first century religious texts were produced freely outside of the context of the Pharisaic–rabbinic tradition. One can speculate whether the observably greater distance of the Johannine community to the Pharisaic–rabbinic milieu played a role here.

The Gospel of *Matthew* is wholly based upon Mark. Besides this, use was made of a Jewish-Christian primal source from which in particular the teachings of Jesus were added. In the light of what has already been said, this can signify either that Matthew, too, was originally intended for non-Jews and the Matthaean source text was reworked for completeness, or that Matthew is a Jewish-Christian reaction to the Gospel of Mark and that the Matthaean source texts were intentionally inserted. In hindsight the latter is the more probable: it would explain the intentionally divergent structure of Matthew with its Jewish-Christian accents and the critical attitude towards both the Pharisees and the 'heathen'. The reaction against the latter two tallies in turn with the basic premise that Matthew could only have been composed after the Gospel of Mark had already materialized. Matthew's emergence could best be situated in the eighties or nineties, when a quite centralistic Pharisaic–rabbinic regime was in power and there was considerable tension in the relationship with non-Jewish churches.

With the insertion of the Jewish-Christian source into the structure of Mark, what we have called the third, Jewish-Christian phase of Matthew emerged. If this insertion was indeed a conscious statement of position, then this also gives clues as to the context in which this occurred. We have proposed a relationship between the primal source of Matthew, on the one hand, and the *Didache* and the Epistle of James, on the other. Precisely at the point of the two mentioned lines of distinction—with the Pharisees and with non-Jewish Christians—there is a certain amount of concord between these writings. The *Didache*, like Matthew, reacts against the Pharisee as 'hypocrites'; James, like Matthew, puts an heavy accent on the keeping of the law. Nonetheless, there are also differences in emphasis, as mentioned at the end of Chapter 8. In all events, it appears that the third phase of Matthew originated in a Jewish-Christian context akin to that of James and the *Didache*.

In stating this, however, only half of the story of Matthew is told. We have repeatedly drawn attention to the ambivalent character of this Gospel. Alongside prominent Jewish-Christian accents, it also exhibits an orientation towards non-Jews with clear anti-Jewish implications. Again, within a wider context this time, we raise the question as to which circumstances can account for this situation. We are reminded even more strongly that the Gospel texts with which we are familiar are each the product of a community with an eventful history.

The last phase of Matthew must have emerged from a non-Jewish church of uncertain location. Whatever its provenance, this church must have represented a group that initially did not feel repelled by the pronounced Jewish-Christian character of the Gospel. The extra emphasis upon the prophets gives the impression that the legal side of the Gospel was repressed so that the statement 'not to annul but to fulfil' (Mt. 5.17) was altered so as to apply to 'the law *and the prophets*'. A following step of decisive importance was a revision in an anti-Jewish sense, to be distinguished from the anti-Pharisaic emphasis that still fits entirely within the third, Jewish-Christian phase. We have listed certain striking anti-Jewish passages: the rumour that Jesus' body was stolen, the exclamation about Jesus' blood, the moral of the parable of the tenants of the vineyard, the venemous finale of the healing on the Shabbat, in agreement with Mark's version, and the conclusion of the report about the centurion of Capernaum (Mt. 28.15; 27.34; 21.43; 12.14; 8.12). These passages can be seen as defining a position in relation to the Jews so that the standpoint of the evangelist is made clear to the reader. They generate a tendency to read the other anti-Pharisaic passages throughout the whole of the Gospel as anti-Jewish as well.

At this point, a comparison with John is important. In both cases, a Jewish-Christian polemic against fellow-Jews is transposed to an explicit non-Jewish framework and acquires a strong anti-Jewish effect. The result is the confusing *combination of intra-Jewish and anti-Jewish polemics*. There are, however, two important distinctions: the Johannine diabolizing of the opponents and the generalization of opponents to 'the Jews' are both lacking in Matthew. The virulence of the Johannine anti-Judaism is thus brought out more sharply.

Finally, the synoptic relatedness of Mark and Matthew to Luke reflects a broader, shared context. Apparently, from the beginning Mark was intended for a non-Jewish public, and Luke, which is based upon Mark, exhibits affinity with the Pauline churches. The picture is painted of a climate in which non-Jewish churches participated in the Jewish-Christian tradition, and one is reminded of the mutual understanding that was originally present between Pauline and Jewish churches. On the other hand, Paul demonstrates that he took the apostolic tradition of Jesus' words completely seriously. It is thus conceivable that the synoptic tradition in its amorphous, oral form was shared by Jewish and Pauline churches alike, whereby a basis was created for the broader acceptance of the Gospel of Mark.

In this climate it is understandable that Matthew was originally adopted by the non-Jewish churches, even more so since this Gospel was based upon Mark and since the *Didache*, a related Jewish-Christian document, also takes non-Jews into account. This Pauline–Jewish-Christian milieu, however, fell apart, and the Pauline churches that were a part of it suffered a schism. The final text of Matthew should probably be seen as the product of the anti-Jewish faction of this originally broader milieu, a product that, perhaps precisely because of the striking Jewish-Christian material it also contains, turned out to be much more anti-Jewish than Mark.

Gnostic Gospels
Gnostic writings can be useful for filling in the picture of first-century movements. The *Gospel of Thomas* and the *Gospel of Philip* are of particular significance because they exhibit the clearest continuity with the synoptic tradition and Jewish-Christian elements. They must have acquired their definite form around the end of the second and half way through the third century, respectively.

The *Gospel of Thomas* comprises a long series of loosely connected sayings of Jesus without the customary narrative framework of the canonical Gospels. This form is seen as an ancient manner of passing on Jesus' words, the same form that the presumed synoptic sayings source, *Q*, would have had. Furthermore, various sayings are closely related to the synoptic tradition, but have often a more concise form. It is not impossible that words of Jesus are preserved here that are not found elsewhere or of which the form encountered elsewhere is less original. A number of the aphorisms, however, are clearly later and are inspired by lines of thought unfamiliar to the synoptic tradition. Thus, after several lovely short sayings about the splinter and the beam, about fasting and Shabbat, we read the following: 'Jesus said: I took my place in the midst of the world, and I appeared to them in the flesh; I found them all drunk...' (*Gos. Thom.* 26–28). An undeniable estrangement from Judaism is reflected in the following: 'You do not know who I am from what I say to you, but *you have become as the Jews*; for they love the tree and hate its fruit or love the fruit but hate the tree' (43). Remarkably, women are presented as 'masculine', that is, sexless, in order to be able to be partakers in 'life' (114).

The *Gospel of Philip* is conspicuous for the attention it gives to names and their significance. These are sometimes explained etymologically from Hebrew or Aramaic (*Gos. Phil.* col. 62.13; 63.22), but more often allegorically. A main theme is the recurring extrapolation of the deeper reality of names, elements, or sacraments from their externals, usually with a mystifying twist: 'Through water and fire the whole place is cleansed—the visible through the visible, the hidden through the hidden. Some things are hidden through the visible things. There is water in water, there is fire in anointment' (57.22-27). Often reference is made to the 'Hebrews'—here the designation for the Jews—as a group with which there was a previous relation: '*When we were Hebrews*, we were orphans and had only our mother, but when we became Christians, we had both a father and a mother' (52.21-24). With these last words possibly Eve, God and Mary or Wisdom are intended.

Undeniably both works contain elements that are akin to the synoptic tradition. Just as clearly there is the all-determinant, 'evasive' tendency to make things mystical, which transposes related text material into an alienating framework. In a more radical manner than in the Gospel of John, the groups here speaking differentiate themselves from the Jewish-Christian and Pauline milieus. Furthermore, the texts apparently circulated only after a consensus had already been reached on the New Testament canon. Their significance lies in their reminder to us that authentic traditions existed outside of the growing canon. On the other hand, they indicate as well that the consensus concerning the canon arose early and with inherent authority.

Conclusion: The Canon of the New Testament
None of the canonical Gospels derives directly from Jewish-Christian circles, but all four have a Jewish-Christian background, the first three through the broadly rooted synoptic tradition, and the fourth in the more isolated Johannine context. The isolation of John disappeared when the Gospel sailed into non-Jewish seas; its by then well-developed sharp anti-Jewish accentuations appealed to both Gnostic and orthodox Christians. Matthew and Mark each underwent a final last redaction in a non-Jewish milieu where the anti-Jewish position dominated.

Luke is the only Gospel that shows no evidence of an anti-Jewish revision, but, in contrast, emphasizes continuity with Judaism. Together with Acts, this Gospel was written by a non-Jewish disciple of Paul, who, in a time of strongly increasing tensions, described the idyllic initial period of a unified church for Jews and non-Jews. The depiction gave us cause to wonder whether this was not a conscious correction of the dominant climate of the time. Finally, the writings of Paul are not only the oldest of the New Testament, but are also the most direct witness to the movement that began with the gospel of Jesus and within a generation fanned out to be the good news for Jews and Greeks alike.

Meanwhile the Jewish churches in Galilee and Judaea transmitted the message of Jesus further within their own tradition. Most of their writings have been lost so that information about them must be gathered from outsiders or opponents. In a lost corner of the New Testament, between the Epistle to the Hebrews and Revelation, the Epistles of Jude and James, possibly brothers of Jesus, were preserved as silent, but unique testimonies to the Jewish birthplace of Christianity.

The canon of the New Testament grew in a non-Jewish, more or less Pauline milieu. The oldest core was possibly the Pauline canon, comprising the letters of this apostle to the nations and the writings of his fellow-worker Luke. Nonetheless, the anti-Jewish reading, apparent in Ignatius's letters and in the final texts of Mark and Matthew, became dominant. John did not originally belong to this environment, but was later incorporated into it; his virulent antagonism towards the Jews corresponded to the anti-Jewish reading given to Paul and the synoptic Gospels. Jude, James and Revelation were only recognized as canonical one or two centuries later, perhaps because of their assumed apostolic reputation. Their Jewish-Christian identity, however, became neutralized within the latter framework. The *Didache* and related books fell outside of the canon due to a lack of apostolic credit, nor did the Gnostic writings have a chance of being included in the canon due to their opposition to the apostolic tradition. The anti-Jewish and anti-Gnostic delineation of the proto-orthodox church created a preference for *apostolic texts read anti-Jewishly*.

Dealing with Anti-Judaism in the New Testament

From the survey given, in so far as it is correct, the reader can derive diverse implications. The result will be different for an agnostic opponent of anti-Semitism than for a practising Jew and again different for a

Christian. If Christians want to reread the New Testament with a new sensitivity 'after Auschwitz', they will be confronted with painful questions. How is one to treat a New Testament that as a whole has an anti-Jewish encasement? What is one to do with the passages in Matthew in which the Jews are rejected, and with the sharp anti-Judaism of John? Though some declare that they no longer can read such passages aloud with a clear conscience, it remains true that both simple believers and prominent theologians draw their deepest inspiration from the Gospel of John, which is of old the Gospel lesson for the high holidays and remains the cornerstone of christological dogmas.

The depth of this dilemma is expressed by Gregory Baum, an American Roman Catholic theologian of non-religious Jewish descent. In his book *The Jews and the Gospel* (1961), he attempted to consider seriously the question of whether the New Testament contained anti-Jewish statements. He was moved to do so after reading the passionate indictment by the Jewish historian Jules Isaac, *Jésus et Israël* (1948), who singled out the beginning of church anti-Judaism in Matthew and John. Baum's answer was to state that the New Testament was God's revealed source of salvation and *could* not proclaim hate towards the Jewish people. Where one presumes to find such in the text, it must be blamed on confusion caused by the interpretation of the church fathers and later exegetes. Baum could not, however, maintain his position. In his introduction to the book of Rosemary Ruether, *Faith and Fratricide* (1974), Baum admits that he had been too optimistic in his earlier work, and that the New Testament indeed does contain anti-Judaism. The question remains, How can Christians read the New Testament as a document of God's revelation?

The present author is of the opinion that this question can only be answered by means of a question that must precede it: *exactly where* do we encounter anti-Judaism in the New Testament? This question has been the point of departure for this book, and in successive chapters the road towards an answer has been traced: *to read with as much honesty and differentiation as possible*. Reading honestly involves that we do not shield the New Testament on the basis of some a priori conviction, that we thus allow ourselves to be open to the unpleasant possibility that cherished Bible portions might not be infallible on this point. To read with differentiation means that the New Testament should not be rejected as a whole as an anti-Jewish book because of disappointment over this fallibility, but that, with patience, sobriety and good sense, we sound out and distinguish from one another those portions that need to be regarded in this way and that do not. Rosemary Ruether's book itself is not above critique in this respect. She approaches the New Testament in its totality as the earliest expression of anti-Judaism and states that this is the direct corollary of confessing Jesus to be the Messiah. Her position would make every one who broke bread in Jesus' name—from the first disciples onwards—anti-Jewish! The portions in her book about the church fathers and the Middle Ages are undergirded in a much better fashion.

Our study has brought a series of gradations to light in the early Christian attitude towards the Jews and Judaism. Jesus and his disciples maintained a somewhat eccentric position within Judaism, but one of great involvement, and the Jewish churches continued to disseminate Jesus' gospel within the framework of the law. Paul struggled for one unified church of Jews and non-Jews who would respect each other's individual characteristics, and the two volumes of Luke are a deliberate, later token of support of this. In Mark and Matthew the message of Jesus eventually came to be encased in a framework implying aversion for the Jews, and in John this antipathy is sharpened into hatred. To that more limited extent Ruether's position is correct.

This variegated result is disenchanting. There is no basis for a mass collective indictment, nor for a gallant defence. Like all human endeavours in the area of religion and culture, the New Testament is an inextricable blending of grandeur and failure. The writer of each Gospel and of each epistle saw himself as the mirror of a light that is too great to be contained. The thickness of the layer of dust and smudges on each mirror is not the same and these affect the clarity of the reflection. None of the mirrors offers more than an image of what it has received. Does not the apostle himself write, 'For now we see through a glass darkly,' and, 'Hope that is seen is not hope; for how can one hope for something which he has already seen?' (1 Cor. 13.12; Rom. 8.24; cf. Heb. 11.1). The question for Christians reading with hope is not so much whether, but to which extent they can read the New Testament as a document of God's revelation.

The same is also applicable to the Old Testament, even apart from the general question of its value within the Christian perspective. A story like that of the flood, where all life is annihilated because humankind had corrupted the earth, confronts an honestly thinking person with major questions (Gen. 6). What about the terrible dilemma of Abraham when God ordered him to offer his son, 'his only one, his beloved' (Gen. 22.2)? What are we to think of the commandment that a 'rebellious son' is to be stoned, just as someone who unintentionally violated the Shabbat (Deut. 21.18-21; Num. 15.32-36)?

Various attitudes are possible here, and that was also the case in early Judaism. The *Book of Jubilees* prescribes point-blank the death sentence for everyone who does 'anything' on Shabbat, such as talking about work or drawing water (*Jub.* 50.8). Striving for humaneness in jurisdiction (see pp. 55-56), the Pharisees and rabbis decided that only he who in defiance of an explicit warning intentionally violates the Shabbat is guilty of death, and that the intentionally rebellious son 'never has existed and never will' (*t. Sanh.* 11.3, 6; *Sifre Numbers*, *shalah* 114, p. 123). Nonetheless, these difficult passages were not skipped over: 'Then why is it written (about the rebellious son)? In order that you study it and become a better person' (*b. Sanh.* 71a).

The rabbis' approach to the Torah is also conceivable for Christians in their reading of the New Testament. Would it not be possible to honestly admit to having difficulties with certain passages, without deleting these from the Bible or removing them from the list of texts to be read aloud? The anti-Jewish effect of John's Gospel is not neutralized by leaving the book closed. Due to the prevailing interpretation of John, shared by friend and foe alike, the texts continue to have their own effect anyway, with this difference: both when read uncritically and when left unread, their effect is not verifiable, and, therefore, not correctable. This is the profound significance of 'studying it and becoming a better person'. On the other hand, the 'difficult' passages should not be read aloud without supplying an explanation concerning the time and context from which they emerged. This honest and discerning information helps the readers to take a proper distance from the content without rejecting it entirely.

The historical approach that we have followed in the preceding chapters can be of great help to us here. The diversity is not only between the various parts of the New Testament, but also within them. This is not in the last place true of the Gospel of John. Distinction has been made between the layers in the stories of healing on the Shabbat and the anti-Jewish framework in which these were encased (see pp. 316-17). Because it is possible to take the deepest layer of the story seriously and more or less ignore the anti-Jewish framework in which it has been placed, one can read the latter as belonging to a later phase of the Gospel. This phenomenon can be observed more often. The announcement that it was the Jews who sent priests and Levites to John the Baptist is not only peculiar but also unnecessary for understanding the story (Jn 1.19). It is an eloquent example of how the evangelist projected the conflict with the Jews from his own time back on to an early phase of the Gospel. There are also passages and chapters where this later layer of conflict apparently was not superimposed, such as the stories of the Samaritan woman and of Lazarus, which on other grounds we noted to be older sections (Jn 4; 11–12). If we read the Gospel with an awareness of its possible history, it could be that the original message will be heard in a purer form.

In the Gospel of Matthew, the stark contrast between the Jewish-Christian and the anti-Jewish phases begs, as it were, for a historically differentiated manner of reading. Only then can one fully do justice to the statement of Jesus that he came 'to *fulfil* the law and the prophets', without veiling the painful fact that anti-Jewish texts are also present.

At the deepest level, the question is how the early Christian authors, on the one hand, and their contemporary Christian readers, on the other, have dealt with or should deal with the fundamental duality of the correspondence with and the distinction from the Jews. We spoke of this in the introduction and are now able to pursue it further. The issue need not remain purely theoretical: a historical example is available within the Pauline tradition. The schism there revealed two manners of dealing with the duality, two manners of reading Paul's letters and the Gospels. The Ignatian option, which gained the upper hand, took over the Jewish and Jewish-Christian elements, but emphasized the difference with the Jews and *repressed the consciousness of affinity*. In this way the duality became ambivalence, the tense two-facedness towards the Jews that unfortunately still characterizes much of orthodox Christianity.

In contrast, within the option of the Lukan minority, the differences between Jews and non-Jews and between Jewish and non-Jewish Christians were accepted within a broader perspective of kinship. The author of Luke and Acts did not need, therefore, to obscure the growing intolerance of Jewish-Christians towards the non-Jewish brothers, nor to relinquish the pluriform vision of Paul. This author's subtly written two-volumed work granted to later readers the hopeful example of the account of a Christian faith not based upon a denial of Judaism.

Reading in an Open Community

Encouraged by the hopeful example of Luke and Acts, we conclude this book with a contemplation of the church as a Scripture-reading community. In this it is a full sister of the synagogue, where, as we saw in Chapter 2, the reading of the Torah is the most distinctive characteristic.

In this context we return to our observations about liturgical reading presented in the Introduction. Reading the Scriptures in the liturgy creates a meaningful structure within time. Within the framework of weekly meetings, portions from the Scriptures—in this context called the Holy Scriptures—are read, in which the reading congregation as a whole and each individual gradually comes to recognize themselves. The stories of the creation, the patriarchs, the exodus, the revelation at Sinai and the wilderness journey, as well as the prophetic descriptions of entry into the promised land and of kingship, exile and return, become the story of the reading congregation from week to week. Before long, the early church added to these the Gospel stories and the epistles, sometimes also Revelation (Col. 4.16; Rev. 1.3). *A reading congregation defines itself through the writings that it reads.*

The time perspective evoked by this manner of reading generates a double unity: that of the reading congregation and that of the Scriptures that are read. Weekly, in the gathering around the reading of the Scriptures, the essence of the church renews itself, as the synagogue does as well. Subsequently, through the regular meetings, this community also creates a unity of the divergent writings that it reads. The whole of the Scriptures is a read unity. Its holiness is based on its being read aloud in the congregation. *The canon of holy writings emerges from the reading of the congregation.*

Of old, the liturgical reading of Scripture also entails a demarcation. Thus it was that the early church distinguished itself from the Gnostic groups where the Old Testament and church authority were rejected and where their own esoteric writings were read alongside generally accepted Christian texts. The church refused to accept these writings and thereby also the community that believed in them. Thus it was also that Marcion, who shared with the Gnostics the rejection of the Old Testament, was excommunicated by the proto-orthodox church. The church unhestitatingly decided to continue the reading of the Old Testament alongside the accepted Gospels and other apostolic writings.

That this was indeed the case is testified to by the 'picture books' of the ancient church—mosaics and paintings. Among the mosaics on the side wall of the Santa Maria Maggiore in Rome (fifth century) just as many scenes from the Old Testament as from the New are depicted. The eclipse of the reading of the Old Testament did not begin until the Middle Ages. The rejection of Marcion confirms that the church canon first and foremost contained the Old Testament; this must also have been the case in the oldest 'Pauline canon'. *Through the reading of the Old Testament, the church maintained her original link with the synagogue.*

This continuity is but one side of the coin, for the reading community that was to become the church also defined itself as being separate from the synagogue. Besides the Law, the Prophets and the Psalms, which it shared with the synagogue, the church also read the Gospels and other apostolic writings as 'Holy Writ'. In its essential form of a community that reads Scriptures, the church expressed thus the fundamental duality of its affinity with and distinction from the synagogue. Not only does it, in fellowship with the synagogue, read that which it came to call the 'Old' Testament: *in contrast to the synagogue, the church reads the 'New' Testament as well.*

The question again is, what importance did the Scripture-reading church attach to this duality of kinship and distinction? A remarkable answer is to be found in another church mosaic in Rome, above the entrance to the Santa Sabina, also from the fifth century. On both sides there is the noble figure of a woman as an allegory of the two forms of the church, elucidated by the comment ECCLESIA EX CIRCVMCISIONE —ECCLESIA EX GENTIBVS, 'The church of the circumcision—the church of the nations'. A similar scene from the same time is located in the apsis of the Santa Pudenziana. Thus apparently in the fifth century in Rome the ideal that Paul and the apostles of Jerusalem once had agreed upon still persisted (Gal. 2.9). *A non-Jewish church that reads the Scriptures in open communion with a Jewish church preserves the awareness of its affinity with the Jews.*

A disparate answer, apparently the negative application of what has just been related, became popular in the Middle Ages and is depicted as such in stone in a number of churches in the Rhineland, including those in Treves and Strasbourg. There are indications, however, that this scene also originated in antiquity. Here again there are two figures of women, but this time a triumphant church confronting a defeated, blindfolded synagogue; hereby the attitude of the (proto-)orthodox church has been fixed in stone. *A church that sees itself as the glorious successor to the synagogue represses its affinity with Judaism.*

It is not only a matter of what the church reads, but also of how it reads. The history of the Pauline tradition can again serve as a guideline. Marcion retained the core of the Pauline collection, the Pauline and Lukan writings, but rejected the Old Testament. This placed the writings of Paul and Luke in a totally different, anti-Jewish framework. The majority decided to expand the Pauline canon on the basis of a continued reading of the Old Testament; nonetheless, an anti-Jewish reading of Paul and other apostolic writings had already taken root among the same proto-orthodox majority, as can be seen in the case of Ignatius, the bishop of Antioch. *Retention of the Old Testament is a necessary but not a sufficient prerequisite for correcting an anti-Jewish reading of the New Testament.*

The truth of this statement is apparent from the canon that began to delineate itself during these happenings. To the core of Pauline and Lukan writings, which make up just half of the final total, were added Mark, Matthew and John, so that by the middle of the second century there were 'four Gospels'. The text then could not have been much different from that of our oldest manuscripts, that is, it comprised Mark, with its incidental anti-Jewish additions, Matthew, with its contrast between Jewish-Christian and anti-Jewish portions, and John, which on the whole was edited in a sharply anti-Jewish manner. The Ignatian majority then read the Pauline writings anti-Jewishly, and by implication also the Lukan writings. *The proto-orthodox church read not only the Old, but also the New Testament in an anti-Jewish framework.*

The writings of the church fathers provide ample witness to the anti-Jewish reading of the Old Testament. An early document in this field, the *Dialogue with Trypho the Jew* by Justin (also mid second century), is one grand argument on the basis of the Old Testament to prove the church's being in the right. Though this is in itself understandable, the point is that Justin places the non-Jewish church and its practices as 'the true Israel according to the Spirit' diametrically opposed to the Jews and their law (*Dial.* 11-12). The Old Testament is read exclusively from the point of view of the non-Jewish church and its way of life. *The anti-Jewish reading practice of the church is founded in its exclusive demarcation with regard to the Jews.*

Such an exclusive manner of reading was not new: it occurred also within Judaism. In fact it is based upon the general human tendency to view one's own group as absolute. The Qumran texts exhibit the dualistic mentality of a group of people who read the Scriptures in an exclusive manner and place themselves in opposition to their fellow-Jews. This mentality is expressed in the manner in which they celebrated the Shabbat and feast days, applied the purity and marriage laws, and interpreted the history of their own time. They considered their interpretation of the Scriptures and the law to be divinely inspired and indisputable. *Judaism as well contains groups that read the Scriptures as a closed community of the elect.*

In this the Pharisees manifested a different attitude, summarized in the adage of Hillel against a mentality like that of the Essenes: 'Do not separate yourself from the community' (*m. Ab.* 2.4). Their approach to internal disagreement is not that of the Essenes. The schools of Shammai and Hillel had whole series of disagreements about purity and marriage laws; nonetheless, they visited one another as guests and married into each other's families (*t. Yeb.* 1.10-13). The final prevalence of the Hillellites did not mean that the Shammaite tradition was abolished: 'A heavenly voice came which said: both opinions are words of the living God, but the decision is according to the school of Hillel' (*y. Ber.* 1.3b; *b. 'Erub.* 13). This should be taken as a sagacious legend, for the Talmud teaches that the revelation of an heavenly voice does not decide in matters of halakah. In a famous dispute, the Shammaite R. Eliezer called upon all sorts of miracles and even upon a heavenly voice, but the Hillelite R. Yoshua said: 'She (the Torah) is not in heaven' (Deut. 30.12). The matter was settled in a human manner, and 'heaven' acquiesced (*b. B. Meṣ.* 59b). It is not by coincidence that these traditions are all handed down within *the Hillelite tradition whose interpretation of Judaism represents a pluriform conception of the Scripture-reading congregation.*

The benevolent attitude of the Hillelites extended to the non-Jews as well. The Hillelites were open for proselytes and recognized the possibility that non-Jews would share in the world to come, while the Shammaites maintained a closed attitude, in which only godlessness was to be expected from non-Jews. The indications of participation in the synagogue services of a notable number of non-Jewish 'God fearers' in Asia Minor, Syria and Palestine (see p. 88) also witness to this openness. *The Hillelites and other broad-minded Jews read the Scriptures in an open fellowship with God-fearing non-Jews.*

This open-heartedness entailed that one's own community was not viewed as absolute but was seen within the perspective of God's mercy that will extend to all of humankind at the end of time. This is expressed in the following tradition:

> Every dispute for the sake of Heaven shall endure, but when it is not for the sake of Heaven it shall not endure.—What is such a dispute for the sake of Heaven? That is *the dispute between Shammai and Hillel.* [...] Every assembly (*knēsiyâ*) for the sake of Heaven shall endure, but when it is not for the sake of Heaven, it shall not endure.—What is such an assembly for the sake of Heaven? That is *the assembly of our fathers before Sinai* [...] (*ARN* A40/B46, fol. 64b-65a; cf. *m. Ab.* 5.17).

This saying characterizes the Hillelite tradition, which passes on the opponent's opinion along with its own and allows the two to coexist side by side until the Judgment Day. The second part expresses that they did not even take the 'assembly' of Israel that received the revelation from Sinai to be absolute. The right of existence of that assembly relies on their invocation of 'Heaven', the God who redeemed Israel and gave it his Torah. *The Hillelite tradition sees Israel as a community that continues to exist as long it reads the Torah 'for the sake of Heaven'.*

The preceding statement is vulnerable and needs to be protected under certain circumstances. In no way should we entertain the illusion that such statements are detached from actual history. Reading in an open community does not mean that one should be blind to the reality of evil, including that present in human conduct. The history of the Jewish community in Hellenistic-Roman Alexandria, once a paragon of refinement and tolerance, proves the reality of this vulnerability (see pp. 36-38). The openness and susceptibility with which Jews themselves formulate their religious congregation does not give others the right to place charges against them, let alone to attack them. It is not without reason that the Hillelites continued to hand down the more distrustful and assertive standpoint of the Shammaites along with their own. *Reading Scriptures in an open community entails that, if necessary, one takes up arms to combat evil and injustice.*

Reading the Bible in an exclusive manner within a closed community is not a Christian patent but is based on the general human tendency of self-protection, and it also occurred in early Judaism. Likewise, reading in an open community is not the prerogative of the Hillelite rabbis, although it cannot be coincidental that the most open-minded reading in ancient Christian circles shows resemblances to the Hillelite tradition. Reading always entails interpreting, which means understanding a text within a new context. Communal reading means that one relates the reading congregation to that context as well. There is correlation between the delineation of the community and the context within which it reads. *Those who read within a broad perspective also view themselves as members of an open community, and vice versa.*

It is thus not surprising that in this regard the varieties of early Christianity are analogous to those of Judaism. Comparable to the community reflected in the Qumran Scrolls, the Johannine writings reveal a closed community that views matters dualistically and exclusively, diabolizes opponents and assumes its own interpretation to be absolute. Transmitting this tradition within a demarcated anti-Jewish framework led, according to our analysis, to the development of Christian hatred of the Jews. On another level, from the middle of the first century onwards, a line began to be drawn between Jewish and non-Jewish churches. On both sides reading was done not so much dualistically as from the context of a sharpened distinction between Jews and non-Jews. This is somewhat comparable to the Shammaite attitude. Finally, in early Christian circles there was also a tradition that consciously exerted effort to read as an open community, taking into account the differences between Jews and non-Jews and even those between believing and non-believing Jews. *The Pauline–Lukan tradition is akin to the Hillelite tradition in both form and content.*

At the end of Chapter 4, we have seen how Paul in Romans 9–11 depicts the congregation of Israel standing in front of Sinai, where it received the Torah and where it conducts its own dialogue with God over the ultimately correct interpretation. The fact that Israel was refractory does not annul its having been chosen: in the end 'all Israel shall be saved'. Paul, a former disciple of Gamaliel and an apostle of Jesus to the non-Jews, conceived of two simultaneous 'elections': that of the multi-membered body of Christ alongside that of the one people of Israel. Neither of the two 'assemblies' cancels the other, both rightfully appeal to the words of the living God. Not before the end of time will it become apparent what in God's name is a correct judgment in the matter. The passage closes appropriately with a song of praise to God's inscrutable wisdom. *Paul views the community of Israel (synagōgē) and the church composed of Jews and non-Jews* (ekklēsia) *as two open communities within the perspective of God's history.*

That, too, is a vulnerable statement. Who can pretend to stand above both ways of believing, above the faithfulness to the Torah of Moses and above the trust in Jesus, God's Messiah? A higher position than being a member of one of the two communities, or a member of both, as Paul himself was, is not attainable for a human, and even then her or his knowledge would be only partial. Beyond the confession of Israel or of the church no human pronouncement is possible, and that which goes beyond, surpasses all understanding. On principle, the agnostic or sceptic does not commit himself and does not utter such exalted words, and his or her statements by axiom remain within human limitations. Only a radical atheist takes it upon himself to pass final judgment. *A right to decisive evaluation concerning the truth of one religion or another is not reserved for humankind.*

This leads us back to the rabbinical adage about the different assemblies that continue to exist if they are 'for the sake of Heaven'. The saying must have been known in one form or the other to the author of Acts. Let us return to the report of the incident where the Sadducean high priest and his temple administration judged the apostles of Jesus to be a heretical messianic movement and threatened them with death, which was averted by the intervention of Gamaliel. Of particular significance is the fact that this episode has a strategic place in the whole of Luke–Acts. The apostles are arraigned by the high priest, as Jesus was earlier, and Paul later. They are then released due to Gamaliel's intervention. Gamaliel was a well-known figure in his day, and it cannot be a coincidence that our author also reports that he was Paul's teacher (Acts 23.3). Finally, even the last reported conversation of Paul in Rome is a dispute with an open end due to the fact that the Jewish leaders were not in agreement about what he brought forward (see p. 230).

Further confirmation of the assumption that the Lukan author was familiar with the Hillelite maxim is to be found in its terminology. The word that we translated as 'meeting' is *kᵉnēsiyâ*; it is related to *knesset*, which occurs more often, also being used for 'synagogue'. Incidentally, *kᵉnēsiyâ* is also the modern Hebrew word for 'church', and we can thus see it as a synonym of the Greek *ekklēsia* (see pp. 24-25). Before this word came to signify 'church' pre-eminently, however, it meant 'meeting' in the general sense. This appears to be reflected in the Greek word *boulē* used by Gamaliel in this passage. Though usually translated as 'plan' or 'council', not incorrectly, it would be more understandably rendered 'council' or just 'assembly'.

In the midst of the arraignments against Jesus' gospel by the Sadducees and their consorts, the author of the story, this disciple of Paul, let the plea for release come from the leading Pharisee from the line of Hillel. *Through Gamaliel's speech, 'Luke' confirms his testimony to a 'church' assembled around Jesus that is not opposed to, but is side by side with Israel*:

> When they heard this they were enraged and took counsel to execute them. But a Pharisee in the council named Gamaliel, a teacher of the law, held in honour by all the people, stood up and ordered the men to be put outside for a while. And he said to them, 'Men of Israel, take care what you do with these men. For before these days Theudas arose, giving himself out to be somebody...but he was slain and all who followed him were dispersed and came to nothing. After him Judas the Galilean arose...he also perished... So in the present case I tell you, keep away from these men and let them alone; for if this assembly or this undertaking is of men, it will fall apart; but if it is of God, you will not be able to make it fall apart. You might even be found opposing God!' (Acts 5.33-39).

ACCOUNTING FOR THE METHODOLOGY

The preceding is an interpretational description of the New Testament with unrelenting attention for the relationship to Judaism. It is an expansion of an originally intended monograph on *anti-Judaism in the New Testament*. By broadening the perspective, the New Testamental traces of anti-Judaism are perceived as a part of the general attitude towards the Jews. Through this, as explained in the Introduction, both the Jewish origin of Christianity and early Christian anti-Judaism are exposed. The result is somewhat of an 'introduction to the New Testament' from an unusual angle.

Customarily, the New Testament is viewed only as the oldest collection of Christian writings, or as the earliest Christian document. The fact that Jews also play a role, not only as interlocutors and opponents, but primarily as main characters, is of secondary importance in this approach. Nowadays almost no one denies that the gospel emerged from a Jewish context and was propagated as such by Jesus and his first followers. This fact, however, usually remains a coincidental detail. Thus the possibility that certain writings portray considerable tension with and even hatred towards the Jews is at most an interesting but far from determinant aspect.

In this volume, such aspects are in the foreground. This is not done arbitrarily nor due to the indulgence of a personal preference, for from the earliest beginnings of Christianity, the relationship to Judaism was an issue. The entirety of nascent Christianity is inconceivable apart from this connection. Thus the whole of the emergence of the New Testament must be viewed in direct relationship to the development of the church, and these both in a continuous relationship to the history of the Jews and their literature.

At the beginning of the nineteenth century, such a broad design was envisaged during the first phase of historical criticism. The attempt ran aground, however, due to insurmountable barriers. In the first place, the inherited dichotomy between Judaism and Christianity prevented a merging of Jewish and Christian expertise. The separation between Christian 'historical criticism' and its Jewish counterpart, the *Wissenschaft des Judentums*, began to diminish only during the second half of the twentieth century. Secondly, scholars are scattered among historical and literary specializations. This book assumes fundamental coherence of these specializations and scientific traditions.

With the progressive fragmentation into historical and literary specializations, awareness of the correlation between the history of ancient writings and of the communities from which they emerged also dwindled. A significant methodological aspect of this book is, therefore, the observation of the documents together with their historical context. Primary attention is given to this in the initial and final chapters. Theoretically speaking, we hereby take into account that we possess these writings only through the selective processes of history, that our knowledge of the society of that time is limited by the irony of history, and that we can only counter this by our own enlightened irony of the hermeneutical circle. Information on the historical context is acquired primarily from literary documents, but adequate interpretation of the documents is only possible through a multifaceted image of the historical context. This is true as well of the coming into being of the New Testament, in its components and its entirety. The New Testament is, therefore, continually observed in relationship to the Jewish society of its day.

As a consequence, in our approach to the texts there can never be a fundamental contrast between historical and literary analytical methods such as close reading, structural analysis, etc. On the contrary, literary analysis assumes always, however indirectly, the workings of a human brain within a particular situation and therefore forms in our viewpoint an indispensable component of historical criticism in a broader sense.

We operate thus along the overlapping peripheries of the traditional fields of Jewish studies, New Testament and Church History. For those interested in Jewish history, this book will therefore at times seem too 'Christian'. Those interested only in the roots of anti-Semitism will be confronted with a mass of religious and theological data, not to mention the numerous Jewish and other sources with which one solely interested in Christian matters is faced. It is more than a rearrangement of the subjects of theology: a paradigm shift is implied in several directions. The extent to which this has succeeded remains, of course, to be seen.

We have learned to think of Judaism and Christianity as two religiously and theologically mutually exclusive blocks. Historically viewed, this is an impossibility. This conception is primarily a mediaeval creation whose roots go back to the Byzantine period. In the fourth century, non-Jewish Christianity crystallized opposite to rabbinic Judaism, which had reached maturity in the meantime. Thus there came an end to a process of growth of several centuries in which, from a great variety of movements and groups, not only these two main groups emerged, but also their most important documents. The many Jewish, Christian and Jewish-Christian groups and sects that had existed until that time gradually disappeared from history, together with their writings. Thus a proportionate amount of witnesses to this creative, pre-classical period of Judaism and Christianity slipped away from us.

The traditional image of Judaism, primarily formed by the rabbinic tradition, is but partially applicable to the circumstances in the first century, certainly as far as the Jewish environment is concerned from which the earliest layers of the New Testament emerged. Information from the writings from Qumran forms an indispensable supplement and teaches us how pluriform Judaism of that day was and what kinds of 'eccentric' milieus it could include.

On the other hand, the traditional image of the beginnings of Christianity needs adjustment. Christians are accustomed to viewing Jesus and his disciples as a phenomenon totally unique in their day, which if not literally then certainly figuratively fell from the sky. One must, in constrast, attempt to picture devout Jewish milieus where the 'consolation of Israel' was impatiently anticipated with fasting, prayer and attentive reading of the prophetical books. It was in such an environment that Jesus must have been formed and where the gospel emerged that he and his disciples propagated.

The simultaneous correction of both of these conceptions presumes furthermore a critical and integrated relationship between theology and historiography and involves a revision of scientific models in our postmodern era. On the one hand, the intimate involvement of the researcher with his or her religious object is as unavoidable as it is essential to arriving at a congenial and pure manner of reading. On the other hand, it is imperative that the readers see both themselves and the authors of 'Jewish' and 'Christian' sources as historically determined subjects. The history of anti-Semitism as a secular phenomenon is largely that of Christian and Jewish groups and individuals whose motives are unfathomable without direct knowledge of their religious documents. Perhaps the political collapse of radical materialism and the expansion of the power of religious fundamentalism provide extra incentives to think through anew the positive and negative significance of 'the theological factor' in history.

The correction of these conceptions makes the customary distinction between 'Jewish' and 'Christian' texts in the first centuries untenable. We must learn to live with the fact that the initial phase of the gospel tradition is part and parcel of Jewish history. I have become convinced that such an approach can render a wealth in new insights and in fact a completely novel impulse to synoptic, Pauline, Johannine and patristic studies, not to mention the various Judaistic, rabbinic and Talmudic disciplines.

Regarding the style of this book, scientific terminology and methodology have been avoided. Discussions with colleagues remain hereby in most cases implicit. I am keenly aware of the inherent disadvantages of this approach because this book contains many ideas and insights as yet not published elsewhere. Though a complete bibliography has not been provided, the reader is offered the literature that appeared to be the most important; some of the author's more recent publications have been added here. Alongside the drawback of the inescapable limitation involved, a synthesis like the present one offers the advantage of versatile thinking from the perspective of a greater whole—a rare commodity in our age of affluence.

Conversely, the discussion of the texts is done in extensive detail. In that respect, this book is more of an interpretative commentary on the New Testament than a summarizing introduction. One drawback to traditional introductions is hereby avoided: the impression of there being fixed historical and literary 'facts', as though each introduction could be other than a résumé of interpretations. Our method entails as well that various themes usually reserved for the 'Theology of the New Testament' are treated extensively. In Chapter 3, for example, the problem of the historical Jesus is approached both from a historical and a theological angle. The discussion in the final chapter on the formation of the canon is also both theologically and historically relevant.

The translations from Greek, Latin, Hebrew and Aramaic are the author's own. The editions mentioned refer to the originals further specified in the list of sources.

A few remarks should be made on the terminology. The customary usage of 'Old' and 'New Testament' has been maintained, in spite of the known objections: the Old is not antiquated, neither did the New come in its place. 'First and Second Testament' has been suggested, but the objection is that it does not express that which is new, which in the viewpoint of Jesus and his disciples certainly did come. In view of 'liturgical reading' discussed in the final chapter, the author takes the customary terms to be both understandable and acceptable.

Due to modern religious–political developments around the name of the 'Holy Land', precisely that designation has been used frequently. As adjective for this period in antiquity, the Roman administrative term 'Palestinian' has been used.

BIBLIOGRAPHY

The author acknowledges the permission from the Regents of the University of California for copyright access to the CD ROM files of the Thesaurus Linguae Graecae.

General Works

Charlesworth, James H. (ed.), *The Old Testament Pseudepigrapha*. I. *Apocalyptic Literature and Testaments*; II. *Expansions of the 'Old Testament' and Legends, Wisdom and Philosophical Literature, Prayers, Psalms, and Odes, Fragments of Lost Judeo-Hellenistic Works* (Garden City, NY: Doubleday; London: Darton, Longman & Todd, 1983–85).

García Martínez, Florentino, *The Dead Sea Scrolls: Translated: The Qumran Texts in English* (Leiden: E.J. Brill, 1994).

Hennecke, E., and W. Schneemelcher, *Neutestamentliche Apokryphen in deutscher Übersetzung* (2 vols.; Tübingen: J.C.B. Mohr [Paul Siebeck], 1987–89).

Johnson, Luke T., *The Writings of the New Testament: An Interpretation* (London: SCM Press, 1986).

Köster, Helmut, *Ancient Christian Gospels: Their History and Development* (London: SCM Press, 1983).

Kümmel, Werner Georg, *Einleitung in das Neue Testament* (Heidelberg: Quelle & Meyer, 21st edn, 1983); ET by A.J. Mattill Jr, in collaboration with the author, of 14th edn (1965): *Introduction to the New Testament* (London: SCM Press, 1966).

Sandmel, Samuel, *Judaism and Christian Beginnings* (New York: Oxford University Press, 1978).

Strack, Hermann L., and Paul Billerbeck, *Kommentar zum Neuen Testament aus Talmud und Midrasch* (4 vols.; Munich: Beck, 1922–74).

Vielhauer, Philipp, *Geschichte der urchristlichen Literatur: Einleitung in das Neue Testament, die Apokryphen und die Apostolischen Vätern* (Berlin: W. de Gruyter, 4th edn, 1985).

Editions of the Rabbinic Texts

Buber, S., *Midrasch Tehillim: Oder, Haggadische Erklarung der Psalmen* (Trier: S. Mayer, 1892–93).

Finkelstein, L. (ed.), *Sifre on Deuteronomy* (repr.; New York: Jewish Publication Society of America, 1969).

Fisch, S., *Midrash haggadol on the Pentateuch* (Manchester: Manchester University Press, 1940).

Friedmann, M. (ed.), *Seder Eliahu Rabba and Seder Eliahu Zura (Tanna d'Be Eliahu); Pseudo-Seder Eliahu Zuta* (According to a MS edited with commentaries and additions; Jerusalem: Wahrmann Books, 3rd edn, 1969).

Horovitz, H.S. (ed.), *Siphre ad Numeros adjecto Siphre zutta / cum variis lectionibus et adnotationibus* (repr.; Jerusalem: Wahrmann, 1966 [1917]).

Horovitz, H.S., and L. Finkelstein (eds.), *Sifre on Deuteronomy* (New York: The Jewish Theological Seminary of America, 1969).

Horovitz, H.S., and I.A. Rabin (eds.), *Mechilta d'Rabbi Ismael* (Frankfurt a M: Kauffmann, 1931).

Lichtenstein, H. (ed.), *'Megillat Taanit'*, *HUCA* 8–9 (1931–32), pp. 257-351.

Lieberman, S. (ed.), *The Tosefta according to Codex Vienna, with variants from Codex Erfurt, Genizah mss. and Editio princeps (Venice 1521)* (New York: Jewish Theological Seminary of America, 1955–57).

Mandelbaum, B. (ed.), *Pesikta de-Rab Kahana: according to an Oxford manuscript: with varients from all known manuscripts and Genizoth fragments and parallel passages with commentary and introduction* (New York: Jewish Theological Seminary of America, 1962).

Margulies, M., *Midrash Haggadol on the Pentateuch: Exodus* (Jerusalem: Mosad Harav Kook, 3rd edn, 1976).

Schechter, S. (ed.), *Massekhet 'Avot de-Rabi Natan* (Vienna: Ch.D. Lippe, 1887).

Theodor, J., and Ch. Albeck (eds.), *Midrash bereshit rabba: Critical edition with notes and commentary* (repr.; Jerusalem: Shalem, 1996 [1965]).

Urbach, E.E. (ed.), *Sefer Pitron Torah: A Collection of Midrashim and Interpretations* (Jerusalem: Magnes Press, 1978).

Weiss, I.H. (ed.), *Sifra' de-vey Rav : hu' sefer Torat kohanim* (Vienna: Shlosberg, 1862).

Introduction: Reading the New Testament Anew

Eckert, Willehad, Paul Levinson and Martin Nathan Peter Stöhr (eds.), *Antijudaismus im Neuen Testament? Exegetische und systematische Beiträge* (Abhandlungen zum christlichen-jüdisch Dialog, 2; Munich: Chr. Kaiser Verlag, 1967).

Evans, Craig A., and Donald A. Hagner, *Anti-Semitism and Early Christianity: Issues of Polemic and Faith* (Minneapolis: Fortress Press, 1993).

Farmer, William R. (ed.), *Anti-Judaism and the Gospels* (Harrisburg, PA: Trinity Press International, 1999).

Fleischner, Eva (ed.), *Auschwitz: Beginning of a New Era? Reflections on the Holocaust* (New York: Ktav; The Cathedral Church of St John the Divine; Anti-Defamation League of B'nai B'rith, 1977).

Ginzel, Günther Bernd (ed.), *Auschwitz als Herausforderung für Juden und Christen* (Heidelberg: Lambert Schneider, 1980).

Klappert, Bertold, and Helmut Starck, *Umkehr und Erneuerung; Erläuterungen zum Synodalbeschluss der Rheinischen Landessynode 1980 'Zur Erneuerung des Verhältnisses von Christen und Juden'* (Neukirchen–Vluyn: Neukirchener Verlag, 1980).

Richardson, Peter, and David Granskou (eds.), *Anti-Judaism in Early Christianity* (Waterloo, ON: Wilfrid Laurier University Press, 1986).

Rosenzweig, Franz, 'Die Einheit der Bibel' and 'Das Formgeheimnis der biblischen

Erzählungen', in F. Rosenzweig and M. Buber, *Die Schrift und ihre Verdeutschung* (Berlin: Schocken, 1936), pp. 46-54, 239-61 (ET by L. Rosenwald with E. Fox: *Scripture and Translation* [Bloomington: Indiana University Press, 1994]).

Chapters 1 and 2: Judaism in the Graeco-Roman World, Jewish Religious Life

Alon, Gedalyahu, *Jews, Judaism and the Classical World: Studies in Jewish History in the Times of the Second Temple and the Talmud* (Jerusalem: Magnes Press, 1977).

—*The Jews in their Land in the Talmudic Age*, I–II (Jerusalem: Magnes Press, 1980–84).

Barclay, John M.G., *Jews in the Mediterranean Diaspora from Alexander to Trajan (323 BCE–117 CE)* (Edinburgh: T. & T. Clark, 1996).

Epstein, J.N., *Introduction to Tannaitic Literature: Mishna, Tosephta and Halakhic Midrashim* (ed. E.Z. Melamed, Jerusalem: Magnes Press; Tel Aviv: Dvir, 1957) (Hebrew).

—*Mavo le-nosah haMishna; nosah haMishna we-gilguleha lemi-yeme haAmoraim he-rishonim we-ad defuse R. Yomtov Lippmann Heller* (repr.; Jerusalem: n. pub., 1963–64 [1948]).

Frye, R.N., *The Heritage of Persia* (London: Weidenfeld & Nicolson, 1962).

Grabbe, L.L., *Judaism from Cyrus to Hadrian*. I. *The Persian and Greek Periods*; II. *The Roman Period* (Minneapolis: Fortress Press, 1992).

Heinemann, Isaak, *Philons griechische und jüdische Bildung; kulturvergleichende Untersuchungen zu Philons Darstellung der jüdischen Gesetze* (repr.; Hildesheim: Georg Olms, 1973 [1929–32]).

Hengel, Martin, *Judentum und Hellenismus: Studien zu ihrer Begegnung unter besonderer Berücksichtigung Palästinas bis zur Mitte des 2. Jahrhunderts* (WUNT, 10; Tübingen: J.C.B. Mohr [Paul Siebeck], 1969) (ET by J. Bowden: *Judaism and Hellenism: Studies in their Encounter in Palestine during the Early Hellenistic Period* [Philadelphia: Fortress Press, 1981]).

Horbury, William, *Jews and Christians in Contact and Controversy* (Edinburgh: T. & T. Clark, 1998).

Horst, P.W. van der, 'Jews and Christians in Aphrodisias in the Light of their Relations in Other Cities of Asia Minor', *Nederlands Theologisch Tijdschrift* 43 (1989), pp. 106-21.

Jaubert, Annie, *La date de la Cène: Calendrier biblique et liturgie chrétienne* (Paris: Lecoffre, 1957) (ET: *The Date of the Last Supper* [Staten Island, NY: Alba House, 1965]).

Momigliano, Arnaldo, *Alien Wisdom: The Limits of Hellenization* (Cambridge: Cambridge University Press, 1975).

—*Essays in Ancient and Modern Historiography* (Oxford: Oxford University Press, 1977).

—*Studies in Historiography* (London: Weidenfeld & Nicolson, 1966).

Mulder, Martin J. (ed.), *Mikra: Text, Translation, Reading and Interpretation of the Hebrew Bible in Ancient Judaism and Early Christianity* (CRINT, 2.1; Assen: Van Gorcum; Philadelphia: Fortress Press, 1988).

Safrai, Shmuel (ed.), *The Literature of the Sages. First Part: Oral Tora, Halakha, Mishna, Tosefta, Talmud, External Tractates* (CRINT, 2.3a; Assen: Van Gorcum; Philadelphia: Fortress Press, 1987).

Safrai, Shmuel, and Menahem Stern (eds.), *The Jewish People in the First Century: His-*

torical Geography, Political History, Social, Cultural and Religious Life and Institutions (CRINT, 1.1–2; Assen: Van Gorcum, 1974–76).

Sanders, E.P., *Jewish Law between Jesus and the Mishnah: Five Studies* (London: SCM Press, 1990).

—*Judaism: Practice and Belief, 64 B.C.E.–66 C.E.* (London: SCM Press, 1992).

Schürer, Emil, *The History of the Jewish People in the Age of Jesus Christ*, I–III.2 (rev. and ed. by G. Vermes, F. Millar, M. Black and M. Goodman; Edinburgh: T. & T. Clark, 1973–87).

Smallwood, Mary, *The Jews under Roman Rule; from Pompey to Diocletian: A Study in Political Relations* (repr.; Leiden: E.J. Brill, 1981).

Stemberger, Günter, *Einleitung in Talmud und Midrasch* (Munich: Beck, 1992) (ET by N.M.A. Bockmuehl: *Introduction to the Talmud and Midrash* [Minneapolis: Fortress Press, 1992]).

Sterling, Gregory E., *Historiography and Self-Definition: Josephos, Luke, and Apologetic Historiography* (NovTSup, 64; Leiden: E.J. Brill, 1992).

Stern, Menahem, *Greek and Latin Authors on Jews and Judaism* (3 vols.; Jerusalem: Magnes Press, 1974–84).

Stone, Michael E. (ed.), *Jewish Writings of the Second Temple Period: Apocrypha, Pseudepigrapha, Qumran Sectarian Writings, Philo, Josephus* (CRINT, 2.2; Assen Van Gorcum; Philadelphia: Fortress Press, 1984).

Tarn, W.W., and G.T. Griffith, *Hellenistic Civilisation* (London: Edward Arnold, 3rd edn, 1953).

Tcherikover, Victor, *Hellenistic Civilisation and the Jews* (Philadelphia: Jewish Publication Society, 1959; repr.; New York: Atheneum, 1977 [1959]).

Tomson, Peter J., 'The Names Israel and Jew in Ancient Judaism and in the New Testament', *Bijdragen* 47 (1986), pp. 120-40, 266-89.

—'Jewish Purity Laws as Viewed by the Church Fathers and by the Early Followers of Jesus', in M.J.H.M. Poorthuis and J. Schwartz, *Purity and Holiness: The Heritage of Leviticus* (Jewish and Christian Perspectives, 2; Leiden: E.J. Brill, 2000), pp. 73-92.

Trebilco, Paul R., *Jewish Communities in Asia Minor* (Cambridge: Cambridge University Press, 1991).

Urbach, Ephraim E., *The Sages: Their Concepts and Beliefs* (2 vols.; Jerusalem: Magnes Press, 2nd edn, 1978).

VanderKam, James C., *The Dead Sea Scrolls Today* (Grand Rapids: Eerdmans, 1994).

Chapter 3: Jesus

Bultmann, Rudolf, *Jesus* (repr.; Tübingen: J.C.B. Mohr [Paul Siebeck], 1951 [1929]).

—*Die Geschichte der synoptischen Tradition* (Göttingen: Vandenhoeck & Ruprecht, 1979) (ET by J. Marsh: *The History of the Synoptic Tradition* [New York: Harper & Row, 1963]).

Dahl, Niels A., *Jesus in the Memory of the Early Church: Essays* (Minneapolis: Augsburg, 1976).

Dibelius, Martin, *Die Formgeschichte des Evangeliums* (ed. G. Bornkamm; Tübingen: J.C.B. Mohr [Paul Siebeck], 3rd edn, 1959 [1919]) (ET from 2nd edn in collaboration with the author by B.L. Woolf: *From Tradition to Gospel* [London: Nicholson & Watson, 1934]).

Evans, Craig A., 'Predictions of the Destruction of the Herodian Temple in the Pseud-epigrapha, Qumran, and Related Texts', *JSP* 10 (1992), pp. 89-147.

Flusser, David, *Die rabbinischen Gleichnisse und der Gleichniserzähler Jesus*. I. *Das Wesen der Gleichnisse* (Bern: Peter Lang, 1981).

—*Jesus: In Selbstzeugnissen und Bilddokumenten* (Hamburg: Rowolt, 1968).

—*Judaism and the Origins of Christianity* (Jerusalem: Magnes Press, 1988).

Jeremias, Joachim, *Die Abendmahlsworte Jesu* (Göttingen: Vandenhoeck & Ruprecht, 3rd edn, 1960).

—*Neutestamentliche Theologie*. I. *Die Verkündigung Jesu* (Gütersloh: Gerd Mohn, 2nd edn, 1973).

Kähler, Martin, *Der sogenannte historische Jesus und der geschichtliche, biblische Christ-us* (ed. E. Wolff; Munich: Chr. KaiserVerlag, 2nd edn, 1956 [1892]) (ET with intro. by C.E. Braaten: *The So-Called Historical Jesus and the Historic Biblical Christ* [Philadelphia: Fortress Press, 1988]).

Klausner, Joseph, *Jesus von Nazareth: Seine Zeit, sein Leben und seine Lehre* (Jerusalem, 3rd edn, 1957 [1934]) (ET from the original Hebrew by H. Danby: *Jesus of Nazareth: His Life, Times, and Teaching* [New York: Macmillan, 1925]).

Safrai, Shmuel, 'Yeshu weha-tenua he-hassidit', in A. Oppenheimer, I. Gafni and D. Schwartz, *The Jews in the Hellenistic-Roman World: Studies in Memory of Menahem Stern* (Jerusalem: Shazar Center, 1996), pp. 413-36 (Hebrew).

Sanders, E.P., *The Historical Figure of Jesus* (London: Allan Lane; Penguin, 1993).

Schweitzer, Albert, *Geschichte der Leben-Jesu-Forschung* (Tübingen: J.C.B. Mohr [Paul Siebeck], 6th edn, 1951 [1913]) (ET by W. Montgomery: *The Quest of the Historical Jesus: A Critical Study of its Progress from Reimarus to Wrede* [new introd. by J.M. Robinson; New York: Macmillan, 1968]).

Tomson, Peter J., 'The Core of Jesus' Evangel: *euaggelisasthai ptôchois* (Isa 61:1)', in C.M. Tuckett (ed.), *The Scriptures in the Gospels* (BETL, 131; Leuven: Leuven University Press; Peeters, 1997), pp. 647-58.

Chapter 4: Paul

Dahl, Niels A. *Studies in Paul: Theology for the Early Christian Mission* (Minneapolis: Augsburg, 1977).

Davies, W.D., *Paul and Rabbinic Judaism* (London: SPCK, 3rd edn, 1971 [1948]).

Donfried, Karl P., *The Romans Debate: Revised and Expanded Edition* (Edinburgh: T. & T. Clark, 1991).

Engberg-Pedersen, Troels (ed.), *Paul in his Hellenistic Context* (Studies of the New Testament and its World; Edinburgh: T. & T. Clark, 1994).

Flusser, David, 'The Dead Sea Sect and Pre-Pauline Christianity', in *Scripta Hieroso-lymitana 4* (Jerusalem: Magnes Press, 1958), pp. 215-66 (repr. in *idem, Judaism and the Origins of Christianity* [Jerusalem: Magnes Press, 1988]).

Schweitzer, Albert, *Geschichte der paulinischen Forschung von der Reformation bis auf der Gegenwart* (Tübingen: J.C.B. Mohr [Paul Siebeck], 1911) (ET *Paul and his Inter-preters, a Critical History* [New York: Schocken Books, 1964]).

—*Die Mystik des Apostels Paulus* (Tübingen: J.C.B. Mohr [Paul Siebeck], 1930) (repr. (Uni Taschenbücher, 1981); ET by W. Montgomery: *The Mysticism of Paul the Apostle* [Baltimore: The Johns Hopkins University Press, 1998]).

Stendahl, Krister, *Paul among Jews and Gentiles, and Other Essays* (London: SPCK, 1977).

Tomson, Peter J., *Paul and the Jewish Law: Halakha in the Letters of the Apostle to the Gentiles* (CRINT, 3.1; Assen: Van Gorcum; Minneapolis: Fortress Press, 1990).

—'Paul's Jewish Background in View of his Law Teaching in 1 Cor 7', in J.D.G. Dunn (ed.), *Paul and the Mosaic Law* (Tübingen: J.C.B. Mohr [Paul Siebeck], 1996), pp. 251-70.

Chapter 5: Luke and Acts

Alon, Gedalyahu, 'The Levitical Uncleanness of Gentiles', in *idem, Jews, Judaism and the Classical World: Studies in Jewish History in the Times of the Second Temple and Talmud* (Jerusalem: Magnes, 1977), pp. 146-89.

Bockmuehl, Markus N.A., 'The Noachide Commandments and New Testament Ethics, with Special Reference to Acts 15 and Pauline Halakhah', *RB* 102 (1995), pp. 72-101.

Cadbury, Henry J., *The Making of Luke–Acts* (repr.; London: SPCK, 1958 [1927]).

Fitzmyer, Joseph A., *The Gospel According to St. Luke* (2 vols.; AB, 28; Garden City, NY: Doubleday, 1981–85).

Flusser, David, and Safrai Shmuel, 'Das Aposteldekret und die Noachitischen Gebote', in E. Brocke and H.J. Barkenings (eds.), *'Wer Tora vermehrt, mehrt Leben': Festgabe für Heinz Kremers zum 60. Geburtstag* (Neukirchen–Vluyn: Neukirchener Verlag, 1986), pp. 173-92.

Hengel, Martin, *Between Jesus and Paul: Studies in the Earliest History of Christianity* (trans. John Bowden; Philadelphia: Fortress Press, 1983).

—*Zur urchristlichen Geschichtsschreibung* (Stuttgart: Calwer Verlag, 1979).

—'Zwischen Jesus und Paulus; die "Hellenisten", die "Sieben" und Stephanus (Apg 6,1-15; 7,54–8,3)', *ZTK* 72 (1975), pp. 151-206.

Hill, Craig G., *Hellenists and Hebrews: Reappraising Division within the Earliest Church* (Minneapolis: Fortress Press, 1992).

Jervell, Jacob, *Die Apostelgeschichte* (MeyerK, 3; Göttingen: Vandenhoeck & Ruprecht, 17th edn, 1998).

—*Luke and the People of God; A New Look at Luke–Acts* (Minneapolis: Augsburg, 1972).

Keck, Leander E., and Louis J. Martyn (ed.), *Studies in Luke–Acts* (Nashville: Abingdon Press, 1966).

Koet, Bart-Jan, *Five Studies on Interpretation of Scripture in Luke–Acts* (Studia NT Auxilia, 14; Leuven: Peeters, 1989).

Mason, Steve, 'Chief Priests, Sadducees, Pharisees and Sanhedrin in Acts', in R. Bauckham (ed.), *The Book of Acts in its Palestinian Setting* (Carlisle: Paternoster Press; Grand Rapids: Eerdmans, 1995), pp. 115-77.

Sanders, Jack T., *The Jews in Luke–Acts* (London: SCM Press, 1987).

Tomson, Peter J., 'Gamaliel's Counsel and the Apologetic Strategy of Luke–Acts', in J. Verheyden (ed.), *The Unity of Luke–Acts* (BETL, 142; Leuven: Leuven University Press; Leuven: Peeters, 1999), pp. 585-604.

Chapter 6: Mark and Matthew

Conybeare, F., 'The Eusebian Form of the Text Matth. 28,19', *ZNW* 2 (1901), pp. 275-88.

Davies, W.D., and Dale C. Allison Jr, *A Critical and Exegetical Commentary on the Gospel According to St. Matthew* (3 vols.; Edinburgh: T. & T. Clark, 1988–1997).

Flusser, David, 'The Conclusion of Matthew', *ASTI* 5 (1967), pp. 110-20.

Klijn, A.F.J., *Jewish-Christian Gospel Tradition* (VCSup, 17; Leiden: E.J. Brill, 1992).

Klijn, A.F.J., and G.J. Reilink, *Patristic Evidence for Jewish-Christian Sects* (NovTSup, 36; Leiden: E.J. Brill, 1973).

Luz, Ulrich, 'Antijudaismus im Matthäusevangelium als historisches und theologisches Problem', *EvT* 53 (1993), pp. 310-27.

—*Das Evangelium nach Matthäus* (EKKNT, 1-3; Zürich etc. [Benzinger etc.] 1985-).

—'Das Matthäusevangelium und die Perspektive einer biblischen Theologie', in Dwight R. Daniels *e.a.*, *'Gesetz' als Thema Biblischer Theologie* (Jahrbuch für Biblische Theologie, 4; Neukirchen–Vluyn: Neukirchener Verlag, 1989), pp. 233-48.

Pesch, R. *Das Markusevangelium* (HTKNT; Freiburg: Herder, 3rd edn, 1980).

Schelkle, Karl Hermann, 'Die Selbstverfluchung Israels nach Matthäus 27,23-25', in W.P. Eckert (ed.), *Antijudaismus in Neuen Testament? Exegetische und systematische Beiträge* (Abhandlungen zum christlichen-jüdisch Dialog, 2; Munich: Chr. Kaiser Verlag, 1967), pp. 148-56.

Chapter 7: John

Barrett, C.K., *Essays on John* (London: SPCK, 1982).

Bauer, Walter, *Das Johannesevangelium* (HNT, 6; Tübingen: J.C.B. Mohr [Paul Siebeck], 1933).

Black, Matthew, 'The Arrest and Trial of Jesus and the Date of the Last Supper', in A.J.B. Higgins (ed.), *Studies in Memory of T.W. Manson* (Manchester: Manchester University Press, 1959), pp. 19-33.

Brown, Raymond E., *The Community of the Beloved Disciple* (London: Geoffrey Chapman, 1979).

—*The Gospel According to John*, I–II (AB, 29, 29a; Garden City, NY: Doubleday, 1966, 1970).

Bultmann, Rudolf, *Das Evangelium des Johannes* (Kritisch-Exegetische Kommentare zum Neuen Testament; Göttingen: Vandenhoeck & Ruprecht, 1941).

Jaubert, Annie, *La date de la Cène: Calendrier biblique et liturgie chrétienne* (Paris: Lecoffre, 1957).

Leistner, Reinhold, *Antijudaismus im Johannesevangelium? Darstellung des Problems in der neueren Auslegungsgeschichte und Untersuchung der Leidensgeschichte* (Theologie und Wirklichkeit, 3; Bern: Peter Lang, 1974).

Martyn, J. Louis, *The Gospel of John in Christian History: Essays for Interpreters* (New York: Paulist Press, 1978).

Tomson, Peter J., ' "Jews" in the Gospel of John as Compared with the Synoptics, the Palestinian Talmud, and Some Apocryphal Gospels', in R. Bieringer, D. Pollefeyt and F. Vanneuville (eds.), *Anti-Judaism in the Gospel of John and Jewish-Christian Dialogue* (forthcoming).

Chapter 8: Letters of the Jewish Churches

Alon, Gedalyahu, 'Ha-halakha ba-Torat 12 ha-Shelihim' (1939–40), in *idem*, *Studies in Jewish History in the Times of the Second Temple, the Mishna and the Talmud*, I (Tel Aviv: Ha-kibbutz ha-meuhad, 1958), pp. 274-94 (Hebrew).

Audet, Jean-Paul, *La Didachè: Instructions des apôtres* (Paris: Lecoffre, 1958).

Bauckham, Richard, *Jude and the Relatives of Jesus in the Early Church* (Edinburgh: T. & T. Clark, 1990).

—*The Climax of Prophecy: Studies on the Book of Revelation* (Edinburgh: T. & T. Clark, 1993).

Charles, R.H., *The Revelation of St. John* (ICC; 2 vols.; Edinburgh: T. & T. Clark, 1920).

Flusser, David, 'Qumran und die Zwölf', in C.J. Bleeker (ed.), *Initiatio: Contributions to the Theme of the Study-Conference of the International Association for the History of Religions held at Strasburg, Sept. 17th to 22nd 1964* (NumenSup = Studies in the History of Religions, 10; Leiden: E.J. Brill, 1965), pp. 134-46.

—'Shte derakhim hen', in *idem, Jewish Sources in Early Christianity: Studies and Essays* (Jerusalem: Poalim, 1979), pp. 235-52 (Hebrew).

Kraft, Heinrich, *Die Offenbarung des Johannes* (HNT, 16a; Tübingen: J.C.B. Mohr [Paul Siebeck], 1974).

Mussner, Franz, *Der Jakobusbrief* (HTKNT, 13.1; Freiburg: Herder, 3rd edn, 1975).

Wengst, Klaus *Didache (Apostellehre), Barnabasbrief, Zweiter Klemensbrief, Schrift an Diognet* (Schriften des Urchristentums, 2; Darmstadt: Wissenschaftliche Buchgesell-schaft, 1984).

Chapter 9: The New Testament and the Jews

Bauer, Walter, *Rechtgläubigkeit und Ketzerei im ältesten Christentum* (BHT, 10, Tübingen: J.C.B. Mohr [Paul Siebeck], 1934) (ET by Philadelphia Seminar on Christian Origins, ed. R.A. Kraft and G. Krodel: *Orthodoxy and Heresy in Earliest Christianity* [Philadelphia: Fortress Press, 1971]).

Baum, Greory, *The Jews and the Gospel: Is the New Testament AntiSemitic? A Re-Examination of the New Testament* (Glen Rock, NJ: Paulist Press, 1965).

—'Introduction', in R.R. Ruether, *Faith and Fratricide: The Theological Roots of Anti-semitism* (New York: Seabury, 1974), pp. 1-22.

Gager, John G., *The Origins of Anti-Semitism* (Oxford: Oxford University Press, 1983).

Horbury, William, 'Old Testament Interpretation in the Writings of the Church Fathers', in Martin J. Mulder (ed.), *Mikra: Text, Translation, Reading and Interpretation of the Hebrew Bible in Ancient Judaism and Early Christianity* (CRINT, 2.1; Assen: Van Gorcum; Philadelphia: Fortress Press, 1988), pp. 727-87.

Isaac, Jules, *Jésus et Israël* (Paris: Albin Michel, 1948) (ET by S. Gran: *Jesus and Israel* [New York: Holt, Rinehart & Winston, 1971]).

Parkes, James, *The Conflict of the Church and the Synagogue: A Study in the Origins of Antisemitism* (repr.; New York: Athenaeum, 1977 [1934]).

Poliakov, Léon, *Histoire de l'antisémitisme* (4 vols.; Paris: Calmann-Lévy, 1966–77) (ET by Richard Howard, Nathalie Gerardi, Miriam Kochan and George Klin; *The History of Anti-Semitism* [London: Routledge & Kegan Paul, 1974–85]).

Richardson, Peter, *Israel in the Apostolic Church* (SNTSMS, 10; Cambridge: Cambridge University Press, 1969).

Ruether, Rosemary Radford, *Faith and Fratricide: The Theological Roots of Antisemitism* (New York: Seabury, 1974).

Simon, Marcel, *Verus Israel: Étude sur les relations entre chrétiens et juifs dans l'empire romain (135–425)* (Paris: De Boccard, 2nd edn, 1964 [1948]) (ET by H. McKeating:

Verus Israel: A Study of the Relations between Christians and Jews in the Roman Empire, 135–425 [Oxford: Oxford University Press, 1986]).

Tomson, Peter J., 'The New Testament Canon as the Embodiment of Evolving Christian Attitudes towards the Jews', in A. van der Kooij and K. van der Toorn, *Canonization and Decanonization: Papers Presented to the International Conference of the Leiden Institute for the Study of Religions (LISOR), held at Leiden, 9-10 January 1997* (Leiden: E.J. Brill, 1998), pp. 107-32.

Zahn, Theodor, *Geschichte des neutestamentlichen Kanons* (Leipzig: Deichert, 1888–92).

INDEX OF REFERENCES

OLD TESTAMENT

'If this be from Heaven...'

EARLY CHRISTIAN REFERENCES

EARLY CHRISTIAN SOURCES